SHAKESPEARE AND THE HUNT

Shakespeare and the Hunt is the first book-length study of Shakespeare's works in relation to the culture of the hunt in Elizabethan and Jacobean society. The book explores topics generally unfamiliar to Shakespeareans, such as the variety of kinds of hunting in the period, the formal rituals of the hunt, the roles of Queen Elizabeth and King James as hunters, the practice of organized poaching, and the arguments both for and against hunting. Situating Shakespeare's works in this rich cultural context, Berry illuminates the plays from fresh angles. He explores, for example, the role of poaching in *The Merry Wives of Windsor*, the paradox of pastoral hunting in *As You Like It*; the intertwining of hunting and politics in *The Tempest*; and the gendered language of falconry in *The Taming of the Shrew*.

EDWARD BERRY is Professor of English at the University of Victoria, British Columbia. His books include *Patterns of Decay: Shakespeare's Early Histories* (1975), *Shakespeare's Comic Rites* (Cambridge University Press, 1984) and *The Making of Sir Philip Sidney* (1998). He also co-edited *True Rites and Maimed Rites: Ritual and Anti-Ritual in Shakespeare and His Age* (1992).

SHAKESPEARE AND THE HUNT

HUNT

A Cultural and Social Study

EDWARD BERRY

CAMBRIDGE
UNIVERSITY PRESS

PUBLISHED BY THE PRESS SYNDICATE OF THE UNIVERSITY OF CAMBRIDGE
The Pitt Building, Trumpington Street, Cambridge, United Kingdom

CAMBRIDGE UNIVERSITY PRESS
The Edinburgh Building, Cambridge CB2 2RU, UK
40 West 20th Street, New York, NY 10011-4211, USA
10 Stamford Road, Oakleigh, VIC 3166, Australia
Ruiz de Alarcón 13, 28014 Madrid, Spain
Dock House, The Waterfront, Cape Town 8001, South Africa

http://www.cambridge.org

First published 2001

Printed in the United Kingdom at the University Press, Cambridge

Typeface Monotype Baskerville 11/12.5   *System* QuarkXPress™   [SE]

A catalogue record for this book is available from the British Library

Library of Congress cataloguing in publication data
Berry, Edward I.
Shakespeare and the hunt: a cultural and social study/Edward Berry
p.   cm.
Includes bibliographical references and index
ISBN 0 521 80070 6 (hardback)
1. Shakespeare, William, 1564–1616 – Knowledge – Hunting. 2
Hunting – England – History – 16th century. 3. Hunting – England – History – 17th century
4. Hunting in literature. I. Title
PR3069.H85 B47 2001
822.3′3 – dc21   00–063063

ISBN 0 521 80070 6 hardback

To Margaret

Contents

Illustrations

Preface

The current controversies surrounding the sport of hunting in Britain and North America make it likely that a book on Shakespeare and the hunt will be greeted with suspicion by both proponents and opponents. To readers engaged in the controversies, I should say that, while I have never hunted and have no desire to do so, I am not a vegetarian or a principled opponent of the sport. To readers not engaged in the controversies, and for whom the problems of urban society might make such controversies seem marginal and trivial, I can only appeal to the prominence of the hunt in Elizabethan and Jacobean culture, to the extent of Shakespeare's imaginative involvement in it, and to the continuing significance of the issues – ethical, social, ecological – that surround the killing of animals for sport.

Although the subtitle represents this book as a "cultural and social study," I tend to include social structures within the broad concept of culture throughout. Hence I refer often to a culture of the hunt. Though inexact, the phrase allows me to imagine Elizabethan and Jacobean culture as in some sense a hunting culture, presided over by monarchs who spent much time in the field and for whom hunting was a ritualistic expression of socially pervasive royal power. It is also a notion that allows me to imagine the hunting "fraternity" as a sub-culture within the broad society as a whole – a sub-culture which might itself be divided into such overlapping but sometimes antagonistic groups as hunters and poachers. Finally, the word "culture" allows me to think of the hunt in a broad sense: as a social practice, a symbol, a ritual, a discourse, an ideology. My context for understanding Shakespeare's relationship to the hunt therefore includes the practice of the sport itself, handbooks of hunting, poems and plays, mythology, theology, politics, painting – in short, the entire apparatus of what we usually understand as culture. As with most subjects in the early modern period, the evidence that survives favors high culture over low.

Research into the early modern culture of the hunt poses special challenges. Eye-witness accounts of the sport are rare and sketchy. Descriptions in the handbooks are not only incomplete but also inconsistent. The terminology of the sport, though wonderfully pedantic, is imprecise. And there is little in the way of modern research into either the practice of the hunt or its cultural significance. Hence I owe a special debt of gratitude to previous scholarship in the field – in particular, to D. H. Madden's odd but useful book, *The Diary of Master William Silence* (London: Longmans, Green, 1907); to Richard Marienstras's *New Perspectives on the Shakespearean World*, trans. Janet Lloyd (Cambridge: Cambridge University Press, 1985); and, most significantly, to Roger B. Manning's *Hunters and Poachers* (Oxford: Clarendon Press, 1993).

The book contains eight chapters and touches on nearly every major Shakespearean allusion to hunting. Chapter 1 surveys the theory and practice of the hunt in the period, introduces the major issues surrounding the sport, and suggests, in general, Shakespeare's relationship to it. Chapter 2 examines hunting in *Venus and Adonis* and *Love's Labor's Lost*, with particular attention to the paradoxes of female hunting embodied in the figures of Venus and the Princess of France. Chapter 3 treats the ritual of the hunt as a context for tragedy in *Titus Andronicus* and *Julius Caesar*. Chapter 4 offers a new interpretation of *The Taming of the Shrew* by focusing on the implications of Petruchio's speech on taming Katherine as a falcon and the prominence of the hunting lord in the Induction. Chapter 5 surveys the comic career of Falstaff as both stag and poacher from *1 Henry IV* to *The Merry Wives of Windsor*. Chapter 6 explores the paradox of pastoral hunting in *As You Like It*. Chapter 7 juxtaposes Prospero's hunt of Caliban in *The Tempest* with James I's career as a hunter and the crisis brought on by his assertions of his royal prerogative at the time in which the play was being written. Chapter 8 concludes the study with a brief overview of Shakespeare's conception of hunting.

Throughout the study I quote Shakespeare from G. Blakemore Evans, ed., *The Riverside Shakespeare*, 2nd edn. (Boston: Houghton Mifflin, 1997). In quoting from old texts, I have normalized *u*, *v*, *i*, and *j* to conform with modern practice. I deliberately use the gendered word "man" to represent "human-kind" throughout the work since replacing it with such terms as "people" would tend to erase the patriarchal bias of the period.

I owe thanks to a great many people for their assistance, some of whom I must mention by name. The "onlie begetter" of this project, for which he is in no way to blame, is François Laroque, who prompted my invitation to address the Société Shakespeare Française on the topic of the Shakespearean "green world" and thereby precipitated my frantic search for something new to say on the topic and my discovery of hunting; an early version of the section on *Love's Labor's Lost* was published in the proceedings of this conference (*Shakespeare: Le Monde Vert: Rites et Renouveau* [Paris: Les Belles Lettres, 1995]). I owe thanks as well to the many students who were persuaded to share my esoteric interests; to my colleagues in the 1997 Shakespeare Association Seminar on *As You Like It*, so ably chaired by Christy Desmet; to Patrick Grant, who read part of the study; to Terry Sherwood and Roger B. Manning, who, heroically, read it all; to the University of Victoria for support in the way of research grants and study leave; to my efficient and gracious editor at Cambridge, Sarah Stanton; to my wonderfully supportive but too distant children; and, finally, to Margaret, to whom this book is dedicated.

Glossary

(The definitions below attempt to capture the most common meanings in early modern handbooks of hunting and falconry, but the terminology is imprecise and often inconsistent)

bow and stable hunting the most popular kind of hunting in parks, in which deer were driven towards bow-hunters, waiting in stands

buck a male fallow deer, often one of five years

coursing pursuing hares or other game with greyhounds, guided by sight

doe a female fallow deer

falcon the female of all long-winged hawks

fallow deer a medium-sized deer, most commonly kept and hunted in parks

hart a male red deer, usually one after its fifth year or possessing antlers with ten tines; the noblest animal hunted in Elizabethan England

haggard a mature hawk captured in the wild, usually considered a superior hunter

hind the female of the red deer

par force de chiens the noblest kind of hunting, in which a hart or stag was pursued in open forest by hounds guided by scent, and hunters

rascal a young, lean, or otherwise inferior deer of a herd

red deer the largest animal hunted in England, and prized for *par force* hunting

stag a male red deer, usually one five years old (not always clearly distinguished from the hart)

CHAPTER ONE

Introduction: the culture of the hunt and Shakespeare

In the British Museum, a magnificent Assyrian frieze depicts a royal lion hunt. The climactic moment of the hunt features the king Ashurbanipal killing a wounded lion. The roaring beast, an arrow lodged in its forehead, lunges at the king, who extends his left arm to ward off the attack, and with his right arm plunges a sword through its chest. The faces of king and lion are level with each other, only a foot apart, and they stare directly into each other's eyes. The rigid and almost hieratic pose of the combatants suggests primal conflict: this is the most powerful of the beasts against the most powerful of men. Despite the closeness of the two in magnificence and stature, however, the power of Ashurbanipal is triumphant. He stands erect, utterly unmoved by the assault. His face betrays no emotion, unless it be the slight suggestion of a smile. His extended arms, massive yet calm in their strength, literally stop the lion dead. The frieze, like the hunt it depicts, serves to define and glorify the power of the king.

An Assyrian frieze from the seventh century BC may seem a peculiar starting point for an exploration of the Elizabethan and Jacobean culture of the hunt. Yet its central image, which evokes with such elemental force the dominance of the king over nature, foreshadows one of the most powerful Jacobean representations of the hunt, that of *Henry Frederick, Prince of Wales and Sir John Harington*. In this painting (fig. 1), the stern young prince, with a huntsman, horse, and greyhound just behind him, sheathes his sword after executing a symbolic *coup de grâce* to a fallen deer, its antlers held by the young Lord Harington, who rests on one knee.[1] At the time of the painting, Prince Henry was nine years old.

Despite the two thousand years that separate them, the Assyrian and Jacobean images have much in common: both use the hunt to celebrate royal power and, more specifically, royal power over wild nature. In the painting of Prince Henry, the elemental conflict depicted in the Assyrian frieze has been elaborated and invested with distinctively Jacobean

1 Robert Peake, "Henry Frederick, Prince of Wales and Sir John Harington" (1603).
The nine-year-old prince sheathes his sword after symbolically decapitating a
dead deer.

significance. The beast hunted is no longer the lion but the deer, the noblest of animals routinely pursued as game in a land unhappily deprived of lions, wolves, or, for the most part, boar. The supreme hunter is not the king himself but the prince, whose youth makes the action seem a rite of initiation. The solitary conflict between ruler and animal is replaced by the image of the ruler surrounded by helpful and obedient human and animal companions: friend, huntsman, horse, and dog. The climactic action, moreover, is no longer a stab through the chest but a ceremonial assault upon an animal already dead. Despite these differences, the essential import of the two images remains very much the same: the painting, like the frieze, demonstrates and celebrates royal power. In the portrait of Prince Henry, that power extends to humans, both aristocratic and common, to domesticated animals, to wildlife, to the forested landscape in the background, and, one might add, to the viewer, whose gaze is returned head-on by the stern eyes of the young warrior-prince. In Peake's painting, one might say, the viewer plays the role of the lion in the Assyrian frieze, stopped dead not by the out-thrust arm but by the penetrating gaze of the prince.

From the Middle Ages to the end of the seventeenth century in England, hunting was one of the most significant royal activities and manifestations of royal power. "To read the history of kings," observed the democrat Tom Paine in the eighteenth century, "a man would be almost inclined to suppose that government consisted of stag hunting."[2] During the sixteenth and seventeenth centuries, every English monarch except Edward VI and Queen Mary hunted throughout his or her reign, either regularly or obsessively. As a young king, Henry VIII hunted so often and so hard that one member of the court complained to Wolsey that he spared "no pains to convert the sport of hunting into a martyrdom."[3] Queen Elizabeth was still hunting at the age of sixty-seven, as is shown by a letter from Rowland Whyte to Sir Robert Sidney on 12 September 1600. Whyte, writing from the palace at Oatlands, informs Sidney that "her majesty is well and excellently disposed to hunting, for every second day she is on horseback and continues the sport long."[4] James I so immersed himself in hunting when king of England that his recreation occasioned serious religious, political, and popular protest. Hunting was also an important recreation for Charles I, who was introduced to the sport by his father at the age of four.[5] Charles II remained true to his father and grandfather in his devotion to the sport, continuing to hunt at least until three years before his death at the age of fifty-five.[6] Among the tasks facing Charles during the Restoration was the re-establishment of the royal parks, forests, and herds, many of which had been damaged or destroyed as symbols of royal and aristocratic privilege during the Civil Wars.[7]

Throughout the reigns of the Tudors and Stuarts, then, hunting was an important part of the life of the court, and of the aristocratic households connected with it. It existed in a variety of modes and served a variety of purposes. It provided a regular source of exercise and recreation. It served as entertainment for foreign visitors. It amused the monarch on progress, both as a diversion en route and as a subject for pageantry provided by the owners of estates. It served social purposes as simple as informal recreation (if any action involving a monarch can be called informal), or as complex as court ceremonial. Images of the hunt surrounded the monarchy and nobility of the period, appearing in their plate, their tapestries, their paintings, their statuary, their poems, and their masques. Stirling Castle, the birthplace of James I, still features a statue of the goddess Diana on its exterior wall and a clear view from its interior down to what in James's time was a hunting park below. Queen Elizabeth's palace of Nonsuch included a grove of Diana with a fountain depicting Actaeon turned into a stag.[8]

Although the pictorial tradition of the hunt is rather thin in Tudor and Stuart England, a number of images confirm the importance of the sport as an emblem of monarchical power. Queen Elizabeth was apparently never painted as a huntress, despite her association with Diana, goddess of the hunt, but she appears prominently in three woodcuts in George Gascoigne's 1575 edition of *The Noble Arte of Venerie or Hunting* (two are reproduced as figs. 2 and 3). In the Jacobean court the hunt took on dynastic significance, providing memorable images of many members of the royal family. A 1603 painting of the Princess Elizabeth by Robert Peake shows a hunting scene in the background (fig. 4). Peake's hunting portrait of Prince Henry, previously mentioned, was produced in two versions. A 1617 painting by Paul van Somer features Anne of Denmark in royal hunting attire, standing beside her horse and holding her dogs by a leash (fig. 5). Although James himself seems not to have been painted as a huntsman, his image in the role was kept alive in the 1611 edition of the most important hunting manual in the period, George Gascoigne's *The Noble Arte of Venerie*; in that edition two of the three images of Queen Elizabeth and her ladies-in-waiting that had appeared in the 1575 edition were cut out and replaced with images of James and his pages (one is reproduced as fig. 6).[9]

The continuing popularity of the hunt among the monarchs of

2 Queen Elizabeth at a hunt assembly. From [George Gascoigne], *The Noble Arte of Venerie or Hunting* (1575).

England cannot be explained merely as personal inclination or even as family tradition. The easy substitution of James for Elizabeth in the images of *The Arte of Venerie* highlights the fact that the monarch's role was more important than any personal views he or she might have towards hunting. Because of its legal status, the hunt was deeply intertwined in conceptions of the royal prerogative itself. The very definition

3 Queen Elizabeth taking the assay. From [George Gascoigne], *The Noble Arte of Venerie or Hunting* (1575).

of a forest provided by John Manwood in his *Treatise of the Lawes of the Forest* (1615) suggests the convergence of real and symbolic power in the role of the monarch as hunter: "A forest is a certaine Territorie of wooddy grounds and fruitful pastures, priviledged for wilde beasts and foules of Forest, Chase and Warren, to rest and abide in, in the safe protection of the King, for his princely delight and pleasure . . ."[10] The law

4 Robert Peake, "Elizabeth of Bohemia" (1603). Hunting (right background) is
juxtaposed with intimate conversation (left background).

5 Paul van Somer, "Anne of Denmark" (1617).

of the forests, which originated with the Norman kings and was separate from the common law, gave the monarch sole authority over every forest in the kingdom and all of the so-called beasts of forest, chase, and warren within them. According to this definition, forests were essentially wildlife preserves for the royal hunt. The right to hunt in a forest could

6 James I taking the assay. From [George Gascoigne], *The Noble Arte of Venerie or Hunting* (1611).

only be conferred by the monarch, and even the right to hunt in the boundaries of the forest, the so-called purlieus, was restricted to those of superior wealth and rank. Even the establishment of a private game park required a warrant from the monarch.[11]

Hunting was restricted not only by the forest law but by the innumerable game laws that were enacted throughout the period. Whereas the forest law privileged the monarch over all others, even his greatest peers, the game laws aligned the monarch with the privileged elite whose property and interests they were designed to protect. The game laws, as Roger B. Manning notes, "made crimes of hunting without a sufficient estate, hunting at night or in disguise, breaking into a park, or being in possession of hunting weapons, nets, or hunting dogs."[12] Under James I, in particular, who vigorously asserted his royal prerogative in relation to the hunt, these laws became highly controversial. Throughout the entire period hunting served as a considerable source of social tension, involving in various ways the complex and sometimes conflicting hierarchies of wealth, rank, and ownership of land. Since all hunting was ultimately within the warrant of the monarch, the monarchy was necessarily at the symbolic and legal center of such social conflict.[13] Not until the Game Act of 1671 did the squirearchy begin to dominate the sport as it did throughout the eighteenth century, giving rise to Blackstone's quip that "the forest laws established only one mighty hunter throughout the land, [but] the game laws have raised a little Nimrod in every manor."[14]

The social tensions within the culture of the hunt are apparent even in works that one might expect to represent a stable and coherent point of view. Gascoigne's *The Noble Arte of Venerie* is for the most part a straightforward translation of a French hunting manual, giving directions on the care of dogs, the blowing of horns, and the methods used to hunt fifteen different animals. The dominant tone of the work is celebratory. The 1575 edition features three original woodcuts of Elizabeth as a huntress and a preface, also original with Gascoigne, that justifies hunting in highly conventional terms. In his emphasis upon the nobility of hunting, however, Gascoigne situates himself in a way that reveals the ambiguity of his own relationship to the sport. At the end of a prefatory poem that celebrates hunting, his praise of the nobility of the sport is fraught with ironic tension. Hunting, he concludes, is

> A sport for Noble peeres, a sport for gentle bloods,
> The paine I leave for servants such, as beate the bushie woods,
>   To make their masters sport. Then let the Lords rejoyce,
> Let gentlemen beholde the glee, and take thereof the choyce.
>   For my part (being one) I must needes say my minde,
> That Hunting was ordeyned first, for Men of Noble kinde.
>   And unto them therefore, I recommend the same,
> As exercise that best becommes, their worthy noble name.[15]

Gascoigne reveals in this passage the ironies within his own social position. As a gentleman, he is at one remove from both the servants, who find nothing but pain in the sport, and the nobles, who find only pleasure. The choice he makes, and with self-mocking glee, is to align himself with the nobles.

The ironic self-awareness in this choice suggests the complexity of Gascoigne's own experience, which included an early life of privilege and recklessness, ruinous lawsuits that culminated in debtor's prison, and a disillusioning tour of several years in the military that he drew upon in his satiric poem on war, "Dulce Bellum Inexpertis."[16] Gascoigne returned to England from the Dutch wars in 1574; in 1575 he published *The Noble Arte of Venerie*, presumably as one part of his strategy to secure patronage and to re-establish himself within the Elizabethan court. In this sense, he himself was a kind of "beater" for the nobles he celebrates, and his self-mocking assertion of his position as a gentleman betrays the anxiety brought on by his equivocal social position. As we shall see later, the social and ideological tensions within the *Arte of Venerie* reveal much about the culture of the hunt in the period.

Gascoigne was not the only Elizabethan of equivocal social status attempting to secure privilege through the hunt. Throughout the period, but especially in the reign of James, a knowledge of hunting separated the elite from the would-be elite, and books like the *Arte of Venerie* were popular in part because they gave outsiders access to an esoteric lore from which they were otherwise excluded. Following his French original, Gascoigne is scrupulously careful to use the precise terms of the art, and he expresses some anxiety about the difficulty of getting them right. At the end of the work he lists the terms of venery, including the proper words for such things as the companies, ages, footing, excrements, and noises of beasts. The demands of this arcane language are awesome. One cannot speak of a "fayre Deare," for example, unless it is a roe deer; all others must be referred to as a "great Deare."[17] For the uninitiated, verbal pitfalls were everywhere. Shakespeare both delights in and mocks this wonderful zest for jargon in the conversations of Dull, Nathaniel, and Costard about the deer killed by the Princess in *Love's Labor's Lost*. Ben Jonson, more conventionally satirical, gives us the country gull, Master Stephen, in *Every Man In His Humour*: "why you know, an' a man have not skill in the hawking and hunting languages nowadays, I'll not give a rush for him. They are more studied than the Greek or the Latin. He is for no gallant's company without 'em."[18] Hunting was thus not merely a physical but a verbal sport, and one in which the mastery of words implied both power over nature and society.

In his depiction of hunters, Shakespeare stays realistically within the social boundaries of the Elizabethan and Jacobean hunt. Throughout the plays, as in Elizabethan society, the language, symbolism, and activity of the hunt center upon a social elite. With the exception of a few foresters or keepers, those who hunt in Shakespeare are invariably royalty, aristocracy, or privileged gentry. The only commoners who become significantly involved in the sport are Nathaniel, Holofernes, and Dull in *Love's Labor's Lost*, and their participation is restricted to accounts of a hunt that display endearingly their ignorance and ineptitude. Shakespeare also maintains the social hierarchy in the use of hunting language and allusions to the hunt. Commoners tend not to use hunting metaphors, for example, whereas they flow naturally from the lips of the higher orders. As we shall see later, the class tensions that often characterize the Elizabethan hunt find expression in the plays, but usually indirectly. Shakespeare's monarchs and nobility are never forced to defend the activity as the prerogative of a social elite. Instead, they assume their rightfulness as hunters; the forests and parks are their terrain, and they never feel the need to justify their privilege with appeals to the laws of the forests or the monarch's power. The only exception to this rule, as we shall see in chapter 2, is that of the Princess in *Love's Labor's Lost*, who questions the validity of the sport even as she engages in it.

The elevated status of the hunt in Elizabethan England makes it somewhat difficult to understand Shakespeare's obvious familiarity with and interest in the sport. Shakespeare grew up in the town of Stratford, so it is reasonable to assume that most of his early activities were those of town life; his father, John, was a glover and active in political affairs. The family must have spent some time in the country, however, for, through his wife, John owned a considerable estate at Wilmcote. Stratford, moreover, was surrounded by countryside. Warwickshire and Gloucestershire included numerous parks, among them that of Kenilworth, and the woodlands of the Forest of Arden ranged north of the Avon. At the very least, the young Shakespeare would have had opportunities to be an onlooker at hunts and to participate with other local youths as a beater.

Whether John Shakespeare would have been entitled to hunt is uncertain. Under Queen Elizabeth, the requirement consisted of ownership of land worth 40 shillings a year.[19] Although the annual income of the estate at Wilmcote is not known, the property seems to have been large enough to meet that test; in 1578, when pressed for ready cash, John was able to mortgage the house and 56 acres and, in addition, to convey another 86 acres. At the peak of his prosperity (probably 1565–71), John Shakespeare was a substantial citizen. A note appended to the 1596 application for a coat of arms asserts that during this period he was "a justice of the peace and bailiff, and a Queen's officer; that he had 'Landes and tenementes of good wealth.& Substance,' worth £500; and that he had taken for his wife the daughter of a gentleman of worship."[20] Given the dramatic decline in John's fortunes in the early 1570s, it is possible that young William was reaching puberty at the very time at which his father was losing the privilege of hunting. If so, his position would have been not unlike that of the small gentry, landless gentlemen, and yeomen who, according to Manning, "were the cause of a disproportionate amount of the riotous hunting in early modern England."[21] Perhaps the combination of youth and social resentment made young William a poacher.

As a playwright, Shakespeare would certainly have been exposed to the culture of the hunt, especially because both hunting and theater played important roles at court and at aristocratic festivities. Many members of his audiences would have been avid hunters. Once he became prosperous as a shareholder in his acting company, Shakespeare himself would have probably met the economic requirements for hunting; in May of 1602, he paid £320 for about 120 acres of arable land in Old Stratford. In 1610 this "freehold" was described as "consisting of 107 acres of land, and 20 of pasture." If, as Schoenbaum suggests, the recorded price for properties was habitually understated by a wide margin, then it is likely that such an investment would have yielded a return of at least 40 shillings a year.[22] In view of the essentially urban nature of his existence, however, it is highly unlikely that Shakespeare would have availed himself often of the privilege of hunting, even if he had it.

If Shakespeare achieved the right to hunt in 1602, a Parliamentary act of 1603 would almost certainly have taken the privilege away. And not coincidentally. In order to exclude social climbers like Shakespeare, to keep the sport within the higher gentry and aristocracy, James I initiated changes to the game laws in 1603–4, 1605–6, and 1609–10 that made them much more severely restrictive. Each act provided three categories within which Shakespeare could have been permitted to hunt. The 1603 act required freehold ownership of land worth £10 a year (increased to £40 a year in 1605); copyhold ownership of land worth £30 a year (increased to £80 in 1609); or possession of goods and chattels to the value of £200 (increased to £400 in 1609).[23] If Shakespeare fit within any of these categories, which seems unlikely, it was probably the latter; the recorded purchase price of New Place was only £60 in 1597, however, and that of the London house in the exclusive Blackfriars district only £140 in 1613. As a playwright and shareholder, then, it is unlikely that Shakespeare participated directly in the culture of the hunt. Nonetheless, his company's increasing ties with the world of the court would have given him many opportunities to indulge himself vicariously in its pleasures.

Although frustrating, the uncertainty about whether Shakespeare hunted or was entitled to hunt leads to an interesting conclusion: throughout his life Shakespeare was situated – economically, socially, and geographically – on the margins of the culture of the hunt. He grew up a town boy but had easy access to the country. He prospered in the popular London theater as an actor and shareholder but also cultivated courtly audiences, including James I himself, devoted to the hunt. He sealed his success at his craft by securing a coat of arms for his family and by buying land in and around Stratford, suggesting an affinity with the upwardly mobile in society who, like Master Stephen in *Every Man In His Humour*, struggled to learn the "hawking and hunting languages" because they were "more studied than the Greek or the Latin" and provided access to the company of gallants. If excluded from the privilege of hunting, Shakespeare was never hopelessly removed from that world. If included, he was never placed securely within it, as were the country gentry and aristocracy. He could thus combine a direct or indirect knowledge of the sport with critical detachment.

Whatever his exact social relationship to the hunt, Shakespeare's exploitation of its imagery is unique among dramatists of the period. One poem and eight of the plays include hunting scenes or episodes, and hunting imagery recurs throughout the canon. Shakespeare's plays are exceptional not only in the frequency of their allusions to the hunt but in the impression of technical mastery and experiential knowledge that these allusions convey. Ben Jonson, Shakespeare's closest competitor in numbers of allusions to the hunt, conveys in contrast only a bookish knowledge and is drawn to the subject primarily for topical satire or for courtly celebration of the monarch. Shakespeare's easy mastery of the sport has led some writers, such as D. H. Madden, to assume that he was himself an avid hunter. Madden, whose *Diary of Master William Silence* demonstrates in overwhelming detail Shakespeare's technical knowledge of the hunt, concludes that he was "beyond doubt a sportsman, with the rare skill in the mysteries of woodcraft, loving to recall the very names of the hounds with which he was wont to hunt . . ."[24] Others, however, equally impressed by Shakespeare's easy familiarity with the sport, have come to the opposite conclusion: both Caroline Spurgeon and Matt Cartmill, for example, argue that Shakespeare disliked hunting.[25] We shall examine the question of Shakespeare's "attitude" towards hunting in chapter 8, where I shall attempt to widen the arguments of Spurgeon and Cartmill. To a great extent, this study situates Shakespeare within the anti-hunting discourses of the Elizabethan and Jacobean periods.

The power of the culture of the hunt in Shakespeare's day can be seen at a glance in the county maps of John Speed, where forests are represented by clusters of trees, and parks by circles of fences (fig. 7). Most hunting, it seems, took place in parks, which are prominent features in the landscape of almost all counties; Derbyshire alone had thirty-six.[26] Susan Lasdun counts eight hundred and seventeen parks identified in the county maps made by Christopher Saxton between 1575 and 1580.[27] William Harrison, who lamented the economic and social consequences of such a wasteful use of land, scoffed also at the self-indulgent and frivolous kind of hunting the parks encouraged. Harrison estimates that "the twentieth part of the realm is employed upon deer and conies."[28] When the Duke of Stettin visited England in 1602, he noted that "'there is scarcely any royal residence, or even a nobleman's house, which has not at least one deer park – sometimes two, or even three, may be found.'"[29] Shakespeare's *Love's Labor's Lost*, as we shall see, is set in such a park, and the play evokes the ethos of sophisticated and frivolous cruelty that social critics like Harrison treat with considerably less urbanity than Shakespeare.

The number of parks throughout England testifies to the paramount status of deer hunting throughout the period. Other kinds of hunting were routinely indulged in. Coursing of hare was popular, occasionally being considered even superior to hunting deer.[30] The hunting manuals, moreover, usually provide instruction for hunting other animals, such as conies, badger, fox, and otter, although it is clear that such hunting enjoyed neither the status nor the ceremonial appeal of the deer hunt. Fox hunting, which has come to dominate the mythology of the hunt in modern England, did not begin to achieve its present status until the late seventeenth century, after the massive depletion of deer stocks during the Civil Wars. For most hunters of the sixteenth century, foxes were vermin, to be hunted without ennobling ceremony – as in King Lear's image of Cordelia and himself being "fire[d]" out of a hole "like foxes"

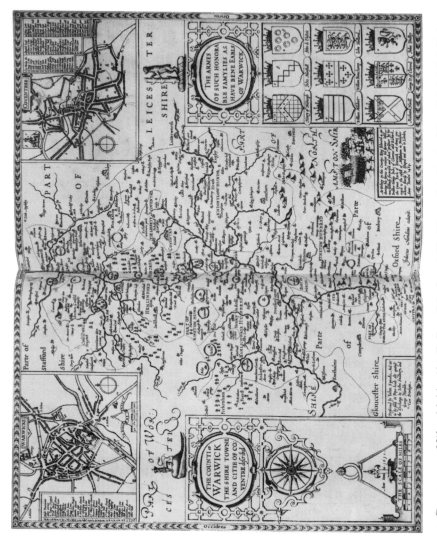

7 County map of Warwickshire (detail). From John Speed, *The Theatre of the Empire of Great Britain* (1611). Parks are shown as fenced enclosures.

(5.3.23). Because of its social importance during the Tudor and Stuart period, its long-standing artistic and literary significance, and its centrality in Shakespeare, the deer hunt will be our focal point throughout this study.

As objects of the chase, deer were arranged into a shifting but more or less hierarchical order, according to size, appearance, age, and gender. The largest and noblest were the red deer. A male red deer, the largest animal hunted in England, was usually called a "hart" after it had reached six years, although sometimes the term was restricted to an animal with at least ten tines. A male red deer of five years was called a "stag." The hunting handbooks, however, do not always distinguish the two categories. The female of the red deer was a "hind." Harts and stags were prized for their size, their magnificent antlers, their power, and their stamina in the hunt. Slightly lower in the hierarchy were the fallow deer, divided into buck and doe. These were the most common deer to be found in parks. Smaller and less impressive physically than the stag, the buck was nonetheless prized for its meat, which some judged superior. Finally, the smallest and least significant were the roe deer, also divided into buck (or roebuck) and doe. Shakespeare's allusions to deer are invariably attuned to their social and cultural connotations. The association of the stag with kingship, for example, affects our perception of both Henry VI and Edward IV in *3 Henry VI*, and of Julius Caesar in the play of the same name. When Falstaff dons horns in *Merry Wives*, the rich comic symbolism evoked by the gesture includes mock-usurpation, since he imagines himself a "Windsor stag" (5.5.12–13).

Three kinds of deer hunting dominated the sport in the period: *par force de chiens*, bow and stable, and coursing with greyhounds.[31] The former was the most physically demanding and, conventionally, the noblest and most masculine kind of hunt. In its royal or ceremonial form, which was highly ritualized, this hunt took place in field and forest and was roughly divided into five stages: the entry of the hunters into the forest; the consumption of an elaborate breakfast in a forest clearing, featuring reports of the huntsmen and the planning of the hunt; the chase of a single deer located earlier by the huntsmen; the baying, death, and dismemberment of the deer, and the rewarding of the dogs; and finally, the return of the hunting party to the court, climaxed with another feast. As its name implies, this kind of hunting depended upon the ability of the dogs to pursue the deer by its scent and to run it to its death. In his book of advice to the young Prince Henry, *Basilicon Doron*, James I praises this kind of hunting, "with running hounds," as "the most honourable and noblest sorte thereof." James dismisses shooting with guns and bows as a "theevish forme" of hunting, and notes that "greyhound hunting," or coursing, "is not so martiall a game."[32]

Although disapproved of by James, bow and stable hunting and coursing, both more appropriate to parks or chases than forests, were also very popular in the period. Shakespeare depicts bow and stable hunting in the Princess's hunt in *Love's Labor's Lost*. In the most common form of such a hunt, deer were driven before stationary hunters armed with cross-bows, who were positioned in ambushes or specially constructed stands. Greyhounds, which hunted by sight rather than scent, were often used in such hunts, both to chase the deer to the waiting hunters and to run down those that had been wounded. Whereas bow and stable hunting required at least the effort of shooting an arrow, coursing in parks was essentially a spectator sport, with observers stationed on stands en route or even in rooms with views of the chase. A description of coursing deer appears in the account of the Queen's visit to Cowdray in 1591: on one evening she watched from a turret while sixteen bucks were pulled down by greyhounds in the clearing below.[33] That morning she had used a cross-bow to kill about three or four of thirty deer enclosed in a paddock; the account does not specify whether she shot at random or whether the deer were driven before her in a rather constricted version of the bow and stable hunt.

Descriptions of hunting in parks suggest that, unlike *par force* hunting, this sport was not considered an end in itself, an action invested with the significance of ritual, but an adjunct to courtly pageantry.[34] The principal objection to the sport, as we have seen in the case of King James, was its easiness. In *The Governor*, Thomas Elyot dismisses bow and stable hunting as serving "well for the pot (as is the common saying)" but as containing "no commendable solace or exercise, in comparison to the other forms of hunting."[35] Theodore Roosevelt, commenting on descriptions in Edward, Duke of York's *The Master of Game*, found such easy kinds of hunting to be "debased," "contemptible," and guilty of "luxurious and effeminate artificiality" – "dismal [parodies] upon the stern hunting life in which the man trusts to his own keen eye, stout thews, and heart of steel for success and safety in the wild warfare waged against wild nature."[36] In their attitudes towards hunting, Roosevelt, Elyot, and James I had much in common.

Accounts of hunting in the period show that, despite its affinities with ritual, the sport could be conducted in a great variety of ways, and much of the evidence is so fragmentary that it is often difficult to discover what kind of hunting is envisaged. At times, the methods must have been very casual indeed, as when Henry VIII indulged in impromptu hunts while traveling on progress around the countryside. A letter from the French ambassador to Francis I in 1541, for example, records that King Henry's "fashion of proceeding in this progress is, wherever there are deer numerous, to enclose 200 or 300 and then send in many greyhounds to kill them, that he may share them among the gentlemen of the country and of his Court . . . "[37] It is difficult to imagine that such impromptu slaughter was accompanied with elaborate ceremony. The ritual attached to the hunt must have varied greatly, depending upon the animal hunted, the rank of the participants, and the occasion of the hunt.

As Roger B. Manning has shown, illegal hunting was also extremely common in the period and extremely disruptive. "Of all the species of disorder in England," Manning observes, "probably only the Civil Wars of the seventeenth century were more injurious to royal government and aristocratic privilege than the phenomenon of large-scale, organized poaching."[38] Illegal hunting of this kind could also take many different forms. The stereotypical image of the poacher that developed in eighteenth and nineteenth-century novels, however, that of a poor tenant setting snares for rabbits in the lord's woods, is of relatively little importance in the period. Such poaching no doubt took place, but the kind that most captured the public eye, and most obsessed the gentry, aristocracy, and, above all, King James, was far more serious and destructive. In such acts of poaching, the ceremonial of the hunt was flagrantly undermined, with riotous bands of hunters storming through a park at night, terrorizing the keepers, massacring deer, and leaving them to rot as an insult to their owner. Manning argues that such riotous hunting was a symbolic substitute for war, a method by which socially rebellious gentry and their followers could vent aggression and pursue their own vendettas.

Poaching of this kind, as we shall see especially when considering *Merry Wives*, substituted for the noble ceremonial of the hunt an inverted mock-ceremonial, of the sort customary in rituals of inversion, such as the charivari. When a gang of hunters went after the deer of Sir Thomas More's father, for example, they "impaled the head of a buck upon a staff with a stick in its mouth facing towards the manor house."[39] Manning suggests that this ritual insult may have been prompted by More's illegal enclosure of land for a park.

Deer could be killed, in sum, by a wide variety of methods and in a wide variety of modes, ranging from the highly ritualized – what Shakespeare calls in *Titus Andronicus* a "solemn hunting" (2.1.112) – through various stages of decreasing formality to casual slaughter or to the grotesque and inverted ritualism of poaching.

Shakespeare, as we have seen, may have been a likely candidate for poaching as an adolescent in Stratford. By far the most popular of the stories of Shakespeare's youth is that in which his very origin as a poet and dramatist is attributed to misadventures in this illicit sport. The story appears in print for the first time in Nicholas Rowe's 1709 edition of the works of Shakespeare. According to Rowe, as a youth Shakespeare fell into the company of some local youths prone to deer-stealing. He was severely prosecuted for that offense by Sir Thomas Lucy of Charlecote, near Stratford, and revenged himself by writing a satirical ballad upon him. This had the unfortunate effect of increasing Sir Thomas's desire to prosecute him, to the extent that he was forced to leave Stratford for London. Another version, by the Reverend William Fulman, written independently of Rowe and several decades earlier, adds the rather garbled information that Shakespeare's revenge extended to depicting Sir Thomas as his "'Justice Clodpate and calls him a great man and that in allusion to his name bore three louses rampant for his arms.'"[40] Fulman refers unmistakably to the pompous Justice Shallow in *Merry Wives*, whose coat of arms, according to Slender, includes a "dozen white luces" (a species of pike), provoking Evans to make the inevitable but unconscious pun: "the dozen white louses do become an old coat well" (1.1.16–20). In *Shakespeare's Lives,* Schoenbaum notes that "on a Lucy tomb at Warwick the three luces on the coat are repeated four times – thus providing the dozen to which Slender refers."[41] Schoenbaum discusses two other less reliable sources, Joshua Barnes and Thomas Jones, before concluding that "the deer-poaching legend has thus come down from several autonomous sources . . . all (it would seem) stemming ulti-mately from Stratford gossip."[42]

Although he is appropriately skeptical about the story, Schoenbaum cannot dismiss it out of hand. The evidence, though not compelling, is substantial enough to warrant serious treatment. The counter-argu-ments, moreover, are inconclusive. That Sir Thomas did not have a legal park but a free warren, for example, does not rule out the story, as Schoenbaum admits, because roe deer, unlike red and fallow deer, were considered beasts of warren. Although Schoenbaum finds it unlikely that Shakespeare would wait fourteen years before satirizing Lucy, he also admits the extreme difficulty of interpreting the passage in *Merry*

Wives without Fulman's gloss. He concludes, finally, that although most responsible modern scholars have rejected the episode as "traditionary romance," some have not; among the exceptions are scholars of the stature of E. K. Chambers, whose account covers the essential evidence.[43] The story, in short, is not easily dismissed. Whether true or not, however, as Roger B. Manning observes, it tells us something important about popular culture in the period: "that poaching was a usual rite of passage for the youth who wanted to assert his manhood or lay claim to genteel status."[44]

It should be clear from all of the examples above, legal or illegal, that the object of killing game in the Elizabethan and Jacobean period was neither the protection nor the sustenance of society. Society did not need to be protected from deer, especially since most of the deer lived within fences and the common farmers whose crops might have been vulnerable were not entitled to hunt in any case. Like some modern hunters, Elizabethan hunters ate what they killed, but the feasting was incidental to the joy of the chase and the status it both required and confirmed. If an Elizabethan lord desired venison, he did not need to hunt for it; a deer could be culled from a herd in his park for dinner at any time by his mere command. The venison collected at a hunt was a trophy, like the antlers, not a necessity; it was consumed in feasting or distributed as a sign of privilege among friends, dependants, and retainers. As Manning observes, "gifts of venison solidified alliances and traditional relationships."[45] In *Merry Wives,* Justice Shallow gives Master Page enough meat for a venison pasty, a gesture not unconnected to his desire to arrange a match between his nephew Silence and Mistress Anne Page. In *Titus Andronicus*, this custom is grossly parodied, with Titus serving Tamora a pasty composed of her sons.

Since hunting could not be justified in terms of social or economic necessity, two other rationales were repeatedly invoked: that of recreation, and that of war. In the *Gentleman's Recreation* (1686), Richard Blome summarizes what he takes to be the conventional encomiums for the sport, highlighting its recreational value:

To Tell you that *Hunting* is a commendable *Recreation*, and hath always been practised and highly prized by all *Degrees* and *Qualities* of *Men*, even by *Kings* and *Princes;* that it is a great preserver of *Health*, a Manly *Exercise*, and an increaser of *Activity;* that it recreates the *Mind*, strengthens the *Limbs*, and whets the *Stomach*; and that no *Musick* is more charming to the *Ears* of *Man*, than a *Pack* of *Hounds* in full *Cry* is to him that delights in *Hunting*, is to tell you that which experimentally is known, and what hath been sufficiently treated of by others . . .[46]

For Blome the hunt is not merely a recreation but a "commendable" recreation, what Nathaniel in *Love's Labor's Lost* calls a "very reverent sport" (4.2.1). As such, it does not merely preserve health, promote manliness, relax the mind, and provide the emotional and esthetic satisfaction of the cry of the hounds; it also confers the social advantage of association with kings and princes.

In law, as we have seen, a forest served only a recreational purpose, that of protecting wildlife for the "princely delight and pleasure" of the monarch. As might be expected, James I was not shy in asserting this right; in an address to Parliament on the need for laws to protect the forests, for example, he mentioned the importance of the forests for the maintenance of the navy, for fuel, and for "sports and pleasure, which is for my honor."[47] Unlike John Evelyn, who in *Sylva* (1664) tried to persuade the aristocracy that planting trees was a nobler recreation than hunting, James argued that trees were important mainly because they served the noble sport of the hunt.[48] The monarch's honor alone could thus be used to justify the hunt. More commonly, however, James defended his controversial activity on the ground of his health, as he did, for example, in a letter to his Privy Council that formalized governmental procedures during his absences in pursuit of the "open air and exercise" necessary "even in strongest bodies."[49] The hunting manuals too make much of health, citing the benefits of early rising, the open air, the avoidance of idleness, and physical exercise in general. This tendency to define hunting as a means towards some other end rather than as an end in itself typifies the mixture of moral earnestness and evasiveness found in rationales for the sport, which allowed most writers to ignore the challenging question of whether killing animals for pleasure alone was justifiable.

For those who pursued the question, the answer was generally affirmative. Implicit in any justification for hunting in the period was the conventional Christian view, outlined usefully by Keith Thomas, which sanctioned hunting as falling within the biblical injunction that nature was to be controlled by man.[50] Although this view did not sanction wanton cruelty to animals, it justified hunting, and was often cited in sermons when the issue arose, even, as we shall see, in sermons by Puritans, whose view towards the sport was generally critical.

As a mode of recreation, hunting was public, ceremonial, and often festive. It could be used as a pageant to celebrate and entertain the Queen, as at Cowdray in 1591 or at Hatfield in 1557, where the young princess was met on the way to a hunt by fifty archers wearing scarlet boots and yellow caps and armed with gilded bows, one of whom "presented her a silver-headed arrow, winged with peacock's feathers."[51] It could be used to impress foreign dignitaries. It could add to the holiday atmosphere of extended festivities, such as weddings and christenings. Roger B. Manning notes that "a popular belief seems to have existed that no celebration or special occasion was complete without a bit of hunting."[52] The sport also provided an opportunity for competition and wagering, either on relatively private occasions or in public festivities, such as the Cotswold games.[53] The association of wagering and marriage festivities with hunting, as we shall see, underlies Shakespeare's depiction of the wager on wives at the end of *The Taming of the Shrew*.

Shakespeare's representations of the hunt often evoke this recreational mode. In *3 Henry VI* kings are allowed to exercise themselves by hunting in captivity. In the *Taming of the Shrew* a noble lord hunts for his personal recreation and amusement. In *Love's Labor's Lost* the Princess is honored by a hunt of the kind that Queen Elizabeth might have arranged for a foreign ambassador. In *A Midsummer Night's Dream*, Theseus and Hippolyta hunt as part of their wedding festivities. In the comedies Shakespeare accentuates the notion of communal bonding implicit in the recreational hunt by repeatedly associating hunting with love and marriage. In the tragedies hunting is more likely to be linked with war or, as in *Titus Andronicus*, developed in such a way that the ritual of communion is grotesquely parodied and inverted. Titus invites Saturninus to a "solemn hunting" (2.1.112) in honor of his marriage, but the forest becomes a setting not for social harmony but for rape, mutilation, and murder.

Far more important than the recreational justification for hunting in the period was the militaristic, which promoted the sport as a training ground in the arts of war. Sir Thomas Cockaine's argument in *A Short Treatise of Hunting* (1591) is typical:

And for the first commendation of Hunting, I find (Gentlemen) by my owne experience in Hunting, that Hunters by their continuall travaile, painfull labour, often watching, and enduring of hunger, of heate, and of cold, are much enabled above others to the service of their Prince and Countrey in the warres, having their bodies for the most part by reason of their continuall exercise in much better health, than other men have, and their minds also by this honest recreation the more fit and the better disposed to all other good exercises.[54]

Machiavelli advises princes never to turn their mind "from the study of war" and to do "a great deal of hunting" in order to harden the body and master the terrain.[55] In the *Governor*, Sir Thomas Elyot carries this argument to an extreme, approving only the kind of hunting that comes closest to war itself. His model is the hunting described in Xenophon's *Cyropaedia*, which includes education in justice and temperance, vigorous exercise, exposure to extreme physical hardship, the use of bows, swords, or hatchets, fasting while hunting, and eating only what was killed. Lamenting the softness of hunting in contemporary England, Elyot recommends the use of "javelins and other weapons, in manner of war."[56] Even James I, who never tired of lecturing his people on his need to hunt for the sake of his health alone, draws upon Xenophon in his *Basilicon Doron* to support his preference for the *par force* hunt as a more "martiall" game than hunting with greyhounds.[57] Robert Peake's painting of Prince Henry demonstrating his prowess before a slain deer embodies this militaristic notion of the hunt, even to the point of implying, in the extreme youth of the prince, an initiatory function. The youth who can achieve mastery over a deer promises to be a warrior.

The military rationales for hunting in the period are invariably nostalgic and anti-technological. Elyot's idealization of Xenophon's description of the hunt in *Cyropaedia*, his attempt to promote the javelin as the most warlike of hunting weapons, James I's aversion to the use of guns as a "theevish forme of hunting" – these are all symptoms of a desire to make of hunting an elemental test of man's power. In some respects this impulse confirms Ortega y Gasset's view of hunting: "in hunting man succeeds, in effect, in annihilating all historical evolution, in separating himself from the present, and in renewing the primitive situation."[58] For Ortega y Gasset this meant strolling in the woods accompanied with no more than a dog and gun. For James I, it meant racing through the forests on horseback, sword at the side, in the midst of a throng of dogs, foresters, and fellow huntsmen.

The obvious institutional power behind the leading justifications for the hunt, which are found in the handbooks for governors, the hunting manuals, the church, and even the speeches and writings of James I himself, should not obscure the fact that hunting was a source of considerable ideological controversy and social tension throughout the period. Although the ideological opposition appears in many different quarters and guises, three main strands are dominant. The first in time and importance is that which might be called broadly the humanist opposition, led by such figures as More, Erasmus, and Agrippa. The second might be called the sentimental opposition, embodied most powerfully in Montaigne, who stands almost alone in his detailed condemnation of the cruelty of the hunt, but whose moral sensitivity resonates in other authors. The third might be called the Puritan opposition, which developed mainly during the reign of James I. Since all three provide a potential backdrop for Shakespeare's treatment of the hunt, they are worth individual attention in some detail.

As Robert P. Adams has shown, the satiric attacks on hunting by early sixteenth-century humanists such as Erasmus and More were closely related to their opposition to war.[59] Instead of celebrating the hunt for its capacity to initiate young men into the strategies and hardships of war, they attacked it for its cruelty and its tendency to brutalize. In *Utopia*, the Utopians regard hunting "as a thynge unworthye to be used of free men," relegating the activity to butchers, who are all slaves, and for whom hunting is a lower occupation than butchery, being unnecessary. The so-called pleasure of the hunt, according to Utopians, is no more than a pleasure in killing or mutilation, and it either reveals a cruel disposition or creates one, the hunter losing his humanity "by longe use of so cruell a pleasure."[60] Erasmus takes a similar view in *Praise of Folly*. [61] Throughout his plays, Shakespeare draws upon this connection between hunting and human violence.

As we shall see when we consider *Titus Andronicus* and *Julius Caesar*, some of Shakespeare's most aggressive images of the hunt probably derive not from legitimate hunting but from poaching, which, as Roger Manning has shown, constituted in the period a kind of symbolic warfare. When King Edward's brothers rescue him from captivity in *3 Henry VI*, they jestingly refer to themselves as poachers, stealing the "Bishop's deer" (4.5.17). In *Titus Andronicus* the attack on Lavinia is conceived as an episode of poaching, in which Lavinia becomes a "doe" taken in secret and "borne . . . cleanly by the keeper's nose" (2.1.93–94). In *As You Like It*, Duke Senior and his men are technically poaching, since they live as outlaws, taking deer from land that is under the authority of Duke Frederick. Justice Shallow accuses Falstaff of poaching his deer in *Merry Wives of Windsor*, and the motif of wild and disorderly hunting runs throughout the play.

The most savage humanist critique of hunting in the sixteenth century is that of Agrippa in *Of the Vanitie and Uncertaintie of Artes and Sciences* (1530). Both more scathing and more systematic than either More or Erasmus, Agrippa finds hunting a "detestable" and "cruell Arte," one that leads men to set "all humanitie apart" and "become salvage beastes." Following Augustine, Agrippa locates the origin of hunting in the act of original sin, which ended forever the peace between men and animals. When God said to the serpent, "I will set hatred betweene thee

and the woman, and betweene thy seede and her seede," asserts
Agrippa, "of this sentence the battail of huntinge tooke his beginning."
Throughout history, then, hunting is a "battle" and a symptom of
human depravity: it is linked to "wicked menne and sinners" like
Nimrod and Cain in the Bible, and to wicked nations like that of the
Thebans. In contemporary Europe, according to Agrippa, kings,
princes, nobles, and even churchmen devote their lives exclusively to
hunting, driving farmers from their farms and herdsmen from their pastures. "Huntinge," he says, "was the beginninge of Tyrannye, because it
findeth no Authoure more meete then him, whiche hathe learned to
dispise God, and nature, in the slaughter and boocherie of wilde beastes,
and in the spillinge of bloude."[62] Agrippa's connection between hunting
and tyranny also appears in the beast fable told by Philisides in Sidney's
Old Arcadia; in this account, the final stage of man's tyranny over the
animals is reached when he turns to killing them not for food but "for
sport."[63] Shakespeare draws most directly upon the association of
hunting with tyranny, as we shall see in chapter 7, in his treatment of
Prospero's hunt of Caliban.

Agrippa's notion that hunting appears only as a consequence of original sin implies that life in Eden was vegetarian. The idea of an original
and lost age of peace between humans and animals was available during
the period in both biblical and classical versions, often interrelated. The
account of creation in the King James version of Genesis seems to imply
a vegetarian regimen (1:28–30), with meat eating sanctioned only with
the establishment of the new covenant after the flood (9:2–4). The image
of the New Jerusalem in Isaiah supports the many conventional depictions of Eden as a peaceable kingdom, in which "the wolf and the lamb
shall feed together" (65:25). In Ovid's *Metamorphoses*, the most popular
classical source for images of the Golden Age, hunting is associated with
the decline of human society that takes place in the age of iron.
Although the account of the four stages of civilization – Golden, Silver,
Bronze, and Iron – offered in Book I does not refer specifically to the
invention of hunting, the narrative implies that humans turned to killing
animals in the Iron Age, an age that also marks the introduction of war.
In Book XV, when Ovid gives voice to Pythagoras, the association
between social decline and hunting becomes explicit. Pythagoras, who
espouses both vegetarianism and the doctrine of transmigration of
souls, argues that neither hunting nor fishing occurred in the Golden
Age. Meat eating began only with the imitation of lions, and was the first

step humans took "on the road to crime."[64] We shall return to such Edenic and Golden Age thinking when considering Prospero's hunt in *The Tempest*.

Montaigne alludes to both Pythagorean and Christian attitudes towards animals in his critique of hunting in the essay "Of Cruelty." His starting point, however, as always, is his observation of his own most intimate feelings and behavior. Noting that he hates cruelty above all other vices, he admits that he cannot bear even to see "a chickins neck pulld off" or to hear the "groane" of "a seely dew-bedabled hare . . . when she is seized upon by the howndes." In discussing the capacity of emotion to overwhelm reason, Montaigne finds the pleasure of sexual passion less compelling than the surprise of the chase: "whereby our reason being amazed, looseth the leasure to prepare her selfe against it: when as after a long questing and beating for some game, the beast doth sodainely start, or rowze up before us, and happily [perhaps] in such a place, where we least expected the same." Montaigne's account of the irresistible excitement of the hunt – the "riding, and the earnestnes of showting, jubeting and hallowing, still ringing in our eares" – captures the primitive quality of the chase that Ortega y Gasset celebrates: "Suddenly the orgiastic element shoots forth, the dionysiac, which flows and boils in the depths of all hunting."[65] Despite his susceptibility to these emotions, Montaigne recoils at the suffering imposed upon the animal: "As for me, I could never so much as endure, without remorce and griefe, to see a poore, silly, and innocent beast pursued and killed, which is harmeles and voide of defence, and of whom we receive no offence at all."

In its remarkable candor and complexity, Montaigne's view of the hunt offers us a unique glimpse into the subjective experience it provided for at least one exceptional figure in the sixteenth century. His aversion to cruelty, however, although rarely articulated in such detail or with such sensitivity to animal suffering, can be found in other writers in the period as well, such as More and Agrippa, or, much later, Margaret Cavendish, Duchess of Newcastle, whose "The Hunting of the Hare" (1653) is the most powerful anti-hunting poem of the early modern period in England.[66] Sometimes, however, the persistent metaphoric identity of animal with human suffering makes it difficult to tell whose pain is really at issue. When Jaques sits beside a stream in *As You Like It*, for example, and moralizes upon the death of the sobbing deer, his language so confuses deer behavior with human behavior that one is tempted to say that the "real" subjects of the passage are not animals at all but human beings. What seems to be sensitivity to animal suffering, in short, may actually be satiric contempt for the human condition. We shall deal with these ambiguities later in relation to *As You Like It* .

An interesting example of this interpretative problem occurs in Gascoigne's *Arte of Venerie*, a hunting manual that paradoxically gives voice to four of the victims themselves. After describing the methods of hunting the hart, hare, fox, and otter, Gascoigne provides poems for each animal, in which the animal itself laments its fate and accuses humans of cruelty, hypocrisy, and immorality. The sudden shift in perspective from technical descriptions of chasing, killing, and dismembering prey to poetic laments spoken by the animals themselves forces the reader to perceive the hunt as a moral problem. Although Matt Cartmill suggests that the device might have been intended as a joke and therefore might imply no true sympathy for the animals themselves, Gascoigne's ambiguous social position and his cynicism towards war are more likely to have made him genuinely ambivalent about the very art that he describes.[67]

Although its significance may sometimes be uncertain, an emerging sympathy for animals is certainly evident in the period, particularly among English Puritans of the middle and late seventeenth century. The theological basis for this view is to be found in the biblical doctrine of stewardship. Keith Thomas quotes John Calvin, who argues that God "will not have us abuse the beasts beyond measure . . . but to nourish them and to have care of them. . . If a man spare neither his horse nor his ox nor his ass, therein he betrayeth the wickedness of his nature. And if he say, 'Tush, I care not, for it is but a brute beast,' I answer again, 'Yea, but it is a creature of God.'"[68] While this view mitigated against cruelty to animals, both wild and domestic, it was rarely used, as in Montaigne or Cavendish, to attack hunting. Both Luther and Calvin accepted hunting as a proper recreation, if conducted in moderation. The Puritan John Downame, in *A Guide to Godlynesse* (1629), lists hunting, hawking, fishing, and fowling among lawful recreations, but courting, gambling, theater-going, and dancing as unlawful. For most Puritans, attending Shakespeare's plays was more likely to lead to sin than killing deer.

Puritans who protested against hunting were less concerned with cruelty to animals than with the social abuses attendant upon the sport – the destruction of property through the wanton pursuit of deer across farmers' fields, the waste of time, and the waste of resources that might have been used to alleviate poverty. In *The Anatomie of Abuses*, Philip Stubbes expresses the Puritan viewpoint with unusual succinctness:

If necessitie or want of other meats inforceth us to seek after their [animals'] lives, it is lawfull to use them in the feare of God, with thanks to his name: but for our pastimes and vain pleasures sake, wee are not in any wise to spoyle or hurt them. Is he a christian man or rather a pseudo-christian, that delighteth in blood? . . . Is hee a Christian that buieth up the corne of the poor, turning it into bread (as many doo) to feed dogs for his pleasure? Is hee a christian that liveth to the hurt of his Neighbour in treading and breaking down his hedges, in casting open his gates in trampling of his corne . . .?[69]

According to Stubbes, hunting should be conducted only in necessity, and in fear and gratitude towards God.

Justifying hunting as a necessity, however, was exceedingly difficult. Gascoigne's otter attacks the hypocrisy of this traditional religious defence by reminding humans of their insatiable gluttony:

> Well yet mee thinkes, I heare him preache this Texte,
> *Howe all that is, was made for use of man:*
> So was it sure, but therewith followes next,
> *This heavie place, expounde it who so can:*
> *The very Scourge and Plague of God his Ban,*
> Will lyght on suche as queyntly can devise
> To eate more meate, than may their mouthes suffise.[70]

Given the fact that hunting was not necessary for food, most Puritans defined recreation itself as a necessity, although Stubbes's position is somewhat ambiguous. Wanton destruction and cruelty, however, are clearly indefensible: not only sinful in themselves but leading to uncharitable actions towards fellow human beings. Under James I the Puritan argument against hunting became part of a broader assault upon the policies and practices of the monarchy, as we shall see when we consider Shakespeare's treatment of Prospero's hunt in *The Tempest*.

The Puritan concern for the poor shows that the opposition to the hunt was not merely ideological but also economic and social. As we have seen, hunting was a highly visible sign of privilege, and the vast parks and forests set aside for the pursuit of that privilege, defined as recreation, could not help but be an irritant, both literally and symbolically, to the less privileged. Unfortunately, the views of commoners on the hunt are rarely recorded, except indirectly, as in the diatribes of Puritan ministers such as Philip Stubbes. Although the wholesale destruction of hunting parks during the Civil Wars had many causes, the most important was probably popular rage against a repressive social custom. The rage was vented not just against parks but the deer within them, symbols of aristocratic privilege. As E. P. Thompson observes, "there was an

ancient enmity between democracy and these gentle creatures."
Thompson shows that in Windsor Forest alone the deer population
declined from 3066 in 1607 to 461 in 1697, despite efforts to replenish the
herds during the Restoration.[71]

In his *Description of England* (1587), William Harrison, whose sympa-
thies inclined strongly in the direction of the Puritan reform movement,
generalizes this kind of local resentment by placing the hunt within a
contemporary social and economic framework. For Harrison, the practice of hunting, particularly as manifested in the keeping of parks, was
dangerously destructive. The keeping of deer, he says, is of no economic
benefit to their owners, for deer cannot be sold and are merely
exchanged as gifts. The reduction of arable land necessary to the
support of parks leads owners to enclose common lands, which impov-
erishes and dislocates the common people and causes under population.
The lack of population means a lack of soldiers, and consequent military weakness for the kingdom. In his chapter entitled "Of Savage
Beasts and Vermins," Harrison notes with admiration the hunting habits
of monarchs of the past: Alexander the Great, for example, hunted tiger,
boar, and lions; Henry I "loved to hunt the lion and the boar"; and
Henry V "thought it a mere scoffery to pursue any fallow deer with
hounds or greyhounds, but supposed himself always to have done a
sufficient act when he had tired them by his own travel on foot and so
killed them with his hands in the upshot of that exercise and end of his
recreation." In contrast to these heroic pursuits, the hunting of fallow
deer and conies in parks, and even the hunting of the stag are "pastimes
more meet for ladies and gentlewomen to exercise . . . than for men of
courage to follow, whose hunting should practice their arms in tasting of
their manhood and dealing with such beasts as efstoons will turn again
and offer them the hardest [danger] rather than their horses' feet, which
many times may carry them with dishonor from the field." Harrison
wittily includes fallow deer and conies among the few remaining "per-
nicious" beasts in England because their great numbers make them as
destructive to arable land as sheep.[72]

For Harrison, then, the traditional argument in favor of hunting, that
it prepares men for war, is subverted in two senses. First, the contemporary practice of hunting, which depends primarily on vast lands
devoted to parks – more of them in England, he observes, than in all
Europe[73] – results in poverty and depopulation, reducing thereby the
potential number of recruits for military service. Second, the debased
form of hunting encouraged by parks "feminizes" men, providing none

of the discipline and hardship that they need as soldiers. Along with Elyot, whose criticism of the "softness" of contemporary hunting practices we have already considered, Harrison finds in hunting a threat to the perpetuation of a military elite; unlike Elyot, he extends his critique to the effect of hunting upon the common people and the nation as a whole.

The conventional linkage between hunting and masculinity that underlies the views of writers such as Elyot, Harrison, and James I was complicated by the fact that aristocratic women routinely hunted and had done so in Britain and on the continent for many centuries. Elizabeth's image appears prominently three times in *The Noble Arte of Venerie*. Lord Henry Berkeley's wife, Katharine, as we shall see in dealing with *The Taming of the Shrew*, acquired a reputation as a remarkable huntress. Manning even records the "unique" example of Catherine Gawen, "a recusant lady who actually led and rode with a poaching gang."[74] In pursuing the hunt throughout her reign, Queen Elizabeth was thus exceptional but not unique among women of the period. In the hunt, as in other activities, gender seems to have been less influential in determining one's social role than social status. The handbooks for women in the period seem to have had no concern with hunting, no admonitions comparable to those that appeared, say, in the Victorian magazine *The Field*, which in 1853 listed "six reasons why ladies should not hunt."[75] Despite the participation of high-ranking women in the hunt, however, the sport had powerfully masculine connotations. The gentler kinds of field sports, such as falconry or bow and stable hunting, were often recommended for women, and their participation in the more demanding kinds, such as *par force* hunting, seems to have carried with it an aura of masculinity.

Although few of Shakespeare's women hunt, those who do reflect Elizabethan customs and attitudes. They are aristocrats or royalty, for example, and their participation in the hunt is accepted by the males as natural and unworthy of comment. The pervasively masculine atmosphere of the hunt is particularly apparent in two cases, those of Hippolyta in *A Midsummer Night's Dream* and Tamora in *Titus Andronicus*. Hippolyta is quite literally an Amazon. Tamora, whose propensity for hunting is linked to her delight in rape, murder, and mutilation, is Queen of the Goths. Although the more "feminine" Lavinia also hunts in *Titus Andronicus*, she does so only to become herself the prey. The most complicated instance of the female hunter in Shakespeare, as we shall see, is that of the Princess in *Love's Labor's Lost*, who disapproves of hunting but still shoots a deer. The fact that few of Shakespeare's women hunt, and that they include an Amazon, an inciter to murder and rape, and a princess with doubts about the sport, suggests a certain "unnaturalness" in female participation in the sport. Women also rarely use the language of the hunt metaphorically in Shakespeare, with the result that their world, like the world of the lower social orders, both male and female, is for the most part insulated from the world of the hunt.

The gender tensions underlying the custom of female hunting may explain why Elizabeth's role as huntress did not become a more central part of her own political mythology or that of the courtiers around her. Elizabeth was often celebrated as Diana, of course, and occasionally the image was exploited in such a way as to highlight Diana's role as goddess of the hunt. The palace at Nonsuch, as mentioned previously, featured a grove of Diana with a fountain depicting Actaeon turned into a stag, and a hunting pageant at Cowdray in 1591 celebrated Elizabeth as Diana the huntress.[76] A widespread use of the image of Diana the huntress, however, might have evoked connotations of a virginal power too aggressive and deadly to be promoted by Elizabeth or to be happily endorsed by her courtiers. As Roy Strong has shown, moreover, the image of Elizabeth as Diana took on imperial connotations at an early stage, so that it was the moon as goddess of the seas that dominated the political mythology of the court; Ralegh's "Ocean to Cynthia," for example, ignores Diana's association with the hunt.

Hunting is of course a pervasive metaphor for the experience of love throughout Western culture, one that finds powerful expression in such works as The Song of Solomon, Virgil's *Aeneid*, Ovid's *Metamorphoses*, Petrarch's *Rime*, and *Gawain and the Green Knight*. The metaphor is capable of almost infinite variation: the male or female might play the role of hunter, for example, or either or both might fall prey to Cupid's arrow, or to their own desires, as in one popular interpretation of Actaeon, devoured by his own hounds. The most common use of the metaphor, however, in Shakespeare and in the tradition as a whole, places the male in the role of hunter and the female in the role of prey. In a hunting poem by William Cornish, for example, composed in the reign of Henry VIII, the male narrator describes, with obvious and sustained sexual innuendo, how he first struck a doe to the ground, then, weary, urged a companion to pursue her and do the same, and then finally discovered the creature with an arrow in her haunch, confirming that his companion's bow was now "well unbent, / Hys bolt may fle no more."[77]

8 Devonshire Hunting Tapestry, 1435–50 (detail). The disemboweling of a doe is
juxtaposed with a hunter's sexual advances.

Medieval and Renaissance art often represents the hunt as a site for
male sexual adventure. One conventional image, it seems, is of aristocratic male hunters fondling common women, as if the poetic convention of the love-chase were so strong it became inevitably realized in
the literal hunt. The fifteenth-century Devonshire Hunting Tapestries
show the prostrate and open carcass of a doe and, immediately and
disturbingly juxtaposed, a nobleman fondling the breast of a miller's
wife or daughter, while the miller looks on (fig. 8). A tapestry in the
Louvre – the month of May in the sixteenth-century series known as
Les Chasses de Maximilien – features, juxtaposed suggestively with preparations for a forest banquet, an aristocratic hunter fondling the breast
of a woman presumably from the village just visible in the background.

The Elizabethan pictorial tradition contains no such images, as far as
I am aware, and it is even possible that under Elizabeth, the Virgin
Queen, the connotations of male sexual aggression that surround the
hunt may have been somewhat suppressed. The images of Elizabeth
provided in Gascoigne's *Arte of Venerie* are devoid of sexuality, as is the
work itself, with the exception of a few inevitable jokes in the section on

antlers. The French original, in contrast, includes a long poem of love, "The Adolescence," which combines hunting with the pastoral in a way that is rare in the period. In this poem, the author, while hunting, comes upon a beautiful shepherd lass, seduces her, and shares her love for many years. Gascoigne excises this poem from his edition with the following comment:

And that which I have left out is nothing else but certayne unsemely verses, which bycause they are more apt for lascivious mindes, than to be enterlaced amongst the noble termes of Venerie, I thought meete to leave them at large, for such as will reade them in French.[78]

Gascoigne is an English patriot – he takes pains to include English terms and customs when they differ from the French – and he writes for a Virgin Queen.

In the opening scene of *Twelfth Night* Shakespeare provides a complex comic variation on the motif of love as a hunt. When Curio attempts to distract Orsino from his melancholy with the suggestion that he hunt the hart, Orsino responds with the inevitable pun:

> Why, so I do, the noblest that I have.
> O, when mine eyes did see Olivia first,
> Methought she purg'd the air of pestilence!
> That instant was I turn'd into a hart,
> And my desires, like fell and cruel hounds,
> E'er since pursue me.   (1.1.17–22)

The tortuous development of his thought suggests the disoriented state of Orsino's mind. The "heart" that he hunts is Olivia, whose virtues are associated with the powerful curative properties traditionally ascribed to the hart.[79] Yet in the very act of hunting he himself is turned into a hart, and, like Actaeon, who had become a traditional emblem of lust, is pursued by his own hounds. The convoluted image of Orsino hunting Olivia while his desires hunt him not only suggests the diseased nature of Orsino's imagination but anticipates the comically morbid intermingling of love and death that characterizes the chief romantic entanglements of the play.[80]

The comic treatment of sexuality in relation to the hunt often focuses on puns and wordplay that link the two activities. Jokes on "dear" and "deer" recur throughout Shakespeare's plays, as do allusions to the horns of the cuckold. Such wordplay runs riot in *Love's Labor's Lost*, especially in the dialogue between Boyet and Rosaline, which features bawdy allusions to shooting, pricks, horns, and hitting the target, much to the delight of Costard, for whom their wit "comes so smoothly off, so obscenely as it were, so fit" (4.1.143). The most blatant comic symbol of the sexuality of the hunt is the figure of Falstaff wearing the stag's horns at the end of *The Merry Wives of Windsor.* The disguise links him simultaneously and paradoxically to the sexual potency of the stag, the impotency of the cuckold, for whom he is a stand-in, and the violence of the hunter, represented by the legendary figure of Herne.

Shakespeare's most obviously tragic treatment of the hunt in relation to male sexual aggression is to be found in *Titus Andronicus*, in which the rape and mutilation of Lavinia by Tamora's sons is portrayed as a grisly parody of a hunt, even to the symbolic dismembering of the victim. In *The Rape of Lucrece*, Lucrece is compared to a frightened doe, and her rape becomes thereby a kind of hunt. *Venus and Adonis* plays out an inversion of this convention, in which the female figure becomes the aggressor and the male the passive victim; although never literally a hunter of Adonis, Venus plays the role of predatory animal. As usual, Shakespeare resists easy generalization: as soon as one begins to stereotype the male and female roles in the hunt, one encounters a reversal that calls the stereotype into question.

Both comic and tragic love occasionally evoke from Shakespeare hunting images from mythology. *Venus and Adonis*, of course, is a sustained treatment of one such myth, in which the violence and eroticism of the hunt are combined. In the Induction to *The Taming of the Shrew*, the lord and his servants offer Sly a chance to hawk, hunt, course, or view a picture of "Adonis painted by a running brook, / And Cytherea all in sedges hid" (Ind.2.50–51). Allusions to Diana are frequent throughout Shakespeare but only occasionally evoke her role as huntress. In a hunting scene in *Titus Andronicus*, Bassianus mocks Tamora as a "Dian" who has "abandoned her holy groves / To see the general hunting in this forest" (2.3.57–59). Diana's victim Actaeon appears more often than Diana herself, but almost exclusively in satiric or comic contexts as a symbol of lust or cuckoldry. Tamora replies to Bassianus's taunt by wishing she could use Diana's power and plant his head with horns like Actaeon's (2.3.61–65), an insult with prophetic overtones, since she later urges her sons to rape Lavinia, thereby transforming Bassianus into a cuckold. As a symbol of cuckoldry, the figure of Actaeon plays a major role in *The Merry Wives of Windsor*, with Ford's potential horns thrust upon Falstaff at the end of the play.

Shakespeare's use of the literary tradition of the hunt re-enforces the notion that his fascination with the sport is experiential rather than

merely bookish. The allusions to myth and classical literature are relatively infrequent, despite the powerful presence of hunting in such
authors as Ovid and Virgil; nor are there significant allusions to the rich
and evocative hunting motifs of medieval romance. To read
Shakespeare in the context of medieval hunting stories such as
Tristram's in Malory or Bercilak's in *Gawain and the Green Knight* is to
become aware of the loss of an enchanted world. Shakespeare's forests
are without unicorns, without figures like St. Eustace, who is converted
at the sight of a stag with Christ's cross between its antlers, and without
boars that represent the Devil. Such mystical images of the hunt are kept
alive to a certain extent in Spenser's imaginative universe, but not in
Shakespeare's.

The position of the hunt in both Shakespeare and in Elizabethan and
Jacobean society was thus complex. As a subject for art, it had a long and
rich tradition, capable of almost infinite elaboration. As a social practice, it embodied distinctive cultural tensions. On the one hand, and most
significantly, it was an activity that drew support from and re-enforced
the patriarchal and authoritarian tendencies within Elizabethan society.
Hunting was sanctioned by the Church. The legal position of the hunt
vested enormous power in the hands of the monarch and in those aristocrats fortunate enough to share in the privilege. The hunt itself, especially in its most ceremonial form, was a ritual celebration of the power
of the monarch. Its dominant social justification was as preparation for
war, a means of perpetuating the power of the landed elite. As such,
moreover, its most potent connotations were masculine. Hence the hunt
can be seen religiously, politically, socially, and sexually as a manifestation of various kinds and levels of patriarchal power.

If this is the dominant paradigm, however, each of its terms was con-
tested. The hunt was a site of controversy. Christianity could be used to
oppose the hunt, as it was in the emergent attitude of sympathy for
animals, or in the Puritans' concerns for the poor. The monarch's
powers in the hunt could be, and were, challenged, as were those of the
aristocracy. The justification of the hunt as preparation for war could be
inverted and made to serve pacifist ends. The ceremony of the hunt
could be undermined ritualistically in poaching, as defiant mockery of
the authority of the aristocracy or monarch. And the notion of masculinity could be extended to include powerful women, as in the case of
Amazonian huntresses like Elizabeth, or used to challenge effete kinds
of hunting as symptoms of a decadent aristocracy.

As a social reality, then, hunting provided Shakespeare with a variable and conflicting set of practices, symbols, and attitudes. Hunting was not a source of social stability but of social tension. As both a potent social institution and traditional symbol, moreover, the hunt crystallized some of the most important tensions characteristic of the period as a whole: tensions in conceptions of the monarchy, of social status, of gender, of power over nature. Given its cultural richness and complexity, and its role as a site of social conflict, it is not surprising that Shakespeare found in the hunt a powerful source of drama.

CHAPTER TWO

Huntresses *in* Venus and Adonis *and* Love's Labor's Lost

The cultural conflict between the martial and sentimental views of the hunt, represented by such figures as James I and Montaigne, is invoked every time an Elizabethan or Jacobean female participates in the sport. Within this patriarchal society, the custom of female hunting involves a paradox: it liberates women to play the most virile of male roles but constrains them by denying their "essential" female nature. It is not surprising, therefore, that the most powerful anti-hunting poem of the period, Margaret Cavendish's "The Hunting of the Hare" (1653) is written by a woman who says of herself elsewhere, "according to the constitution of my *Sex*, I am as fearefull as a Hare."[1] In the activity of the hunt, tenderness, compassion, timidity – the traditionally female emotions – must be suppressed or somehow joined in tension with the traditionally male attributes of strength, fierceness, and courage. The huntress is therefore inevitably a kind of Amazon.

The paradox of the huntress is not explored in contemporary handbooks or in the dominant discourses of the hunt. Huntresses appear frequently in Shakespeare's plays, however, and we shall examine later such figures as Hippolyta in *A Midsummer Night's Dream* and Tamora in *Titus Andronicus*. In this chapter we shall consider two radically different huntresses who dominate their respective works: the goddess Venus in *Venus and Adonis* and the Princess of France in *Love's Labor's Lost*. In one sense, these figures share little in common: the one is the goddess of love, the other a mere princess; the one is at the centre of a tragic narrative, the other at the centre of a comic drama. For this reason, the figures will be treated in separate sections, in relation to their own distinctive works.

Juxtaposing the two characters, however, highlights their common involvement in the culture of the hunt. Both are huntresses, and the works in which they appear are deeply implicated in the conventional metaphor of love as a kind of hunt; the works have often been discussed, indeed, with this metaphor in mind. In both works, moreover, hunting is more than a conventional metaphor for erotic experience. The love-hunts are played out within a distinctive social ambiance. Each of the characters is defined in relation to specific kinds of hunting that have rich cultural meaning: Venus in relation to the hunting of boar, hare, and deer in parks, the Princess in relation to the latter motif alone. As huntresses, the two characters represent some deep social tensions within the bloody customs of the hunt. Caught within these tensions, both characters are forced to confront some unsettling truths about themselves and about the nature of love.

THE "BLOODING" OF VENUS IN *VENUS AND ADONIS*

At the end of November 1996, at Balmoral, Scotland, Prince William, son of Prince Charles and, after his father, heir to the British monarchy, killed his first stag. He was fourteen. In the weeks after the event the British press was filled with cries of moral indignation. A headline announcing a column of commentary in the *Observer* proclaimed, "Balmorality is Plain Obscene." The pursuit of blood sports by the royal family, the article argued, was anachronistic and immoral. In other reports moral outrage was accompanied with laments about the nega-tive effect of hunting on the royal family. William's mother, Diana, Princess of Wales, it was said, was a strong opponent of blood sports, and her son's obvious love of hunting had driven a wedge between the two and had made it impossible for her to be selected as president of the Royal Society for the Prevention of Cruelty to Animals (*Irish Times*, 2 Dec.). In his love for the hunt, it was repeatedly implied, Prince William had been clearly influenced by his father, who accompanied him in this escapade, as did his brother, Harry, and the rather ambiguous and shadowy figure of Tiggy Legge-Bourke, who was not only a keen hunter but William's nanny.

For our purposes, the most curious feature of this event was the fasci-nation in the press with one unknown fact: was Prince William "blooded" after he killed the stag? To think that this fourteen-year-old boy might have had his face daubed with the blood of his first stag as a mark of his initiation into the world of the hunt aroused more than a little discomfort in certain quarters. To think that it might not have hap-pened, however, aroused equal discomfort in others. "The only shame," wrote Andrew Roberts in *The Times*, "was that the countryman prince was apparently not, possibly for reasons of political correctness, 'blooded' in the traditional Highland manner" (1 Dec.). One writer,

Adam Nicolson, was moved to describe his own "blooding" as a youth, which was accomplished in two stages, first, by a decorous stalker, who carefully used his fingers, but later, by the Dionysiac lord of the manor, who scooped up the blood with cupped hands (*Sunday Telegraph*, 1 Dec.). Despite the pressure of the reporters, the royal family never revealed whether the "blooding" actually occurred; most articles simply recorded the lack of certainty. A writer in the *Guardian* (28 Nov.), however, implied rather strongly that the deed had been done: "The prince is believed to have had blood smeared on his forehead by Sandy Masson, the head stalker, in a ritual similar to that faced by his father when he killed his first stag in the 1960s." *The Times* reported without comment that the artist Andre Durand had begun a portrait to commemorate the event, which would show Prince William "dressed in flowing red robes, his face smeared in the stag's spent blood and Balmoral Castle [nestled] sweetly in the snow-capped peaks beyond" (5 Dec.).

The tradition of "blooding" is certainly of ancient origin, although its history, not surprisingly, is obscure. It almost certainly existed in Shakespeare's time. A report from a Venetian ambassador in 1618 describes James I "blooding" his hunting companions as part of a *par force* hunt of the stag:

On his Majesty coming up with the dead game, he dismounts, cuts its throat and opens it, sating the dogs with its blood, as the reward of their exertions. With his own imbrued hands, moreover, he is wont to regale some of his nobility by touching their faces. This blood it is unlawful to remove or wash off, until it fall of its own accord, and the favoured individual thus bedaubed is considered to be dubbed a keen sportsman and chief of the hunt and to have a certificate of his sovereign's cordial good-will.[2]

As described by the Venetian observer, "blooding" was not restricted to one's first kill but was a mark of honor for heroic action, a kind of knighthood conferred to commemorate one's part in the day's victory. Erasmus's satiric description of the hunt in *Praise of Folly* does not mention "blooding," but his account of the ritual dismemberment of the deer suggests a similar initiatory significance: "the standers by, not speakyng a worde, behold it solemnly, as if it were some holy **Misterie**, havyng seen the like yet more than a hundred tymes before. Than (sir) whose happe it be to eate parte of the flesshe, marie he thynkes verily to be made therby halfe a gentilman."[3]

Although it seems to have escaped the attention of critics of the poem, a rite of "blooding" also appears in Shakespeare's *Venus and Adonis*.[4] At the very end of the work, the grief-stricken Venus looks down at the body of Adonis and, in a sudden reversal, identifies herself with the boar. It has killed Adonis out of excess love, she imagines, and she acknowledges that she herself would have done the same. The action that follows is the climax of the narrative: "With this she falleth in the place she stood / And stains her face with his congealed blood" (1121–22). The narrator's description is slightly ambiguous, but it is clear from the ensuing description of Venus's avid examination of the body that she does not fall and bloody her face involuntarily, as in a faint; instead, she drops suddenly but deliberately to the ground and daubs herself with Adonis's "congealed blood." As John Roe observes, the word "congealed" suggests that Venus applies the blood "ceremoniously like dye or paint."[5] In her case, unlike that of James's courtiers, the blood will not later fall off; it is a stain and will endure. As a rite of "blooding," Venus's action is curious indeed: she daubs her own face, making herself both the experienced hunter and the novice, and the blood she uses is that of Adonis, who becomes therefore not only the boar's prey but her own. To understand the significance of this peculiar action, which occurs at the climactic moment of the narrative, it helps to place the poem as a whole within the Elizabethan culture of the hunt.

Shakespeare's main source for *Venus and Adonis* is Ovid's account of the story in Book Ten of *The Metamorphoses*. His most striking departure from this source, as has often been observed, is in making Adonis resistant to Venus's love. Both Ovid's Adonis and Shakespeare's love to hunt, but Ovid's also makes love to Venus, and his account gives no suggestion that the two sources of pleasure are in conflict. In Ovid's version, Venus even tucks up her skirts like Diana and hunts the gentler game with him. For Ovid, Adonis's tragic death is caused not because he prefers hunting to love, but simply because he fails to heed Venus's warning against hunting the boar. In Shakespeare's version of the tale, in contrast, Adonis is an adolescent boy almost prudishly hostile to sexual love and strongly enamored of the hunt. The effect of this redefinition of Adonis's motives is to focus the tragedy on a conflict between two modes of behavior, hunting and love.

Because Venus has far more to say about love than Adonis about hunting, the significance of Adonis's preference makes itself felt mainly indirectly, by implication. In the Elizabethan context, however, especially that of the aristocratic coterie for which the poem was apparently written, Adonis's silences could be to some extent filled in by a shared cultural understanding. Shakespeare's Adonis is an adolescent boy on the verge of manhood, and it is towards his manhood that the poem as a whole seems to drive. Venus wants Adonis to act the part of a man by making love to her: "Thou art no man, though of a man's complexion, / For men will kiss even by their own direction" (215–16). Adonis wants to become a man by killing the boar: "if any love you owe me, / Measure my strangeness with my unripe years; / Before I know myself, seek not to know me" (523–25). Adonis's resistance to Venus is embodied in his resistance to the pun on "know": for him, self-knowledge precedes sexual experience; for her, self-knowledge and sexual experience occur at the same time.

Although some critics find Adonis's rejection of Venus merely prudish or narcissistic, his own formulation leaves open the prospect of sexual love, only deferring it to a later stage in his development.[6] He is not against love, it seems, but against Venus's love at this time; the difference is subtle but important.[7] Even Venus is not altogether opposed to hunting, merely the most dangerous kind of hunting, the hunting of boar. Both characters thus see Adonis's entry into manhood as a desirable end, but they define the experience in antithetical ways. For Venus, it is the act of love that initiates: Adonis will "know" himself when he "knows" her. For Adonis, self-knowledge proceeds from hunting. Although Adonis has presumably hunted before – "hunting he lov'd, but love he laugh'd to scorn" (4) – the killing of the boar thus takes on an initiatory significance. Two modes of initiation are played off against each other throughout the poem in Ovidian fashion, each metamorphosing into the other in ways that ultimately make it difficult to tell them apart.

Adonis's conception of the hunt as part of an initiatory process that culminates in manhood, as a means of knowing the self before committing the self to love, translates into Ovidian terms a conception of adolescent experience grounded in Elizabethan culture. For adolescent males of all social classes, hunting or poaching served an important initiatory and educational function. As works like Elyot's *Governor* and James I's *Basilicon Doron* make clear, boys in the period were introduced early to the hunt as a training ground for war, a test of their ability to master terrain, to endure physical hardship, to show courage, and to kill. In this, young aristocrats emulated their betters. James I, obsessed with hunting as an adult, was already alarmingly "addicted" to the sport, according to a contemporary observer, at the age of nineteen; an early portrait of James shows him as a boy of about fourteen, holding a falcon on his left hand.[8] Charles I was introduced to hunting at the age of four, and note was taken that he took great delight in seeing a buck hunted

9 Memorial brass of John Selwyn, underkeeper of the Royal Park of Oatlands, Surrey (*c.* 1587). The brass was originally affixed to a gravestone, with one of its sides invisible. Presumably, the family was unhappy with one version.

and killed.[9] His young son, later Charles II, provoked admiration when, at the age of eleven, he leapt from his horse, waded through some ditches and killed a hare that had been wounded by his father.[10] The epitome of this adolescent bravado, in its "adult" manifestation, is the monumental brass depicting John Selwyn, underkeeper of the Royal Park of Oatlands, stabbing a stag in the throat while riding it; the brass commemorates a deed said to have been performed before Elizabeth (fig. 9).

Venus and Adonis is dedicated to Henry Wriothesley, Earl of Southampton, who was only nineteen in 1593 when the poem was published.[11] Whether Shakespeare's portrayal of Adonis alludes to the Earl's resistance to a marriage arranged by Lord Burghley is uncertain, but the atmosphere of adolescent male camaraderie in which such young men grew up pervades the poem. "The younger sort," according to Gabriel Harvey, "takes much delight in Shakespeare's Venus and Adonis."[12] From the age of eight to his maturity Southampton was one of Burghley's wards. In his early years, he lived and studied with the other young wards in Burghley's household. At twelve he entered the entirely masculine world of St. John's College, Cambridge; at fifteen he was admitted to the equally masculine and more fashionable world of Gray's Inn. He became close friends with two of Burghley's other wards, the young Earls of Rutland and Essex.

Throughout his life Southampton was closely associated with the world of the hunt. In 1589, when he was sixteen, his steward brought suit on his behalf against one Richard Pitts and his companions for stealing deer and beating the keepers one night at Whiteley Park.[13] Southampton's friend Rutland shared with him his own avidity for the sport. In a letter of 14 July 1590 to Burghley, Rutland included commendations to Southampton, who was sixteen at the time, with the regretful note that he doubted whether he would even kill one buck that summer. In another letter, Burghley had to urge Rutland not to forget his books: "'you will, whan you ar weary of huntyng, recontinew some exercise of huntyng in your book.'"[14] Burghley himself kept parks stocked with game, loved his horses and dogs, and was a skilled rider and archer.[15] Southampton went on to a military career – he was knighted by Essex for his role in the Azores expedition – but was imprisoned by Elizabeth for his role in the Essex rebellion. He was released and restored to favor by James I in 1603, when he was made "Master of the Queen's Game with direction over all Her Majesty's forests and chases." He hunted often with the King and Queen thereafter, and in 1607 was appointed Keeper of the New Forest.[16]

As is well known, Elizabethans conceived of adolescence as a distinct period, with a wide range of stereotyped behaviors and attitudes.[17] For most young male aristocrats, the potential period of adolescence covered roughly the ages of 12 to 26, and was marked at one end by departure from the family home and at the other by marriage and full adult status. The higher the social standing, the more pressure there was to marry early; Burghley attempted to force Southampton to marry his granddaughter, Lady Elizabeth Vere, at the age of sixteen. In most cases young male aristocrats had a period of ten to fourteen years in which to serve as pages in others' households, attend university and the inns of court, travel abroad, fall in and out of love, and hunt. Hunting, of course, continued after marriage, and love often preceded it. The relatively late age of marriage, however, tended to make of the wedding ceremony, with its dominant symbol of sexual consummation, an initiation rite in which mature heterosexual experience and the acquisition of adult social status converged.

Unlike marriage, hunting involved initiation into an essentially masculine society, and at a very early age. John Smyth's history of the Berkeley family links hunting to the period of life he calls "the age of puberty" and the "age of adolescency." Smyth notes the great delight that the young Sir Thomas Berkeley took in hunting in the reign of Edward I, an adolescent enthusiasm that seems to have been passed down to his descendant Henry, Lord Berkeley, who, as a young man in the reign of Edward VI, lived with his mother in London and hunted daily in the fields of Gray's Inn.[18] Adonis's conception of the hunt as an initiatory experience, a way of knowing the self that precedes and, in effect, prepares one for adult heterosexual love, is recognizable within this social context. Hunting was a form of education, a training ground for war, and a means of bonding adolescent males to each other and to the adult fraternity of the chase.

Suggestive evidence for the importance of hunting as an initiatory experience for adolescent males appears in two hunting portraits of the period: one, a painting by Robert Peake that we have considered in chapter 1, shows the nine-year-old Prince Henry sheathing his sword after ritualistically cutting the neck of a deer (fig. 1); the other, the "December" tapestry from the hunting series in the Louvre entitled *Les Chasses de Maximilien*, features a young man, whose beardless face contrasts markedly with the faces of the hunters coming to his aid, killing a boar (fig. 10).[19] In each case the drama of the moment of the kill is heightened by the obvious youthfulness of the protagonist. The portrait of Prince Henry is the less exciting of the two, since the animal is already dead, but an aura of power is evoked by the Prince's imposing sword and intimidating stare. There is no adolescent awkwardness or hesitation in the pose. The attack upon the boar in the "December" tapestry is highly theatrical and highlights the notoriety of the animal as the most dangerous of prey. Compared to this image of the hunt, the tapestries in the series devoted to killing the stag – "September" and "October" – are anticlimactic: in both of them the hunting party is in the foreground, and the pursued stags are visible only in the distance.

Shakespeare's choice of the boar for Adonis's hunt was of course dictated by the myth, and his treatment of the animal, not surprisingly, is more obviously "literary" than his treatment of the hare and the horse, the descriptions of which evoke the countryside around Stratford.[20] In his survey of the medieval conception of the boar, John Cummins calls the animal an "archetype of unrelenting ferocity." In both medieval and Elizabethan hunting manuals the boar is treated as the most dangerous animal hunted. The medieval writer Gaston Phoebus claims to have seen a boar "strike a man and split him from knee to chest, so that he fell dead without a word."[21] In *The Noble Arte of Venerie*, Gascoigne is reluctant even to recommend the boar hunt, in view of its destructive effect upon dogs; the boar, he says, "is the only beast which can dispatch a hounde at one blow."[22]

Hunting the boar, then, is a supreme test of manhood, one that accords fully with the values of those who, like Thomas Elyot, William

10 The December tapestry from *Les Chasses de Maximilien* (mid sixteenth-century). The climax of a boar hunt.

Harrison, and James I, praise only the most "manly" kinds of hunting. James's praise of *par force* hunting and contempt for less "manly" kinds, such as coursing, occurs in *Basilicon Doron*, a book he published in 1599 for the instruction of his young prince Henry, then six years old. Elyot's attempt to resurrect the hunting of deer on foot, following the heroic examples of Alexander the Great and Henry V, also appears in a book devoted to the instruction of boys, *The Book Named the Governor*. Both Elyot and James, moreover, draw upon Xenophon's *Cyropaedia* for their idealization of the initiatory qualities of the hunt, a work that was taught in the grammar schools with great effect, if Sidney's admiration for it in the *Defence of Poetry* is any test. Elyot recommends the reading of the *Cyropaedia* between the ages of fourteen and seventeen.[23] Hence the most prominent rationale for the hunt in the period, that it trained young men for war, invites an initiatory approach to the hunt itself.

Adonis's quest to "know" himself through the boar hunt is thus an initiatory quest. The boy becomes a man in the conquest of death, taking on the warrior-status of the ferocious beast he kills. In this sense the boar is a symbol of Death, as many critics have observed.[24] But the boar's role as an "archetype of unrelenting ferocity" is not restricted to killing. The boar is also a conventional symbol of dangerous virility. In *The Historie of the Foure-Footed Beastes*, for example, Edward Topsell describes the "venerial rage" of the boar in a manner that makes sexuality itself a force of death:

Being inflamed with venerial rage, he so setteth upright the bristles of his neck, that you would take them to be the sharp fins of Dolphins; then champeth he with his mouth, grateth and gnasheth his teeth one against another, and breathing forth his boyling spirit, not only at his eies, but at his foaming white mouth, he desireth nothing but copulation, and if his female endure him quietly, then doth shee satisfie his lust, and kill all his anger; but if she refuse, then doth he either constraine her against her will, or else layeth hir dead upon the earth.[25]

As A. T. Hatto has shown, literary counterparts to this naturalistic tradition appear in many writers, including Boccaccio and Chaucer, both of whom describe Troilus's dream of a boar making love to Criseyde.[26] Shakespeare himself evokes the tradition in *Cymbeline*, where Posthumus expresses his jealous rage in an image of the lustful Jachimo mounting Imogen with a cry "like a full-acorn'd boar" (2.5.16). The notion that the boar kills Adonis merely because he wanted to kiss him also appears often in sixteenth-century verse.[27]

Eros is thus everywhere in this Ovidian poem, and Adonis's adolescent attempt to flee love for boar-hunting is doomed to fail. But

Shakespeare gives the story another twist. Although he is not original in ascribing amorousness to the boar, Shakespeare seems to be unique in ascribing to Adonis himself a reciprocal erotic longing. In a way that Adonis does not foresee, his tragic quest of the boar plays out the implications of the narrator's account of his motives as early as line four: "Hunting he lov'd, but love he laugh'd to scorn." Adonis scorns love but loves hunting. Like Ovid's Hippolytus, as William Keach remarks, Adonis "has committed himself to chastity and redirected all his repressed erotic energies to the hunt."[28]

As an adolescent in pursuit of manhood, barely awakening to sexuality, Adonis does not understand his own motives. "I know not love," he tells Venus, "nor will not know it, / Unless it be a boar, and then I chase it . . ." (409–10). The familiar pun on the word "know" suggests here an unconscious confusion between sexuality and killing, as does the image of the "chase," which is equivocal enough to refer to sexual pursuit or the pursuit of the hunt. The equivocation is later resolved, in Venus's description, at the moment of Adonis's death: "nousling in his flank, the loving swine / Sheath'd unaware the tusk in his soft groin" (1115–16). Although one might be tempted to read these lines dramatically, as merely a projection of Venus's own psychology, both the conventional symbolism of the boar and the development of Adonis throughout the poem serve to confirm the intuitive truth of her words. The initiatory consummation of the boar's "love" for Adonis, and Adonis's unconscious love for the boar, brings forth not only blood but a purple flower, which Venus "cradles" (1185) in her breast as if it were Adonis's child.

As Don Cameron Allen has shown, *Venus and Adonis* rests upon a longstanding metaphoric relationship between love and hunting: love itself is a kind of hunt, a "soft" hunt opposed to the heroic "hard" hunt of dangerous prey such as the boar.[29] Allen's account ignores, however, Shakespeare's Ovidian reversal of that motif, which converts hunting into a kind of love. Although the reversal may be implicit in the metaphoric equation – if love is a hunt, then hunting must be a love – there seems to be no comparable literary tradition behind it.[30] As Matt Cartmill has shown, however, the notion often surfaces in modern discussions of the motivations of hunters. Cartmill quotes William Thompson, who helped to establish the sport of bow-hunting in America, as saying of the deer he has pursued, "I have so loved them that I longed to kill them." According to Cartmill, this "pathological" motif "crops up again and again throughout the literature of hunting:

many hunters deeply and sincerely love the animals they kill, and they identify that love as one of their reasons for wanting to kill them."[31]

Although Adonis too loves his prey, Shakespeare's treatment of the motif is quite different from that described by Cartmill. Adonis is vague and uncertain about his motives, for one thing, driven by his awakening manhood to pursue drives he does not fully understand; the impulse that Cartmill finds pathological is in him innocent, although at the same time dangerous. The prey that Adonis pursues, moreover, is not the shy and seductive deer lusted after by William Thompson but a boar; Adonis's love object is hyperbolically masculine, a symbol of raging virility. The eroticism that in Cartmill's example is associated with traditional notions of male dominance over women is thus in the case of Adonis more complex. From one perspective, as we have seen, "knowing" the boar may be conceived of in heterosexual terms, as the acquisition of an aggressive adult masculinity. From another, however, it may be conceived of in homosexual terms, as an act of masculine self-sufficiency. Both potential outcomes are inimical to Venus's desires, and both are thwarted by Adonis's death.

Although it does not figure in Ovid's account of the myth, the homo-eroticism in Shakespeare's treatment of Adonis is nevertheless Ovidian, as Jonathan Bate has so persuasively argued; in this regard, Ovid's stories of beautiful adolescent boys who, like Narcissus or Cyparissus, flee from heterosexual love are as relevant to Shakespeare's version of the myth as the story of Adonis himself.[32] Here too Shakespeare's imagination seems to have been prompted as much by the Elizabethan culture of the hunt as by the literary tradition. When Venus asks Adonis if he will meet her the next day, he "tells her no, to-morrow he intends / To hunt the boar with certain of his friends" (587–88). The hard hunt of the boar, as we have seen, is the most conventionally masculine kind of hunting. Adonis hunts with boys and men, and one of the traditional functions of such hunting was to bind men to one another, to create a warrior-class set apart from and superior to the "effeminate" society of the court. In this respect the early life of the Earl of Southampton, to whom Shakespeare's poem is dedicated, is a paradigm. He was brought up among boys in Burghley's household and educated among boys and men at Cambridge and the Inns of Court. Burghley's attempt to marry him off at the age of sixteen was thus an intrusion of adult heterosexuality into a dominantly masculine adolescent world.

While the Elizabethan proponents of the hard hunt saw clearly the

danger represented by the love of Venus, whose softness was emasculating, they did not see the danger represented by the love of the boar, a
danger that, as Shakespeare develops it, grows directly out of the initiatory impulse behind the hunt. If young boys are to become not only men
but warriors through the pursuit of the boar, and if that pursuit is driven
by an erotic impulse, then the very love of men that such an initiation
fulfills is inevitably tied to the death of men; the animals hunted are, after
all, only surrogates for the men to be hunted later in war. Although
Shakespeare only hints at this dangerous and destructive eroticism in
Venus and Adonis, it underlies his later representation of the warriors
Coriolanus and Aufidius in *Coriolanus*. The fascination that draws these
two characters to each other seems that of a deadly eroticism, and one
that is expressed in the language of hunting. "He is a lion," Coriolanus
says of Aufidius as he prepares for battle, "That I am proud to hunt"
(1.1.235–36). "Let me twine / Mine arms about that body," says Aufidius,
greeting Coriolanus, "where against / My grained ash an hundred times
hath broke, / And scarr'd the moon with splinters" (4.5.106–09). At the
end of the play, Coriolanus is "entwined" by Aufidius's soldiers, who
encircle and slaughter him like a beast of prey.

To speak of homoeroticism in the case of the "love" of Adonis and
the boar, however, is ultimately misleading, for it implies a rigid catego-
rizing of sexual experience that does not occur in the poem. As we have
seen, the boar functions as a symbol of both homosexual and heterosexual passion. As Bruce R. Smith observes, the "temporary freedom" that
such androgynous figures as Adonis "grant to sexual desire allows it to
flow out in all directions, toward all the sexual objects that beckon in the
romantic landscape."[33] Just how many sexual objects there are in the
landscape of *Venus and Adonis* is shown in Jonathan Bate's account of
Shakespeare's adaptation of his Ovidian sources, which include stories
of incest (Adonis's mother is Myrrha), homosexuality, heterosexuality,
narcissism, and hermaphroditism. Given such a polymorphous poetic
landscape, one is tempted to add bestiality to the list; the "love" that
Adonis pursues, after all, is a boar. To speak of heterosexuality or homosexuality in such a poem is thus inevitably reductive; at issue is eros itself,
which drives the universe. And eros, in this poem, leads only to death.

Venus, of course, believes that eros leads to life, and throughout the
poem she uses all her arts to persuade Adonis of this truth. She appeals
to her beauty, threatens him with the dangers of narcissism, argues that
procreation is not only delightful but a duty, berates him with the
example of his virile and willing horse, maneuvers him into inviting

sexual postures, holds before him the immortality to be won by propa-
gation – yet she fails utterly to convince him. And she fails to convince
the reader. If an unconscious eroticism underlies Adonis's pursuit of the
hunt, an unconscious violence underlies Venus's pursuit of love. She is
as much a "hunter" as Adonis or the boar. In her case the hunt is the traditional hunt of love, and her prey is Adonis. Much of the wit of the
poem lies in Shakespeare's variations on this conventional theme.

The Venus of Ovid's story is not opposed to hunting, as we have
seen; she tucks up her skirts and accompanies Adonis on the chase.
Shakespeare's Venus, however, prefers a more passive approach. She
invites Adonis to be her "deer":

> "Fondling," she saith, "since I have hemm'd thee here
> Within the circuit of this ivory pale,
> I'll be a park, and thou shalt be my deer:
> Feed where thou wilt, on mountain, or in dale;
>   Graze on my lips, and if those hills be dry,
>   Stray lower, where the pleasant fountains lie."   (229–34)

This is a wonderfully seductive vision of love, not the less so because it
wittily parodies the Song of Solomon, in which the bride imagines her
bridegroom a roe or young hart that feeds among the lilies (2.16–17).
From a modern perspective, the image is not only erotic but comically
nurturing: Adonis is invited to graze at will, to luxuriate in her bounty.
An Elizabethan park, however, was by no means a nature preserve in the
modern sense. Deer were coddled in parks – fed and cared for, protected
from winter's harshness – but for one reason only: to be killed by arrows
or run to death by greyhounds. Venus's "ivory pale" is a lovely and inviting "circuit" of death. Her very words of reassurance – "No dog shall
rouse thee, though a thousand bark" (240) – are ominous, since they
make the languor of sexual fulfillment seem suspiciously like the silence
of the grave. Commenting on the "effeminate" custom of hunting in
parks, William Harrison remarks wryly that keeping deer enclosed
makes it difficult to tell "whether our buck or doe are to be reckoned in
wild or tame beasts or not."[34] Parks are killing fields for pet deer.

The deadly eroticism of Venus's delightful park thus derives not
merely from the literary tradition linking love with the hunt but from
the social practice of hunting in Elizabethan parks. Such hunting provided a casual and relaxing form of entertainment, one that could be
easily indulged in as part of the socializing one expected when enter-
taining the Queen on progress or a foreign visitor. Robert Peake's portrait of Princess Elizabeth in 1603 provides a suggestive image of such

an occasion (fig. 4).[35] The painting itself is innocuous, but the links it forges between hunting in parks and intimate affairs of the heart have the potential to be developed in less innocent directions. In this painting the Princess, dressed elaborately in white, stands in an outdoor setting, directly facing the viewer. To our right, in the background, a small bridge across a stream leads the eye to the pales of the park, within which a hunt is in progress, represented by the figures of two horsemen, a huntsman on foot, and deer fleeing across a lawn. To our left, in the background, and juxtaposed exactly with the image on the right, a winding path leads the eye upwards to a small circle of trees enclosing a wooded bower, in which sit two women in close conversation. The absence of sexuality in the painting differentiates this park from the one envisaged by Venus: the young princess is virginal and dressed in white, set off from the landscape in which she finds herself; the conversing women are prim and decorous figures. Peake's choice of background imagery, however, is highly suggestive. For him, pursuing deer within a pale and conversing intimately within a bower are not merely part of the same landscape; they occur at the same time and are visually equivalent. Both activities occur within "circuits" reminiscent of Venus's "circuit of this ivory pale." Venus imagines her arms the pale of a park; Peake displays two "pales," the one devoted to the death of deer, the other, simultaneously, to intimate personal affairs.

Queen Elizabeth's visit to Cowdray in 1591 provides another suggestive gloss on Venus's fantasy of herself as a park. Most country estates had good views of the park, and it was often possible simply to watch a hunt from a window, as one might watch a tennis match from the gallery. At Cowdray Elizabeth watched from a turret in the evening while sixteen bucks were "pulled downe with Greyhoundes, in a laund." That morning, she had been led to a "delicate Bowre" in the park, listened to a "dittie" that celebrated her as an eroticized Diana, received the gift of a crossbow, and killed "three or four" deer that had been "put into a paddock." The erotic ambiance of this kind of hunting, which mingles the death of tame deer with sophisticated courtly compliment, are evoked in the "dittie" sung to Queen Elizabeth as the bow is presented:

> Goddesse and Monarch of (t)his happie Ile,
> vouchsafe this bow which is an huntresse part:
> Your eies are arrows though they seeme to smile
> which never glanst but gald the stateliest hart,
> Strike one, strike all, for none at all can flie,
> They gaze you in the face although they die.[36]

Although the Queen assumes the role of Diana in accepting the bow "which is an huntresse part," the power of her arrow-eyes kills all who behold her, deer or courtiers, with love. It is not difficult to see behind Venus's longing for her timorous deer, the nibbling Adonis, the menacing undercurrent that one detects in the ditty sung before Elizabeth. In both cases, the deer are there to die for love.

Venus's attempt to seduce Adonis by appealing to the eroticism of the hunting park is greeted only by his smile "as in disdain" (241). When she discovers that he intends to hunt the boar, she shifts the ground of her appeal from the hunting of deer in parks to the coursing of hare in open woods and fields. Unlike Ovid's Venus, who actually indulges in such hunting with her lover, Shakespeare's merely urges it upon Adonis, and only then because the hunting of "fearful creatures" (677) such as the "timorous flying hare" (674) is preferable to hunting the boar. In her fear, she thus turns to another soft kind of hunting, one that, although slightly less "effeminate" than hunting in parks with bows, aroused the contempt of such advocates of the martial hunt as Elyot, Harrison, and King James. In the *Governor*, for example, Elyot begrudgingly accepts hare-hunting as a sport for "effeminate" men, such as scholars, and for women who might otherwise be idle:

Hunting of the hare with greyhounds is a right good solace for men that be studious, of them to whom nature hath not given personage or courage apt for the wars. And also for gentlewomen, which fear neither sun nor wind for impairing their beauty. And peradventure they shall be thereat less idle than they should be at home in their chambers.[37]

In the *Basilicon Doron*, James I echoes this point of view, disparaging "greyhound hunting" as "not so martiall a game" as the running of deer with hounds.[38]

In her account of the hare hunt, as in her vision of love in a deer park, Venus projects upon the hare her own erotic fantasies; in doing so, however, her identification of herself with the hare leads her into an argumentative impasse. The hare is of course a traditional symbol of sexuality, and even the popular name that Venus uses, "Wat" (697), alludes to the female genitalia.[39] In this sense the hunt that Venus so vividly urges upon Adonis is the hunt of herself, his willing prey, and critics tend to treat her description in such erotic terms.[40] Although this kind of conventional eroticism is present in the episode, it is less pronounced than one might expect; the subtlest source of wit is less predictable and draws upon the contemporary discourse of hunting. Despite her sexual obsessiveness, Venus's description of the hunt is curiously chaste, and its effect is to dampen her ardor and disrupt her seductive train of thought. As she describes the flight of the hare in its "cranks and crosses with a thousand doubles" (682), it becomes increasingly humanized and its plight increasingly desperate and moving. Even at the beginning of the description the hare is a "poor wretch" (680). By the end, it has been given a name, "poor Wat," has been shown standing pathetically on its "hinder-legs with list'ning ear" (697–98), and, as a "dew-bedabbled wretch" (703), has become, to Venus's own surprise, an emblem of human misery: "For misery is trodden on by many, / And being low, never reliev'd by any" (707–08). [41] She herself is shocked by her conclusion: "To make thee hate the hunting of the boar," she says, "Unlike myself thou hear'st me moralize . . ." (711–12). Distracted by the effect of her own exhortation to hunt the hare, she ends by losing her train of thought altogether: "Where did I leave?" (715).

In "moralizing" the hunt, Venus follows a familiar convention. Emblematic readings of the book of nature were customary even in the hunting manuals themselves. In *The Noble Arte of Venerie*, for example, George Gascoigne praises hunting for its capacity to "represent" other activities, noting that the "nimble Hare, by turning in hir course, / Doth plainly prove that *Pollicie*, sometime surpasseth force." [42] Within the initiatory context of the hunt, in which the danger and hardship of the sport become a test of manhood, Venus's argument in favor of hunting hare, as one might expect, is dangerously "effeminate." The comedy of the hare-hunt thus depends upon the way in which Venus's desperate argument, intended to encourage Adonis towards a harmless kind of hunting and save him from the boar, misfires. She has moralized in the wrong direction. Given the conventional associations of hare-hunting with a lack of virility, it is not surprising that Venus's eloquent description of the hare hunt has no effect at all upon Adonis. His response to Venus's distracted question, "Where did I leave?" is wittily abrupt and dismissive: "No matter where, . . . / Leave me, and then the story aptly ends" (715–16).

More surprising is the effect of her description upon Venus herself, for she is unexpectedly moved to pity the very animal she has been recommending as prey. She not only advocates an "effeminate" kind of hunting; she is psychologically and morally unable to sustain even the thought of killing such a beast. She is beginning to think like Montaigne, in the essay "Of Cruelty," whose translator, Florio, seems to echo Venus's own characterization of the hare as a "dew-bedabbled wretch":

"I cannot well endure a seely dew-bedabled hare to groane, when she is seized upon by the howndes."[43] Her anthropomorphic treatment of the hare and the moral that she draws, with its sympathy for those who are "low" and "trodden on by many," are reminiscent not only of Montaigne but of the Puritans, who saw hunting both as potentially cruel and as an attack upon the poor. Her distraction at the end of this increasingly impassioned speech thus marks her confused awareness that sympathy for the hare has undermined not only the hunting she advocates but the sensual love she represents.

Behind Venus's attempt to seduce Adonis through images of hunting deer in parks and coursing hare in the fields lies a hierarchy of social values within the culture of the hunt itself. In the debate between love and hunting, she positions herself not merely on the side of love but on the side of the debased kinds of hunting that transform a heroic and martial activity, an initiation into manhood, into an ignoble and effeminizing kind of entertainment. The coursing of hares, the shooting of tame deer in parks – these are activities that blur the distinctions between martial values and courtly eroticism, that threaten to turn hunting itself into love. And this is of course exactly what Venus hopes to accomplish. She herself is an agent of metamorphosis, a force devoted to transforming one kind of venery into another. Shakespeare's poem enacts the transformative possibilities on either side of that pun.

Venus's emasculating energy, like that of the boar, manifests itself in paradoxical ways. On the one hand she desires a tame Adonis, attempting to transform him from a hunter of boar into a hunter of deer or hare, or worse, into her own pet deer, grazing on her lips and "sweet bottom grass" (233, 236). On the other hand, she wants him to act the part of a man. "Thou art no man," she complains, "though of a man's complexion, / For men will kiss even by their own direction" (215–16). When she falls upon the ground, she tries to jostle Adonis into the appropriate male position, and when his highly-sexed stallion proves his masculinity with a breeding jennet, she provides Adonis with the moral: "Thy palfrey, as he should, / Welcomes the warm approach of sweet desire" (385–86).

The powerful example of natural passion provided by Adonis's horse has led many critics to adopt Venus's point of view and to find Adonis's resistance priggish or narcissistic. As William Keach argues, however, Venus herself embodies neither in words nor actions the powerful argument for natural passion implied in the majestic and primitive sexuality of the horses.[44] The range of her sexual expression, which mingles comedy and pathos, coyness and direct assault, sophistication and simplicity, is no more "natural" than that of Cleopatra, whose character she anticipates. Underlying all of her varied appeals to love is a manipulative desire for sexual domination that belies her wish that Adonis were a man. What she most desires is a man, but a man who is child-like because under her control. As Heather Dubrow observes, "Venus connects loving Adonis with controlling him, mastering him; indeed, so deep is the connection as to make us suspect that even had he been less reluctant her impulse would have been to assert sovereignty by grasping and entrapping him."[45] Like Adonis, she cannot escape her mythological destiny. What she desires – and as Venus must desire – is another Mars, led prisoner by a "red rose chain" (110). *Venus and Adonis* is a poem about sexual domination, and shadowing the struggle between loving and hunting is the archetypal struggle for mastery between Venus and Mars.

Although fundamentally opposed, Venus and the boar therefore have much in common. Both love Adonis with a love that destroys. Venus herself is described at many points in the poem as a hunter or predatory animal whose sexual aggression is not only unattractive but murderous and devouring. She kisses Adonis's brow like "an empty eagle . . . devouring all in haste" (55–57). She holds him as one holds a hunted bird, "tangled in a net" (67). When they fall to the earth, "their lips together glued," she feeds "glutton-like" upon the "yielding prey," as if she were a vulture (546–51). Even upon Adonis's death she "crops the stalk" (1175) of the flower that has grown from his blood, aware that in doing so she destroys it but excusing herself by remarking that "it is as good / To wither in my breast as in his blood" (1181–82). In her pursuit of Adonis, Venus is in many respects identified with the boar itself. She accosts Adonis at the beginning of the poem as a "bold-fac'd suitor" (6). In her passion, she becomes so "enrag'd" that she plucks him from his horse (29–30), and so "red and hot" that she burns like "coals of glowing fire" (35). She pushes him backward, "as she would be thrust" (41). When he speaks, she "murthers" his words "with a kiss" (54). When Adonis finally yields a kiss, she exhibits symptoms comparable to those that Edward Topsell calls the "venerial rage" of the boar:

> And having felt the sweetness of the spoil,
> With blindfold fury she begins to forage;
> Her face doth reek and smoke, her blood doth boil,
> And careless lust stirs up a desperate courage . . .   (553–56)

When Venus discovers Adonis dead upon the ground, her shock is thus a shock of recognition. She sees in the deadly eroticism of the boar an image of herself:

> "Had I been tooth'd like him, I must confess,
> With kissing him I should have kill'd him first,
> But he is dead, and never did he bless
> My youth with his, the more am I accurs'd."
> With this she falleth in the place she stood,
> And stains her face with his congealed blood. (1117–22)

Although a goddess and eternally young, Venus sees herself now as old, as looking back upon a "youth" that was never blessed with Adonis's love. The true initiation towards which the poem has been driving is now revealed: not Adonis but Venus achieves maturity and self-knowledge, and she does so, not through the blessing of youthful love, but through the deadly eroticism of the hunt. She knows herself, in the violence of her passion, the boar. The mark of that knowledge is the mark of the hunter: the stain of her prey, Adonis, forever upon her face. As the goddess of love, she initiates herself.

In his insightful account of Shakespeare's Ovidianism, Jonathan Bate calls Venus's prophecy, with which the poem concludes, an "etiology of love's anguish."[46] The Ovidian context certainly invites the identification of origins, and Venus herself concludes her prophecy with what seems to be a curse: "Sith in his prime, Death doth my love destroy, / They that love best, their loves shall not enjoy" (1163–64). In a deeper sense, however, the moment is not one of origin but of recognition; Shakespeare works a variation on the Ovidian theme. Venus does not cause the future but merely sees it: "Since thou art dead, lo here I prophesy, / Sorrow on love hereafter shall attend" (1135–36). The catalogue of sorrows she describes – of inconstancy, deception, madness, jealousy, war – is not called into being by Venus but called into consciousness. The sorrows of love are not new to the poem. Mars has already been led by a golden chain, and even the naive Adonis has heard that love is "a life in death, / That laughs and weeps, and all but with a breath" (413–14). The sorrows of love are part of Venus's inescapable nature: she is the goddess of love, eternal and immutable; she has always had and will always have a deep affinity with the boar. Her staining of her face, in short, has an initiatory rather than an etiological significance: the nature of reality is not altered by the act but understood and accepted. Venus now knows who she is; she knows what it means to be Venus.

The poem does not moralize its tragic theme, but merely enacts its paradoxes in a ritual of "blooding," in which the goddess of love plays the roles of initiator and initiate. Despite the long-standing efforts of critics to do so, one cannot read the poem as a cautionary tale, placing blame on either Venus or Adonis. The ultimate fate of both characters is that of Ovidian tragedy: they are doomed to enact their own mythology.

Ovidian tragedy, of course, is not mature Shakespearean tragedy. Adonis dies without insight. Venus's insight must be by definition unredemptive: she cannot be other than she is. The maternal impulse that makes her "cradle" Adonis's flower in her breast (1185), and that earlier made her pursue him to the hunt "like a milch doe, whose swelling dugs do ache" (875), might make her plight sympathetic but is nonetheless tinged by a continuing and deadly self-absorption. "To grow unto himself was his desire," she tells the flower she has torn from its stem, "And so 'tis thine, but know it is as good / To wither in my breast as in his blood" (1180–82). She has not allowed Adonis to "grow unto himself," and now she denies the same impulse to his "child," who is plucked from its source of nourishment and whose fate is to be smothered by her love: "There shall not be one minute in an hour / Wherein I will not kiss my sweet love's flow'r" (1187–88). As Heather Dubrow observes, Venus's plight at the end of the poem involves us in "a seesawing between sympathy and judgment that characterizes the whole poem."[47] To understand the significance of Venus's ritual of "blooding," then, is not to resolve the ambiguity of her character, which is by definition unresolvable, or to simplify our response to it. Attending to her ritual act, however, does illuminate the distinctive nature of her tragedy and heighten what William Keach calls the poem's "surprisingly powerful sense of erotic pathos."[48] For a goddess, insight does not and cannot produce guilt or reformation; the only mark of Venus's initiation as a hunter is the enduring stain of Adonis's blood.

Venus and Adonis is a stylish and sophisticated poem, one that captures the ambiance of the young aristocratic males for whom it was apparently written. This ambiance is on the one hand modishly literary, and much of the delight of the poem springs from the twists and turns, the paradoxes and perversities, of Ovidian themes, many of which depend upon the traditional identification of love with hunting. But the ambiance is also modishly social, deeply implicated in the values and customs of the hunt within which young aristocratic males were so deeply immersed. The zest for country life that so animates the imagery of the poem does not derive merely from Shakespeare's Stratford youth, important though that may be. Adonis's love of the heroic hunt of the boar, Venus's seductive attempts to deflect that love into the soft hunting of deer in parks or hare in the open field, the ritual of "blooding" with which the poem concludes – such episodes achieve their witty resonance in large part because they draw upon the traditions, practices, debates, and values embedded in the Elizabethan world of the hunt. The poem was dedicated to the young Earl of Southampton. It might have pleased as well another hunter, the hunting lord of *The Taming of the Shrew*, who knows and loves his hounds, who enjoys a good joke, and who has a picture of

> Adonis painted by a running brook,
> And Cytherea all in sedges hid,
> Which seem to move and wanton with her breath,
> Even as the waving sedges play with wind.   (Ind.2. 50–53)

"VERY REVERENT SPORT": THE PRINCESS'S HUNT IN *LOVE'S LABOR'S LOST*

The most significant event in *Love's Labor's Lost* is one that is merely reported at the end of the play: the death of the French king. Marcade's sudden and unexpected account of this shocking occurrence stuns the Princess and her companions, disrupts their festive merriment, thwarts the amorous desires of the young suitors, and destroys the anticipated resolution of the comedy. Given the theatrical power of this event, it is not surprising that few readers or viewers remember a second death that also occurs offstage in the play – the death of a deer, killed in act 4 scene 1 by the French King's daughter, the Princess of France. This death, in contrast to that of the King, seems completely insignificant, provoking little attention among the characters of the play and even less among its critics.[49] Yet the death of the deer is in its own way shocking. It occurs not in a distant court but in the very heart of the play's ostensibly restorative green world, the park of Navarre. It results, moreover, not from natural causes – the King dies from lingering illness and old age – but from a sudden act of violence, an act that the Princess herself calls a murder (4.1.8).

The most common critical approach to the play's hunting scene has been to treat it as a metaphor for love. From this perspective the Princess, as a representative of the women, becomes a typical Petrarchan mistress, "killing" the men who worship her. Louis Adrian Montrose, for example, interprets the Princess's reflections on the killing of a deer as indirect reflections of her own attitude towards the King's desire.[50] John Barton's 1978 production of the play, according to Miriam Gilbert, represented the Princess's motives in this way, by making her comments on the deer grow out of her disappointment at not seeing the King.[51] There is much to recommend such interpretations. The convention of the love-hunt was virtually a cliché in the period, and the play's language evokes it. The language of hunting in the scene, as we shall see, bristles with high-spirited sexual wordplay, and even the love-stricken men see themselves later as prey: "the King he is hunting the deer," says Berowne, "I am coursing myself" (4.3.1–2).

The hunting scene, however, is not merely a stage metaphor for love; it is a representation of actual events that would have occurred frequently in the Elizabethan court. For the Elizabethan aristocracy, and for Elizabeth herself, park-hunting was a favorite pastime, a "sport" that was also a festive entertainment; as in Shakespeare's play, it was a common entertainment for visiting nobles and ambassadors. By imitating such an event, the Princess's hunting scene joins the vast repertory of "games" that define the action of *Love's Labor's Lost* – among them, word-games (the stock-in-trade of nearly every character), practical jokes, a masque of Russians, and a pageant of the Nine Worthies. As many critics have noted, the play is not only based on games and entertainments but is to a great extent about them. In this sense, the play both reflects – and reflects upon – the life of the Elizabethan court. In doing so, as John Turner has argued, the play captures the tension within the Elizabethan word *competitor*, which might mean either *partner* or *rival*.[52] The various games of the play embody not only the high spirits and *camaraderie* of the court of Navarre but its tendencies towards narcissism and aggression. Because of this tension, the play's tone sits on the knife-edge between romantic comedy and satire.

In 1591, as we have seen earlier, Queen Elizabeth killed three or four deer in the park at Cowdray after being presented with a crossbow and celebrated in a song as an eroticized Diana. Addressed as the "Goddesse and Monarch of (t)his happie Ile," she was told that her "eies" were "arrows," attracting the fascinated gaze of the stately "harts" that they killed. This is the social atmosphere of the hunting park that Venus invokes in her attempt to seduce Adonis away from the dangerous hunt of the boar. In *Love's Labor's Lost* Venus's fantasy of park hunting becomes literalized. The Princess is taken to the park of Navarre and positioned in a stand to await the deer to be driven before her. Although not as heavily eroticized as the setting that Venus imagines, the park of Navarre is at once a site of love-games and a field of death. Like the eroticized Diana who was celebrated at Cowdray, this Princess "kills" both deer and men.

In *Love's Labor's Lost*, the Princess's hunt holds a unique place among the play's festive entertainments. Although many of the games and pageants of the play are aggressive, including the love-games, the Princess's hunt is the only one that results in the literal death of the competition. While the Princess can compliment both of her two bantering ladies on "a set of wit well played" (5.2.29), no one can do the same for both her and the deer. Hunting, in short, carries the aggressive tendencies of the play's courtly games to a disturbing extreme, suggesting that behind a joke may lie a desire to kill.

An entrance into the distinctive hunting culture evoked by this play is provided by Shakespeare's endearingly pompous curate, Nathaniel. In act 4, Nathaniel, Holofernes the schoolmaster, and Dull the constable engage in a dizzying debate about the nature of the deer the Princess has just killed. While much scholarly effort has been expended on the mock pedantry and misunderstanding that characterize this disagreement, the statement that initiates it, Nathaniel's pious approval of the hunt, has for the most part escaped attention. "Very reverent sport truly," he says, "and done in the testimony of a good conscience" (4.2.1–2). Why, we might ask, does Nathaniel call the Princess's hunting a "reverent" sport, one undertaken with the warrant of a good conscience? And why is a curate's sanctimonious approval a natural way for Shakespeare to open a scene in which a few village worthies chat about the sporting activities of their social betters?

The word "reverent" in Nathaniel's phrase means "worthy of veneration." It contains two complementary ideas – one religious, the other social. The godliness of the sport is emphasized by the phrase "done in the testimony of a good conscience," a phrase that echoes Paul's words to the Corinthians: "For our rejoycing is this, the testimonie of our conscience, that in simplicitie and godlie pureness, and not in fleshlie wisdome, but by the grace of God we have had our conversation in the worlde, and moste of all to you wardes."[53] In his role as village curate, Nathaniel endorses the sport in language appropriate to his calling; as William C. Carroll observes, "virtually everything he says has a biblical or patristic allusion lurking near the surface."[54] Like his colleagues, Nathaniel is an admiring and respectful member of the commonwealth, a sympathetic supporter of the powers that be. He voices complacently the position of the established church and state on hunting. In this he is supported by Holofernes. "Away," says the pedant, as he leads Nathaniel and Dull from the hunt to their festive dinner, "the gentles are at their game, and we will to our recreation" (4.2.165–67). Hunting is a "game" for "gentles," and worthy of veneration.

As we have seen in chapter 1, the religious and social justification of hunting as a recreation sanctioned by God, a result of man's dominion over nature, was opposed in the period on three closely related fronts: by humanists, for whom hunting transformed men into beasts; by Puritans, for whom hunting provoked cruel and destructive behavior both to animals and to the common people; and by others who, like Montaigne, felt instinctive sympathy for animal suffering. Erasmus's satire on hunting in *The Praise of Folly* provides an apt gloss on Nathaniel's words, since he mocks not only the social status of the hunters, who think they inhale exotic perfume even in "the verie stenche of the houndes kennell," but the "reverence" implied in their ritual actions upon the death of a deer. "Ye know your selves," says Folly, "what ceremonies they use about the same."[55]

In *Love's Labor's Lost,* the folly of hunting is voiced by the huntress herself. As the Princess waits, bow in hand, for the hunt to begin, she acknowledges the cruelty of her role, that of playing "the murtherer" in ambush (4.1.8). Her theatrical vocabulary implies that hunting of this kind, as in Elizabeth's hunt at Cowdray, is a form of pageant. She reflects upon the unworthiness of her motives, admitting that she hunts "for praise alone" (34), a statement that suggests the Puritans' emphasis upon the cruel frivolity of the sport. In lines that resonate throughout the play, moreover, she treats the desire for praise in hunting as a symptom of the destructive quest for fame in all human activities:[56]

> And out of question so it is sometimes:
> Glory grows guilty of detested crimes,
> When for fame's sake, for praise, an outward part,
> We bend to that the working of the heart;
> As I for praise alone now seek to spill
> The poor deer's blood, that my heart means no ill.   (4.1.30–35)

Like Erasmus and More, the Princess sees behind the hunt the desire for glory; like the Puritan Philip Stubbes, she emphasizes the lack of charity in her action. She adds to all of these opposing voices, moreover, a distinctive note of sympathy for the deer itself, the suffering of which transcends its mere emblematic meaning. For a brief moment, she edges towards the sentiments of Montaigne.[57]

Through the Princess's own words, then, Shakespeare embeds in his text a familiar satirical perspective on hunting, a perspective, moreover, that provides a framework for the whole of act 4. Although the development of the hunting motif in the several scenes of act 4 is complicated, its central core is the connection between hunting and human vanity, which turns every action into a kind of hunt, an irreverent sport. Behind the vanity, in most cases, lie threats of aggression, often sexual, which are sublimated into attacks of wit. Armado's letter, which Boyet reads for the Princess, concludes with his flamboyant threat to play the "Nemean lion" to Jaquenetta, his helpless prey (4.1.88–89). After the Princess leaves the stage, Boyet and Rosalind remain, and Boyet's "Who is the shooter?" (108) triggers off a verbal sparring match in which "shooters" are likened to "suitors" and hunting to the pursuit of the cuckold's horns; the contest is joined by Maria and Costard and eventually becomes so openly obscene as to elicit Maria's laughing protest, "Come, come, you talk greasily, your lips grow foul" (137). For Rosalind, Boyet, Maria, and Costard, the hunt has no reality except as an excuse for a playful competition in sexual puns, a contest that concludes with Costard awarding victory to himself and the ladies: "Lord, Lord, how the ladies and I have put him down" (141). Costard's phrase "put him down" captures tersely the mixture of sexuality and aggression that characterizes the dialogue as a whole. Sport consists of putting down. The satire of hunting is thus implicated in several respects in the "preposterous reversals" of high and low that Patricia Parker identifies in the language of the play throughout.[58]

   In the next scene, which begins with Nathaniel's comment on the reverence of the sport, the hunt provides an opportunity for the learned commentators to display their knowledge of aristocratic recreations. In this contest the pedantical verbiage of curate and schoolmaster are set against the simple constable's inarticulate yet unshakable conviction. Although one risks a Holofernian pedantry in glossing the wordplay of the scene, to do so highlights further the satire submerged in Nathaniel's phrase "a very reverent sport." The point of debate among the three is the worth of the deer that the Princess has killed; the more fully mature and majestic the animal, the more "reverent" the sport. Holofernes begins by asserting that the deer was "*sanguis*, in blood" (4.2.3–4) – that is, fully mature, in the full vigor of health, and therefore, to adopt Nathaniel's terminology, capable of providing "very reverent sport" and great praise to the Princess. Nathaniel, however, objects that the deer was not fully mature but "a buck of the first head" (10) – that is, a buck about five years old, with its first fully developed antlers. Holofernes then protests with the pedantical Latin expression "*haud credo,*" (11) or, "I cannot believe it," a statement that is apparently misheard by Dull as "old grey doe" and vigorously denied; to kill such a weak specimen would be an act of shame. Dull insists that the deer was a "pricket" (12), a buck of two years – that is, a kill more "reverent" than an old grey doe but not as "reverent" as a buck of the first head.[59]

It is characteristic of the play that this debate is never resolved, and that we never discover the age or value of the Princess's deer. This in itself undermines the idea of pursuing hunting as a means of winning fame or reputation, for, as Falstaff knows, one's honor depends upon the fickleness of others' perceptions. Dull is allowed the final word in his debate with his more learned companions, but only because Holofernes deflects the conversation into another kind of self-display, that of making a poem, a contest in which he is the only competitor and therefore destined to win.

The monstrosity that results – "The preyful Princess pierc'd and prick'd a pretty pleasing pricket" (56) – reduces the question of the deer's age or worth to one of mere verbal convenience, the word "Princess" demanding the alliterative "pricket." The suffering and death of the deer, moreover, are completely trivialized, for its wounds merely provide inspiration for Holofernes' poetic vanity. The sore pricket becomes a "sore," a deer of four years, or adding a letter, a "sorel," one of three years. When the "l" is transformed into the capital "L" representing the Roman numeral fifty, and a second "L" is added to make one hundred, the number of wounds on the deer killed escalates accordingly. Holofernes' epitaph on the death of the deer thus conveys no sense of "reverence," to use Nathaniel's term, but serves merely to feed the vanity of the speaker, whose verbal pyrotechnics suggest the unfeeling violence of the sport itself. As a parody of an epitaph, Holofernes' poem pricks the bubble of reputation both for the unfortunate deer and the Princess, whose kill is lost altogether in the sweet smoke of rhetoric.

For the King of Navarre and his young companions, the hunt provides a setting for their own massacre by love. Berowne opens act 4 scene 3 with a line that frames the action that follows: "The King he is hunting the deer: I am coursing myself" (1–2). When he observes the King entering with a love-sonnet in hand, he remarks to himself, "Shot, by heaven! Proceed, sweet Cupid, thou hast thump'd him with thy bird-bolt under the left pap" (22–24). The entire scene, in which Berowne watches unobserved as each of his companions betrays his love for one of the women, might be called one of ambush, with the final victim being Berowne himself. Having forsworn themselves while hunting, the young men now transform hunting into open warfare, for which it provides the traditional training ground: "Saint Cupid, then!" shouts the King, "and, soldiers, to the field!" (363). The Princess's satiric linkage between hunting and vanity provides an apt gloss not only on the love of the young men but on their initial devotion to their little academe. In the opening line of the play, the King commits himself to the pursuit of "fame, that all hunt after in their lives" (1.1.1). Hunting after fame in books, he becomes eventually both the hunter and the hunted in love. In study and love, the metaphor of the hunt, with its overtones of narcissism and aggression, shapes the overall action of the play. The metaphor situates the literary convention of the love-hunt within the social tensions surrounding the practice of hunting in parks.

One of the play's many paradoxes is that the satirist of the hunt, the Princess, includes herself among the satirized, mocking her own vanity along with all the others. In this she is like Berowne, whose mockery is also self-reflexive. She is like Berowne, too, in the discrepancy between her emotions and her actions. Berowne knows that he will be unable to keep the oath the King asks him to swear at the beginning of the play, yet he pledges his word nonetheless. The Princess knows that she hunts with no purpose but vanity; she acknowledges her compassion for the deer; and yet she kills. She suffers a guilty conscience but participates nonetheless in a social ritual her mind and heart oppose. Her action, ironically, receives the pious blessing of Nathaniel, who finds the hunt "very reverent" and "done in the testimony of a good conscience."

Like most of the heroines of the romantic comedies, the Princess is often idealized by critics, taken to be a clear-sighted, playful, and emotionally mature center of value in the play. She is certainly as close as the play comes to such a character. The killing of the deer, however, underlined by the unconscious irony in Nathaniel's blessing, marks the Princess out as a target among all the others, only for more sophisticated satire. Like Berowne, she is ruefully conscious of her own folly at moments, but this consciousness does not guide her actions. Her satiric assaults on others, moreover, like Berowne's, betray a delight in verbal aggression rather than any desire to educate or reform. In the words of Holofernes' poem, she is a "preyful Princess." When she first meets the King of Navarre, she mocks him for welcoming her not to the court but to the fields (2.1.91). In the scene before the hunt (4.1.), she befuddles the poor forester by accusing him of not recognizing her beauty. In this scene too she orders the seal of Armado's letter broken so that she can mock the contents, despite her knowledge that the letter is addressed not to her but to Jaquenetta.

The Princess characterizes her mockeries as "sport," but her use of the word invokes notions of violence rather than reverence. When she learns that the young men are coming as wooers in the guise of Russians, she proposes the wearing of masks so that "sport by sport" will be "o'erthrown" (5.2.153) and the wooers sent "away with shame" (156). In response to Boyet's observation that having the women avert their faces when the men address them will "kill the speaker's heart," she answers, "Therefore I do it" (149–151). Later in the same scene, she urges the King to watch the pageant of worthies because "that sport best pleases that doth [least] know how" (516). This is so, she continues, because "Their form confounded makes most form in mirth, / When great things laboring perish in their birth" (519–20). Berowne takes this remark as a "right description of our sport" (521). The Princess's image of a mirth that comes from watching "great things laboring" only to "perish in their birth" conveys not only the vanity that drives the festive merriments of all the nobles, a vanity evoked in Hobbes's description of laughter as "sudden glory," but the insidiously life-denying quality of its pleasure. Comedy does not thrive on abortion.

As Louis Adrian Montrose observes, the word "sport" is used throughout the play in relation to activities that, unlike rituals, divide participants into winners and losers.[60] Play in the world of *Love's Labor's Lost* is almost invariably a form of aggression, as in the Princess's delight at the promise of watching the men make fools of themselves in disguise: "There's no such sport as sport by sport o'erthrown, / To make theirs ours and ours none but our own" (5.2.153–54). The contrast is not merely between sport and ritual but between Elizabethan and modern notions of sport. The words that link sport to fair play – "sportsman," "sportsmanship," being a "good sport" – did not enter English until the eighteenth century. In Shakespeare's usage, the word "sport" is far more likely to refer to mere diversion or entertainment than to an organized game with rules and proper decorum. The entertainment, moreover, is as likely to be cruel as innocuous, as when Longaville singles out Costard and Armado to be "our sport" (1.1.179), or when, in *Merry Wives of Windsor*, Master Ford promises his neighbors that they "shall see sport anon" when they capture his wife's lover (3.3.169). Hunting itself seems not to have been called a "sport" in the period. In the titles of handbooks, it is most commonly an art (*The Noble Arte of Venerie*) or a recreation (*The Gentleman's Recreation*). The tension between delightful wit and disturbing verbal aggression that runs throughout the play seems related to a tension within the culture in attitudes towards sport itself, of which the deadly game of hunting is a special case.

The Princess's chief targets throughout the play are the young men. Like Elizabeth at Cowdray, she is the object of male desire, but she kills. Although not an Amazon, like the huntress Hippolyta in *A Midsummer Night's Dream*, she threatens male dominance with her aggressive wit and disturbs the patriarchal order. She kills the deer with a literal arrow and the King with a metaphoric one. Before she goes off to the hunt, the Princess is questioned by Boyet about her admission that she "for praise alone" seeks "to spill / The poor deer's blood, that [her] heart means no ill" (4.1.34–35). "Do not curst wives hold that self-sovereignty / Only for praise' sake," asks Boyet, "when they strive to be / Lords o'er their lords?" (36–38). To which the Princess replies, "Only for praise – and praise we may afford / To any lady that subdues a lord" (34–40). The word "subdues" crystallizes the complex nature of the threat the Princess represents to the adolescent male ego: the mastery of this "curst" wife is at once psychological, physical, and sexual. A similar mastery is evoked in the unconscious innuendoes of Holofernes' song, with its unconventional application of familiar male terms for sexual aggression to the Princess: "The preyful Princess pierc'd and prick'd a pretty pleasing pricket."

The subversive laughter of the Princess comes to a sudden halt upon Marcade's announcement of the French King's death. Although her characterization in this final scene is not entirely clear, there are hints that her father's death shocks the Princess into a new state of mind. She speaks of her "new-sad soul" (5.2.731) and apologizes to the suitors for "the liberal opposition of our spirits" (733). When the King attempts to continue his suit, moreover, she is for once at a loss for words; her mocking wit leaves her, and she can only say "I understand you not, my griefs are double" (752). If there are signs of reform in the Princess's language, however, they are left tantalizingly vague; as David Bevington observes of all the female roles in the play, "essentially complete in themselves, the women remain a mystery."[61]

The ineffectual efforts of the King and Berowne to reform, on the other hand, are certainly clear, and both are required to endure a year's penance for their continuing folly. The King's retreat into a hermitage and Berowne's term in a hospital, "[enforcing] the pained impotent to smile" (854), are intended to produce in them "new-sad" souls that will make them worthy of marriage. Berowne's task in particular is to transform his delightful but ultimately cruel and unfeeling wit into what might be called a "reverent sport," a recreation that cures rather than kills because based on a respect for life. Whether such a transformation can be achieved remains a disturbingly open question. "To move wild laughter in the throat of death?" asks Berowne, "It cannot be, it is impossible: / Mirth cannot move a soul in agony" (855–857).

The event that shocks the aristocrats into perceiving the gap between deadly and curative sport is the death of the French King. The insight has already been embedded, however, in the scene in which the Princess, in "sport," and with no more than self-professed vanity as a goal, kills a deer. The values implied in Berowne's curious description of laughter as "wild" suggest the dangers of the enclosed, hermetic, and ultimately unnatural world of the little academe and its park of tame deer. To "move wild laughter in the throat of death," as the Princess makes clear in her reply to Berowne, is to empathize with human suffering, to use wit not as a means of assault but as a cure. Curative laughter is released by empathy. In the hunting scene, the Princess feels empathy as she prepares to "spill / The poor deer's blood, that [her] heart means no ill" (4.1.34–35). But she kills nonetheless. The play's juxtaposition of two invisible deaths, that of a king and that of a deer, implies a link between human and animal suffering, a link endorsed at the end of the play in the quest to release "wild laughter" through empathy. Although the values finally upheld by the Princess do not imply that animal and human life are of equal value, they do promote the existence of what Montaigne calls a "mutuall bond" between them.[62]

Nathaniel complacently approves of hunting as a "reverent sport." Yet the play as a whole mocks that complacency, insinuating into its language and action disturbing doubts about the prospects for reverence in any "sport," so deeply engrained are the aggressive and narcissistic impulses that characterize the various entertainments at Navarre. The full text of 2 Corinthians, to which Nathaniel's blessing of the hunt alludes, includes not only Paul's assurances to his church that his own conscience is clear, but his exhortations that they avoid the dangers of vanity, act charitably towards their neighbors, and follow the spirit of the New Law, engraved in the heart, rather than the ritualism of the Old Law, preserved in tablets of stone. The contemporary controversy over hunting touches the values of this text, as we have seen, and Shakespeare's ending probes skeptically the capacity of the aristocracy to enact them. The commoners in the play, interestingly, share the folly of their social betters but lack somewhat their aggressive edge. Unlike their superiors, they are not licensed to hunt.

As a "comedy," *Love's Labor's Lost* does not pursue Berowne's doubts about the possibility of moving "wild laughter in the throat of death." The consequences of the death of a father and the death of a deer remain uncertain. To invoke the ghost of the Princess's deer, however, is to learn something about the skeptical overtones of this curious romantic and satirical comedy. Although one cannot help but be exhilarated by the exuberance, playfulness, and *camaraderie* that many readers have emphasized in the language and action of the play, one should not underestimate its critical energy or probative force. Nor should one underestimate, as in its use of hunting as a central metaphor for the life of a contemporary court, the play's close relationship with Elizabethan social experience. In representing the courtly sport of park-hunting, Shakespeare insinuated himself into a contemporary debate with broad social ramifications, one that touched even a royal English huntress who, like the Princess of France, shot deer from ambush and killed courtiers with arrows from her eyes.

Although not explicitly invoked by Shakespeare, the image of Queen Elizabeth hunting at Cowdray, her eyes killing courtiers and her bow killing deer, seems to haunt both *Venus and Adonis* and *Love's Labor's Lost*. Elizabeth, Venus, and the Princess of France are all "preyful princesses," implicated by their Amazonian roles in the deathly eroticism of courtly hunting. The role is one Elizabeth at least seems to have found comfortable; if she experienced ambivalence in any of her numerous hunts throughout her reign, the evidence has gone unrecorded. Shakespeare's huntresses, in contrast, feel within themselves the tension of their Amazonian identity. The goddess Venus is startled to be moved by the plight of a hunted hare and shocked to discover in the death of Adonis her identity with the boar. The stain on her face marks the knowledge of her own inner contradiction. The Princess of France is also a killer, and one moved by the innocence of her prey. In her case, unlike that of Venus, the tension embodied in the role of the huntress is not resolved in tragic or comic paradox but left suspended, as irresolvable, perhaps, as the play in which it appears.

CHAPTER THREE

"*Solemn*" *hunting in* Titus Andronicus *and* Julius Caesar

As Roman tragedies, *Titus Andronicus* and *Julius Caesar* have much in common. Although set in very different periods, they share many of the familiar concerns of the Shakespearean Roman world: with tyrannical political power, with social conflict and civil war, with family values and family honor, and with the idea of Rome as a civilized society. Both of the plays begin with an image of an unstable society, a Rome threatened by internal political dissension following upon recent military triumph; both depict the unraveling of the state into savage anarchy; and both conclude with the Roman polity restored, if only in formal terms, by a powerful ruler.

The two plays share a more curious feature in common, a preoccupation with imagery of the hunt. *Titus Andronicus* includes a literal hunting scene (2.3), in which the hunted creatures are not the panther and hart to which the hunt is ostensibly devoted but Bassianus and Lavinia, who become human prey for the predatory sons of Tamora. The language of hunting spans the play as a whole. Although *Julius Caesar* does not enact a hunt, the central event of the play, the assassination of Caesar, is characterized as a hunt by both Brutus and Antony and is staged in a manner that strongly evokes the death of a stag. The civil war that ensues, moreover, is envisaged by Antony in terms that suggest the wild, anarchic hunting of an Elizabethan poaching raid.

Why should Shakespeare's representation of these two Roman worlds feature the language and imagery of hunting? The choice may have been triggered by brief allusions in his sources. Although the narrative source of *Titus Andronicus* is in dispute, the most likely candidate is *The History of Titus Andronicus*, which is recorded in an eighteenth-century chapbook. In that version of the story, Tamora, the Moor, and her two sons plot to invite the prince to hunt "in the great Forest, on the Banks of the River Tyber, and there murder him." While in the forest, the sons not only murder the prince, but, "like two ravenous Tygers," rape and mutilate Lavinia.[1] If Shakespeare used this story, he converted mere hints of a forest setting into a full-scale representation of a Romanized Elizabethan hunt. In North's translation of Plutarch's *Life of Julius Caesar*, the major source for that play, North includes a single but powerful image from the hunt in his description of the assassination: Caesar, he says, "was hacked and mangeled amonge them, as a wilde beaste taken of hunters."[2] This single image becomes a major symbol in Shakespeare's tragedy. In both plays, then, Shakespeare seems to have seized on incidental allusions to the hunt in his sources and to have amplified them into powerful poetic and theatrical symbols. Neither the specific sources nor the generalized Roman settings explain, however, why he should have done so, or why he should have based his imagery of the hunt on the most elevated and ceremonial kind in the Elizabethan period, what Aaron calls the "solemn hunting" devoted to the hart or stag (2.1.112).[3]

To explain the peculiar prominence of the hunt in both plays, and its distinctive overtones, we must attend to another feature they share in common, a preoccupation with ceremony. As many critics have observed, Shakespeare's conception of Rome is richly ceremonial. *Titus Andronicus* opens with a Roman triumph, the election of an emperor, and the ritual sacrifice of Tamora's son, Alarbus. It ends with a ritual banquet, a cannibalistic feast in which Tamora devours her own sons. As Eugene M. Waith observes, the most important ceremonies in the play are those that "order or partly conceal discordant energies."[4] *Julius Caesar* also begins with a triumph, the celebration of Caesar's victory over Pompey, a ceremony which is combined with the observances of the Feast of the Lupercal.[5] The play includes as well the taking of auguries, the celebration of the Ides of March, and Caesar's funeral. As is often the case in Shakespeare, the ceremonies represented in both plays are deeply problematic; the social ideals behind the ceremonies are never fulfilled but are perverted, travestied, or manipulated for political ends. At the core of both plays is a concern with the most disturbing and paradoxical of ceremonies, that of human sacrifice: the tragic events of *Titus Andronicus* begin with the ritual death of Alarbus, and the civil war of *Julius Caesar* follows upon Brutus's attempt to see himself and the other conspirators as "sacrificers, but not butchers" of Caesar (2.1.166).[6]

The link between hunting and ritual implied by Shakespeare's juxtaposition of the two themes in these plays becomes particularly suggestive in the light of an influential study of the origins of ritual sacrifice. In *Homo Necans*, Walter Burkert not only links hunting to sacrifice but

finds in the hunt the origin of all sacrificial ritual. The introduction of
hunting into human society, according to Burkert, was the crucial and
defining event in the development of humanity. The age of the hunter,
the Paleolithic period, is by far the longest in human history and, according to Burkert and others, has had a profound effect upon the development of the human species and human society. Both human physiology
and the patriarchal order of society, with its gendered division of labor
and child-rearing, owe their origins, in this view, to the needs of a
hunting culture.

For Burkert, the ritualistic behavior characteristic of the hunt in
hunter-gatherer societies – the purifications and abstinences before the
hunt, the ceremonial of the death and dismemberment, the preservation of trophies of various kinds – answers to the shock of killing, a shock
that must be overcome in order for the society to survive. The hunted
animal thus becomes a sacrificial animal, and the ritual of its death
enacts the paradox that life is "nourished and perpetuated by death."
The ceremonies of the death purge feelings of fear and guilt both
through the dynamics of group solidarity and through the symbolic restoration, in the preservation of relics or trophies, of the life that has been
lost. "The shock felt in the act of killing," observes Burkert, "is answered
later by consolidation; guilt is followed by reparation, destruction by
reconstruction."[7]

As Burkert himself acknowledges, any argument of this kind is bound
to be speculative, depending as it does on the fragmentary evidence of
pre-history, sweeping generalizations about the historical practice of the
hunt in very different cultures, and a functional view of ritual that is
open to challenge. His conception of hunting ritual, nonetheless, provides a touchstone against which to test Elizabethan custom and
Shakespeare's representations of it. Such a touchstone is particularly
useful in the absence of Tudor or Jacobean attempts to explain or justify
the obsessive attention to ritual detail that characterized the practice of
the hunt. The hunting manuals all insist upon a meticulous observance
of custom, especially in the killing of the noblest of animals, the hart,
yet none of them poses the question, why.

The entirety of a hunt may be considered a ritual structure, one that
corresponds in a broad sense to the tripartite rhythm that Van Gennep
and others associate with seasonal rites and rites of passage.[8]
Characteristically, the hunters begin in the social world of the court,
proceed into the forest, and return to the court for a feast. Each part of
the event has its own ceremonies. Gascoigne's *Noble Arte of Venerie*, for

example, features illustrations of Queen Elizabeth presiding over the ceremonial feast in the forest before the hunt (fig. 2) and receiving the ceremonial presentation of the fumets, or excrement, of a deer from the chief huntsman as evidence of the worthiness of the animal to be hunted.[9] The climactic moments of the hunt, as made clear in the descriptions in the handbooks of the sport, are those of the death and, especially, the dismemberment of the animal, an event that features elaborate ceremonial behavior. Although the hunting manuals are generally of one accord in their descriptions of the dismemberment of the hart or stag, their accounts of the kill naturally differ. The pursuit of a wild animal to the death with dogs and horses does not lend itself to ceremonial behavior. Death is difficult to control and may come in many guises. The tendency in the manuals, and certainly in the artistic representations of the scene, is to stylize the kill, and to emphasize the role of the ruler or noblest personage, to whom by rights it belongs. This is done by focusing on the decapitation of the deer, which occurs after its death. The quintessential statement of this ritualistic assertion of royal privilege occurs, as we have seen, in Peake's painting of Henry, Prince of Wales (fig. 1).

For our purposes the most representative description of the death and dismemberment of the hart occurs in Gascoigne's *Noble Arte of Venerie*, published in 1575 and reprinted in 1611. The ritual of breaking up the hart is so important to Gascoigne that he recounts it in two versions: first, following his French source, he describes the method used in France; then, after alerting the reader to the fact that French custom differs in part from English, he describes the distinctive features of the English method.[10] In describing the event, I shall assume that unless Gascoigne indicates otherwise the French and English versions are sufficiently similar to be treated as one.

The death of the hart is first marked by the sounding of the horns and the "whooping" of what Gascoigne calls "a deade note" to call the hunters together (126). Once the hunters are assembled, the hounds are brought to the deer and permitted, for a short time, to "byte and teare him about the necke"; they are then coupled to await their reward. In England, as Gascoigne illustrates by a woodcut of Queen Elizabeth (fig. 3), the chief person takes the "assaye of the Deare with a sharpe knyfe" (133), slitting along the brisket of the deer towards the belly while the deer is held by the kneeling chief huntsman; this is done to test the "goodnesse of the flesh" (134). Next, the deer's head is cut off, usually "by the chiefe personage. For they take delight to cut off his heade with

their woodknyves, skaynes, or swordes, to trye their edge, and the goodnesse or strength of their arme" (134). The head is then "cabaged,"
which removes the antlers for a trophy and the brains and other morsels
for the hounds. At this stage too certain "deintie morsels," which include
the tongue, ears, and "doulcets" (testicles), are put in "a faire hand-
kercher altogether, for the Prince or chiefe" (134). In France these
morsels are roasted and eaten on the spot as carbonados, with much
rejoicing of the nobles, who offer rewards to the best of their hounds and
huntsmen.

The dismembering of the deer then proceeds in two stages. First, the
huntsman removes the skin in a precise order, beginning with a slit at the
throat. After this is accomplished, the huntsman must pause for a hearty
draught of wine, "for if he shoulde breake up the Deare before he
drinke, the Venison would stinke and putrifie" (128). The breaking up of
the deer is also done in a precise order, with particular parts given to the
huntsman who harbored, or roused, the deer, and to the chief personage. At this point Gasgoigne adds a substantial paragraph to his source,
describing in meticulous detail the "ceremonie" the English use "in
taking out the shoulder." The ceremony tests the skill of the huntsman:
"If . . . he touch the shoulder or any part of the legge, with any other
thing than his knyfe, untill he have taken it out, it is a forfayture, and he
is thought to be no handsome woodman" (134–35). In *Merry Wives*,
Falstaff, imagining himself a Windsor stag, sees himself the victim of
such a ceremony, divided between Mistress Ford and Mistress Page:
"Divide me like a brib'd buck, each a haunch. I will keep my sides to
myself, my shoulders for the fellow of this walk – and my horns I
bequeath your husbands" (5.5.24–27). The image suggests that even
poachers divided their "brib'd" deer with a consciousness of the customary ritual.

The ceremony of the breaking up of the hart also includes the
rewarding of the hounds. The honor of assembling them is given to the
"Prince or chiefe," who begins "to blow and to hallow." After the other
huntsmen have also blown, the hounds are set loose upon the food,
which is spread on the deer skin. When they have almost finished eating,
a huntsman holding the deer's head hallows them to the hunt again. He
shows them the head, "lifting it up and downe before them to make them
baye it: and when he hath drawne them al about him baying shall cast
downe the heade amongst them that they may take [?] their pleasure
thereon" (132). Finally, he leads them back to the skin, and prepares them
for the kennel. Although Gascoigne does not describe it, the ceremony

almost certainly concludes with a procession homeward. William Twiti's directions for the return are as follows: "Carry the head home before the Lord; and the heart, tail, and gullet should be carried home on a forked branch, and you should blow the menée at the door of the hall."[11]

The foregoing account of the ceremonial death and dismemberment of a stag provides only a rough idea of its general nature. Because Gascoigne mixes French and English custom, his account is not always clear. Nor is it necessarily complete. Since the ceremony is to a great extent customary, moreover, it was probably subject to local variation. All of this said, however, Gascoigne's description conforms so closely to others in the period and exercised such influence upon Elizabethan readers that it provides us with our closest approximation of the actual event.

What are we to make of this ritual? In the absence of either an Elizabethan or modern anthropological account, how can we explain its significance? More specifically, what is there about the ritual that might explain its presence in Shakespeare's imagination as he envisaged the Roman worlds of *Titus Andronicus* and *Julius Caesar*? Four elements, it seems to me, are especially important: the respectful imposition of human order upon wild nature; the centrality of the chief personage; the emphasis upon hierarchical solidarity among all participants; and, in the reward of the hounds, the disciplined re-enactment of savage violence. Let us examine each of these elements in turn.

The meticulous observances that accompany the dismemberment of the deer and the rewarding of the hounds can be attributed, of course, to practical necessity: efficiency demands that an animal be butchered methodically, and the continuity of the hunt depends upon re-enforcing the instincts of the dogs. The emphasis upon the specific observances to be followed and their precise ordering, however, far exceeds what practical necessity requires. The taking of the assay; the decapitation with a sword; the use of specific knives (owned by the huntsmen themselves); the precise parts removed as specific rewards; the precise order of the cutting; the explicit acknowledgment of "some ceremony" in the cutting out of the shoulder, with punishments imposed if it is done improperly – all of these suggest a very powerful need to "civilize" the event by marking off the boundaries between art and nature. The ceremony as a whole represents the domination of man over nature, the imposition of a specifically human order upon the wildness of the animal. In this it is a microcosm of the entire ceremony of the hunt in which the death of the animal acknowledges human power.

When one considers the inherent messiness of dismemberment, the emphasis upon its artfulness is striking. Although the event is called the "breaking up" of the hart, the language of dismemberment is more like that of carving at table than that of butchery. Gascoigne's most graphic verbs, for example, are "cut" and "slit," and his most common expressions are the euphemistic "take off," "take from," or "take out" – as in "we use some ceremonie in taking out the shoulder." A hunting manual of 1614, *A Jewell for Gentrie* by T. S., actually refers to the dismemberment as "carving the hart" (G2v). Shakespeare himself uses "carving" as a synonym for "breaking up" in *Love's Labor's Lost* (4.1.57).

In many societies this imposition of human upon natural order is accompanied by ritual acknowledgment of the limitations of human power, of the dependency of civilization upon nature. Often these ritual gestures signify as well a reverence for the animal that has been killed and ritual gestures of reparation or atonement. Burkert's theory of sacrifice, as we have seen, draws heavily upon such a pattern as central to the ritual event, which assuages the guilt of the kill. Given Elizabethan attitudes towards animals, which were by no means reverential but assumed human uniqueness and rightful ascendancy, one would not expect to find in the ceremonies of the hunt a strongly reverential dimension or acknowledgment of guilt.[12] In the Elizabethan context, however, the very provision of a ceremony implies a respectful, if not reverential, acknowledgment of the worth of the animal.

The animal with the most symbolic potency in the Elizabethan hunt was the one treated with the highest degree of ritual, the hart. The hart was a potentially dangerous fighter, physically magnificent, and sexually powerful. It was, in short, the wild counterpart to a warrior prince. Hence the ritual dismemberment of the hart gathers into it some of the chivalric notions that linger on in the Elizabethan period. The dead animal is honored in death by the ceremonies that it deserves. This is not so much a question of sympathy for the animal but of respect for its status. The adversary is honored by being symbolically killed by the "chief personage" of the hunt.

The second element, the centrality of the "chief personage," follows from the first. If a specifically human order is to be imposed on wild nature, then that order must replicate the hierarchy of human society, as imagined by Elizabethans. In Gascoigne's treatise, the dominance of the Queen herself is overwhelming. She appears in a woodcut taking the assay, attired in a costume that in its artifice alone demonstrates the absolute authority of the human to the natural world. In the texts cited, the "chief personage" not only takes the assay but cuts off the head, receives the special delicacies, blows for the hounds to be rewarded, and leads the procession homeward, preceded by the trophy of the hunt. The animal is hers, as is the forest or park, hers. The ceremony of the breaking of the hart thus crystallizes the exalted conception of the monarch's power that is manifest in all the laws of the forest. In no other activity – political, religious, or social – was the Queen's authority so absolute as in the hunt.

Not only does the centrality of the "chief personage" assert the supremacy of the monarch; it imposes on all present, human and beast, a third element, that of the conventional social and biological hierarchy. Each participant has rights, responsibilities, and rewards that are established hierarchically. The nobles (in the French version) are depicted chatting gaily as they reward "theyr best favoured houndes and huntesmen before them" (128); the alliterative balance of "houndes" and "huntesmen" suggests ironically a rather more democratic than hierarchical attitude on the part of the nobility. The huntsman who breaks up the deer has the privilege of pausing for drink. The huntsmen responsible for the hounds are able to sit and drink while the varlets of the kennel reward the hounds. The bloodhound that harbored the deer has the privilege of the first reward at the hands of its master. And the list could go on, with even the knives arranged in importance according to the worth of their task. The ritual of the hunt is thus a rite of incorporation, binding the human community to itself in a hierarchy of social order that parallels the order of nature.

The fourth and final element, the disciplined re-enactment of savage violence in the rewarding of the hounds, seems to run counter to the impulses towards the imposition of civilized order we have already examined. In one sense, it does. As domesticated animals, the dogs are intermediate creatures, poised between civilized humanity and wild nature. The success of the hunt depends upon both their innate savagery and their imposed discipline. In releasing that savagery, the ritual acknowledges its importance both literally and symbolically: the hunt must be re-enacted so that the dogs will associate the action with their reward. At this point the ceremony becomes highly theatrical, with the horns sounded yet again, the hounds running, the deer's head held aloft before the yapping pack, and then thrown to the ground for them to be torn apart.

This is a richly suggestive ceremony. It seems significant in at least two ways. First, it dramatizes the wild and vicious instincts upon which the hunt depends, instincts that man controls by subjecting the dogs to his will. From this perspective the ritual endorses the conventional Elizabethan separation between human and animal nature. The stag is hunted with dogs; as Gervase Markham puts it, hunting is "a curious search or conquest of one Beast over an other, pursued by a naturall instinct of enmitie, and accomplished by the diversities and distinction of smells onlie . . ."[13] In this sense, the image of the savage pack, led by the basest of senses, the smell, represents another version of wild nature subjected to the ordering power of human civilization. Second, and perhaps more speculatively, the rewarding of the hounds represents a subterranean acknowledgment of the deeper human motives that underlie the hunt: the instinct to chase and kill, which Montaigne acknowledges so powerfully in the essay "Of Cruelty."[14] In this sense, the theatrical re-enactment of the hunt as unbridled savagery perhaps permits a catharsis of emotions aroused by the hunt itself. Once this catharsis is achieved, the hunters leave the world of nature for the civilized world and the feast.

Overall, then, the ritual dismemberment of the hart may be said to enact human domination over wild nature while at the same time acknowledging implicitly the wildness in human nature itself. As hunters, humans live in order to kill, and kill in order to live. In a hunter-gatherer society, the ritual of the hunt has real meaning and is tied to a real human need, the need for food; in Elizabethan society, however, no one needed to hunt in order to live. In the high culture of the Elizabethan hunt, indeed, hunting "for the pot" was considered vulgar. In Elizabethan culture, therefore, the ritual of the hunt was extremely artificial. It is difficult to sustain the notion of ritual sacrifice when the hunter simply kills for sport, and when forests themselves, as John Manwood puts it, are places for deer to "rest and abide in, in the safe protection of the King, for his princely delight and pleasure."[15] In the context of "princely delight" the very notion of a ceremonial, or, as Aaron calls it, a "solemn hunting," is suspect.

The ease with which the ritual of the hunt could be debunked in the period is suggested by Erasmus's witty travesty of the ceremony of dismemberment in the *Praise of Folly*. In this short passage Erasmus brings together several of the motifs we have been exploring: the highly ritualistic nature of the action; the solidarity achieved through participation in the event; the hierarchical aspiration towards nobility that underlies this participation; and the ironic incongruity between this aspiration and the savage impulses released by the hunt itself. I quote Folly's speech in the Elizabethan translation, by Thomas Chaloner:

For as touchyng the death of a deare, or other wilde beast, ye know your selves, what ceremonies they use about the same. Every poore man maie cutte out an oxe, or a shepe, wheras suche venaison maie not be dismembred but of a gentilman: who bareheadded, and set on knees, with a knife prepared proprely to that use, (for every kynde of knife is not allowable) also with certaine iestures, cuttes a sunder certaine partes of the wild-beast, in a certaine order verie circumstantly. Whiche duryng, the standers by, not speakyng a worde, behold it solemnly, as if it were some holy **Misterie**, havyng seen the like yet more than a hundred tymes before. Than (sir) whose happe it be to eate parte of the flesshe, marie he thynkes verily to be made therby halfe a gentilman. So therfore, wheras these hunters through continuall chasyng and eatyng of theyr venerie, gaine nothyng, but in a manner dooe them selfes also degenerate into wilde and salvage propretees, ye maie see yet, how through this errour of mine, thei repute thyr lyves ledde in more than princely pleasure.[16]

For Erasmus, the breaking up of the deer parodies the ritual of the Mass. The huntsman becomes a priest, bareheaded and kneeling, wielding his ritual implement in the precise ritual order; the onlookers become worshippers, solemnly participating in a "holy Misterie," with some fortunate enough to partake in the ritual communion, eating of the flesh of the animal and, through grace, elevating themselves to become "halfe a gentilman." This is an unholy communion, however, a barbarous rite of incorporation, for although thinking of themselves as princes, the hunters degenerate into wild and savage beasts. Erasmus, then, breaks apart the ritual paradox, making the ritual of the hunt not a symbol of the artful and civilized domination of wild nature by humanity but of human bestiality. For Erasmus, as for other humanists, this incongruity between the ritual of the hunt and the bestial reality is not merely symbolic but causal: hunting bestializes human beings.

Titus Andronicus may be said to begin where Erasmus leaves off. As part of the festivities to mark the double wedding of Bassianus and Lavinia and Saturninus and Tamora, Titus offers to provide what Aaron later calls a "solemn hunting" (2.1.112). On the morning after the marriages, the court will hunt the panther and the hart. That Titus turns to the ceremonial hunt for courtly entertainment is not surprising: he is a warrior, for one thing, and, like Theseus and Hippolyta in *A Midsummer Night's Dream*, sees the hunt as a festive extension of his martial role. More importantly, Titus has what might be called a ritualistic or ceremonial impulse that characterizes his actions throughout the play. In the opening scene of the play he yields to his sons' insistence upon sacrificing Tamora's first-born son, despite her powerful plea for human compassion. "Religiously," he says, his sons "ask for sacrifice" – to which

Tamora replies, "O cruel, irreligious piety!" (1.1.124,130). The sacrifice that ensues, gleefully described by Titus's son Lucius, is not merely abhorrent because it constitutes a pagan ritual of dismemberment and burning but because the motives behind it are undisguisedly vicious and revengeful. "See, lord and father," exults Lucius,

> how we have perform'd
> Our Roman rites. Alarbus' limbs are lopp'd,
> And entrails feed the sacrificing fire,
> Whose smoke like incense doth perfume the sky.   (1.1.142–45)

The language with which Lucius describes the dismemberment of the body has none of the delicacy of the hunting manuals: he goes out to "hew [Alarbus's] limbs" (1.1.97) and returns exulting that he has "lopp'd" them.

It is clear, then, to all but Titus, that his sons do not "religiously" ask a sacrifice; they ask vengefully for sacrifice, exploiting ritual as a cover for their own barbarous impulses. The ceremonial form becomes a travesty, even in the imagined Roman world of the play, by serving merely to disguise the desire for bloody revenge. This dichotomy between ritual action and reality, so artfully developed by Erasmus in his satire upon the hunt, escapes Titus. He sees the ritual as the reality itself and is committed to ceremony as the true external manifestation of inner belief. The human paradoxes imposed by such ritualism become evident when he must decide whether to sanction the burial of the son he himself has killed in a rage for his disobedience. At that point he becomes entangled in a ritual dilemma created by his own action: he cannot allow a proper burial for one who has dishonored the family, yet he cannot bring himself to oppose his other sons or his own paternal feelings. He allows the burial rites. He thus violates the ritual demands of his honor for the sake of his own child, although he has previously refused to violate the demands of ritual sacrifice for the sake of Tamora's child. What might be called Titus's ritual naiveté is again apparent at the end of the opening scene, as he takes optimistic solace from the double marriages intended to resolve the discord between Bassianus and Saturninus and offers his own courtly gesture to greet Saturninus the next morning with "horn and hound" (1.1.494).

Act 2 scene 2 begins with the entrance of Titus and his three sons, "*making a noise with hounds and horns*" (s.d.), a direction that implies the presence of dogs on stage. With joyful exuberance, Titus celebrates the beauty of the day, the fields, and the forest, and awakens Saturninus and the court with the noises of the hunt:

The hunt is up, the [morn] is bright and grey,
The fields are fragrant and the woods are green.
Uncouple here and let us make a bay,
And wake the Emperor and his lovely bride,
And rouse the Prince, and ring a hunter's peal,
That all the court may echo with the noise.   (2.2.1–6)

Beneath this festive show lie ironies of which Titus is unaware. He himself admits to having been "troubled in [his] sleep this night" (l.9), so his exuberance belies an inner anxiety. The description of the beauties of the day and the natural world, as we shall see later when we examine the observations of other characters, is highly subjective and suggests his own inner need for harmony.[17] The Emperor's "lovely bride," moreover, is the vengeful Tamora.

More sinister ironies are implied in the action itself, which, like the hunt in *A Midsummer Night's Dream*, joins festivity with latent aggression. Titus's noisy salute is a hunting variant of the customary *reveille* by which newlyweds were awakened the morning after their marriage. The action itself, however, the uncoupling of hounds and making a bay, pushes merriment to the edge of assault. It mimics the final stage of the hunt, when the hounds are released and the exhausted and encircled animal stands at bay to meet its death.[18] Titus's gleeful *aubade* is thus unconsciously a murderous attack, foreshadowing later events. When Titus's madness later prompts him to shoot arrows to the heavens, Marcus fulfills the sinister implications of this festive gesture by ordering the arrows to be aimed at the court itself. At the grotesque banquet with which Titus finally achieves his revenge, moreover, Saturninus's stepsons are devoured in pasties, which for festive occasions were commonly filled with venison.

The most pressing and tangible irony in the scene preparing for the hunt occurs in the final lines, when Demetrius and Chiron confirm their plan to rape Lavinia. "Chiron," says Demetrius, "we hunt not, we, with horse nor hound, / But hope to pluck a dainty doe to ground" (2.2.25–26). The scene that begins with a festive image of the hunt as a celebration of human bonding and the joys of nature ends with an image of murderous sexual violence. Chiron and Demetrius need no animal intermediaries between themselves and the wild prey they hunt; they are beasts themselves, the predators for whom sexual attack and violent death are interchangeable. In this they degrade even the imagery of Aaron, who earlier likened them to human hunters, singling out a deer to be run to death, or hunted *par force*: "Single you thither then this

dainty doe, / And strike her home by force, if not by words" (2.1.117–18).
The allusion to *par force* hunting, the most "solemn" or ceremonial kind,
heightens the perversity of their deed. Long afterwards, Demetrius
remembers the event nostalgically as a great hunt: "I would we had a
thousand Roman dames / At such a bay, by turn to serve our lust"
(4.2.41–42). In his crafty madness, Titus calls the sons and mother "a pair
of cursed hell-hounds and their dame" (5.2.144). The "hunting" of
Demetrius and Chiron, one might say, plays out the latent violence of
Titus's festive call to the hunt, transforming the playful baying at newlyweds into rape, mutilation, and murder.

   Although Titus's "solemn hunting" takes place in the forest, the symbolic opposition implied by such a setting – a contrast between Rome
and wilderness, civilization and barbarism – is evoked only to be dissolved. As we have observed already, the Rome of the Andronici is
already at the point of barbarism and includes within its civilized boundaries ritual slaughter of an enemy and the impetuous murder of a son.
With an ease afforded by the bareness of the Elizabethan stage,
Shakespeare turns the image of the forest inward, making its landscape
a projection of the forces that lie within the characters. For Aaron, who
urges Chiron and Demetrius on to rape and murder, the "woods are
ruthless, dreadful, deaf, and dull" (2.1.128). For Tamora, the landscape
alters with her mind: "the birds chaunt melody on every bush" (2.3.12)
when she woos Aaron to take advantage of their solitude, yet when she
accuses Bassianus and Lavinia of attacking her the same setting becomes
a "barren detested vale" in which "nothing breeds, / Unless the nightly
owl or fatal raven" (2.3.93,96–97). For Titus, the "fragrant" fields and
"green" woods of his joyful *aubade* become finally the "ruthless, vast, and
gloomy woods" described by Ovid as the backdrop for the rape of
Philomel. "Ay, such a place there is where we did hunt," he cries, as he
reads the passage marked by Lavinia,

> (O had we never, never hunted there!),
> Pattern'd by that the poet here describes,
> By nature made for murthers and for rapes.   (4.1.54–58)

Unlike King Lear's mad interrogation of nature and the gods, Titus's
stops short of the ultimate question, of what there is in nature that causes
these hard hearts.

   That Titus looks to Ovid for answers is not surprising, for the scene of
the "solemn hunting" centers upon two Ovidean myths, both of which
involve the hunt: those of Philomel and Actaeon. The scene begins with
yet another classical hunting story, that of Dido and Aeneas, whose

hunting is interrupted by a storm that forces them to take shelter in a cave. The source of this allusion is Tamora, who, in her attempt to seduce Aaron, plays "Dido" to his "wand'ring prince" (2.3.22), inciting him to imagine them both "curtain'd with a counsel-keeping cave," "wreathed in the other's arms," and possessed of "a golden slumber,"

> Whiles hounds and horns and sweet melodious birds
> Be unto us as is a nurse's song
> Of lullaby to bring her babe asleep.   (2.3.24–29)

To this Aaron replies that although Venus may "govern" *her* desires, Saturn dominates his (30–31); he proceeds to inform her of his plans for Bassianus's murder and Lavinia's rape. Like a travesty of Aeneas, Aaron abandons love for the higher destiny of war.

Having been deprived of a Virgilian role by Aaron's uncooperativeness, Tamora is immediately assigned an equally grotesque antithesis, that of Diana, goddess of chastity and the hunt. When Bassianus and Lavinia see Tamora alone with Aaron, they suspect romantic intrigue, and Bassianus slyly asks Tamora whether she might be not "Rome's royal Emperess" but Diana herself, "Who hath abandoned her holy groves / To see the general hunting in this forest" (55, 58–59). Stung by this obvious insult, Tamora transforms Bassianus into Actaeon:

> Had I the pow'r that some say Dian had,
> Thy temples should be planted presently
> With horns, as was Actaeon's, and the hounds
> Should drive upon thy new-transformed limbs,
> Unmannerly intruder as thou art!   (61–65)

The spontaneous insult provides a metaphoric structure for the events that ensue. When Lavinia is raped, Bassianus is indeed given the cuckold's horns, and by an action that Tamora encourages. When Bassianus is killed, by Chiron and Demetrius, he falls prey to characters who, if not hounds, are tigers, and is thrown like an animal into a pit. Aaron has earlier implied a likeness between Bassianus's death and that of a hunted animal in his observation to Tamora that her sons will "wash their hands in Bassianus' blood" (2.3.45); here the imagery of human sacrifice merges with the ritual that marks the death of the deer. The grotesque and nightmarish world of the play has more affinity with Ovid than Virgil. Whereas Shakespeare's travesty of Dido and Aeneas undermines the Virgilian possibilities in his story, his use of Ovid, here and throughout, exaggerates the ironic horrors of stories already macabre.[19]

Unlike the stories of Dido and Actaeon, that of Philomel does not center on the hunt; an allusion to hunting within the story, however, might have triggered off the grisly symmetry of Shakespeare's ending. In Ovid, when Philomel goes into hiding after her rape and mutilation, her sister, Procne, searches for her in disguise, wearing over her shoulder the deer-skin of a Bacchante and carrying a lance. Later, when in revenge she seizes Tereus's son, Itys, she does so "like some tigress on the Ganges' banks, dragging an unweaned fawn through the thick forest."[20] The child is then hacked to bits, with some parts boiled and some roasted, and served up to his father. In Shakespeare's version Philomel herself, Lavinia, becomes a doe, and her rape and mutilation recall the death and dismemberment of a deer. The hunt to avenge this deed is led by Titus, who dismembers Chiron and Demetrius and serves them up to Tamora as a "pasty." Shakespeare's substitution of a pasty for the boiled and roasted meat of his source suggests his desire to keep the irony of the hunting theme alive, for, as the *Oxford English Dictionary* makes clear, pasties were often made of venison. The ceremonial nature of this feast would increase the likelihood of such meat, for venison was considered a special delicacy, as is clear from accounts such as William Harrison's.[21]

The assault on Lavinia is motivated primarily by the lust of Chiron and Demetrius. Once they are persuaded by Aaron to join forces, however, the crime becomes not merely personal but political and familial. The hunt becomes an attack upon the Andronici. When Lavinia pleads with Tamora to save her, "for my father's sake," Tamora replies,

> Even for his sake am I pitiless.
> Remember, boys, I pour'd forth tears in vain
> To save your brother from the sacrifice,
> But fierce Andronicus would not relent.　　(2.3.158,162–65)

The assault on Lavinia, then, becomes an act of retaliation, a "sacrifice" that atones for the death of Tamora's eldest son. As such, her violation serves as a constant reminder of the original sacrifice. The revenge is not exactly symmetrical: Alarbus is killed, dismembered, and burned; Lavinia is raped and mutilated. In the Roman logic of the play, however, as witnessed by the reactions of both Titus and Lavinia, rape is a fate worse than death. The play's central visual symbol, moreover, is that of Lavinia's maimed body. Before Alarbus is sacrificed, Lucius asks "that we may hew his limbs" (1.1.97); afterwards, he exultantly tells his father that the "limbs are lopp'd" (1.1.143). When Marcus first encounters the maimed Lavinia, he asks "what stern ungentle hands" have "lopp'd and

hew'd" her (2.4.16–17). At the end of the play, upon his capture of
Aaron, Lucius must endure the description of his own sister having been
"wash'd, and cut, and trimm'd" – a "trim sport for them which had the
doing of it" (5.1.95–96).

Lavinia is thus not merely a "doe" but one that belongs to Titus
Andronicus. When Marcus describes how he found the violated Lavinia
"straying in the park, / Seeking to hide herself, as doth the deer / That
hath receiv'd some unrecuring wound," Titus responds, "It was my dear,
and he that wounded her / Hath hurt me more than had he kill'd me
dead" (3.1.88–92). By shifting the locale from forest to park, Shakespeare
accentuates both the sense of ownership and the sense of pathos. The
attack upon Titus's daughter is an attack upon him, her loss of honor a
loss of his own.

In the metaphoric terms of the hunt, Titus has been the victim of
poaching; someone has attacked his "deer." Demetrius himself views the
attack upon Lavinia in precisely this way, when in anticipation of the
chase he reminds Aaron and Chiron of the pleasures of poaching. The
exchange joins images of illicit hunting and illicit sexuality:

> *Dem.* What, hast not thou full often strook a doe,
> And borne her cleanly by the keeper's nose?
> *Aar.* Why then it seems some certain snatch or so
> Would serve your turns.
> *Chi.*   Ay, so the turn were served.
> *Dem.* Aaron, thou hast hit it.
> *Aar.*   Would you had hit it too!
>
> (2.1.93–97)

The viciously jocular puns on "strook," "snatch," and "hit" all serve to
link the joys of sexual violence not merely to the violence of the hunt
but to the special pleasures of poaching.

Aaron, Chiron, and Demetrius can thus be seen as nightmare versions
of Elizabethan poachers. They are swaggerers. They delight in wanton
destruction. They use the hunt to take revenge against an enemy, as an
act of symbolic warfare. They make a trophy of the victim, confronting
the enemy with a reminder of their power over his property. And of
course their action begets a corresponding revenge-action, the killing of
Chiron and Demetrius as animals, to be served up in a pasty.

Tensions within the Elizabethan culture of the hunt, then, underlie
the representation of violence in *Titus Andronicus*. The conflict between
civilization and bestiality enacted and ideally resolved in the ritual dismemberment of the hart is played out with Erasmian effect: the sacrifice

of the hunt reveals the beasts within the hunters. In the case of Titus, Shakespeare focuses on the ironic breaking apart of this ritual tension, with his noble but naive aspirations towards ceremony themselves precipitating the social descent into savagery. The "irreligious piety" of Titus's initial attempt to ritualize savage revenge through the lopping and burning of Tamora's first-born son fuels another revenge of murder, rape, and dismemberment, which fuels yet another revenge of murder, dismemberment, and cannibalistic feasting. The festive yet "solemn" hunting celebrating the marriage of Saturninus and Tamora becomes transformed into the wild and parodic rites of poaching, with humans as both predators and prey. In the play's final abhorrent actions, the hunt theme reaches its logical conclusion: Tamora the tigress eats her sons, and Titus kills his own "dear" Lavinia. In *Praise of Folly*, the hunters become savage beasts. In *Titus Andronicus*, these same beasts end by devouring themselves.

In *Julius Caesar*, Brutus, like Titus, is a ceremonialist. His complicity in the plot against Caesar depends upon his ability to persuade himself that the assassination is not a murder but a solemn sacrifice. A staunch republican, whose ancestors drove Tarquin "from the streets of Rome . . . when he was call'd a king" (2.1.53–54), Brutus justifies the assassination of Caesar as an act of "pity to the general wrong of Rome" (3.1.170). "What villain touch'd his body," he asks, "that did stab / And not for justice?" (4.3.20–21). For Brutus, as for Titus, personal, familial, and civic honor require the imaginative conversion of live human beings into mere ceremonial victims, sacrifices to the common good. In both cases the motives of the sacrificers are tainted, and their action does not redress the "general wrong of Rome" but intensifies it.[22]

The most powerful statement of Brutus's ceremonialism occurs, ironically, in his dispute with Cassius over the necessity of killing Antony along with Caesar. Cassius rightly perceives Antony as a serious political threat and advocates his murder as the necessary corollary of Caesar's. Brutus counters with a visionary but confused mixture of political strategy and political principle. He turns first to the issue of Antony:

> Our course will seem too bloody, Caius Cassius,
> To cut the head off and then hack the limbs –
> Like wrath in death and envy afterwards;
> For Antony is but a limb of Caesar.   (2.1.162–65)

At this point the question remains a political one, that of the potential impact of the murder of Antony upon the people. Brutus is capable of thinking tactically, and even during the assassination, as we shall see, he reveals a sensitivity to the symbolic nature of political action. Unfortunately, however, his tactical thinking is invariably wrong, and Cassius, confusing moral with political authority, invariably yields to it.

The source of Brutus's political misjudgment, it seems, is his moral sensitivity, which finds expression as this speech continues and he turns to the murder of Caesar himself:

> Let's be sacrificers, but not butchers, Caius.
> We all stand up against the spirit of Caesar,
> And in the spirit of men there is no blood;
> O that we then could come by Caesar's spirit,
> And not dismember Caesar! But, alas,
> Caesar must bleed for it! And, gentle friends,
> Let's kill him boldly, but not wrathfully;
> Let's carve him as a dish fit for the gods,
> Not hew him as a carcass fit for hounds;
> And let our hearts, as subtle masters do,
> Stir up their servants to an act of rage,
> And after seem to chide 'em.   (166–77)

Unlike Cassius, Brutus shows genuine moral feeling for the deed he is about to commit, and for this he is celebrated at the end of the play by Antony himself.

Brutus's attempt to define assassination as a moral, even a religious act, however, is intellectually and morally evasive. He first attempts to distinguish sacrificial killing, the death of the spirit, from butchery, the death of the body, but then must admit that the only way to the spirit is through the body: "alas, / Caesar must bleed for it!" Having conceded the necessity of blood, Brutus then focuses on the method of bloodshed, distinguishing between the sacrificial "carving" accorded to a noble dish and the "hewing" accorded to a carcass for hounds.[23] Yet even here he must admit the devious psychology upon which the distinction rests: that one can stir oneself to an act of rage and then pretend to reprove oneself by respectful action – that one can, in short, stir oneself to murderous rage, and then convert the action into one of solemn sacrifice.

The deviousness that underlies this last image – of stirring one's servants to a rage and then pretending to chide them – continues as Brutus returns once more to the political effect of their action:

> This shall make
> Our purpose necessary, and not envious;
> Which so appearing to the common eyes,
> We shall be call'd purgers, not murderers.   (177–80)

His final remark is to belittle the political threat represented by Antony:

> And for Mark Antony, think not of him;
> For he can do no more than Caesar's arm
> When Caesar's head is off.　　　　　　　　　　(181–83)

The movement of thought throughout the speech is from amoral political strategy to religious sacrifice and back to amoral political strategy.
Either Brutus is guilty of intellectual and moral confusion or he is pretending to think politically for the sake of Cassius.

The contrast between "carving" and "hewing," and the notion of an
act of killing that requires not only rage but the suppression of rage both
anticipate the imagery of the death and dismemberment of the hart that
will later dominate the scene of the assassination itself. As we have seen
earlier, the dismembering of a stag is a ceremonial and potentially
sacrificial act, an act that in both *A Jewell for Gentrie* and *Love's Labor's Lost*
is described as "carving"; it is also an act of respect or even reverence
for the worth of the dead animal, which dies so that humans may live.
As René Girard observes of Brutus's image, "in the carving metaphor
all aspects of culture seem harmoniously blended, the differential and
the spiritual, the spatial, the ethical, and the aesthetic."[24] Brutus's reductive alternative to this ceremony, the brutal "hewing" of a "carcass fit for
hounds," ironically anticipates Antony's later description of the savage
nature of the assassination itself. Brutus's image of stirring up "servants"
to rage that must be later suppressed recalls the dependency of the hunt
on the ferocity of the hounds, which not only characterizes the process
of the pursuit and the attack but is re-enacted in the ritual of their
reward.

The underlying issue in these allusions to the hunt is the one we have
already observed in Erasmus's *Praise of Folly*: Is the hunt a solemn
sacrifice, or is it a mere act of savage bestiality? And, more precisely, does
the act of hunting itself, with all its ceremony, simply encourage humans
to suppress their humanity, to become no more than beasts themselves?
Brutus's attempt to "carve" rather than "hew" Caesar is an attempt,
through ceremony, to legitimize and sanctify the act of killing. In this,
Brutus is like Burkert's Paleolithic hunters, for whom the shock of the
kill requires a ritual form within which it may be overcome. Both Brutus
and Titus Andronicus are basically good men who recoil from the
bloody acts that "justice" requires of them, and whose recoil is marked
by the desire to transform the bloodshed into a sacrificial rite.

Brutus's image of the assassination as a solemn sacrifice is important not merely because it reflects his inner motivations but because it prepares for the event itself, which is the climactic moment of the play. In this scene Brutus becomes a kind of priest, who attempts to translate his ritualistic conception of the meaning of the plot into stage action. In this, Brutus fails, for, whether we imagine the killing of Caesar to be staged ritualistically or with frenzied brutality, the contrast between Brutus's bloodless aspirations and the bloodiness of the deed cannot help but unnerve an audience. Despite his aspirations to spiritualize the action, the "sacrifice" becomes the very "savage spectacle" (3.1.223) he sought to avoid. The encircling of Caesar by the conspirators; their thrusting forward of petitions, which makes Caesar think of fawning dogs (45–46); the multitude of the wounds; the bathing of the conspirators' hands "up to the elbows" (107) in Caesar's blood – the actions of Brutus's "sacrifice" undermine his ritual purpose.

After the event, when Antony enters and looks down at the corpse of Caesar, he converts the underlying symbolism of the scene into explicit verbal statement:

> Here wast thou bay'd, brave hart,
> Here didst thou fall, and here thy hunters stand,
> Sign'd in thy spoil, and crimson'd in thy lethe.
> O world! thou wast the forest to this hart,
> And this indeed, O world, the heart of thee.
> How like a deer, strooken by many princes,
> Dost thou here lie![25]   (3.1.204–10)

The link between Caesar and a hunted animal, as we have seen, is foreshadowed in North's Plutarch, in which he is described as "hacked and mangeled amonge them, as a wilde beaste taken of hunters." In specifying that the "wilde beaste" is a hart, Antony both ennobles and creates sympathy for the subject, since the hart is the most magnificent and royal of the animals hunted, and not itself a predator. The image may also have sprung to mind because of the common tradition that harts belonging to Caesar had been found alive throughout Europe hundreds of years after his death, with collars around their necks indicating his ownership.[26]

Antony's description of Caesar's death as that of a hart reverses Brutus's earlier attempt to ritualize and thereby sanitize it. In juxtaposing the two men's opposed views of the same event, Shakespeare exploits tensions that underlie the Elizabethan hunt itself. Antony's image of the hunters "signed" and "crimsoned" in the life-blood of the deer, like Brutus's earlier exhortation to the conspirators to "bathe our hands in Caesar's blood / Up to the elbows" (3.1.106–7), derives from

the customary action of "blooding" at the end of a hunt. The notion of
"blooding" may have indeed inspired the episode, since nothing like it
occurs in the source descriptions of Caesar's assassination.[27] Both characters see the conspirators' action as symbolic, but for both the symbolism points in opposite directions. For Brutus, the bloody hands signify
"peace, freedom, and liberty" (3.1.110); for Antony, the "purpled hands"
that "do reek and smoke" (3.1.158) signify utter bestiality.

In the discourse of the hunt, one might locate this conflict in the opposition between the views of James I and those of Erasmus. For James,
daubing his courtiers' faces with the blood of a deer was a ritual sign of
their valor, to be worn proudly and displayed until the stain wore off.
King James also used the blood of a deer killed in the hunt for curative
purposes, as when he "killed a buck in Eltham Park, and bathed his bare
feet and legs in the blood, as a cure for the gout."[28] For Erasmus, the
bloodshed of the hunt had no ritualistic or curative value but merely
incited human bestiality. Brutus's attempt to ritualize the death of
Caesar arouses discomfort in Cassius, whose views are more pragmatic
than spiritual. When Brutus exhorts the conspirators to "bathe our
hands in Caesar's blood," Cassius responds with the curt directive,
"stoop, then, and wash" (3.1.111). Bathing suggests ritualistic immersion;
washing, ironically, mere cleansing. The public display of bloody hands
is for Brutus a ritual demonstration of the conspirators' honor; for
Cassius, however, it is mere theater: "How many ages hence / Shall this
our lofty scene be acted over" (111–12).

Antony's image of Caesar as a deer struck "by many princes" might
also be situated in cultural anxieties surrounding the ritual of the hunt.
On the one hand, the word "princes" euphemistically elevates the action
of the conspirators, masking Antony's true opinion for the sake of his
own safety. The use of the plural form of the word, however, conveys a
subtle irony, for the killing of a stag was almost certainly not a group
action.[29]

The moral ambiguities that lie within the killing of the hart surface in
George Gascoigne's account of the event. In order to illustrate the great
danger in killing a hart, Gascoigne recounts the story of the Emperor
Basil, who, although heroically victorious in many battles, was slain by a
hart as he attacked it. The tragic irony in the Emperor's death – that a
great warrior should be slain by a "fearefull beast" forced to defend itself
– leads Gascoigne to moralize the event as "a mirrour to al Princes" not
to proffer "undeserved injuries" or to "constrayne the simple sakelesse
man to stand in his owne defence." Having drawn his moral, however,

Gascoigne realizes to his dismay that, if taken seriously, it would undermine the very idea of hunting. So he is forced to backtrack:

> I woulde not have my wordes wrested to this construction, that it were unlaw-
> full to kill a Deare or such beasts of venerie: for so should I both speake agaynst
> the purpose which I have taken in hande, and agayne I should seeme to argue
> against Gods ordinances, since it seemeth that suche beastes have bene created
> to the use of man and for his recreation: but as by all Fables some good moral-
> itie may be gathered, so by all Histories and examples, some good allegorie and
> comparison may be made.[30]

In chapter 1 we have already observed Gascoigne's complex attitude
towards the hunt. In this instance, the death of a hart becomes the
source of a moral tension remarkably similar to that evoked by
Shakespeare in his treatment of the death of Caesar. Gascoigne's ambivalence is expressed in two contradictory attitudes: either the hart is innocent and the deed reprehensible, or the hart is innocent but a legitimate
sacrifice to human need. In Shakespeare's play, Antony takes the former
view, Brutus the latter.

As soon as the conspirators leave, Antony bursts through the sentimental image of the stricken deer, an image which insulates the conspirators from the real horror of their action and protects him from their
fury. In soliloquy, he vents his passion for revenge: "O pardon me, thou
bleeding piece of earth, / That I am meek and gentle with these butchers!" (3.1.254–55). Brutus's hopeful imagery is thus turned against him;
his attempt to create a solemn ritual, to be perceived as a sacrificer, not
a butcher, has achieved the opposite effect. By the end of Antony's
speech, the roles of Brutus and Caesar have been reversed, and Caesar's
spirit becomes a hunter, pursuing the conspirators for his revenge:

> And Caesar's spirit, ranging for revenge,
> With Ate by his side come hot from hell,
> Shall in these confines with a monarch's voice
> Cry "Havoc!" and let slip the dogs of war,
> That this foul deed shall smell above the earth
> With carrion men, groaning for burial.   (270–75)

The image is terrifying for a number of reasons, not the least of which
is the fact that Antony himself not merely prophesies the dreadful civil
war but deliberately incites it. Caesar's "spirit" lives within him, and he
urges the hounds to violence.

Antony's ferocious call for vengeance combines the language of
hunting and of war, and thus depends upon the long-standing convergence of the two activities in vindications of the hunt as a preparation

in the arts of war. The word "range," according to the *Oxford English Dictionary*, is used of both persons and animals, and in the latter case, especially, of "hunting dogs searching for game." The word "confines," an odd choice for a civil war that will later encompass the Mediterranean, suggests the enclosed space of a park. The cry "havoc," primarily a military term, a call for utter destruction of the enemy, takes on overtones of hunting through the association with letting slip "the dogs of war"; Roger B. Manning notes that the term is "occasionally used in Star Chamber complaints to describe poachers who wantonly killed more deer than they could possibly carry away, leaving many carcasses behind to spoil."[31] In *Coriolanus*, Menenius uses the term in the context of the hunt: "Do not cry havoc where you should but hunt / With modest warrant" (3.1.273–74). The notion that Caesar is a "spirit" hunter might link his avenging ghost to the mythological figure of Herne the hunter, whose wildly destructive night-hunts, suggestive of poaching raids, are alluded to in *The Merry Wives of Windsor*. The image of the hunt that underlies this passage is thus not that of the "solemn" or ceremonial hunt, but that of a revenge-hunt, an act of poaching.

The social context invoked by Antony's lines may be illustrated by one of the more dramatic instances of such poaching warfare in the period – an attack in 1572 by the Earl of Leicester upon his enemy, Henry, eleventh Lord Berkeley, that implicated the Queen. While on progress, accompanied by Leicester, Elizabeth arrived at Berkeley Castle. Lord Berkeley, absent at the time, was an avid hunter and kept a herd of red deer in the adjoining park. Leicester and the Queen decided to hunt them. "Such slaughter was made" during their brief stay at the Castle that "27 stagges were slayne in the Toiles in one day, and many others in that and the next stollen and havocked." Furious at this insult, Berkeley destroyed his own park. A few months later, however, he received a "secret freindly advertizement from the Court" relating Elizabeth's warning to him to beware of Leicester's designs. Leicester had "drawn" the Queen to the Castle, according to this report, and, contrary to her desire, "purposely had caused that slaughter of his deere." Leicester, the report said, "might have a further plott against his [Berkeley's] head and that Castle, whereto he had taken noe small liking, and affirmed to have good title thereto . . ."[32]

More was at stake in this affair than appears at first glance. Berkeley's absence was probably a deliberate slight, for Elizabeth's main purpose in the visit was to warn him that the followers of his brother-in-law, the recently executed fourth duke of Norfolk, should end their resistance;

the slaughter of his deer was thus an emblem of royal power. By traveling with Leicester, moreover, Elizabeth was also signaling her support of
his side in his dispute with Berkeley over the Lisle inheritance. The attack
upon Berkeley's deer was thus part of a long-standing feud between
powerful nobles. The attack itself had significant consequences: it
"reverberated through the Vale of Berkeley and precipitated a poaching
war lasting nearly fifty years between Lord Berkeley's gamekeepers and
the adherents of Sir Thomas Throckmorton, Leicester's henchman in
Gloucestershire."[33] In Elizabethan England, then, as in the Rome
invoked by Mark Antony, the language of civil war and the language of
wild hunting converge.[34]

Under Antony's direction the war of revenge that he envisages takes
on overtones of a hunt. The scene in which he and Octavius, like deathly
accountants, decide who is "prick'd to die" depends so heavily upon rep-
etitions of the word "prick" or "prick'd" (three times in sixteen lines,
4.1.1–16) that it may allude to the special role of "prickers" in the hunt,
whose job it was to goad the chosen animals to their death.[35] Later, when
Brutus mocks him before Philippi, Antony converts his earlier image of
Caesar as a hart stricken by many princes into that of a man bitten to
death by sycophantic apes and dogs:

> You show'd your [teeth] like apes, and fawn'd like hounds,
> And bow'd like bondmen, kissing Caesar's feet;
> Whilst damned Casca, like a cur, behind
> Strook Caesar on the neck. O you flatterers!   (5.1.41–44)

Both Brutus and Cassius see themselves finally as prey. As he awaits the
battle at Philippi, Cassius observes fatalistically that the eagles that have
heretofore perched on his foremost banner have flown away and been
replaced by "ravens, crows, and kites" looking at them as if they were
"sickly prey" (5.1.84, 86). When he later has himself killed by Pindarus,
Cassius calls attention to the irony in the weapon used: "Caesar, thou art
reveng'd, / Even with the sword that kill'd thee" (5.3.45–46). Brutus too
notes the irony of his own suicide: "Caesar, now be still, / I kill'd not thee
with half so good a will" (5.5.50–51). Brutus takes his life, moreover,
shortly after he likens his end to that of a driven animal:

> Our enemies have beat us to the pit.
> It is more worthy to leap in ourselves
> Than tarry till they push us.   (5.5.23–25)

In true Roman fashion, both conspirators take their own lives, having
been gradually transformed from hunters of Caesar into Caesar's prey

and finally into hunters of themselves. Although rather more decorously tragic than the final actions of Tamora and Titus in *Titus Andronicus*, these deaths too show predators finally preying upon themselves.

In both *Titus Andronicus* and *Julius Caesar*, Shakespeare exploits the conventional image of the hunt as a ritual of death and dismemberment, a means of civilizing bloodshed. In both plays the contrast between a civilized and barbaric Rome is articulated in the equivocal ritualism of the hunt – a ritualism that for Elizabethans was itself a source of ideological conflict. In both plays, Shakespeare explodes the ritual ideal of civilized violence by depicting the inner tensions and hypocrisies that characterize it, even in high-minded ceremonialists like Titus and Brutus. The ceremonial ideal ultimately finds only parodic expression in the wild and anarchic vendettas of poaching. The anti-ceremonial thrust of both plays recalls the satiric perspective of Erasmus, for whom the ritual of the hunt itself accentuates the human tendency towards cruelty and violence, transforming men into beasts.

Shakespeare's plays, unlike Erasmus's satire, are not directed at hunting. They exploit an Erasmian view of the hunt, one might say, to probe the discordances between the ceremonial ideals of a high civilization and the savage realities that underlie them. This tension is a familiar one in Shakespeare, appearing in theatrical moments as diverse as Henry V's soliloquy on ceremony the night before Agincourt (4.1.225–84), Othello's attempt to see Desdemona's murder as a sacrifice (5.2.65), and King Lear's anguished action of ripping off his clothes to find the "poor, bare, fork'd animal" beneath (3.4.107–8). The ritual of the hunt, with its uniquely literal attempt to bring the bestial within the order of civilization, provided Shakespeare with a vivid set of images for a problem he pursued throughout his career: the tragic inability of ceremonial ideals to withstand the violent impulses within human nature.

CHAPTER FOUR

The "manning" of Katherine:
falconry in The Taming of the Shrew

Since at least the end of the nineteenth century, when G. B. Shaw lamented that "no man with any decency of feeling" could sit out the play "in the company of a woman" and not be "extremely ashamed of the lord-of-creation moral" of its ending, *The Taming of the Shrew* has been a critical and theatrical problem.[1] How are we to enjoy a play that not only centers upon the brutal farce of "taming" a woman but concludes with the woman's own celebration of the doctrine of the tamer? As the critical and theatrical traditions suggest, the question permits a variety of possible answers. We can consign the play to the shelf, at least theoretically (it continues to be performed and discussed). More realistically, we can take the shame out of the ending by overturning or at least softening its apparent "lord-of-creation moral": we can show Katherine as remaining essentially untamed; or as having achieved the upper hand herself; or, more romantically, as having fulfilled herself through marriage. As Lynda E. Boose has wittily observed, the latter option in particular, which emphasizes affection more than submission, has become the most popular way to "save the play from its own ending."[2]

There are other options. We can keep the play and its ending, according to Robert B. Heilman, if we simply remember that the play is a farce, that farce "anesthetizes" us from thought or emotion, and that the repressive patriarchal doctrine which the play celebrates, like that of the divine right of kings and other bizarre Elizabethan notions, can be easily ignored as archaic and irrelevant. The problem with this view, however, anesthesia aside, is that the play resists either generic or ideological taming. Even Heilman, who begins by reducing the play emphatically to farce, admits later that both Katherine and Petruchio are given "a good deal of intelligence and feeling that they would not have in elementary farce."[3] Peter Saccio, in another discussion of the play as farce, avoids this trap but only by defining the play as a humane or "kindly" farce.[4] Once we begin to move from farce towards romantic comedy, however, the anesthesia of farce begins to evaporate and the problem of taming returns.

The ideological problem of the ending is as vexing as the generic. Here too the critical drift is towards romanticizing the ending. As John C. Bean and others have observed, if read historically the doctrine enunciated in Katherine's final speech is far less repressive than its counterpart in the closely related play, *The Taming of A Shrew*, and can be positioned at the liberal end of the spectrum of Elizabethan views on marriage. Historicizing the speech, in short, can soften the edges of its apparent antifeminism and sanction readings that stress mutuality and affection. Solving the problem of the ending in this way, however, as Bean shrewdly perceives, merely poses a new problem, that of the manner in which the ending is achieved: Katherine's speech is uttered at Petruchio's command and after a long period of brutal and coercive "taming." In her final performance, observes Bean, Katherine "still has some of the vestiges of a trained bear."[5] That she voices a relatively progressive view of marital relations is in this context hardly reassuring.

The more liberal and romantic our reading of the play, it seems, the more difficult becomes its title and the more problematic the main action of the play. How can we reconcile the practice of taming with even the most mildly progressive gestures of the play, as in its tendency to move beyond farce and to liberalize contemporary doctrines of marriage? The problem, moreover, is not merely that of reconciling Shakespeare with contemporary views. Fletcher's sequel to the play, *The Woman's Prize or the Tamer Tamed*, which features the taming of Petruchio by his second wife and concludes with a homily on mutuality in marriage, shows that *The Taming of the Shrew* was at the very least controversial and capable of evoking protest among Elizabethan and Jacobean audiences. In addition, there is the problem of reconciling the *Shrew* with the rest of Shakespeare; although his other plays often reflect patriarchal attitudes towards women and marriage, none does so with such apparently zestful brutality as this one.

The difficulty posed by the play may help explain why, although it is often acknowledged, the metaphor of taming in the title is rarely considered at any length. Instead of basing their interpretations of Petruchio's courtship of Katherine on the taming of falcons, the metaphor that Petruchio himself uses, critics tend to prefer other, more benign metaphors. For Joel Fineman, Petruchio follows the logic of homeopathic medicine, by which he holds "his own lunatic self up as mirror of Kate's unnatural nature."[6] For Peter Saccio Petruchio is a teacher of games; he "teaches" Katherine "to play."[7] The metaphor of game is important for many critics, including Marianne Novy, who in adopting it acknowledges the irony that "the leader of the game" is always Petruchio.[8]

Each of these metaphors, it is fair to say, has some warrant in the text, and each evokes certain real qualities in the relationship between the two characters. The tendency in using them, however, as Novy observes in the case of "game," is to soften and romanticize the process, to imply a mutuality that only begins to appear, if at all, at the very end of the play. To respond adequately to this play, we must come to terms with its central metaphor, articulated both by Shakespeare and by Petruchio, that of taming falcons. The metaphor appears not only in the title of the play but in Petruchio's crucial soliloquy in act 4 scene 1, in which he rationalizes his approach to courtship by means of a detailed and technical description of the process of taming a falcon. If we understand the full implications of the metaphor, and of the social context it evokes, we might discover, by a circuitous route, a way of "saving the play from its own ending" without either evading or romanticizing its main action, that of "taming" a woman.

As a play about taming, and especially taming in the context of hunting, the *Shrew* is implicitly about "man's" dominion over nature. The right to tame animals, like the right to hunt them, derives from God's exhortation in Genesis to "subdue" the earth and to "rule over the fish of the sea and over the foule of the heaven, and over everie beast that moveth upon the earth."[9] As Gervase Markham rather smugly notes, in defending the legitimacy of recreational hunting, "a man so good and vertuous as the true *Husband-man* is, should not be deprived any comfort, or felicity, which the earth, or the creatures of the earth can affoord unto him, being indeed the right Lord and Master (next under God) of them both . . ." The very notion of taming, in this context, implies the rightful domination of man over nature in a double sense: the tamed animal, the dog or falcon, becomes man's weapon against the wild prey. In an age like our own, in which hunting is dominated by technology, it is difficult to appreciate the extent to which Elizabethan hunting emphasized the discipline and control of animals. So accustomed is Markham to the use of dogs in the chase, in fact, that he defines hunting itself simply as "a curious search or conquest of one Beast over an other."[10] The training of a beast to subordinate its own instincts to man's will is a triumph of human ingenuity. "Suche and so great is the singular skill of man," says George Turbervile of the successful training of a falcon, "when by arte he is resolved, to alter the prescribed order of nature, which by industrie and payne we see is brought to passe and effect."[11]

Throughout the *Taming of the Shrew*, Petruchio is shown in constant relation with animals and servants. He dominates them both with farcical brutality, and with boisterous and good natured tyranny. In his first appearance in the play, he wrings Grumio's ears after a heated exchange over the meaning of his equivocal order to "knock me here soundly" (1.2.8). He appears at his wedding on a horse both ill-caparisoned and wracked with disease: "possess'd with the glanders and like to mose in the chine, troubled with the lampass, infected with the fashions, full of windgalls, sped with spavins, ray'd with the yellows," and more (3.2.50–53). On the journey to his home, he beats Grumio because the horse stumbles in the mire. Once arrived, he rages at his servants for their lack of attendance, strikes both the servant who attempts to take off his boots and the servant who brings water to him, throws over the table of food, and beats all the other servants in sight.

Some of these violent antics can be explained as ploys to "educate" Katherine into an awareness of his power, which extends over all the people, property, and animals he controls:

> I will be master of what is mine own.
> She is my goods, my chattels, she is my house,
> My household stuff, my field, my barn,
> My horse, my ox, my ass, my any thing . . .   (3.2.229–32).

Petruchio's impetuous rages and outrageous posturing cannot be explained away, however, as mere "educational" theater. The opening knock-about with Grumio has no other witnesses and creates a "personality" that informs the more overtly theatrical gestures that follow. Petruchio's braggadocio may be calculated in part, and may partly disguise an inner humanity, but it expresses nonetheless his own powerful sense of self: "Have I not in my time heard lions roar?" (1.2.200). He sets out to master Katherine not only for the money but for the challenge; the wooing has about it the stereotypically masculine love of the dare and the competitiveness that accompanies it. For Petruchio, marriage is a sporting event. His energy, his noise, his self-assertiveness, his violent physicality, his swaggering relish of the life of a soldier amidst the "Loud 'larums, neighing steeds, and trumpets' clang" (1.2.206) – all bespeak his affinity with the aggressively masculine culture of the hunt.

Petruchio is not nearly as rough physically on Katherine as he is on his servants and animals. He never hits her. As Anne Barton observes, moreover, if we compare him to the usual husband in shrew-taming stories, who is prone to bind, beat, or bleed his wife, or wrap her in the salted skin of a dead horse, he seems "almost a model of intelligence and humanity."[12] This is so, ironically, not because Petruchio is a model husband but because he is a model tamer of hawks. His guide to courtship is not a book of sonnets or a handbook on marriage but a book of falconry: he adapts the methods of taming and training a hawk to the task of domesticating Katherine. Since we will be dealing closely with the language of falconry in the play, I shall quote the entire speech in which he declares this intention and italicize the technical terms:

> Thus have I politicly begun my reign,
> And 'tis my hope to end successfully.
> My *falcon* now is sharp and passing empty,
> And till she *stoop*, she must not be *full-gorg'd*,
> For then she never looks upon her *lure*.
> Another way I have to *man* my *haggard*,
> To make her come, and know her keeper's call,
> That is, to *watch* her, as we *watch* these *kites*
> That *bate* and beat and will not be obedient.
> She eat no meat to-day, nor none shall eat;
> Last night she slept not, nor to-night she shall not;
> As with the meat, some undeserved fault
> I'll find about the making of the bed,
> And here I'll fling the pillow, there the bolster,
> This way the coverlet, another way the sheets.
> Ay, and amid this hurly I intend
> That all is done in reverend care of her,
> And in conclusion, she shall watch all night,
> And if she chance to nod I'll rail and brawl,
> And with the clamor keep her still awake.
> This is a way to kill a wife with kindness,
> And thus I'll curb her mad and headstrong humor.
> He that knows better how to tame a shrew,
> Now let him speak; 'tis charity to shew.   (4.1.188–211)

As this speech demonstrates, Petruchio has mastered the jargon of falconry; he uses easily and naturally terms like "stoop," "lure," "man," "watch," and "bate." He knows that the tamer must keep the hawk hungry and sleepless, and that the tamer's ultimate goal is a bird that returns obediently to the call. More strikingly, he has mastered the paradoxical psychology coupling cruelty and kindness that underlies the process: "amid this hurly I intend / That all is done in reverend care of her." He perceives, moreover, that the goal of taming is power: "Thus have I politicly begun my reign." He is a benignly Machiavellian falconer, a sporting parody of Richard III, determined "to kill a wife with kindness." The phrase captures perfectly the paradoxical nature of the falconer's art.

Shakespeare's use of the language of falconry to characterize Petruchio's "taming" of Katherine must have had considerable impact upon contemporary audiences. When John Fletcher came to write his sequel to *The Taming of the Shrew*, entitled *The Woman's Prize or The Tamer Tamed* (1611), he acknowledged Shakespeare's metaphor by having his own "shrew," Maria, subvert it to her own purposes:

> Hang these tame hearted Eyasses, that no sooner
> See the Lure out, and heare their husbands halla,
> But cry like Kites upon 'em: The free Haggard
> (Which is that woman, that has wing, and knowes it,
> Spirit, and plume) will make an hundred checks,
> To shew her freedome, saile in ev'ry ayre,
> And look out ev'ry pleasure; not regarding
> Lure, nor Quarry, till her pitch command
> What she desires, making her foundred keeper
> Be glad to fling out traines, and golden ones,
> To take her down again.[13]

In contrasting herself to a tamed hawk, Maria sees herself as a "free Haggard" that flies at will and is drawn back to her tamer only with the lure of "golden" rewards. Having alluded to his Shakespearean original in this passage, Fletcher drops the metaphor of falconry and develops his lovers' conflict in the more conventional imagery of siege warfare. In Shakespeare's play, Katherine is tamed like a falcon; in Fletcher's, Maria wins a war.

The paradoxical effect of falcon-taming is foreshadowed in Petruchio's witty pun on the word "stoop" (191). In its technical sense the word conveys the astonishing speed and power of the falcon itself, referring to the "swift swoop or thunderbolt descent of the falcon on the quarry from above."[14] In its common meaning, in contrast, it refers to a lowering of the self, as in a gesture of submission. The "stooping" of the falcon thus expresses simultaneously its own and its master's power: the falcon fulfills its instinctual will, one might say, by lowering itself. Such a gesture of victorious submission occurs at the very end of the play when

Katherine, having outdone the other wives, offers to stoop and place her hand below Petruchio's foot. "'Tis my hope to end successfully," Petruchio tells us in his soliloquy, "And till she stoop, she must not be full-gorg'd." In such a context, the comic convention of the feast that ends the play takes on new meaning. Katherine feasts after she has "stooped" to defeat the other wives and "stooped" to honor her husband.

For Petruchio, Katherine is a "haggard . . . falcon" (4.1.193,190). The name "falcon," although used variously in the manuals, refers most commonly to "the female of all long-winged hawks."[15] Katherine is thus placed among the noblest of hunting birds, those that tower above their prey, not those that pursue it from the side or below. As a "haggard," she is a mature bird captured in the wild, not an "eyas," a bird stolen from the nest before it has learned to hunt. The haggard is often considered superior to the eyas because of its wild and hardy nature. Symon Latham, for example, ranks the haggard falcon above all other birds of prey.[16] As Edmund Bert observes, however, because the haggard has "lived long at liberty, having many things at her command, . . . she is therefore the harder to be brought to subjection and obedience."[17] As a haggard falcon, Katherine is a challenge worthy of her powerful lord.

As the numerous books on the subject make clear, taming a haggard falcon is an excruciatingly difficult art. The goal is "subjection and obedience," as Edmund Bert puts it, the complete subordination of the will of the bird to that of its master. The difficulty lies not only in securing obedience but in securing it in such a way that the bird is not destroyed as a hunter in the process. Taming requires that the bird suppress some of its most basic instincts, such as the fear of man, while at the same time fulfilling others, such as the will to hunt, only at the direction of the master. At its best, the sport aspires towards a union of two wills, animal and human, each devoted to the same exhilarating and instinctive end, the pursuit of prey. Any such union must be one-sided, however, for ultimate power resides with the falconer alone. In the language of the sport the falconer does not merely "train" his bird but "makes" it; the process of taming results in a new identity, a new creation. Edmund Bert exemplifies the pride of such a maker: "I have made so many and so extraordinary good Hawkes, as they could not be bettered both for flying and good conditions."[18]

Taming a falcon is necessarily a variable and fluid process, but it can be divided roughly into three general stages: the "manning," the training to the lure, and, climactically, the test of unrestricted flight.

Petruchio's "taming" of Katherine follows a similar pattern. The bulk of the "courtship" – including the first meeting, the wedding debacle, and the stay at Petruchio's – consists of "manning," the most difficult, intense, and time consuming part of the job. The trip home, including the meeting on the road with old Vincentio, might be considered Katherine's training to the lure. The final banquet, in which Katherine demonstrates her new status as an obedient wife, is the test of unrestricted flight towards which the entire exercise drives. Viewing Petruchio's "courtship" of Katherine from the perspective of falcon-taming illuminates the inner logic of his sometimes bizarre and puzzling behavior.

According to Frederick II of Hohenstaufen, taming a falcon "consists chiefly in persuading her to live quietly among men."[19] The first stage of the process, that of "manning," is devoted to making the hawk "acquainted" with the tamer. To achieve this end, the hawk, temporarily blinded by hooding or "seeling" the eyes, is placed on the wrist of the falconer, fed very sparingly, and kept awake for about three nights. The hawk's natural tendency is to escape, to "bate," but each time it tries it is returned firmly but affectionately to the wrist. Markham summarizes the process in a way that suggests the subtlety of its psychology:

All Hawkes generally are manned after one manner, that is to say, by watching and keeping them from sleep, by a continuall carrying of them upon your fist, and by a most familiar broaking and playing with them, with the wing of a dead Fowle or such like, and by often gazing and looking of them in the face with a loving and gentle countenance, and so making them acquainted with the man.[20]

As Markham's description suggests, the process drives the opposing forces of discipline and affection to paradoxical extremes. On the one hand, the bird is subjected to cruel deprivations, such as lack of food and what T. H. White calls the "secret cruelty" of sleeplessness.[21] On the other hand, it is treated with ostentatious care and affection. The final result is exhaustion and absolute submission.

Petruchio's treatment of Katherine, which throughout the play combines outrageous cruelty with ostentatious expressions of affection, killing her with kindness, imitates the method of the falconer. In their first meeting he trades insult for insult but refrains from violence even when she strikes him. Throughout their exchange, moreover, he keeps up a barrage of affectionate praise, celebrating the virtues he hopes to create as if her very "shrewishness" embodied them. He simply refuses to be put off:

Kath. I chafe you if I tarry. Let me go.
Pet. No, not a whit, I find you passing gentle:
'Twas told me you were rough and coy and sullen,
And now I find report a very liar;
For thou art pleasant, gamesome, passing courteous,
But slow in speech, yet sweet as spring-time flowers.   (2.1.241–46)

At the wedding ceremony he adopts a similar technique. As he seizes Katherine to take her home with him, refusing her the ceremony of the wedding feast, he declares in one breath that she is "my horse, my ox, my ass, my any thing," and in the next that he will chivalrously protect her against the "thieves" who beset them: "Fear not, sweet wench, they shall not touch thee, Kate! / I'll buckler thee against a million" (3.2.232, 238–39). He is both brute and chivalric hero.

At Petruchio's country house Katherine experiences complete bewilderment. Sleeplessness, lack of food, and lectures on continency take their toll. "She, poor soul," says the sympathetic Curtius, "Knows not which way to stand, to look, to speak, / And sits as one new risen from a dream" (4.1.184–86). Her greatest shock, however, comes from what we might call the falconer's paradox:

But I, who never knew how to entreat,
Nor never needed that I should entreat,
Am starv'd for meat, giddy from lack of sleep,
With oaths kept waking, and with brawling fed;
And that which spites me more than all these wants,
He does it under name of perfect love;
As who should say, if I should sleep or eat,
'Twere deadly sickness, or else present death.   (4.3.7–14)

Petruchio intends that "all is done in reverend care of her"; Katherine is here utterly mystified because his brutal actions carry the "name of perfect love." The falconer, says Edmund Bert, must show the falcon he dominates both "diligent care" and "loving respect."[22]

Perhaps the most striking sign of this paradoxical combination of cruelty and kindness is Petruchio's use of Katherine's name to assert both the imperiousness of his will and his affection. Katherine's very first words to him consist of a vain attempt to assert her identity by denying that her name is Kate: "They do call me Katherine that do talk of me" (2.1.184). Throughout the play she never calls herself anything but "Katherine." With only a few insignificant exceptions, moreover, she is "Katherine" or the equivalent "Katherina" to everyone else in the play. Petruchio uses "Katherine," however, only three times: once with ironic intent, in their first meeting (2.1.267), and twice in the final scene of the play, when he commands her to step on her cap (5.2.121) and lecture the wives on obedience (5.2.130). The formality of the latter instances suggest that he is engaged in a subtle form of bribery, a sign of a lingering doubt about the strength of Katherine's conversion. For the remainder of the play – at least sixty times, by my count – Petruchio re-creates Katherine's identity by imposing upon her his own version of her name, a version that in its intimacy puts him immediately in the position of a husband and master.

The most forceful attack on her sense of identity occurs in their first meeting, the point at which the tamer's power must be asserted unequivocally. In overwhelming her with the name "Kate" – he uses the name eleven times in five lines – Petruchio probably takes his cue from Baptista, who has referred to her by the intimate family name a moment before.[23] He therefore usurps the patriarchal role. As Katherine's taming proceeds and she becomes increasingly pliant, Petruchio's tone becomes increasingly affectionate, the name "Kate" becoming less wittily insulting and more endearing. It remains to the end, however, Petruchio's chosen name, not Katherine's, symbolizing not only his affection but his power even in the famous "kiss me, Kate" which marks both their public embrace and their final union at the end of the play (5.1.143; 5.2.180). The falconer thus not only "makes" his falcon but names it, as Adam "gave names unto all cattel, and to the foule of the heaven, and to everie beast of the field."[24] The continuing power of Petruchio's naming can be felt, ironically, in the language of most critics of the play, who follow Petruchio's choice, not Katherine's.

As the many allusions to affection between hawk and tamer in the manuals of falconry suggest, the process of taming is erotically charged, making the metaphor peculiarly apt for Petruchio's "courtship" of Katherine. The most highly prized hawks were female, and, although women of the gentry and above often hunted with hawks, the trainers and authors of manuals seem to have been invariably male. Whenever a hawk is mentioned in the manuals, it is almost always a "she," the falconer invariably a "he." The result is a persistent rhetoric of sexual attraction and domination throughout the entire process, the first and most difficult stage of which even goes by the provocative name of "manning." As George Turbervile puts it, a falcon is "made and manned" by a trainer who should take such "syngular delyght" in his bird that "hee may seeme to bee in love."[25] Edmund Bert advises the falconer to make the hawk "much in love with thy sweet and milde using her."[26]

The complex combination of cruel discipline, courtesy, and eroticism required in the taming of a falcon gives to Shakespeare's metaphor of taming far greater subtlety than one often finds in the critical and stage traditions. Neither the handbooks on falconry nor the play itself represents a view of the tamer like that imagined by G. B. Shaw, who sees Petruchio as a "coarse, thick-skinned money hunter, who sets to work to tame his wife exactly as brutal people tame animals or children – that is, by breaking their spirit by domineering cruelty." Nor does the metaphor of taming sanction the long-standing stage custom which provides Petruchio with a whip.[27] The whole point of taming a falcon is not to break its spirit but to attract, focus, and control its wild energy.

Once the falconer has induced submission to his own will, the hawk is gradually exposed to human society and to the normal disruptions of social experience which it must learn to tolerate if it is to be taken into the fields and among people. "Manning" thus involves not only the submission of the hawk to "man" but its submission to one man above all others, its refusal to be distracted from this peculiar allegiance by any external temptations. The customary practice of hooding the eyes lessens the danger of distraction by sight, but since the bird must eventually use its eyes to hunt, it must learn to look without distraction. The bird must be exposed to the world yet remain fixated upon the will of its master. T. H. White's goshawk was much upset by the cars, cyclists, and crowds it encountered on its first outing.[28]

The importance of training a falcon to live at the same time in the world and apart from it, to tolerate society but to act only upon the will of the master, helps to explain a peculiarity in Petruchio's "courtship" of Katherine: his repeated manipulation of tests that pit her loyalties to family and society against her devotion to him. Each of these tests requires that she accept his will, no matter how absurd or arbitrary, and defy the conventions and conventional ties that threaten to distract her. Among her own family, she must forgo a proper wedding ceremony, enduring a misattired bridegroom, a travesty of a church service, and the culminating insult of Petruchio's refusal to attend the feast. At Petruchio's country house she must endure humiliation before the servants and the haberdasher, whose attempts to provide her with respectable clothing are foiled by her husband. Even at the very end of the play, when Petruchio has won his will, he demands, and receives, a kiss in the streets. These tests are too obviously social to be explained simply as arbitrary manifestations of Petruchio's authority. As Camille Wells Slights observes, however, critics contradict each other in explaining their rationale, with some holding that Petruchio is trying "to rescue Kate from a repressive society" and others that he is trying "to teach her by negative example how insupportable such antisocial eccentricity is."[29] If viewed from the perspective of falconry, Petruchio's social tests have a single unifying purpose: to assert the absolute power of the master, whose will must become the unchallenged source of all authority, and to assert that power even in the face of the most compelling demands from the world at large.

Once the falcon is "manned," it is gradually trained to hunt and to return to the call of the falconer. To ensure that the hawk does not escape, the falconer attaches a fine cord, or "creance," to the bird before encouraging it to fly to a lure. If the hawk returns when called, it is rewarded with meat. With success, the falconer gradually increases the length of the cord, providing greater and greater distances for flight and return. Petruchio follows a similar method. When he is convinced that Katherine is "manned," he agrees to take her to visit her family, thus exposing her to the world outside. On the road, he tests her obedience by commenting on the brightness of the shining moon. When she objects, insisting that "it is the sun that shines so bright," he starts to turn around; she reverses herself immediately, however, affirming that the sun is not the sun when he says it is not and, slyly, that "the moon changes even as your mind." Her reversal convinces both Petruchio and Hortensio that she has been successfully "manned." "Petruchio," gasps Hortensio, "go thy ways, the field is won" (4.5.5–23).

The proof of Petruchio's victory lies in the mutual sport that both he and Katherine take in confusing old Vincentio, who enters at that moment. By now Katherine needs no orders to follow Petruchio's will. When he addresses Vincentio as if he were a "gentlewoman," she treats him as such without a pause to gather her wits, even embellishing her performance for their mutual delight; when required to reverse Vincentio's gender, she responds with equally instinctual ease. She has taken the lure, in the form of an innocent and disinterested stranger, and has demonstrated not only obedience but the spirited love of the sport that shows she is ready for public competition.[30]

In many readings and productions, the play takes a decidedly romantic turn at this moment. Because Katherine plays her new role before Vincentio with such obvious delight and theatrical exuberance, one cannot help but feel the joy and exhilaration of the sport. From the vantage point of falconry, however, such loving and responsive behavior is the mark of successful taming. A well trained hawk, says Symon

Latham, one that should be rewarded and treated with special kindness, is one that is "familiar," "lovingly reclaimed," gives "care to you, and to your voice," comes quickly when called, and when she comes seems "eager and hot to cease [seize] upon that which you shall throw or give unto her, and be familiar with your selfe, without starting or staring about her, or otherwise to be coie or waiward"; when she does the falconer's will, moreover, she looks up for the fist "and willingly and redily" jumps onto it.[31] The bond between falconer and successfully trained falcon thus blurs the boundaries between free will and subjection, pleasure and obedience; the bird's apparent delight in service creates the illusion of complete independence. The bond not only unites falcon and falconer against the prey which is the object of their pursuit but against any competitor who might seek to better them at their own game.

In Elizabethan and Jacobean England falconry was a competitive sport. The mere possession of such exotic and valuable properties as hawks fueled competitive energies, with owners and their falconers vying over methods of training and care and the quality and abilities of their favorite birds. Shakespeare evokes this general atmosphere in the very opening of the play, when the lord and the huntsman debate the various abilities of their hounds. But falconry was also competitive in a much more direct and obvious sense. Matches were held, wagers laid, and great sums won or lost, as moralists often lamented. A telling theatrical example of this custom is provided in Thomas Heywood's *A Woman Killed with Kindness* (1603). In the opening scene of the play, which depicts the wedding feast of Anne and John Frankford, Sir Charles Mountford proposes a hawking match the next day at Chevy Chase with the bride's brother, Sir Francis Acton; the wager is set at a hundred pounds, with an additional hundred on the dogs. The match takes place and, after a heated, complex, and technical dispute over whose hawk and dogs are victorious, a fight ensues, in which Sir Charles kills two of Sir Francis's men. In this case a friendly hawking match ends in murder. A desire to mitigate the anti-social tendencies in such competitions, one suspects, must have been in part responsible for the fanfare which accompanied Robert Dover's celebration of the Cotswold Games in 1636. The book of poems published in honor of these games, which includes figures such as Drayton, Jonson, and Heywood, portrays them as the heroic reincarnation of the ancient Olympics. In the Cotswold Games, both coursing and hawking were formal competitive events, with prizes awarded to the winners.[32]

The wager that takes place at the end of *The Taming of the Shrew* is thus

the logical culmination of the process of taming. The banquet at
Baptista's house evokes the sporting atmosphere of the hunt. Hortensio
and his Widow begin the festive competition by taunting Petruchio with
insinuations about Katherine's shrewishness. When Katherine takes
offense, the conflict becomes a metaphoric hunt, with Petruchio and
Hortensio imitating the orders that a huntsman gives to his dog in the
chase: "To her, Kate," "To her, widow!" (5.2.33–34).[33] "A hundred
marks," says Petruchio, "my Kate does put her down" (5.2.35). When
Bianca is in turn attacked, she shifts the metaphor to birding and leads
the women from the room: "Am I your bird? I mean to shift my bush, /
and then pursue me as you draw your bow" (5.2.46–47). Once introduced, the metaphor of the hunt expands to encompass not only the
immediate conflict but virtually the entire action of the play:

> *Pet.*   Here, Signior Tranio,
> This bird you aim'd at, though you hit her not;
> Therefore a health to all that shot and miss'd.
> *Tra.* O, sir, Lucentio slipp'd me like his greyhound,
> Which runs himself, and catches for his master.
> *Pet.* A good swift simile, but something currish.
> *Tra.* 'Tis well, sir, that you hunted for yourself;
> 'Tis thought your deer does hold you at a bay.
> *Bap.* O, O, Petruchio, Tranio hits you now.
> *Luc.* I thank thee for that gird, good Tranio.
> *Hor.* Confess, confess, hath he not hit you here?
> *Pet.* 'A has a little gall'd me, I confess;
> And as the jest did glance away from me,
> 'Tis ten to one it maim'd you [two] outright.   (5.2.49–62)

Fowling, coursing, stag-hunting – the language of the hunt, used
throughout to characterize the taming of Katherine, at this point
expands to encompass the play's entire treatment of courtship.

The play thus ends as it begins, by invoking the atmosphere of the
hunt.[34] Petruchio, finding himself at this point hunted and at bay,
decides to gamble upon his wife's obedience. The challenge is whether
the wives will return upon the call of their husbands, a test of obedience
that mimics precisely the test required of a hawk trained to the lure. The
wager, moreover, links Katherine's "taming" explicitly to that of hawks.
"Twenty crowns!" exclaims Petruchio in response to Lucentio's offer,
"I'll venture so much of my hawk or hound, / But twenty times so much
upon my wife" (5.2.71–73). He accepts an offer of a hundred crowns, and
wins. Katherine, it seems, has been "manned" and "made."

Viewing the main action of the play as an instance of falcon-taming thus seems to lead to a reductive conclusion. Petruchio is more than falconer, we might want to object, Katherine more than falcon, and the play more than farce. The metaphor of taming is capable of a more romantic interpretation, indeed, and one is provided by Margaret Loftus Ranald. Ranald's interpretation provides a useful test for my own reading not only because it represents a rigorous and sustained attempt to situate the play within the context of falconry but because it develops from the metaphor romantic implications. Through the metaphor of falconry, Ranald argues, the play subverts the "antifeminist genre" of "the wifebeating farce," reinterpreting "that traditionally male-oriented view of marriage which requires the molding of a wife, by force if necessary, into total submission to her husband." The play celebrates instead the "success of the relationship of equality between the sexes personified by Kate and Petruchio."[35]

Ranald's argument, like my own, depends to a great extent upon the most striking feature of the process of taming a hawk, its goal of "mutual respect between bird and keeper."[36] She develops at length, and with considerable sensitivity, the parallelism between the two activities, that of taming a hawk and courting Katherine. In Katherine's final speech, she argues, Shakespeare conveys "the ideal matrimonial situation. Both keeper and falcon, husband and wife, have their own areas of superiority, but when both work together at a given hunting task they are incomparable."[37] Although she does not exploit it, Ranald's argument carries a nicely ironic paradox: that Shakespeare humanizes marriage by treating the relationship between husband and wife as that between falconer and falcon. The play achieves a liberal view of marriage, in short, because the taming of falcons was so humane.

It may be true, regrettably, that the treatment of hawks was more humane than the treatment of wives in Elizabethan England; Shakespeare implies, certainly, that the hunting lord's treatment of his hounds is at least as humane as his treatment of Christopher Sly. To use words such as "mutual agreement," "mutuality," or "equality" to characterize the relationship between tamed hawk and lord, however, is to lose sight of the actual nature of the relationship. To tame a hawk is to achieve mastery over it, to secure its obedience. The process requires affection, as we have seen, and it ends, if successful, with mutual respect and mutual exhilaration in the hunt. But affection, respect, and exhilaration of this sort have nothing to do with equality. The bird has simply learned to fulfill its instinctual desires by expressing them upon the command and under the control of its master. It hunts, but not of its own will. The art of training a falcon, George Turbervile reminds us, testifies to "the singular skill of man."[38] Ranald's "positive evaluation of falconry as a model for marriage," as Frances E. Dolan observes, "downplays the significant disparities between the two parties," ignoring the fact that the bond between bird and man is "hardly between equals."[39]

The difficulty of reconciling the metaphor of falconry with a liberal reading of the play is illustrated by Brian Morris's attempt to develop the familiar motif of Petruchio as Katherine's teacher. Morris's admirably wide-ranging introduction to the Arden edition includes separate sections on Petruchio's role as falconer and as educator. In the former, he notes how the last two acts of the play "focus intensively on the single action of manning a wild hawk, translating it relentlessly into human terms"; in the latter, he discusses Petruchio as an innovator in "educational methodology." To see Petruchio as a teacher, Morris must argue that education is always paradoxical, designed on the one hand "to liberate" individuals and on the other to reduce them "to social conformity." "To some extent," he observes, education is "always a taming procedure, at odds with the very human desire for liberty." In *The Taming of the Shrew*, he concludes, the "tension between these contrary impulses" is "uncomfortably evident." Although the admission of discomfort acknowledges the ultimate irreconcilability of teaching and taming, it does not keep Morris from romanticizing the final union of pupil and teacher. When Katherine kisses Petruchio in the streets at the end of act 5 scene 1, according to Morris, her words demonstrate "a mutuality, a gentle and loving concern for union which shows that the teaching is over, the pupil has graduated, and all that is left is love."[40] How the discomfort vanishes is never explained.

The entire thrust of the metaphor of falconry in *The Taming of the Shrew*, as we have seen, is to identify Petruchio as tamer and Katherine as hawk. To treat taming as education is to blur the boundaries between activities that are fundamentally at odds. As the manuals of falconry make clear, hawks are not tamed by free choice. They are "killed with kindness." Hence the language applied to the successfully tamed hawk is that of creation. One "makes" a hawk. Katherine herself is similarly "made." She is "manned," exposed to the lure, and, finally, tested in competition. For her owner, she becomes not only a creature of delight, capable of imagining and fulfilling his desires without even the necessity of command, but, like other hunting animals, an instrument of playful aggression. She can beat the competition.

As critics such as John C. Bean have shown, the notion of "mutuality" in marriage can be found in the more enlightened Elizabethan treatments of marriage.[41] The liberalizing of doctrines of marriage that occurred in the Elizabethan and Jacobean periods, however, depended essentially upon Christian theology. Underlying the Puritan emphasis upon marriage as a kind of friendship, for example, was the notion that husbands and wives, although not physically, intellectually, or socially equal, were equal in the eyes of God, equally capable of salvation.[42] Such a view of marriage does not necessarily challenge the patriarchal social order, especially because of the biblical injunctions that sustain it, but it does not accommodate metaphors of taming animals. As Keith Thomas has amply demonstrated, fundamental to all thinking about animals in the period was acceptance of the Christian notion that only human beings have immortal souls.[43] In such a context, to compare a wife to a tamed hawk is not to liberalize marriage. The humanizing of marriage, then, depends upon a theology that divorces humans from animals; the metaphor of falconry identifies humans with animals, or, more precisely, wives with falcons.

If focusing on the reductive implications of the metaphor of taming seems too cynical, we might consider the play's satiric depiction of other marital and familial relationships. Baptista seems a kind man and caring father, but his views of marriage are in essence simply economic. He is embarrassingly eager to foist Katherine upon Petruchio, so much so that he is willing to take an unusual business risk: "Faith gentlemen, now I play a merchant's part, / And venture madly on a desperate mart" (2.1.326–27). As for Bianca, he assures Tranio and Gremio that "deeds must win the prize," but for him the word "deeds" means contracts, not worthy actions: "he of both / That can assure my daughter greatest dower / Shall have my Bianca's love" (2.1.342–44). In contrast to Baptista, Lucentio is delightfully romantic, but his romanticism is as automatic and conventional as Baptista's mercantilism; the two incongruous discourses – of mercantile and romantic love – are played off against each other for broadly comic effect. If the relationship between Katherine and Petruchio looks good at the end of the play, it is not because it embodies a Shakespearean ideal of marriage but because the alternatives are so absurd.

The name for the kind of comedy that treats humans as animals is farce, a label that seems both inadequate and inescapable in response to this play. The label is ultimately inadequate, it seems to me, not so much because it obscures the play's richness of characterization or romantic tone but because it ignores its metadramatic nature. If we are given something close to farce in the courtship of Petruchio and Katherine, it is farce made self-conscious. The relationship is framed by our aware-ness that we are watching a play-within-a play, an entertainment for Christopher Sly. In this sense the play might be called, paradoxically, a self-reflexive farce, one in which farce recoils upon itself and in the process becomes intellectually provocative. True farce is notoriously anti-intellectual, of course, the kind of comedy that depends upon slap-stick, horseplay, caricatures, broad verbal humor, and ludicrous situa-tions – all of which appear in the play. Farce is also notoriously reductive, implying a "debased" view of life, in which instinct is all, and in which success, if it comes, depends upon cunning, physical strength, and an obsessive and child-like egotism. *The Taming of the Shrew* is reductive in much the same way, it seems to me, but self-consciously so. In this sense the farce of taming Katherine might be considered an experiment or hypothesis in human relations, requiring us to confront, in comic terms, the full implications of a traditional metaphor. What does it mean to "tame" a wife? Or, as Petruchio himself demands of the audience, "He that knows better how to tame a shrew, / Now let him speak; 'tis charity to shew" (4.1.210–11). The self-conscious farce of taming the shrew works like a peculiarly mad version of scientific reductionism: it pares life down to its most basic drives, de-humanizing individual relationships in order to reveal their essential natures.

This concentration on essentials, which underlies the entire represen-tation of falconry in the relationship between Katherine and Petruchio, climaxes in Katherine's final speech (5.2.136–79). The bulk of this speech is in this respect of little consequence, although it has attracted most of the commentary. Katherine spends most of her time wittily and theatri-cally developing the conventional images and arguments in favor of benign patriarchal marriage: a woman's beauty is marred by frowns; the husband is lord, life, and keeper; the wife owes the duty of obedience to her husband; her place is in the home, under his protection and author-ity; and so forth. In this part of the speech one recognizes the theatrical delight in her new role displayed earlier in her address to old Vincentio.

More revealing, and more essentially true to the dynamics of Katherine's taming, is her conclusion, which centers upon the brute fact of weakness:

My mind hath been as big as one of yours,
My heart as great, my reason haply more,
To bandy word for word and frown for frown;
But now I see our lances are but straws,
Our strength as weak, our weakness past compare,
That seeming to be most which we indeed least are.   (5.2.170–75)

Everything that Katherine says about wifely duties and obligations derives from this recognition and acceptance of Petruchio's greater strength. The formal rhetoric of benign patriarchal marriage which she elaborates with such gusto is here revealed as an ideological result of female weakness. This admission is the one part of her speech that grows directly out of the play's experience. Petruchio has simply overwhelmed Katherine, and the pleasure she takes in her new role is coupled with the rueful acceptance of defeat. The play ends, in short, with the metaphor of taming carried unflinchingly to its logical conclusion.

The most insidious implications of this metaphor lie not in its mere elevation of male power but in the very "humanity" with which such power is invested. As Petruchio and the manuals of falconry develop it, the metaphor actually enables us to imagine the very Katherine who appears in productions and critical essays of the romantic kind. She is not brutalized in body or cowed in spirit. She is vibrant, alert, so ready for competition that she performs far beyond the expectations of her master or the demands of the occasion. She carries with her a sense of play, as if in following orders she herself is achieving the fulfillment of her own desires, as if her very freedom were to be found in obedience itself. The very "romantic" spirit which Katherine demonstrates at the end of the play, in short, if read in the context of the metaphor of taming, is not a mark of true independence and mutuality but of successful taming. Katherine seems a more vibrant and fulfilled human being from this perspective because she behaves like an ideal hawk. Since man was "appointed by God to have dominion over the beasts," observes C. S. Lewis, "the tame animal is . . . in the deepest sense the only 'natural' animal – the only one we see occupying the place it was meant to occupy."[44] The metaphor of falconry is insidious precisely because the relationship between tamer and bird is so intensely and lovingly "human."

If we accept such a reading of the play, one that takes the metaphor of taming to its reductive extreme, do any consolations remain? Is there any way, to adopt Shaw's Victorian phrasing, for a "man" with "decency of feeling" to attend this play, with or without the company of a woman?

Not if we look for serious "mutuality" in marriage, it seems to me, or even for the anesthesia of pure farce. Consolation is to be found, if at all, only in more desperate measures. If we value the resistance of wives to patriarchal coercion, for example, we might take some solace in the behavior of Bianca and the widow, neither of whom respond on call to the commands of their husbands. Bianca's behavior is itself characterized in the language of hawking. At the beginning of the play, both Gremio and Tranio protest at Bianca's being "mew'd" up, caged like a falcon, because of Baptista's desire to marry Katherine first (1.1.87, 183). When Hortensio discovers her affection for the disguised Lucentio, he likens her to a hawk that is distracted by every decoy, that casts its "wand'ring eyes on every stale" (3.1.90), and later he renounces his love for this "proud disdainful haggard" (4.2.39). He leaves Bianca in the futile hope of finding a more docile and obedient bird in the widow. The irony of the play's ending depends upon a sharp contrast between the birds that merely seem tame and the one who is. If one prefers wild to "manned" hawks, then there is perhaps some consolation to be found in the continuing wildness of the widow and Bianca.

A more likely source of consolation is to be found in Katherine herself. In many productions of the play, actresses playing Katherine have undermined her apparent subjection by signaling, usually through a wink to the audience, her secret resistance to the role that she accepts for the moment. Such a gesture is sanctioned by the motif of "seeming" which runs throughout this metadramatic play. The motif cuts two ways: if Bianca "seems" a docile wife at first, Katherine may "seem" so at the end. Petruchio's decision to use the name "Katherine" twice in calling her to him at this point, as we have seen earlier, suggests a certain anxiety about her obedience. The play's final line, moreover, is Lucentio's "'Tis a wonder, by your leave, she will be tam'd so" (5.2.189).

This male anxiety about the possibility of relapse is one that audiences familiar with falconry would take for granted. From the vantage point of falconry, the issue is not so much whether Katherine has been truly tamed – her speech gives no reason to believe otherwise – but how long she will remain so. In this context, Petruchio's nervousness and Lucentio's wonder are predictable responses to the situation. As all of the manuals make clear, tamed hawks require vigilant care. The more valuable they are as hawks, moreover, the more likely they are to seek their freedom. The falconer therefore always flirts with disaster, encouraging in his hawk the most highly spirited and soaring flight, making himself vulnerable to the possibility that wildness will reassert itself and the hawk be lost forever. Symon Latham, for example, warns his readers about the special need to remain watchful over haggards:

Now must it needes bee that these kindes of *Hawkes* have, and evermore will have some wildnesse in them, which disposition, although I have formerly shewd you how to alter and change, and to keepe them loving and familiar with you: yet that being wrought and effected by art you must beware that nature do not get the upper hand, or beare the greatest swaie, for if it doe, then your skill failes you, and your art deserves no commendation.[45]

In the language of the play, as we have seen, Katherine is a "haggard"; any falconer would know that such hawks "evermore will have some wildnesse in them." The metaphor of taming a haggard thus carries with it a continuing potential for escape, a continuing male anxiety. We too may wonder, with Lucentio, that Katherine "will be tam'd so."

But perhaps there is a more radical way to save the play from its own ending – by probing more fully than is customary the implications of its beginning. The play opens with an Induction, which features a hunting lord's practical joke at the expense of the tinker and beggar, Christopher Sly. The motif of taming is introduced upon the first appearance of this lord, for he enters "*from hunting, with his* Train," and to the sound of horns(Ind.i.16.s.d.). He has just returned from hunting deer with his hounds, and for the next fifteen lines he gives directions to his huntsman for their care. The dialogue between lord and huntsman establishes at the outset of the play the atmosphere of the hunt, and their concern for their dogs later modulates into the "taming" of Christopher Sly which, for the brief period of a joke, transforms his identity. The scene as a whole, as has often been observed, mirrors the major action of the play, with the lord transforming Sly from a "monstrous beast" (Ind.1.34) to a nobleman and Petruchio transforming Katherine from a shrew to an obedient wife.

In the brief exchange between the lord and his huntsman (Ind.1.30), Shakespeare evokes the ethos of the hunt that underlies the role of Petruchio throughout the play.[46] Like Petruchio, the lord is a forceful man: he "charges" his young huntsman to care for the hounds and calls him, with affectionate brusqueness, a "fool" for preferring the wrong dog. Like Petruchio, too, he has a playful wit, for it is he who instigates the jest against Sly and directs the various performances. As striking as his mastery over his world, however, is his care for those dependent upon his power. He takes pains to protect Sly against the "over-merry spleen" of his servants, "which otherwise would grow into extremes" (Ind.i.137–38), and his care for his dogs accords with the best models of the manuals of the hunt. The pack as a whole, he tells his huntsman, is to be "tendered" well; poor Merriman, "embossed" (foaming at the mouth) from an exhausting chase, is to be given special attention, as is Clowder, who is to be coupled with "the deep-mouth'd brach," perhaps because he is a young hound and requires the stability of a mature bitch, or perhaps because the music of their voices is harmonious.

Training even a domesticated animal for the hunt requires affection, discipline, and reinforcement. The hunting lord's hounds, for example, would have been taught first to respond to the "hallow" of both voice and horn and then gradually introduced to the hunt itself by the method preferred by their trainer. In *The Noble Arte of Venerie*, George Gascoigne recommends "entering" the hound first to the hare, since it is easily weaned from such hunting to that of the stag; he admits, however, that they can be also "entered" to fat or wounded stags, for they are easily pursued. In their first attempts the young dogs benefit from the guidance of mature dogs in the pack. Their desire to hunt is reinforced by immediate reward at the end of the hunt, the neck of the hart being flayed for that purpose.[47] As we have seen in chapter 3, the hunting instincts even of mature hounds must be reinforced with every kill, the rewarding consisting of an abbreviated mimicry of the hunt itself, with each dog being allotted its rightful share in the carcass. Successfully trained hunting dogs achieve a difficult balance between obedience to man and instinctual wildness; they pursue and kill, but only on command.

Moralistic objections to the hunt often focused on the lavish indulgence of hounds, which were usually treated better by aristocrats than the common people themselves. Keith Thomas quotes an early Stuart commentator who complains that when masters returned from the hunt they would often show "more care for their dogs than of their servants and make them lie down by them, and often the servant is beaten for the dog; you may see in some men's houses fair and fat dogs to run up and down and men pale and wan to walk feebly."[48] The care recommended in Gascoigne's *Noble Arte of Venerie* is typical. The kennels are to be spacious, well aired, clean, heated by a fireplace, provided with running water, lightened by whited walls and windows, and each dog is to be assigned a "little bedstead" on rollers, so that when it returns from the chase it can be rolled "as neare the fire as you wil." After a chase in inclement weather, the hounds are to receive special care: their coats are to be warmed, brushed and cleaned and, if necessary, their feet are to be washed with a mixture of water, salt, egg yolks, vinegar and herbs. Although the *Noble Arte of Venerie* defines a "good keeper of hounds" as

"gratious, curteous, and gentle, loving his dogs of a naturall disposition,"[49] the care of the animals was not disinterested, for they were
essential instruments in the hunt. "Sup them well, and look unto them
all," says Shakespeare's lord of his hounds, "To-morrow I intend to hunt
again" (Ind.i.28–29).

Intertwined with the lord's directions to his huntsman about the care
of his hounds is a jocular debate about the abilities of the various dogs.
The lord praises Silver for picking up a cold scent at the hedge-corner,
but the huntsman counters with the example of Belman, who "twice today picked out the dullest scent" and is the "better dog" (Ind.i.24–25).
The lord in turn objects, praising Echo, despite his slowness, as "worth
a dozen such" (Ind.i.27). Such bantering is as characteristic of the
culture of the hunt as the lord's care of his hounds. Were the hunter and
his huntsman social equals and the dogs from different packs, bets might
be placed. The careful appraisal of the virtues of the hounds, the competitive ranking of one against the other – these activities are as much a
part of the sport as the chase itself. This competitive male spirit, as we
have seen, is one of the driving forces of the taming plot, especially of
the wager that brings it to a close.

The world that Shakespeare evokes at the opening of the play, then,
is the bantering, playfully aggressive and stereotypically masculine world
of the hunt. Its presiding spirit is a lord, who dominates both the social
and natural orders as master of his hounds, his servants, and drunken
tinkers. He rules with rough care, affection, and wit. The "dream" that
he creates in jest for Christopher Sly is not an arbitrary fantasy but one
that projects the distinctive ethos of his own world. In his offers to Sly he
lists the usual accoutrements of a nobleman – servants, music, a soft and
lustful bed – but his vision of a lord's life climaxes with the prospect of
riding, hawking, and hunting:

> Or wilt thou ride? Thy horses shall be trapp'd,
> Their harness studded all with gold and pearl.
> Dost thou love hawking? Thou hast hawks will soar
> Above the morning lark. Or wilt thou hunt?
> Thy hounds shall make the welkin answer them
> And fetch shrill echoes from the hollow earth.   (Ind.ii.41–46)

Even the titillating pictures offered by the lord and his servants feature
eroticized versions of the hunt, with Venus in pursuit of Adonis, and
Apollo chasing Daphne. Sly is presented with a vision of life as lived and
imagined not by any lord but by a hunting lord.

To have this life, even in the brief unreality of a dream, Sly must do two things. He must repudiate his former identity: "Upon my life, I am a lord indeed, / And not a tinker, nor Christopher Sly" (Ind. ii. 72–73). He must also repress his sexual desire for his "wife," the indulgence of which would jeopardize his cure: "But I would be loath to fall into my dreams again. I will therefore tarry in despite of the flesh and the blood" (Ind.ii.126–28). The bargain he makes, trading the drunken life of a tinker for the dream life of a lord, makes him analogous to a hound or bird of prey: he is "tamed." For the price of a few instincts and a name, he receives the treatment of a lord, which is guaranteed for as long as he continues to provide amusement. His first reward is the performance of a play. Why does he see a play that involves the taming of a shrew?

Throughout his career Shakespeare invariably connects his plays-within-plays to the character of the rulers or nobles who request them. The practice surely imitates normal custom, for one would expect the person who pays the players to choose the nature of the entertainment. In *A Midsummer Night's Dream,* Theseus is given his choice of entertainments, such as it is, and selects "Pyramus and Thisbe," having rejected others as too familiar or as "not sorting with a nuptial ceremony" (5.1.55); in its tragical-comical rendition of the violence of love, the playlet sorts rather more well with the nuptial ceremony than its audience imagines. In *Love's Labor's Lost,* Holofernes, having been ordered by Navarre to entertain the Princess, chooses the pageant of the Nine Worthies as most "fit" for the audience and the occasion (5.1.123); both the theme and the performance of the entertainment mock the aspirations of the young male aristocrats who have commissioned it. In *Hamlet,* the visiting actors receive instructions from the prince for a play that is designed to "catch the conscience of the King" (2.2.605). In *The Tempest,* finally, Prospero designs and choreographs his own entertainment; the masque that he presents before Ferdinand and Miranda not only blesses the betrothed couple but embodies his idealized celebration of chaste love.

With these analogues in mind, it is not difficult to see the play performed at the request of the hunting lord in *The Taming of the Shrew* as a projection of his own values. The performance focuses on Christopher Sly, of course, as the guest of honor. The lord prepares the actors for his eccentric habits and warns them that he has never seen a play. When the play is announced, the messenger tells Sly that a comedy has been selected upon the recommendation of the doctor, as an antidote to his melancholy. Implicit in these preparations is the notion that the performance will speak both to the hunting lord who has called for it and to the lord who is his guest; the hunting lord's life has become Sly's fantasy.

It should come as no surprise, then, that the play which ensues depicts the successful courtship of another hunting lord, one who tames a wife by using the methods of a falconer and who triumphs over wooers whose methods are contemptibly sentimental or mercenary or both. The fantasy projected before Christopher Sly is not his own fantasy but that of the hunting lord himself. The play he witnesses shows the triumph of the culture of the hunt over the mercantile and romantic culture embodied in the courtships of Bianca and the widow, and over a woman who needs to be tamed. It is a play that catches the conscience of a hunting lord.

The device of the Induction, then, allows us to experience *The Taming of the Shrew* as an image not of *the* world but of *a* world – a world characterized by a distinctive social atmosphere and inhabited by distinctive social types with their own ways of thinking and behaving in society. This is not our world, we may say, but it is also no more than a self-consciously farcical and satirical slice of Shakespeare's. The ironic framework established by the Induction lends support to Coppélia Kahn's unconventional and brilliantly provocative argument that the play is a satire and its target "the male urge to control woman." From Kahn's perspective, Petruchio's outrageous exaggerations of the typical attributes of male supremacy – his oaths, his brutality, his arbitrariness and irrationality, his reduction of Katherine to the status of an animal – are a source of satiric laughter.[50] The dominant motifs of hunting and taming throughout the play locate this male braggadocio in the culture of the hunt.

The metadramatic potential of the Induction has only recently begun to be realized on stage. From 1754 to 1844 Garrick's *Catherine and Petruchio* was the sole version performed, and it eliminated both the Induction and the subplot. Even after 1844, when Shakespeare's text became the basis for performances, the Induction was omitted more often than not until the 1950s, when a series of productions stressed its potential to distance the audience from the farcical action of the taming and to highlight theatrically the notions of role-playing and illusion. Emphasis on the Induction, of course, can provide very different theatrical meanings. Graham Holderness, for example, contrasts the effects achieved in John Barton's Royal Shakespeare Company production of 1960 with those achieved in Di Trevis's Royal Shakespeare Company touring production in 1985. The former, he shows, used the Induction to emphasize harmony and reconciliation at the end of the play, whereas the latter created a Brechtian effect, distancing audiences from the drama they

had just seen. In Barton's version, the prominence of the Induction and
Christopher Sly highlighted a cheerful romanticism in the main plot; in
Di Trevis's, it highlighted the link between Sly and Katherine, who
appeared alone on stage at the end as victims of their capricious lords.[51]
It is not difficult to imagine a production that could present the play-
within-the-play as a version of life seen through the eyes of a hunting
lord.

As Leah Marcus has shown, most of the recent productions of the
play that have exploited the Induction have merged the text of *The Shrew*
with that of *A Shrew*, in which the Sly framework is much more system-
atically deployed. In *A Shrew*, Sly not only interrupts the proceedings on
several occasions, the lord at his side, but is returned to the streets at the
end. The play closes with his awakening from a "dream" and determining to put his new knowledge to use by taming his wife. Productions that
frame the taming plot with the misadventures of Sly, Marcus observes,
deflect its "reality" by making shrew-taming "the compensatory fantasy
of a socially underprivileged male." According to Marcus, this reading
of the play, which depends upon a text that most editors dismiss as a
"bad" quarto, represents the recovery of an interpretative possibility
foreclosed by editors who have traditionally preferred their texts authoritative and their women obedient. Modern texts of the play, edited so as
to exclude consideration of *A Shrew*, enforce patriarchy by representing
Katherine's taming as "real"; theatrical productions, adapting the
framework of *A Shrew*, cast the whole patriarchal system constructed by
the taming plot into "doubt and unreality."[52]

Although Marcus's appeal to re-open consideration of the text of *A
Shrew* is convincing, her argument depends upon two questionable
assumptions: that any metadramatic irony is evoked from the play only
by the full Sly framework, and that the irony is necessarily focused on Sly
alone. Even the text of *The Shrew*, it seems to me, implies sustained irony
in the use of the framework. Although Sly interrupts the proceedings
only once, the Induction as a whole is rich enough to carry its ironies
throughout, especially since, as we have observed, the final scene of the
play restates its dominant motifs of hunting, taming, and joking. The
absence of stage directions, moreover, makes it possible either to keep
both Sly and the lord on stage throughout the play or to double the parts
of the lord and Petruchio; either choice would keep alive the ironies of
the Induction. To say that *The Shrew* represents a "real" taming because
the play does not close upon Christopher Sly thus overstates the case

considerably. The difference between the two texts is one of degree, not kind.

The emphasis upon Sly's "fantasy" created both by Marcus and the productions she cites, moreover, fails to address the role of his host, the hunting lord. In either version of the text, the fantasy is Sly's only because the lord directs the actors to present a play. In *A Shrew*, moreover, the role of the lord is even more emphatic than in *The Shrew*. In the former version he explicitly selects the play, greeting the player's proposal with, "the taming of a shrew, that's excellent sure" (1.65); he converses with Sly during each interruption; and he orders Sly returned to the street at the end. Sly may interpret the play as a "compensatory fantasy," but it is a fantasy selected by the hunting lord and developed by players devoted to his entertainment.

To see the taming of Katherine as the wish-fulfillment fantasy of a hunting lord, of course, does not necessarily resolve the problem of the ending. One can imagine a production of the play, indeed – one at court, perhaps – that would give full weight to the Induction and highlight the motifs of taming and hunting throughout, not to satirize the swaggering masculinity of the world of the hunt but to celebrate it with playful mockery. In such a case, male members of an audience sharp enough to perceive the mockery could indulge simultaneously in a wish-fulfillment fantasy of taming and a rueful acknowledgment of their own braggadocio. At the very least, however, acknowledgment of the ironic treatment of the culture of the hunt throughout the play makes it impossible to take the taming of Katherine straight. It complicates our perspective on the taming, forcing us to see its most insidious implications as emblems not of reality itself but of the social world of the hunt. By disallowing the reductive extremes of stark antifeminism or evasive romanticism, it brings the play within the more familiar patriarchal boundaries of Shakespearean comedy.

To appreciate the distinctive social world evoked by Shakespeare's Induction, and by the "play" that ensues, it might be useful to consider the life of a true Elizabethan hunting lord, one for whom Petruchio's taming of Katherine would have provided a welcome "compensatory fantasy." In the early seventeenth century, John Smyth of Nibley, having served for many years as steward of the manors of the great Berkeley estate, wrote a history of the family from 1066 to 1628.[53] Smyth's own employer was Henry Lord Berkeley (1534–1613). If we attend closely to

Smyth's family history of Lord Henry, his wife, and one of their falcons, we can uncover a remarkably immediate social context, and perhaps even a new "source" for the atmosphere of the hunting world that so deeply permeates Shakespeare's play.

In the long section devoted to the life of his employer, Smyth at one point recalls his lord's fondness for falconry, and his own delight, as a young, new employee, in watching Lord Henry's famous pair of haggard falcons soar out of sight. The falcons "lasted twelve or more years," notes Smyth, and were

famous with all great faulconers in many counties, and prized at excessive rates, esteemed for high and round flying, free stooping, and all other good conditions, inferior to none in Christendome; whom my self in my younger years waiting upon his son Thomas, then not twelve years old, at Binly Brooke, have in the height of their pitch, lost the sight of, in a cleer evening . . . (363)

Since Lord Henry's son Thomas turned twelve in 1587, and since the falcons lasted "twelve or more years," these magnificent and superbly trained birds were almost certainly famous throughout the territories favored by Lord Henry – Gloucestershire, Warwickshire, and London among them – during the years in which Shakespeare must have composed *The Taming of the Shrew*.[54]

Lord Henry's falcons are of particular interest because they had evocative names. One, which we shall ignore, was called Stella, perhaps after the heroine of Sidney's *Astrophil and Stella*.[55] The other was named Kate, probably after its mistress, Lady Berkeley, whose name was Katharine. As we have seen, this name resounds in various forms throughout Shakespeare's play – 8 times as Katherina, 19 times as Katherine, and 71 times as Kate. The name does not occur in any of the works usually proposed as sources for the play. Around 1590, then, we have the coincidence of three Kates: one is a falcon, one owns a falcon, and one is tamed as a falcon in a comedy.

I begin with Smyth's image of a soaring haggard falcon because, as we have seen, *The Taming of the Shrew* develops the idea of taming primarily through metaphors from falconry. In the case of Lady Katharine, the association between wife and falcon was more than metaphoric. Lady Katharine was an avid falconer herself. Although Smyth says nothing about her relationship to the falcon named Kate, a comment he makes about her general treatment of hunting birds suggests that it may well have been close: she "kept commonly a cast or two of merlins, which sometimes she mewed in her own chamber; which falconry cost her husband each yeare one or two gownes and kirtles spoiled by their mutings" (285). Since Lady Katharine went so far as to keep molting falcons in her chamber, she might even have played an active role in their taming; if so, she would have been unusual indeed, for, although hunting with falcons was common among aristocratic women in the period, contemporary handbooks on falconry never refer to women as trainers. In any event, Smyth's anecdote implies an exceptional intimacy, perhaps an implicit kind of identification, between Lady Katharine and her birds of prey.

Like many other female aristocrats, Lady Katharine hunted not only with falcons but with dogs. She was known, indeed, as an extraordinary huntress. She was a strong woman, "somewhat tall," according to Smyth, and "of pace the most stately and upright all times of her age that ever I beheld" (382). In hunting she used both a cross bow and a long bow, and in her younger days was "amongst her servants soe good an Archer at butts, as her side by her was not the weaker" (285). Smyth expresses wonder at her physical courage, as when she refused to "take notice of the paine" while watching a surgeon cut off her finger (385).

Lady Katharine was exceptional in other respects as well. As a Howard, she was a member of one of the most prominent, cultivated, and troubled families in the kingdom. She had remarkable intellectual interests and abilities and had received an extraordinary education. Smyth describes her as

of speech passing Eloquent and ready; whom in many years I could never observe to misplace or seem to recall one mistaken, misplaced or mispronounced word or sillable; And as ready and significant under her pen; forty of whose letters at least at severall times I have received; her invention as quick as her first thoughts, And her words as ready as her invention; Skillfull in the french, but perfect in the Italian tongue, wherein shee most desired her daughters to bee instructed; At the lute shee played admirably, and in her private chamber would often singe thereto, to the ravishment of the hearers . . . (382–83)

Like Shakespeare's heroine, Lady Katharine is eloquent, outspoken, and quick-witted; she is also a master at the very instrument that Katherine breaks across Hortensio's head (2.1.142.s.d.). In "her elder years," observes Smyth, Lady Katharine studied natural philosophy and astronomy, and she often discussed the rules of Latin grammar with him to "continue her knowledge in the latin tongue."

Although he admired Lady Katharine for her intelligence, learning, and spirit, Smyth clearly found her difficult. To illustrate her character, he quotes a letter she wrote to him in May 1595, which conveys an impression of strong, manipulative control of both Lord Henry and the household (383–84). After reading Lady Katharine's letter, it comes as no surprise that she and her husband had a rather stormy marriage. Smyth calls attention to her proud bearing. She was "of stomacke great and haughty, no way diminishing the greatnes of her birth and marriage by omission of any ceremony, at diet or publike prayers; whose book I have usually observed presented to her with the lowest courtesies that might bee, and on the knees of her gentlewoman . . . " (382). She seems to have been more intelligent than her husband and was certainly more highly educated. Smyth notes that Lord Henry reproached himself for his own lack of education and, when appointed Justice of the Peace for Gloucester, he "brought his servant Thomas Duport into equall authority with him, whereby his own unaptnes was less perceived, and the buisines of the Country not worse discharged" (287).

For Smyth, the conventions of the patriarchy counted for more than mere ability, and he minces no words about Lady Katharine's domineering tendencies as a wife. Despite occasional expressions of wonder at Lady Katharine's abilities and power in the household, Smyth's overall judgment of her is strongly patriarchal and censorious. He speaks the dominant language of the day. Lady Katharine's spending far exceeded her income, an offense that must have rankled with the man who was largely responsible for keeping the finances of the household in order. More offensive than her spending habits, however, which were shared by her husband, was her desire to "rule her husbands affaires." Smyth's judgment of this aspiration is worth quoting at length:

It cannot bee said That any apparant vice was in this lady, But it may bee said of a wife as of money, they are as they are used, helpers or hurters; money is a good servant but a bad master: And sure it is that shee much coveted to rule her husbands affaires at home and abroad, And to bee informed of the particular passages of each of them, which somtimes brought forth harshnes at home, and turning off of such servants as shee observed refractory to her intentions therein.

Not only did she use the servants as spies, but she took regularly without her husband's knowledge a percentage of the fines levied upon his tenants, a practice that Smyth notes was "by us all disliked, but by none of us to bee helped" (386–87).

Smyth concludes his account of his mistress by drawing a conventional moral from her behavior, one that Petruchio himself seems to live by:

Most just it is that all Toll should come into the right Tolldish: For the most part it falleth out That where wives will rule all they marre all, words I lately heard from wise lords in the Starchamber in the cases of the lady Lake, the Countesse of Suffolke, and some others: These verses are ancient;

> Concerning wives, take this an certaine rule
> That if at first, you let them have the rule
> Your self with them at last shall bear no rule
> Except you let them evermore to rule.   (387)

Highly educated, eloquent, quick-witted, unconventional in behavior, Lady Katharine "awed" the household, ruled over her husband, and manipulated his financial affairs. She was the kind of woman who could prompt even a steward to quote poetry.

As one would expect from his "ancient" verses, Smyth assigns the blame for this inversion of the patriarchal order to Lord Henry, who abrogated his responsibilities as a husband. In a section entitled "The Application and use of his life," in which he draws from Lord Henry's life morals that might be useful for his heirs, Smyth singles out his inability to control his wife as one of his major faults. From Lord Henry's treatment of Lady Katharine, Smyth observes, the family "may learne That nothing is more necessary in the person of a master of a family, according as his estate and greatnes shall bee, then Majesty," and he urges "every master" to "remember Esops fable of the frogs, how contemptibly they esteemed their heavy and blockish king" (411). Smyth sees this marital misrule, moreover, as of more than local significance. Noting Lord Henry's "sufferings and losses by [too] indulgently following the wills and Counsells" of both his mother and Lady Katharine, Smyth reminds the family

That when Eve went about to expound the text shee mistooke the text and hurt her husband: And that English wives challenge more liberty and enclyne to more soveraignty then those of other nations: That female counsells are to bee suspected, as proceeding from an unproper sphear . . . And that prodegy of witt whose excellencies have conquered both example and imitation [*marginal note: Sir Walter Raleigh*], hath told his son that wives were ordained to continue the generation of men; To obey, not to rule their affairs: that they are like marchants in a common wealth, the greatest good or the worst of evills that can happen to a man; And to ballence them and their Counsells thereafter. (413–14)

For Smyth, Lady Katharine represented not only an imperious mistress, one who domineered over her husband and manipulated his servants, but a threat to the patriarchy itself. The stridency and repetitiousness of his attacks suggest the degree of anxiety that such a figure could arouse in the period. Smyth's response to marital relations within the household may explain why the epithet he chooses for Lord Henry is "Henry the harmlesse" (265).

Lord Henry, who clearly failed in his role of wife-tamer, seems to have had three dominant passions in his life: lawsuits, gambling, and hunting. The lawsuits, although they take up much of Smyth's narrative, shed no light on his resemblance to Petruchio, except perhaps that they illustrate a disputatious nature and a tendency towards impetuous anger, which was easily dissolved "when the cause [was] removed" (413). The love of gambling is more suggestive, since Petruchio shows himself willing to take risks in his courtship of Katherine and, more importantly, since, in the final scene of the play, Petruchio proposes a wager to test the wives' obedience. Smyth notes admiringly that Lord Henry's "longe and slender lady-like-hand knew a dye as well and how to handle it as any of his ranke and time" (363).

Lord Henry's "chief delights," however, and those which link him most directly to both the hunting lord and Petruchio in *The Taming of the Shrew*, are in hunting and hawking:

> But his cheife delights wherein hee spent near three parts of the yeare, were, to his great charges, in hunting the hare fox and deere, red and fallow, not wanting choice of as good hunting horses as yearly hee could buy at faires in the North; And in hawking both at river and at land: And as his hounds were held inferior to no mans, (through the great choice of whelps which with much care hee yearly bred of his choicest braches, and his continuall huntings,) soe were his hawks of severall sorts; which if hee sent not a man to fetch from beyond seas, as three or fower times I remember hee did, yet had hee the choice as soone as they were brought over into England, keeping a man lodging in London, in some years a month or more, to bee sure of his choice at their first landing. (363)

It is easy to recognize in this description the hunting lord of *The Taming of the Shrew*, who enters the play "*from hunting*," instructs his huntsman to "tender well" all his hounds, gives precise directions for the care of "Brach Merriman" and "Clowder," and admires Silver so much that he "would not lose the dog for twenty pound" (Ind.1.16–21). Shakespeare's emphasis upon the lord's care of his dogs captures a familiar attribute of the type, but it is worth noting that Smyth mentions Lord Henry's pride in his dogs several times (282, 285). Petruchio, whose taming of Katherine parallels the hunting lord's joke upon Christopher Sly, continues the play's hunting motif with his swaggering, his taming methods drawn from falconry, and his numerous hunting jests in the final scene (5.2.49–62). The ethos that characterizes the hunting lord of the

Induction, Petruchio, and Lord Henry is that of the Elizabethan culture of the hunt.

It would be difficult to imagine a better example of an Elizabethan hunting lord than Lord Henry, whose "chief delight" lay in the sport. In his early years he hawked en route to his various properties, leading his 150 servants in livery between "Yate, Mangottesfeild, London, Callowdon, and other places" (284). In July 1558 he initiated a pattern of hunting that was to last throughout most of his life. When he arrived at Callowdon, near Coventry,

the first worke done was the sending for his buckhounds to Yate in Gloucestershire: His hounds being come Away goes hee and his wife a progres of buck hunting to the parks of Barkewell, Groby, Bradgate, Leicester forrest, Toley, and others on that side his house: And after a small repose, Then to the parks of Kenilworth, Ashby, Wedgenocke, and others, on the other side his house: And this was the course of this lord (more or lesse) for the thirty next somers at least: not omitting his own at Callowdon and in the county of Gloucester. (285)

Lord Henry hunted not only often but with abandon. In about 1560 he "extreamly heated himself by chasing on foot a tame Deere in Yate Parke," an escapade that caused an immoderate nose-bleed which he tried to stop by thrusting "his whole face into a bason of cold water"; the action caused in turn a "flush and fulnes of his nose . . . [which] could never bee remedied" (287). In his "middle age," he indulged in nostalgia for such episodes, and would "often comfortably remember" his near escapes from death, two of which involved falling from horses while galloping at full speed in pursuit of his hounds and deer (380). Even Lord Henry's political and legal affairs were intertwined with hunting, as when, in an episode recounted in chapter 3 (92–93), Queen Elizabeth joined the Earl of Leicester in a riotous slaughter of his deer in Worthy Park.

A case can be made, then, for Lord Henry, Lady Katharine, and their falcon as raw material from which Shakespeare fashioned his central characters. Lady Katharine was an independent, intelligent, and powerful woman, a huntress and falconer, a dominant force in household affairs, and a perceived threat not only to marital tranquillity but to the entire structure of patriarchal values. Lord Henry, or "Henry the harmless," was not only the husband of a difficult wife named Katharine and the owner of a "famous" falcon named Kate but the epitome of an Elizabethan hunting lord – a falconer and stag-hunter, a man who lavished care on his dogs, who hawked while traveling, who roamed the hills of Warwickshire every summer for thirty years chasing deer, who, if Smyth is to be believed, spent "three parts of the year" hunting (363). The relationship between Lord Henry and Lady Katharine, moreover, seems complicated in much the same way as that between Petruchio and Katherine. Despite the evidence of conflict provided by Smyth, the couple lived, traveled, and hunted together from their marriage in 1554 until Lady Katharine's death in 1596, when her husband gave her an impressive funeral at Coventry. She bore Lord Henry six children, only three of whom survived into adulthood. The relationship is thus compatible with the mixture of conflict and affection that Shakespeare depicts in Petruchio and Katherine, and in his hunting couple, Theseus and Hippolyta, in *A Midsummer Night's Dream*. Smyth's description of Lord Henry's inability to control his wife, and the ironic title of "Henry the harmless" that highlights it, suggest that this hunting lord might have found in Petruchio's successful taming of his wife a delightful wish-fulfillment fantasy.

If one finds the parallels between the Berkeley family and *The Taming of the Shrew* suggestive, a question still remains: Is there evidence that Shakespeare would have known, or known of this couple and their "famous" falcons? The likelihood that Shakespeare knew of the falcons, of course, increases with the likelihood that he knew of their owners.

Lord Henry was often in London. In the mid-1550s he and Lady Katharine lived with his mother in the city, and he achieved a kind of notoriety through his hunting, gambling, lawsuits, extravagance, and 150 liveried servants. Under Elizabeth the couple continued to spend wildly beyond their means, the victims, according to Smyth, of captains, scholars, poets, and cast-off courtiers. Even as late as 1595, when Lord Henry was negotiating over the marriage of his son, Thomas, Lady Katharine attempted to keep her husband out of London, fearing his susceptibility to the influence of "younge crafty Courtiers" (384). Lady Katharine's controversial family and Lord Henry's lawsuits would have kept them both in the public eye throughout their lives, and Lord Henry spent much time pursuing his legal affairs in London. A single feud with Sir Thomas Throckmorton, for example, led Lord Henry to file numerous complaints in the Court of Star Chamber between 1576 and 1596, charging Throckmorton and "eighty-eight of his kinsmen, gamekeepers, servants, tenants, and allies" with unlawful hunting.[56] Throughout his life, then, Lord Henry's presence as a hunting lord would have been manifest in London: he hunted there himself, imported his falcons there, and, as Justice Shallow threatens to do to Falstaff in *Merry Wives*, he brought his enemies to the Star Chamber on charges of poaching. His only "notorious vice," Smyth notes ironically, was that "hee was too great a lover of law, knowing it noe better" (409). It is difficult to imagine Shakespeare or his audiences unaware of or uninterested in the activities of the Berkeleys.

Although many opportunities existed for close observation of the couple in London, Shakespeare would almost certainly have encountered them as a boy in Stratford and remained aware of their activities through his close relationship with the region throughout his life. When he died, Lord Henry had holdings in the counties of Gloucester, Somerset, Warwick, Leicester, and Sussex. Throughout his life he traveled regularly with his family from one estate to another. Smyth's account suggests that one of his favorite residences, and certainly one in which he spent a great deal of time, was Callowdon, an estate in the liberties of Coventry, about twenty-five miles from Stratford. Binly Brook, where Smyth watched the falcon Kate soar out of sight, ran through the estate. Every summer from 1558 until at least 1588, according to Smyth, Lord Henry hunted in the parks surrounding this estate – "Barkewell, Groby, Bradgate, Leicester forrest, Toley, and others" towards the north, and "Kenilworth, Ashby, Wedgenocke, and others" towards the south (285). Kenilworth was about fifteen miles from Stratford, Wedgenocke Park less than ten. Shakespeare could not easily have been unaware of these activities, especially given the highly public nature of Elizabethan hunting and the size of the Berkeleys' retinue.

As far as the falcon named Kate is concerned, Smyth observes that both she and Stella were "famous with all great faulconers in many counties." He recalls seeing the birds in 1586 or 1587 at Binly Brook, near Callowdon. Since Lord Henry hawked nearly all the time and everywhere – in London, on his many estates, en route from one place to another – Shakespeare would have had many opportunities to learn of the feats of these birds. Since they lived for at least twelve years, as we have seen, the falcons were almost certainly famous at the time that he composed *The Taming of the Shrew*.

Shakespeare's interest in the Berkeley family would have been accentuated by Lord Henry's association with the world of the theater. He himself had a troupe of actors, Lord Berkeley's Men, for which we have records from 1581 to 1610. The troupe seems to have performed mainly in the country, since only one record, an account of a brawl with Inns of Court men in 1581, links them to London. But Shakespeare is likely to have been aware of at least two of their performances, since they took place at Stratford-upon-Avon in 1580–81 and 1582–83, when he was between the ages of sixteen and twenty.[57]

An even closer connection between Lord Henry and Shakespeare seems likely through the Russell family of Strensham, a village in Worcestershire not far from Stratford. Sir Thomas Russell was a Protestant member of Parliament and an adviser to Bishop Sandys. During 1569 and 1570, according to Smyth, Lord Henry and his wife and family "sojourned" for an extensive period with Sir Thomas (376). At this time Shakespeare would have been five or six years old and living in Stratford, less than thirty miles away. Sir Thomas's second son, born in 1570, was also named Thomas, and he eventually became one of the overseers of Shakespeare's will. When Thomas was four, his father died, and his mother married soon after a cousin of Lord Henry – another Henry, Sir Henry Berkeley of Bruton, Somerset. Thomas grew up in their household with his stepbrothers and later went to Queen's College, Oxford. Although we do not know when he first met Shakespeare, Thomas had property in Alderminster, Worcestershire, only four miles south of Stratford, and by 1597 / 8 he was identified as residing in that place.[58]

Although highly speculative, there is also a possible connection between Lord Henry and Lady Katharine Berkeley and the first performance of *A Midsummer Night's Dream*. When in her letter to John Smyth in 1595 Lady Katharine expressed her anxieties over her husband's going to London to negotiate their son's marriage, the son in question was Thomas Berkeley, and the potential bride, Elizabeth Carey, daughter of Sir George Carey, and the granddaughter of Henry, Lord Hunsdon, the Queen's Lord Chamberlain. Shakespeare's company at this time was the Lord Chamberlain's Men. The marriage took place on 19 February 1596. Many scholars have suggested that *A Midsummer Night's Dream* was composed for this wedding and first performed at the event.[59] If so, and there is admittedly no evidence that the play was performed for any special occasion, the hunting of Theseus and Hippolyta might have taken on a special meaning. Their paradoxical love, combining affection and aggression, is embodied in the voices of their hounds, which astonish Hippolyta with "so musical a discord, such sweet thunder" (4.1.118).

Speculations aside, there seems to be sufficient evidence in the foregoing account of the activities and relationships of the Berkeleys in London and the nearby counties to establish the probability of

Shakespeare's interest in and perhaps even intimate knowledge of the family. The Berkeleys were much in the public eye, were famous for their prowess in hunting and hawking, resided often in the environs of Stratford and London, and were connected – through their acting company, their misadventures with scholars, poets and cast-off courtiers, and the Russell family – with individuals to whom Shakespeare would have had ready access.

If Lord Henry and Lady Katharine are somehow the "originals" of Petruchio and Katherine in *The Taming of the Shrew*, their shadowy presence in the play is unlikely to be explained by a sustained allegorical intent on the part of Shakespeare. It is far more likely that stories of Lord Henry, Lady Katharine, and their falcons were simply engrained in Shakespeare's imagination – some deriving from his boyhood in Stratford, some from his own travels in the region as an adult, and some from his experiences in London. From such a perspective, one can imagine Shakespeare shaping his plot and characters independently of these "sources" but aware of their potential recognition, on occasion, by knowing members of an audience; one can imagine as well individual performances exploiting this allusive potential in many different ways, both satiric and celebratory. If such is the case, the lives of the Berkeleys simply become another source for Shakespeare's drama, a living source, filtered through his imagination along with the literary documents which we more customarily privilege with the title. This "source" takes on added interest when one considers that, in none of the most commonly proposed sources or analogues of *The Taming of the Shrew* – whether in folklore, oral tradition, or literary document – do hunting and falconry figure as a significant motif.[60]

Critics agree that one of the most striking features of *The Taming of the Shrew* is its evocation of the Warwickshire countryside. Ann Thompson notes that "the whole atmosphere of rural Warwickshire with its hunting lords, drunken tinkers and fat alewives is clearly drawn (perhaps somewhat rosily) from [Shakespeare's] own youthful experience." She observes as well that, "despite the Paduan setting, Petruchio and Katherine's marriage seems to take place in a world of country courtship practices and sports (hunting, falconry) readily comprehensible to a Warwickshire tinker."[61] When we consider the importance of this Warwickshire atmosphere, and its absence from any other known sources, the activities of the Berkeleys become as suggestive a backdrop for the play as Gascoigne's *Supposes* or folktales of tricking artisans or taming shrews. Even if the argument for the Berkeleys as a "source" fails to convince, the social atmosphere that their lives so vividly evoke tells us much about the imaginative world of Shakespeare's play.

If we attend to the culture of the hunt, as represented both within and outside *The Taming of the Shrew*, it might be possible to acknowledge the insidiously oppressive nature of Katherine's taming and at the same time "save the play from its own ending." Even from the limited perspective of the hunting lord, the taming of Katherine has ironic potential, for any falconer knows that the most highly trained hawk might suddenly revert to wild behavior. From the wider perspective of the audience, the entire play-within-the-play might become ironical, the taming of Katherine a wish-fulfillment fantasy of a hunting lord, a man whose imagination is infected with the values of his "sport." The lives of the Berkeleys and their falcon named Kate help us to reconstruct a part of that world with great particularity. Seen as a response to its distinctive ethos, the play might become more familiarly Shakespearean, in its sly social criticism, its metadramatic energy, and in its satiric framing of the more blatant and unreflective symptoms of the male dominance of the time. Perhaps a modern setting of the play with the culture of the hunt in mind could offer us a new and unsentimental way of appreciating its rich comic texture.

CHAPTER FIVE

The "rascal" Falstaff in Windsor

In act 5 scene 4 of *1 Henry IV* Prince Hal kills Hotspur in single combat on the field at Shrewsbury. While doing what he calls "fair rites of tenderness" (98) to honor Hotspur's corpse, Hal spies Falstaff on the ground, dead. He responds with a speech filled with wordplay. He calls Falstaff an "old" acquaintance. He muses on the incongruity of Falstaff's bulk: "Could not all this flesh / Keep in a little life?" He salutes Falstaff as "poor Jack," the name both a familiar and affectionate substitute for "John" and a synonym for "knave." He weighs his loss both morally and emotionally: "I could have better spar'd a better man" (102–4). The wit of the lines brings together affection and moral judgment, playfulness and regret, crystallizing Hal's complex relationship to his companion throughout the play.

As his speech draws to a close, Hal introduces a novel metaphor for Falstaff, transforming him from a man into a deer:

> Death hath not strook so fat a deer to-day,
> Though many dearer, in this bloody fray.
> Embowell'd will I see thee by and by,
> Till then in blood by noble Percy lie. (5.4.107–10)

For a brief moment, the bodies on the field at Shrewsbury become a quarry of deer and Falstaff the fattest among them. The metaphor triggers off yet another pun – "though many dearer" – and sustains its force in the word "embowell'd" and the phrase "in blood." Emboweling in preparation for salting or cooking was the inevitable fate of a dead deer, especially a fat one in the prime of life, one "in blood."[1] To compare Falstaff to a deer "in blood" is to subject him to a triple thrust of wit. As a man, Falstaff is ignoble, and therefore not "in blood." The chief mark of his ignobility at this moment, moreover, which Hal himself does not perceive, is his retention of his blood: he does not lie in blood but is "in," or full of, blood. As a deer, finally, Falstaff is hardly "in blood"; although old and fat, he is by no means in his prime, and Hal's irony acknowledges that fact.

The appropriate metaphor for Falstaff is not that of a deer "in blood" but a "rascal." Although the term is often used in the period in a general sense, to mean a "rogue" or "knave," it also carried a technical meaning, as "the young, lean, or inferior deer of a herd, distinguished from the full-grown antlered bucks or stags" (*OED*). Shakespeare plays on both meanings of the term earlier in the play when Hal calls Falstaff a "fat-kidney'd rascal" (2.2.5–6), an "oily rascal" who is "known as well as Paul's" (2.4.526), and an "impudent, emboss'd rascal" (3.3.157). The latter phrase, "emboss'd rascal," captures both Falstaff's swollen girth and breathlessness, for the word "embossed" refers not only to something molded or carved in relief but to a hunted animal, in this case a "rascal," foaming at the mouth from exhaustion.[2] As a deer, then, Falstaff is as paradoxical as he is as a man. He is a rascal, an inferior specimen, but neither young nor lean; he is an old fat rascal. He himself notes the incongruity of the metaphor in *2 Henry IV* when Doll Tearsheet calls him a "muddy rascal." He replies, "You make fat rascals, Mistress Doll" (2.4.39–41).

Because they are inferior specimens, rascals are less likely to be killed than deer "in blood." Hotspur dies at the end of *1 Henry IV*, but Falstaff, the rascal, feigns death, wounds Hotspur, and gains honor. Arising from the ground after Hal's exit, he gasps in outrage at the implications of Hal's metaphor: "Embowell'd! if thou embowel me to-day, I'll give you leave to powder me and eat me too tomorrow" (5.4.111–13). Hal's fat rascal comes back to life, desperate to prevent the emboweling and salting that would lead to his being eaten. The dead Percy becomes food "for worms" (87), but the live Falstaff refuses to become venison. As has often been observed, the "resurrection" of Falstaff is reminiscent of the ritualistic English folk drama, in which a challenger is first killed by the hero and then resurrected by a doctor. The metamorphosis of Falstaff into a deer at this point accentuates the ritualistic quality of the moment, for the participants in such folk-plays often wear or carry parts of animals, such as skins or tails. In the horn dance of Abbots Bromley, indeed, the dancers carry the horns of reindeer.[3]

Although Falstaff is called a "rascal" several times in the play, the metaphor is hardly significant enough to warrant its centrality in the "death" of Falstaff at Shrewsbury. As John Dover Wilson has shown, Falstaff is characterized throughout *1 Henry IV* primarily through the language of the taverns, and particularly that of feasting on meat.[4] Falstaff is Sir Loin-of-Beef. "Call in ribs, call in tallow" (2.4.111), says Hal of the man he later calls "my sweet beef" (3.3.177). He is also "that roasted manningtree ox with the pudding in his belly" (2.4.452–53). As befits the lord of the Boar's Head Tavern, moreover, he is the boar himself: "guts" (2.4.452), "chops" (1.2.136), "brawn" (2.4.110). In *2 Henry IV* Hal asks, "doth the old boar feed in the old frank?" (2.2.146–47), and Doll calls him her "whoreson little tidy bartholomew boar-pig" (2.4.231). All of these metaphors associate Falstaff with domesticated meat, not venison. Elizabethan social custom, indeed, makes venison a somewhat unlikely choice for Falstaff. Although the numerous complaints about the marketing of poached deer make clear that venison would have been available at least occasionally in the tavern world of London, it could not easily be made into a symbol of that world or of the traditional holidays that the play exploits. Venison connoted a higher social world than the one we customarily associate with Falstaff; the meat was normally reserved for gifts among the gentry and for formal occasions such as the Lord Mayor's feast.[5] Given these associations, it is not surprising that Hal's reference to Falstaff as a deer at the end of *1 Henry IV* is the only significant instance of its kind in either the *Henry IV* plays or in *Henry V*.

Why, then, should the metaphor of Falstaff as deer engage Shakespeare's imagination at this climactic moment in *1 Henry IV*? One answer, I suspect, lies in a poem that could well be a submerged source for the play, the ballad "The Hunting of the Cheviot," more commonly known as "Chevy Chase." The ballad was of ancient origin and was well known throughout the Elizabethan period. Sidney, for example, praises it in the *Defence of Poetry* as an example of the power of primitive lyric poetry: "Certainly, I must confess my own barbarousness, I never heard the old song of Percy and Douglas that I found not my heart moved more than with a trumpet; and yet is it sung but by some blind crowder, with no rougher voice than rude style . . ."[6] Although the evidence is only circumstantial, both the overall plot of the ballad and certain details suggest that it might have been in Shakespeare's mind when conceiving the battle of Shrewsbury.

"Chevy Chase" recounts in fictitious form the battle of Otterburn. The ballad account is historically anomalous in a manner suggestive for the *Henry IV* plays, for it sets the battle not in the reign of Richard II where it belongs but in that of Henry IV. The plot of the ballad has little relationship to Shakespeare's play, but mysterious echoes of names and events make it seem a fantasy on the themes of the Henriad. The protagonists of "Chevy Chase" are Percy and Douglas. The battle is initiated when Percy crosses the Scottish border to hunt deer, hoping to encounter his enemy Douglas on the other side. Percy and his men hunt all morning, and by noon a hundred fat harts have been killed. When Percy goes to see the breaking of the deer, Douglas appears and challenges him. Percy answers his challenge with defiance, and Douglas replies in turn with an offer of single combat. When one of Percy's men refuses to sit by and watch, a general battle breaks forth, and Douglas is killed by an arrow as he fights with Percy. Percy honors him in death and is then killed himself. The ballad ends with both armies virtually destroyed and with Henry IV vowing to avenge Percy's death at Holmedon. In this brief and ancient ballad, then, we find a kaleidoscope of elements that appear in *1 Henry IV*: a border raid, a challenge of single combat between two heroic protagonists, a refusal of one soldier to allow single combat to proceed, opposition between characters called Percy and Douglas, and a victor honoring his dead opponent. The ballad ends, moreover, with Henry IV looking forward to avenging his dead hero at the battle of Holmedon, the very battle with which Shakespeare's play begins.

Even more curious are certain verbal echoes that link ballad to play. Three times in the ballad the fatness of the harts is emphasized. They are the "fattiste hartes in all Cheviat" (st. 2).[7] By noontime "a hondrith fat hartës ded ther lay" (st. 7). Percy taunts Douglas by saying, "The fattiste hartës in all Chyviat / we have kyld, and cast to carry them away" (st. 17). The imagery of fat harts dead on the field is oddly close to Hal's "Death hath not strook so fat a deer to-day" (5.4.107). In honoring Douglas in death, moreover, Percy uses words that recall Hal's of Falstaff. Holding the dead man's hand, Percy comments, "For a better man, of hart nare of hande, / was nat in all the north contrë" (st. 39); Hal's words are "I could have better spar'd a better man" (5.4.104). In the ballad, finally, when Henry IV vows to avenge Percy's death, his use of the word "brook" links his speech to Hotspur's own dying words in Shakespeare's play. Henry IV says, "But Persë, and I brook my lyffe, / thy deth well quyte shall be" (st. 62). Hotspur, also thinking of whether his death has been well recompensed, says, "I better brook the loss of brittle life / Than those proud titles thou has won of me" (5.4.78–79).[8]

Although probably inadequate to establish "Chevy Chase" as a definite source for *1 Henry IV*, the many resemblances between the two works seem more than coincidental. The sheer arbitrariness and obliquity of the echoes, however, if that is what they are, forestall any attempt to explain them as conscious allusions. If the ballad was in Shakespeare's mind as he composed his play, it was likely to have been present at a barely conscious level, with fragments of the narrative, setting, and language reassembling themselves by a process of association. If such a scenario seems plausible, we may ask why these memories should have been triggered off by Falstaff's mock-death at the battle of Shrewsbury.

Part of the answer, of course, is provided by the detailed resemblances we have already examined: the names of the characters, the battlefield setting, the situation of two great heroes fighting in single combat. At a deeper and perhaps less conscious level, however, the two episodes are linked in a way that will eventually lead to the Falstaff of *The Merry Wives of Windsor*. The link is that between hunting and war, and, more precisely, between poaching and social rebellion.

In the ballad of "Chevy Chase," Percy's hunting raid has as its object not merely the killing of deer but the humiliation of Douglas, the chief ranger of the parks and chases of Scotland, under whose protection the deer exist. "Who gave youe leave to hunte in this Chyviat chays," asks Douglas when he accosts Percy, "in the spyt of myn and of me" (st. 15). The poem as a whole, moreover, treats the hunting raid and the battle as symbolic equivalents. The battle itself is introduced as a continuation of the hunt (st. 24), and is identified with the hunt in the final stanza:

> Ihesue Crist our balys [torments] bete [assuage],
>   and to the blys us brynge!
> Thus was the hountynge of the Chivyat:
>   God send us alle good endyng!   (st. 68)

The ballad, in short, depends upon the same symbolism that underlies Elizabethan poaching. In slaughtering his deer, Percy is destroying Douglas's honor, thereby symbolically slaughtering both him and his army. As Roger B. Manning's account of the ballad makes clear, the action is both a literal instigator of war and its symbolic equivalent.[9]

Shakespeare's imagination works in a similar manner. In an Elizabethan context, the field of battle, unlike the world of the taverns, does not evoke images of boar or beef; it evokes images of the hunt. The field of a hunt, like the field of a battle, was often filled with corpses, and with the victors surveying the nobility of those that had been killed. The hunt was not merely associated with war but was even conducted as a kind of war itself.[10] For Hal, the battlefield at Shrewsbury, littered with corpses, becomes a quarry of deer and the "dead" Falstaff the fattest of the lot.

Although both Hal and Hotspur aspire to elevate the battle of Shrewsbury into chivalric warfare, the conflict actually pits rebels against a rebel-king who peoples the field with counterfeits wearing his own armor. The men killed at Shrewsbury, like the deer killed at Chevy Chase, are not ceremoniously hunted but poached. Rebellion is to chivalric warfare what poaching is to the ceremonial hunt. In this sense, Falstaff may be considered a poacher, since he steals from Hal the honor of killing Hotspur. From this perspective, Hal's fat rascal avenges himself upon the "hunt" of war by stabbing the noblest hunter in the thigh and carrying him home as a trophy. Falstaff will not be eaten. The hunted becomes the hunter, and sheer animal vitality triumphs. The fat rascal survives and prospers.

Although the man Falstaff gets his comeuppance at the end of *2 Henry IV*, when the newly crowned Henry V rejects and banishes him, the fate of the fat rascal Falstaff, the dear deer of Shrewsbury, is suspended until he meets the wives of Windsor. In *The Merry Wives*, the metaphor that surfaces momentarily upon Falstaff's "death" at Shrewsbury appears throughout the play. In Windsor, the rascal Falstaff plays the roles of a literal poacher of deer, a metaphoric poacher of wives, Herne the Hunter, and a Windsor stag. To appreciate the significance of these roles, it is necessary to consider not merely the figure of Falstaff but his place within the play as a whole.

The Merry Wives poses special problems for critics. The date of composition, the occasion for which the play might have been written, the relationship between the Quarto and Folio texts are all uncertain and the subject of continuing controversy.[11] The anomalous position of the play among Shakespeare's comedies, moreover, has encouraged a kind of disparagement by exclusion: *The Merry Wives*, it seems, offers neither the delights of the romantic comedies, with their exotic locales, their vibrant heroines, or their marvelous plots, nor the wit, energy, and gritty realism of the Falstaffian history plays. A recent interest in local history and local readings of plays, however, has begun to provide a context within which to appreciate the play's most distinctive qualities, the most important of which is its depiction of Elizabethan town life. The Windsor of the play, as R. S. White observes, is "solidly rooted in its specified town planning, its diurnal activities, its local customs."[12] In a lively and insightful essay, "Falstaff and the Comic Community," Anne Barton stresses the dramatic significance of that distinctive world, observing that "Windsor itself, as a corporate entity, is the true protagonist of the comedy, not Falstaff, the shadowy lovers, or even the merry wives themselves, who uphold its values so well."[13]

Although I shall later want to qualify Barton's characterization of the wives as mere upholders of Windsor's values, I believe she captures the single quality that makes this play most distinctive and is most important to its critical appreciation: *The Merry Wives* is the one Shakespearean comedy that represents the social dynamics of Elizabethan town life. In placing a generalized "Windsor" at the center of the play, moreover, Shakespeare not only achieves a high degree of comic realism but subjects the very social practices he imitates to comic scrutiny. In this way the play provides not only a representative image of an Elizabethan community, "Windsor," but a comic meditation on some of the forces that drive Elizabethan communal life, forces for which poaching becomes a central metaphor. In so doing, the play also turns our gaze upon its own form – upon the capacity of comedy to resolve social tensions of the kind it imitates. The play thus reflects the customs of Elizabethan town life, reflects upon them, and probes their adaptability to traditional comic form.

The most important fact about Windsor is conflict. The opening words of the play, Shallow's "I will make a Star chamber matter of it" (1.1.1–2), are only the first of many demands for retribution – so many that, as Linda Anderson observes, the play seems "not merely concerned with revenge" but "obsessed with it."[14] Each plot of the play develops a different kind of social conflict and a different mode of attempted resolution. Shallow wants to bring Falstaff to the Star Chamber for poaching his deer, although he still hankers after the sword-fights of his youth. Slender accuses Falstaff's men of stealing his purse. Evans and Caius attempt to fight a duel over Anne Page, but are thwarted by the jocular peacemaking of the Host, who becomes in turn the victim of their revenge, the "theft" of his horses. Mistress Page and her husband compete against each other as matchmakers for Anne, both attempting to arrange a secret marriage, a legal but strongly anti-social bit of trickery. Falstaff arouses the wrath of Pistol and Bardolph by dismissing them, the wrath of Mistress Ford and Mistress Page by insulting them, and the wrath of Master Ford by threatening to cuckold him – all actions that precipitate counter-plots of revenge. Pistol and Bardolph become informers against Falstaff, while Master Ford attempts to entrap him, using his own wife as bait and, according to Mistress Quickly, beating her "black and blue" (4.5.112) when his efforts fail. The merry wives, finally, devise a series of informal punishments which climax in Falstaff's humiliation before the entire community. In the range and variety of conflicts and attempted resolutions, the play provides a casebook of

conflict in an Elizabethan town. Local and national law, the private code
of the duel, trickery, neighborly intervention, and public humiliation are
all part of the social repertory of the citizens of Windsor.

From a modern perspective, what is most striking about the various
attempts to resolve conflict is their dependence upon informal and communal methods of "justice." Although Shallow and Slender threaten the
use of the national and local legal system, they are thwarted in their
designs, and social peace is essentially left in the hands of the community itself. To resolve disputes, the citizens of Windsor take the "law" into
their own collective hands. Since the play opens with Shallow's
ineffectual attempt to bring Falstaff before the Star Chamber and ends
with Falstaff punished by the community, we might say that the plot itself
replaces legalistic with informal and communal methods of achieving
peace.

Keeping order in Windsor is both a local and a highly collaborative
activity. Evans attempts to settle Slender's complaint against Falstaff's
men with a panel of "three umpires" – Page, the host of the Garter, and
himself (1.1.137). Page holds a dinner of venison pasty in hopes that
Shallow, Slender, Falstaff, and his men will "drink down all unkindness"
(1.1.196–97). Mistress Page and Mistress Ford band together in their punishments of Falstaff. Page, Shallow, and Slender join the Host in prevent-
ing the duel between Caius and Evans. In her indiscriminate good will
as a match-maker, Mistress Quickly scrambles to keep everyone happy,
parodying the role of peacemaker. In his efforts to catch Falstaff in the
act of courting his wife, Ford brings Page, Caius, and Evans as witnesses,
hoping to transform the shame of cuckoldry into communal applause:
"to these violent proceedings all my neighbors shall cry aim" (3.2.43–44).
The erstwhile opponents, Caius and Evans, join forces to revenge themselves against the Host. And the play climaxes in a scene that shows
almost the entire community united against Falstaff. In a society that
seems as obsessively driven by the bourgeois motive of economic gain as
that of revenge, it is worth observing that the resolution of conflict
involves the whole community in ways that largely transcend differences
in wealth and social status.

When placed against the backdrop of what we know about
Elizabethan town life in the late sixteenth and early seventeenth centuries, the play's preoccupation with conflict, and with informal, communal modes of conflict resolution, sharpens in focus. In the 1590s most
Elizabethan towns experienced serious social and economic disorder,
brought on by a wide variety of causes, among them harvest failure,

plague, and overseas war. In the early seventeenth century demographic change, enclosure, and an increase in class divisions accentuated by Puritanism continued this destabilizing trend. Partly in response to these social tensions, the civic authorities and moralists of the period seem almost obsessed with fears of civil disorder.[15]

In a way that is difficult for moderns to appreciate, this anxiety about civic order was expressed within a social system that had few legal and institutional resources. The national system of law enforcement and local administration, for example, depended upon "the diligence and co-operation of essentially amateur, unpaid local officers,"[16] such as Justice Shallow. For this and other reasons – including the desire for independence and local control – informal, local mediation of disputes was usually preferred to legal means: "Local gentlemen, clergymen and prominent neighbors were commonly involved in mediation of this kind and local officers could also take a hand."[17] At the level of the town and village, according to Keith Wrightson, "'order' meant little more than conformity to a fairly malleable local custom which was considerably more flexible than statute law."[18] In cases not amenable to informal mediation, the community had available numerous traditional sanctions, ranging from the relatively benign method of gossip to more violent methods, such as the charivari.

In order to be effective, these communal methods of conflict resolution depended upon the small size of the towns, which fostered among individuals, for better and worse, close involvement in each other's affairs. Informal peacemaking also required a reasonable consensus about the nature of social relations in the community. Central to this consensus, according to Mildred Campbell, was an ideal of "good neighborhood": "Neighborliness stands perhaps first in the criteria by which the social and ethical standing of an individual in a country community was measured."[19] Keith Wrightson offers a definition of this social ideal, which he sees as complementary with two other social norms, paternalism and deference. Neighborliness, he observes, "involved a mutual recognition of reciprocal obligations of a practical kind and a degree of normative consensus as to the nature of proper behaviour between neighbors . . . it was essentially a horizontal relationship, one which implied a degree of equality and mutuality between partners to the relationship, irrespective of distinctions of wealth or social standing."[20] In general, neighborliness was manifested in a willingness, among other things, to lend implements or money (without interest), to share in parish administration, to help at shearing or harvest time,

to assist the needy, to engage in genial social relations, to mediate disputes, and to promote harmonious social relations.[21]

Such a social ideal, of course, was commonly much diluted when put
into practice, and the informal power and responsibility it conferred on
individuals and groups could have negative and sometimes dangerous
implications. A good example of the equivocal nature of "good neighborhood," as we shall see in some detail later, is the charivari, an informal method of social punishment that could be coercive not only to
offenders but to those in the community who might have prevented the
offense. In some charivaris, for example, a neighbor served as a surrogate victim, as if the neighborhood itself were somehow implicated in
the offense.[22] Neighborliness was thus not a matter of choice but an
obligation, involving, in some cases, both the offender and the peacemaker in a network of socially coercive behavior. In cases of extreme
conflict, "good neighborhood" might be difficult to distinguish from
social violence.

A comic representation of the way in which "good neighborhood"
might have worked in Elizabethan towns is provided in the opening
scene of *The Merry Wives*, which serves as an overture to the play as a
whole. The scene begins with Justice Shallow's threat to make a Star
Chamber matter out of Falstaff's poaching of his deer. Sir Hugh Evans,
as a good neighbor and cleric, attempts to mediate – "I am of the
church, and will be glad to do my benevolence to make atonements and
compremises between you" (1.1.32–34) – but Shallow insists that "the
Council shall hear it, it is a riot" (35), and then sputters that if he were
only young again, "the sword should end it" (40–41). Evans's reply to this
threat gives us, in a thick Welsh accent, the cryptic insight of the fool, an
insight, as we shall see, that the remainder of the play explores: "It is
petter that friends is the sword, and end it" (42–43). The opening
moments of the play thus outline three potential modes of conflict resolution: the socially (and personally) anachronistic method of the duel,
the law, and the informal mediation of neighbors.

Shallow is too old for sword-fights and, initially, too stubborn for informal mediation. He is Justice of the Peace and Coram, and *Custa-lorum*,
too, and he wants the law. His opening confrontation with Falstaff,
however, demonstrates the limitations of this approach. Falstaff knows
the law and how to evade it. This becomes most obviously clear in
Slender's accusations against Bardolph, Nym and Pistol for stealing his
purse. Because he was too drunk at the time to make a positive identification, Slender's charge cannot hold up, and Falstaff can conclude,

triumphantly, "You hear all these matters denied, gentlemen; you hear it" (186–87). Slender's only recourse at this point is to restrict himself henceforth to getting drunk in "honest, civil, godly company" (182). The law will do him no good.

Shallow's charge of poaching involves subtler matters of law and a subtler evasiveness. Since the nature of Falstaff's triumph in this matter tends to escape critical notice, it is worth special attention. The chief theatrical question raised by the episode is why, after so insistent a demand for a trial in the Star Chamber, Shallow (or Shakespeare) lets the matter drop. Although the issue is not resolved in this scene, it is never referred to again. The image of Falstaff as a poacher is obviously important, however, for it reappears in his disguise as Herne the hunter at the end of the play.

To understand the significance of the episode, one must consider the legal treatment of poaching in the period. In its most destructive and dangerous form, the offense had nothing to do with the occasional desire of a commoner for meat; it constituted instead both a symbolic and real assault by one member of the gentry against another and often involved serious injury, destruction of property, and loss of honor, or what Evans calls "disparagements" (31). For such offenses, usually treated as a form of riot in the courts, recourse to the Court of Star Chamber was fairly common and appropriate.[23] In the case of Falstaff, the motive for the poaching is unclear. Both the theatrical and social contexts imply that drunken sport was the most likely motive, with perhaps the addition of a riotous challenge to Shallow and the social order in general. Since Falstaff needs money, however, the motive might also have been economic. Commercial poaching became a major problem at the turn of the century, and inns and alehouses were well-known distribution points in the illicit trade; speaking in Star Chamber in 1616, James I complained "of Ale-houses, for receipt of Stealers of my Deer."[24] Much of the venison sold illegally in London, moreover, came from the grounds of Windsor Castle.[25] Whatever Falstaff's motives, it is clear that Falstaff has not only "beaten" Shallow's men, "kill'd" his deer, and "broke open" his lodge (111–12), but assaulted his dignity: "If he were twenty Sir John Falstaffs, he shall not abuse Robert Shallow, esquire" (2–4). The raid, in short, constitutes a symbolic assault.[26]

Why, then, does Shallow let the matter drop? Because Falstaff outmaneuvers him procedurally by admitting his crime outright. When Shallow demands "this shall be answer'd," Falstaff's replies give him little choice but to allow Page's efforts at informal mediation:

Fal. I will answer it straight: I have done all this. That is now answered.
Shal. The Council shall know this.
Fal. 'Twere better for you if it were known in counsel. You'll be laugh'd at.

(114–19)

Implicit in this exchange is not only the recognition of both men that Falstaff might have influence at court but that Shallow would disgrace himself by invoking the Star Chamber for a relatively minor offense. Crucial to the legal process in cases of poaching was a distinction between those who admitted the crime and those who did not. Admission downgraded the offense from a felony, at least technically punishable by death, to a misdemeanor, an offense with less severe consequences.[27] By admitting the offense, Falstaff has reduced its severity significantly. Since the Court of the Star Chamber was seriously overburdened with litigation during this period, and since Justices of the Peace like Shallow were under the Court's authority and had numerous formal and informal means to settle such disputes, the likelihood of the Court looking sympathetically upon such a case would have been very small indeed.[28] In such circumstances, Shallow would be well advised to follow Falstaff's advice and keep his own counsel. In his quest for justice, Shallow is thus driven back upon his own and the community's resources.

The scene concludes, therefore, not with a summons to the Star Chamber but with an invitation to a dinner of venison pasty. "Come," says Page, having taken over the peacemaker's role from Evans, "we have a hot venison pasty to dinner. Come, gentlemen, I hope we shall drink down all unkindness" (195–97). Shakespeare does not stage this dinner, but it seems a very curious affair. Conventionally in Shakespearean comedy, as in Elizabethan society, feasting marks the resolution of conflict and binds society together in a rite of incorporation; in this case, however, the feast seems at best premature, for Falstaff's conflict with Shallow and Slender has not been resolved. This feast, one might say, includes hostility within the festive form itself, as if eating together might bring the kind of peace that a feast would ordinarily celebrate.

Even more curious is the meal itself, which consists of venison. Where did it come from? Literally, the deer is a gift from Shallow to Page, presumably a neighborly gesture intended to foster their proposed family alliance; metaphorically, however, it might be called an inadvertent gift from Falstaff, for, as Shallow's apology to Page makes clear, the deer is one that Falstaff poached: "I wish'd your venison better, it was ill kill'd" (82–83). Shallow's statement probably applies in two senses: the deer was killed illegally and, as a consequence, not properly drained of blood. So the very food itself symbolizes the conflict it is meant to resolve. In a precisely literal way, conflict feeds the community, suggesting that Falstaff's relationship with the community is less parasitic than symbiotic. Instead of marking the end of conflict, the festive form "contains" it, in both senses of the word: conflict is both included and kept in check by the feast. That conflict is not ended by such events becomes clear later, when Ford cites his wife's behavior at the dinner to bolster his suspicions against Falstaff (2.1.234–36).

Perhaps the best gloss on this paradoxical interdependency between peace and conflict, order and disorder is Evans's cryptic response to Shallow's threat of the sword, alluded to earlier: "it is petter that friends is the sword, and end it." The statement captures the essence of "good neighborhood" as depicted in the play. It suggests, on the one hand, that the best way to resolve conflict of this kind is not through the sword, or even the Star Chamber, as Shallow proposes, but through members of the community, through friends. Evans's peculiar turn of phrase, however, suggests a deeper meaning, establishing an identity between "friends" and "the sword," as if in taking the place of a duel, the friends themselves were engaged in a surrogate act of violence: "the friends *is* the sword." As we have seen, this paradoxical identification of peace and violence occurs implicitly at Page's dinner of venison pasty; it recurs throughout the play, moreover, in ways that challenge conventional distinctions between order and disorder, harmony and conflict. Evans himself, ironically, the cleric and man of peace who offers to "make atonements and comprimises" (1.1.33–34) between Shallow and Falstaff, will later enact the paradox when he prepares to meet Caius in a duel. In its linkage of friendship and force, and more broadly, festivity and violence, the play mirrors in comic form the dynamics of conflict in Elizabethan towns. As Keith Wrightson observes, "such equilibrium as local society possessed was the product of a constant dynamism in its social relations and the impetus of this dynamic came, as often as not, from conflict."[29]

Falstaff poses a special threat to Windsor society because he is an alien, displaced both geographically and socially. A fallen knight, a former frequenter of the world of the court, he resides temporarily in the Garter Inn, the name of which, like the allusion to the Garter ceremonies at the end of the play, casts an ironic shadow on his present condition. His counterpart as an alien threat to the social order of Windsor is Fenton, who also represents the foreign values of the court. Although the comparison may seem strange at first, the two interlopers are curiously alike. Both do not belong in Windsor. Both have squandered their money and, as Page says of Fenton, have "kept company with the wild Prince and Poins" (3.2.72–73). Both are attracted to the women of Windsor for economic reasons. Both become "lovers," and, as such, become involved in intrigues to fulfill their desires. Once they take on the role of lover, moreover, their initial economic motivation becomes complicated by sexual and romantic inclinations: disguised as Herne the Hunter, Falstaff revels at the prospect of bedding both of the merry wives, while Fenton eventually persuades Anne that his love is genuinely disinterested and that he would wed her without dowry, which he does. The Host's appreciation of Fenton – "he speaks holiday, he smells April and May" (3.2.68–69) – suggests that the young wooer represents a benign reincarnation of the old Falstaff, just as Anne represents a more admirable and radical independence even than that manifested by her mother, who is said by Mistress Quickly to have the freedom of her house (2.2.116–20). Falstaff's comment on the couple's successful elopement at the end of the play makes Fenton himself a poacher: "When night-dogs run, all sorts of deer are chas'd" (5.5.238). While Falstaff gets fairy pinches for his poaching, Fenton gets Anne, the blessing of her parents, and the money his elopement had put at risk.

Antagonism between the aristocratic world of the court and the bourgeois world of Windsor runs throughout the play; given the proximity of the castle to the town, the tension probably had a basis in social fact. The local patriotism of Windsorites might have been accentuated at the turn of the century, moreover, because of their concerted but unsuccessful effort to persuade the Queen to renew their charter.[30] As disruptive agents from the court, both Falstaff and Fenton might be said to turn the bourgeois world of Windsor upside down. "He is of too high a region," says Page of Fenton, "he knows too much" (3.2.73–74). It is important to recognize, however, that the society of Windsor actually needs the two wily intruders, in much the same way that the little circle of feasters at Page's house needs Falstaff's poaching. Without Fenton, after all, Anne Page would be doomed to marry Evans or Caius, either prospect a fate worse than being "set quick i'th'earth, / And bowl'd to death with turnips!" (3.4.86–87). Without Falstaff, Ford's obsessive jealousy, for which he is already famous, would doubtless seek out other victims, to the misery of his long-suffering wife. The courtly interlopers do not so much turn the world of Windsor upside down as release disorders already simmering within it; they are catalysts for existing social and personal tensions.

As "foreigners," both Fenton and Falstaff have something in common with two other characters – Evans, the Welsh preacher, and Caius, the French physician. Although to some degree accepted by Windsor society, they remain outsiders, to be treated as comic butts partly for their bizarre behavior, but more consistently for their linguistic deficiencies. Joan Rees's observation about Evans might serve for both characters: "[he] is absorbed into his small town community, certainly, but without honour, dignity or even language, save for a ridiculous version of the tongue of his masters."[31] Although both characters are relatively simple as comic types, they occupy complex social positions. Vocationally they are important to the community: Evans is a "curer of souls," as Shallow observes, Caius a "curer of bodies" (2.3.39). As would have been true in the world outside the play, however, their social status is ambiguous. They are on good terms with the village notables, for example, and Caius has connections at court, but at the same time Shallow, Page, and the Host feel free to make fools of them. The aborted duel provides yet another example of the linkage between festivity and social coercion in the play, for it combines well-meaning merriment, aggression, and public humiliation. Even the Host's act of "good neighborhood" in ordering the combatants disarmed contains an image of violence: "Disarm them, and let them question. Let them keep their limbs whole and hack our English" (3.1.76–78). Like Falstaff's deer, the English language becomes a sacrificial victim, to be hacked and hewn in the interest of social peace. As in Page's dinner of venison pasty, there is no thought here of ending conflict, merely of diverting it into less destructive social forms. As hackers of English, moreover, the two men serve as perpetual outlets for the festive aggression of the community as a whole. They too are "contained" by the community.

The play's most striking instance of trickery as an informal means of social control is provided by the titular heroines of the play, the merry wives. In basing the Falstaff plot upon their witty stratagems, Shakespeare adapts to comic purposes, and subjects to implicit comic scrutiny, a popular form of social control that goes by many names – "rough music," riding, skimmington, and charivari being the most common.[32] Although the charivari took extremely varied forms throughout Europe and England, its essential feature was the public humiliation, by means of raucous noise and symbolic action, of individuals considered guilty of violating social norms. A charivari licensed both festive and derisive laughter, and often included such ritualistic features as processions of armed men, the wearing or display of animals' horns or heads, and mock proclamations, songs, and other kinds of verbal horseplay. The victim or a surrogate was often paraded through the streets on a horse or a wooden pole called a "stang," and subjected to verbal and physical abuse. The social offenses punished in this manner were almost invariably domestic, and in sixteenth-century England the majority occurred because a wife had physically assaulted or dominated her husband, a situation that almost invariably implied cuckoldry. In such cases the victim might vary: sometimes it was the wife, sometimes the husband, sometimes a surrogate, such as, in one instance, "'the next nearest neighbour to the church'"[33] – the latter choice implying, as we have already observed, the coercive nature of the notion of good neighborliness that underlies the entire custom.

Although the forms of charivari are too varied to allow a single instance to stand as a typical example, one cited by Martin Ingram captures some of the essential features. The event took place on 27 May, 1618, in the small market town of Calne, Wiltshire. Thomas Mills, a cutler, and his wife Agnes, the object of the attack, deposed that, after an earlier and smaller group of men and boys was turned away,

about noon came again from Calne to Quemerford another drummer named William Wiatt, and with him three or four hundred men, some like soldiers armed with pieces and other weapons, and a man riding upon a horse, having a white night cap upon his head, two shoeing horns hanging by his ears, a counterfeit beard upon his chin made of a deer's tail, a smock upon the top of his garments, and he rode upon a red horse with a pair of pots under him, and in them some quantity of brewing grains, which he used to cast upon the press of people, rushing over thick upon him in the way as he passed; and he and all his company made a stand when they came just against this examinate's house, and then the gunners shot off their pieces, pipes and horns were sounded, together with lowbells and other smaller bells which the company had amongst them, and rams' horns and bucks' horns, carried upon forks, were then and there lifted up and shown . . .

"Stones were thrown at the windows," continues Ingram, "an entry forced, and Agnes Mills was dragged out of the house, thrown into a wet hole, trampled, beaten, and covered with mud and filth. Her tormentors, however, failed in their final object of riding her behind the horseman to Calne to 'wash her in the cucking stool.'"[34] Agnes's crime, it seems, was having beaten her husband, a crime common enough for Ingram to observe that "the great majority" of such events "in early modern England took place because a wife had physically assaulted her husband or otherwise dominated him."[35]

From this description it is possible to imagine something of the social and psychological impulses behind this potentially dangerous form of social control. Raucous, festive, derisive – the event combines festivity and punishment, creating group solidarity through the expression of righteous aggression. Ingram notes that the custom could range from mild satire to vicious assault, with the individuals sometimes reintegrated into the society and sometimes forced to leave. The basic method, a public humiliation symbolically appropriate to the offense involved, was by no means restricted to popular forms of "justice" but was a popular expression of a pattern already employed in the official punishments of church and state, as in the carting of criminals, the shaming of penitents, and the staging of public executions. As E. P. Thompson observes, "until the early nineteenth century, publicity was of the essence of punishment."[36]

The social significance of any given charivari would depend upon the specific nature of the occasion and its participants. During the sixteenth century the civic authorities seem to have encouraged and sometimes participated in such events, presumably because they were under local control and seen to complement the work of the legal and church hierarchies. By their very nature, however, charivaris were dangerously unstable and could lead to flagrant abuse, not only by causing serious harm to the victim, but, through riotous behavior and the destruction of property, by inciting further social conflict. Individuals, moreover, could subvert such events to their own purposes, using them to settle old scores either against the victim or other neighbors, or merely to vent lawless and destructive energies. It is even possible that such events were inadvertently subversive of their own apparent ends, by creating among women, the usual victims, oppositional attitudes towards patriarchal authority.[37] In the seventeenth century moralistic opposition to charivaris increased, and by 1700 they were declared illegal, although they persisted until the twentieth century.

The equivocal status of such events, which were part festivity and part violent assault, is suggested by the fact that participants commonly referred to them as "sports."[38] Shakespeare's Windsor resonates with a similar use of the term, which is used repeatedly to characterize acts of festive social control that involve public humiliation. Shallow tempts Page to join in the mockery of Evans and Caius with "we have sport in hand" (2.1.197). When Ford invites Page home with him, in hopes of entrapping his unfaithful wife, he promises "you shall have sport" (3.2.80–81); later he assures his witnesses that they may "make sport" at him if his suspicions are wrong (3.3.150), a promise he reiterates during the second search: "If I find not what I seek . . . let me be forever your table-sport" (4.2.161–62). The most evocative use of the term occurs in relation to the charivari against Falstaff: Page calls the event a "public sport" (4.4.13), and asks later that "Heaven prosper our sport!" (5.2.12); Mistress Page, perhaps usurping the role of peacemaker played by her husband in the opening scene, brings the charivari and play to an end by inviting all the participants to "laugh this sport o'er by a country fire" (5.5.242).

Although many details of the charivari are absent from Shakespeare's play, the essence of the form has been preserved in the structure of Falstaff's experience. Falstaff offends against the domestic and social order by attempting to seduce Mistress Page and Mistress Ford, thereby cuckolding their husbands, and in return the society as a whole subjects him to public and symbolically appropriate humiliation. It is important to note, however, as will become clear later, that Falstaff's charivari proceeds in two stages. In the first stage, he is subjected to two symbolic punishments of a relatively private sort, under the exclusive control of the wives: he is first hidden in a buck basket and dumped into the Thames, and then disguised as the old woman of Brainford and beaten. Taken by themselves, these episodes hardly require consideration of the charivari, for such revenge-tricks appear in many plays. In the second stage, however, which takes place under Herne's oak at midnight, Falstaff is subjected to symbolic punishment and public humiliation at the hands of the entire community, children included. This climactic episode, with its mixture of festive and derisive laughter, its use of disguise (including the wearing of the antlers of a stag), its mocking songs and wordplay, its physical abuse, and its raucous noise, adapts the social custom of the charivari to comic theater.

By invoking the charivari, Shakespeare not only brings into the drama the social resonances of a customary popular form; he subjects the form itself to the critique of comedy. For a contemporary Elizabethan audience, Shakespeare's most dramatic departure from social convention would have been the reversal of gender roles in the relationship between punisher and punished. Although the vast majority of charivaris were directed at aggressive and sexually threatening women, the victim in this play is a man. The agents of social justice that undo him, moreover, are strong, aggressive, and sexually secure women. In adapting the charivari, then, Shakespeare has taken a ritual form that threatened women with patriarchal punishment and inverted it, making it a means whereby women achieve their comic revenge. In this sense, the play confers upon married women some of the license of the unmarried and disguised heroines of the romantic comedies. In the *Merry Wives*, the women are subject to the patriarchy, as wives, yet they find in what Mistress Page calls the "sport" (5.5.242) of the charivari a form that enables them to assert a temporary power and freedom. The clash between comic and social form, between matriarchal license and patriarchal restraint, invites among audiences critical reflections upon popular forms of social justice.

The comic revenge inflicted upon Falstaff by the wives is developed in such a way as to accentuate its anti-patriarchal implications. The motives for the revenge, for one thing, are distinctly personal, an expression of the individuality and friendship of the two women; neither woman responds to Falstaff's overtures as an assault upon the good name of her husband, or upon the domestic order. Their outrage springs from his assault upon themselves. Their revenge, moreover, cuts a wide swath. In the first instance, it is directed against Falstaff alone. Falstaff, however, is also a surrogate for Ford; he is not only a potential cuckold-maker but a salaried representative of the potential cuckold himself. In serving the will of a man named Ford, Falstaff is dumped in a "ford" – "I have my belly full of ford" (3.5.36–37), he laments – beaten as someone from "Brainford," and forced to wear the horns that Ford sees upon his own head.[39] He is also hidden in a "buck" basket, which Ford punningly identifies with his own cuckolding: "Buck! I would I could wash myself of the buck! Buck, buck, buck!" (3.3.157–58). The wives make clear, in addition, that behind the individual targets of both the seducer and the jealous husband lies the patriarchy. "Heaven forgive me!" shouts Mistress Page as she reads Falstaff's letter of seduction, "Why, I'll exhibit a bill in the parliament for the putting down of men" (2.1.28–30). This modulation from the particular threat to the general is itself characteristic of the charivari, which can attack either the offender or a surrogate, and which in practice treats the offender as a representative of womankind.

Falstaff's misadventures at the hands of the women, therefore, are appropriately gendered. His first punishment is to be taken out of Ford's house in a buck basket and dumped into a muddy ditch. In 1618, we recall, Agnes Mills was "thrown into a wet hole, trampled, beaten, and covered with mud and filth." In Agnes's case the symbolic intent, it seems, was to cover her with filth that represented her crime, filth being closely allied to sexual misbehavior, and then to cleanse her symbolically "in the cucking stool." Something of the same motif seems embedded in Falstaff's punishment, for although Mistress Ford directs that he be dumped into "the muddy ditch close by the Thames side" (3.3.15–16), the punishment is also linked to the bleaching of sheets, and the victim actually ends up in the Thames itself, as he reports later, drenched and with a bellyfull of water.

The episode is comical for many reasons, not the least of which is its feminist attack on domesticity. Cleanliness is next to godliness, and Falstaff's soul needs whitening as much as Mistress Ford's dirty linen. The comedy is heightened by Falstaff's unaccustomed prissiness as a wooer. In his overtures to Mistress Ford he assumes the role of an effete courtier, and his Sidneyan posturing – "'Have I caught thee, my heavenly jewel?'" (3.3.43) – bespeaks a fastidiousness that will be severely tested by a buck basket of foul linen. The messy business of dealing with soiled linen is women's work, of course, as Mistress Ford reminds her husband in the midst of his questioning about the destination of the buck basket: "Why, what have you to do whither they bear it? You were best meddle with buck-washing" (3.3.154–56). Falstaff is forced to meddle with buck-washing, and one result, as he tells Ford, is an assault upon his olfactory senses – "the rankest compound of villainous smell that ever offended nostril" (3.5.92–93).

Falstaff's second punishment is just as clearly conceived as a woman's revenge. This time he is disguised, says Mistress Ford, as "my maid's aunt, the fat woman of Brainford" (4.2.75–76). This woman is not merely fat, having a gown large enough to fit Falstaff, but she is old and detested by Master Ford, who believes she is a witch: "He cannot abide the old woman of Brainford. He swears she's a witch, forbade her my house, and hath threat'ned to beat her" (4.2.85–87). And Ford is as good as his word. He beats the disguised Falstaff out the door while hurling insults: "you witch, you rag, you baggage, you poulcat, you runnion! out, out! I'll conjure you, I'll fortune-tell you!" (4.2.184–86). In this instance, Falstaff is not merely dirtied by contact with woman's work; he is beaten by taking on the role of a woman who is in some ways a female counterpart. She is old; she is fat; she is unmarried; she is not of the town of Windsor. Whereas Falstaff can overcome these limitations, after a fashion, the woman of Brainford is victimized by them, as Falstaff discovers feelingly. Simple, whose name suggests his capacity as a speaker of unconscious truth, calls the woman "the wise woman of Brainford" (4.5.26–27), and Slender enters the inn later to seek out her advice. Falstaff admits to the Host that there was a wise woman with him, and "one that hath taught me more wit than ever I learn'd before in my life" (4.5.59–61).

Falstaff's words are belied by the rapidity with which he accepts another assignation, and his failure to learn justifies the escalation of private trick into the public ritual with which the play concludes. The modulation between specifically female and more generally communal sanctions occurs when the wives, having satisfied their desire for private revenge, decide to inform their husbands of their actions and to defer to them for any further vengeance. "If they can find in their hearts the poor unvirtuous fat knight shall be any further afflicted," says Mistress Page, "we two will still be the ministers" (4.2.216–19). Mistress Ford anticipates the likely response of their husbands, and accepts its merit: "I'll warrant they'll have him publicly sham'd, and methinks there would be no period to the jest, should he not be publicly shamed" (4.2.220–22). What Master Page later calls a "public sport" (4.4.13) no longer expresses the individuality of the wives but the outrage of the husbands and the community as a whole. As in the romantic comedies, the female protagonists of this play willingly relinquish the power of their own festive liberty in the interest of traditional community values. It is important to recognize, however, that in doing so they take on the untraditional role of "ministers" of the charivari, and that the charivari itself remains untraditional in being directed against a male. While one cannot call this theatrical gesture revolutionary, it suggests the possibility of progressive social change within the patriarchy, as it both absorbs and is modified by potentially rebellious female energies. As elsewhere in the play's vision of social harmony, the final situation of the wives implies an unstable equilibrium, a continuing social tension that has both destructive and creative potential.

The "public sport" directed against Falstaff at the end of the play is designed to chasten rebellious energies at their most dangerously antisocial. The sport combines the two forms of symbolic assault embodied in the charivari and poaching. As a man, in disguise as Herne the Hunter, Falstaff is subjected to the raucous humiliation of the charivari. As a deer, he is poached. If he is a "Windsor stag" (5.5.12–13), as he says he is, and if, as has been argued, the scene is set in the Little Park of Windsor Castle, then the townsfolk are "poaching" the Queen's deer.[40] When the townsfolk conduct their hunt, they resemble a band of poachers: they assemble at night, they wear disguise, they blow hunting horns, they chase their chosen victim, and they encircle him in preparation for the "kill." Their motive, as in poaching, is not venison but punishment and humiliation. As he kneels in abject terror, Falstaff embodies in a single image the fate of the butchered deer and the dishonored landowner in a poaching raid. The play begins with Falstaff poaching Shallow's deer and ends with the townsfolk poaching the rascal Falstaff.

Shakespeare's merger of the charivari with poaching is not surprising. As forms of extra-legal social control, they both have much in common. They bring together bands of people acting in festive and punitive consort; they feature raucous behavior and noise; they attack their victims often through surrogates – deer, neighbors, or spouses. Some instances of poaching were themselves designed as charivari, as when the inhabitants of seven villages in Nottinghamshire, including a bailiff, parson, and schoolmaster, joined in a raucous and festive massacre of George Wastnes's deer, in retaliation for his allowing deer to damage tenants' crops and the manorial woods.[41] The form of charivari that has most in common with Falstaff's punishment, indeed, enacts symbolically a hunt. In the Devon stag-hunt, a surrogate figure disguised as a deer is chased through the streets and symbolically but realistically "killed" on the victim's doorstep.[42]

Falstaff's disguise, however, makes of him a complex and equivocal symbol.[43] On the one hand, he is associated with the destructive energies of nature. He wears the costume of Herne the hunter, an image that links him not only to his own activities as a poacher of deer and women but to the folklore of Windsor, which tells of a hunter who hanged himself on Windsor oak and haunts the place, and to the legendary figure of Herne, the savage Celtic god who leads wild hunts at night. The antlers he wears also link him to Actaeon, who, as John M. Steadman has shown, had become a conventional emblem of lust.[44] Falstaff himself glories in the role of the stag, whose sexual prowess he emulates: "For me, I am here a Windsor stag, and the fattest, I think, i' th' forest. Send me a cool rut-time, Jove, or who can blame me to piss my tallow?" (5.5.12–15).

Although the symbolism of Falstaff's disguise centers upon destructive sexuality, the horns he wears are deeply equivocal, for they represent not only sexual potency but, in relation to the cuckold, emasculation. The horns are thus paradoxically a symbol of sexual power and weakness, just as Falstaff is both a potential cuckold-maker and a surrogate for the potential cuckold, Ford. In one disguise, then, Falstaff plays the role of both male victimizer and male victim. By making Falstaff so obviously a surrogate for Ford, Shakespeare calls attention to the ways in which the victims of the charivari, even if guilty of breaching social norms themselves, may well be scapegoats for social tensions that lie outside their control.

When measured against reports of charivaris, the treatment of

Falstaff is relatively benign. Nonetheless, he is burnt with tapers, pinched by "fairies," made the butt of derisive laughter, and exposed as a fool before the entire community. It is difficult to imagine a stage representation of the event that would not create sympathy for Falstaff, especially since the action mimics the form of the hunt, with horns sounding offstage, the antlered Falstaff hurling himself face-down on the ground, and the "fairies" encircling, pinching, and burning him with tapers. In that sense the central image of the punishment is the ritual killing of the hart or stag, an image that Shakespeare always treats with pathos, most notably in the death of Caesar in *Julius Caesar*. Having begun the play as an "ill-killer" of deer, Falstaff ends it as a deer himself, the poacher brought down by another extra-legal "sport." The pathos is tinged with irony, however. Falstaff's mock-death parodies that of the heroic Talbot in *1 Henry VI*, who rallies his encircled troops to act like "English deer . . . in blood, / Not rascal-like, to fall down with a pinch" (4.2.48–49). Although he sees himself as a Windsor stag in blood, Falstaff falls down even before he is pinched.

Of the two possible ways to end this charivari against Falstaff – expulsion from the community or reintegration – Shakespeare chose the latter. In keeping with the realistic tone of the play, however, and the nature of his comic victim, Shakespeare provides no gestures towards conversion on Falstaff's part and no feast as a ritual of social communion, merely a "posset" by a "country fire" (5.5.171, 242). Although nonplussed by his experience, which includes a barrage of taunts from the wives, husbands, and Evans, Falstaff remains resilient, able to vent his frustration by assaults upon the Welsh preacher, whose linguistic infelicities make him a safe and enduring object of attack: "Have I lived to stand at the taunt of one that makes fritters of English? This is enough to be the decay of lust and late-walking through the realm" (5.5.142–45). Falstaff draws strength not only from the thrusts of his wit but from the image of virility that his escapade has somewhat unexpectedly thrust upon him. The discovery of the marriage of Anne and Fenton, moreover, affords him a final laugh at his tormentors. His quip at their expense precipitates not only Mistress Page's neighborly invitation to "laugh this sport o'er by a country fire" (5.5.242) but the comical swaggering of Master Ford, whose final taunt ends the play: "Sir John, / To Master [Brook] you yet shall hold your word, / For he to-night shall lie with Mistress Ford" (5.5.244–45). The allusion to honor, and the sardonic use of the title, "Sir John," highlight the degree to which Falstaff continues to threaten both Ford's sexual and social status.

Charivaris, the civic authorities feared, could have unforeseen consequences. In the midst of the well-designed plot against Falstaff, Anne Page and Fenton elope, to the dismay not only of Slender and Caius, both of whom discover that they have married boys, but of Mistress Ford and her husband, whose separate and competing plots have been foiled. In this victory of Anne and Fenton over the older generation, Shakespeare further complicates the motif of the charivari with the conventions of comedy. As we have seen, Fenton and Falstaff are in a curious way mirror images. At the end of the play, however, their fates diverge sharply. While the town joins together to punish the threat of rampant sexuality ironically represented by the aging Falstaff, another illicit suitor, who "capers," "dances," and "has eyes of youth" (3.2.67), is secretly marrying Anne Page. At the end of the play both Falstaff and Fenton stand before the community as social rebels, but Falstaff stands alone and humiliated, while Fenton stands with Anne, his equal in rebellion, and triumphant. By admitting his poaching at the very beginning of the play, Falstaff evades punishment; by admitting his marriage at the end, Fenton gets a reward. Whereas Falstaff's degraded version of court life threatens the community of Windsor, Fenton's, equally and more permanently rebellious, renews it. Although Anne's rebellion against the marriage market goes no farther than a husband of her choice, this in itself is a significant social gesture, and one that goes beyond the more domesticated rebelliousness of Mistress Ford and Mistress Page.

To pursue this vein, however, and to draw political, social, or economic conclusions from the ending of *The Merry Wives*, is to enforce a closure that the play itself resists. Critics who take such a tack generally see the play as socially conservative, and its conclusion as a celebration of Windsor's ability to resolve conflict without significant social change.[45] One could mount a progressive, if not radical, challenge to this apparent consensus by accentuating the recognitions of the protagonists, the residual power of the wives, and the infusion of new values into the community by the elopement of Anne and Fenton. Either view, however, risks oversimplifying the complexity of the social vision that makes the play most distinctive. Although it is the protagonist of the play, the community of Windsor is finally neither celebrated nor attacked, merely embodied with comic realism – a realism that cuts to the paradoxical quick of town life in a way that is difficult to generalize in political terms. If the play tests the popular custom of the charivari against the festive expectations of comic form, it also tests the capacity of comedy to resolve the social tensions that give rise to such customs.

The comic irresolution of the play's final scene is appropriately embodied in the figure of Mistress Quickly, whose actions throughout the play travesty the notion of "good neighborhood."[46] She is the go-between, the peace-maker, whose indiscriminate good will serves Caius, Shallow, Fenton, and Falstaff. Her motives are obscure, especially to herself. Busybody, trickster, bawd, prude, she is as happy fostering illicit marriages as she is furthering the punishment of Falstaff for lechery. Although her achievements are uncertain at best – Fenton and Anne prosper through their own device, and Falstaff is foiled through the devices of Mistress Page and Mistress Ford – her energy and resiliency make her irrepressible. As the Fairy Queen, she achieves a comic apotheosis, ensuring through her fairy power the virtue of Windsor Castle and the Order of the Garter and bringing Falstaff to "trial-fire" (5.5.84) for his lechery. She and her fairies disappear, ironically, before the outcome of her own plots to marry Caius, Shallow, and Fenton is known. Any social order that depends upon such a presiding spirit is unlikely to be stable.

The play ends more or less as it began, with a "posset" and "a country fire" taking the place of a dinner of "venison pasty" as the backdrop for attempted social reconciliation. One thing has changed, permanently: Anne Page and Fenton are married. The charivari against Falstaff, moreover, and the revelations of the young lovers have provoked a social catharsis, leaving the citizens, for the moment, at least, emotionally purged and enlightened. Essentially, however, the town remains as it was. Whether outsiders like Falstaff and Fenton will eventually be assimilated, or even uneasily "contained," as are Caius and Evans, is left uncertain; perhaps they will both return to a more courtly environment. Whether Ford's obsession has been broken is also unclear, especially in view of his final taunt against Falstaff. Shallow's complaints against Falstaff are unresolved, as are the Host's against Caius and Evans, whose revenge has left him without his horses. The future roles of the wives, too, are left somewhat in doubt: Ford's concluding taunt not only mocks Falstaff but asserts his sexual mastery over his wife, and even Page invites Falstaff to "laugh at my wife" (5.5.172) in anticipation of his success in the wedding plot. The play's vision of social life, while comic, is distinctly unsentimental, suggesting the resiliency of the community and its capacity to absorb conflict, but suggesting as well that conflict is only absorbed, never resolved, and that social tensions are paradoxically both creative and destructive of social order. The town of Windsor will survive, but any peace it achieves will be restless and unstable, for "good neighborhood" carries the motto that "friends is the sword" and is nourished by "ill-killed" deer, whether poached from Shallow or pinched by fairies in Windsor Forest.

The Merry Wives is not a play about hunting. But the town of Windsor, as befits a royal seat located near both the Little and Great Parks of Windsor Castle and the immense tract of Windsor Forest, is touched at many levels by the culture of the hunt. Its gentry give venison to cement relationships, threaten poachers with the Star Chamber, go birding, imagine themselves with buck's antlers when anxious about cuckoldry, and devise charivari that make full use of the ritual of the hunt. When confronted with an alien poacher, the citizens unite, transforming the hunter into the hunted. And the mark of their unity, ironically, the charivari, is itself poaching in another guise – a kind of rough justice, a symbolic assault by means of which the offender is harassed and humiliated for social deviance. In its representation of Falstaff as the "stag" of Windsor Forest, the comedy of *The Merry Wives* captures something of the rough humor of poaching, in which society both destroys and renews itself in the "killing" of rascals.

CHAPTER SIX

Pastoral hunting in As You Like It

If, as Paul Alpers suggests, the central and defining fiction of pastoral is the representation of "herdsmen and their lives," then it is not surprising that hunting appears infrequently in the genre.[1] The life of the shepherd, as conceived by pastoral poets, centers upon the tending of flocks, and both the activities and values associated with that life contrast sharply with those associated with the life of a hunter. The hunter spends time in vigorous action, the shepherd in patient watching, whiling away the hours in contemplation, discussion, and song. The hunter lives to kill animals; the shepherd, although required to slaughter lambs on occasion, lives to nurture and protect them. The hunter enters wild nature and assaults it; the shepherd lives within domesticated nature, intertwining his own life with that of the animals he tends.

Despite these sharp contrasts in the two modes of life, Virgil allows at least a little space for hunting in his *Eclogues*. In the Second Eclogue, for example, the shepherd Corydon sings of his frustrated love for the absent Alexis. In his song he yearningly envisions the simple but joyful life they could lead together: "If only you could bring yourself to live with me under some humble roof in the homely countryside, to shoot the stag, and drive a herd of goats with a green marshmallow switch!" The implied equivalency between shooting the stag and driving a herd of goats suggests that for Virgil, as for Corydon, the two activities coexist as part of the natural rhythm of a shepherd's life, a rhythm that includes both the nurturing and killing of animals. In Eclogue I, Tityrus speaks of taking "new-weaned lambs" to the marketplace; in Eclogue II, as we have seen, Corydon imagines killing stags for food. In Eclogue I, Tityrus promises to "stain" an altar with "the blood of a young lamb" to honor the man who has made his leisure possible; in Eclogue VII, Corydon promises a boar's head and stag's antlers to the goddess Diana.[2] Although the bloodshed of both hunting and shepherding is kept discreetly in the background, both activities are treated as part of the natural routine of a shepherd's life. For Virgil, the life of a shepherd includes occasional hunting.

In Spenser's *Shepheardes Calender*, in contrast, hunting is scarcely mentioned. The sole reference to an actual hunt occurs in the December Eclogue, when Colin briefly recalls chasing "the trembling Pricket" and hunting "the hartlesse hare" as a youth (27–28), an image that recalls the conventional association between hunting, especially poaching, with adolescence. With this single exception, Spenser's shepherds live without hunting. The rural landscape, although filled with flowers, brambles, hills, dales, grazing lambs, greenwood, and even an occasional wolf or fox, provides no sustenance from deer or hare. Even the goddess Cynthia, invoked in the April Eclogue to celebrate Queen Elizabeth, does not appear as a huntress. Aside from Colin's momentary nostalgia for his youthful escapades, the only image of the hunt that appears in the work captures not the normal rhythms of the shepherd's life in nature but the searing and destructive heat of July. In this astrological image, the sun of the July Eclogue "hunts" the "rampant Lyon" with "Dogge of noysome breath, / Whose balefull barking bringes in hast / pyne, plagues, and dreery death" (21–24).[3] In Virgilian pastoral, hunting is a minor but unexceptional part of the shepherd's life; in Spenserian pastoral, hunting is virtually irrelevant, appearing only as a fleeting memory or as an astrological sign.

The reason for this difference probably lies in the social and legal position of hunting in the two cultures. Virgil could assume that a shepherd might hunt deer or boar, but Spenser certainly could not. For the Romans, both the forests and the wild beasts were *res nullius* (belonging to no one); even wild animals that inhabited private land were not legally the property of the owner.[4] For Elizabethans, shepherds could not hunt, at least legally, for hunting was restricted by the Game Laws to those of wealth and social standing. Hence any allusion in pastoral to hunting hare or deer might imply that characters intended to represent natural innocence were actually poachers. To associate hunting with shepherds as Virgil does, moreover, would be to characterize it as a necessity rather than a sport. If they hunt at all, shepherds hunt for sustenance. The dominant Elizabethan and Jacobean attitudes towards the hunt, however, express contempt for what Elyot calls hunting "for the pot."[5] Hunting is admirable not because it sustains human life but because it provides a "manly" recreation suitable for future warriors.

The social tensions that divide hunting from the pastoral in the Elizabethan period are evident in Sidney's treatment of hunting in the

Arcadia. In the *Old Arcadia*, hunting does not appear in the narrative at all, and appears in the eclogues only twice, both times in relation to Philisides, who is not a shepherd, but an exile, and, in addition, Sidney's own persona. The first allusion to hunting is insignificant: the old shepherd, Geron, advises Philisides to "hunt fearefull beastes" as a means of overcoming love-melancholy. The second is both significant and strongly negative: Philisides himself sings a beast fable, "On Ister Bank," that depicts hunting as the final stage in the development of man's tyranny over the beasts. The climactic moment of that process occurs when man turns from killing for food to killing for sport: "At length for glutton taste he did them kill: / At last for sport their sillie lives did spill."[6]

When Sidney revised the *Old Arcadia*, transforming it from pastoral romance into a kind of epic, he brought hunting within the narrative as an aristocratic sport. In a brief episode, Kalander, as a noble host, takes Pyrocles and Musidorus stag-hunting. Kalander recalls his youthful joys as a hunter, and Sidney describes the chase from beginning to end. Although Sidney treats the death of the stag in a way that hints at his own critical attitude towards the hunt – the "poor beast" weeps to show "the unkindness he took of man's cruelty" – he also praises Kalander for his compassion in despatching the deer quickly.[7] Nothing in the episode as a whole indicates that the hunt is unworthy of Kalander's hospitality or the participation of his young guests. For Sidney, then, attitudes towards the hunt are generically marked. In the pastoral *Arcadia*, hunting is either ignored or condemned outright as a mark of tyranny; in the heroic revisions, hunting is accepted as a lively, if slightly disturbing, aristocratic entertainment.

If treated as an aristocratic sport, the hunt itself may evoke traditional pastoral attitudes. In Drayton's *The Muses Elizium*, for example, Silvius, the forester, celebrates the life of the hunter for its reveling in the beauties of nature:

> I am the Prince of sports, the Forrest is my Fee,
> He's not upon the Earth for pleasure lives like me;
> The Morne no sooner puts her Rosye Mantle on,
> But from my quyet Lodge I instantly am gone,
> When the melodious Birds from every Bush and Bryer
> Of the wilde spacious Wasts, make a continuall quire . . .

The list of joys continues with flowered meadows, soft breezes, dryads, fairies, bubbling brooks, groves, and more.[8]

Even the hunting manuals occasionally strike the same note. In *The Master of Game*, Edward Duke of York asserts that "hunters live in this world more joyfully than any other men." When the hunter "riseth in the morning," he "sees a sweet and fair morn and clear weather and bright, and he heareth the song of the small birds, the which sing so sweetly with great melody and full of love." With the rising of the sun, "he shall see fresh dew upon the small twigs and grasses."⁹ Such celebrations of nature are not restricted to the rising of the hunters; they appear as well in descriptions of the assembly, in which the hunters enjoy a woodland feast and review the plans for the pursuit. In the *Noble Arte of Venerie*, George Gascoigne even provides a poetic description of the assembly, which centers upon a contrast between its natural pleasures and the unhealthy artifice of the court. The setting is a "pleasant gladsome greene" with a stream nearby. The colors of the ground provide a tapestry, the aromas of the flowers, perfume. It is a place "where pleasure dwels at large, / Which Princes seeke in Pallaces, with payne and costly charge."¹⁰

The difficulty with this aristocratic "pastoralizing" of the hunt is that the joys of nature are incidental to the main business of the day, the pursuit and killing of deer. This fact produces some ironic incongruities. Immediately after describing the hunter's joy in the beauties of nature, for example, Edward Duke of York turns to joys of a rather less pastoral kind: "And when the hart be overcome and shall be at bay he [the hunter] shall have pleasure. And after, when the hart is spayed and dead, he undoeth him and maketh his curée and enquireth or rewardeth his hounds, and so he shall have great pleasure . . ."¹¹ Even in Gascoigne's poetic description of the assembly, the description of the beauties of the place yields to a fanciful battle for supremacy between the cooks and butlers, as if peace and harmony were inappropriate to the festive setting. The only hunting manual in the period that gestures toward the traditional pastoral experience is Gascoigne's French source, *La Venerie de Jaques Du Fouilloux*. Du Fouilloux includes a long poem, "L'Adolescence de Jacques du Fouilloux," in which the hero, an adolescent hunter and a persona for the author himself, encounters while hunting a group of shepherdesses tending their flocks. He falls in love with one of them, courts her, and wins her, and the two experience the joys of love in an idyllic pastoral setting. In *La Venerie,* then, the hunt provides a setting for a pastoral experience, but the two modes of activity remain completely separate. For Gascoigne, the inclusion of an amorous pastoral episode merely degrades the hunt. He refuses to translate "L'Adolescence de Jaques du Fouilloux" because these "unseemly verses . . . are more apt for lascivious mindes, than to be enterlaced amongst the noble termes of

Venerie."[12] The insistence upon the nobility of the terms of venery suggests that Gascoigne feared not merely the moral taint of lascivious love but the social taint of mixing shepherd lasses with aristocratic hunters.

The closest one comes in Elizabethan England to a pastoral version of the hunt is in the ballads, folk-customs, and plays associated with Robin Hood. The celebration of the greenwood that characterizes these materials evokes the joys of a simple, spartan life in the forest, a life made festive by an abundance of venison and communal merry-making. The ballad "A Gest of Robyn Hoode," for example, evokes the surge of relief that Robin feels after returning to Sherwood Forest after a stay in the court:

> Whan he came to grenë wode,
>   In a mery mornynge,
> There he herde the notës small
>   Of byrdës small
> Of byrdës mery syngynge.
>
> 'It is ferre gone,' sayd Robyn,
>   'That I was last here;
> Me lyste a lytell for to shote
>   At the donnë dere.'
>
> Robyn slewe a full grete harte;
>   His horne than gan he blow,
> That all the outlawes of that forest
>   That horne coud they knowe,
>
> And gadred them togyder,
>   In a lytell throwe.[13]

In this version of the greenwood, the pleasures of the merry morning and the small birds singing harmonize with the pleasure of shooting a deer, and the deer itself will provide the communal meal bringing Robin together once more with his merry band.

As versions of pastoral hunting, however, the Robin Hood stories were deeply implicated in social conflict. In his traditional form, Robin is a commoner and an outlaw, carrying out from his sanctuary in the forest attacks upon the rich, the church, and the civil authorities. Hunting in this context is poaching; in the ballad just quoted, Robin actually serves the King one of his own deer. Hence the Robin Hood stories may celebrate life in the greenwood and the delights of pursuing the stag, but they do so in a way that subverts the aristocratic culture of the hunt. Some of the popularity of the Robin Hood stories, one suspects, derives not merely from his protests against social injustice but from his direct assault on the King's control of the forests and the deer. It is therefore not surprising that in the Elizabethan and Jacobean periods bands of poachers, including both gentry and commoners, sometimes linked themselves to Robin Hood and his merry men.[14]

The gentrification of the Robin Hood materials that took place during the sixteenth century drained away their subversive potential. In Munday's play, *The Downfall of Robert Hood, Earle of Huntingdon*, for example, Robin is a nobleman (Robert, Earl of Huntingdon), forced into the forest by injustice; he takes the name of Robin Hood upon becoming an outlaw. His love, Matilda, becomes Maid Marian, and lives with him in the forest, scrupulously retaining her virginity until he is able to make her his lawful wife. The pleasures of the forest life are many. In one scene Robin sleeps on a green bank while Marian strews him with flowers. In another, Robin evokes a pastoral contrast between the greenwood and the court: "*Marian*, thou seest though courtly pleasurs want, / Yet country sport, in Sherewodde is not scant." Instead of instrumental music, they have the songs of "winged quiristers." Instead of rich tapestries, they have "natures best imbrothery." Instead of mirrors, they have the "Christall brooke." "What in wealth we want," Robin concludes, "we have in flowers, / And what wee loose in halles, we finde in bowers."[15] The play as a whole concludes with Robin welcoming the King himself to his bower. Munday's elevation of Robin not only sentimentalizes the treatment of nature and love but transforms the social context of the hunt. No longer does it represent a commoner's assault against social privilege. The Earl has hunted deer before, presumably, and will do so again when returned to his rightful position; his pursuit of deer as an outlaw in Sherwood Forest merely converts an aristocratic sport into a temporary means of survival. His hunting thus represents only a superficial threat to aristocratic and royal privilege.

The relationship between hunting and the pastoral in the Elizabethan and Jacobean periods is thus fraught with literary and social tension. To treat the hunt within the traditional pastoral context is to threaten the traditional values that the shepherd's life represents, which center upon the nurturing, not the destruction of animals, and to threaten an aggressive radicalizing of the form by making law-abiding shepherds into poachers; as politically oriented studies of the pastoral tend to show, the form itself seems to have displaced or contained serious political and social subversion rather than provided a forum for it.[16] To step outside the pastoral, and to "pastoralize" the hunt itself is to introduce still other problems, among them the inevitable prominence of the kill and the subversive implications of the greenwood motif, as celebrated in the stories of Robin Hood. It is within this complicated literary and social context, it seems to me, that we can best understand the treatment of the hunt in *As You Like It*.

The genteel and "masculine" status of hunting is reflected in the play by a delicate separation between the worlds of hunters and shepherds and an implied hierarchy which advantages the former. Duke Senior and his men survive by hunting deer, and their activities and imaginations center on the forest itself. Duke Senior's first words concern the hunt, and Jaques first makes his presence felt in Amiens' description of him weeping over a wounded deer. The Duke and his men are dining in the forest when Orlando, who will later become one of the Duke's foresters, accosts them in search of food. Towards the end of the play, the Duke's men mark a successful hunt with festive song and merriment. The shepherds in the play, in contrast, whether "real" like Corin or "artificial" like Silvius and Phebe, exist in what Rosalind calls "the skirts of the forest" (3.2.336), an image that subtly feminizes the pastoral landscape. Rosalind and Celia buy a shepherd's cottage from Corin's landlord, and, with the exception of their meetings with Orlando, both the women and Touchstone spend their time among shepherds. Until the end of the play, the two social realms are kept separate for the most part, with only occasional exchanges between them.

The social superiority of the hunters' life is implied in Shakespeare's play in the fact that the hunters comprise an aristocratic elite, exiled temporarily in Arden, whereas the shepherds – even Silvius and Phebe – are common people and permanent residents. At the end of the play the hunters, sans Jaques, will return to the world of the court, their social status untouched by exile; they have not become shepherds but have merely exchanged one form of hunting for another. In exile they hunt out of necessity; in power they are privileged to hunt for sport. When they next enter Arden, they may do so to hunt not on foot but *par force*. Although Charles the wrestler likens the Duke's way of life to that of "the old Robin Hood of England" (1.1.116), the carnivalesque potential in that gesture is not fulfilled. Duke Senior does not attack passers-by, does not make incursions into the corrupt society to protect the innocent or fight against injustice, does not engage in sporting contests of prowess, does not, in short, live anything like the traditional life of Robin Hood or do anything to recover his power. Even his hunting, as we shall see, is never connected to poaching. Like many other banished rulers, Duke Senior continues to live in exile the life of a Duke, only in straitened circumstances. He recovers his dukedom only because, in keeping with the play's title, his usurping brother experiences a miraculous conversion.

Rosalind's banishment, not to mention her love for Orlando, forces upon her a rather more adventuresome change in role. She is on the one hand associated with the hunt. The leader of the band of hunters, Duke Senior, is her father, and she enters Arden with a boar spear in her hand (1.3.118). But she is also associated with the shepherd's life, and her social position is thereby compromised in a way that her father's is not. She buys a shepherd's cottage and becomes the confidante of a lovelorn shepherd and the object of a love-sick shepherdess's affections. When she resumes her proper social position at the end of the play, she rejoins the world of hunters. A figure who mediates between both the hunters' and the shepherds' worlds, she quite literally brings them together at the end of the play.

Since Rosalind plays the role of a shepherd in her mock courting with Orlando, their meetings bring together imaginatively the roles of shepherd and forester. Although Orlando seems never to hunt, the role of forester fits well with the "Herculean" qualities that enable him to defeat Charles the wrestler and to kill the lioness that threatens Oliver. Although temporarily besotted with a love-melancholy that Rosalind promises to cure, Orlando is thus associated with "manliness." By disguising Rosalind as a shepherd, Shakespeare creates a delicately gendered difference between the two lovers, even when Rosalind too is "male." She would have no excuse at all for fainting at the sight of Orlando's blood if she were disguised as a hunter. The subversive effects of Rosalind's masculine disguise are thus qualified somewhat not only by its temporary nature but by the specific masculine role she assumes. Although transgressive in her male disguise, Rosalind does not take on the more boisterous and aggressively masculine attributes of a figure like Maid Marian, who often joins Robin Hood in the hunt.

Shakespeare's treatment of the Robin Hood materials is thus by no means socially subversive. Duke Senior is associated with the aristocratic and courtly world of the hunt, and dissociated from the socially compromising world of shepherds or, worse, of genuine outlaws. The disguised Rosalind certainly conveys subversive energies, but even her boar spear yields to a shepherd's staff when she settles in Arden. In bringing together the worlds of hunters and shepherds, Shakespeare subtly perpetuates the divisions within Tudor and Stuart society that kept the two worlds apart. The introduction of hunting into the pastoral world works not so much to make possible a critical perspective on the court but to bring true courtly and country values into harmony with each other.

A similar evasion of social conflict occurs in Shakespeare's treatment of setting. *As You Like It* takes place, for the most part, in the Forest of Arden. Forest settings of virtually any kind would have carried a high political charge for contemporary audiences. Throughout the Elizabethan and Jacobean periods, the forests of England were sites of social, economic, and political conflict. Both the forests themselves and the purlieus around them were often inhabited by poor people, vagabonds and squatters driven off farms elsewhere by the conversion of agricultural land to sheep-grazing. Some were drawn to the forests by the development of mining, which created employment not only in the industry itself but in the cutting of wood to fuel it. The illegal enclosure of forest lands by neighboring landowners, moreover, aroused opposition from those who eked out a living by gathering wood, working in mines, or raising sheep, hogs, or cattle, activities which by tradition provided certain rights of access to forest land. The conflicts that resulted from these competing demands often pitted local commoners against gentry, aristocracy, and monarchy, sometimes in violent protest. To write plays sympathetic to "outlaws" dwelling in the forests of Elizabethan England was thus to enter highly political terrain.[17]

Critics of *As You Like It* commonly assert that Shakespeare's Arden is not a realistic locale but a landscape of the mind. The incongruous flora and fauna of the place lend support to this notion. Arden contains, among other things, an oak tree, a palm tree, olive trees, a lioness, and a green and gilded snake. At some level Shakespeare surely wants to disrupt expectations of social realism and to create a world in which the imagination is given free rein. This said, it must be admitted that the geographical oddities are few and far between, and that the dominant impression of Arden in the play is familiarly local and English, recognizable as a version of Shakespeare's own Warwickshire.[18] The Ardennes of Lodge's *Rosalynde*, in contrast, a place with fountains, groves like arbors, amphitheaters, and lemon trees, bears no resemblance to the actual Ardennes of France.[19]

If Shakespeare intends Arden as a landscape of the imagination, he is curiously insistent about identifying the locale. The word "forest," for example, appears twenty-three times in *As You Like It*, but no more than three times in any other play. The forest is specifically identified as

"Arden," moreover, four times – most provocatively in the exchange between Rosalind and Touchstone upon their first arrival:

> *Ros.* Well, this is the forest of Arden.
> *Touch.* Ay, now am I in Arden, the more fool I.   (2.4.15–16)

The metatheatrical gesture in these lines towards the empty stage as a hopelessly inadequate representation of a forest plays on the notion that Arden, with its palm trees and lionesses, exists essentially in the mind's eye, as the spatial equivalent, perhaps, to Touchstone's pregnant phrase, "much virtue in If" (5.4.103). For some members of Shakespeare's audience, however, this gesture towards the imagination would have taken on yet another dimension. The empty stage is from this point of view a perfect representation of the forest of Arden because in Elizabethan times it was a "Utopia" in the original sense, a "No-place." In the literal and legal meaning of the term, a "forest" of Arden did not exist. In John Manwood's authoritative definition, "A forest is a certaine Territorie of wooddy grounds and fruitfull pastures, priviledged for wild beasts and foules of Forest, Chase and Warren, to rest and abide in, in the safe protection of the King, for his princely delight and pleasure . . ."[20] The so-called forest of Arden had not been a true forest – a royal hunting preserve, subject to the special laws of the forest – from before the time of Henry II.[21] The play is thus rather insistently set in a place that does not exist.

Nor was the area of Arden even heavily wooded in Shakespeare's day. By the early sixteenth century the vast forests of early medieval Arden had yielded to mixed woodland and pasture. The economy was mainly pastoral. In his *Itineraries*, John Leland describes the region as "muche enclosyd, plentifull of gres [grass], but no great plenty of corne."[22] Throughout the century, increased enclosure, the destruction of timber, the conversion of woodland to arable or pasture land, population growth in wooded areas, the development of dairy farming, and the introduction of mining all diminished the woodland available. In 1586 William Camden could still describe the region as mainly woodland, but he noted that it was "not without pastures, corn fields and iron mines."[23] These physical changes in the landscape were both the cause and effect of social and economic transformation. The "rising prices" and "rapid economic change" characteristic of the sixteenth century, notes Ann Hughes, had a "social cost in the Arden, bringing increasing polarisation within local society and the creation of a landless proletariat."[24] The woodlands that remained were under the control of local landowners.

Had Duke Senior and his men been exiled in this region they would probably have lived and hunted in a local nobleman's park.

In his study of five contiguous parishes in Arden during the period 1570 to 1674, V. Skipp provides a picture of the region distinctly at odds with Shakespeare's. Throughout the sixteenth century, the region consisted of about one-third arable land and two-thirds woodland-pasture, so Shakespeare's depiction of a pastoral environment is at least generally accurate. Skipp estimates, however, that as early as 1550 only 9 per cent of the region was common wasteland, with the rest in the possession of private landowners. Skipp's Arden, moreover, increased in population by the astonishing figure of 38 per cent from about 1570 to 1600, many of the immigrants being landless cottagers who eked out a living while the landed husbandmen profited. Shakespeare's Arden, in contrast, is virtually unoccupied and consists of deep forest with the cottages of shepherds on the outskirts. In Shakespeare's Arden life on the land is simple but good. In Skipp's, the food shortages produced mainly by the tremendous influx of population resulted in severe dearth in the 1590s and a genuine crisis, with a sharp drop in population, in the years 1613 to 1619.[25] Against this backdrop of actual life in Arden during the period, Shakespeare's title takes on added meaning.

Shakespeare does allude briefly to this general social context, first in Corin's remarks about his cruel master, a man "of churlish disposition," who "little reaks to find the way to heaven / By doing deeds of hospitality" (2.4.80–82), and secondly, in Orlando's words as he accosts the Duke and his men at their "banquet." When Orlando discovers that he has encountered "civilized" men, he identifies himself as being "inland bred" and therefore knowing "some nurture" (2.7.96–97). He asks pardon for his rudeness by saying, "I thought that all things had been savage here, / And therefore put I on the countenance / Of stern command'ment" (2.7.107–09). What Orlando expects is the rough behavior of the occupants of the squatters' communities that grew up within Elizabethan forests, the kind of people John Norden encountered in the survey he published in 1607. The inhabitants of these scattered hamlets, Norden observes, are "'given to little or no kind of labour, living very hardly with oaten bread, sour whey, and goats' milk, dwelling far from any church or chapel, and are as ignorant of God or of any civil course of life as the very savages amongst the infidels.'"[26] Although Shakespeare evokes a brief image of such a life, the allusion simply marks the absence of the harsh reality it represents. Nor does Corin's master make an appearance.

The economic and social tensions generated by the conflicting forces we have observed created considerable social unrest. Much of the unrest was agricultural, but the forces at work affected both farming and wooded regions. Many counties, among them Warwickshire and Oxfordshire, experienced extensive enclosures during the 1580s and 1590s. In Arden, according to Alasdair Hawkyard, "repeated and sustained efforts by improving landlords to enclose . . . woodland during the Tudor period were bitterly resented by their tenants, and as a result the Forest of Arden was one of the most disaffected agrarian regions in the Midlands, intermittent commissions of enquiry ordered by the Crown providing neither solution nor more than temporary alleviation."[27] In neighboring Oxfordshire, an anti-enclosure rebellion was planned in 1596, for which the chief conspirators were executed for treason. The leader, a carpenter named Bartholomew Steere, who professed devotion to the cause of the common people, had visions of Utopian reform that find no expression in Shakespeare's Arden. Steere is reported to have declared that the world "'would never be well untill some of the gentlemen were knockt downe," that the commoners of Spain had "lyved merrily there" since rising and killing all the gentlemen, and that he cared "not for work, for we shall have a merrier world shortly . . . I will work one day and play the other."[28] Poverty, unrest, rebellion, desperate visions of Cockaigne – these images from Arden and nearby Oxfordshire represent a mode of existence far removed from that of Shakespeare's play.

If Shakespeare's version of Arden is a kind of "no-place," it also exists in a kind of "no-time." Although Charles the Wrestler alludes to the Golden Age, the presence of hunting alone in the play excludes that possibility. More likely is the allusion to Robin Hood and his merry band, for medieval Arden was at least heavily wooded. The mix of woodland and pasture, however, suggests that the Arden of the play is vaguely contemporary, although somehow immune to the social pressures that were transforming its character. In a sense rather broader than Orlando intends, "there's no clock in the forest" (3.2.301). The image of the forest that remains – of babbling brooks, ancient oaks, deer, pastures, and shepherd's cottages – seems an evocation of contemporary Arden as we might like it. In *Poly-Olbion*, published about fifteen years after Shakespeare's play, Michael Drayton treats Arden with nostalgia as a symbol of an England that is being destroyed. Drayton locates Warwickshire in the heart of England, Arden in the heart of Warwickshire, and his muse in the heart of Arden. Although he celebrates the beauty of Arden and its variety of wildlife – he describes the songs of the birds and the majestic tragedy of a stag hunt – Drayton's evocation of the place is suffused with nostalgia. The magnificent forests in which the goddess Diana used to hunt are no longer. "For, when the world found out the fitnesse of my soyle," the Forest herself complains,

> The gripple wretch began immediatly to spoyle
> My tall and goodly woods, and did my grounds inclose:
> By which, in little time my bounds I came to lose.[29]

Drayton responds to Arden with a nostalgia localized in space and in the dim recesses of time, a time before enclosure. The contrast between past and present implies a political judgment. Shakespeare, in contrast, remains more subtly evasive, evoking an Arden that seems to have only one definitive attribute: an exclusion of contemporary social reality. The shadowy allusions to that reality serve as reminders of an absence. Shakespeare's most striking gesture towards social realism is an absentee landlord, Corin's cruel master, who never appears in the play.[30]

Despite his political evasiveness, Shakespeare not only includes but foregrounds the problem of the hunt. The image of the sobbing deer that introduces audiences to the forest of Arden in act 2 scene 1 has proved to be one of the most resonant of the play. The image itself is by no means original with Shakespeare. It appears in the hunting manuals, lending a note of pathos to descriptions of the death of the deer, and has a long poetic and iconographic history. Almost always, the image is strongly anthropomorphic, the actual experience of the deer serving as a mere vehicle for human grief. The *locus classicus* for such treatment is Book 4 of Virgil's *Aeneid*, in which the unhappy Dido, left by Aeneas, rages throughout the town – in Surrey's translation, "like the striken hinde . . . / Amid whose side the mortall arrow stickes." Surrey represents himself by means of the same image in another poem that describes his unhappiness in love:

> Then as the striken dere withdrawes him selfe alone,
> So do I seke some secrete place where I may make my mone.
> There do my flowing eyes shew forth my melting hart,
> So that the stremes of those two welles right well declare my smart.[31]

Shakespeare's treatment of this convention is so unlike that of his predecessors and contemporaries, and so much more complicated, that it repays considerable attention. In bringing the hunt into the pastoral, Shakespeare achieves a complex and paradoxical effect: on the one hand, he "pastoralizes" hunting based on necessity by suggesting its essential harmony with nature; on the other, however, he reveals the tragic undercurrents within that accommodation. In his treatment of the hunt, as in his treatment of other aspects of the pastoral experience, Shakespeare achieves a measure of pastoral optimism by subjecting that very optimism to skeptical scrutiny. An appreciation of the nature and significance of this achievement requires a rather painstaking analysis of the play's language of the hunt.

The first mention of hunting occurs, as we have seen, in act 2 scene 1, when Duke Senior and the First Lord discuss the reactions of Jaques to a sobbing deer. Although the episode focuses upon Jaques, it is important to recognize that the fact of animal suffering is presented to us through three different characters: Duke Senior, who introduces the topic of the hunt; the First Lord, who develops it by describing the suffering of the deer itself; and, finally and indirectly, Jaques, whose moralizings are reported by the First Lord. Although the three perspectives shade into one another, they are nonetheless distinct. Each represents a different way of coming to terms with the brutal fact that their lives in undeserved exile depend upon the violent death of wild animals.

Duke Senior, who finds "Sermons in stones, and good in every thing" (2.1.17), and whose benign stoicism seems at the moral center of the play, introduces the episode by suggesting a hunt to his companions: "Come, shall we go and kill us venison?" His very next words, however, express reservations:

> And yet it irks me the poor dappled fools,
> Being native burghers of this desert city,
> Should in their own confines with forked heads
> Have their round haunches gor'd.   (2.1.21–25)

This is emphatically a speech of sympathy for the suffering of the deer the Duke is about to hunt, and as such it strikes a note absent completely from Shakespeare's source, Lodge's *Rosalynde*. Duke Senior is saddened that the deer whose forest he occupies should be wounded and killed by the "forked heads" of their arrows.

The complex metaphoric structure of the Duke's lines, however, radically complicates this simple and powerful response. Although its burden is sympathy for the animal, the speech as a whole does not turn the Duke into a vegetarian or prevent the hunt. Instead, it represents a series of strategies, at once rhetorical and psychological, to repress the disturbing consequences of the Duke's twinge of conscience. The Duke begins with the antiseptic desire to "kill" some "venison," ignoring the fact that between killing and venison must come violent death and butchering; to kill a steak is to evade the moral consequences of one's action. The use of the word "venison" is even more evasive in Elizabethan English than it would be in modern English because the word was used of any wild meat and was only gradually coming to be restricted to the meat of deer. To kill venison is not to enact the Duke's own philosophy, in which the cold and winter's wind "feelingly persuade me what I am" (2.1.11).

The Duke's instinctive evasiveness, however, lasts only a moment; he is immediately stricken by the thought of the "poor dappled fools" he is about to pursue. The word "fool" is a term of endearment used often with great emotional power by Shakespeare, as in King Lear's "My poor fool is dead"; the image of deer as fools, as we shall see, recurs through-out the play. In Duke Senior's speech, the image not only humanizes the deer but associates it with the innocence and closeness to God of the "natural" fool, whose motley is hinted at in the dappling of the deer's coat. To pursue the implications of this metaphor, however, would end the hunt altogether: one does not kill helpless and innocent fools. In the space of two lines, it seems, the Duke has veered from a total indifference to the brutalities of the hunt to a sentimentality that threatens hunting itself.

In the next line, however, the Duke re-conceives the image. This time the deer become not fools but "native burghers," a term that subtly works against the incipient sentimentality of "fools," evoking as it does a hint of social condescension: the social, intellectual and emotional relationship between Dukes and fools, who might be their daily compan-ions and critics, is potentially closer than that between Dukes and bur-ghers, who are their distant subjects. To say, moreover, that either burghers or deer live in "their own confines" is to ignore the social real-ities of the burghers' political dependency upon Dukes and the deers' dependency, in Elizabethan England, upon protected reserves. The metaphoric identification of the deer in their forest with burghers in their native "city" creates a complicated series of overlapping images in the final lines of the Duke's speech. The most obvious way to read the lines, one promoted by most editors, is to interpret the "forked heads" as forked arrows (which were common in the period) and to imagine deer wounded in the haunches – a kind of wounding, as A. Stuart Daley sug-gests, that would almost inevitably cause a very painful death.[32] Since haunches were never a target in hunting, however, and since they are among the more desirable cuts of venison, it is possible that the Duke is jumping ahead again to the meal itself, envisaging his court using forks to feed themselves on venison. A third possibility, unlikely in the context but recommended by a number of critics, turns the violence against the deer themselves, their antlers goring the haunches of their opponents, as in the rutting season. A final possibility, difficult to justify in relation to the Duke's psychology but linguistically persuasive, is to see in the image a sly and familiar sexual innuendo, whereby the "burghers" become cuckolds, their forked heads produced by the "goring" of their wives' haunches.

The tendency of most editors and critics, of course, is to reduce this proliferation of meanings. At some level, however, they are all evoked by the language of the passage itself. If allowed full scope, the complex resonances that result enable us to appreciate how a sensitive moral being like the Duke can evade the moral consequences of the hunt. If suffering deer cannot be dismissed as venison or sentimentalized as "fools," they can be sympathetically distanced as "burghers." By the alchemy of the metaphor of "forked heads," moreover, Shakespeare implicates both society and nature in a cycle of violence that, although it might "irk" our sensitive spirits, seems inevitable. Deer are gored by hunters' arrows, yet that goring produces sustenance for humans, who use forks to gore them yet again. Burghers' wives are gored by illicit lovers, providing forked heads for the husbands, yet illicit sex is a potentially creative act and an inevitable fact of life. The deer themselves gore each other in the rutting season, an action that joins together the creativity of sex with violent aggression and potential death. To see ourselves feelingly what we are, it seems, is to locate ourselves within these paradoxes – paradoxes that join human with animal life. Although "irked" by animal suffering, in short, the Duke accepts it, as he does the other facts of life that persuade him feelingly what he is.

Jaques, as we shall see, does not accept animal suffering. Before his moralizing is reported, however, the First Lord responds in his own way to Duke Senior's words, painting a picture of a scene that he himself observed. As Jaques was lying beside a brook and underneath an ancient oak, the Lord says,

> a poor sequest'red stag,
> That from the hunter's aim had ta'en a hurt,
> Did come to languish; and indeed, my lord,
> The wretched animal heav'd forth such groans
> That their discharge did stretch his leathern coat
> Almost to bursting, and the big round tears

> Cours'd one another down his innocent nose
> In piteous chase; and thus the hairy fool,
> Much marked of the melancholy Jaques,
> Stood on th'extremest verge of the swift brook,
> Augmenting it with tears. (2.1.33–43)

This is the closest one comes in the play, and perhaps in Shakespeare as a whole, to the shock of empathy evoked by Gascoigne's poetic adoption of the voice of a hart in the *Noble Arte of Venerie* or Durer's drawing of the mournful head of a stag, pierced by an arrow.[33] As Linda Woodbridge observes, the passage contains the "seeds of an animal rights argument."[34] The image achieves its emotional effect in part through dramatic shifts in focus. We see first the "hunter's aim" and the generalized languishing it causes. Then we move imaginatively inside the suffering, experiencing it through the minutely observed details of the loud groans, the bursting coat, and the tears coursing down the nose. Finally, we stand back to view the scene as a whole – Jaques' melancholy attention, the swift brook, the weeping deer – as an all-encompassing image of grief.

As in the case of Duke Senior's lines, however, the images of the First Lord evoke a more complex and less potentially sentimental experience than pure empathy for a suffering animal. In some respects, indeed, the First Lord's language works against the elemental experience of an animal's pain at the hands of a hunter, encouraging us to perceive such suffering as an inevitable fact of life, not as the simple result of a violent assault. The First Lord's view of the stag, for example, is anthropomorphic. The stag is first "sequest'red," a word that may mean "removed from office" as well as "cut off from congenial surroundings." Like a man, it wears a "leathern coat" and is likened to a "hairy fool," one that, like Touchstone, is "Much marked of the melancholy Jaques" (2.1.41). The suffering deer thus becomes in certain respects not only a suffering human but, as was the case in Duke Senior's lines, an endearingly innocent human, a fool, and perhaps even a fool wearing an animal skin, as was the custom in folk-dances and folk-plays of the period. The human responsible for the actual grief of the deer, in contrast, is virtually invisible and harmless. It is not that he has wounded the deer, but that the stag has "ta'en a hurt" from "the hunter's aim." The stag itself is therefore complicit in its own wounding, which is occasioned not by the hunter but by his disembodied "aim." Underlying the First Lord's sympathy, then, is an apparent evasion both of human violence and of animal suffering: the "aim" causes wounding, and the pain that results can only be imagined in human terms, as the innocent suffering of a "fool." The sympathy experienced for a deer wounded by an attacking hunter is paradoxically evoked as sympathy for innocent humanity.

The First Lord's sentiments ultimately imply not only the innocence of humanity but the guilt of nature. In "taking" the hunter's aim, as we have seen, the stag itself seems complicit in its own undoing. The deer is "sequest'red," moreover, as the lines later attributed to Jaques make clear, not because it has been singled out by the hunter but because it has been abandoned by the other deer. The grief of the deer itself, moreover, implies a world of inner violence, with groans "discharge[d]" and even tears themselves as hunters: they "Cours'd one another down his innocent nose / In piteous chase." Having pursued each other as dogs pursue a hare, the tears flow into a brook which is not only "swift" but, as depicted earlier by the First Lord, violent: it "brawls along this wood" (32). If we look for the cause of this stag's suffering in human action, then, we look in vain. Its suffering arouses genuine human grief – the First Lord is no hypocrite – but implicit in that grief is a view that paradoxically juxtaposes images of human innocence with natural violence.

The natural violence, however, is also paradoxically human violence. The images we have examined, after all, are human images – of sequestering, of discharging, of coursing, of brawling. So although these images locate violence within the world of nature, they confuse that world with the world of man. In the same way one can say that the image of the fool, especially that of a "hairy" fool, is a liminal image, one that occupies the ambiguous borderland between the human and the animal.

One may be tempted simply to call such thinking anthropomorphic, and to find in it a "colonizing" and assimilationist mentality. In part, this is true. Despite the instinctive sympathy of Duke Senior and the First Lord for the animals that they kill, the language of both shows that they can only feel animal suffering when it is imagined as human suffering, a response that might be said to deny the reality and authenticity of animal experience. The guilt of human violence against innocent nature, moreover, is unconsciously evaded by minimizing human agency and imputing violence to nature itself – in its "brawling" brooks, its "coursing" tears, its "forked heads." The evasion circles back upon itself, however, for the very violence attributed to nature is only capable of articulation in human terms – only humans brawl, course, or make forked implements. The anthropomorphism, in short, has a double effect: on the one hand, it assimilates animal experience into human experience, but on the other, it assimilates human into animal experience. If deer are like humans, humans are also like deer. Both have a capacity for violence, and both have a capacity for suffering.

The central imaginative link between the two realms is provided by the image of the "natural" fool, an image that conveys a mysterious innocence existing at the boundary between man and nature. With the image of the "natural," the tendency to humanize nature becomes indistinguishable from the tendency to naturalize humanity. The figure of the fool defies categorization, calling in question the conventional distinctions between human and animal that neutralize the violence of the hunt. In their focus on the figure of the fool, both passages suggest a new way of thinking about the human relationship with nature, one that, in its paradoxical inclusion of innocence and violence, resists the extremes of indifference or sentimentality. The implied attitude seems similar to that expressed by the modern philosopher, Ortega y Gasset, who observes that *"every good hunter is uneasy in the depths of his conscience when faced with the death he is about to inflict on the enchanting animal"* because "man has never really known exactly what an animal is."[35] The language of Duke Senior and the First Lord captures this indeterminacy.

Whereas the responses of Duke Senior and the First Lord implicitly sanction the very activity that "irks" them by creating a vision of the entire social and natural world as participating in violence, that of Jaques (44–66) is altogether more disturbing. At first, this seems not to be the case. The "moralizings" that the First Lord reports are entirely conventional and emblematic, each image of the deer representing a particular human vice or folly. The deer makes its "testament" as "worldlings" do, bequeathing its tears to a stream that needs no more water. The treatment of a deer's death as a funeral is itself conventional, as P. J. Frankis has shown, citing examples from Drayton and Sidney and the medieval lyric *The testament of the bucke*.[36] The deer's loneliness enacts a familiar proverb: "'thus misery doth part / The flux of company.'" And the sight of a well-fed and "careless herd" passing by indifferently provokes thoughts of those "fat and greasy citizens" who ignore a "poor and broken bankrupt." In one sense, these anthropomorphic images can be said to work reciprocally, as do those of Duke Senior and the First Lord: if the deer are imbued with human motivations and behavior, such as the indifference to suffering of "fat and greasy citizens," then these same citizens are acting like deer. Jaques' emphasis on folly and vice might be said to complement and extend the emphasis on physical violence provided by Duke Senior and the First Lord. The interwining of society and nature implied in each of these visions is captured in the

First Lord's comment that Jaques' moralizings "pierceth through / The body of [the] country, city, court, / Yea, and of this our life." For Jaques, it seems, there are no distinctions: folly, vice, and misery unite the entire body of our life.

Despite its tendency to complement and extend the vision of Duke Senior and the First Lord, Jaques' moralizing is as a whole more paradoxical and disturbing than the compassion of the other two. Although the implications of his emblems are potentially reciprocal, as we have seen, characterizing both the human and the natural world in the same terms, their conventional quality distracts attention from the animal itself. In contrast to Duke Senior and the First Lord, whose images rely on precise observation of nature and a mysterious and vital likeness between animal and human experience, Jaques seems not to see the animals at all but to look through them at the underlying folly and misery of human experience. The deer serve merely as emblems for human behavior. His moralizing does not break out of the tradition of the beast fables or the emblem books. Such detachment is itself implicated in violence by the language of the First Lord, who notes that "most invectively" Jaques "pierceth through . . . the body . . . of this our life." Like the forked arrows of the hunters, Jaques' invectives work to destroy their targets.

One may see in Jaques' conventional moralizing, then, tendencies noted by many critics in general interpretations of his character – tendencies towards conventional posturing, indifference to genuine suffering, and a reductive and aggressive cynicism. His melancholy moralizing can thus be dismissed as mere self-indulgence. The First Lord's description of this melancholy scene does not end with Jaques' moralizings, however, but with his final assault on humanity and a final image of his behavior. The climax of the episode comes with Jaques' attack on the tyranny of their own life in the wilderness. In the report of the First Lord, Jaques swears

> that we
> Are mere usurpers, tyrants, and what's worse,
> To fright the animals and to kill them up
> In their assign'd and native dwelling-place.   (60–63)

If Jaques' conventional emblems distract from animal suffering, focusing instead upon the follies of human life in society, this final statement confronts us not only with the reality of animal suffering but with the fact of human responsibility. The evasiveness in the responses of Duke

Senior and the First Lord is here replaced by an unequivocal moral judgment.

This judgment, moreover, is joined with feeling. Our final image of Jaques is of him "weeping and commenting / Upon the sobbing deer" (65–66). Although there is much in Jaques' behavior throughout the play that suggests self-indulgent posturing, in his contemplation of the stag, as the First Lord makes clear, Jaques believes himself to be alone. Overall, then, Jaques' response to the sobbing deer seems contradictory. On the one hand his conventional moralizing seems to reflect at best an indifference to animal suffering, as such, or at worst a cynicism that unites the whole world, humans and animals, in folly, vice, and misery; empathy for the animal is precluded in either case. On the other hand, his unequivocal attack on human tyranny and his own weeping upon the sobbing deer suggest a deep emotional identification with the animal, based upon a split between human evil and animal innocence.

With this final and disturbing image of the stag as innocent victim of human tyranny, the episode comes to an end. The implications of Jaques' moralizing and weeping are left suspended. Instead of pursuing the questions raised by Jaques' emotional attack on human tyranny, the Duke merely dismisses them as amusing symptoms of his melancholy. "I love to cope him in these sullen fits," he says, "For then he's full of matter" (68–69). The Duke is thus distracted from his earlier desire to "go and kill us venison," but only because he prefers the amusement of the melancholy Jaques. He is utterly unmoved by the scene that the First Lord has painted before him. The violence of the hunt will continue to "irk" him, presumably, but not enough to abandon hunting or to think deeply about its human significance. Duke Senior, like Jaques, has a fondness for moralizing. Unlike Jaques, however, he not only finds "tongues in trees, books in the running brooks," and "sermons in stones," but "good in every thing" (16–17).

Amiens admires Duke Senior's optimism. "Happy is your Grace," he says, "That can translate the stubbornness of fortune / Into so quiet and so sweet a style" (18–20). The lines are richly evocative and might be taken as a comment on the action of the play itself – Shakespeare translating the misfortunes of his characters into the quiet and sweet style of a redemptive pastoral. The peculiar dangers of this kind of translation are evasiveness and sentimentality, just as those of Jaques' translations are cynicism and self-indulgence. If in writing *As You Like It* Shakespeare set about translating the stubbornness of fortune into the quiet and sweet style of redemptive pastoral, he deliberately complicated his task not by including villains – they are easily converted – but by including Jaques and Touchstone, who resist conversion and are neither quiet nor sweet. Neither character appears in Shakespeare's source, Lodge's *Rosalynde.* He also complicated his vision of pastoral, as we have seen in the image of the sobbing deer, not only by including the hunt but by highlighting through Jaques its violation of the bond between humans and nature. The resonance of Jaques' image of tyranny never quite goes away – Shakespeare admits the untranslatable – but for the most part Shakespeare's treatment of the hunt follows that of Duke Senior himself. He translates the violence of the hunt into a quiet and sweet style of pastoral. Shakespeare's treatment of hunting throughout the play can be seen as a complex series of negotiations to overcome indirectly the irreconcilable conflict that Jaques depicts between human morality and the hunt. In one sense, we may say that these constitute a series of evasions, strategies that render the culpable innocuous. If they are evasions, however, they are knowing evasions, for they are prompted by Shakespeare's own decision to thrust the issue of the hunt into the limelight. Neither Jaques nor an anti-hunting perspective exists in his source, Lodge's *Rosalynde.* These evasions characterize not only Shakespeare's treatment of the elemental violence of the hunt itself but of the controversies surrounding the hunt in the period.

Perhaps the most obvious way in which Shakespeare counteracts Jaques' conviction of human tyranny is by representing the Duke's hunting as a necessity, forced upon him and his men by their exile in Arden. Despite the Duke's rather suspicious zest – "Come, shall we go and kill us venison?" – he and his men kill not for pleasure but to live. And yet it still "irks" them. In the dominant hunting culture in the period, of course, hunting "for the pot" was treated with contempt. Hunting was a recreation, a sport, to be justified for its promotion of warlike virtues. Its aristocratic and noble character, indeed, could only be justified if it were divorced from any contact with mercenary or domestic gain. From the perspective of the royal and aristocratic sport of hunting, Jaques' critique is difficult to answer, and the humanist tradition of opposition to aristocratic hunting as leading to war and tyranny depended upon that difficulty. From the perspective of simple human survival, however, Jaques' anti-hunting sentiments seem merely silly and Duke Senior's hunting easily defensible, with or without the moral qualms that continue to "irk" him. Whether Duke Senior will resume hunting for pleasure once restored to his dukedom is a question Shakespeare leaves unanswered.

For Elizabethans sensitive to the controversies surrounding hunting, Shakespeare's portrait of aristocrats hunting for necessity would have had a special impact. His allusions to hunting throughout the play, indeed, seem calculated to remind his audience of the conventions of aristocratic hunting by overturning them. As Daley has shown, for example, the Duke does not engage in aristocratic *par force* hunting, associated with the recreational and "military" hunt, but in stalking with the bow and arrow, a humbler kind of hunting, necessary in exile.[37]

The same ironic inversion of hunting conventions underlies Shakespeare's representation of the Duke's "banquet." In Lodge, this is an opulent affair. The banished King, Gerismond, "that day in honour of his Birth made a Feast to all his bolde yeomen, and frolickt it with store of wine and venison, sitting all at a long table under the shadowe of lymon trees."[38] In Shakespeare the proximity of the "banquet" to the discussion of the hunt links it to the customary "assembly" held at the beginning of a hunt, celebrated in hunting manuals such as Gascoigne's *Noble Arte of Venerie* and in tapestries such as *Les Chasses de Maximilien*. The feasting at such assemblies, as depicted in these works, was astonishingly opulent and required the immense logistical support necessary to bring tables, viands, cooking implements, and wines into a forest glade. The depiction in the *Arte of Venerie* of Queen Elizabeth attending such a picnic captures the ambiance of such events (fig. 2). Although such affairs may seem "pastoral" in design, they connote less a harmony between civilization and nature than an invasion of nature by civilization. In *As You Like It*, in contrast, the word "banquet" is ironically intended, and the simple repast of fruit stands in opposition to the elaborate picnics conventionally associated with the culture of the hunt. The contrasting significance of the two kinds of banquet is also apparent in their social function. The traditional assembly joins the hunters together to select their prey and to plan the method of pursuit. For Orlando, however, the Duke's "banquet" is a means of nurturing Adam, and his language calls attention to the difference between such banqueting and the traditional hunters' feast:

> Then but forbear your food a little while,
> Whiles, like a doe, I go to find my fawn,
> And give it food.   (2.7.127–29)

This same tendency to soften or "pastoralize" the customs of the contemporary hunt characterizes the brief depiction of a return from the hunt in act 4 scene 2. The procession that takes place in this scene is based upon the actual practice of the hunt, which traditionally culminated in a ceremonial return to the home or lodge of the chief lord. The leader of the procession would have been the lord of the hunt or a surrogate. The head of the deer would have been carried at the front of the procession, the deer's carcass, in sections, carried behind. Although there is no conclusive evidence to show that songs were sung, the practice is highly likely, and one can assume as well an atmosphere of festive merriment; whether the chief hunter would have worn the skin of the deer, as is done in this case and in many of the folk customs, is uncertain. The arrival home was announced by the sound of the hunters' horns, and the day was ended, traditionally, with a feast. Jaques' characterization of the event as a triumphal procession seems to capture its spirit. In Munday's *The Death of Robert, Earl of Huntington,* Friar Tuck carries "*a Stag's head, dauncing,*" as part of a procession returning from a hunt in which a stag wearing Caesar's collar has been killed.[39] Although both Shakespeare and Munday allude to actual hunting behavior, both episodes may also incorporate closely related folk customs, such as the Horn Dance of Abbots Bromley, or the festive procession led by a buck's head to honor the feast of St. Paul at St. Paul's Cathedral.[40]

In transposing the return from the hunt to the stage in act 4 scene 2, Shakespeare retains its processional and festive nature, yet evokes complex overtones that almost certainly go beyond the original custom. For one thing, the event is directed by Jaques, who has not participated in the hunt and who has been described earlier, as we have seen, weeping over the fate of a wounded deer. Jaques' comments, therefore, although not opposed to the celebration, place it in an ironical framework. The irony is extended by an apparent allusion to Elyot's treatment of hunting in *The Governor*. Elyot recommends only the kind of hunting that comes closest to imitating war. In this spirit, he urges upon hunters a ceremony imitating that of the Roman conquerors. Those who "show most prowess and activity" in such warlike hunting, he says, should be given "a garland or some other like token . . . in sign of victory, and with a joyful manner . . . be brought in the presence of him that is chief in the company; there to receive condign praise for their good endeavour."[41] Jaques' directions mock this attitude. He instructs the hunters that the forester who killed the deer be presented "to the Duke like a Roman conqueror," with the "deer's horns [set] upon his head, for a branch of victory." The conventional view of the hunt as a training ground for the skills of war is thus undermined by Jaques in the bathetic contrast between Roman conqueror and killer of deer. The inescapable association of the deer's horns with those of the cuckold, moreover, convert this image of conquest into an image of sexual impotence. Jaques' final subversive gesture is to dismiss the hunters' song as mere noise: "Sing it. 'Tis no matter how it be in tune, so it make noise enough" (8–9). The celebration of the hunt is thus framed by a sardonic debunking of the whole endeavor. Although he does not weep over the body of this deer, Jaques remains deeply alienated from the idea of the hunt and contemptuous of the hunters themselves. For audiences, Jaques' framing comments are difficult to reconcile, emotionally or intellectually, with the festive spectacle that ensues.

The representation of the hunters' song depends upon an existing custom, as is made clear by Jaques' request, "Have you no song, forester, for this purpose?" No songs of this type survive, however, and extensive work by editors and musicologists has failed to identify a source for the one performed on stage. The song may well be Shakespeare's invention. In the First Folio, it reads as follows:

> What shall he have that kild the Deare?
> His Leather skin, and hornes to weare:
> Then sing him home, the rest shall beare this burthen;
> Take thou no scorne to weare the horne,
> It was a crest ere thou wast borne,
> Thy fathers father wore it,
> And thy father bore it,
> The horne, the horne, the lusty horne,
> Is not a thing to laugh to scorne.   (4.2)

I quote the version in the First Folio because there has been considerable debate among editors about the clause "the rest shall beare this burthen" in the third line. Some take it as part of the song, an implied stage direction indicating that, while the victorious hunter wears the horns, the rest will carry the burden of the slaughtered deer. Others, including the Riverside editors, detach it from the text of the song, treating it as a stage direction requiring the rest of the hunters to sing the ensuing "burden," or refrain. Whichever meaning one chooses, the total context of the scene suggests a single action: the victorious hunter, wearing the horns of the deer, and even its skin, leads a triumphant and merry procession of hunters singing a traditional song.

Although the song centers upon the inevitable joke on cuckoldry, the performance as a whole works against Jaques' corrosive debunkery of the hunt in several ways. In the song's version of the triumph, the victorious hunter is given not only the horns to wear but the "leather skin."

Such a costume works against Jaques' mockery of the "Roman conqueror," evoking instead the popular festivities, such as the charivari or
horn dance, in which the figure of the deer can represent not only cuckoldry but virility. This image of the deer, indeed, might be said to reconcile Jaques' conflicting images of contempt, the Roman conqueror and
the cuckold, bringing the two paradoxically together in a festive assertion of man's union with nature: in his identification with the deer, the
hero is at once conqueror and victim, cuckolder and cuckold. The horns
of the cuckold themselves enact this paradox, of course, for they represent both the phallic power of the seducer and the impotency of the
deceived husband. The allusion to the "leather skin," moreover, suggests
the material necessity that underlies this particular hunt; the skin worn
in dance as a costume will be eventually worn as clothing, perhaps even
as the "leathern coat" alluded to earlier in the First Lord's image of the
wounded stag:

> The wretched animal heav'd forth such groans
> That their discharge did stretch his leathern coat
> Almost to bursting . . .   (2.1.36–38)

The costume of the skin, moreover, relates the episode to such folk traditions as the Plough Plays, in which the Fool figure was often a leader
and wore a coat of skins. As we have already seen, in the earlier description of the wounded deer this "leathern coat" links the deer to the figure
of the fool. The image of the leader cavorting as a deer thus implies not
only the triumph of the hunt but a sympathetic identification with the
animal itself. Both hunter and deer are "fools" in "leathern coats."

Similarly, the equivocal directions, "the rest shall beare this burthen,"
can be seen as a gesture of reconciliation. If read as printed in the First
Folio, as part of the song rather than as a separable stage direction, the
clause can fulfill both of the functions that editors usually treat as mutu-
ally exclusive alternatives. The opening singer, the Second Lord, can
direct the message to the rest of the Lords, who both carry the carcass
of the deer and join in the refrain that follows. In such a case, the physical burden – and perhaps even the moral burden – imposed upon the
hunters by the kill is relieved by the singing of the song, as is customary
in work-songs. Music, then, becomes another reconciler of conflict – the
reality of the deer's death and the burden it imposes translated into
harmony. In this sense the ritual progression of the hunt achieves the
same effect as the ritual progression of the couples at the end of the play:

in both cases tensions and discords are momentarily suspended in the reconciling medium of music.

The words of the "burden" are themselves devoted to reconciliation and acceptance of one's place in nature. The hunter who wears the deer's horn, along with men in general, is offered the consolation that it is "no scorn to wear the horn," a sentiment that answers Jaques' earlier contempt. The horn is an emblem of the male condition, a "crest" that is passed down through each patriarchal generation and must be accepted and worn with grace; it makes men a part of nature. Even in these lines, which focus so insistently on the lamentable fact of cuckoldry, the alternative symbolism of the horn emerges at the end: "the lusty horn / Is not a thing to laugh to scorn." The "crest" is thus an ambiguous one, representing both impotency and sexual virility. It is worn by the best hunter of the day.

As already mentioned, it is difficult to relate this scene precisely to the custom of the procession homeward because the social evidence is so scanty. Examined in its own terms, the dramatic episode might be said to continue the evasive strategies outlined earlier, and to continue to place them in irreconcilable conflict with Jaques' anti-hunting perspective. The entire thrust of the song and procession, one might say, is to harmonize man and nature, to "pastoralize" the hunt, even at a moment which celebrates the bloody triumph of man over nature. The "burden" of guilt is lifted in song. The carcass of the deer is in full view, its skin and horns worn as trophies of victory. Yet these trophies are not for mere display but for use; in the context of exile, they fulfill essential human needs. And they are worn not merely as emblems of victory but as acknowledgments of a union between man and animal – one that encompasses both sexual power and sexual powerlessness. The entire thrust of the song and procession, in short, is to convert what for Jaques is discordant "noise" into harmony. Although the Duke is not present at the song, he is the ultimate goal of the procession, and its spirit seems to capture his own response to the natural elements, as forces that "'feelingly persuade me what I am'" (2.1.11). In this "pastoralizing" of the hunt, it seems to me, Shakespeare avoids sentimentality but continuously evades, even while representing it, the radical threat embodied in Jaques' alternative vision. This is not hunting without blood, but it is nonetheless hunting "as you like it."

In representing life as we like it, then, Shakespeare slides away from the social and political conflict that the inclusion of hunting within the pastoral invited. The only way in which he engages in the contemporary controversies surrounding hunting and the forests is through the Duke's discomfort with and Jaques' emotional protest against the killing of deer. Including hunting within the pastoral is most tellingly difficult for Shakespeare because it evokes the essential problem in the human relationship with nature, a problem evaded by conventional pastoral, that of violent and murderous conflict. The dilemma for the pastoral represented by this conflict is left unresolved, insofar as Jaques remains unchanged and unsocialized at the end of the play, determined merely to seek wisdom of an old hermit who lives in Arden rather than to return to the court.

Although Shakespeare allows Jaques' pessimistic vision of the tyranny of man over nature to haunt the play, he nonetheless, through Duke Senior, the First Lord, the song of the huntsmen, and, implicitly, through Orlando, presents a vision of the hunt that ties human and animal life together in bonds that include both violence and kindness. As we have seen, this unsentimental but tolerant and accepting vision of reciprocity is expressed in a number of different ways in the representation of the hunt. Perhaps its most significant emblem, however, is that of Orlando's heroic action both in putting aside his desire for vengeance against his wicked brother, Oliver, and in killing the lioness that threatens his brother's life (4.3.104–32). As Richard Knowles has shown, the episode almost certainly alludes to Hercules's killing of the Nemean lion, and in this sense celebrates the heroism of Orlando.[42] The contrast between the Nemean lion, however, and the beast that threatens Oliver, is striking: the one is large, violently aggressive, and male; the other is a "sucked and hungry lioness" (126), with "udders all drawn dry" (114) – a female that needs food because it has been suckling its cubs. In this small episode Shakespeare achieves a complex and unsentimental awareness of the animal and human worlds as implicated in both nurturing and killing.

Both Orlando and the lioness are engaged in a protective and nurturing action – the one to save the life of his brother, the other to save the life of its cubs. Yet for both creatures this benign and "kindly" purpose requires killing. Orlando, we might say, saves his brother through exalted reason, whereas the animal tries to feed its young through mere instinct. But the two actions are balanced in such a way that distinguishing them becomes difficult. Even Oliver, who has been saved from the lioness, refers not to its murderous instinct but to the "royal disposition" that leads it to "prey on nothing that doth seem as dead" (117–18). We might apply to the episode Montaigne's challenge to human arrogance in the

Apology for Raymond Sebond: "there is no likely-hood, we should imagine, that beastes doe the very same things by a naturall inclination, and forced genuitie, which we doe of our owne free-wil and industrie. Of the very same effects we must conclude alike faculties; and by the richest effects infer the noblest faculties, and consequently acknowledge, that the same discourse and way, wee hold in working, the very same, or per-happes some other better, doe beasts hold."[43] Even the "green and gilded snake" of this scene suggests, in its union of natural and courtly symbols, a commingling of human and natural life that includes on both sides beauty and danger.

The breaking down of boundaries between human and animal life implied in Shakespeare's language of the hunt throughout *As You Like It* may derive in part from Shakespeare's continuing fascination with Ovid, whose descriptions of metamorphoses embody a materialist conception of the underlying unity of all of nature. The "recurring materialist theme of the *Metamorphoses*," as Robert Pogue Harrison observes, is the "preformal kinship of all creation, which enables human beings to be transformed into animals, trees, flowers, and other forest phenomena."[44] Whether Shakespeare's vision is materialist in any but a superficial sense is of course doubtful. But the depth and intricacy of his metaphoric rela-tions between animals and humans in *As You Like It* can hardly be explained in merely linguistic terms. The metaphoric relations between human and animal in Shakespeare are also metamorphic. A deer is like a man in wearing a leathern coat, and a man is like a deer in wearing one as well, and in folk festivals a man may become a deer by wearing the deer's leathern coat, which is no more than a skin. Even Jaques' opposition to hunting has an Ovidean precedent, for in Book 15 of the *Metamorphoses* Pythagoras inveighs at length against the killing and eating of animals.

Although Shakespeare shies away from the political and social conflict potentially embodied in the hunt, he thus engages directly the debate about man's relation to nature as it figured in conceptions of the hunt. He uses the image of the hunt to challenge the sentimental idealism that often characterizes conventional pastoral and the greenworld motif. He uses it as well to challenge implicitly the notion of hunting for sport. More subtly and ambivalently, he uses it to underline, through Jaques' sentimental extremism, the moral dilemma posed by the human depen-dence upon animal food. Although the play as a whole implies an accep-tance of man's role as a killer, it does so, as we have seen, by implying a mutuality in the relationship between man and nature. In so doing,

Shakespeare breaks down the boundaries erected between human and animal life by the conventional Christianity of his day, which easily justified animal suffering and death, even in sport, on the ground that the Bible gives humans lordship over the animals, and that God provides only humans with immortal souls. Shakespeare's blurring of these boundaries carries to an extreme tendencies implicit in the metaphoric linkage of animal and human life that runs throughout the Western tradition. Although Shakespeare does not give the deer a literal voice, as does Gascoigne in the *Arte of Venerie*, his metaphors imply a community among humans and animals rarely to be found in conventional Elizabethan Christianity.

This new attitude towards animal suffering bears a remarkable affinity to that expressed by Montaigne in the essay "Of Cruelty." "As for me," Montaigne remarks, "I could never so much as endure, without remorce and griefe, to see a poore, silly, and innocent beast pursued and killed, which is harmeles and voide of defence, and of whom we receive no offence at all." The example he uses to illustrate his distress is, as in Shakespeare, a weeping deer – a stag that, exhausted from the chase, "findes his strength to faile-him," and, "having no other remedie left him, doth yeelde and bequeath himself unto us that pursue him, with teares suing to us for mercie." When he considers "the neere resemblance betweene us and beastes," he says, "truely I abate much of our presumption, and am easily removed from that imaginary Soveraigntie, that some give and ascribe unto us above all other creatures." "*Unto men we owe Justice,*" he concludes, "*and to all other creatures, that are capable of it, grace and benignitie.* There is a kinde of enter-changeable commerce, and mutuall bond betweene them and us."[45]

In its depiction of hunting, *As You Like It* may be called a politically evasive play, subversive only in the offhand dismissiveness of its title, which suggests that the playwright offers us the evasions we enjoy, knowing full well that real forests offer other visions. In contrast, however, it may be called an ecologically progressive play, one that by introducing the hunt into the pastoral world implicitly criticizes hunting for sport, and accepts hunting for necessity only if it involves a reverence for life and recognition of all the bonds that tie animals and humans together. The complex metaphoric relationships between humans and animals that characterize Shakespeare's treatment of the hunt throughout the play provide an experiential grounding for Montaigne's belief in "a kinde of enter-changeable commerce, and mutuall bond betweene them and us." Although progressive in its own time, this belief would be undermined in the late seventeenth century by Cartesian rationalism, which denied not only reason to animals but feelings and sensations.[46]

In his treatment of what might be called the ecology of pastoral hunting, Shakespeare develops a hard-edged or unsentimental vision of the hunt by creating images of harmony between the human and natural world that implicate both in the destructive and creative paradoxes of mortal experience. Such a vision of the hunt carries with it an implicit social critique. In *As You Like It*, pastoral hunting implies not only opposition to the culture of hunting for sport but, as in Montaigne, the need for a new attitude of sympathy and respect for wild nature. In Jaques' uncompromising extremism, furthermore, Shakespeare provides a haunting reminder that even such a benign and progressive attitude as Montaigne's cannot disguise the fundamental and always disturbing fact that humans kill in order to live. By challenging the traditional culture of the hunt and the attitude towards nature that sustained it, Shakespeare achieves a measure of social disturbance even while offering a vision of the world as we like it.

CHAPTER SEVEN

Political hunting: Prospero and James I

In act 4 scene 1 of *The Tempest* Prospero celebrates the betrothal of Ferdinand and Miranda with "some vanity" of his "art" (41), a masque presided over by Juno, the goddess of marriage, and Ceres, the goddess of the harvest. In the middle of the performance, however, he suddenly remembers the threat posed by Caliban, Stephano, and Trinculo, who are at this moment on their way to assassinate him and make themselves lords of the island. He abruptly breaks off the masque and, deeply troubled, tries to reassure Ferdinand and Miranda, who wonder at his altered state of mind. He then directs Ariel to trap the conspirators by tempting them with *"glistering apparel"* (193.s.d.), a ruse that easily distracts Stephano and Trinculo, much to Caliban's dismay. As they start to carry away their loot, the three conspirators are set upon by spirits, who, urged on by Prospero and Ariel, chase them away. The scene concludes at this point, with Prospero assuring Ariel that their labors are nearly at an end and that his promised freedom is imminent. At the beginning of the next scene, prompted by Ariel's sympathy for the suffering of his enemies, Prospero announces that he will turn away from vengeance, forgive his enemies, and renounce his magical art.

Prospero's chase of the conspirators is Shakespeare's final representation of the hunt:

> *A noise of hunters heard. Enter divers SPIRITS in shape of dogs and hounds, hunting*
> *them about; Prospero and Ariel setting them on.*
> *Pros.* Hey, Mountain, hey!
> *Ari.* Silver! there it goes, Silver!
> *Pros.* Fury, Fury! there, Tyrant, there! hark, hark!
>   [*Caliban, Stephano, and Trinculo are driven out.*]
> Go, charge my goblins that they grind their joints
> With dry convulsions, shorten up their sinews
> With aged cramps, and more pinch-spotted make them
> Than pard or cat o'mountain.

Ari   Hark, they roar!
Pros. Let them be hunted soundly. At this hour
Lies at my mercy all mine enemies.   (4.1.254–63)

Prospero orders the attack, with Ariel as chief huntsman. The lesser spirits are dogs, each with a distinctive name. The *"noise of hunters"* presumably includes the sound of the horn, the barking of the dogs, and the hallowing of the hunters themselves. Although the fierce confusion of the hunt is evoked in sound, language, and action, its ultimate goal, the death of the hunted, is in this instance deflected. Prospero orders the conspirators to be "hunted soundly," a phrase that suggests thrashing more than killing. His directions, moreover, extend to physical torment but not to death. While this restriction insulates the audience somewhat from the full implications of the action, it can have no such effect on Caliban, Stephano, and Trinculo, who hear behind them as they run the terrifying sound of dogs, horns, and hunters.

The masque scene in which this hunt occurs has received much attention from critics, as have the other obviously allegorical episodes in the play, such as the opening storm, the appearance of the harpies, and the game of chess played by Ferdinand and Miranda. For the most part, however, the significance of the hunt itself has been ignored. Why, we might ask, at this climactic moment in the play, should Prospero's final attack upon his enemies take the symbolic form of a hunt? Potential answers to this question will lead us in many directions – into the dynamics of the play itself, into Shakespeare's previous representations of the hunt, into conventional humanist attitudes towards the hunt, and into the politics of the hunt in the court of James I. Exploration of each of these contexts should ultimately convince us that Prospero's hunting of the conspirators is as rich and complex a symbol as any other that the play provides.

The most startling feature of Prospero's response to the threat posed by Caliban and his cohorts is its extremity. As soon as he remembers their plot, Prospero becomes so deeply moved that Miranda herself remarks, "Never till this day / Saw I him touch'd with anger, so distemper'd" (4.1.144–45). The melancholy vision of the "revels" speech leaves him unconsoled, his "old brain troubled" (159). And as he attends to Caliban, he thinks bitterly of his slave's degenerate and degenerating nature:

> A devil, a born devil, on whose nature
> Nurture can never stick; on whom my pains,

> Humanely taken, all, all lost, quite lost;
> And as with age his body uglier grows,
> So his mind cankers.   (188–92)

Prospero's response to such hopelessness is not despair but violent revenge: "I will plague them all, / Even to roaring" (192–93). The hunt, then, is presented not as a methodical plan, a corrective punishment, but as a spontaneous invention, a symptom of inner rage.

The violence of Prospero's reaction to the threat represented by the conspirators cannot be explained or justified in relation to the seriousness of the threat itself. Prospero is a great magician; Caliban, Stephano, and Trinculo are mere playthings of his art. Given Prospero's power, the rebellion should be a mere nuisance. If we are to explain Prospero's rage, therefore, we must consider not who these figures are but what their action represents. They are potential assassins and usurpers, and their attempt to seize power is the fourth such attempt to which the play alludes. Before the play begins, two usurpations have taken place: in Milan, Antonio usurped Prospero's position as Duke, and on the island, Prospero usurped Caliban's rightful title, at least according to Caliban. As the play proceeds, Prospero himself tempts Antonio and Sebastian into another plot of usurpation against Alonzo. The action of the conspirators, then, is part of the play's continuing exploration of the quest for political power. In the light of what seems an endless cycle of attempted usurpations, Prospero's rage against Caliban and his cohorts suggests his still unsuppressed fury against Antonio, whose usurpation initiated the cycle. In this sense it is less Caliban who angers him than the reality of usurpation itself, an implication that seems present in Prospero's juxtaposition of his punishment of Caliban with that of his other enemies: "Let them be hunted soundly. At this hour / Lies at my mercy all mine enemies."

Prospero's rage, however, is more deeply self-directed than this analysis suggests. The masque episode, as has often been observed, recapitulates symbolically the original action that caused the loss of Prospero's dukedom. In Milan, having devoted himself to the liberal arts, and having grown careless of his political role, Prospero made himself vulnerable to usurpation. For this he blames himself. By dedicating himself to the "bettering" of his mind, he tells Miranda, he "awak'd" in his "false brother . . . an evil nature" (1.2.90–93). Now, thirteen years later, having withdrawn again from his political responsibilities into "some vanity" of his "art" (4.1.41), an idealistic celebration of the future of Miranda and Ferdinand, he jeopardizes both them and himself by neglecting the danger of assassination and usurpation. Prospero's anger, then, is the anger of disillusionment, not only with Caliban, and by extension Antonio, but with himself. The price of political power, it seems, is constant vigilance, which he finds it impossible to maintain. Although Prospero recovers himself in time to avert the danger, the play's conclusion is sufficiently realistic to suggest the ongoing nature of the problem.

Such a reading of the masque scene as a whole can be accommodated to many of the various discourses within which the play has been interpreted. Prospero's dangerous tendency to lose himself in a world of art, to project upon experience his own conceptions, and to respond with impatience or vengeful rage when the world does not answer to his desires – this dynamic may be articulated in the language of art, of theater, of magic, of politics, of colonialism, and of paternity, to mention only the more common interpretative contexts. The multivalency of the play's language, indeed, creates a layering of complementary discourses, not all of which can be sustained by even the most expansive critical or theatrical interpretation.

Central to this interpretative complexity, and to any interpretation of the hunt, is Caliban, the history of whose representations suggests both the inevitability and falsity of reducing the play's proliferation of meanings. The figure has been as much constrained by critics and directors as by Prospero. Both on stage and in criticism he has been seen as, among other things, a native American, a monster, an animal, a devil, and a projection of the instinctual drives of Prospero himself.[1] Each of the above images has a certain validity, responds to something within the text, yet if applied consistently oversimplifies the role. Many of the discourses within which Caliban is defined are complementary, but not all: he cannot be played as both a native American and an animal, for example, yet the language of the play alludes to both roles. By its very nature, critical or theatrical interpretation tends to dissolve the essential mystery of the character.

The play invites us to imagine Caliban not in a fixed role but as a being who resists categorization, who inhabits the liminal realm between the human and bestial, both within the mind and in the world at large. As a liminal creature, he remains forever beyond our grasp: we cannot know who or what he is. He is at once essential to human survival and dangerous. He is both a human product and an autonomous being. He is responsive to beauty yet brutish in his instincts and behavior. He is capable of language but incapable, it seems, of "civilization." To hunt Caliban, then, is to hunt that which is irredeemably "other," beyond even Prospero's self-interested imaginings. To hunt Caliban, however, is also to hunt Stephano and Trinculo, who are refreshingly familiar and simply human. Any interpretation of Prospero's hunting, therefore, must begin with the fact that, whatever the identity of Caliban, the hunting is directed towards human subjects. The blurring of categories introduced by the figure of Caliban extends the gesture into the wider context of varying kinds and degrees of bestiality. To hunt the conspirators, it seems, is to hunt not only men but certain elements in both human and external nature.

To see in Prospero's rage against the conspirators not only an immediate response to the threat that they represent but a reflection of his rage towards Antonio, towards himself, towards all that resists the fulfillment of his imaginative desires, does not explain the particular image of the hunt. Prospero's desires for retribution take different symbolic forms throughout the play: he creates elsewhere a tempest, for example, and a banquet that vanishes in an onslaught of harpies. Why does his rage against Caliban and his confederates take the particular symbolic form of a hunt?

One obvious place to look for an answer to this question is in Shakespeare's own mythology of the hunt, a mythology that had evolved over a lifetime in the theater. As we have seen throughout this study, Shakespeare routinely links hunting to violence against humans, especially the violence of war, and most of his allusions to hunting in this context focus on savage and vengeful fury. Richard of Gloucester's furious desire to "hunt" young Clifford during the battle of Towton is typical: "Nay, Warwick, single out some other chase, / For I myself will hunt this wolf to death" (*3 Henry VI.* 2.4.12–13). Richard's gesture, of course, is not the same as Prospero's. Richard merely invokes an expressive metaphor, for one thing, whereas Prospero literalizes the metaphor by imitating an actual hunt. The goal of "hunters" such as Richard, moreover, is straightforward and literal: they seek to kill the human that they have redefined as prey. Prospero's response to Caliban may be similarly violent and furious, but he stops short of killing, seeking only to torment his victim. In this sense, there are no literal or exact precedents in Shakespeare for Prospero's action. Nonetheless, his hunt participates in a linkage of hunting, anger, and violence that runs throughout the plays.

Shakespeare uses hunting imagery not only to express the perspective of the hunter but of the prey. Sometimes such imagery connotes the rape of injured innocence, as in the case of Lucrece, Lavinia, and Lady

Macduff and her children. In others, it simply evokes the pathos of the helpless victim, whether innocent of wrongdoing or guilty: Julius Caesar, Falstaff, and Talbot are all like bayed stags when surrounded by those who want to kill or punish them. Even the hunting of vermin can occasion a flash of sympathetic identification, as when Lear tells Cordelia that "He that parts us shall bring a brand from heaven, / And fire us hence like foxes" (5.3.22–23). In view of the frequency of such images in Shakespeare, it is remarkable that there are no counter-examples, no instances in which the hunt is used simply as a metaphor of righteous pursuit, without an undercurrent of sympathy for the hunted that compromises the notion of just punishment.

In its association of the hunter with rage and violent assault, then, and with the hunted as a sympathetic victim, the chase of the conspirators in *The Tempest* might be considered a culmination of Shakespeare's negative representations of the sport. Prospero's attack is partly justified, of course, since the conspirators seek to kill him, but his anger propels him beyond rational justice into the sphere of violent revenge. In this regard the names of his dogs take on a precise significance – the one is Fury, the other Tyrant. As a symptom of Prospero's potentially dangerous aspirations towards transcendent power, the hunting episode is comparable to the speech in which he renounces his magic, which, by virtue of its allusions to the witchcraft of Medea, hints at the diabolic potential within his magic. The significance of both dramatic moments is not to undermine the value of Prospero's magic or, in the case of the hunting episode, to legitimize Caliban's desire to kill Prospero, but to call attention to Prospero's own inner potential to do harm. His renunciation of his magic follows upon his renunciation of revenge, which in turn follows upon the furious hunt of the conspirators. Before he returns to Milan, Prospero not only renounces his magic but acknowledges, if grudgingly, a bond with Caliban: "this thing of darkness I / Acknowledge mine" (5.1.275–76).

Shakespeare's treatment of the hunt in *The Tempest* is not merely self-referential; as in the case of the many other allegorical episodes in the play, it carries a wealth of conventional meaning. As we have seen in previous chapters, certain strands in both Reformation and humanist thought provide powerful critiques of hunting. One of these critiques focuses on the tendency of hunting to fuel violent behavior, to turn the very hunters themselves, as Erasmus's Folly observes, into savage beasts.[2] Such fury is often politicized, linking hunting to tyranny. In his commentaries on the Book of Genesis, for example, Calvin couples the notions of bestiality and tyranny and associates both with the Old Testament figure of Nimrod, "a mighty hunter before the Lord" (Genesis.10.9).[3] Both Sidney – in Philiside's song, "Ister Bank" – and Agrippa attack hunting as the historical origin of tyranny.[4] For Agrippa, contemporary kings, princes, and even prelates "doo seeke daily, to have some thinge to conquere, and hunte," turning their destructive instincts against both defenseless animals and humans.[5]

Agrippa's diatribe seems particularly relevant to *The Tempest* because of his unusual concern with hunting as an attack upon nature itself. Most writers in the anti-hunting tradition focus on the negative effect that hunting has upon humans: either upon the commoners who are victimized by the practice or upon the hunters who are brutalized. For Agrippa, however, to hunt is not merely to persecute humans but to "exercise tyranny againste beastes." It is "a cruell Arte, and altogeather tragicall, whose pleasure is in deathe, and bloude . . ." Many hunters, he observes, "have runne into so great madnesse, that they became enimies to nature."[6] Agrippa's advocacy of respect for nature, even bestial nature, provides a useful perspective on the role of Caliban and on the "rough magic" with which Prospero attempts to control nature.

At the end of his discourse on hunting, Agrippa recalls the condition of Eden, when humans and animals lived in tranquillity, disharmony beginning only with original sin: "And so, togeather with sinne, the anoyaunce, the persecution, and the flighte of livinge creatures entred in, and the Artes of Huntinge were devised."[7] This contrast between a brief age of innocence and a long and continuing history of hunting is also found in authors, like Ovid, who portray the degeneration of human history from the Golden to the Iron Age. Underlying both Agrippa's and Ovid's versions of the cruelty of the hunt is a notion of kinship between all living things, a kinship that has been violated historically in the falling away from a Golden Age or an Eden. A similar contrast between a peaceable kingdom and perpetual conflict also underlies the sudden shift in *The Tempest* away from the idealized vision of natural harmony represented by Iris, Ceres, and Juno to the fury of Prospero's hunt. It is as if we plunge in one moment from a golden to an iron age. And in the same moment we replace an image of Prospero as a benign and even godlike ruler with Prospero as a furious tyrant.

Given our inevitable anthropocentrism, the image of Prospero hunting the conspirators is particularly disturbing because it reduces humans to the status of animals. The anti-hunting literature we have been exploring, however, suggests that even if one interprets Caliban as other than human the image should also disturb. From this perspective the hunt evokes Prospero's destructive impatience with nature as it is, an impatience that characterizes his relationships throughout the play not only with Caliban but with Ariel, who also yearns for freedom. As a magician, Prospero aspires towards the absolute domination of nature, an impulse that becomes most clearly apparent in the speech in which he glories in his dangerous powers before renouncing them forever. At the end of the play this renunciation is accompanied by the freeing of Ariel into the air and, probably, the release of Caliban to the freedom of the island. When Prospero acknowledges Caliban as his own – "this thing of darkness I / Acknowledge mine" – he thus suggests a begrudging acceptance of that which he finds unregenerate in all nature, to which he himself is inevitably bound.

The association of hunting with cruelty is central to Montaigne's essay "Of Cruelty." Montaigne's views on the hunt are particularly significant in relation to *The Tempest* because two of his essays – "Of Cannibals," and "Of Cruelty" – are clearly echoed in the play. The former allusion, appearing in Gonzalo's naive attempt to imagine a golden age, has been much studied; the latter, however, has received little attention. This allusion is unmistakable, however, as Eleanor Prosser has demonstrated, and occurs at what might be considered the climax of the play, the point at which Prospero turns from vengeance to forgiveness:

> Though with their high wrongs I am strook to th' quick,
> Yet with my nobler reason, 'gainst my fury
> Do I take part. The rarer action is
> In virtue than in vengeance.
>
> (5.1.25–28)

Montaigne's passage, which contains many verbal echoes, ranks virtue as *"much more noble"* than mere "inclinations unto goodnesse."[8] Virtue is demonstrated not by those whose good nature shields them from the temptation of revenge, but by those who feel injury, desire revenge, and yet control their passion through reason.

The event that immediately precedes Prospero's renunciation of vengeance, and by less than thirty lines in the text, is his furious hunt of Caliban, Stephano, and Trinculo. Despite the proximity of Prospero's wild chase to the passage in question, however, neither Prosser nor other scholars who cite "Of Cruelty" as a source mention the importance of hunting to the essay.[9] Montaigne's most telling example of uncontrollable and irrational fury in "Of Cruelty" is the hunt. Admitting his own complicity in the irresistible appeal of the chase – the "showting, jubeting and hallowing, still ringing in our eares" – Montaigne goes on to deplore the various kinds of torture Roman tyrants and other rulers have inflicted upon criminals, urging that if such inhuman outrages must take place for deterrent effect they should be visited not upon the living bodies but upon the corpses of the offenders.[10] The topic of cruelty to humans leads him to that of cruelty to beasts, which he also finds abhorrent. His conclusion, which has served as a touchstone for Shakespearean values throughout this study, seems implicit in the ending of *The Tempest*:

there [is] a kinde of respect, and a general duty of humanitie, which tieth us, not only unto brute beasts that have life and sense, and are Sensitives, but unto trees and plants, which are but Vegetatives. *Unto men we owe Justice, and to all other creatures, that are capable of it, grace and benignitie* [Florio's italics]. There is a kinde of enter-changeable commerce, and mutuall bond betweene them and us.[11]

In Montaigne's essay "Of Cruelty," then, Shakespeare found not only the notion that the "rarer action" lies in a virtue that proceeds from struggle rather than in one that proceeds from mere innocence. He found there an image of the hunt used as an example of tempestuous passion, irrational and uncontrollable. He found a protest against cruel punishments of men, even of men guilty of the most heinous crimes. He found a protest against cruelty to animals that focuses on the hunt. And he found a notion of a "mutuall bond" joining human, animal and vegetative nature. It is even possible that Shakespeare found in Montaigne's essay the germ of Caliban's final desire to "be wise hereafter, / And seek for grace" (5.1.295–96), for the ambiguity of the word "grace" seems to echo "*Unto men we owe Justice, and to all other creatures, that are capable of it, grace and benignitie.*" Montaigne's "Of Cruelty" thus implies not only a powerful endorsement of the bonds that tie humans to one another in sympathy but an unconventional endorsement of the bonds between the human and the natural world. In Prospero's struggle to forgive Antonio, to release Ariel, and to accept Caliban, we may perhaps see the glimmering of both of those ideas.

Thus far the context we have explored in attempting to understand the hunting episode in *The Tempest* has been strictly literary: Shakespeare's own depictions of hunter and hunted, and the anti-hunting tradition represented in writers such as Agrippa and Montaigne. There is another and at least equally immediate context for the episode, however, that of the politics surrounding the hunt in the court of James I. The king was an obsessive hunter, and his hunting occasioned considerable protest both within and outside the court. Since any association between James I and Prospero at his most tyrannical seems unlikely on the face of it, however, for reasons of censorship if for no other, one must proceed cautiously. I shall therefore turn first to broad questions of the play's relationship to court politics, and then to the particular question of James's hunting and its political implications, focusing on those features that seem most relevant to Prospero's hunt in *The Tempest*.

As Stephen Orgel observes, despite the fact that *The Tempest* was performed at court both in 1611 and in 1613, there is no evidence to suggest that the play was written or modified for court performance.[12] There is little doubt, however, that it is deeply implicated in court issues, as numerous critics have made clear. The play's concern with the union of kingdoms, peaceful succession, appropriate diplomatic marriages of children, the need for discipline in promising heirs – these and other topics have been traced plausibly to the court environment surrounding the play. Recent studies have also shown the relevance to the play of more overtly subversive and popular discourses, such as those of treason, both domestic and political, and colonialism.[13] One cannot read criticism of the play or accounts of James I, moreover, without being struck by the startling resemblances between Prospero and the king, both of whom share, in addition to absolute political authority, a preoccupation with the occult, a delight in masques, a tendency to neglect their duties, a concern with the political marriages of progeny, and a proneness to fits of rage. While much of this contextual criticism has been illuminating, the sheer proliferation of relevant perspectives has not resulted in substantial agreement about those that are most significant or about the overall political positioning of the play. The more we learn about the immediate context, it seems, the more complicated both the history and the play become.

To understand the political significance of Prospero's furious hunt, we must consider the threat of royal absolutism as it was embodied in both the Parliamentary crisis of 1610 and in James's obsession with hunting. The Parliamentary crisis arose out of continuing debates over supply and the royal prerogative.[14] The debates of 1610 took place in the context of the "great contract," by which the king had agreed to forfeit certain claims upon his subjects in exchange for a grant of annual revenue. From the viewpoint of the Crown, desperately in need of money, the main purpose of the session was to secure a grant of subsidies. From the viewpoint of many members of the Commons, however, the main purpose, as Elizabeth Read Foster puts it, was "the expression and preparation of grievances, ecclesiastical and temporal."[15]

The question of the royal prerogative that dominated the Parliament of 1610 emerged from the king's attempt to enhance his revenues by increasing impositions on imported and exported goods. Since such impositions had traditionally served mainly a regulatory purpose, the king's desire to treat them as royal revenue aroused much opposition in the Commons. Such a move was treated as an illegitimate extension of the royal prerogative. The king was therefore called upon to defend his prerogative, which he did with the absolutist theories that he had enunciated over a lifetime. The Commons defended its position, with various members making provocative statements that challenged the prerogative. The recalcitrance of the Commons precipitated a major debate: could the Crown levy additional customs duties without the consent of Parliament? Because the king tried at one point to silence the arguments against him, on the ground that the debate itself undermined his prerogative, the conflict raised the further and fundamental question of the right to free speech in the Commons. The problem of the levy was left unresolved, the great contract collapsed, and the king dissolved Parliament in February 1611. The great contract failed, according to Elizabeth Read Foster, mainly because of the Commons' distrust of the Crown. "The King will not acknowledge his prerogative to be inferior to law," commented the Earl of Huntingdon, "'and therefore no good assurance and tie can be made but his prerogative will be above it."[16]

The anxious question that ran throughout the entire session, from the viewpoint of the Commons, is whether the king's absolutist inclinations could be contained. On this score the arguments put forward by the crown, including those made by the king in person, were not reassuring. In two major speeches the king enunciated his prerogative in language that took the absolutist position to extremes. On 21 March 1610, in a speech later published in his *Works*, James addressed directly what he took to be the major question posed by the Commons, whether he intended to continue ruling "according to the ancient forme of this State, and the Lawes of this Kingdome" or whether he intended not to limit himself "within those bounds, but to alter the same when [he] thought convenient, by the absolute power of a King." To many, his answer was not reassuring. "The State of MONARCHIE," James had declared, "is the supremest thing upon earth: For Kings are not onely GODS Lieutenants upon earth, and sit upon GODS throne, but even by GOD himselfe they are called Gods."[17] In his speech of 21 May he took the absolutist position to its logical conclusion: "If a king be resolute to be a tyrant, all you can do will not hinder him. You may pray to God that he may be good and thank God if he be."[18] As both the king's words and the reaction of auditors such as John Chamberlain make clear, the shadow under which the 1610 debate was conducted was that of future tyranny.[19]

In the midst of the debates, shortly after 14 May, the news arrived that the French king, Henri IV, had been assassinated. James, like his subjects, was stunned by the news, and he reacted with fear and horror at the prospect of his own death in a like manner. Immediate precautions were taken to protect the king, and especially to guard him carefully while hunting. A few days after the assassination he was seen riding through London with an armed guard.[20] In Parliament, fears for the king's safety became intertwined with conflicts over his prerogative.

The 1610 debates in Parliament thus provide an illuminating context within which to view the potential for tyranny implicit in Prospero's attack upon Caliban, Stephano, and Trinculo. In both instances, a ruler is beset by internal dissension and by disputes over prerogative; Caliban's position, after all, is that the island belongs to him. In both instances, a ruler is subject to fits of rage when challenged and to hyperbolic assertions of supreme authority. In both instances, a ruler is fearful of assassination. In both instances, finally, a ruler defines his power in relation to hunting. The intertwining of hunting with potential tyranny that characterizes Shakespeare's treatment of Prospero, as we shall see, is also to be found in the person and politics of King James.

At the age of eighteen James had already established his reputation as an obsessive hunter, the French envoy, M. de Fontenay, observing that "he loves the chase above all the pleasures of this world, living in the saddle for six hours on end." Later in the same letter, Fontenay criticizes James in a way that was to become familiar throughout his entire reign, noting that he was "too idle and too little concerned about business, too addicted to his pleasure, principally that of the chase."[21] In his first progress after his coronation as King of England, laments Francis Osborne in his memoirs, James was wearing a garment "as greene as the grasse he trod on, with a fether in his cap, and a horne instead of a sword by his side: how sutable to his age, calling, or person, I leave to others to judge from his pictures . . ."[22]

James hunted throughout his career – in middle and old age, in sickness and in health. He hunted en route to the estates of his nobles while on progress and was entertained with hunting when he arrived. He hunted at his own vast parks and forests, such as Royston and Newmarket, and even established formal procedures to be followed by

his government while he was away from court and in the field.[23] Hunting
was intertwined with nearly all his private and public activities. He conducted court business and wrote letters in the midst of hunting trips. He
cheered sick nobles with the prospects of hearing once again the "wild
hallow" of the hunt. When his daughter Princess Mary died of a fever
in 1607, he sent the Earl of Salisbury to console the Queen while he went
hunting at Cheshunt Park.[24] James himself died, appropriately, after
catching a tertian ague, according to Sir Anthony Weldon, on the last
hunt of the year "as wel as of his life."[25]

James's voluminous correspondence records his obsession with
hunting, most revealingly in his metaphoric identification of the sport
with politics. This identification occurs most consistently in his letters to
his first minister, Robert Cecil, between 1604 and 1610. Perhaps the most
striking feature of this correspondence is the salutation with which
James begins every letter: "my little beagle." Whether James alludes to
hunting in such letters or not, their imaginative framework, whatever the
political topic, is that of the hunt: James's chief minister, responsible for
implementing his political will, is his favorite hunting dog, his little
beagle. The metaphor, moreover, is often carried beyond the salutation,
as in the following letter, in which James orders Cecil to prepare
Theobalds for his hunting while on progress:

My little beagle,
   It is now time that ye prepare the woods and park of Theobalds for me. Your
part thereof will only be to harbour me good stags, for I know ye mind to
provide for no other entertainment for me there than as many stags as I shall
kill with my own hunting. Yet ye have that advantage that I trust so much to
your nose that when I hear you cry it I will halloo to you as freely as to the
deepest-mouthed hound in all the kennel. And since ye have been so much used
these three months past to hunt cold scents through the dry beaten ways of
London, ye need not doubt but it will be easy for you to harbour a great stag
amongst the sweet groves about your house. Only beware of drawing too greed-
ily in the lyam, for ye know how that trick hath already galled your neck.[26]

The psychology and tone of this letter are typical. The nickname
"beagle" is affectionate, and the letter captures James's pleasure in both
Cecil and the hunting he will provide. There is no mistaking the implications of the metaphor, however: James is master, Cecil a favorite dog.
Cecil "hunts" the king's prey in London and harbours stags for him at
Theobalds, but he must never forget that he is on a leash, which will
"gall" his neck if he shows signs of pursuing his own will rather than the
king's. The metaphor thus captures implicitly James's absolutist notions

of kingship: he is the hunter, his enemies the prey, and his agents his hounds, trained in obedience to his will. Even the Council as a whole is praised in a later letter as a "good kennel that all run well."[27]

Although most of James's metaphoric identifications of hunting with political affairs focus on tracking and pursuing, on one occasion the end latent in the metaphor, that of violent death, is actually pronounced. Presumably alluding to an episode involving witches and prophets at Hinchingbrooke in January of 1605, James informs his "little beagle" that he has been "out of privy intelligence" with him since they last parted because he has been "kept so busy with hunting of witches, prophets, Puritans, dead cats, and hares."[28] In view of James's harsh attitudes and policies towards witches and Puritans, the use of the hunting metaphor in this instance is genuinely ominous. The leveling effect created by James's syntax is also disturbingly suggestive, for it reduces all of the items to the value of dead cats, an allusion so absurd in context that it must hint at some meaning now lost. In the privacy of his correspondence, then, James saw his political affairs in general through the eyes of a hunter and his enemies in particular as prey, sometimes as prey to be literally destroyed.

By the time of the Parliamentary crisis of 1610, James had become notorious for his personal obsession with hunting, his lavish expenditures on the sport, and his incessant efforts to limit it and punish illegal hunting through royal proclamations and the Game Acts. Although the Parliamentary debates of that year did not explicitly include the issue of hunting, James himself was driven to include it as yet another potential threat to his prerogative. In the same speech in which he declared that the state of monarchy was "the supremest thing upon earth," and that kings were "not onely Gods Lieutenants upon earth" but were called "Gods" even by "God himselfe,"[29] James exhorted Parliament to attend to the protection of the forests and game. He chided the members for their casting out of a bill for the preservation of woods in the last session, accusing them of "frowardnesse" and reminding them of the general need for fuel, and timber for the navy, and of his own pleasure in the hunt: "yee know my delight in Hunting and Hawking, and many of your selves are of the same minde." He rebuked them too for unsatisfactory bills passed in the previous session, 1605–06, regarding the preservation of pheasant and partridge and the unlawful hunting of deer and conies.[30]

Hunting was of course only one of several issues touched upon in this speech. Given the nature of Parliament's grievances and his own desperate need for the grant of funds, however, it is remarkable that he gave the issue any attention at all. Even more remarkable is the aggressive and hectoring tone of his remarks, which reveal a good deal of tension surrounding the subject, even among those who might seem predisposed in its favor. The tone of the king's remarks lends support to Francis Osborne's bitter comment, in his memoirs, that in James's reign "one man might with more safety have killed another, than a raskall-deare, . . . [so] tragicall was this sylvan prince against dear-killers, and indulgent to man-slayers."[31] James's pursuit of protection for his favorite recreation, in short, was as vigorous and uncompromising in this speech as his defence of the royal prerogative in general. For James, it seems, kings were both Gods and hunters.

James's passion for the hunt aroused controversy at all levels of society. At the heart of the matter was the same problem that we have encountered in the Parliamentary conflict of 1610: fears of James's extension of the royal prerogative. In reacting against the neglect of the game laws by his predecessors, as Chester and Ethyn Kirby have demonstrated, James sought to restore a "moribund prerogative, a claim to the personal control of the game everywhere in England and to the right of hunting wherever the king pleased."[32] According to Roger B. Manning, "the increased emphasis on the prosecution of hunting offences in Star Chamber and other equity courts certainly represented a revival of the royal prerogative in ways that the Tudor monarchs had never contemplated . . ."[33]

James's son, Charles I, was also a hunter. Although far less obsessive about the sport than his father, he was at least as committed to the royal prerogative, and he continued his father's aggressive policies: restricting hunting to a privileged elite, prosecuting unlawful hunting, and maintaining and extending royal parks and forests. The forces set in motion by James I, in short, accelerated under Charles I, and the results were disastrous. In September 1641 there were popular attacks against Windsor Forest, attacks which Manning notes displayed "a distinct anti-monarchical bias," and which continued for several years. Throughout the Civil Wars, moreover, parks and forests were routinely destroyed and deer slaughtered, at least in part as protests against the monarchy and noble privilege. Manning concludes that "James I and Charles I had made the royal hunting reserves a symbol of royal tyranny."[34]

When Prospero first hunted Caliban, Stephano and Trinculo on stage in 1611, then, he did so in a political atmosphere in which hunting and the threat of tyranny were intertwined. In this sense the hunting scene in *The Tempest* might be said to crystallize a deep cultural anxiety about James's rule, with Prospero's regression to the primitive tyranny of the hunt as a means of "punishing" his conspirators playing out fears of a hunter-king that were being expressed in Parliament, in letters, and on the streets of London. From this perspective, Prospero's decision to renounce vengeance, abjure his magic, and release Ariel and (probably) Caliban to their natural elements might provide a wish-fulfillment fantasy of personal reformation and social reconciliation. If so, the fantasy seems seriously qualified by the many irresolutions of the play's ending, which include hints of Prospero's own pessimism and recalcitrance.

If conceived as an indirect comment on James's rule, the hunting scene may seem difficult to reconcile with the political realities of state censorship and court performance. On 29 March 1608, for example, the French ambassador reported that because two plays had offended the king all the London theaters were shut down and threatened with permanent closure. In one of the plays, the ambassador observes, James himself had been represented cursing and swearing because he had been robbed of a bird and beaten a gentleman who had called off his hounds from the scent.[35] The episode shows that in 1608 James's hunting was a likely topic for satire, but its message on censorship is more difficult to extract. On the one hand, it reveals the vulnerability of actors to immediate and arbitrary political reprisals; on the other, it suggests that even the most flagrant mockery of the king could escape prosecution (and attract audiences).

In addressing the question of censorship, it is important to keep in mind that we are dealing not only with scripts but with performances before both a courtly and popular audience. Both modes of representation are open to alteration of various kinds – ranging from subtle nuance to complete inversion of meaning. It is easy to imagine, for example, radically different treatments of the hunting episode in a court and a popular setting: in the former the episode could have been omitted, or truncated, or treated as farce; in the latter it could have been used to insinuate satirical possibilities. The scene itself, of course, is rich enough to support various interpretations, theatrical or critical, ranging from sympathetic approval of Prospero's firmness against usurpation to anxious horror at his anger and cruelty. Given James's attitudes and susceptibility to drink, it is even arguable that the king at least might not have found anything offensive even in the most forbidding of theatrical realizations of the scene. The many variables in performance, then, can be seen to multiply the variables in textual interpretation. In this respect the hunting episode more than meets the test of "functional ambiguity" developed by Annabel Patterson in her study of censorship in the period.[36]

Ambiguity is different from overt subversiveness of the kind that Curt Breight finds, for example, in his article on the discourse of treason in the play. Although Breight's insistence on "the theatre's wide range of ideological possibilities" provides a useful corrective to the more influential view of conservative ideological containment, his attempt to read the play as "a politically radical intervention in a dominant con-temporary discourse" is not very persuasive.[37] More in keeping with the realities of censorship and the complexities of Shakespeare's dramatic methods are interpretations that recognize the ideological containment implied in Shakespeare's dramatic form, a form that begins and ends with Prospero in authority but at the same time enables the expression of doubts, anxieties, and criticism. Critics as far apart as Donna B. Hamilton and Paul Brown, for example, have in this respect come to similar conclusions. For Hamilton, Shakespeare's overall strategy in the representation of Prospero, and by implication, James, is epideictic, a mode of praise that contains within itself the possibility of criticism and instruction. For Brown, the play expresses the tensions within the ideol-ogy of early colonialism but without resolving them. In Hamilton's argu-ment, the play functions much as one of Jonson's masques was intended to function, as an idealized but instructive portrait of the king and court. In this sense, Shakespeare might have represented the potential within the king, and within absolute rule in general, for acts of tyranny, but rep-resented as well the overcoming of that temptation, in the disciplined decision to seek virtue rather than vengeance. Although plausible enough, I find this line of argument less convincing than that of func-tional ambiguity because it implies a strong degree of didacticism on the part of the author and the centrality of James and the court as an intended audience.

The most plausible position, it seems to me, is to assert not only Shakespeare's immersion in the culture of his day, including the culture of the hunt and the Jacobean court, but to allow him a measure of inde-pendence as a playwright. The story told in *The Tempest* includes far more than Jacobean political issues, and even those issues are broadly framed. Illuminating contexts for the "hunting" of Prospero may thus be found in Agrippa's attacks on hunting; in the "hunting" of King James in sport and politics; in the proverbial role of Nimrod as great hunter; in myths of the Iron Age; in the use of dogs against natives by Spaniards in the new world; in the persecution of native peoples, in Scotland, Ireland, or the New World; and in the persecution of "masterless men" in Elizabethan England. A local reading need not be reductive. Given the working conditions of an Elizabethan dramatist, in fact, one begins to suspect that, whether by accident or design, the habit of functional ambiguity was in large part responsible for the endlessly widening ripples of meaning that we associate with Shakespeare's art in particular. In this sense, his very immersion in the immediate particulars of cultural experience, and the threats that such immersion entailed, might be in part responsible for the very "universality" that has been traditionally claimed for his works.

Although Shakespeare develops Prospero's hunt primarily as a political symbol, moreover, it is well to remember that the implications of the episode extend beyond a narrow conception of politics. The liminal status of one of the conspirators, Caliban, as we have observed, aligns Shakespeare's treatment of the hunt at least partly with that of Agrippa and Montaigne, both of whom are concerned with the welfare of animals in a literal sense. The very liminality of Caliban, his apparent position at the boundaries of the human and the animal world, opens up the possibility of literalizing the metaphor of the hunt and extending the question of cruelty into the realm of nature itself. As Jonathan Bate reminds us, *The Tempest* is not only a political play but a play about the relationship of culture to nature.[38] At the end of the play Prospero renounces his power over nature as dangerous, frees Ariel to the elements, and probably leaves Caliban to his island. However one interprets these actions, they do not imply a tyrannical attitude towards nature. Nor is it easy to reconcile them with the passion of the hunt.

Prospero's begrudging acceptance of Caliban and his final release of both Caliban and Ariel challenge the conventional notion of man's right to absolute dominion over nature. Shakespeare's treatment of Caliban and Ariel is curiously reminiscent of his treatment of the weeping deer in *As You Like It*. In both cases he blurs the boundaries between the natural and the human world, suggesting that they are parts of a continuum, not separate and unbridgeable categories. Ariel exists at the boundaries between spirit and matter, Caliban at the boundaries between the human and bestial. They both possess an external reality, as objective beings, but also an internal reality, as capacities within Prospero himself. Ariel is "my spirit," the means by which Prospero executes his magic; Caliban is "mine," the means by which he caters to his bodily needs. The acknowledgment of the ultimate freedom and autonomy of these creatures at the end of the play suggests a heightened emphasis on the kinship between living things that stretches the traditional conception of man's relationship to nature. In this kinship lies Prospero's redefinition of his "so potent art" as a "rough magic" that must be renounced (5.1.50). The "vanity" of Prospero's art leads to a furious and tyrannical hunt.

James I, ironically, can be called an early conservationist. He enlarged the forests and parks of England, protected and increased the wildlife, even sometimes in opposition to his own officers, for whom the collection of revenues through timber was the highest priority. As is true of some modern hunters, however, his passion for environmentalism derived from the simple desire to kill; nowhere does he ever express a need to preserve and protect the natural environment for the sake of nature itself. For him, forests existed to serve the recreation of the king. This kind of "tyranny" was not in Shakespeare's day a significant political issue; opposition to James's forest policies was not based on the innate value of wild nature. Shakespeare's play, however, at least hints towards a more modern attitude, one that was shortly to be undermined, ironically, by the development of Baconian science and Cartesian rationalism. To release Ariel to the air and Caliban to his island is to give up a coercive power over elemental nature, to recognize its own autonomy. This is not to sentimentalize nature, for both Ariel and Caliban can only be left to their own devices if left in their own sphere; in society, both must be controlled. Nor does the gesture towards release sentimentalize Prospero or the play. The release is hard earned, reluctant, and, like the play's other hopeful gestures towards a "brave new world," carries with it a skepticism born of tragic experience.

The Tempest thus participates in the Jacobean culture of the hunt in many ways. It crystallizes in a single, powerful symbol Shakespeare's continuing preoccupation with the violence of the hunt. It situates Prospero's furious chase of the conspirators within a long tradition of thought linking the origins of the hunt with the origins of tyranny. It alludes to contemporary anxieties about tyranny in the court of King James, anxieties that were deeply intertwined with the various manifestations of the king's obsession with the hunt as a symbol of royal power. Drawing on Montaigne's novel and progressive feelings of sympathy for brute creation, moreover, the play implies a need to return Caliban and Ariel to their natural elements, to resist the human desire to tyrannize over nature itself. In this sense the play poses, but does not resolve, the very modern conundrum, that human purposes require subordinating a wild nature that is better off left alone.

CHAPTER EIGHT

Conclusion: Shakespeare on the culture of the hunt

Both the absence of an intellectual biography and the elusiveness of the plays make it difficult to write convincingly about Shakespeare's attitudes or opinions. One is tempted to resort to Keats's conception of "negative capability" or to Barthes' denial of the very concept of authorship and to abandon the quest altogether. The theme of hunting poses a particular challenge, since none of the works is centrally "about" hunting, and the allusions to and representations of the hunt are therefore incidental to broader questions of human experience. Even when the plays give prominence to the sport, moreover, as does *Love's Labor's Lost*, they do not express a specific agenda or a didactic point of view: Shakespeare is not G. B. Shaw.

Given the elusiveness of Shakespearean dramatic form, it becomes not only difficult to extrapolate authorial views but seductively easy to impose our own. It is not surprising, therefore, that two impressive scholars of the hunt, D. H. Madden and Matt Cartmill, find in Shakespeare confirmation of their own views. Madden, impressed by Shakespeare's easy technical mastery of the hunt, concludes that he was "beyond doubt a sportsman, with the rare skill in the mysteries of woodcraft, loving to recall the very names of the hounds with which he was wont to hunt"; Cartmill, noting that Shakespeare consistently links hunting to rape and murder, observes that among his characters, "a distaste for the hunt is a sign of common decency."[1] The quest to discover the recurrent themes and patterns of language through which implied authorial attitudes are revealed is inevitably subjective.

It should be clear already, from our detailed exploration of Shakespeare's many allusions to the hunt, that my own view inclines strongly towards Cartmill's. Individually, each of the works implies a critique of the culture of the hunt; collectively, the recurrent patterns of the critique imply a coherent authorial point of view. In *Venus and Adonis*, hunting is a metaphor for both destructive male aggression, as an initiation into war, and for destructive female aggression, as an initiation into sexuality. The same themes recur in *Titus Andronicus*, where rape, mutilation and murder comprise the sport of a hunting party. In both *Titus Andronicus* and *Julius Caesar*, moreover, the attempt to ritualize killing, as in the hunt, serves only to heighten the ironic gap between the aspiration towards sacrifice and the reality of savage butchery. In the comic world of *Merry Wives*, predation also serves as a metaphor for human experience, although with more benign, if not wholly innocuous, effect; as a poacher of deer and women, Falstaff is finally hunted down himself, the victim of the social violence of the charivari. In *Love's Labor's Lost*, the cruelty of the hunt is acknowledged by the hunter herself, the Princess of France, and serves as a touchstone for the unfeeling sportfulness of an aristocratic court. In *As You Like It*, a play that does more to foreground the plight of hunted animals than any other in the canon, Duke Senior's regrets and Jaques' tears for a dying deer accentuate the paradoxes in the notion of pastoral hunting. In *The Taming of the Shrew* a hunting lord and a falconer embody the male braggadocio in patriarchal rule, with the falcon Kate providing a wish-fulfillment fantasy of successful taming. In *The Tempest*, finally, the hunting of Caliban, Stephano, and Trinculo becomes a metaphor for the tyrannical potential of Prospero's art.

The most powerful challenge to the notion that Shakespeare's conception of the hunt is negative, it seems to me, comes from the brief hunting episode in *A Midsummer Night's Dream*, an episode that has so far escaped our attention. Surely, we might argue, at least here we find a festive hunt, a moment that replicates the positive ideology that resonates through the handbooks on hunting and the remarks of James I. As would have been common in the Elizabethan period, Theseus and Hippolyta celebrate their wedding with a hunt. They take delight in the beauty of the morning and admire together the music of the hounds. The event seems entirely joyful and decorous: the participants are warriors but in love; the dogs are beasts but disciplined and musical. In this brief moment, the hunt seems to become a positive symbol of social order, uniting man and woman, human and beast, and prefiguring the harmonious resolutions that characterize the ending of the play. Is it possible that in this single episode Shakespeare allows his audience to revel in the conventional pleasures of the hunt?

Before considering the episode in detail, it might be helpful to consider a benchmark for festive representations of the hunt, a speech that occurs at the beginning of Greene's *Friar Bacon and Friar Bungay*. In this speech, Prince Edward's friend Lacy describes the joy of a hunt that the two men have just completed:

> Alate we ran the deer, and through the lawns
> Stripp'd with our nags the lofty frolic bucks
> That scudded 'fore the teasers like the wind.
> Ne'er was the deer of merry Fressingfield
> So lustily pull'd down by jolly mates,
> Nor shar'd the farmers such fat venison,
> So frankly dealt, this hundred years before . . .[2]

"Frolic" is the governing word in this description. The hunt is a festive game, shared with equal delight by the nags, the bucks themselves, the teasers (the hounds that rouse the game), the mates, and even the farmers, whose trampled fields are more than compensated by the gift of venison. In such a portrait the hunt becomes a festive rite, expressing the social and natural communion in which Fressingfield manifests its true and "merry" identity. This is an idealized version of the positive attitudes towards the hunt popularized by the handbooks on the sport. Lacy's description is utterly without irony and contains no recognition of the various kinds of opposition to hunting – social, religious, political, ethical – that we have considered throughout this study.

The hunting episode in *A Midsummer Night's Dream* evokes a general atmosphere reminiscent of Lacy's celebration. The focus is not the kill but the delightful music of the hounds. Theseus begins by expressing his desire to hear the "musical confusion / Of hounds and echo in conjunction" (4.1.110–11). His words bring memories of her own hunting to Hippolyta's mind, and she tells of accompanying Hercules and Cadmus once when, in "a wood of Crete they bay'd the bear / With hounds of Sparta" (113–14). The sound of these hounds, she says, was incomparable: "I never heard / So musical a discord, such sweet thunder" (117–18). In reply, Theseus asserts the superiority of his hounds to any she has yet heard; they are "bred out of the Spartan kind" (119), and are "match'd in mouth like bells, / Each under each" (123–24). "A cry more tuneable," he assures her,

> Was never hollow'd to, nor cheer'd with horn,
> In Crete, in Sparta, nor in Thessaly.
> Judge when you hear.   (124–27)

Before Hippolyta can judge, however, they discover the sleeping lovers and "set aside" their "purpos'd hunting" so that all of the couples, "three and three," may return to Athens to hold "a feast in great solemnity"

(183–85). As in *Friar Bacon and Friar Bungay*, it seems, the characters are sympathetic and the context is ceremonial, joyful, and comic; the hunt becomes an emblem not of violence but of social and natural concord.

Qualifying the comic delight of this scene, however, are several underlying sources of tension. The relationship between Theseus and Hippolyta, for example, seems appropriately symbolized by the paradox of festive hunting. Both are powerful and aggressive figures, linked to the energetic and "masculine" activity of the hunt; Hippolyta is literally an Amazon. Their conversation about hunting is subtly competitive – both characters see hunting as a symbol of personal power – and hints at the likelihood of continuing tension in a relationship that began with wooing by the sword. Theseus is proud of his hounds, yet Hippolyta counters that pride with her own evocations of hunting with figures superior to Theseus: Hercules and Cadmus, whose prey was not the relatively harmless deer but the more deadly and challenging bear. Having won Hippolyta with the sword, Theseus must continue to woo her with heroic assertions of masculine prowess; she resists, but with a self-assertiveness muted to accord with her new marital role. For both characters the violence of the battlefield seems merely sublimated in the sporting competition of the hunt. In this sense their relationship prefigures that of Petruchio and Katherine in *The Taming of the Shrew*.

Theseus's delight in the music of his hounds might be taken as an emblem of this sublimation, for it transforms violent discord into a source of esthetic pleasure. Yet even the magic of this transformation is shadowed by a hint of satire. In his pride in the music of his hounds, Theseus plays the role of a familiar social type. To the dismay of Puritans, hunters in the period lavished great sums on the breeding and care of their dogs, and, like Theseus, they often had voices more in mind than speed or scenting ability. In *Country Contentments*, for example, Gervase Markham gives directions for creating a consort of hounds:

If you would have your Kennell for sweetnesse of cry, then you must compound it of some large dogges, that have deepe solempe mouthes . . .,which must as it were beare the base in the consort, then a double number of roaring, and loud ringing mouthes, which must beare the counter tenor, then som hollow plaine sweete mouthes, which must beare the meane or middle part: and so with these three parts of musique you shall make your cry perfect . . .[3]

Theseus himself recognizes one negative effect of breeding hounds for music when he notes that, although his hounds are "match'd in mouth like bells," they are "slow in pursuit" (123).

The concord of these slow hounds, like the harmony created within

A Midsummer Night's Dream as a whole, is deeply paradoxical. It marks a high civilization – Theseus delights in the music of the hunt rather than in the kill – but a fragile one, in which naturally opposed forces are poised momentarily in delicate equilibrium. Theseus's pride in his dominion over nature is itself ironic, given the instability of the fairy world that lies beyond his control. The beauty he achieves through his hounds, moreover, like the concord of his own marriage, masks underlying violence; the song of the hounds, no matter how delightful, as the eighteenth-century poet William Somervile later observed, is ultimately the sound of the beast, "Op'ning in concerts of harmonious joy, / But breathing death."[4]

The mythological subtexts underlying the roles of Theseus and Hippolyta also hint at a latent violence associated with hunting that shadows the festive nature of the moment. Hippolyta's account of hunting with Hercules and Cadmus seems to have been Shakespeare's own invention. In the context of the hunt, allusions to both characters are ironic: Hercules, the slayer of the Nemean lion, is also, in at least one account, the slayer of Hippolyta herself; Cadmus is the grandfather of Actaeon, a hunter who is destroyed by his own hounds. Theseus himself is celebrated as a hunter in mythology. He participates, for example, in Meleager's hunt of the Calydonian boar in the *Metamorphoses*.[5] More significantly, he and Hippolyta will later have a son, Hippolytus, who achieves fame as a hunter and worshipper of the goddess of the hunt, Artemis. Through the treachery of his stepmother, Phaedra, however, Hippolytus will be cursed and banished by his own father. One might argue, of course, that Shakespeare excludes these ominous subtexts from the play, but the centrality of the hunt to the episode in question surely pulls them towards the surface. For audiences with a knowledge of the mythology behind the characters, Theseus's wedding hunt has subtle tragic overtones.

The comic paradox of a festive hunt holds together in this scene because of an absence: the event that would unravel the paradox, the kill, never takes place. The hunt is interrupted by the discovery of the young lovers lying asleep on the ground. The movement from hunting to awakening the lovers represents a kind of modulation or metamorphosis whereby the latent violence of the hunt becomes transformed into life-giving love. The lovers are themselves awakened by the hunting horns; they have become Theseus's prey. This is truly a festive hunt, then. But its festivity depends upon an interruption of the true end of the hunt, death, and its replacement by marriage and social renewal.

Unlike Greene, who creates a stereotypically perfect scene of hunting, a joyful communion of man and nature in which even the prey participates, Shakespeare creates a festive hunt that is shadowed by reminders of violence and death. Within the comic contours of the episode, in short, lie the major hunting themes that Shakespeare was to explore in tragic, ironic, and satirical contexts throughout his career: sexual violence, war, patriarchal power, and the domination of nature. To underline these themes, of course, as the present line of argument has required, is to destroy the delicate comic balance of the scene. But their presence shows that even Shakespeare's most benign representation of the hunt carries critical and potentially tragic overtones.

As a poet and dramatist who moved between the worlds of Stratford and London, and whose audiences ranged from commoners to monarchs, Shakespeare would have been highly sensitive to the social and political implications of the topic of hunting. In general, as we have seen, the Elizabethan and Jacobean gentry, aristocracy, and monarchy were emotionally and intellectually committed to a positive ideology of the hunt. One would expect this fact to register upon any writer with social and economic ambitions. In this regard, Ben Jonson provides a useful foil to Shakespeare. Jonson's tendency to idealize the hunt is apparent in at least two plays – *Cynthia's Revels* and *The Sad Shepherd* – and throughout the poems and masques.

As the name implies, *Cynthia's Revels* celebrates Cynthia, or Diana, the goddess of the moon and the hunt, a figure who represents an idealized conception of Queen Elizabeth. The play also celebrates an idealized image of Jonson himself, as Crites the poet and masque-maker, and seems to have been designed to enable Jonson to offer the Queen "his services as a maker of court entertainments."[6] Not surprisingly, the play's few allusions to the hunt are favorable. Although the Diana of the play is accused of injustice in her punishment of Actaeon (the Earl of Essex in the allegory behind the play), she defends herself as appropriately "austere." This "austerity" is captured in images that celebrate the just power of the huntress. As "Queen and huntress, chaste and fair," she is asked to "give unto the flying hart / Space to breathe, how short soever," forgoing her proper role as huntress only for the temporary occasion of her revels. One of the four cardinal properties of her court, moreover, is "Good Audacity," whose symbol is *divae viragini* [divine female warrior], which expresses her "hardy courage in chase of savage beasts, which harbour in woods and wilderness."[7] Although Jonson's treatment of Elizabeth's role as huntress is symbolic, the symbolism carries with it an acceptance and promotion of the ideology of the royal hunt.

Jonson's plays occasionally include satiric thrusts at hunters, but they never attack the sport itself – merely the social pretensions and eccentricities of contemporary social types. Master Stephen, the country gull in *Every Man In His Humour*, wants to learn the "hawking and hunting languages" because they "are more studied than the Greek or the Latin" and provide access to the company of gallants. Puntarvolo, in *Every Man Out of His Humour*, a hunter devoted to "singularity," loves his dogs, hawks and wife equally and "has dialogues and discourses between his horse, himself, and his dog."[8] His is a harmless eccentricity, not one that threatens the true ethos of the sport.

An idealization of the hunt runs throughout the poems, particularly in those that, like "To Penshurst" and "To Sir Robert Wroth," praise the country life. "Penshurst" describes the King's impromptu visit to the estate while out hunting, a visit that celebrates the King's graciousness and the readiness of his hosts to receive him. In "To Sir Robert Wroth," the country estate conjures up visions of the Golden Age, a notion that for Jonson and Wroth, unlike Ovid, includes the joys of hunting. The aristocratic bias of the latter poem is revealed in the dissociation of hunting from any need for food: the true nobility of Wroth and his friends is demonstrated by the fact that they hunt "more for the exercise, then fare."[9] In this, they align themselves not only with the aristocratic ideology of the hunt but with the views of James I, who time and again stressed his need to hunt for the sake of his health.

In the masque *Time Vindicated*, the role of Diana, originally appearing as goddess of the hunt in *Cynthia's Revels*, reappears. When she is forced to defend her favors to the two hunters, Hippolytus and Cephalus, against Love's report to Time, Diana says that she has brought the youths forth

> To make them fitter so to serve the Time
> By labor, riding, and those ancient arts
> That first enabled men unto the wars.

Saturn yields to this assertion of her chaste purpose, and the Chorus celebrates hunting as the noblest exercise, one that promotes health, aids the faculties, chases away ill habits, and, as long as hunters follow the example of King James, protects Peace.[10] In developing his theme in this masque, Jonson interestingly attempts to reconcile James's commitment to pacifism with the traditional view of the sport as a training ground for

war. One can see in this maneuver, by which peace becomes paradoxically the end of an activity that promotes war, an anticipation of later
defenses of the hunt, which find in it less a preparation for war than a
surrogate, deflecting energies that might otherwise kill men. In his poem
The Chase (1735), for example, William Somervile praises the hunt as "the
sport of kings; / Image of war, without its guilt."[11]

Jonson, in short, was wedded to the courtly ideology of the hunt in
ways that Shakespeare was not. In contrast, Shakespeare's treatment of
the courtly ethos of the hunt, as we have seen, is deftly ironic. In the
reign of Elizabeth, he writes not of a "Queen and huntress, chaste and
fair," but of a Princess of France, whose ambivalence about hunting is
displayed in a setting distinctly reminiscent of Elizabeth's own progresses. In the reign of James I, he writes not of a King who pursues the
hunt only for the sake of his health but of a Duke who vents his rage at
rebellious subjects by symbolically hunting them. In neither case is
Shakespeare's flirtation with satire of the monarch necessarily dangerous. The allusions are oblique, tonally complex, and easily deflected in
the dynamics of stage representation. But their presence suggests, in a
small but focused way, the broad differences between Jonson and
Shakespeare in their orientation towards the world of the court. As a city
boy of modest means and, later, a masque writer for the Jacobean court,
Ben Jonson lacked Shakespeare's familiarity with hunting, his potential
access to it economically, and his ability to insulate himself from the
courtly ideology that sustained it. Shakespeare, unlike Jonson, wrote no
country-house poems or masques idealizing the world of the hunt; nor
are his occasional satiric thrusts against this world centered upon the
pretensions of those who, without the aristocratic credentials, yearn to
be part of it. Shakespeare's critical energies go to the heart of the courtly
ideology itself.

Central to Shakespeare's treatment of the hunt is its affinity with the
violence of war. In this sense, his imagery of hunting seems to grow out
of the humanist opposition to the sport, articulated most powerfully, as
we have seen, by writers such as More, Erasmus, and Agrippa.
Throughout the canon the link between hunting and war tends to
appear more directly in metaphors than in full scenes, metaphors that
focus not on positive qualities, such as military virtue or prowess, but on
savage, murderous violence. Caroline Spurgeon, for example, discovered that in only one out of thirty-nine hunting images was the sport
"pictured as a gay and joyous pastime, and described from the point of
view of the sportsman."[12] Her single positive image comes from the

English herald in *King John* as he attempts to persuade the citizens of Angiers to open their gates to the English army:

> And like a jolly troop of huntsmen come
> Our lusty English, all with purpled hands,
> Dy'd in the dying slaughter of their foes.
> Open your gates and give the victors way. (2.1.321–24)

Although the image identifies the exultation of military victory with that of successful hunters, whose "purpled hands" are emblems of conquest, the thrust of the passage as a whole is rather heavily ironic. In the context of the herald's rhetoric, the image of "purpled hands" is not "jolly" at all but savagely ominous, conveying the implied threat that these hunters are now likely to dip their hands in the blood of the people of Angiers.

Most of Shakespeare's metaphoric links between hunting and war emphasize the murderous violence of individual combat. In such instances, the discipline imposed by the ceremonial hunt, with its elaborate etiquette, is not transferred to military action, despite the fact that both the hunt and battle were subject to elaborate chivalric codes. Instead, the image connotes unfettered violence and murderous blood-lust. And there are many such images, so many that they might be said to represent a Shakespearean convention in the depiction of war. In *2 Henry VI* York seeks vengeance against old Clifford on the battlefield, telling Warwick to seek out "some other chase, / For I myself must hunt this deer to death" (5.2.14–15). In *3 Henry VI* Richard of Gloucester uses virtually the same phrase in relation to young Clifford, who is now the object of revenge for having killed both York and young Rutland. "Nay, Warwick," Richard says as Clifford runs off, "single out some other chase, / For I myself will hunt this wolf to death" (2.4.12–13). The substitution of wolf for deer suggests the increasing brutality of the civil wars and of the men who pursue them. In *Troilus and Cressida*, Ulysses's treatment of the enemy as an animal to be hunted is rather more dispassionate, respectfully chivalric, and understated: "There is no tarrying here, the hart Achilles / Keeps thicket" (2.3.258–59). In the same play, however, Hector pursues an unnamed Greek warrior for the sake of his armor: "Wilt thou not, beast, abide? / Why then fly on, I'll hunt thee for thy hide" (5.6.30–31). In this instance, the chivalric and hunting codes intersect, with both the pursuit of armor and the pursuit of a hide being ignoble motives. In contrast to this venal conception of the hunt is that of *Coriolanus*, whose hatred of his enemy, Aufidius, acknowledges his worth as a warrior: "He is a lion / That I am proud to hunt" (1.1.235–36). Coriolanus is later betrayed by Aufidius, ironically, and dies encircled by assassins in a manner suggestive of the baying of a stag.

The impulse to kill in battle, then, is repeatedly associated with the hunt. The nuances of the comparison vary greatly, ranging from murderous revenge to chivalric acknowledgment of the worth of an adversary, suggesting the diversity of motives that might also characterize the hunt itself. In each case, however, the metaphors suggest the centrality in both hunting and warfare of a powerful drive to kill. In that sense, the use of hunting metaphors undermines the chivalric ideology so often used to sustain both warfare and hunting. From this vantage point neither activity can be called truly recreational or sporting. Although one cannot conclude that Shakespeare followed the humanists in deploring hunting as a cause of war, one can conclude that he implied a deep affinity between the two, not only in the centrality of death to both activities but in the motivations of the hunter-warriors.

Perhaps the only truly sympathetic association of hunting with warfare in Shakespeare occurs, ironically, in the comparison made by the encircled Talbot in *1 Henry VI* between his plight and that of an English stag. Here the hunt is seen not from the vantage point of the attacking hunter but from that of the desperate prey:

> How are we park'd and bounded in a pale,
> A little herd of England's timorous deer,
> Maz'd with a yelping kennel of French curs!
> If we be English deer, be then in blood,
> Not rascal-like, to fall down with a pinch,
> But rather, moody-mad; and desperate stags,
> Turn on the bloody hounds with heads of steel,
> And make the cowards stand aloof at bay.   (4.2.45–52)

The powerful effect of this passage depends upon the way in which Talbot converts an image suggestive of bow and stable hunting – that of a herd of fallow deer being driven within a park – into an image suggestive of *par force* hunting, with the magnificent bayed stag turning on its attackers. In so doing he not only demeans the French as attacking curs but converts the initial English mood of bewildered fright into one of enraged and desperate aggression. This image of a helpless animal surrounded by attacking predators haunts Shakespeare's imagination and recurs throughout the plays; helplessness of this kind can become transformed into a desperate moral power, as happens in the taunting of York in *3 Henry VI* or in the blinding of Gloucester in *King Lear*.

The closest Shakespeare comes to direct engagement with the conventional argument that hunting prepares young men for war is in *Cymbeline*, which features a hunting scene involving Belarius and his two "sons," Guiderius and Arviragus. As outlaws, the three men hunt out of necessity, so that their hunting is of a more primitive kind than would be customary among Elizabethan aristocrats. Since the boys eventually prove themselves as valiant warriors in battle against the Romans, one might expect their success to be attributed not merely to their noble blood but to their youthful training in the hunt; this is the convention that Spenser follows in his praise of Sidney in "Astrophel." Curiously, however, the opposite seems true. Arviragus, for example, has nothing but contempt for their life as hunters:

> We have seen nothing.
> We are beastly: subtle as the fox for prey,
> Like warlike as the wolf for what we eat;
> Our valor is to chase what flies.   (3.3.39–42)

When confronted for the first time with war itself, Arviragus is drawn instinctively to battle by his noble blood but dismisses the value of his training as a hunter:

> What thing is't that I never
> Did see man die, scarce ever look'd on blood,
> But that of coward hares, hot goats, and venison!   (4.4.35–37)

One might attribute these anti-hunting sentiments to Arviragus's youthful impatience for actual combat and to his innate nobility, which causes him to excel in warfare instinctively, without the need for any training that the hunt might provide. Such a viewpoint, however, would have been unconventional in the period. Spenser provides an instructive contrast in the *Faerie Queene*. In Book VI, Canto ii, the noble youth Tristram, having been forced to grow up in the forest and having therefore learned the ways of the hunt, puts his skills to good use by killing a discourteous knight, a deed that brings him to the attention of Calidore, who rewards him by making him his squire. Like Sidney in Spenser's "Astrophel," Tristram prepares himself for the role of warrior by pursuing the hunt as a young man. Whereas Spenser stays within the convention, Shakespeare works against it. In *Cymbeline* certain virtues of the warrior are celebrated through the characters of Guiderius and Arviragus, but the origin of these virtues is seen to rest in innate nobility alone. In the totality of the play, this unconventional dissociation of hunting from military prowess is a minor matter, but it is worth noting that the dissociation was also un-Jacobean; in *Basilicon Doron*, King James himself had proclaimed in print the military value of the hunt. In *Cymbeline*, as in *The Tempest*, Shakespeare seems to have missed an obvious opportunity to align his play with prominent royal views in support of hunting.

Common to the humanist argument against the hunt is the paradox that pursuing beasts ultimately bestializes men. In view of Shakespeare's repeated analogies between hunting and war, one might assume an underlying sympathy for this Erasmian position. As is usually the case in Shakespeare, however, the issue is dealt with indirectly; no character expresses a view on the subject. Characters who exhibit what might be called bestial tendencies in war are associated with the hunt – the language of the chase comes naturally to their lips on the battlefield – but the drama leaves open the question as to whether they have become violent warriors because they are hunters or whether innate tendencies towards violence simply find expression in both activities.

The closest Shakespeare comes to commentary on the psychological effect of repeated acts of violence is in *Henry V*. Encouraging his troops during the siege of Harfleur, Henry urges the nobles to "imitate the action of the tiger; / Stiffen the sinews, [conjure] up the blood, / Disguise fair nature with hard-favor'd rage" (3.1.6–8). At the end of this speech the yeomen are also included and the entire attack becomes metaphorically a hunt:

> I see you stand like greyhounds in the slips,
> [Straining] upon the start. The game's afoot!
> Follow your spirit; and upon this charge
> Cry, 'God for Harry, England, and Saint George!'   (31–34)

The exhortation is rhetorically complex, with Henry attempting to ennoble his troops by paradoxically bestializing them. The nobles become tigers; the yeomen, who are given "noble lustre" (30) in their eyes, become noble dogs, greyhounds. The image of tigerish hunting with which the speech begins is ultimately transformed into an English hunt, with the king and his mounted nobles letting slip the dogs of war.

In the present context, the most significant image in the address is that of imitating the action of the tiger, an image that suggests that savage violence is a mask, to be put on or off at will. The apparent implication of such an image is that violent action does not become habitual, that hunting and war are in a sense theatrical activities, in which humans may play temporarily the role of beasts and escape morally and psychologically unscathed. This is precisely the view of the hunt offered by the most important modern philosopher of hunting, Ortega y Gasset, who defines the sport as a conscious and artificial re-enactment of the primitive confrontation of man and beast, which depends upon "an imitation of the animal."[13] Ortega y Gasset does not explore the question as to whether such acts of imitation have the capacity to brutalize the actor. In *Henry V*, however, an argument for the brutalizing effect of war – and by extension, the hunt – appears in the long and eloquent speech by the Duke of Burgundy, in which he laments the destruction of France. The land has become wild, he says, and the people, even children, have grown "like savages – as soldiers will / That nothing do but meditate on blood – / To swearing and stern looks, defus'd attire, / And everything that seems unnatural" (5.2.59–62). Characteristically, Shakespeare does not resolve the discordant views implied by Henry V and the Duke of Burgundy; nor does he engage them in direct debate. That he mixes the language of hunting and war to frame the issue, however, suggests an imaginative awareness of the contemporary debate.

In sum, Shakespeare's representation of war is deeply affected by the traditional association of war with the hunt. His representation of the contemporary debate surrounding the hunt, however, is oblique. Whether hunting prepares men for war is left an open question, although the examples of Arviragus and Guiderius in *Cymbeline* suggest a skeptical response. Whether hunting causes cruelty or merely expresses it is also left an open question, although there is no doubt that Shakespeare identifies the two in representations of war. Hunting metaphors abound in battle, and not usually in chivalric contexts, where the formality and discipline of the hunt might carry over into the etiquette of chivalric war, but in contexts accentuating violent bloodshed and confusion. Although the contemporary ideology of both hunting and war treated them as highly ritualized activities, Shakespeare's allusions to hunting occur most often when war loses its ritualism and degenerates into anarchic violence.

In promoting the courtly ideology of the hunt, Ben Jonson was ironically led to promote an aggressive and powerful role for women. Under Elizabeth, who hunted throughout her reign, Jonson created the role of "Queen and huntress, chaste and fair." Under James, whose Queen was painted in hunting attire, with horse and leashed dogs by her side, he created a second Diana, who appears in the masque *Time Vindicated*, and who, like the Diana of *Cynthia's Revels*, promotes the values of the hunt.

Under Charles I, whose Queen, Henrietta Maria, was painted at least twice in readiness for the hunt, Jonson created the role of Maid Marian in the *Sad Shepherd*, who delights in the hunt *par force*.[14] By treating his female hunters within the aristocratic ideology of the court, the Jonson who seems almost misogynistic in such plays as *Volpone* or *Epicoene* appears to move towards a celebration of female power.

The implications of Shakespeare's treatment of female hunters is difficult to assess. The aristocratic ethos of the sport, as we have seen, is strongly "masculine," both in Shakespeare and Elizabethan society. Virility, military prowess, sexual aggression, bravado – these are the stereotypical qualities that tend to be linked to the hunt. At their most benign, they appear in such characters as Theseus and Petruchio, whose swagger has a kind of charm; at their most savage, they appear in such characters as Tamora's sons in *Titus Andronicus*, or, far more subtly, Brutus in *Julius Caesar*, for whom the ritual of the hunt justifies the suppression of human feeling. Shakespeare's skeptical and satiric treatment of the hunt is in many respects a skeptical and satiric treatment of the stereotypical male ethos.

While the satiric undercurrents in the treatment of male hunters are relatively straightforward, the implications of the roles of the few female hunters are less clear. Shakespeare follows Elizabethan custom in showing females as aggressive hunters. In this sense, he can be said to challenge, as the custom itself challenged, at least for aristocratic women, the stereotypical dichotomy between hard, unfeeling males and soft, tender females. In the context of Shakespearean hunting, however, female aggression is not a sign of liberation. In the case of Tamora, for example, hunting is a figure for human depravity. In the case of the more benign hunting female, Hippolyta, her Amazonian status does not protect her from being defeated in war by Theseus, the male hunter overcoming the female. Although Katherine in *Taming of the Shrew* is not portrayed as a hunter, her metaphoric role as haggard falcon makes her a hunter too, one ultimately tamed to do her master's will. Shakespeare's female hunters may seem aggressive and powerful, for good or ill, but in either case their power is ultimately constrained by patriarchal control.

The most interesting and problematic example of the female hunter in Shakespeare is that of the Princess in *Love's Labor's Lost*, whose reluctance to hunt springs from a tender compassion for the deer's plight. Although such sensitivity is stereotypically female, it is shared, in *As You Like It*, by both Duke Senior and Jaques. The Princess's sensitivity, moreover, is not translated into action. She pauses to reflect, but she goes on to kill. And in her case Duke Senior's justification for hunting, the need for food, provides no excuse: the hunt is mere sport, and the sport, park hunting, notoriously easy and effete. As we have seen, the Princess's suppression of her "natural" instincts in the interest of deadly social sport becomes a figure for life in the aristocratic court of Navarre. Since the young men are also suppressing their natural instincts, however, in attempting to rise above love, the general problem is shared by both male and female.

Insofar as Shakespeare's few hunting females are characterized in relation to the hunt, then, they are brought within the governing male ethos of the sport. If they are hunters, they exemplify, "naturally" or through the suppression of compassion, the stereotypically male attributes of aggression and dominance; this is true even of metaphoric hunters such as Venus. At their worst these attributes make the women monsters of depravity (Tamora); at their best, as in the case of Hippolyta or the falcon Kate, they give them a strong-willed independence that stretches but does not break the limits of patriarchal marriage. Even Tamora is ultimately undone by the male hunter, Titus, who serves up her sons as a venison pasty. In this sense all of Shakespeare's female hunters are ultimately subject to male domination, whether benign or merciless. Lavinia, raped and mutilated as a defenseless "deer" in *Titus Andronicus*, is thus not unique in being victimized by the hunting ethos; her fate merely stands at the grimly absurdist end of the spectrum. The only huntress whose power seems unchallenged is Venus, and she is a goddess.

In his allusions to hunting, as we have seen throughout this study, Shakespeare tends to draw upon the cultural critique of the hunt found in such writers as Erasmus, More, Agrippa, and Montaigne. As we saw in chapter 1, another mode of opposition was available to Shakespeare, that of the Puritans, exemplified by such writers as Philip Stubbes, who objected to hunting in part because of its cruelty to animals but mainly because of its disastrous social effects upon the poor, whose lands were destroyed and whose incomes were depleted so that hounds could live in heated kennels. This kind of social protest towards the sport seems almost invisible in Shakespeare. The testing of the hunt that runs throughout *As You Like It* includes no reference to the protests of the poor against landlords eager to expand their hunting parks at the expense of forest or common land. Nathaniel in *Love's Labor's Lost* is an Anglican curate, devoted to the hunt as a "reverent sport," not a Puritan preacher; nor is Dull a simple farmer whose crops are destroyed by deer who forage outside Navarre's park. The commoners of *Love's Labor's Lost* are as enamored of the hunt as their social superiors and, although excluded from direct participation in the sport, are as keen to compete vicariously. Their vicarious enjoyment of the pursuits of their betters evokes a subtle satiric irony rather than direct social protest. Shakespeare's satiric energy, if we can call it that, is focused more on the internal dynamics of the court world than on potential opposition from outside and below.

Ironically, discordant voices muted or unheard in Shakespeare were to have a major impact on the development of the hunt within a few short years of his death. To some extent, these voices may be detected in the brief moments of Prospero's hunt, where the latent threat of tyranny crystallizes negative views towards the royal hunt that later found expressions in the Civil Wars. But other, more impersonal forces were also at work in Jacobean society to alter profoundly the culture of the hunt: among them, wide-scale destruction or enclosure of forest land, dislocation and repression of the woodland poor, quarrels between gentry and monarchy over the control of forest land, increasing restrictions on the right to hunt, and glaring inequities in the distribution of wealth, symbolized in the expenditures on parks, horses, and dogs. By the end of the seventeenth century, these social tensions, stretched to the breaking point in the Civil Wars, had radically altered the culture of the hunt.

The historical moment in which Shakespeare's images of the hunt resonated with deep cultural meaning was thus a brief one. Within fifty years of his death the forests and parks of England were in such a parlous state that writers like Pepys struggled to renew them through campaigns of planting – more for shipbuilding and industry, however, than for the king's recreation. The parks, their fences destroyed and their deer slaughtered in the Civil Wars, were rebuilt and re-stocked with foreign animals during the Restoration, but with disappointing results; despite these efforts, as E. P. Thompson shows, in Windsor Forest alone the deer population declined from 3066 in 1607 to 461 in 1697.[15] Though it lingered on at court, the hunt, like the monarchy itself, had lost much of its royal potency. Formerly a ritual of kingship, the hunt became increasingly a sport of the squirearchy. Even the prey became less royal, the scarcity of deer, especially the traditional symbol of royalty, the red deer, encouraging the substitution of the verminous and once contemptible fox. The image of the poacher, formerly that of a member of a wild band of night hunters, slaughtering deer not out of need but out of social vengeance, became increasingly that of the isolated and poor countryman, eking out his living with an occasional rabbit for the pot. And the sympathy for the deer itself, which flickers momentarily in writers like Montaigne, Agrippa, and Shakespeare, was eventually reduced to a sentimental fantasy by the harsh philosophy of Descartes, which made of living animals insentient machines.

Although the Elizabethan culture of the hunt was soon swallowed up by history, Shakespeare's images of hunting raise questions that continue to perplex contemporary Western societies – societies in which, like his own only more so, the practical necessity for the hunt is long gone, and in which a once meaningful ritual has become mere sport. At the center of Shakespeare's evocations of the hunt lie questions about the origins and cultivation of violence, about sexuality, about male and female identity, about social bonding and political power, about ritual and emotion, and about human ties to nature. Although Shakespeare does not answer these questions – his very elusiveness seems one secret of his continuing theatrical life – he probes them energetically, forcing us to consider, even in the flash of a metaphor, what it is to be a hunter and what to be a hunter's prey.

Notes

1 Two versions of this painting exist: the original, reproduced here, painted in 1603 by Robert Peake, featuring as the prince's companion the young John, 2nd Lord Harington, and a copy, painted probably in 1606–07, replacing Lord Harington with the young Robert Devereux, 3rd Earl of Essex. Both young men were educated in the company of the prince and became his close companions. Both portraits are reproduced in Oliver Millar, *The Tudor, Stuart and Early Georgian Pictures in the Collection of Her Majesty the Queen*, 2 vols. (London: Phaidon, 1963); see vol. I, plate 6, and vol. II, plate 36. Although Millar and other art historians refer to the deer as a stag (a fully mature red deer), it has some characteristics of the fallow deer and was probably not painted from life. As Julius S. Held argues, a bloody gash on the deer's neck indicates that the Prince is not preparing to administer the *coup de grâce*, as has often been claimed, but sheathing his sword after having tested its edge and the strength of his arm in the manner recommended in [George Gascoigne's] *The Noble Arte of Venerie or Hunting* (1575), p. 134; the severing of the head will be left to others. See Held's "Le Roi à la Ciasse," *The Art Bulletin* 40 (1958): 144–45.

2 Quoted in Keith Thomas, *Man and the Natural World* (London: Allen Lane, 1983), 184.

3 Frederick Chamberlain, *The Private Character of Henry the Eighth* (New York: Ives Washburn, 1931), 140.

4 Joseph Strutt, *The Sports and Pastimes of the People of England*, ed. J. Charles Cox (London: Methuen, 1903), 9.

5 Charles Carlton, *Charles I* (London: Routledge and Kegan Paul, 1983), 3, 129.

6 Antonia Fraser, *King Charles II* (London: Weidenfeld and Nicolson, 1979), 292, 420.

7 E. P. Thompson, *Whigs and Hunters: The Origin of the Black Act* (London: Allen Lane, 1975), 40. For a useful survey of the changes to forests, chases, and parks in England, see Leonard Cantor, *The Changing English Countryside, 1400–1700* (London: Routledge and Kegan Paul, 1987), 96–118.

8 John Nichols, *The Progresses and Public Processions of Queen Elizabeth*, 3 vols. (London: 1823), I: 74n.

9 *The Noble Arte of Venerie or Hunting* (1575) has been ascribed to George Turbervile, but Charles and Ruth Prouty show conclusively that the work is Gascoigne's; see "George Gascoigne, *The Noble Arte of Venerie*, and Queen Elizabeth at Kenilworth," in *Joseph Quincy Adams Memorial Studies*, ed. James G. McManaway, Giles E. Dawson, and Edwin E. Willoughby (Washington[DC]: 1948), 650–55. Although a few sections of the work are original with Gascoigne, *The Noble Arte of Venerie* is essentially a translation of the 1573 edition of Jacques du Fouilloux, *La Venérie*, itself a compendium of earlier French hunting manuals. For reviews of the most important English manuals in the period, see D. H. Madden, *The Diary of Master William Silence* (London: Longmans, Green, 1907), 364–71, and Marcia Vale, ed., *The Gentleman's Recreations* (Cambridge: D. S. Brewer, 1977), 30–33.

10 John Manwood, *A Treatise of the Lawes of the Forest* (1615; facs. rpt. Amsterdam: Walter J. Johnson, 1976), 18–18v. Manwood's definition is not entirely accurate: forests were unenclosed game preserves but were not necessarily wooded. For a useful discussion of the forest and game laws and the controversies surrounding them, see Roger B. Manning, *Hunters and Poachers* (Oxford: Clarendon Press, 1993), 57–82.

11 Manwood, *Lawes of the Forest*, 25v–26.

12 Manning, *Hunters and Poachers*, 59.

13 For a discussion of Stuart attempts to expand the royal prerogative through the game laws, see Chester and Ethyn Kirby, "The Stuart Game Prerogative," *English Historical Review* 46 (1931): 239–54.

14 Quoted in P. B. Munsche, *Gentlemen and Poachers: The English Game Laws 1671–1831* (Cambridge: Cambridge University Press, 1981), 14; Munsche provides a useful account of the development of the laws surrounding the hunt.

15 [Gascoigne], *Arte of Venerie*, A4v.

16 For accounts of Gascoigne's life, see C. T. Prouty, *George Gascoigne* (1942; rpt. New York: Benjamin Blom, 1966) and Ronald C. Johnson, *George Gascoigne* (New York: Twayne, 1972).

17 [Gascoigne], *Arte of Venerie*, 236.

18 G. A. Wilkes, ed., *The Complete Plays of Ben Jonson*, 4 vols. (Oxford: Clarendon Press, 1981), I: 185.

19 Manning, *Hunters and Poachers*, 60. The law dates from the reign of Richard II; see *Statutes of the Realm*, 9 vols. (1810–22), II, 65, 13 Rich. II, st. 1, c. 13.

20 S. Schoenbaum, *William Shakespeare: A Documentary Life* (Oxford: Clarendon Press, 1975), 137, 167.

21 Manning, *Hunters and Poachers*, 60.

22 Schoenbaum, *William Shakespeare*, 188, 173.

23 Manning, *Hunters and Poachers*, 60. See *Statutes of the Realm*, IV, 1055, 1 Jac. I c. 27; IV, 1088, 3 Jac. I c. 13; and IV, 1167, 7 Jac. I c. 11.

24 Madden, *Diary of Master William Silence*, vii; Madden provides no evidence to show that Shakespeare would have been legally entitled to hunt.

25 Caroline F. E. Spurgeon, *Shakespeare's Imagery* (Cambridge: Cambridge University Press, 1968), 30–33, 100–05; Matt Cartmill, *A View to a Death in the*

Morning: Hunting and Nature through History (Cambridge, Mass.: Harvard University Press, 1993), 78–79.

26 Nigel Nicolson and Alasdair Hawkyard, *The Counties of Britain: A Tudor Atlas by John Speed* (London: Pavilion Books, 1988), 61.

27 Susan Lasdun, *The English Park: Royal, Private and Public* (London: 1991), 32–33.

28 William Harrison, *The Description of England*, ed. Georges Edelen (Ithaca, N.Y.: Cornell University Press, 1968), 254, 256.

29 Cited in Vale, ed., *The Gentleman's Recreations*, 29.

30 See, for example, T. S., *A Jewell for Gentrie* (1614; rpt. Amsterdam: Walter J. Johnson, 1977), F3v. This author, depending upon William Twiti's *The Art of Hunting* (1327), asserts that the hare is not only the king of all beasts of venery but the best sport.

31 For useful descriptions of all of these methods of hunting, see John Cummins, *The Hound and the Hawk: The Art of Medieval Hunting* (London: Weidenfeld and Nicolson, 1988), 32–67; although Cummins describes medieval customs, the essential nature of the hunt remained unchanged in the sixteenth and seventeenth centuries. The terminology used to describe the various kinds of hunting is vague in Shakespeare's period. Cummins' term "bow and stable" is not used, as far as I can tell, and "*par force*," when used, is often translated as "at force." The term "stable," Cummins suggests, probably refers not to the line of awaiting hunters but to the line of beaters whose job it was to herd the deer in the right direction (50–51). For additional descriptions of Elizabethan deer hunting, see Madden, *Diary of Master William Silence*, 11–65, 221–40.

32 *The Workes* (1616; rpt. Hildesheim: Georg Olms Verlag, 1971), 185–86.

33 Jean Wilson, *Entertainments for Elizabeth I* (Woodbridge, England: D. S. Brewer, 1980), 89–90.

34 For a lively survey of the use of parks in Shakespearean and Restoration drama, see Anne Barton, "Parks and Ardens," *Proceedings of the British Academy* 80 (1993): 13–104.

35 Sir Thomas Elyot, *The Book Named the Governor*, ed. S. E. Lehmberg (London: Dent, 1962), 68.

36 W. A. Baillie-Grohman and F. Baillie-Grohman, eds., *The Master of Game* (New York: Duffield, 1909), xxiii.

37 Chamberlain, *Henry the Eighth*, 181.

38 Manning, *Hunters and Poachers*, 194.

39 Ibid., 41.

40 Quoted from Schoenbaum, *Shakespeare's Lives* (Oxford: Clarendon Press, 1970), 109; Schoenbaum provides a detailed account of the various versions of the story, 108–14.

41 Ibid., 110.

42 Ibid., 111.

43 Ibid., 114, 716–17; E. K. Chambers, *William Shakespeare: A Study of Facts and Problems*, 2 vols. (Oxford: Clarendon Press, 1930), 1: 18–21.

44 Manning, *Hunters and Poachers*, 183.

45 Ibid., 10.

46 Richard Blome, *Gentleman's Recreation* (1686), 67.

47 Elizabeth Read Foster, ed., *Proceedings in Parliament 1610*, 2 vols. (New Haven: Yale University Press, 1966), 1: 51.

48 John Evelyn, *Sylva* (1664; rpt. Menston, England: Scolar Press, 1972), 115.

49 G. P. V. Akrigg, ed., *Letters of King James VI and I* (Berkeley: University of California Press, 1984), 246.

50 Thomas, *Man and the Natural World*, 153, 160–61.

51 Nichols, *Progresses*, 1: 17; the report notes that "Sir Thomas Pope had the *devising* of this show."

52 Manning, *Hunters and Poachers*, 19.

53 See *Annalia Dubrensia* (1636; rpt. Menston, Yorkshire, England: Scolar Press, 1973). In his introductory note, Bent Juel-Jensen indicates that Robert Dover "took over and revived" the games in about 1611; their date of origin is uncertain.

54 Sir Thomas Cockaine, *A Short Treatise of Hunting (1591)*, Shakespeare Association Facsimiles No.5 (Oxford University Press, 1932), A3–A3v.

55 Niccolò Machiavelli, *The Prince*, ed. and trans., Robert M. Adams, 2nd edn.(New York: W. W. Norton, 1992), 41.

56 Elyot, *Governor*, 66–67.

57 James I, *The Workes* (1616; rpt. Hildesheim: Georg Olms Verlag, 1971), 185–86. Praise for the martial hunt is also to be found in Plato's *Laws*, in which the noblest hunting is "the hunting of four-footed prey that employs horses, dogs, and the bodies of the hunters themselves. In this type the hunters use running, blows, and missiles thrown by their own hands to prevail over all their prey, and this is the type that should be practiced by whoever cultivates the courage that is divine" (Trans. Thomas L. Pangle [Basic Books: New York, 1980]), 217.

58 José Ortega y Gasset, *Meditations on Hunting*, trans. Howard B. Wescott (New York: Charles Scribners, 1972), 135.

59 Robert P. Adams, *The Better Part of Valor* (Seattle: University of Washington Press, 1962), 15, 45–47, 145–46. See also Claus Uhlig, "'The Sobbing Deer': *As You Like It*, II.i.21–66 and the Historical Context," *Renaissance Drama* 3 (1970): 79–109; Uhlig sketches the development of this humanist tradition from its origin in John of Salisbury's *Policraticus* to Pope's *Windsor Forest*.

60 Thomas More, *Utopia*, trans. Ralph Robinson (1551; facs. rpt. Amsterdam: Da Capo Press, 1969), M2–M2v.

61 Desiderius Erasmus, *Chaloner: The Praise of Folie*, ed. Clarence H. Miller, *Early English Text Society* (London: Oxford University Press, 1965), 54.

62 Henry Cornelius Agrippa, *Of the Vanitie and Uncertaintie of Artes and Sciences*, ed. Catherine M. Dunn (Northridge: California State University, 1974), 260–63.

63 Sir Philip Sidney, *The Countess of Pembroke's Arcadia (The Old Arcadia)*, ed. Jean Robertson (Oxford: Clarendon Press, 1973), 259.

64 Ovid, *Metamorphoses*, trans. Mary M. Innes (Baltimore: Penguin Books, 1955), 31–33, 337.

65 Ortega y Gasset, *Meditations on Hunting*, 89.
66 Cavendish's poem is printed in *Kissing the Rod: An Anthology of Seventeenth-Century Women's Verse*, ed. Germaine Greer, et. al. (London: Virago Press, 1988), 168–72.
67 Cartmill, *A View to a Death*, 82–83; Cartmill identifies the author erroneously as Turbervile. Gascoigne's ambivalence is supported by the fact that three of the four subversive poems – those of the hare, fox, and badger – do not appear in the French original, and the fourth, that of the hart, is expanded from 99 to 133 lines (see *Arte of Venerie*, 135–40).
68 Thomas, *Man and the Natural World*, 154.
69 Philip Stubbes, *The Anatomie of Abuses* (1583; facs. rpt. Amsterdam: Da Capo Press, 1972), P5.
70 [Gascoigne], *Arte of Venerie*, chapter 76, p. 358 (the text's pagination is erroneous).
71 Thompson, *Whigs and Hunters*, 56.
72 Harrison, *Description*, 253–63, 326–29. For a useful treatment of Harrison's religious inclinations, see Annabel Patterson, *Reading Holinshed's Chronicles* (Chicago: University of Chicago Press, 1994), 26–27, 58–70.
73 Harrison, *Description*, 259.
74 *Hunters and Poachers*, 224.
75 *The Field* 3(1853): 342.
76 For Nonsuch, see Nichols, *Progresses*, 1: 74n; for Cowdray, see Wilson, *Entertainments for Elizabeth I*, 89–90.
77 John Stevens, *Music and Poetry in the Early Tudor Court* (Cambridge: Cambridge University Press, 1979), 401.
78 [Gascoigne], *Arte of Venerie*, 140.
79 These are common to the hunting manuals. In the *Arte of Venerie*, for example, George Gascoigne cites the bone in the heart of the hart as a cure for trembling of the heart; the pizzle as a cure for the bloody flux; the head as an antidote to poisons; the horn as a cure for worms; and the marrow or grease as a cure for the gout (39–40).
80 For the medieval traditions behind this version of the hunt of love, see Marcelle Thiébaux, *The Stag of Love* (Ithaca, NY: Cornell University Press, 1974); Thiébaux cites Orsino's speech on p. 245.

2 HUNTRESSES IN *VENUS AND ADONIS* AND *LOVE'S LABOR'S LOST*

1 See *Kissing the Rod: An Anthology of Seventeenth-Century Women's Verse*, ed. Germaine Greer, et. al. (London: Virago Press, 1988), 172.
2 *Calendar of State Papers, Venetian*, 15 (10 July, 1618), 260.
3 Desiderius Erasmus, *Chaloner: The Praise of Folie*, ed. Clarence H. Miller, *Early English Text Society* (London: Oxford University Press, 1965), 54.
4 For a useful anthology of criticism on the poem, which includes a wide-ranging introductory survey, see Philip C. Kolin, ed., *Venus and Adonis: Critical Essays* (New York: Garland Publishing, 1997).

5 William Shakespeare, *The Poems*, ed. John Roe (Cambridge: Cambridge University Press, 1992), 135n. 1122.

6 Coppélia Kahn, for example, in *Man's Estate* (Berkeley: University of California Press, 1981), sees Adonis's claim that he is too young to love as merely a mask for his refusal to love at all (29); for her, Adonis is fatally narcissistic and his tragedy represents the idea that "for a man, sexual love of woman is vital to masculinity"(42). Although Adonis's adolescent narcissism is important to the poem, Kahn's formulation, as I hope will become clear, oversimplifies the characters of Adonis and Venus and the conception of love developed throughout.

7 In *Hunting in Middle English Literature* (Woodbridge, Suffolk: Boydell Press, 1993), Anne Rooney discusses the medieval tradition of the chaste hunter in ways that are suggestive for Adonis. She cites, in particular, a story curiously like that of Adonis, Marie de France's *Guigemar*, in which the hero, who spurns love but loves to hunt, wounds a mysterious white hind, only to have the arrow rebound and pierce his thigh. When Guigemar later falls in love, he leaves the hunt behind. In this story, as in others, according to Rooney, love of the hunt is linked to sexual immaturity (50–51).

8 G. P. V. Akrigg, ed., *Letters of King James VI and I* (Berkeley: University of California Press, 1984), 8. The portrait, by Arnold Bronckorst and dated *c.* 1580, is in the Scottish National Portrait Gallery, Edinburgh.

9 Charles Carlton, *Charles I* (London: Routledge and Kegan Paul, 1983), 3.

10 Ronald Hutton, *Charles the Second* (Oxford: Clarendon Press, 1989), 3.

11 For an account of the relationship between Shakespeare and the Earl, see G. P. V. Akrigg, *Shakespeare and the Earl of Southampton* (London: Hamish Hamilton, 1968). See also the provocative but unconvincingly abstract attempt by Patrick M. Murphy to read *Venus and Adonis* as a critique of the custom of wardship under which Southampton suffered: "Wriothesley's Resistance: Wardship Practices, and Ovidian Narratives in Shakespeare's *Venus and Adonis*," in *Venus and Adonis*, ed. Kolin, 323–43.

12 Quoted in Shakespeare, *The Poems*, ed. Roe, 13n.

13 Charlotte Carmichael Stopes, *The Life of Henry, Third Earl of Southampton, Shakespeare's Patron* (Cambridge: Cambridge University Press, 1922), 27.

14 *Calendar of State Papers, Domestic*. Edward VI. vol. II: 1581–90, 680 (14 July 1590); Akrigg, *Southampton*, 27.

15 B. W. Beckingsale, *Burghley, Tudor Statesman* (London: Macmillan, 1967), 276–77.

16 Akrigg, *Southampton*, 66, 136, 144.

17 For a brief review of Elizabethan adolescent and courtship customs, see Edward Berry, *Shakespeare's Comic Rites* (Cambridge: Cambridge University Press, 1984), 26–32.

18 *Berkeley Manuscripts: Abstracts and Extracts of Smyth's Lives of the Berkeleys*, ed. Thomas Dudley Fosbroke (London: John Nichols, 1821), 113, 186.

19 If, as a recent study of *Les Chasses* tentatively suggests, the young man is the young Ferdinand I, he would have been about thirty when the work was

being done. Both the identification and dates, however, are subject to doubt; see Arnout Balis, et al., *Les Chasses de Maximilien* (Paris: Editions de la Réunion des musées nationaux, 1993), 122.

20 Evidence of boar hunting is difficult to find and ambiguous. If the sport existed at all, it was certainly rare. See Joseph Strutt, *The Sports and Pastimes of the People of England*, ed. J. Charles Cox (London: Methuen, 1903), 14, and William Harrison, *The Description of England*, ed. Georges Edelen (Ithaca, N.Y.: Cornell University Press, 1968), 328. Roger B. Manning observes that if James I hunted a wild boar in Windsor Forest in 1617, it must have been put there for his pleasure; see *Hunters and Poachers* (Oxford: Clarendon Press, 1993), 23.

21 Quoted in John Cummins, *The Hound and the Hawk: The Art of Medieval Hunting* (London: Weidenfeld and Nicolson, 1988), 97. Cummins's book includes a useful survey of the nature of the medieval boar hunt and its symbolism (96–108). See also Rooney, *Hunting in Middle English Literature*, 78–85; Rooney argues that the "boar-hunter is a paragon of military prowess"(85).

22 [George Gascoigne], *The Noble Arte of Venerie or Hunting* (1575), 149.

23 Sir Thomas Elyot, *The Book Named the Governor*, ed. S. E. Lehmberg (London: Dent, 1962), 37.

24 For a brief review of interpretations of the boar, see Philip C. Kolin, "Venus and/or Adonis Among the Critics," in *Venus and Adonis*, ed. Kolin, 45–50.

25 Edward Topsell, *The Historie of the Foure-Footed Beastes* (1607; facs. rpt. Amsterdam: Da Capo Press, 1973), 697.

26 A. T. Hatto, "'Venus and Adonis' – and the Boar," *Modern Language Review* 41 (1946): 353–61.

27 Douglas Bush, *Mythology and the Renaissance Tradition in English Poetry* (1932; rpt. New York: Pageant Book Co., 1957), 138n.

28 William Keach, *Elizabethan Erotic Narratives* (New Brunswick, N.J.: Rutgers University Press, 1977), 81.

29 Don Cameron Allen, "On *Venus and Adonis*," in *Elizabethan and Jacobean Studies Presented to Frank Percy Wilson*, ed. Herbert Davis and Helen Gardner (Oxford: Clarendon Press, 1959), 100–11. W. R. Streitberger qualifies and extends Allen's argument usefully by placing Adonis's development in the context of Elizabethan adolescence. He, too, however, ignores the erotic implications of Adonis's love of the hunt, which he interprets as a desire for a healthy and moral life, as defined by such writers as Thomas Elyot. See W. R. Streitberger, "Ideal Conduct in *Venus and Adonis*," in *Venus and Adonis*, ed. Kolin, 171–79.

30 Marcelle Thiébaux notes that the medieval *Ovide Moralisé* treats Adonis's death as "a self-induced punishment for his excessive indulgence in hunting, a wicked pastime anyway which, taken allegorically, represents his lechery"(296); see "The Mouth of the Boar as a Symbol in Medieval Literature," *Romance Philology* 22 (1969): 281–99. There is no evidence that this interpretation influenced Shakespeare's.

31 Matt Cartmill, *A View to a Death in the Morning: Hunting and Nature through History* (Cambridge, Mass.: Harvard University Press, 1993), 238.

32 Jonathan Bate, *Shakespeare and Ovid* (Oxford: Clarendon Press, 1993), 60–65.

33 Bruce R. Smith, *Homosexual Desire in Shakespeare's England* (Chicago: University of Chicago Press, 1991), 136.

34 Harrison, *Description of England*, 254.

35 In an article confirming the identity of the portrait's subject as Elizabeth of Bohemia, Mark Weiss suggests that it was executed in conjunction with the painting of Prince Henry and Sir John Harington at the ritual death of the deer. Sir John was a close friend of Prince Henry's, and Elizabeth was sent to live with Lord and Lady Harington in Warwickshire. According to Weiss, close inspection of the two paintings reveals, in addition, that they represent the same deer, hound, and horse. See Mark Weiss, "Elizabeth of Bohemia by Robert Peake," *Apollo* 132 (1990): 407–10.

36 Jean Wilson, *Entertainments for Elizabeth I* (Woodbridge, England: D. S. Brewer, 1980), 89–90.

37 Elyot, *Governor*, 68.

38 James I, *The Workes* (1616; rpt. Hildesheim: Georg Olms Verlag, 1971), 185–86.

39 For brief but useful reviews of the traditions surrounding the hare, see Cummins, *Hound and the Hawk*, 110–19, and Beryl Rowland, *Animals with Human Faces* (Knoxville: University of Tennessee Press, 1973), 88–93.

40 See, for example, Allen, "On *Venus and Adonis*," 109.

41 Margaret Cavendish's "The Hunting of the Hare," which presents the hunt from the terrified hare's point of view, echoes Venus's description; see *Kissing the Rod*, 171.

42 [Gascoigne], *Arte of Venerie*, A4v.

43 Michel de Montaigne, *The Essays*, trans. John Florio (1603; facs. rpt. Menston, England: Scolar Press, 1969), 247, 249 (the latter page has been numbered erroneously as 237).

44 Keach, *Elizabethan Erotic Narratives*, 65.

45 Heather Dubrow, *Captive Victors: Shakespeare's Narrative Poems and Sonnets* (Ithaca, New York: Cornell University Press, 1987), 25–26.

46 Bate, *Shakespeare and Ovid*, 58.

47 Dubrow, *Captive Victors*, 42.

48 Keach, *Elizabethan Erotic Narratives*, 84.

49 See, however, Louis Adrian Montrose, *"Curious-Knotted Garden": The Form, Themes, and Contexts of Shakespeare's* Love's Labour's Lost (Salzburg: University of Salzburg, 1977), 109–12. Montrose's approach to the hunt complements my own, I believe, although he restricts himself to brief comments on its symbolic and metaphoric significance and does not develop its relationship to criticisms of hunting in Elizabethan society.

50 Ibid., 110.

51 Miriam Gilbert, *Love's Labour's Lost* (Manchester: Manchester University Press, 1993), 99; if I understand Gilbert correctly, this production also

represented the Princess as deciding not to hunt, an interpretation for which I can find no support in the text.

52 Graham Holderness, Nick Potter, and John Turner, *Shakespeare: Out of Court* (London: Macmillan, 1990), 19–48.

53 *The Geneva Bible*, ed. Lloyd E. Berry (1560; facs. rpt. Madison: University of Wisconsin Press, 1969), *2 Corinthians*: i. 12.

54 William C. Carroll, *The Great Feast of Language in* Love's Labour's Lost (Princeton: Princeton University Press, 1976), 39.

55 Desiderius Erasmus, *Chaloner: The Praise of Folie*, ed. Clarence H. Miller, *Early English Text Society* (London: Oxford University Press, 1965), 54.

56 William C. Carroll discusses the speech as "choric commentary"; see *Great Feast of Language*, 91.

57 In a useful article that links Queen Elizabeth in detail to the Princess of France, Maurice Hunt suggests that the Princess's reluctance to hunt is "stereotypically feminine"(183). Hunt fails to consider the broad anti-hunting context within which the Princess's remarks are made; nor is he able to associate Elizabeth herself with such a negative view of hunting. See "The Double Figure of Elizabeth in *Love's Labor's Lost*," *Essays in Literature* 19 (1992): 173–92.

58 Patricia Parker, "Preposterous Reversals: *Love's Labor's Lost*," *Modern Language Quarterly* 54 (1993): 435–82. Parker demonstrates the ways in which the highbrow verbal comedy of the play is repeatedly "contaminated or brought low by the 'low matter' of the bodily and sexual"(437).

59 The terminology is conventional. John Manwood names a buck of the first year, a "Fawne"; of the second, a "Pricket"; of the third, a "Sorell"; of the fourth, a "Sore"; of the fifth, a "Bucke of the first head"; and of the sixth, a "Bucke, or, a great Bucke"(*Lawes of the Forest*, 43v).

60 Montrose, "*Curious-Knotted Garden*," 67–90.

61 David Bevington, "'Jack Hath Not Jill': Failed Courtship in Lyly and Shakespeare," *Shakespeare Survey* 42(1989): 6.

62 Montaigne, *Essays*, 251.

3 "SOLEMN" HUNTING IN *TITUS ANDRONICUS* AND *JULIUS CAESAR*

1 Geoffrey Bullough, ed., *Narrative and Dramatic Sources of Shakespeare*, 8 vols. (London: Routledge and Kegan Paul, 1957),VI: 40, 42. For a review of the debate on sources, see *Titus Andronicus*, ed. Alan Hughes (Cambridge: Cambridge University Press, 1994), 6–9.

2 Bullough, *Narrative and Dramatic Sources*, V:86.

3 The words "hart" and "stag" tend to be used interchangeably in descriptions of the hunt, since both were highly respected and hunted in the same ceremonial manner. The author of one handbook, for example, advises that "in the hunting of the Hart or Stag, being of all the most princely and royal chase, it giveth an exceeding grace unto a huntsman to use the tearmes fit and proper unto the same" (T. S., *A Jewell for Gentrie* [1614; rpt. Amsterdam:

Walter J. Johnson, 1977], F2). Technically, the hart was the larger and nobler of the two. John Manwood observes that "of all other beasts of venery, the Hart is the most noblest, and the most worthiest beast, and taketh the first place"(*A Treatise of the Lawes of the Forest* [1615; facs. rpt. Amsterdam: Walter J. Johnson, 1976], 41v).

4 "The Ceremonies of *Titus Andronicus*," in *Mirror Up To Shakespeare*, ed. J. C. Gray (Toronto: University of Toronto Press, 1984), 160; see also Stephen X. Mead, "The Crisis of Ritual in *Titus Andronicus*," *Exemplaria* 6 (1994): 459–79; Mead reads the play as "a crisis of community-binding ritual"(463).

5 For an illuminating study of the importance of this feast to the ritualism of the play, see Naomi Conn Liebler, *Shakespeare's Festive Tragedy* (London: Routledge, 1995), 85–111; Liebler sees in the Rome of the play a conflict between a traditional religious order and an emerging secular and political one.

6 For insightful accounts of both plays in relation to the commonplace Elizabethan horror of human sacrifice, which was intensified both by Reformation debates about the Mass and by colonial encounters abroad, see Richard Marienstras, *New Perspectives on the Shakespearean World*, trans. Janet Lloyd (Cambridge: Cambridge University Press, 1985), 40–72.

7 Walter Burkert, *Homo Necans: The Anthropology of Ancient Greek Sacrificial Ritual and Myth*, trans. Peter Bing (Berkeley: University of California Press, 1983), 38.

8 See Arnold Van Gennep, *The Rites of Passage*, trans. Monika B. Vizedom and Gabrielle L. Caffee (Chicago: University of Chicago Press, 1960).

9 See [George Gascoigne], *The Noble Arte of Venerie or Hunting* (1575), 90, 95.

10 [Gascoigne], *Arte of Venerie*, 126–35; further citations to this edition are indicated parenthetically.

11 William Twiti, *The Art of Hunting (1327)*, ed. Bror Danielsson, *Stockholm Studies in English 37* (Stockholm: Almqvist and Wiksell, 1977), 51. Stage representations of this event suggest that it was widespread in the period; see my treatment of the procession homeward in *As You Like It* (p. 181).

12 See Keith Thomas, *Man and the Natural World* (London: Allen Lane, 1983), 17–50.

13 *Countrey Contentments* (1615; facs. rpt. Amsterdam: Theatrum Orbis Terrarum, 1973), 3.

14 Michel De Montaigne, *The Essays*, trans. John Florio (1603; facs. rpt. Menston, England: Scolar Press, 1969), 248. See also Richard Marienstras's insightful treatment of the ritual of the hunt in *New Perspectives*, 11–39.

15 *Lawes of the Forest*, 18–18v.

16 *Chaloner: The Praise of Folie*, ed. Clarence H. Miller, *Early English Text Society* (London: Oxford University Press, 1965), 54.

17 As Anne Barton observes, both the setting and nature of this hunt are ambiguous; see "Parks and Ardens," *Proceedings of the British Academy 80* (1993): 55–56. At different times, the hunt seems to take place in a forest, chase, and park; to some characters, the place is cheerful, to some, ominous.

The sport combines, oddly, the pursuit of a panther into a pit and the *par force* pursuit of a stag. The confusion seems appropriate in a play that dissolves the boundaries between the civilized and barbarian.

18 For the custom of the *reveille*, see John Brand, *Observations on Popular Antiquities* (London: Chatto and Windus, 1877), 403–05. For a description of making a bay, see [Gascoigne], *Arte of Venerie*, 124–27.

19 For an enlightening discussion of the displacement of the Virgilian by the Ovidian myth throughout the play, see Heather James, "Cultural Disintegration in *Titus Andronicus*: Mutilating Titus, Vergil and Rome," *Themes in Drama* 13 (1991): 123–40.

20 Ovid, *Metamorphoses*, trans. Mary M. Innes (Baltimore: Penguin Books, 1955), 152.

21 William Harrison, *The Description of England*, ed. Georges Edelen (Ithaca, N.Y.: Cornell University Press, 1968), 132.

22 The most influential study of *Julius Caesar* from this perspective is that of Brents Stirling in *Unity in Shakespearian Tragedy* (New York: Columbia University Press, 1956), 40–54.

23 The image of a carcass hewn and thrown to the hounds probably refers to the fox, marten or gray; see D. H. Madden, *The Diary of Master William Silence* (London: Longmans, Green, 1907), 63.

24 René Girard, *A Theater of Envy: William Shakespeare* (New York: Oxford University Press, 1991), 213. Girard's theory of the sacrificial crisis fits *Julius Caesar* unusually well; in his view, Cassius's mimetic envy of Caesar precipitates an act of foundational violence, which fails because it does not encompass the total community (185–226). Girard's conception of the origin of sacrifice is interestingly juxtaposed with Burkert's in Robert G. Hamerton-Kelly, ed., *Violent Origins* (Stanford: Stanford University Press, 1987).

25 Arthur Humphreys notes that the word "spoil" was a "hunting term for the cutting up of the quarry, from Old French *espoille*, Latin *spolium*, the skin stripped from the dead animal." His commentary on the passage as a whole is helpful; see *Julius Caesar*, ed. Arthur Humphreys, *The World's Classics* (Oxford: Oxford University Press, 1994), 170n.206.

26 Allusions to the tradition occur in Wyatt's sonnet, "Whoso List to Hunt" and in [Gascoigne], *Arte of Venerie*, 43. For a richly documented study of the tradition, see Michael Bath, *The Image of the Stag: Iconographic Themes in Western Art* (Baden-Baden: Verlag Valentin Koerner, 1992), 23–64.

27 For an account of the importance of blood to the spectacle of the play, see Leo Kirschbaum, "Shakespeare's Stage Blood," in *Shakespeare: Julius Caesar*, ed. Peter Ure (London: Macmillan, 1969), 152–59; Kirschbaum's article was originally published in *PMLA* 64(1949).

28 For the rite of "blooding," see above, pp. 39–41. The account of bathing occurs in a letter of 12 June, 1619 from Nathaniel Brent to Sir Thomas Edmondes; see *Calendar of State Papers, Domestic, 1619–23* (London: 1858), x: 53. Reports of the medicinal and cosmetic value of bathing in deer's blood are common in the hunting manuals; Gervase Markham, for example, says

that the blood of the stag is "excellent for all kinde of Fluxes, and to make the skin white and smooth"; see *Countrey Contentments*, 28.

29 Who actually kills the stag is not described in most of the manuals. They tend to imply, however, that the killing is done by a single individual. The *Noble Arte* illustrates the event with a woodcut showing a hart at bay and a single huntsman, sword drawn; see chapter 41. It is quite possible, of course, that the dogs themselves would often kill the animal. Sir Thomas Cockaine seems to imply as much in his description of the death: "When you have killed the Stagge with your hounds . . ."(c3); see *A Short Treatise of Hunting (1591), Shakespeare Association Facsimiles No.5* (Oxford University Press, 1932). Antony's use of the word "princes" would become doubly ironic in such a case.

30 *Arte of Venerie*, 124–25. The French original includes the story of the Emperor and a general moral on the variability of fortune but lacks any acknowledgment of the moral difficulty that disturbs Gascoigne; see Jaques Du Fouilloux, *La Venerie de Jaques du Fouilloux* (Paris: Abel l'Angelier, 1606), 52.

31 *Hunters and Poachers*, 48.

32 John Smyth, *The Lives of the Berkeleys*, ed. John Maclean, 3 vols. (Gloucester: John Bellows, 1883–85), II: 378–79.

33 Manning, *Hunters and Poachers*, 137.

34 For an account of the complex mixture of politics, religion, and economics in a massacre of deer in 1642, see Dan Beaver, "The Great Deer Massacre: Animals, Honor, and Communication in Early Modern England," *Journal of British Studies* 38 (1999): 187–216.

35 Madden, *Diary of Master William Silence*, 31–32.

4 THE "MANNING" OF KATHERINE: FALCONRY IN *THE TAMING OF THE SHREW*

1 Edwin Wilson, ed., *Shaw on Shakespeare* (New York: E. P. Dutton, 1961), 188.

2 Lynda E. Boose, "Scolding Brides and Bridling Scolds: Taming the Woman's Unruly Member," *Shakespeare Quarterly* 42 (1991): 181n. Boose's own essay powerfully challenges this consensus by placing the play in the context of the barbaric custom of bridling scolds. For reasons that should become clear, although I much admire Boose's essay, I find that the taming of falcons provides a more immediate context for the play than the bridling of scolds. Boose provides a helpful list of criticism dealing with issues of gender. For a more recent and more general survey of criticism, and a helpful contextual guide, see Frances E. Dolan, *William Shakespeare*, The Taming of the Shrew: *Texts and Contexts* (New York: St. Martin's Press, 1996). The most thorough survey of the theatrical tradition is to be found in Tori Haring-Smith, *From Farce to Metadrama: A Stage History of 'The Taming of the Shrew,' 1594–1983* (Westport, Conn.: Greenwood Press, 1985); see also Graham Holderness, *The Taming of the Shrew* (Manchester: Manchester University Press), 1989.

3 Robert B. Heilman, "The 'Taming' Untamed, or the Return of the Shrew," *Modern Language Quarterly* 27 (1966): 157.

4 Peter Saccio, "Shrewd and Kindly Farce," *Shakespeare Survey* 37 (1984): 33–40.

5 John C. Bean, "Comic Structure and the Humanizing of Kate in *The Taming of the Shrew*," in *The Woman's Part: Feminist Criticism of Shakespeare*, ed. Carolyn Ruth Swift Lenz et al. (1980), 74.

6 Joel Fineman, "The Turn of the Shrew," in *Shakespeare and the Question of Theory*, ed. Patricia Parker and Geoffrey Hartman (New York: Methuen, 1985), 141.

7 Saccio, "Shrewd and Kindly Farce," 37.

8 Marianne Novy, *Love's Argument* (Chapel Hill: University of North Carolina Press, 1984), 62.

9 *The Geneva Bible*, ed. Lloyd E. Berry (1560; facs. rpt. Madison: University of Wisconsin Press, 1969), 1.28.

10 Gervase Markham, *Countrey Contentments* (1615; facs. rpt. Amsterdam: Da Capo Press, 1973), 2–3.

11 George Turbervile, *The Booke of Faulconrie or Hauking* (1575; facs. rpt. Amsterdam: Theatrum Orbis Terrarum, 1969), 6.

12 Anne Barton, "Introduction" to *The Taming of the Shrew*, in *The Riverside Shakespeare*, ed. G. Blakemore Evans (Boston: Houghton Mifflin, 1974), 106.

13 Fredson Bowers, ed., *The Dramatic Works in the Beaumont and Fletcher Canon*, vol. IV (Cambridge: Cambridge University Press, 1979), 1.2.147–57.

14 The definition is from the very useful glossary provided in Frederick II of Hohenstaufen, *The Art of Falconry*, ed. and trans., Casey A. Wood and F. Marjorie Fyfe (Stanford: Stanford University Press, 1943).

15 Ibid.

16 Symon Latham, *Lathams Falconry* (1615; facs. rpt. Amsterdam: Theatrum Orbis Terrarum, 1976), 4; for a useful survey of Shakespeare's treatment of falconry, see Maurice Pope, "Shakespeare's Falconry," *Shakespeare Survey* 44 (1991): 131–43.

17 Edmund Bert, *An Approved Treatise of Hawkes and Hawking* (1619; facs. rpt. Amsterdam: Theatrum Orbis Terrarum, 1968), 3.

18 Bert, *Hawkes and Hawking*, 7.

19 Frederick II of Hohenstaufen, *Art of Falconry*, 157.

20 Markham, *Countrey Contentments*, 88–89. The word "broaking," if such it is (the "b" is difficult to decipher) presumably comes from the verb "to broke," which means to negotiate or bargain; or perhaps the word is "stroaking." George R. Hibbard quotes the passage, with the word as "stroaking," in *"The Taming of the Shrew*: A Social Comedy," *Tennessee Studies in Literature*, Special Issue No. 2 (1964): 15–28; Hibbard's insightful article focuses on the play as a realistic and satiric depiction of the marriage market in Elizabethan England.

21 T. H. White, *The Goshawk* (London: Jonathan Cape, 1951), 16. White's account of his own, ultimately unsuccessful, attempt to train a hawk by

Elizabethan methods conveys forcefully the complex and intense relationship between man and bird.

22 Bert, *Hawkes and Hawking*, 41, 49.

23 Laurie E. Maguire makes this point in her insightful discussion of Shakespeare's several Kates: "'Household Kates': Chez Petruchio, Percy and Plantagenet," in *Gloriana's Face*, ed. S. P. Cerasano and Marion Wynne-Davies (Detroit: Wayne State University Press, 1992), 133.

24 *The Geneva Bible*, Genesis 2.20.

25 Turbervile, *Booke of Faulconrie or Hauking*, 130, 142.

26 Bert, *Hawkes and Hawking*, 52.

27 Wilson, ed., *Shaw on Shakespeare*, 186. The stage tradition of the whip seems to have originated with Garrick in the nineteenth century; see Haring-Smith, *From Farce to Metadrama*, 29. A delightful variation on the whip motif occurs in the 1929 film of the play featuring Douglas Fairbanks, Jr. and Mary Pickford: Petruchio carries a big whip but is eventually cowed by Katherine, who carries a small one.

28 White, *Goshawk*, 102.

29 Camille Wells Slights, "The Raw and the Cooked in *The Taming of the Shrew*," *Journal of English and Germanic Philology* 88 (1989): 180; although I am not finally persuaded by Slights's article, she presents a thoughtful case for Petruchio as teaching Katherine "that she can create her own identity"(181).

30 In the Arden edition of the play, Brian Morris also sees this episode in relation to the training of a falcon. For Morris, however, it is merely one of a series of tests of obedience that culminates in Katherine's final speech; he does not distinguish between the process of training and the practice of the sport itself, which occurs in the final scene of the play (see *The Taming of the Shrew* [London: Methuen, 1981], 127–28).

31 Latham, *Lathams Falconry*, 24–25.

32 See *Annalia Dubrensia. Upon the yeerely celebration of Mr. Robert Dovers Olimpick Games upon Cotswold-Hills* (London: 1636).

33 This is the gloss provided by H. J. Oliver; see *The Taming of the Shrew* (Oxford: Oxford University Press, 1994), 223n.33. In *The Noble Arte of Venerie or Hunting* (1575), George Gascoigne directs the hunters to start the chase of a "harbored" deer by crying "To him, to him, thats he thats he"(106).

34 For further development of connections between the induction and the ending, see Dorothea Kehler, "Echoes of the Induction in *The Taming of the Shrew*," *Renaissance Papers* (1986): 31–42.

35 Margaret Loftus Ranald, *Shakespeare and His Social Context* (New York: AMS Press, 1987), 117.

36 Ibid., 119.

37 Ibid., 132.

38 Turbervile, *Booke of Faulconrie*, 6.

39 Dolan, The Taming of the Shrew: *Texts and Contexts*, 307–08; Dolan provides a brief discussion of the role of falconry in the play and excerpts from the books on falconry by Turbervile and Latham (304–12).

40 Morris, ed., *The Taming of the Shrew*, 128, 133, 143.

41 Bean, "Comic Structure," 65–78.

42 See William and Malleville Haller, "The Puritan Art of Love," *Huntington Library Quarterly* 5 (1942), 250–51.

43 Thomas, *Man and the Natural World*, 32–33.

44 Quoted in Matt Cartmill, *A View to a Death in the Morning: Hunting and Nature through History* (Cambridge, Mass.: Harvard University Press, 1993), 51.

45 Latham, *Lathams Falconry*, 35.

46 For a radically different reading of this episode, see P. J. Gabriner, "Hierarchy, Harmony and Happiness: Another Look at the Hunting Dogs in the 'Induction' to *The Taming of the Shrew*," in *Reclamations of Shakespeare*, ed. A. J. Hoenselaars (Amsterdam: Rodopi, 1994), 201–10. Gabriner interprets the dogs as "an emblem of the comic ideal, in which individual voices are neither eliminated nor merged into one, but are rather so ranged within a natural order that mutual harmony and social happiness become possible"; they therefore represent the natural hierarchical order into which Katherine is "liberated" by Petruchio (210).

47 [Gascoigne], *Arte of Venerie*, 32–38.

48 Thomas, *Man and the Natural World* (London: Allen Lane, 1983), 103.

49 [Gascoigne], *Arte of Venerie*, 34, 30.

50 Coppélia Kahn, *Man's Estate* (Berkeley: University of California Press, 1981), 104, 117.

51 Holderness, *The Taming of the Shrew*, 26–48; for the earlier stage history, see Haring-Smith, *From Farce to Metadrama*.

52 Leah Marcus, "The Shakespearean Editor as Shrew-Tamer," *English Literary Renaissance* 22 (1992): 178, 198–99.

53 John Smyth was born in 1567 and joined the household of Lord Henry Berkeley in 1584 to attend upon the son and heir, Thomas, then nine years old. He joined William Ligon and young Thomas for studies at Magdalen College, Oxford, for three years and then studied at the Middle Temple. He rejoined the household in 1596, serving in various capacities, and died in 1640. Although the title-page indicates that his history ends in 1618, Smyth must have added to it after that date, for in some instances it extends to 1628. I use the following edition of the work throughout this chapter, citing page references to volume II (1883) parenthetically: John Smyth, *The Lives of the Berkeleys*, ed. John Maclean, 3 vols. (Gloucester: John Bellows, 1883–85). For a summary of Smyth's life, see the preface to volume I. Smyth's account of the family, including the members for whom he worked, is remarkably candid and lends credence to his dedicatory statement of purpose: "In a playne and home-bred stile cleere from passion or partiallity, Ile freely write the truth I know."

54 Most editors now consider the mysterious play entitled *The Taming of A Shrew* to be dependent upon Shakespeare's *The Taming of the Shrew*. If they are correct, then *The Shrew* must have been written before 1594, when *A Shrew* was published; generally, editors suggest 1592 or somewhat earlier for

Shakespeare's work. For an excellent introduction to the play, including the question of date, see the edition of Ann Thompson (Cambridge: Cambridge University Press, 1984). The argument for the Berkeleys as a "source" does not depend upon a specific date for Shakespeare's play or a specific relationship between it and *A Shrew*.

55 See H. R. Woudhuysen, *Sir Philip Sidney and the Circulation of Manuscripts 1558–1640* (Oxford: Clarendon Press, 1996); Woudhuysen argues that the Queen's College copy of the *Old Arcadia* was probably made for Henry Berkeley, whose connections to the Sidney family were close enough to allow some talk of marriage between his daughters and Philip and Robert Sidney in 1573. Woudhuysen suggests "that few would call a bird Stella unless they had a particular interest in Sidney and his literary works"(326).

56 Manning, *Hunters and Poachers*, 141; see also 139–43.

57 E. K. Chambers, *The Elizabethan Stage*, 4 vols. (Oxford: Clarendon Press, 1923), II: 103–04.

58 Mark Eccles, *Shakespeare in Warwickshire* (Madison: University of Wisconsin Press, 1961), 116–17. The first to provide a detailed account of Thomas Russell was Leslie Hotson; see *I, William Shakespeare* (New York: Oxford University Press, 1938).

59 See the Arden edition of *A Midsummer Night's Dream*, ed. Harold F. Brooks (Bristol: Methuen, 1979), liii–lvii.

60 For discussions of the sources, see Geoffrey Bullough, ed., *Narrative and Dramatic Sources of Shakespeare*, 8 vols. (London: Routledge and Kegan Paul, 1957), II: 57–68, and Thompson, *Shrew*, 9–17.

61 Ibid., 11, 13.

5 THE "RASCAL" FALSTAFF IN WINDSOR

1 The pun is clear from Holoferne's lines in *Love's Labor's Lost* describing the deer the Princess has killed: "The deer was (as you know) *sanguis*, in blood, ripe as the pomewater . . ."(4.2.3–4).

2 Although the *Oxford English Dictionary* places the first appearance of the latter meaning of "embossed" no earlier than 1641, it is used in this sense in reference to a stag hunt by Florio in Montaigne's essay, "Of Cruelty," published in 1603; see *The Essays*, trans. John Florio (1603; facs. rpt. Menston, England: Scolar Press, 1969), 249 (the page is marked erroneously, 237).

3 The most influential treatment of Falstaff's resurrection from this perspective has been C. L. Barber's; see *Shakespeare's Festive Comedy* (1959; rpt. Cleveland: World Publishing Company, 1968), 205–13. For an account of the folk-plays, see E. K. Chambers, *The English Folk-Play* (1933; rpt. New York: Russell and Russell, 1964), and Alan Brody, *The English Mummers and Their Plays* (Philadelphia: University of Pennsylvania Press, 1970); Brody includes photographs of the Bromley horn dancers (figs. 5, 6).

4 J. Dover Wilson, *The Fortunes of Falstaff* (Cambridge: Cambridge University Press, 1964), 25–31.

5 See Roger B. Manning, *Hunters and Poachers* (Oxford: Clarendon Press, 1993), 10, and William Harrison, *The Description of England*, ed. Georges Edelen (Ithaca, N.Y.: Cornell University Press, 1968), 132. Harrison notes that if "the inferior sort of artificers and husbandmen" come upon a piece of venison and a cup of wine" at a feast, they imagine themselves to have "fared so well as the Lord Mayor of London."

6 Katherine Duncan-Jones and Jan Van Dorsten, eds., *Miscellaneous Prose of Sir Philip Sidney* (Oxford: Clarendon Press, 1973), 97; a crowder is a fiddler.

7 John E. Housman, ed., *British Popular Ballads* (New York: Barnes and Noble,1952), 177; further citations to this edition are indicated parenthetically by stanza.

8 It is possible that the ballad is also echoed in the witches' prophecy in *Macbeth*. The witches tell Macbeth that "none of woman born" shall "harm" him (4.1.80–81). In the ballad, Percy meets Douglas's challenge with the assertion that he has never feared single combat with any man: "Nethar in Ynglonde, Skottlonde, nar France, / nor for no man of a woman born, / But, and fortune be my chance, / I dar met him, on man for on" (st. 21). He repeats the words in stanza 35.

9 Manning, *Hunters and Poachers*, 49.

10 An extreme version of this tendency may be seen in the Coburg Hunting Chronicle of the Emperor Maximilian, written in 1499–1500. Images from the Chronicle are reproduced in William A. Baillie-Grohman, *Sport in Art*, 2nd edn. (London: Simpkin, Marshall, Hamilton, Kent and Co., 1919); figure 113, for example, which depicts the weighing of stags, shows about fifteen corpses meticulously lined up according to size in an enclosed field full of dogs, hunters, horses, and carts.

11 The Oxford editor, T. W. Craik, provides a useful survey of these issues in *The Merry Wives of Windsor* (Oxford: Clarendon Press, 1989), 1–13, 48–63. See also Leah Marcus's convincing treatment of the Quarto and Folio as independent texts in "Levelling Shakespeare: Local Customs and Local Texts," *Shakespeare Quarterly* 42 (1991): 168–78, and Barbara Freedman's thoughtful challenge to the conventional arguments surrounding the questions of date and occasion: "Shakespearean Chronology, Ideological Complicity, and Floating Texts: Something is Rotten in Windsor," *Shakespeare Quarterly* 45 (1994): 190–210. Arthur F. Kinney has extended Marcus's approach to the texts of the play; see "Textual Signs in *The Merry Wives of Windsor*," *Yearbook of English Studies* 23 (1993): 206–34. In view of Marcus's argument, I should note that my interpretation is directed primarily to the Folio text, which highlights the locale of Windsor. The edition of the play in *The Riverside Shakespeare*, which I cite parenthetically throughout this study, is based on the Folio.

12 R. S. White, *The Merry Wives of Windsor* (New York: Harvester Wheatsheaf, 1991), 2.

13 Anne Barton, "Falstaff and the Comic Community," in *Shakespeare's "Rough Magic"*, ed. Peter Erickson, and Coppélia Kahn (Newark: University of Delaware Press, 1985), 142.

14 Linda Anderson, *A Kind of Wild Justice* (Newark: University of Delaware Press, 1987), 68.

15 For the generalizations in this paragraph, see Peter Clark, "A Crisis Contained? The Condition of English Towns in the 1590s," *The European Crisis of the 1590s*, ed. Peter Clark (London: Allen and Unwin, 1985), 45; David Underdown, *Revel, Riot, and Rebellion* (Oxford: Clarendon Press, 1985), 33; and Keith Wrightson, *English Society 1580–1680* (London: Hutchinson, 1982), 149–82.

16 Wrightson, *English Society*, 150.

17 Ibid., 157.

18 Keith Wrightson, "Two Concepts of Order: Justices, Constables and Jurymen in Seventeenth-Century England," in *An Ungovernable People*, ed. John Brewer, and John Styles (London: Hutchinson, 1980), 24.

19 Mildred Campbell, *The English Yeoman* (1942; rpt. The Hague: Krips Reprint Company, 1960), 382.

20 Wrightson, *English Society*, 51.

21 Ibid., 51–57.

22 See Martin Ingram, "Ridings, Rough Music and the 'Reform of Popular Culture' in Early Modern England," *Past and Present* 105 (1984): 86, and Susan Dwyer Amussen, *An Ordered Society* (Oxford: Basil Blackwell, 1988), 50.

23 Manning, *Hunters and Poachers*, 68

24 *The Political Works of James I*, ed. Charles H. McIlwain (Cambridge, Mass.: Harvard University Press, 1918), 342.

25 Manning, *Hunters and Poachers*, 160, 164, 167.

26 If Shallow represents Sir Thomas Lucy, as seems to be the case, and if the satire commemorates Shakespeare's own poaching as a youth, then the episode includes an additional kind of symbolic assault, identifying Shakespeare, delightfully, with Falstaff; see above, p. 20.

27 Manning, *Hunters and Poachers*, 188.

28 Resolutions in the Privy Council for 1582 and 1589 attempted rather ineffectually to shift the burden of private complaints to other courts, unless they concerned, as stated in the 1582 resolution, "'the preservacion of her Majesties peace or shalbe of some publicke consequence to touche the government of the Realme'"; see Sir William Holdsworth, *A History of English Law* (London: Methuen, 1903), 1: 498.

29 Wrightson, *English Society*, 61.

30 Rosemary Kegl, "'The Adoption of Abominable Terms': The Insults that Shape Windsor's Middle Class," *ELH* 61 (1994): 265. Kegl also provides a useful account of the ineffectuality of Shallow and Evans as representatives of legal and ecclesiastical authority.

31 Joan Rees, "Shakespeare's Welshmen," in *Literature and Nationalism*, ed. Vincent Newey, and Ann Thompson (Liverpool: Liverpool University Press, 1991), 38.

32 Other critics have noted the relevance of charivari to the play; for especially helpful comments, see François Laroque, "Ovidian Transformations and Folk Festivities in *A Midsummer Night's Dream*, *The Merry Wives of Windsor*, and

As You Like It," *Cahiers Elisabethains* 25 (1984): 23–36, and C. Gallenca, "Ritual and Folk Custom in *The Merry Wives of Windsor*," *Cahiers Elisabethains* 27 (1985): 27–41. As far as I am aware, no critic has dealt with the play's reflections upon charivari, or with the tensions created by adapting such a social form to comic ends.

33　Ingram, "Ridings," 86.

34　Ibid., 82.

35　Ibid., 86.

36　E. P. Thompson, *Customs in Common* (New York: New Press, 1991), 480.

37　Natalie Zemon Davis, *Society and Culture in Early Modern France* (Stanford: Stanford University Press, 1975), 140.

38　Ingram, "Ridings," 96.

39　For an insightful treatment of the complex relationship between the two characters, see William C. Carroll, *The Metamorphoses of Shakespearean Comedy* (Princeton: Princeton University Press, 1985), 183–202.

40　In his reproduction of Norden's 1607 map of Windsor Castle, William Green situates Herne's Oak within the Little Park; see *Shakespeare's* The Merry Wives of Windsor (Princeton: Princeton University Press, 1962), fig. 2.

41　Manning, *Hunters and Poachers*, 153; see also 157 and 218–19.

42　See Thompson, *Customs*, 470–71, and Theo Brown, "The 'Stag-Hunt' in Devon," *Folklore* 63 (1952): 104–9. Although probably of ancient origin, this brutal sport is not recorded until well after the Elizabethan period.

43　Jeanne Addison Roberts treats the ambiguity of Falstaff's role in the final scene with particular insight; see *Shakespeare's English Comedy* (Lincoln: University of Nebraska Press, 1979), 110–16.

44　John M. Steadman, "Falstaff as Actaeon: A Dramatic Emblem," *Shakespeare Quarterly* 14 (1963): 231–44.

45　G. R. Hibbard, for example, sees the play as endorsing "the values of the Elizabethan bourgeoisie, the class from which its author came and to which he belonged"; see his edition, *The Merry Wives of Windsor* (Middlesex: Penguin Books, 1973), 14. George K. Hunter takes a similar view, arguing that Shakespeare implicitly endorses the efforts of Windsor to resist social change; see "Bourgeois Comedy: Shakespeare and Dekker," in *Shakespeare and His Contemporaries*, ed. E. A. J. Honigmann (Manchester: University of Manchester Press, 1986), 14. Peter Erickson sees the image of the Garter and the triumph of Fenton as justifying the aristocracy, although he concludes that male anxiety about female rule prevents Shakespeare from endorsing the power of the state; see "The Order of the Garter, the Cult of Elizabeth, and Class-Gender Tension in *The Merry Wives of Windsor*," in *Shakespeare Reproduced*, ed. Jean E. Howard, and Marion F. O'Connor (New York: Methuen, 1987), 126–34. Rosemary Kegl notes that the restoration of order by the wives reinforces "the play's more general sense that town gentlemen are the ideal custodians of both the town and the nation" ("Adoption," 272).

46　Both the Quarto and Folio texts assign the role of Fairy Queen in act 5 scene

5 to Mistress Quickly. During the preparations for the scene, however, Mistress Page says that "My Nan shall be the queen of all the fairies, / Finely attired in a robe of white"(4.4.71–72). The discrepancy has led some directors to substitute Anne for Quickly in the role; see Peter Evans, "'To the Oak, to the Oak!' The Finale of *The Merry Wives of Windsor*," *Theatre Notebook* 40(1986): 106–14.

6 PASTORAL HUNTING IN *AS YOU LIKE IT*

1 Paul Alpers, *What Is Pastoral?* (Chicago: University of Chicago Press, 1996), 22.

2 I quote from *The Pastoral Poems*, trans. E. V. Rieu (Harmondsworth, Middlesex: Penguin, 1949), 33, 21, 83. For a general discussion of Roman hunting in the time of Virgil, see J. K. Anderson, *Hunting in the Ancient World* (Berkeley: University of California Press, 1985), 83–100; Anderson restricts himself to the hunting of gentlemen and nobles and does not indicate whether there were restrictions placed on the hunting of common people, as there were in the Elizabethan period.

3 *The Works of Edmund Spenser: A Variorum Edition*, ed. Edwin Greenlaw et al., 11 vols. (Baltimore: Johns Hopkins Press, 1943), VII.

4 For the legal position of wild animals among the Romans, see C. M. C. Green, "Did the Romans Hunt?," *Classical Antiquity* 15 (1996): 222–60. See also Robert Pogue Harrison, *Forests: The Shadow of Civilization* (Chicago: University of Chicago Press, 1992), 49. Harrison observes: "The public Roman domain – the domain of its civic jurisdiction – included the sacred city as well as the patricians' rural estates, but it did not extend past the edge of the forests. The forests were in fact commonly referred to as the *locus neminis*, or 'place of no one'(it is probable that even the Latin word *nemus*, or woodlands, comes from *nemo*, meaning 'no one')."

5 Sir Thomas Elyot, *The Book Named the Governor*, ed. S. E. Lehmberg (London: Dent, 1962), 68.

6 William A. Ringler, Jr., ed., *The Poems of Sir Philip Sidney* (Oxford: Clarendon Press, 1962), 25, 103.

7 Sir Philip Sidney, *The Countess of Pembroke's Arcadia (The New Arcadia)*, ed. Victor Skretkowicz (Oxford: Clarendon Press, 1987), 54.

8 Michael Drayton, *The Works of Michael Drayton*, ed. J. William Hebel (Oxford: Basil Blackwell, 1961), III: 294.

9 Edward, Duke of York, *The Master of Game*, ed. Wm. A. and F. Baillie-Grohman (London: Chatto and Windus, 1909), 8–9.

10 [George Gascoigne], *The Noble Arte of Venerie or Hunting* (1575), 90.

11 Edward, Duke of York, *Master of Game*, 10.

12 [Gascoigne], *Arte of Venerie*, 140.

13 Francis James Child, ed., *English and Scottish Popular Ballads*, 5 vols. (Boston: Houghton, Mifflin, 1888), III: 78.

14 Manning, *Hunters and Poachers*, 20–22.

15 Anthony Munday, *The Huntingdon Plays: A Critical Edition of The Downfall and The Death of Robert, Earl of Huntingdon*, ed. John Carney Meagher (New York: Garland Publishing, 1980), 199–200.

16 See, for example, Louis Adrian Montrose, "'Eliza, Queene of shepheardes,' and the Pastoral of Power," *English Literary Renaissance* 10 (1980): 153–82, and Annabel Patterson, *Pastoral and Ideology* (Berkeley: University of California Press, 1987). Patterson's account of Spenser's pastorals allows more room for social and political criticism than Montrose's, but even she finds Spenserian pastoral ambivalent rather than subversive.

17 For social protests in the forests, see Peter Stallybrass, "'Drunk with the Cup of Liberty': Robin Hood, the carnivalesque, and the rhetoric of violence in early modern England," in *The Violence of Representation*, ed. Nancy Armstrong and Leonard Tennenhouse (London: Routledge, 1989).

18 For a useful survey of the forest and pasture settings in the play, see A. Stuart Daley, "Where are the Woods in *As You Like It?*," *Shakespeare Quarterly* 34 (1983): 172–80.

19 Thomas Lodge, *Rosalynde*, ed. Geoffrey Bullough, vol. II, *Narrative and Dramatic Sources of Shakespeare* (London: Routledge and Kegan Paul, 1958), 180, 183.

20 John Manwood, *A Treatise of the Lawes of the Forest* (1615; facs. rpt. Amsterdam: Walter J. Johnson, 1976), 18–18v.

21 J. Charles Cox, *The Royal Forests of England* (London: Methuen, 1905), 229.

22 Lucy Toulmin Smith, ed., *Leland's Itinerary in England and Wales*, 5 vols. (London: Centaur Press, 1964), II: 47.

23 Quoted in William Cooper, *Henley-in-Arden* (Birmingham: Cornish Bros., 1946), xi.

24 Ann Hughes, *Politics, Society and Civil War in Warwickshire, 1620–1660* (Cambridge: Cambridge University Press, 1987), 5.

25 V. Skipp, *Crisis and Development: An Ecological Case Study of the Forest of Arden, 1570–1674* (Cambridge: Cambridge University Press, 1978); see especially 18, 33, 41, 51, 68. For general surveys of conflicts in pastoral and sylvan societies, focusing mainly on the seventeenth century, see Roger B. Manning, *Village Revolts* (Oxford: Clarendon Press, 1988), 255–83; Buchanan Sharp, *In Contempt of All Authority: Rural Artisans and Riot in the West of England, 1586–1660* (Berkeley: University of California Press, 1980); and Andrew Charlesworth, ed., *An Atlas of Rural Protest in Britain 1548–1900* (London: Croom Helm, 1983).

26 Quoted in Joan Thirsk, ed., *The Agrarian History of England and Wales* (Cambridge: Cambridge University Press, 1967), IV: 411.

27 Nigel Nicolson and Alasdair Hawkyard, *The Counties of Britain: A Tudor Atlas by John Speed* (London: Pavilion Books, 1988), 177.

28 Quoted in Manning, *Village Revolts*, 224; see also 220–29.

29 Drayton, *Works*, IV, 276.

30 For a contrary view, see Richard Wilson, "'Like old Robin Hood': *As You Like It* and the Enclosure Riots," *Shakespeare Quarterly* 43 (1992): 1–19. Wilson,

whose article contains much useful information about the social context surrounding the play, argues that "the play is powerfully inflected by narratives of popular resistance"(4) but that its subversive possibilities are contained by a conservative ending. For an illuminating critique of Wilson's argument, and of New Historicist approaches generally, see Andrew Barnaby, "The Political Conscious of Shakespeare's *As You Like It*," *Studies in English Literature* 36 (1996): 373–95. Even Barnaby, whose views I share, finds in the social critique of the play only an endorsement of traditional social ideals. The play's most progressive gestures, I hope to show, are not political but ecological.

31 Henry Howard, Earl of Surrey, *Poems*, ed. Emrys Jones (Oxford: Clarendon Press, 1964), 65, 15. For a brief survey of the literary tradition, see Arthur Sherbo, "Cowper's 'Stricken Deer' and the Literary Tradition," *Bulletin of Research in the Humanities* 85 (1982): 336–340.

32 A. Stuart Daley, "The Idea of Hunting in *As You like It*," *Shakespeare Studies* 21 (1993): 83.

33 The image is reproduced in Matt Cartmill, *A View to a Death in the Morning: Hunting and Nature through History* (Cambridge, Mass.: Harvard University Press, 1993), 81.

34 *The Scythe of Saturn: Shakespeare and Magical Thinking* (Urbana: University of Illinois Press, 1994), 189. I discovered Woodbridge's complementary reading of this episode after formulating my own argument. For an account of the scene against the background of humanist attacks upon hunting, see Claus Uhlig, " 'The Sobbing Deer': *As You Like It*, II.i.21–66 and the Historical Context," *Renaissance Drama* 3 (1970): 79–109.

35 José Ortega y Gasset, *Meditations on Hunting*, trans. Howard B. Wescott (New York: Charles Scribners, 1972), 102.

36 P. J. Frankis, "The Testament of the Deer in Shakespeare," *Neuphilologische Mitteilungen* 59 (1958): 65–68.

37 Daley, "Idea of Hunting," 88–89.

38 Lodge, *Rosalynde*, 196.

39 Munday, *Huntingdon Plays*, 304–05.

40 William Twiti's directions for the procession homeward are as follows: "Carry the head home before the Lord; and the heart, tail, and gullet should be carried home on a forked branch, and you should blow the menée at the door of the hall" (*The Art of Hunting [1327]*, ed. Broc Danielsson, *Stockholm Studies in English 37* [Stockholm: Almqvist and Wiksell, 1977], 51. For the Horn Dance of Abbots Bromley, in which men dance carrying antlers, see Ronald Hutton, *The Rise and Fall of Merry England: The Ritual Year 1400–1700* (Oxford: Oxford University Press, 1994), 47–48 and Jon Raven, *The Folklore of Staffordshire* (London: B. T. Batsford, 1978), 114–16. The Feast of St. Paul at St. Paul's Cathedral features a procession in which the head of a buck is carried before the cross in procession and then taken outside the West door of the church, where horns blow its death; see John Stow, *A Survey of London*, ed. Charles L. Kingsford, 2 vols. (1603; rpt. Oxford: Clarendon Press, 1971), I: 334–35.

41 Elyot, *Governor*, 67–68.
42 Richard Knowles, "Myth and Type in *As You Like It*," *English Literary History* 33 (1966): 5–6.
43 Michel De Montaigne, *The Essays*, trans. John Florio (1603; facs. rpt. Menston, England: Scolar Press, 1969), 265.
44 Harrison, *Forests*, 26.
45 Montaigne, *Essays*, 249–51. In a later work, "The Hunting of the Hare"(1653), Margaret Cavendish develops a similar critique of hunting; the poem concludes with an attack on the cruelty and arrogance in the hunter's presumption that God made "all *Creatures* for his sake alone . . . to *Tyrannize* upon"(lines 103–06); see *Kissing the Rod: An Anthology of Seventeenth-Century Women's Verse*, ed. Germaine Greer, et al. (London: Virago Press, 1988), 170.
46 See Cartmill, *A View to a Death*, 92–111 and Thomas, *Natural World*, 33–36.

7 POLITICAL HUNTING: PROSPERO AND JAMES I

1 For an illuminating survey of representations of Caliban, see Alden T. Vaughan and Virginia Mason Vaughan, *Shakespeare's Caliban: A Cultural History* (Cambridge: Cambridge University Press, 1991).
2 Desiderius Erasmus, *Chaloner: The Praise of Folie*, ed. Clarence H. Miller, *Early English Text Society* (London: Oxford University Press, 1965), 54.
3 Jean Calvin, *Commentaries on the First Book of Moses Called Genesis*, trans. John King, 2 vols. (Edinburgh: Calvin Translation Society, 1847), 1: 317.
4 Sir Philip Sidney, *The Countess of Pembroke's Arcadia (The Old Arcadia)*, ed. Jean Robertson (Oxford: Clarendon Press, 1973), 254–59; Henry Cornelius Agrippa, *Of the Vanitie and Uncertaintie of Artes and Sciences*, ed. Catherine M. Dunn (Northridge: California State University, 1974), 262.
5 Agrippa, *Vanitie*, 262.
6 Ibid., 260.
7 Ibid., 263.
8 Michel De Montaigne, *The Essays*, trans. John Florio (1603; facs. rpt. Menston, England: Scolar Press, 1969), 243; I use Prosser's italics throughout to highlight verbal resemblances. Stephen Orgel follows Prosser in noting the close similarity between the two passages; see his edition of *The Tempest* (Oxford: Clarendon Press, 1987), 189n.27–8.
9 See, for example, Arthur Kirsch, "Montaigne and *The Tempest*," in *Cultural Exchange between European Nations during the Renaissance*, ed. Gunnar Sorelius and Michael Srigley (Uppsala: Uppsala University, 1994), 111–21, and Ben Ross Schneider Jr., "'Are We Being Historical Yet?': Colonialist Interpretations of Shakespeare's *Tempest*," *Shakespeare Studies* 23 (1995): 125–26.
10 Montaigne, *The Essays*, 248.
11 Ibid., 251.
12 Orgel, ed., *The Tempest*, 1–4.

13 For studies that feature the world of the court, see David M. Bergeron, *Shakespeare's Romances and the Royal Family* (Lawrence: University of Kansas Press, 1985), 178–202, Donna B. Hamilton, *Virgil and "The Tempest"* (Columbus: Ohio State University Press, 1990), and Gary Schmidgall, *Shakespeare and the Courtly Aesthetic* (Berkeley: University of California Press, 1981). For studies of treason and colonialism see Curt Breight, "'Treason doth never prosper': *The Tempest* and the Discourse of Treason," *Shakespeare Quarterly* 41 (1990): 1–28, Frances E. Dolan, "The Subordinate('s) Plot: Petty Treason and the Forms of Domestic Rebellion," *Shakespeare Quarterly* 43 (1992): 317–40, Paul Brown, "'This thing of darkness I acknowledge mine': *The Tempest* and the discourse of colonialism," in *Political Shakespeare*, ed. Jonathan Dollimore and Alan Sinfield (Manchester: Manchester University Press, 1994), 48–71, and Meredith Anne Skura, "The Case of Colonialism in *The Tempest*," in *Caliban*, ed. Harold Bloom (New York: Chelsea House, 1992), 221–48; the latter article, which first appeared in *Shakespeare Quarterly* in 1989, contains a useful critique of the vast critical literature devoted to colonialism.

14 I am much indebted to Donna B. Hamilton's thoughtful book, *Virgil and "The Tempest"* (Columbus: Ohio State University Press, 1990), which first drew my attention to this context.

15 Elizabeth Read Foster, ed., *Proceedings in Parliament 1610*, 2 vols. (New Haven: Yale University Press, 1966), I: xv.

16 Quoted in Foster, ed., *Parliament 1610*, vol. 1, xx.

17 James I, *The Political Works of James I*, ed. Charles H. McIlwain (Cambridge, Mass.: Harvard University Press, 1918), 307.

18 Foster, ed., *Parliament 1610*, vol. II, 101, 103.

19 For Chamberlain's comments, see Wallace Notestein, *The House of Commons 1604–1610* (New Haven: Yale University Press, 1971), 325.

20 D. Harris Willson, *King James VI and I* (London: Jonathan Cape, 1956), 279.

21 Quoted in Caroline Bingham, *James VI of Scotland* (London: Weidenfeld and Nicolson, 1979), 75–76.

22 Robert Ashton, ed., *James I by his Contemporaries* (London: Hutchinson, 1969), 250.

23 G. P. V. Akrigg, ed., *Letters of King James VI and I* (Berkeley: University of California Press, 1984), 245–49.

24 The letters are quoted in Bergeron, *Shakespeare's Romances*, 39.

25 Ashton, ed., *James I*, 271.

26 Ibid., 232–33; Akrigg dates the letter [July? 1604].

27 Ibid., 294; Akrigg dates the letter [19? October 1607].

28 Ibid., 250; Akrigg dates the letter [Early 1605?].

29 McIlwain, ed., *Political Works of James I*, 307.

30 Ibid., 324.

31 Quoted in Ashton, ed., *James I*, 250.

32 Kirby, "Stuart Game Prerogative," 240.

33 Roger B. Manning, *Hunters and Poachers* (Oxford: Clarendon Press, 1993), 65.

34 Ibid., 208.
35 E. K. Chambers, *The Elizabethan Stage*, 4 vols. (Oxford: Clarendon Press, 1923), II: 53.
36 Annabel Patterson, *Censorship and Interpretation* (Madison: University of Wisconsin Press, 1984); see especially, 3–23.
37 Curt Breight, "Discourse of Treason," 15n.38.
38 Jonathan Bate, "Caliban and Ariel Write Back," *Shakespeare Survey* 48 (1995): 155–62.

8 CONCLUSION: SHAKESPEARE ON THE CULTURE OF THE HUNT

 1 D. H. Madden, *The Diary of Master William Silence* (London: Longmans, Green, 1907), ii; Matt Cartmill, *A View to a Death in the Morning: Hunting and Nature through History* (Cambridge, Mass.: Harvard University Press, 1993), 79. Caroline F. E. Spurgeon's study of Shakespeare's imagery of the hunt supports Cartmill's view; see *Shakespeare's Imagery* (Cambridge: Cambridge University Press, 1968), 30–33, 100–05.
 2 Robert Greene, *Friar Bacon and Friar Bungay*, ed. Daniel Seltzer (Lincoln: University of Nebraska Press, 1963), I: 3–11.
 3 Gervase Markham, *Countrey Contentments* (1615; facs. rpt. Amsterdam: Theatrum Orbis Terrarum, 1973), 7.
 4 William Somervile, *The Chase* (London: George Redway, 1896), 6.
 5 Ovid, *Metamorphoses*, trans. Mary M. Innes (Baltimore: Penguin Books, 1955), 186–90.
 6 David Riggs, *Ben Jonson: A Life* (Cambridge, Mass.: Harvard University Press, 1989), 70.
 7 G. A. Wilkes, ed., *The Complete Plays of Ben Jonson*, 4 vols. (Oxford: Clarendon Press, 1981), II: 110, 99, 106.
 8 Ibid., vol. I: 185, 312.
 9 William B. Hunter, Jr., ed., *The Complete Poetry of Ben Jonson* (Garden City, New York: Anchor Books, 1963), 82. The same point is made of James I in the masque, *The Gypsies Metamorphosed*. The gypsy captain, echoing James's own views as he reads his palm, prophesies that he will love "To hunt the brave stag not so much for the food / As the weal of your body and the health o' your blood"; see Stephen Orgel, ed., *Ben Jonson: The Complete Masques* (New Haven: Yale University Press, 1969), 328.
10 Ibid., 406–08.
11 William Somervile, *The Chase* (London: George Redway, 1896), 2.
12 Spurgeon, *Shakespeare's Imagery*, 101–02.
13 José Ortega y Gasset, *Meditations on Hunting*, trans. Howard B. Wescott (New York: Charles Scribners, 1972), 142.
14 For reproductions of the portraits of Henrietta Maria, see Oliver Millar, *Van Dyck in England* (London: National Portrait Gallery, 1982), 22 (figs. 19 and 20).
15 E. P. Thompson, *Whigs and Hunters: The Origin of the Black Act* (London: Allen Lane, 1975), 56.

Index

The Resurrection of Sarah Tinfield

SHARON BROCK HELDMAN

Cover design by
Georgia Bateman

Self Published
createspace.com

Print Date July 2013

ISBN-13: 978-1484138847
ISBN-10: 1484138848

Thank You, Lord.
Without You, I can do nothing.
With You, I can do all things.

Thank you family and friends.
You proofed and read
and with great enthusiasm
told me you loved my book.

"Yea, though I walk

through the valley

of the shadow of death,

I will fear no evil,

for thou art with me."

Psalm 23:4a (KJV)

CHAPTER 1

Chip smiled. A trip to Borders had never been so delightful. Carefully, he laid his treasure on the counter next to the cash register—a leather-bound set of the complete works of Shakespeare—just one of Sarah's Christmas presents. Holiday music filled the store as did the unmistakable and wonderful aroma of cinnamon coffee—the flavor of the day. He loved Christmas! They both loved Christmas, Sarah and he; and secrets and mystery gifts were part of the tradition. Sarah would be ecstatic with this gift—the books—but it was only part of her present from Chip. He looked at his watch— 12/24/2003 - 3:30 p.m.—plenty of time to make it home before the arrival of Sarah's grand piano!

The joy of gift giving was, however, only part of his elation. Chip, slim and trim, stepped back from the counter as the clerk rang up his purchase, and turned his dark brown eyes toward the front entrance. He gazed at the large poster resting upon an easel at the front door, right in the best spot for all to see, coming and going. *"Nicely done,"* he thought, *"very, very nice!"* The red letters at the top had a nearly neon effect: Novel of the Season! In black, in an absolutely perfect font—clear and pronounced—there was the title of the book: *The Street of Petetra.* A tantalizing short summary of the plot was centered below, but Chip did not have to read it. He knew. He knew it like the back of his hand. He suppressed an urge to tell the young man behind the counter, "I know that author. We're like…this. I worked with him to get his book published, you know…the account executive. Yes, Herman Lichten and I are pretty good friends!"

Instead, far too reserved for any such speech, with his set of six hefty volumes in a colorful holiday bag, looking spiffy in his dress khakis, white shirt and red and green speckled tie, he walked past the poster, stopping for just a moment to scrutinize it one more time. The name of the publisher was visible, printed smaller at the bottom of the placard; but, never mind, it did not matter. The person closest

1

to the publishing of Herman Lichten's best seller was standing right there, basking in the glory of success! Payce Publishing was the publisher and Chip Finfield had been the account executive. The book, already, after six weeks on the market, was a sensational success!

Stepping lightly, he left the store, humming the tune about the partridge in a pear tree. Come May, Payce would work with Mr. Lichten again on a second book. The future looked to be bright for all three: Payce Publishing, Herman Lichten and Chester "Chip" Finfield.

It was Christmas Eve. Tonight he and Sarah would celebrate it together as man and wife for the eighth time. His heart and spirit were always uplifted at every thought of his dear Sarah. Still madly in love he was, and greatly cheered, anticipating their evening together, enjoying Sarah's culinary cleverness, singing at the piano, watching "It's a Wonderful Life," reading the Christmas story from Luke and sharing secretly strategized and meaningful gifts—always a time of great surprise. How he loved his Sarah! Wouldn't she be astonished when the piano arrived! He rushed home through the late-shopper traffic. She would be waiting, as always, at the door, even today. Kerrigan employees never worked on Christmas Eve.

"Merry Christmas!" he said out loud, loosening his holiday tie. "I'm glad to be alive!"

❧ ❧ ❧ ❧ ❧

In May—May the 10th, to be exact—at the direction of Richard Payce, President/CEO of Payce Publishing, Chip called Herman Lichten, setting up a time to move ahead with his new book. The next day, Herman arrived at the corporate headquarters, and Gina, after announcing his arrival by phone, ushered him into Chip's fine office on the third floor. Pleasantries were offered as the two unlikely friends stood looking out over the famous Payce Publishing fountain. Then they sat.

"Well, well," Chip started, "what a party, eh? We had no idea—any of us—that your book would explode like it has!"

Across from him sat an old man, dressed in a red and black plaid shirt and overalls, older in his appearance than in actual age. At seventy, Mr. Lichten, with his thick silvery gray hair and slightly bent frame, seemed to be more like a man of eighty. Chip liked this old man with his bushy mustache and equally bushy eyebrows, and his weathered and wrinkled face. He and Herman liked and respected each other equally. Once upon a time he had been a homeless man; now he lived rent free in a dingy and dreary section of town, in a building owned by the Payces, in a run-down apartment at the back and up a long flight of steel steps. It had been Mildred, Chip's mother, who had brought about such a union, engineering the move of Herman to the unused apartment in Payce's Wentworth Building. It was not out of the ordinary for warm-hearted Mildred to have reached out to this destitute person whom she had repeatedly encountered near the train station on her weekly trip downtown to get her hair done!

Thus, he had become more than a client to Chip, and over the many months since meeting him, Chip had wiggled his way into Herman's heart—and a bit into his past—discovering that the man had lived an interesting but hard life. They were true friends now. Mr. Lichten enjoyed Chip's company as well and repeatedly made it clear that he was delighted to be working with him.

"All set to get going on that second book, Herman? I've got a contract right here, ready to go." Chip turned the new contract toward Herman so that his guest could review it.

But something was on Herman's mind. Chip had sensed it with the first handshake. He loosened his tie, unbuttoned his shirt, smoothed back his light brown hair, and waited.

"Chester," the old man said, speaking very deliberately, as always, "I'm having a problem with the royalty payments from *The Street of Petetra*. I'm not the greatest mathematician in the world, but with the help of my little calculator, I can see that what's being deposited is not the agreed-upon amount."

"No!" Chip said, completely taken off guard and hardly believing it to be true. "You sure?"

"It comes out to nine, twelve and fifteen, Chester, not ten, twelve and fifteen. Do you recall?"

Yes, Chip recalled—distinctly. The Payces had fought for nine; Chip had waged war—and won—for ten percent.

"Herman, count on me to look into this! Just a second...maybe I can even check that right now."

Chatting lightly, he turned to his computer, typing away dexterously. It only took a few moments to find out that someone else would have to do the digging.

"You don't worry about this. I'll dig around and make sure it gets fixed. Let's talk now about this contract for your new book. That's why you're here, right? What do you say?"

Herman Lichten, to some extent feeble of body, was not feeble of mind. His penetrating eyes looked back at Chip from under shaggy eyebrows, a deep furrow between them. Speaking slowly in his raspy voice, he said, "I'll not sign another contract, Chester, until this money business is resolved." He leaned forward in his chair, resting against one of the arms. In quieter tones he went on. "You know, Chester, I don't really like the Payces—not the father, not Son No. 1, not Son No. 2. I haven't trusted them from my first encounter with them. I thank them for the apartment—actually, I thank Mildred—but in a month or so, now that I'm set financially, I'll be moving out. Chester, if it weren't for you, I wouldn't even consider Payce again. You...are scrupulous. I recognized that from the start and have counted on it. They...are not. Not one of them. Get this straight for me, will you?"

Chip leaned back in his impressive leather chair, tapping his fingers on the arm. This was unexpected. This meeting was supposed to result in a shiny new contract for Lichten's second book. Though he shared Herman's opinion of the Payces, he did not want to lose this account—nor the dear friendship that had been cultivated over the months of being thrown closely together.

"Can you trust me to take care of this, enough to sign this new contract today? You know I'm going to take care of you."

Herman Lichten's eyes narrowed and his expression left no doubt as to his inflexibility.

"I will not sign with you on Book No. 2 until the beady-eyed owner of this company makes things right on Book No. 1."

He stood, put out his hand to shake Chip's, and before another word could be uttered, shuffled out of the room, his leather boots dragging on the carpet.

Grabbing his cell phone and his fine charcoal gray sport jacket at the same time, Chip left for home. Richard Payce was out of the office, but as Chip drove, he reached him on his cell phone.

"Richard, it's Chip."

"Chip! How's it going?" Mr. Payce responded gustily.

"Richard, I just met with Lichten and he's telling me that the royalty payments on *The Street of Petetra* have not been right since the start. They are not agreeing with the amount on his contract. The first two-fifty thousand is set at nine instead of ten. Do you know anything about that?"

"Of course not! He's probably figuring it wrong. He's old and a little sketchy in the brain."

"Not really. After spending as much time with him as I have, I can assure you that he is sharp...sharp enough."

"Chip, get that new contract, for goodness sake! Tomorrow. Our friend, Mr. Lichten, has made more money in the last six weeks than he has made in his whole life!"

"True, yet a contract is a contract. I'll need to do some investigating. I'll talk with Chris."

"You do whatever, but you get a contract. Call Robert—or Raymond, since he was in that final meeting—and explain. One of them can put a corrected one together—if by chance the old man is right. Have them do it, Chip. You're not legal. You're sales. Get one of the boys on it, and get it done bright and early. Do you know anything about the next book?"

"He wouldn't talk to me about it, Richard." Chip's words were curt and pointed. "He wants *The Street of Petetra* straightened out first."

"Well, get to work! This is not just your boss talking to you, Chip, you understand. This is your stepdad. I'm looking out for you, too, you know."

How he hated to hear Richard refer to himself as his *stepdad!* Chip's mother, a widow of ten years, stricken with unexplainable infatuation for Richard Payce (except that he had treated her like a queen at the start), had married him in a little chapel in Florida four years before. No amount of pleading on the part of Chip, whose intuition on the subject had kicked in with intensity, nor on the part of Sarah, could change her mind. Mildred Ruth Finfield became Mrs. Richard Payce, enraptured with great love for a very selfish man. There was nothing her son could do. The marriage, nonetheless, had landed him a lucrative position with Payce Publishing. Richard promptly brought him on board, gave him an exquisite office overlooking the picturesque Payce fountain—and a staggering salary! Chip's wages, already well into six figures at his former job, nearly doubled overnight.

Yet, with all the glory and with all the wealth that had come his way, Chip despised any verbal references to his being part of the Payce clan. As an employee, he endured; as a relative, he shunned every possible link to such a collection of harsh, not-to-be-trusted people. After just a few weeks of association with them at birthdays and holidays, Sarah could not tolerate them. "Loathsome people," she had indignantly murmured on the ride home from a birthday party.

On Day One, in the presence of the whole family, his voice booming over the reception chatter, Richard had suggested that Chip call him *Dad*. Chip pretended not to hear. Inwardly, he scoffed at such an idea and not once since, had he referred to Richard as *Dad*. For Chip, the only earthly father with that honor was his own precious dad, now gone from this earth fourteen years, buried in a little cemetery twenty-five miles northwest of town. No, he would not call him *Dad*, and he would continue to hate any insinuation that it might be so. His voice inflections as he responded to Richard tonight were entirely on a professional level.

"I'm on this," he said dully. "I just needed to run the royalty thing by you."

"You didn't think I'd do something like that on purpose, now did you?" Mr. Payce said laughing heartily.

"Just thought I'd check. I thought you should be aware of what's going on."

"Like I said, he's making more money than he ever saw. Remind him of that, Chip. Chip? Chip? You still there?"

"I'm here."

"Give him this message, too, Chip. Tell him that Richard says that it's better to bend than to break. Did you hear me, Chip? Call Raymond. No, I'll call him. I'll talk to you tomorrow."

The news the next day was not good. Mr. Lichten was absolutely correct in his accusation of being short changed. The accountant bristled at what could be interpreted as an allegation of error.

"Chris, how could this happen?" Chip's tone was accusatory.

She swiveled on her chair and turned away from him.

"I don't know," was her very catty reply.

"What do you mean, you don't know? Isn't this all done by computer? This is a computerized formula, Chris. What does the percentage show?"

"The percentage that is entered is the percentage I was told to put in."

Chip settled down.

"Now, Chris, that can't be. Everyone involved was in on that long discussion and we all left the meeting with a precise figure in our heads— first two-fifty at ten percent. All of us."

"Chip, I do what I'm told."

"No, Chris, we do what a signed and legal contract says."

"Yes we do, and there you and I agree."

A startled expression passed over his face.

"What are you saying?"

"I'm saying that you should look at the contract."

The conversation was over, for Chip was already out the door, on his way to the second floor file room. Unlocking the correct cabinet, he quickly flipped through the folders until he spied the label, **THE STREET OF PETETRA**. He yanked it out, already fearing what he might find. He punched the metal cabinet. He punched it again. It was all very clear to him now.

It had been Raymond, Son No. 2, who had met with Lichten for the final signing. They had sent Chip to another client that day, and while he was gone, Herman's contract was signed, sealed and delivered—and craftily and purposely altered. He had signed for a lesser royalty amount.

In a near rage, Chip took the stairs two at a time, and rushed to the office where Richard, looking crisp in his monogrammed white shirt, sat studying something on his monitor. His glasses were pushed down to the end of his long nose. Chip calmly closed the door, went to the side chair next to Richard's magnificent desk and sat down. His eyes narrowed as he looked squarely at the CEO who had now turned slightly to look at him.

"How could you do such a thing, Richard?" Chip growled.

Richard knew the subject. He did not have to ask, "How could I do what?" He was a man of hard heart, having no chinks in his armor, unable to flinch at wrong.

"I told you, Chip. Herman Lichten is a rich man because of Payce Publishing and he is greedy for more. If it weren't for your mother's unswerving insistence, I'd end his free rent arrangement!"

"This is not about Herman Lichten's character. This is about yours....and Robert's and Raymond's, for that matter. How can you look at yourself in the mirror in the morning without throwing up?"

Richard found Chip's statement amusing. He laughed boisterously.

"It's business, son," he said, leaning back in his chair and still laughing. He hurried on, not allowing Chip to speak. "Pure and simple, it's business. Now, I have to admit that I didn't think the old man capable of figuring out such a small difference. So, he did, and now what? Is he going to hold out on us for that?" Richard stood, stretched and moved to where he could look out on the lovely Payce grounds. "He can't go anywhere else," he said condescendingly. "He doesn't know how. He'll get eaten alive and I can make sure that it'll turn out worse than this little hiccup. Can't you see that we did him a huge favor by publishing his book? And now, he has a second one. What's he going to do—refuse to work with us? How foolish that would be when Payce has put him on the Top Ten list."

"Well, Richard, you might be surprised at Mr. Lichten. His ability to handle his affairs is not in question. Don't forget that he was smart enough to refuse the Option Clause."

"Yes, he did. No telling how he knew about that."

"He was a brilliant professor of geology, Richard! He's plenty smart! Yesterday, he stared me straight in the eye and said that there would be no contract if the money thing was not straightened out. Now, he said that with the belief that this error was a mistake." Chip's voice lowered. "What will he think when he finds out it was deliberate?"

Richard Payce, lately much more portly than only a few months before, patted his stomach and then stuck his thumbs behind his belt. His grin prepared Chip for what followed.

"You don't mean *when*, right? You mean *if*. Yes, yes, I knew you did. Now, Chip, let's give you an opportunity to prove yourself. What possible solutions do we have?"

"In my opinion, only one," Chip replied without hesitation.

"And that is?"

Would harm be done, Chip considered, telling Herman Lichten that the wrong contract had *inadvertently* been presented to him for signature? He could then sign a new one, Payce could make up the difference in royalties, and a contract on the new book could be obtained. No, Chip quickly decided; he could not do that with a clear conscience. Perhaps, though, if he went to Herman and apologized for being absent at the signing of the contract, when he most certainly should have been present—given the fact that he had been the account exec—and that he now had a corrected document for him to sign, would that be honest? For a moment he weighed such a move in light of his godly principles of truth and integrity, and then gave approval in his heart. He spoke this idea in answer to Mr. Payce's question. Richard applauded loudly and obnoxiously.

"Good answer. Done! Now, go get a brand new contract! I'm leaving for Palm Springs for a couple of days. I'll be expecting a shiny new contract on my desk Monday morning."

Chip rose and walked to the door. He stood with his hand on the door knob and his back to Richard Payce for a long moment. "You make it nearly impossible for me to do my job," he scowled just above a whisper. "I hear that Palm Springs is a great place to retire!"

Richard slapped the desk and roared with laughter.

ໄ຺ໄ຺ໄ຺ໄ຺ໄ຺

On the evening of May 12, 2004, as Chip walked up the heavy steel stairs to Herman Lichten's less-than-fine apartment in the drab and mostly empty Wentworth Building, each step resounding with a noisy clang, he counted them. There were twenty-seven. It was a long climb for an old man. Maybe though, Chip considered, it had been good for the author's health.

Payce Publishing owned this run-down storefront on the east side of town. On the lower level, overstock and overprints were piled in boxes everywhere, without order. The second level contained a three-room apartment at the back and four empty offices in the front—home to old fashioned metal desks and cabinets and piles of trash. Chip had been here before—often. The relationship between Herman Lichten and Chip Finfield had gone beyond a professional one. The old man and this Payce employee were good friends now.

The first fifteen minutes inside the small tidy abode was evidence of the closeness between them. Chip joked with Herman, reminding him that he was a rich man now and could go live in a pricey condo high above the city, overlooking the lake. Herman chuckled with his reply.

"Then I'd have nothing in the bank. No money for food. I couldn't buy my daily ice cream cone at Smitty's. In fact, I'd be too far away from Smitty's!"

"You keep talking about that ice cream. When are you going to take me over there?"

"We'll have to see about that," Herman answered.

The two enjoyed coffee together; then Chip slowly worked the conversation around to the business at hand.

"I bring you good tidings."

"Of great joy, I hope."

"Herman, do you remember that I was not there when the contract was signed?"

"Yes, I do and I remember that I asked about it."

"Well, I should have been. Where is your copy of the contract?"

"I'll get it."

He found it readily. Chip turned to Page Two.

"Raymond did not give you a good contract. Look at the percentage."

"Well, what do you know! I did sign for that, didn't I," the old man said slowly. "I never looked at this. I just assumed that it said ten percent because that's what we agreed upon."

"Hey, that's perfectly understandable. You're sharp, Herman! Some folk would have never caught that. Well, I have a new corrected one for you. We'll fix this Petetra thing up and you'll get the back royalties as well. You can trust me on that. Here...look at this corrected document. Look it over and sign it. I'll take care of everything right away," Chip promised. "I left everything else the same as it was...the direct deposit, beneficiary, etc."

A faraway look came upon the author's face as he reached for a pen and smoothed out the legal paper before him. He was not weighing the signing of the contract; no, his ponderings went far deeper than that. In his raspy voice, much more quiet than usual, Herman spoke.

"I wish I was dealing with just you, Chester. You're smart enough to be doing this for yourself. I wish you had a company of your own. I trust **you** implicitly. You know, I'm not so strong and healthy anymore and I must think about me. I don't trust Richard Payce and I do not like him. I have known other men like Richard Payce in my lifetime. He is a greedy, ruthless man."

Chip knew it was true but he could not bring himself to verbally agree with the statement. How insightful this old man was! For this very reason he was a great writer, capturing the personalities and moral inner recesses of his characters. Richard Payce, though often evidencing an almost juvenile side, **was** ruthless. Chip Finfield had seen it again and again, this crafty and evil way of dealing with anyone who got in Richard's way. He had seen him *slaughter* the lives of those people—clients and competitors—one way or another, their emotions, their character, their money, yes, and even their physical, tangible wellbeing…without remorse or regret.

"I'd like to disagree," was Chip's careful reply.

"Be that as it may, Chester Finfield, I do not like him or his sons. Why don't you break away? Start out on your own. I'll wait."

Today was not the day to divulge his secret. Chip wished he could but thought better of it. No, today, hopefully he would retrieve the contract for Payce Publishing for Mr. Lichten's second book, and then take the future one step at a time. However, locked tight in the glove compartment of his Jaguar was the finished paperwork for Finfield Publishing, Inc. Long and rigorously he had worked, behind the scenes, during every free moment, and with Sarah's exuberant blessing and assistance, taking steps to enable him to walk away from Payce. Things were ready. Today. On Monday, his letter of resignation would be on Richard's desk.

"Chip, you're lost in thought. Tell me, have you ever thought of starting up on your own?"

"Oh, yeah, I do. I do seriously. And…and, I will."

"When? I'll wait!"

"Now, Herman, I've come with a new contract for you to sign, the one for the new book. We need to do that. Take your time looking it over. In fact, if you want until tomorrow, fine. Come to the office tomorrow and we'll wrap it up. I'd like to wrap it up tonight, if possible; but if not, we can wait."

"Chester, before I can do that I need to ask you a question. I've been kicking it around—ask, don't ask—but I'm gonna ask. I know I don't need to preface it by requesting a truthful answer."

Chip squirmed because he was pretty sure he knew the old man's question already.

"This mistake," Herman began, "this mistake on the Petetra book contract, was that really a mistake or was it deliberate?"

No words would come. What could be said anyway? Chip stood and went to lean against the apartment door, his hands in his pockets, his ankles crossed, his face down. After a minute or two, he came and sat down again. Herman searched his facial expression.

"You don't need to answer," he said with kindness. "I know. I knew immediately when you placed your explanation before me."

"I told you the truth," Chip calmly and sincerely stated. "It would not have happened if things would have gone as they should have gone and if I would have been in that meeting. I am the account executive and Raymond should not have been the one to wrap things up."

"You know, I believe you wholeheartedly, but you will understand then when I declare that I will not do further business with Payce Publishing. Period."

"Now you are putting me in a tough spot."

"No," Herman said, taking his time to proceed. "No, Richard has put you in a tough spot. Now **you** must decide what your next move will be." Now it was Herman's turn to get up from his chair. He took a peppermint from a dish on the counter and offered one to Chip. As he made his way back to his chair he began to talk.

"Chester, I'm going to tell you something very confidential. Can it be confidential?"

"No Payces?"

"No Payces," he replied, groaning as he sat down.

"Well, if it has to do with the royalties or the new contract, I can't promise that."

For several long minutes, Herman sat with his arms folded, not taking his eyes off of the Payce employee who sat across from him. He moved not a muscle except for the on-and-off squinting of his eyes. Finally, he talked. His tone, as well as his choice of words, gave evidence of a man of literary strength.

"Be patient with me. I have something crucial to say, but first, let me articulate a few other factors on my mind." Mr. Lichten leaned forward, drawing Chip into the narrative he was about to launch. His voice was raspy as always, but his words tumbled out with great strength. "The name of my next book is *The Dishonor of Sir Quiglee*. Strangely, it is the story of an evil and greedy man who looks out only for himself—a knight—and the captivating chronicle of his downfall. The first time I met Richard Payce and heard the words that flowed from his mouth and even his very voice inflections, I recognized in him my malevolent character, Sir Quiglee. You know that I am not a great mind. I have a good mind, but not a great one. I hardly knew how to go about getting my book published. In fact, it would undoubtedly be stashed away in my cabinets had it not been for the series of coincidences that put me in this apartment, and for your dedication—and...I must not fail to mention the lovely Mildred. I've been as pleased as a person could be who doesn't know much about this kind of thing, but as I told you, you are the one who has made it work. I like you and trust you implicitly. What you don't know, Chester—and I have purposely withheld this information— what you don't know is that I have more than merely a second book written."

"You do?" Chip asked, his eyes widening, his eyebrows raised.

"Yes, sir. This one"—and he picked up the hard copy of *The Street of Petetra* from the shelf behind him—"is the first of...twelve, written at my leisure over the last two years."

Trying not to expose his extreme shock, Chip drew in a deep breath and leaned forward, planting his elbows on the white flecked Formica tabletop. He rested his chin on his folded hands.

"Twelve? Eleven more?"

"Yes, sir."

"You are saying that you have written twelve books in the last two years," Chip said, reaffirming what he had just heard.

"Yes, sir. I've had an overabundance of free time and I own a ferocious imagination."

"I can hardly believe such a thing! Are they all like Petetra— futuristic fantasies and mysteries?"

"Some of the future; some of bygone days."

"All handwritten?"

"All handwritten."

"Twelve handwritten manuscripts! Well, Herman, you just amaze me! You are to be vigorously congratulated and complimented! Mr. Lichten," Chip declared, smacking the table, "that is an amazing accomplishment!" Chuckling, Chip enthusiastically added, "You are truly a fine man and a gifted writer."

Nothing in Chip's words or inflections, and for that matter, in his heart, was spawned from, as they say, *The Old Dollar Sign*. If all of Herman's books gleamed as literary works as did the first one, Herman Lichten, author, was indeed a much better human specimen than even the writer himself was able to recognize. The first book was genius, captivating young and old alike. Surely the rest would be the same. And Chip understood exactly why the old man was sharing this new information.

"Chester," he said with deliberation not to be mistaken, "I'm through with Payce. Even if I never publish another book, I have enough money to last me till I die. Yet, Chester," he said, now speaking in a passionate tone, "I'd like to publish them. Such pleasure there is in writing and finding out that they give others equal pleasure. I'll just wait till you're on your own."

Chip stared at the floor, clamping his teeth down on his bottom lip, thinking, thinking. How he wished he could reach down into his pocket and hand one of his new Finfield Publishing, Inc. business cards to Herman. They were hot off the press. This, however, was most assuredly not the time! Besides, Sarah must be the first one to see them.

Herman was continuing his gentle plea. "You just told me that someday you're going to make the break. I'll wait. We'll do business, Chester."

"Hold on," Chip said, holding up his hand, "At this moment, the immediate future is a blur, one without clear lines."

Herman interrupted. "It's simple. I sign a preliminary paper with you. We do business."

This meeting was not going as planned and Chip was becoming uncomfortable.

"You must remember that I, too, have a contract, Herman. My contract with Payce is up at the end of May 14th, the day after to-morrow, in fact. That is the day, I may as well tell you, that I plan to resign…quit…on the spot. I'm not going to go into all the reasons why. But there are confidentiality agreements and clauses I must honor—a year, two years, I can't remember at the moment. I could not legally publish your books since you are one of Payce's current clients. Not until my agreements with them are honored will I be free."

"Then, I'll wait."

"No, Herman. I will agree to nothing. I won't discuss your books with you until I am legally and morally free to do so. What you do in the meantime is up to you. If you don't want to sign this contract, that's up to you. The one thing I do advise you to do is sign the new contract for *The Street of Petetra.*"

"I'll sign that one. I won't sign the other one."

"If that's what you want."

"Chester," Herman said as he wrote his name at the bottom of the last page. "I'm going to ask you to do something for me. Will you?"

"If I can."

"Take the books with you tonight...."

"Why on earth for?" Chip broke in. "A lot can happen in a year. No. No, Herman, I can't do that. You wait."

"I'm moving out tomorrow, Chester, but I'm not moving to the lakefront." Herman chuckled.

"You're moving out?" Chip asked. "I didn't know that. I didn't know that, Herman. You haven't said anything about moving."

"Just found out this morning."

Chip's face twisted with questions.

"What do you mean?"

"I just happened to see the Payce janitor this morning—oh, what do they call them now?—maintenance engineer or something. You know, Luis. He was rummaging around downstairs as I was leaving. Just sort of casually, he mentioned...the wrecking ball."

"The wrecking ball! What is that supposed to mean?"

"I'm sure he was speaking figuratively."

"They're going to tear the place down? I'm sure I haven't heard anything about it." Chip's voice lowered. "But there's a lot I don't hear."

"Well, as I said, maybe he was using it as a figure of speech. Either way, he told me I had to be out on the 13th. That's tomorrow."

Chip paced back and forth in the small kitchen.

"Well, that's just crazy!"

"Chester, after having no home for so long, such news upsets me not at all."

"Where will you go? Do you have somewhere to go?"

"I've got no plans, but this time, at least, I've got money." Mr. Lichten shot a sincere smile at Chip. "I don't know where I'll end up but that's why I'm asking you to take the books...for safe keeping."

"How in the world are you going to move? I'll come by and help you."

"No need, Chester. All of this," Mr. Lichten said with a wave of his hand, "belongs to the Payces. What I own will fit in that suitcase...see over there? Don't be worrying about me. After tomorrow I won't have a home, but Herman Lichten is no longer a homeless man!" Clamping his large weathered hand down upon Chip's shoulder, he added, "Aw, Chester. I've been grateful for this roof over my head. You might imagine how much so in the middle of January!"

Chip's grim face told the story of his dissatisfaction with such short notice for the author. Surely they deemed him a lesser person! Softening a bit, he reached up for the old man's hand and patted it.

"I guess when you look at it that way, you're right. You've had heat and water. And...you've have the frig and the stove...and I guess it has been a perfect environment for writing, I'd say."

"Never used the stove. The frig, yes, but not the stove. Being out on the street can produce a pretty simple man."

"What? You never cooked?"

"Never. I mostly eat food cold. I heat up my canned food and coffee in the microwave. That's it."

A heavy sigh sounded from Chip's troubled spirit. Herman Lichten...moving away. Herman Lichten...stiffed by the Payces. Herman Lichten...taking life in stride. Where would he go?

"Do you have any family anywhere? I never felt free to ask."

"I had a wife. She left me, divorced me, and then died. No kids. A nephew in Idaho somewhere. Aw, Chester, I've got bucks in my pocket now. I can move in anywhere and I have a feeling it won't be too far away from you. In a big way, Chester, **you** are my family."

"I know," Chip said quietly. "Wow...my mother probably knows nothing of this either. It's an evil menagerie over there."

"Please, Chester, back to the books. Do this for me. I'll come by and get them from you as soon as I settle in somewhere. Maybe by then we can do business." He pulled his chair close to Chip's and whispered, "No one besides you and I know anything about the other ten! Here, let me show you where I've hidden them from those Payce boys who sneak around my apartment now and then."

"Now, Herman, I don't think they'd have any reason to do that."

"Ah, the Payce boys don't need a reason. They always leave obvious signs that they have been here. I guess it's a power thing. I just let them rummage. They've never been smart enough to stumble across the books."

Herman opened the lower kitchen cabinet beside the sink. It was filled with canned food, napkins, potato chips, and many boxes of cereal. He reached down and pulled out a box of Cheerios.

"Here," he said with apparent satisfaction and triumph, "here is *The Dishonor of Sir Quiglee*. Pulling out another box—raisin bran— he announced, "And here, Chester, is *Brave Bonnie Augustine!*"

Chip was duly amused and somewhat dumbfounded. What a

great hiding place!

"More Cheerios," Herman announced. "Honey nut. This is *Silver Cobblestones.*"

"I guess I can safely assume that the rest of what I see is not cereal! And what have you hidden in the potato chip bag there?"

"Nothing in the chips! Please, Chester, I'm just asking that you keep my books safe for a few weeks or so—oh, maybe a month or two at the most."

It was not a simple request, though undoubtedly Herman saw it as one. Chip was resigning on the 14th. Possessing Mr. Lichten's sure-to-be-successful novels could prove quite problematic were that fact to become known. Yet, it would be for a short time only. He could tuck them away at home—somewhere.

"You're certain you will not do this new book—*The Dishonor of Sir Quiglee*—with Payce?"

Herman Lichten shook his head slowly and with finality. He went to the counter, cleared away the silverware awaiting washing, tore a blank piece of paper from the back of his phonebook, and began to write.

"And you're certain that no one else knows about these books?" Chip wanted to know.

"No one. Just you…and me."

Chip sighed.

"I'll take them, but you must promise to stay in touch. Let me give you another business card. I'll write my personal cell phone number on the back. You keep that close and make your plans so you're picking those books up in a month or two, okay?"

"Here, Chester, just in case. Read this." Chip took the paper and scanned it quickly as Herman went on expressively. "You never know. I'm getting up there, you know, and if something happens to me before I can get back to you, I want them to belong to you. I have no one else. I'd give them to your mother for her kindness to me, but she, I'm sorry to say, is a Payce. It would not do for her to know of them. **You** are my friend, Chester. If something happens to me, I want those books to be yours. I don't care if they get published. Just in case, Chester, I want you to have them. I like visualizing you reading them to your children."

"Herman, this says you're selling them to me for $1.00 each. What's that all about?"

"What? You don't have $11.00 in cash on you?" Herman laughed with gusto and put his arm around Chip. "Aw, Chester, you don't really have to give me the money. I just want everything legal. For now, they're yours. I'll buy them back by the end of summer."

Chip shook his head, not quite believing all that was taking place. He pulled out a ten and a five and laid them on the table.

"There. You owe me four!"

❧ ❧ ❧ ❧ ❧

When Chip left the run down building and its now contented resident, he left with four contracts in his briefcase—the old incorrect one for *The Street of Petetra*, signed back in July of 2003; a corrected one for the same book, signed and dated May 12, 2004; the contract for Herman's second book, rejected and unsigned; and a primitive, but legal one, written on a piece of paper ripped from the back of Herman's phone book—a bill of sale, so to speak—making Chester Finfield the owner of eleven pieces of literature written by the now famous Herman Lichten.

The exit from the Wentworth Building was not one of great exuberance. Chip's resignation in two days—likely to be ugly—hung over him like a thick black cloud, nearly blotting out any joy he could possibly be experiencing at the start of a new life, a new enterprise. Added to that was his displeasure at the uncivil handling of removing Herman from his apartment. And then, there was the unpleasant task of informing Richard Payce that the second book of Mr. Lichten would not be running on Payce Publishing presses.

On the way home, his cell phone rang. A blend of gloom and righteous indignation fell upon him as he read the name of the caller. It was Richard.

"Robert tells me he drew up a new contract. Did you get a contract from the old man?" Mr. Payce asked roughly.

"Yes," Chip replied, "and no." He sent up a quick and desperate prayer for the peace of God upon his trembling heart.

"And that means what?"

"He signed a new and corrected contract for Petetra, but he will not sign for the second book. He is resolute."

There was no immediate reply. Chip heard the giggle of a woman in the background and he recognized that it was not his mother's laugh. He waited. Richard finally went on, obviously with food in his mouth.

"Sooo…Herman Lichten, who lives free-of-charge in my Wentworth Building, is resolute. Is that correct? Did I hear you right?"

"Yes, Richard. He will not sign…not today, not tomorrow."

"Well, at least I will have the last laugh."

Chip wondered what exactly he meant, but he did not ask.

"You lay everything on my desk tonight and I'll deal with this when I get back on Monday."

"I'll have them on your desk by Monday. I'm going home now."

"You know, son, you're making a whopping mistake by aligning with the old man and not with the company. The old man is a foolish old man. We'll see about him."

The phone snapped shut.

"Goodbye, Richard...Dad," Chip murmured, his voice thick with cynicism. "For a measly one percent you lost the great author, Herman Lichten...and you lost me."

He turned on to the state highway toward home.

Five minutes later, Mr. Lichten left his humble apartment, without thought of locking his door. He never locked it. Why would he? The outer doors of the Wentworth Building always locked automatically when he left the building. He ambled down the stairs. It was a perfect night for ice cream, a warm one for May. He'd make one more hurried trip to Smitty's before leaving his now familiar neighborhood at the crack of dawn. In the dark of ten o'clock, he left the building, pulled shut the rusty front door, listening for the customary sound of the lock.

In that same darkness, not five minutes later, there came a car, moving smoothly and silently. Dark figures exited the car with equal stealth. The front entrance of the old building opened, the hinges grinding as it did. A man, standing in the shadows across the street, put out his cigarette with one twist of the foot and disinterestedly watched the progressing acts of the play. He watched until the men ran from the building and nearly soundlessly drove away; then, opening his door, he made his way upstairs to his shabby apartment.

CHAPTER 2

Tom had always claimed publicly that it was really Sarah who ran his multi-million dollar enterprise. It was no secret that he leaned upon her remarkable adeptness at taking charge of the global affairs in his many absences. When one day, though, he told her privately that he could not do what he did without her, the smile of fulfillment crossed her lips. For Mrs. Finfield—as Tom Kerrigan, President/CEO always called her—the job had been an overwhelming delight and had provided her with responsibility that spurred her on to tackle more and more. The money was wonderful, the challenges invigorating, and the opportunity to learn and grow, far beyond her expectations! The corporate ambience and her private luxurious office overlooking the rich green grounds and the interstate gave each day an extra reason to bounce out of bed. She loved her job at Kerrigan Corp.

Then, out of nowhere death came to 12006 Timber Lane, the prestigious home of Sarah and Chester "Chip" Finfield, II, snatching the life from one and rendering virtual death to the heart of the other left behind. Sarah withdrew from the world. Without hesitation, she severed all ties: Kerrigan, friends, church…and relatives, such as they were. Chip was dead. Life had draped itself with black. In her solitary state, the visions of the brass and glass, mahogany and marble at One Kerrigan Drive abruptly disappeared. Thoughts and memories of her employment were painted upon walls of inner personal rooms no longer frequented by the grieving woman. No more did the dreams of computers, polished conference rooms and international visitors follow her into sleep. Names and phone numbers of customers—old and new—ceased to be at instant recall. After a whole year, even Tom's face faded. It mattered not at all whether or not he remembered her.

Shoulders aching and eyes tired from peering into a thick April fog for much of the last twenty minutes, she pulled her car into the drive. Taking her purse and the small bag of groceries, with her eyes down, she made her way up the curved brick walkway, wearily climbed the stairs and entered her sprawling ranch house.

The Saturday night routine continued. Groceries were put in their proper place in Sarah's grand, luxurious kitchen, a peanut butter and jelly sandwich made and a glass of milk poured. Heartlessly then, she curled up on the family room couch, nibbled at the food, and then, tucked half of the sandwich into a baggie, as always, for Sunday evening.

It was bedtime. Sarah Finfield took no notice of the exquisite Queen Anne bedroom as she readied for another night alone. Blessed oblivion would soon take her away where it was safe, off into slumber within her room of pale teal, moss and forest green—off to the land of deep rest where no memories could haunt.

A knock on the rustic wooden door unnerved her, tightening her chest. Her hand gripped the door handle to the master bath. No one ever came to her door—she had skillfully engineered that fact into place. Her days were spent in the grateful solitude that had come by not answering the door chimes and by ignoring the ringing of the phone. But why would someone be here at this hour of the night? She looked at the clock. It was eight thirty. She leaned her head back against the door and closed her eyes.

Another knock. This time it was the door knocker and this time it was with insistence. Whoever it was, knew she was home. Next came the rapping of a key against the window pane. Sarah froze. Surely the glass would break! She would not answer. They would go away. Silence fell. Sarah tiptoed to a front bedroom window, peering out into the night. In the fog and darkness she could see nothing.

Inching her way back to her room, fearing that the night guest would hear her stirring, she moved silently across the floor. On the edge of the bed, she sat listening. In a moment, another knock came, this time from the back door. Then another more determined bang sounded, followed by another silence. Her mind raced. It was night and it was dark. Who wanted to see her at this hour? She could think of no one.

Sarah was disquieted, to be sure. Someone had barged into her tranquil life and had disturbed the norm she had successfully established. Her simple existence pleased her. Intruders were most certainly not welcome.

A shout from the front porch shattered the silence. Sarah flinched.

"Lady! Ladeeee! Mrs. Finfield!" the pleading voice rang out. "I need to talk to you, Mrs. Finfield!"

It was the voice of a woman. A young woman. The voice was unfamiliar to her. Should she go to the door?

"Lady! Pleeeease come to the door!"

Sarah arose. Although leery, she moved toward the front door, bolstered by remains of strength of days gone by. She turned the porch light on. The knocking ceased.

She opened the door a crack. Outside, standing in the cloud that had enveloped the whole valley, stood a girl Sarah thought to be about twenty. Greatly animated, she spoke to Sarah, waving her arms about, pointing as she talked.

"I was on my way home...I live down there, in the big brown house...and I saw a car in your drive and it wasn't yours. It was dark and I'm not sure what kind of car it was. I'm not a busybody at all, really, but I see your car there every time I walk by or drive by. It's never in the garage...not that it's any of my business. Well, anyway, tonight...my boyfriend and I...tonight we were coming from town, you know, walking down the west path through the woods behind your house and we saw three men, three grown men, with a flashlight, standing beneath that window. Around there!" She pointed towards the other side of the garage.

"My boyfriend whispered that something was not right about it. I don't know how to tell you this but they were walking around your house for a long time. We couldn't see them when they came in front here, but I don't think they went into your house—at least, we didn't see any lights go on. We stayed in the darkness of the woods until they left. They may have seen us or heard us, for that matter. I don't know. Then we knocked on your door and you were not home. That was about an hour ago."

The girl talked on, barely taking time for a breath, her short brown hair moving in the slight wind, and with each word, the report seemed more feasible. Sarah steadied herself against the door frame.

"Well, thank you for coming to tell me. I'll check into it in the morning."

"If you'd like, Tony and I could stay a while until you check. He's out in the car. Out there. We went to my house to get his car." She turned and motioned towards the darkness.

Sarah responded quickly. Someone enter her hiding place?

"Oh, no. That's not necessary. I'm sure they have gone by now."

"Mrs. Finfield...you are Mrs. Finfield, right?" the girl said, her face fully expressive. "I see your name on the mailbox."

"Yes, I am Mrs. Finfield."

"Mrs. Finfield, you don't have to be afraid of us. I live right down there. You can see my house in the winter when the leaves are gone. I'd feel much better about it if you would at least go and turn on all of your lights."

Sarah capitulated.

"I'll turn them on then if it will make you feel better. Thank you for coming to tell me."

"Oh, I'll just wait! Go turn them on while I wait!"

The girl was not twenty. Getting a better look at her and ob-serving her animated behavior told Sarah that her night visitor was closer to sixteen—perhaps seventeen. She was insistent. The once stalwart Mrs. Finfield went through the immense ranch house, turn-ing lights on here and there, her hands trembling slightly. At the back door, she flipped the switch for the back yard lantern, and tried the door. It was locked.

"Is everything okay?" the teenager asked as Sarah returned.

"Everything seems to be fine. I certainly can't imagine why any-one would be creeping around this house," she said in a near whisper. "I certainly have nothing anyone would want."

"You know, people creep around for more reasons than trying to steal what you own, if you know what I mean. And you know, this isn't exactly a low class neighborhood, if you know what I mean. And, Mrs. Finfield, another thing, robbers don't usually travel in threes." She hesitated. "I don't think they do, do they? Well, I've done my duty. I guess we'll go."

By this time, the boyfriend had joined her at the bottom of the stairs. Even through the mist, his fine clothes and dark handsome features were distinct. Sarah eyed the couple dubiously.

"Well, thank you for coming by. I do appreciate it. I'm sure there is nothing to worry about."

The girl stopped beside the yard light. "They **were** here," she said, sensing Sarah's suspicion.

"Oh, I believe you. I really do but I have not the slightest idea why someone would be hanging around. Perhaps the morning will shed some light."

"My name is Annette Cappetti," the young lady offered, "and this is Tony."

"Well, Annette and Tony, thank you both," Sarah stated cau-tiously and rather coldly guiding the conversation to a finish. She shoved the heavy door shut.

The coming of someone to her house had wearied her nearly as much as had the thought of three men trespassing on her property.

Exhausted, she fell across her mahogany Queen Anne bed, her thin legs dangling off the edge. An interruption in her normal routine was unacceptable. Oh, that this might be the end of it! In her heart, she knew better. Offering a short prayer, she begged the God she once knew well, that she might be left alone.

The next day arrived as other Sundays had arrived, the day appearing with a light blue sky streaked with gold and pale pink. Outside Sarah's window the soft morning breeze brought relief from the hazy weather of the night before. The sweet dawn was relegated to the outside, however; heavy, dark green drapes over a layer of fine crushed voile sheers performed their duty, hiding the daybreak from Mrs. Finfield who lay beneath her pale green comforter pulled close to her chin. In days past, Sarah had been a morning person, up at the crack of dawn, as they say, done with her chores before most people had begun. How she despised sleeping in! Yet today, she slumbered on. The blankets had hardly been disturbed. Her weary body clung to the bed like a rock.

A sound from somewhere beyond slumber-land disturbed her sleep and Sarah sat upright. Immediately she swung her feet over the side of the bed, put on her glasses and looked at the time. With a groan, she badgered herself for staying in bed until almost ten o'clock. The 9:58 train whistled in the distance as it wound its way along the White Rock River.

The incident of the previous night had not faded even slightly, and as Sarah moved about, showering, dressing, brushing her long brown hair, she gave careful consideration to Annette's report of the men seen near the house. Sarah was a bright woman, intuitive, discerning, able to take charge, and above all, not easily pushed around. Her present state of withdrawal from society had not dulled her keen God-given senses; but today, standing there in front of the full length mirror, pulling her hair into a long ponytail, she admitted that she had not a clue as to who the men might be and what on earth they might want. Anything was possible, she assumed; she allowed herself to give careful thought to all possibilities.

Perhaps Annette's story had been exaggerated. Such a spirited child she was! What could anyone see in such a fog? Sarah had not even been able to see her car in the drive when she looked out of the front window. And too, Annette and Tony had been in back where there was no lighting. How could they possibly have made out the forms of three *anybodies!*

Furthermore, what if Annette and Tony themselves were not to be trusted? Before last night, she had never laid eyes on this neighbor girl or on the boyfriend. It was conceivable that there was a scheme in the minds of the two. Sarah rejected this idea for the time being, but reserved the right to think on it again later.

What would three men want with her or with her house? Was there wisdom in the thought that thieves usually work alone? If so, why would three men be moving about her house in the black of night? The Finfield house was a fine one, somewhat secluded by the surrounding woods, and located in the prestigious Sharenne Woods area of Timber Ridge. The homes here were magnificent and pricey. It would not take much figuring to deduce that the belongings of these homeowners would be in proportion to the real estate value.

Apart from a determination to further investigate in the daylight last night's strange occurrence, Sarah knew in her heart this Sunday would pass exactly as all Sundays had for these last dreadful months. A poached egg, wheat toast and coffee would be her morning fare. Having set breakfast in motion, she made her way to the back entry, unlocked the door and shoved it open. She stepped outside onto the deck which reached out into the shaded yard. Chipmunks and squirrels scurried to a hiding place where they could watch the figure standing near the doorway. Who was she, they wondered? Was it really the lady of the house? Yes, it was the lady of the house, still tall and thin, still crowned with thick shiny brown hair, skin still soft and clear, still beautiful; yet, all living things in Sarah's backyard were puzzled by the gray circles beneath the eyes and the stooped shoulders of this one who stood quiet and forlorn where once the bright and high-spirited Sarah Finfield had regularly greeted the mornings.

Hints of spring were everywhere. The faint heavenly fragrance of moist earth touched Sarah with unexpected comfort. This was her first venture out on to the rustic deck in almost a year, out where so much delight had been hers in days past. The winter had made its mark on the wooden deck furniture, not having been safely stored away in the shed as Chip and she had always been careful to do. Little piles of leaves, dull and brown, covered the cushions and the stairs, and were pressed against railings of the deck. She folded her arms and viewed the woods that lined the large back yard. The sweeping willows were wearing gold and swaying gently in the wind. Forsythia branches, red with life, showed signs of bursting forth with their tiny yellow flowers. Small buds clung to the maples. A chipmunk ran past her. She drew in a breath of the post-winter air and nearly smiled; but the outward show of pleasure lasted but a moment. Her lips tightened. She must not linger. Her only purpose was to investigate the reported trespassing.

No signs of an attempted break-in were visible. It was impossible, however, to ascertain if any changes had taken place in the yard; Sarah had not laid eyes on the area behind the house for almost a year now. How would she know if someone had been there? Yet, there did not appear to be any tampering with the lock or the door frame. Had Annette and Tony scared off the prowlers?—if indeed there had been prowlers. Dull and uncaring, Sarah went back in, closed the door and locked it.

For the first time since Death had knocked at her door, she experienced a measure of helplessness. Though suffering deep depression and the death of her own spirit, until this moment life had been manageable. There had been no crises and no insurmountable circumstances. Routine had become her master. No day was different from the next. Emotion had long since disappeared. Tears were extinct. Existing was what she did best. Yet, in all of its dullness, until last night, life had dished out no impossibilities. Today, as she jabbed aimlessly at her egg, the drapes and curtains, as always, shutting out most of the light of day, the realization grew that if intruders had tried once, they might very well try again.

By noon, Sarah had completed her daily chores; living alone generated little need for housework. Though always clean, however, the house was never out of the state of dimness. Only slightly were the drapes and curtains ever open. In the living room, before the fireplace, where Sarah spent most of her time, a brass floor lamp was often the only source of light in the entire house. As was her usual custom, she sat herself down on the plaid loveseat which was positioned perpendicular to the fireplace. Directly across were two large, soft leather recliners. A heavy cedar chest served as a coffee table in between. Farthest from the fireplace—and parallel to it—sat a matching couch. This was Sarah's haven.

The Finfield great room, large and exuding the atmosphere of a hunting lodge, was lined with shelves on the outside wall, reaching high to the cathedral ceiling—valuable and treasured books on the top shelves and hundreds of record albums filling the lower ones. On each side of the fireplace, an exquisite brass eagle's head was skillfully blended into the stone work. A grand piano with a deep, shiny black finish stood in one corner opposite the fireplace, a paneled wall of signed Norman Rockwell paintings behind it. Elegant dining room furniture filled the north end of the room, large framed oil paintings of the sea creating a warm atmosphere. Once a place of comfort and warmth and joy, the room now appeared austere, except for the little haven offered by the furniture arrangement before the grand stone fireplace, and the soft glow of the brass lamp.

This spot was now the refuge of Sarah Finfield, the place to which she retreated day after dreadful day, in seclusion from a world outside which she did not want to see. Here within the walls of the gray ranch trimmed with deep Rhubarb red, Sarah Finfield, woman of twenty-eight, lived out a life of solitude. Tall, slender Sarah, a beautiful woman, (though she never thought of herself as so), spent her long days stretched out upon the tartan plaid sofa or loveseat, book in hand, her long, thick brown hair drawn back into a barrette or clip and pulled forward over a shoulder. Unaware of it, she had settled into a life of grief and anguish, riddled with the aftermath of shock.

On this Sunday, sheltered by the dullness that surrounded her, the once vibrant woman of the business world pulled herself into a curled-up position, satisfied to be withdrawn from all beyond her doors. The leather-bound copy of Hamlet lay upon a cushion propped against her drawn up knees. In a few moments, Shakespeare would take the young widow away, off to where the players are fictitious and the end of the story, a whim of mortal man.

Footsteps on the front porch alerted Sarah before a knock on the door reached her ears.

"Annette," she murmured, jaw clenched, not considering any other alternatives. Another knock, somewhat more resolute, sounded. She closed her eyes. Anger kept her from going to the door. She remained perfectly still, curled up before the fireplace.

"Mrs. Finfield? Mrs. Finfield! It's Annette, Mrs. Finfield!"

Sarah opened her eyes and stared into the air, greatly irritated.

"Mrs. Finfield! Are you there?" Annette knocked again.

Impatiently, and knowing that her visitor would not be going away, Sarah Finfield arose, turned her book upside down on the cedar chest and gracefully stalked to the door.

Opening the door slightly and heaving a sigh, she said, "What is it, Annette?"

"I just wanted to see...I hope you don't mind...how you are today. How are you?"

"I'm...just...fine, Annette," she replied coolly and very quietly, her irritation obvious.

"I worried about you all night. I tell you, that was some scary happenings! I kept thinking 'Why were those men stalking and sneaking around your house?' My father said I should mind my own business, but the way I see it, this **is** my business. How could I just let this go! I mean, you could be in danger. I would never forgive myself if something happened to you!"

It did not please Sarah to be informed that Annette's story had reached the ears of her father and who could know who else.

"I don't think there is a thing to worry about, Annette. I think it must have been some people from church seeing if I was at home."

"Church people? You think? I don't know…."

"It's the only explanation," Sarah broke in. "Everything seems to be fine this morning. I checked out back and I see no signs of anything funny. No footprints. No tampering. I wouldn't worry a bit more. But, thank you, Annette," Sarah said nodding her head meaningfully, "for asking about me."

Annette stood looking out upon the sloping front yard, her hands in her jacket pockets. Upon her face were more questions. She was weighing the whole situation. Sarah wished she would weigh it somewhere else, but it was obvious that the young girl was not leaving soon.

Still staring into the distance, Annette slowly shook her head. "They didn't seem like church people, not that I know that much about church people. But they were snooping, poking around and mumbling."

"Where were you when you saw them?"

"Well, like I told you, we were coming down the west path, not the one that leads to the lake, but the shortcut from town. We were coming from the dance. It was foggy and…." Annette stopped, her face inquiring. "Could I come in, do you think?"

"Well," replied Sarah, abruptly unnerved and aggravated, "I…." She searched for firm words to halt such a possibility. "I can't think that we have anything else to discuss."

"Oh, are you busy? I'm sorry. I just thought it would be good to discuss this thing thoroughly. It's pretty important, Mrs. Finfield, don't you think, you being alone the way you are, you know?"

Sarah frowned. How did she know she was alone?

"Listen," she said as gently as she could, "I will be fine. Please don't worry anymore about this. I'll be safe. Perhaps I will install new locks."

"On all four doors?"

It surprised Mrs. Finfield that Annette had such a ready reference to the amount of doors needing protection. She squinted at Annette's face, searching for a clue.

"Do you need help with them? Tony can put them in for you. In fact, would you like for us to pick them up? We're going in to town in a little while to the pharmacy. I'd be glad to get locks for you. You just tell me what to get."

"Uh, no, Annette. It's not necessary. I'll take care of it."

"You know, it was odd last night. When we came out of the woods, I first saw two men at your back door and then as we walked down that way," she continued, pointing, "I saw the other man at the side door of the garage. He was trying the door and trying it pretty hard. It's a good thing that you keep it all locked up when you go. My dad doesn't. He says that thieves will get in if they want to. Can you believe that? He never locks our doors."

The conversation was over as far as Mrs. Finfield was concerned. Annette was turning out to be a pest. With an affirmation that she would be *just fine*, Sarah began to close the door.

"Listen, Mrs. Finfield," Annette half whispered in a voice tinted with intrigue, "those men, by the looks of it, were **not** friends of yours. Sneaking around with a flashlight, in front, in back, at the side! You best not take it lightly!" she said dramatically, leaning in toward Sarah. "They were up to no good. And listen, this is my phone number. The first numbers are the same as yours and everyone else's around here. The last four are 4...6...6...4. You know where I live, right? You know, you go down Pine Cone Creek Trail around the bend and the first house on the right, you know, the one set way back with the big willow in the front. That's it. You never know. You might need me before it's over with."

With a wrinkled brow, Sarah scanned the bright face of this new and basically unwelcome person in her life. Why was she so concerned? There was an element of sincerity in the tone of voice and the facial expression, but why? This was a high school girl. Did highschoolers usually show such interest in the welfare of others? Or was there more? Was Sarah being fed a line?

"What grade are you in, Annette?"

"I'm a senior."

"Are you new to the neighborhood? I don't recall seeing you before?"

"We moved down there three months ago," Annette replied, and then added almost sadly, "and you probably have never seen me because you are never outside. I walk by every day for the school bus."

"Well, that is true, but I can't help asking what it is that makes you so interested in all of this?"

"I don't know. This is how I am and I know you're alone. We moved in three months ago and the Dickersons told us about you." Sarah let her talk. "I guess I feel sorry for you. I wouldn't want to live alone, I know that. I like people. I wish there were more houses in Sharenne Woods. I'm glad the Dickersons live just down the road. And you."

"And what have the Dickersons told you about me?"

"Well, just that…your husband has recently died?"

There was more to the story, Sarah could tell, by the question mark at the end of Annette's sentence. No doubt, the Dickersons had given a generous supply of information to more than just Annette's family. Filthy rich, Alan Dickerson toted his prestige by being the *town crier* of Timber Ridge. He had always disgusted Sarah. His manner was unmanly in her opinion. Town Crier was too kind of a title. Town Gossip fit him more accurately.

Sarah heard Annette say that she was sorry about Mr. Finfield. A lock snapped into place around her heart. It was time to put an end to this relationship.

"Please, Annette, don't bother yourself on my account. I'm doing wonderfully well—I really am—and I'm sure I'll go on being fine," she exclaimed convincingly. "You were very kind to alert me, but now, you can let it go. I'm sure that there's nothing further to worry about. Okay?"

"Sure, it's okay. If that's what you want. But, Mrs. Finfield, I will be keeping my eyes open," the girl stated firmly, "and if I see anything else, I'll let you know—I mean if I just happen to see something. Remember, too, you can call me. 4664, remember?"

Sarah closed the door wishing that the sound of it meant the end of this invasion into her carefully guarded privacy. Experience whispered that it had not. For weeks, yes, even long months, success had been hers in the silencing of family and friends. Sarah Finfield would see to it that her solitude continued undisturbed. This teenager, Annette, would be silenced politely as had all the rest. Chit chat nauseated Sarah. Conversation meant vulnerability and most probably the necessity to discuss that which had torn her soul and hidden her away from the world.

The twenty-eight year old Sarah Finfield, soon to be twenty-nine, with a slight shiver, tucked a shawl around her drawn up knees and took her book into her long fingers. She opened it to where her marker had been left, but for a moment before she began to read, though she did her best to repress it, the devastating remembrance of a day nearly twelve months before flashed before her like a multimedia presentation, one chilling snapshot after the other. Quickly, she squeezed shut her eyes hoping to block the scenes as she sucked in a panicky breath. The muscles in her neck stiffened. As a thousand times before, anger and grief, indescribable humiliation and despair passed over her very slender body. If only the slow motion replays would finally cease! Time was putting up a brave attempt to mute the vividness of them, but contact with other people somehow caused the gruesome truth to sharpen. In a thousand years she vowed that she would never speak openly of the event that had shattered her hopes and disfigured her views on the meaning of life. Protect her seclusion, that's what she must do. Her lips hardened. Annette must not be allowed to plunge her into another period of hopeless days. Had she been firm enough? Only time would tell.

It was time to escape once again, to block the memories, to run and hide.

"Back to Shakespeare," she mumbled. "Now, where was I?"

Aimlessly, she scanned the page to find her place. There. There it was. Claudius was speaking.

"When sorrows come, they come not single spies. But in battalions."

CHAPTER 3

The soft clatter of rain dripping from the branches above onto the umbrellas around her and the monotone voice of Reverend Fitch reached Sarah's ears, sending shiver after shiver over her thin frame.

"Yea, though I walk through the valley of the shadow of death, I will fear no evil for Thou art with me."

There were four headstones. Sarah, looking particularly slender in her long black coat, planted her feet in a place where the chiseled letters on the third would not be in her line of vision. Too recently she had stood at this very spot, heart consumed with grief, face impassive, tearlessly saying goodbye to her dearest friend. On that day, against the protests of the people gathered with her beneath the oaks, she had remained behind, requesting all to allow her to be alone. There, with the sun streaking the hazy air with its long shafts, her still-life eyes had rested upon the gothic letters staring back at her from the cold, marble slab. The haughty finger of death etched similar ones upon her broken heart as well.

CHESTER "CHIP" ELLIOTT FINFIELD, II
May 15, 1975 – May 15, 2004

She had turned—though today she had no recollection of doing so—and walked to the top of the hill overlooking the town of Meredith Grange. Steadying herself against the black iron fence, she had made a decision to die. Life would not be worth living now. Chip was gone.

"…goodness and mercy shall follow me all the days of my life and I shall dwell…."

Brought back to the present, Sarah's eyes wandered to the inscription upon the first stone: "Chester Elliott Finfield." There beneath the cold ground lay her dear, kind father-in-law. Beside him, by nightfall, would rest his wife. The name, *Mildred Ruth Finfield*

Payce, looked down upon the dreadful opening in the earth, the yawn of death, and told the story of a second marriage. The date etched below was May 18, 2005.

"I am the resurrection and the life," the reverend's quoting of Scripture continued. "He that believeth in Me though he were dead, yet shall he live and whosoever liveth and believeth in Me...."— Sarah shuddered but her face showed no emotion—"shall never die." Her mind mumbled the words, "Sorrow upon sorrow."

A hand upon her shoulder returned her to the scene. The rain had stopped though still it fell from the oaks above. Reverend Fitch, Mildred's pastor, was at the end of his prayer, uttering his final "Amen." Folk whispered condolences and walked through the wet grass to their cars parked along the winding lane.

"This is difficult. This is very difficult." The male voice was familiar. There was no need for Sarah to turn her head. "Sarah, you will come to the church for the meal."

"No, Raymond" she said, leaving no room for any doubt as to her sincerity. She pulled her shoulder away.

"Everyone would like to see you. It's been a long time of silence."

She did not respond to the frustration evident in the speaker's voice. She had given her answer. She would not go.

"You can't go on living like this. It's like you're dead."

Sighing deeply, she responded, "No, Raymond, I'm going home."

"Well, have it your way," he almost whined, "but very soon, we will meet again. You are going to have to help us out at the office."

Sarah turned away from this second son of Richard Payce, unwilling to interact with such a weakling—a puppet-on-a-string! *"Help them out with what!"* she asked herself as she hurried toward the road. Not quite to her car, she looked up. Inwardly, she groaned. Robert, the elder brother, was leaning against it, clad in a splendid suit—no doubt Hugo Boss—his arms folded. What did handsome Robert want—more on the same subject? Her distaste for a conversation with him surpassed the short one with Raymond. She stopped and closed her eyes.

"You are a sight for sore eyes, Mrs. Finfield," Robert called out to her, with a cocky smile. Sarah opened her eyes and looked squarely at the two finely dressed brothers—for Raymond had found a spot next to Robert to lean against the car. Her face showed absolutely no signs of reacting to Robert's statement. She did not move. Robert slowly sauntered toward her.

"I've missed you, Sarah," he called out to her, theatrically. "You've kept yourself from the family. You have isolated yourself."

Still, Sarah spoke no words, though a response was in her mind and on her lips.

"Listen, we all mourn Chip's death. You're not alone. But we have to go on. And what should we do now? Mourn Mother's death for weeks?"

"Oh, please Robert! How dare you refer to her as Mother!" Sarah replied with a bland chuckle of unbelief. "She was not your mother and you never accepted her as a Payce. So don't be pretending that there was some affection on your part."

Sarah's pert correctness did not stop him. "You are right. Yet, she was a grand woman. No one can argue with that. But my point," he said, evading Sarah's, "is that no matter what has gone on before, we must all keep trekking. It's water over the dam."

With a final glance of distaste, Sarah moved toward her car. As she did, her eyes swept over the row of gravestones and lingered upon the fourth one. Her face remained expressionless. The blank stone beside Chip's was for her. Oh, to be laid to rest beneath the sod! Robert stepped beneath her umbrella and took her elbow.

"Sarah, Sarah. Will we never be friends? At least before, we tolerated each other. Let's be acquaintances at least. Let's be able to talk. In fact, I need to talk with you about some business matters. Very, very important business matters."

Wrinkles appeared on Sarah Finfield's brow.

"What business matters could you possibly have to talk to me about?" she asked in near unbelief.

"Herman…Lichten."

Planting her feet firmly upon the wet ground, Sarah turned to fully face him and once again pulled from his grip.

"What…about him?" Sarah was exceedingly aggravated.

"I think you know."

"I know nothing except that Payce published his book, *The Street of Petetra*, and that it has been a raging success. Chip made it a practice not to discuss business with me."

"We're missing some very crucial things. Crucial, Sarah. Very crucial."

"Robert, I'm telling you, I know nothing about Herman or the book. What could there possibly be that remains to be discussed! The book has been on the market for months and selling very well!"

"There's more, and you and I need to sit down and go over this to see if we can uncover the facts."

"Not today, Robert," she snapped.

"When?"

"Not today. Of course, not today."

Robert frowned and pompously shook his head. "This is of great magnitude, Sarah!"

"But not today," Sarah said decisively, shaking her head, her eyes closed.

"This perpetual mourning for the dead is ridiculous!"

Now halfway to her car, she hesitated and turned to face the scene from which she had just come. The rain had made an ugly mess of the site. The three people she had cherished more than any others—beside her own parents who had left this earth and been laid to rest in Missouri when she was but nine years old—lay side by side there beneath the soggy earth. Death, in its finality, had severed the best of love and the greatest of strength from her. She stared at the blank marble slab that would one day mark her final resting place. She should be there now, she was woefully thinking to herself. A far-away gaze fell upon her drawn face.

"The dead cannot mourn the dead," she murmured.

"You're a fool if that's what you think. You're not dead. You're refusing to face up to your aliveness, that's all. You're hiding, Sarah. Chip is gone and there's nothing you can do about it. His father and mother are gone and there's nothing you can do about that either. It's a choice you're making. You're not dead. You're not one bit dead!"

Sarah did not move nor did her eyes leave off staring at the gravestones. Her voice was dull and monotone. "I must be dead, Robert. I don't despise you as intensely as I did when Chip was alive."

Her words brought on a chuckle and snort from Robert's brother as he made his way to his car. Sarah watched his Porsche until it crept through the black wrought iron gate. Robert began to make his way to his shiny pearl white Escalade. His anger could be detected in his gait.

"Sometime soon I will be by," he warned in threatening tones. "One way or another, you and I will talk."

She heard the slam of his door, the roar of his engine and his hasty departure. For a moment, she closed her eyes and then, with one final glance at the last page of the life of Mildred Finfield, Sarah walked to her car and gracefully climbed inside. The crowd—about 30 mourners—had gone their way. Drained as a result of the sorrowful death of her mother-in-law and the necessity of attending a funeral with people, most of whom she deplored, she pulled shut her door, leaned her head back and sighed. Soon, she started the car and followed the winding road lined with flowering dogwoods and lilacs until she reached the main road. A strong and desperate yearning to be at home consumed her. Her eyes peering into the rays of the sun which poked through the charcoal gray clouds ahead, Sarah made a commitment to herself to forever remain in the safety of Timber Lane.

Deep sadness gathered in her heart. Her mind wandered to years gone by. Memories of Chester and Mildred resulted in ones of Chip, thoughts and pictures that she had worked very hard to dull. However, to avoid some private reflection on Mother Payce seemed without decency. Furthermore, it would be impossible; the woman directly and also by example, had touched her daughter-in-law in ways that could never be measured.

It pleased Sarah that Mildred's first married name was used. It would have been better had the Payce name been omitted altogether. How unfortunate that the marriage had ever taken place! Chip had cautioned his mother, being open and honest about his intuitions. Mildred, after ten years the widow, had married Richard Payce with minimal blessing from her only child; Chip—and Sarah—had eventually laid aside their disapprovals, and had decided on a cold winter night, snuggled beneath the down comforter, that they must give their full support to Mildred if this was what she wanted. Marital bliss was to last one mere month. Subsequently, Mildred's life was one of playacting and pathetic struggling to *make things work*, colored with an unending sense that she was somehow at fault for the indifference that soon evidenced itself on Richard's part. Mildred had pretended that all was well and her playacting had fooled Chip and Sarah for a long time.

Sarah could not cry today. Crying had long since disappeared from her broken life. Sorrow, however, gripped her innermost being as she thought upon the beautiful woman whose body had moments before been placed in a grave. Young Sarah had aspired to be like Mildred, the warm and caring wife, the seamstress and cook, the gardener. The woman for whom they mourned today had slowly weakened in every way through the four years of marriage to a dispassionate man. The recent death of her son had dealt the final blow to an excellent woman of sixty-four.

Pulling into her driveway, Annette came to mind. Would she be perched upon the wooden railing in front of the house as had often been her practice? Honoring Sarah's request to, in essence, *leave her alone*, Annette had not bothered her once since their last conversation. However, she had continued to make her presence known almost daily, sitting cross-legged in the front yard or investigating the area surrounding the house on the way to the bus stop in the morning. Twice, as Sarah half suspected would be the case today, she had stayed for a very long time with her legs dangling over the edge of the gray railing, seemingly content to be on watch for something. At first, the sightings of her had been accidental. Sarah would be on her way out of the door to deposit the garbage or retrieve the mail, but fortunately, before she actually opened the door, her hand on the handle, she would spot brown-haired Annette through the sidelight, sauntering towards the house across the lawn or at rest upon the railing or bottom step. The garbage or mail could wait.

This was a deeply puzzling situation. There seemed to be no explanation as to the sudden entrance of this teenager into Sarah's life or for the unusual interest in her welfare. Sarah pledged to herself that she would have privacy, at any cost. The thought of spending time with anyone was distasteful. Annette would need to *go her own way*. Robert and Raymond must be avoided. Sarah, just for a moment, closed her eyes at the pleasant thought of isolation.

Gratefully, Annette was nowhere to be seen as the car pulled closer to the garage. With abruptness, Sarah gathered her purse and hurried from the car to the house, her eyes deliberately avoiding even a simple glance at the garage. Soon she must move somewhere else. It would not do to stay here. *"Why have I stayed this long?"* she wondered.

In a moment, she found safety behind the front door, her heart sighing in incredible relief at the sound of the heavy oak against the jamb. "Oh, that I could be alone forever! I will see to it," she promised herself. "It's my life. I will make the rules."

The tired thin woman walked to her bedroom, her bare feet moving almost noiselessly on the Brazilian cherry hardwood in the hallway. There, surrounded by exquisite paintings of thick forests and sailboats on seas of green, she prepared herself for an afternoon alone.

Until the cool early evening, the fragile solitude remained unbroken. With her peanut butter sandwich and a half glass of milk, she settled into her place on the couch, her book propped against a pillow. Now and then, a thought of Chip arose and she suppressed it with near desperation. Willfully, she became increasingly more absorbed in the words of the genius William Shakespeare, hiding herself in his archaic vocabulary. There she found herself obscured in the shadows of the castle, watching the wild pacing of young Hamlet and shuddering with each passionate word from his lips.

At the sound of a vehicle in the driveway, Sarah jumped to her feet and ran to where she could look out between the draperies. At the sight of Raymond Payce's car, her face stiffened. She closed her eyes and braced herself for the unpleasant. The knock at the door came, each clap of the brass knocker jolting her nerves. Resolutely, she gripped the door handle and pulled the door open.

"Sarah, Sarah, it's me, Robert. You thought it was Raymond, right? I borrowed his nice little car. Sarah, everyone is now at the house and I've come to retrieve you."

Here, once again, was Robert Payce, plunked unbidden into her life—handsome, controlling and conniving Robert. Looking GQ in his outrageously expensive suit and shoes, he moved past her and on into the family room where the remains of her tranquility lay evident. Sarah followed. He politely made himself at home, asking if she minded if he sat down for a while, uninterested as to what her answer might be. Sarah sat down across from him and folded her hands in her lap. *"Robert. Raymond. Richard,"* she mused, *"I wonder which one I loathe the most."* She could tolerate Raymond, Mr. Payce's other son, but only because he was evil out of stupidity. Her attention returned to Robert.

"I had to take Father home. Did you notice that he became ill?"

"No, I didn't."

"The doctor says his dizziness is a result of grief. But, he's a tough old bird. He'll be at it again soon. In fact, he felt able enough to go to the church for the luncheon."

Sarah bit her lip. Mr. Payce was not grieving. He had put Mildred to rest years before and filled his time with the women of Payce Publishing. She chose to remain silent.

"Well, just talking briefly with you at the graveside did my heart good. As pretty...as always! We're all missing you, Sarah...Dad, Gayle, Lois...the whole gang!" His next words were spoken with dramatic inflection, characteristic of Robert. "You are the sunshine that we find nowhere else in this world. You're robbing us of that sunshine, do you know that?"

"Oh, please, Robert," she responded, annoyed at his artificial flattery.

"It's been hard for you, I know. Losing Chip and...losing him the way you did, well, you know what I mean. That was a staggering blow. I can understand a withdrawal from the world. I really can."

"You really can't," Sarah silently retorted, *"but just go on."*

"My goodness! You two were so, well, so much in love. I've never seen anything like it in my life," he said with a laugh. "Yes, I can certainly see how it could affect you the way it has. Tell me, Sarah, are you doing all right? I mean, no one ever sees you or hears from you and we all wonder if things are okay. Money? Health? Mental health?" He smiled, finding himself clever.

Sarah had looked at him as he spoke, attempting courtesy for some reason, but when it became obvious that he expected an answer for such ignorant questions, her eyes moved away and rested upon the gold-framed photo of her as an eight year old. She wished she was still that little girl, hair in unkempt pigtails and a front tooth missing. She remembered smiling at her father as he fiddled with the camera, making jokes at his clumsiness. She could remember, too, his arms about her, big strong arms, enclosing her with safety from harm and evil.

"Life never turns out the way anyone thinks it will," her faint words came, not intended to be spoken.

"Perhaps you're right."

"I'm doing well, Robert, and you are kind to ask. The Payce/Finfield thing, you are quite aware, has not been a pleasant one."

"Sarah, I know that you have only tolerated us but that should be in the past now. I feel responsible for you in some way."

It had been a long time since Sarah had laughed, but Robert's last remark nearly produced a snicker. No Payce would ever be responsible for her. She had only tolerated all of them—Richard, Raymond and Robert—mostly for Mildred's sake. Family gatherings had been abhorrent to her, yet she had graciously attended each one; it was expected. The Payces had become *family* at the marriage of Mildred Finfield and Richard Payce. Chip had been given a prominent place in Payce Publishing at the same time, earning money beyond his wildest dreams. Stress and conflict had escalated during those years of employment, yet Chip had stayed on, handling each problematic conflict with wisdom and determination. At his death, however, Sarah wasted no time cutting all ties...familial and financial. Absolutely no doubt lingered in anyone's mind that she did not consider herself a Payce relation. With a twinge of remorse, she remembered that her decision had necessitated some shunning of Mildred who dauntlessly maintained an allegiance to her crumbled marriage.

"I know you have no need of money...the insurance policy and...well, Father, he surely took care of Chip." The voice inflection gave away Robert's difficulty with that subject. "And no doubt Kerrigan took fine care of you."

Sarah stood and walked to the roll-top desk in the corner, turned and leaned against it, unhappy that Robert did not appear to be leaving any time soon. She scanned the face of this man who had unexplainably found it easy to make himself comfortable in a home he had rarely frequented before. Robert was undeniably handsome, a man of forty five, bearing a likeness, in her opinion—though Chip adamantly disagreed—to Cary Grant. His face was broad and strong, his complexion dark, his hair almost black. Many had been the time when Sarah had observed him returning from hunting with Chip in the Payce woods in Minnesota and noticed how good looking the two were, hair askew, faces red with cold, pheasants or rabbits held high with pride; but Sarah's lack of love and respect for Robert was something that would never change.

"Listen," she finally spoke with her chin lifted, "I am a strong woman. I don't need anyone. I need no sympathy or help. As you've said, I am financially stable and more. I'm doing well. You must all accept the fact that you and I no longer have any ties."

"Oh, Sarah, you don't mean that! You must not shut us out altogether."

"I don't look at it as shutting you out. I look upon it as a new story. This story," she said quietly, pointing to herself and shaking her head, "has no Payces in it. Please let it rest, Robert. I don't want to get into it with you. Perhaps there is a tad of sincere concern for me in your heart, but please, go and pass along the news that...that it's a new story—and remember, there are no characters with the last name of Payce within the pages. That's the way it has to be. That's the way it's going to be. No malice. Just my decision."

Now it was Robert's turn to stare off into the room, fixing his eyes upon the many signed and dated Norman Rockwell paintings upon the dark paneled wall. As he viewed each one, his face showed the gathering of thoughts and a determination to triumph.

"Sarah, Sarah," he began very slowly and quietly, but with marked emphasis. "You are proud. My, you are proud! Your pride makes me disdain you and admire you at the same time. Your pride makes me want to strike you and at the same time, be responsible to care for you. Your pride makes me want to walk out the door and do as you ask and at the same time, to stay close...in case you need me." Anger moved into Sarah's quiet eyes. "No," Robert blurted, "you will let me finish. What do I have to lose? You are appealing and attractive." He arose and began to walk back and forth.

"You say you need no one. Of course you don't and you know what? I believe you." He stopped near to her and stared into her eyes. "You're an unbelievable woman, Sarah Finfield, yet I feel myself hurting in here that you find me so despicable that you will not allow for friendship, just enough so that someday when you need something that Sarah Finfield cannot take care of, you'll think to yourself, 'Who can I call?' and you'll think of me."

A healthy caution arose in her mind, but Sarah was without emotion, not budging at the closeness of his face to hers. It was not unthinkable that Robert, in his present state, might get out of hand. She watched his changing thoughts as they one by one registered upon his face.

"I'll go," he said, placing his forefinger beneath her chin, "but, Sarah, let me tell you something. Sometimes it's wiser to bend in the wind than to break." With eyes slightly squinted, he looked deep into her face, a face filled with puzzlement at this somewhat threatening proverb. What would make Robert go from being an acquaintance to being a foe? She did not know.

As Sarah returned his intense stare, she became acutely aware that she was not up for a fight. Not today. Maybe never. A life of battle for any cause interested her not at all. She fixed her eyes upon the red bound book resting upside down upon the chest, Robert's finger still under her chin. If only he would go.

"Robert, if you don't mind...."

He set his front teeth together and tightened his lips. His strong protruding jaw was captivating. A tiny smile crept around his lips and eyes. Robert Payce had something on his mind. There was battle in his eyes.

"I came to be friends. I came to take you back to join the family, but I can see that was foolish!" Softly, he brushed her cheek with his knuckles. "But, since I am here, I may as well reiterate that there are business related issues to be unraveled."

"Then that is why you came, Robert," Sarah sneered.

He moved slightly closer.

"I came as a friend. There are, however, things of great magnitude to discuss."

It was time to move. She slipped away from him, putting the couch between them.

"*The Street of Petetra*," she said with weariness. "The old man's book. This has nothing to do with me."

"It has to do with Chip," he replied, removing his tie, folding it and placing it in his jacket pocket.

"In what way?"

"Lichten was his account."

"And?"

"Things are missing, Sarah, things that Chip might have had with him when he left Lichten's the last time, invaluable things that belong to us."

"You mean the night of the mystery fire, right?" Sarah asked curtly.

"Yes. Yes. Then your husband up and died leaving some extremely significant loose ends."

"I know of nothing. What are you looking for?"

"That does not concern you."

"Well, yes, yes, it does, if you're standing here intimating that I know something about all of this."

"I am not at liberty to tell you what we are looking for, but we must find it."

"So, what do you think? That I have this *whatever* you are looking for?"

"You could."

"I'm sure I don't."

"Come on, Sarah! Have you really gone through his things?"

She had not. The boxes lined many shelves in the storage room at the bottom of the basement stairs. Even now, the thought of handling the contents of the numerous containers clutched her heart like a vise.

"Chip was not in the habit of bringing work home," she replied dryly, "as you well know."

"I know, but in this particular case, he very well could have brought this stuff home the night of the fire. Let me look through the boxes and this will be the end of it."

"I'd rather not today."

"This should make you happy," he reasoned forcefully. "You'd be done with us awful Payces once and for all. I know exactly what I'm looking for. In ten minutes, I'll be out of here."

"If that's true, then, it's right where you left it a year ago—Chip's office belongings, as well. I haven't done anything with them. And his briefcase is in the foyer closet. You're welcome to look."

Robert touched her nose and was on his way. He'd been at this house a few times before and he headed for the stairs.

"What I am looking for wouldn't fit in his briefcase...yet, who knows? I might find a clue in it. You may have to come to the office and search Chip's files," he yelled as he descended.

When the basement search had ended—unsuccessfully—Robert returned to the entry, with excessive grumbling, and went immediately to the front closet. The briefcase would be his next target.

"You'll do some probing for us, Sarah, will you not?"

Her face evidencing intolerance, Sarah answered quietly, but firmly, "What? Do you mean at the office?"

"Yes."

"No, certainly not. Surely Andrew can dig you out. I'm not going to help you. You're a big company with a wealth of support at your disposal. I'm telling you right now that I want no part of coming to the office for any amount of time. I would think you could understand that."

His mind was upon the contents of the case. Frustrated, he peeled back the papers one by one, scanning them, shaking his head.

"There's nothing here. I don't get it." Abruptly he closed the briefcase and returned it to the shelf. Then, as Sarah was fully expecting, he approached her. He held her by the upper arms with his large hands. "Well, I would think you could understand how important this is. You know how Chip worked. You worked here with him. He's got stuff hidden. Somewhere. What we're looking for is not small. It is sizable. You must help us, Sarah." He hesitated and sucked in an exaggerated breath. "Let's not do the legal thing, Sarah," he said with a melodramatic shake of his head.

Sarah smiled. "You've got to be kidding," she said quietly in disbelief. "What? Are you going to take me to court because I won't help you with your computer system and with work that my husband did for you as your employee a year ago? And why now, Robert, after one whole year? It makes no sense. I don't have what you want and I don't know where to get it!"

"I don't get you, Sarah. I'm asking for a half an hour, an hour, and you resist? Why? We've been good to you! Why are you so adamant? Have we been so horrible that you won't do this much for us? Just come and try," he cajoled with accompanying hand gestures. "Do some investigating."

Sarah shook her head leaving no doubts as to her answer. He grasped her arms once again.

The history of Payce Publishing vs. Chip tore through her mind like a video tape on fast forward. Perhaps at this moment it was more the Payce-versus-Sarah story that was playing. The Payces had abused Chip. And without cause. They had mistrusted him. Also without cause. She had struggled with bitterness towards the three Payces for how they had taken advantage of him. Her anger had sometimes been directed at Chip himself. She had always wished with all her heart that he would make a move, find another place where he would be appreciated for his work ethic and where his talents would be tapped; she had been giddy with joy when he had completed all the necessary steps to start his own publishing firm—all the way down to the beige business cards with teal and coffee brown printing. Now, though it had been death that had accomplished it, Sarah was ecstatic to have Payce Publishing out of her life. No amount of pleading or logical talk would convince her to enter the publisher's doors. She felt the grip tighten upon her arms and gave Robert a warning with her eyes. He relaxed his hold but did not let go. With his jaw set, he fought with himself what his course of action should be.

"Sarah," he whispered close to her ear, "it's better to bend... than to break."

"How professional! A threat. You are a thug in fine clothing," Sarah said, her steady voice surprising her. With her eyes looking back into his fiery, handsome eyes, she went on. "I'm not sure what your masked threat is all about, but I want you to go. You are not welcome here, nor are your father or your brother. Tell me you get that. For a few moments I entertained the possibility that perhaps I've been a bit hard on you; but, with your talk of bending and breaking, and with your rude grip on my arms, I see only the same abrasiveness that the Finfields have endured from the Payces for years." With one quick twist, she freed herself from his hold on her. "No, Robert, you'll have to make it on your own. You made it through the Cassidine affair with flying colors. You're big boys. Surely your success in this matter does not hinge upon the aid of a grieving widow."

"Well, well, Sarah," he said with slight chuckle, "I can't wait to get back to the house so that I can tell one and all that Sarah Finfield truly is not dead at all. She's up for the fight." He laid his hand on her shoulder, a touch from which she instantly withdrew. She hurried away and with a firm pull, opened the massive front door.

"It's time for you to go, Robert Payce."

"Then, you will not cooperate?"

"There is no reason to."

"You're right, we're big boys. And we've got big lawyers, too."

"Are you threatening me?" asked Sarah in unbelief. "You must be kidding. I think that you'll find a way without that."

Robert took a deep breath and smiled, looking down into her tired face.

"You invigorate me. Isn't that the weirdest thing? Just know this: We'll find what we're looking for, no matter what it takes. I just hope you don't get hurt in the process...and yes, I'm threatening you."

The instant the door slammed shut, Sarah stumbled to her bed and collapsed upon it, facedown. Anger stung her heart because after the serene months of near solitude, a rush of interferences was intruding, unbidden. The mantle clock struck eight. The cuckoo concurred a few moments later. Outside, the rapidly darkening night brought on a discomfiting wind. The conversations with Robert began to replay. With heavy eyes, she pondered his words and expressions as they came to mind. Then came visions of Mildred's peaceful countenance, looking asleep in the casket, at rest for the first time in years. She thought on the funeral and the graveside service. The vision of the fourth headstone—void of an inscription—brought, oddly, a measure of serenity.

With the tick-tock of the cuckoo clock lulling away the burrs of the day, Sarah remembered her overturned book and her unfinished glass of milk, the symbols of her quiet life, no doubt warm and unpleasant by now. Was this the way it was to be? Annette and Tony, Robert and Raymond, mysterious men stalking her house in the night? With a long and deep sigh, Sarah spoke repair to her soul. In a few days, life would return to normal again. She visualized a "**FOR SALE**" sign in the front yard. She must move. It would not do to stay here. Another sigh and she arose, tidied the family room, and then prepared for bed. Yes, life would become tranquil once again. Most certainly it would. Wrapped in the beautiful sheets and comforter, Sarah breathed relief that the Payces had at last become a part of a past for which she had longed for many a year.

"Goodbye, Robert. Goodbye, Raymond. Goodbye, Richard. This day brings some good after all." Sarah clicked off the light. "I hope." A siren's wail sounded from the state road. She shivered. "I wonder."

A faint, curious intuition disquieted her.

CHAPTER 4

Life indeed did become tranquil once again. As Sarah had hoped, the days went by with no sign of the undesirable Payces; and that which she dreaded the most—more persistent invasion on Annette's part—did not occur either. May went its way without incident. June entered; Sarah began to feel at ease once again.

Her style of life altered not at all from day to day. Never did she visit the outside, the beautiful wooded property that surrounded her home, except, that is, for the morning when the toaster acted up and produced a houseful of smoke. That day, as she threw open the kitchen door, she got her first lingering glimpse of the back yard for over a year. Spring had burst forth without her. Her eyes slowly scanning the beauty, she viewed the near-summer scene without emotion. Then, with absence of sentimentality, she pulled shut the door and took her morning fare to her spot upon the couch.

All of life returned to solitude and tranquility. The same young man who had mowed the lawn last year started in once again and Sarah, once again, made arrangements to pay him by mail. All other bills continued to go to the accountant—Chip's accountant, a woman Sarah had never met in person. Her phone went unanswered. She never left the house, that is, except on Saturdays. On Saturday evenings, in the late dusk hours, she routinely journeyed to Shelton for groceries and then hurried home, anxious to hide away in front of the fireplace in the great family room. Having completed the reading of Hamlet, she then searched the towering book shelves for another book in which to submerge. It made no difference one way or the other. She pulled down the first of two wide volumes dedicated to the writings of the Civil War. It was as good as anything else.

On a day in mid-June, when white and fluffy clouds lined the horizon every way the eye could see and robins hopped about on the soft green grass, Sarah Finfield, book in hand, her finger marking the page where now she was reading, set out to retrieve the mail from the box by the road. As her foot reached the first step, her eye caught the movement of a running figure, coming from down the road, but too close for Sarah to duck back in. Annette flew down the gravel like a deer, a smile across her face. Her destination was clear. She was headed diagonally across the sweeping front yard to the porch.

"Mrs. Finfield! You will never know how good it is to see you!" The spirited teen waited to catch her breath. "I have wondered and wondered about you, but I wanted to honor your request. I have not bothered you for weeks now and I know that's exactly what you wanted, and I can really hardly blame you at all after all that you have been through. Most people, I think, want to be alone and take some time off from the world. My father told me that I shouldn't bother you because you need time to grieve. And you know what else he said?—he's so smart—he said that one of the problems with the world today is that people don't grieve when their loved ones die. Used to be, widows wore black for a week or a month or a year. Now everyone goes to the funeral in bright colors, the family jokes and laughs at the wake, and they have a big fun party after the grave thing happens. Don't you think? It sounds right to me."

Sarah folded her arms, peering into Annette's expressive face and searching for clues. The teen talked on.

"Well, anyway, I'm doing so good. School is great. Cheerleading is great. Tony is great. I'm graduating in one week. I wish you'd come. My mother won't come. She says she doesn't fit in with all those people. Dad says she's got a poor self-image. I don't know, but I know she'll not be there. Oh, well, Tony's mother and dad will be there and they like me a lot. Dad will come but he'll be griping about everything. Oh, well. Well, how are you? Are you doing better?"

Sarah stood absolutely still, marveling at the speed with which this girl attacked words. She took a deep breath and responded with some kindness.

"I am fine, Annette."

"Do you see those incredible clouds? Look over there. Here, you have to come out a little more. Look over the horizon at that line of them. Are they incredible or what! I just can't believe this day! It's warm and sunny and the sky is full of mashed potatoes!"

Sarah took a few steps to behold the majestic sight, and then went to the mailbox at the road. Annette was right. They were unusual clouds. *Thunderboomers* had been Chip's name for them.

"If I didn't know better," Annette said very pensively, as Sarah returned to the porch, "I'd almost believe there's a God! Oh, Mrs. Finfield. I wish sometimes that you would let me come in and talk to you. Most of the time I think it's because I hate to think of you so alone all of the time, but now and then," Annette said, her voice trailing a bit, "it's because I need someone to talk to and when that happens, for some reason, I think of you. Isn't that strange?"

Annette had done it. She had gone beyond the easy-to-answer conversation and had made it uncomfortable to be casual. How inappropriate now to say, "Well, Annette, thanks for stopping by... I really need to go." Why would such a bubbly child need to find someone to talk to? Did she not have friends galore, teachers who liked her, aunts and uncles who adored her? What about grandparents? And what about her *very smart* dad? Who could tell, but here she stood saying that when she wanted to talk to someone, she was drawn to Sarah. How could she respond to that?

She waited for loquacious Annette to take up her speed talking again, but she did not. Instead, with a wrinkled forehead, she looked up from the bottom of the stairs into the face of the taken-off-guard widow and said nothing. As Sarah leafed through her mail, she felt her cheeks grow warm under the youthful gaze of the girl. The grocery flyer was there. The regular letter from the church was there, undoubtedly accompanied by last week's bulletin.

Annette was now staring off at the cumulus gatherings in the west but then turned toward Sarah who was fully absorbed in her mail. A blue air mail letter had seized her attention. It was from Mexico. Her heart stopped at the name in the corner. A letter from Scott Dolan? Why would she be receiving a letter from Scott? News of Chip's death must have finally reached him.

She looked up for a moment, abruptly brought back to the present by the retreating form of her teenaged *friend*. Annette, showing a measure of disappointment upon her face, turned to wave a fond farewell to Sarah.

"I'll probably see you again somewhere along the way," she called out. "I hope things are well for you. Next time you see me, I'll be a graduate. See you!" With that she began her jog once again. As Sarah waved halfheartedly, Annette disappeared behind the Russian olive hedge.

She was perfectly relieved that she was gone. Fingering the air mail letter in her hands, she considered the mystery of its arrival. She perused the thick black writing upon the air form. It left no doubt as to the identity of the writer. A gust of wind announcing a change in the weather brought with it recollections of an era long gone. A fleeting thought of Annette came and went. Sarah retreated inside.

It was not out of the ordinary for mail that reached the home of Sarah Finfield to remain unopened. In the days immediately following Chip's death, all letters and cards were stashed in the cabinet below the kitchen telephone. There they remained till this day. Sarah refused sympathy. She pushed away any leanings toward emotion, shutting out her friends because they threatened to keep alive the memory of the death of her husband. Notes, full of pity, frightened her. So, there most of the mail still remained—out of sight, out of mind.

This letter today, though, spawned curiosity. The last occurrence of Scott in the Sarah saga was nine years before when he called the night before leaving for the missionfield. Since then, he had crossed her mind once in a while, but except for grapevine news that he had married Chloe Kelleher, Scott had exited her life.

Walking to the atrium doors in the dining room which overlooked the back yard, and opening the wood blinds, Sarah stared out upon the unkempt yard. With the letter in her hands, she allowed her mind to wander back to her college days. The joy of those years would forever remain imprinted upon her heart. Mental photographs came of the Sweet Shop, the bookstore and the women's lounge. It was easy to place people in those photos. Scott was in many of them. A snapshot of The Balcony came into view. She could see herself in a blue and white sailor dress. She could see Scott standing in jeans and tee shirt, his tall, lanky body browned by the sun. It was a warm, sunny day. They were close, looking out over the valley and the river, a brisk wind blowing their hair behind them. There was a kiss and a question, a promise and a ring. Scott's gaze as he spoke could never be erased. For a moment, Sarah closed her eyes and yielded to the rush of memories. Then, with deliberation, she closed the blinds, turned away and made her way to the kitchen. Emotion waned. She placed the letter in the plastic bucket in the kitchen closet with the rest—unopened. A letter from Scott was off limits.

July was ushered in with warm days and warm nights. It had always been a favorite month for Sarah. Hot weather inspired her, and Chip had felt the same. Together they had worked feverishly in the yards, combining wooden beams and wildflowers, brick paths and rock gardens. Two summers ago, they had labored night after night, designing and creating a lighted fountain and waterfall for the back. Then, as a reward, they often took whole Saturdays to bike into the northern hills or to drive to a beautiful nearby preserve to swim and hike. They loved the sounds and smells of the summer months. Hardly ever was the air conditioning turned on. At night, an exhaust fan in the laundry room pulled the sweet summer air through the bedroom sliders and across their bed.

But it was as though last summer had never happened and the outlook was the same for this year. Sarah would be shut up once again inside. So, instead of an evening silhouette of Sarah Finfield crouching to feed a squirrel from her hand, time was painting pictures of a shadowed figure, curled up upon a forest green and navy Tartan plaid couch, reading the moments away. Gone was the brilliant and exciting businesswoman who daily brightened the world with a mad dash to the car, juggling coffee cup and briefcase. Sarah's soft and enchanting green eyes, now obscured within a countenance of apathy, never had occasion to bless, to inspire. Contentment, curious and unexplained, sustained her listless way of life and each night, without emotion, she dropped into an immediate slumber as her head touched the pillow.

On a summer night well into July, however, she awoke from a sound sleep. At first, she lay still, wondering what it was that had disturbed her. Turning her head, she squinted at the clock. It was three thirty.

"This is odd," she said to herself, rolling over and curling up beneath the sheet. For ten minutes, she alternated between eyes closed, trying to slumber once again, and eyes opened, looking at the clock. Speaking aloud, she commented again on the oddness of her inability to sleep. She listened but heard no sounds. Pulling the bedroom curtains slightly apart, she peered out into the darkness, seeing nothing but the black of night. At three forty five, she walked the length of the house from her bedroom to the kitchen, poured a glass of milk, drank it and returned to her bed.

"Well," she whispered with agitation, "let's try this once more." Sleep came.

As the mantle clock announced ten o'clock in the morning, an insistent pounding of a fist upon the door sounded through the house. Sarah awoke with a jolt. No one would knock so ferociously except the neighbor girl. Growling at the clock for telling such a tale of lateness, she pulled her robe about her and headed down the hallway. With a firm pull she opened the door. Annette had begun to chatter before the actual sight of Sarah met her eyes.

"Have you seen your garage door! Not the overhead one, the one on the side of the garage! Come, I'll show you."

Sarah wanted to say, "Wait, Annette, tell me right here," but the young girl was flying down the stairs and across the front yard. It was unlike Sarah to be seen outside in her robe, yet heaven and earth could not make her go through the garage. Hesitating a moment, she followed after Annette, unnerved.

The disconcerting sight at once explained Sarah's middle-of-the-night awakening. Upon the cement garage floor laid the splintered pieces of a brutally bashed door. One sole-of-the-foot kick had done the job. Her arms folded, Sarah's narrowed eyes cast troubled glances here and there.

"You'd better look inside," Annette suggested.

"You look, Annette," Sarah responded, turning away from the house. "Would you look?"

"It looks okay to me," shouted the girl from within the garage, "but how would I know? You should come in and look around. If they stole something, I'd never know!"

There was nothing to steal from the garage. Chip, the two days before his death, had worked at dry-walling the entire three-car garage, leaving the walls—and the whole garage—nicely finished but quite bare of everything except the garden tools hanging in their organized row. Apart from his car, he had moved the remaining few items to the new brick shed that he had recently built—all but the paint cans which, in order to keep them from freezing, were in the two overhead cabinets near the kitchen door.

"No, Annette. I'll look later."

Sarah stared at the cement pad beneath her feet, her eyes darkened with apparent anger, realizing that the wise thing to do at that moment would be to look inside; but she could not.

"What do you think, Mrs. Finfield? Did they just want in the garage or did they get stopped in their tracks before they went as far as they wanted to?"

"I don't know, Annette."

"Did you hear anything last night? By the way, why didn't the alarm go off? Or did it?"

"You ask too many questions!"

"I'm sorry. But, really, it should have gone off, right?"

"Please, Annette, not now." Information about the security system was not Annette's business.

"Well, okay, but that does puzzle me."

Why was this neighbor girl so interested in this? In her heart, Sarah did not really suspect her, but what was the answer to that question? As several times before, she suspiciously searched Annette's face for even a veiled sign of evil.

"Annette, I know you want to help, although I'm not sure why. Listen, I do thank you for telling me about this, but I think you can go now. I can take it from here."

"I'll go, but did you hear something last night."

"I did hear something," Sarah said very quietly.

"You actually heard it?"

"Something woke me up. I assume it was this."

"What did you do?"

"I got up."

"Did you turn on the light?"

"Yes, in the kitchen. That must have scared them off."

"I wonder" mused Annette, "why we both keep saying *them.*"

"Did I?"

"Yes. I did, too! Scary, I'd say. Probably because Tony and I saw those three guys that night."

"Listen," pled Sarah, grasping Annette's arm, "you must promise not to talk to anyone about this...not your parents, not Tony, not anyone." A puzzled brow was Annette's reply. "I just know that it complicates matters when a lot of people are in on something like this. I don't know what is happening, but since they didn't get into the inside door, I'm sure it's okay. It's thieves. They'll leave me alone now."

"Do you mean to tell me that you are not going to do anything about this!"

"I'll get the door fixed," Sarah replied, attempting to sound calm.

"You should call the police, shouldn't you? Right now!"

"No, not this time."

Annette's eyes widened as she uttered a firm disagreement.

"You have to call them! This is the second offense!"

"What can they do? Listen, I'm just going to get the door fixed."

With an exasperated sigh, Annette wisely said, "Whoever fixes it will need an explanation. And what will you tell them?"

"I'll clean up the mess and call a professional to put in a new door. He will not expect an explanation."

It was time for her young neighbor to go, in Sarah's mind; Annette, however, had more to say.

"Tony could do it for you. He's a budding carpenter."

"Annette! Look at me and listen to me. I just told you I don't want anyone else to know about this."

"He'll know as much as a carpenter you get from somewhere else and he won't charge you."

"Annette!"

"Well, okay. Are you going to be all right? Gosh, I feel so bad being the one to discover this stuff all the time."

"Annette, I really do need to take care of some things," Sarah said in a nearly pleading tone. "I'm sorry. I need to go inside."

"I know. I ask too many questions." She turned to go. Her youthful expression said, "Oh, well."

"Thank you for letting me know." Sarah was about to say, "Maybe I'll see you tomorrow," but checked herself in time. Annette would no doubt show up without an invitation anyway.

For a moment, she lingered at the front door after thanking Annette for her help. With a slow sweeping glance, she surveyed her surroundings. Were there any clues? Were there any cars parked down the long road or across the field? Was anyone watching all of this from some secluded spot?

With a far off expression, she let the muggy summer air ruffle her hair. The smell of cut grass filled her nostrils. She was not all right. This second attempt to gain entrance to her home, whether the target had been the garage or the house itself, was begetting fear. Without doubt, the prowlers would...there it was again—the plural!

She quickly closed the door. Her anger evidenced itself in her footsteps as she made her way to find the Yellow Pages in the office. One prowler or two...or even three—what did that matter? Was it not extremely nervy to try to break in with the her at home? Was this happening because the news was out that "the lady in the gray ranch lives there all alone?" Or was there something else going on?

Anger initiated a plan of action and by noon, a carpenter had promised to come to replace the door. A thought of leaving a light on at night came and went; she would not bow to these scoundrels. As the clock tolled midnight, however, there lay a sleepless woman upon her Queen Anne bed. Only in the wee hours did fitful short-lived sleep come, but when dawn arrived, casting its ever-increasing shaft of light through the crack in the drapes, Sarah was awake to witness the event.

The day following was Saturday and as could be expected, she spent no little amount of time thinking about her weekly trip to Shelton. Torn between her intense determination not to allow any thug to be the cause of even the slightest alteration in her life and an idea that leaving the house alone and dark was inviting trouble, she wandered about, wondering what to do. Gray shadows darkened her face beneath the eyes. Tired in every way, she went about the daily chores. The carpenter had promised to deal with the door by the time the day was through. Her ear was tuned to the cuckoo clock and footsteps. At six, she heard them both. The brass door knocker sounded.

"I take it you are the carpenter," she said.

"Yes. I am Adam Cook."

Adam Cook's blond hair stuck out from beneath his Home Depot cap. Behind his ear was a carpenter's pencil and in his hand was a stack of blank estimate sheets on a metal clipboard. The red letters on his gray tee shirt read, "Adam Cook Carpentry." He was wearing blue jeans and heavy work boots.

"I appreciate you coming on short notice," Sarah said, looking up into the face of this obviously strong and able carpenter.

"Well, it actually worked out well. I was going to be installing a hot water heater a couple of miles from here and something came up for them. Not sure what. You called two minutes after they called."

Sarah stepped outside, closing the door behind her, and led the way to the side of the garage.

"Well, here it is. The door—what's left of it—is inside propped against the wall."

"What happened here?" Adam asked. "Looks like a tractor barged through here the way this jamb looks."

She had expected an uncomfortable first few minutes and now that it was here she did not know what to say. She waited. Adam went on.

"Let's take a look at the door. That will help me chart a course."

He stepped inside, turned on the light, examined the door, and once again joined Sarah outside.

"Well, it wasn't a tractor that did it. That I know. Are you aware that it was a foot...that did this to your door?"

Sarah stared at the ground, searching her vocabulary for words. Whether she said *yes* or said *no* the result would be the same. The conversation could only go one direction.

"Yes," she said, raising her eyes to look at Adam.

Adam's expression was interesting. It encompassed curiosity, unbelief, concern and respect for his customer's privacy. He stretched out his arm and leaned against the gray cedar siding and sort of squinted at Sarah.

"Was this a break-in? Or perhaps...a drunk somebody? I guess it's none of my business apart from the fact that I'd like to get you safe again."

Desiring so much to appear cool and collected, Sarah replied calmly, "Someone broke in."

"Did he get into the house?" Adam wanted to know.

"No, I believe he must have been scared off."

"What would have scared him off, Mrs. Finfield? Were you home when this happened?"

"Yes. It was the middle of the night."

"How do you know?"

"Something woke me up though my bedroom is far enough away that I really didn't know what. I got up...it was about three...and went to the kitchen." This was a whole lot more conversation than Sarah wished for. She must end it. "All I know is that they must have been scared off when I turned on the kitchen light."

"They?"

"They. He. I don't know. Anyway, the whole thing is behind me now. I just want the door fixed."

"See if I have this right. You're telling me that you were home when this happened," Adam said, reaffirming what he was sure he had heard.

Sarah was feeling trapped. How much should she say? How much did she have to say? After all, this was the carpenter, not a police officer.

"I...We...," she stuttered, "Yes, we were home."

"What did the police have to say?"

"Uh, I...We...didn't call them." Standing up tall and straight, Sarah rallied her strength and said, "Why call them? Why call them? It was over and done with. And now I just want my door fixed. When can you do this?"

"I can do it right away. I notice, ma'am, that you have an excellent security system according to this. Did the alarm not go off?"

"The garage is not hooked in. My husband finished installing the system in the house, but things came up that kept him from finishing the garage."

"He's doing it himself?"

"He was."

"Well, I'm thinking it odd that someone would do this with the ADT placard plainly displayed. It's almost like he—or they—knew that this door is unprotected."

"Well, I don't know. Maybe they took a chance knowing that it would take the police a good while to get here. I don't know. What I do know is that I just want this done and over with. Can you take care of this for me very soon, all of it?" Sarah asked.

"Yep, I can. "

Adam ceased his questioning. He was just the carpenter.

"I should secure the door temporarily while I order a new one— if you want one just like this. Do you need to use this side door?"

"No. No I don't. Not at all. And yes, I'd like the new one to be just like this one since it matches the other service door."

"Okay. I'll nail this all up for now and put the door in place but you won't be able to open it. Is that okay?"

Adam went inside and retrieved the door.

"Nice car," he said, stepping outside.

He did not see Sarah shudder.

❧ ❧ ❧ ❧ ❧

A week passed and Adam returned with a new door. It was Friday, July 15th. He pulled his silver truck up close to the side of the garage but went first to let Sarah know that he was there. It was late afternoon. She came to the door.

"Mrs. Finfield, I've got the door and I'll just get to putting it in, if that's okay with you."

"I'll walk out with you," Sarah said.

Adam took the new door from the back of his truck and leaned it against the side of the garage.

"Here it is. It's just like the other one."

"Now that I am looking at it, I'm wondering if we need a stronger door. If the last one got kicked in, apparently somewhat easily, what's to keep it from happening again?"

"It's true what you say. We could make both service doors more secure. That would help, but you know, if a culprit wants in, he'll get in one way or another. My big concern is that this was done while you and your husband were at home. I don't get it."

"Well, Mr. Cook, let's just go ahead and put this door in. Okay?"

"Yep. It should all be done in an hour or so."

"I appreciate it. I just want it done as soon as possible." Sarah turned to leave. Adam detained her with another question.

"Is your husband home right now? I have a couple of suggestions to run by you."

Sarah paced back and forth in her head. Why was this becoming so complicated? *Just fix the door, Mr. Cook,* she muttered to herself, aggravation rising.

"Can you just do the door? I'll hope for the best, okay? Is that okay?"

"Yep, it is. I'll have it done in an hour or so and come knock when I'm done."

Heart weary, Sarah started back across the yard, her head down, her footsteps hasty. Adam wondered why she did not just go through the garage into the house, but along with his growing number of other questions, he laid it aside and prepared to work.

When the door was in place, he climbed into his truck. Making a big circle, he pulled into the driveway and stopped where he could admire the fine points of the Finfield home. Resting his elbow on the steering wheel and biting his thumbnail, he studied each aspect of the beautiful house. He liked the red trim and he liked charcoal siding and the gray brick. The metal casement windows and the shake shingles were the finishing touch. If ever he could afford to build a new house—and actually draw it up—it would look very much like this one, even down to the striking landscaping and brick walkways.

"Nice car. Nice house," he said, gathering up the paperwork, and as he quietly climbed down from the truck, he added, "but something is fishy. It looks all shut up like a tomb. Never you mind, Adam."

He walked up the winding brick path toward the house.

"Hello, Adam Cook!" he heard someone call from behind him. Turning to see who it was, he found himself looking upon a teenaged girl bouncing across the lawn. Sarah saw her, too, through the crack in the draperies. She looked up at the ceiling and cringed. She must move quickly.

"Do I know you?" Adam asked.

"Silly, your name is on your truck!" Annette chuckled. "So you're the carpenter!"

"And I'm guessing you're the daughter."

The front door opened. Sarah took charge.

"Annette is a neighbor who stops by now and then." She dared not give Annette another opportunity to talk for surely everything she knew about Sarah Finfield, the widow, would be revealed within minutes. She must break up the party!

"Adam, why don't you come inside so we can finish up?"

Oblivious to any awkwardness, Adam walked past Sarah and into the foyer. Nicely, but leaving no doubt as to her wishes, she said to Annette, "I've got to take care of this, Annette. Maybe later this week stop by."

"Oh, I understand. I'll go." Walking backwards toward the road she closed out today's encounter with Sarah. "Your door is fixed, right?" she half shouted from across the lawn. "You'll leave a light on tonight, right? I wish you weren't by yourself. Please remember to call me if you need help. Remember…4664."

The teenager, naïve and harmless, meant no trouble, but she had rattled off too much information in one breath. There was no question as to whether or not Adam heard. He was right inside the door. Sarah did not respond. She shoved on the door. It closed. Now there was an awkward silence. Finally, Sarah asked him to sit in the family room. There, with an annoying quiver unnerving her, she took out her checkbook, inquired as to the charges, wrote a check, tore it from the pad, and folded it in half, all in a condition of great physical and mental fatigue. Too much had happened today. She was out of practice for trauma and people and decisions and unexpected situations. If she could just get through the next minutes without more questions! No doubt, however, Adam would have more to say.

"Here's a check, Adam. Thank you so much for coming. You do good work. And fast."

"Oh, it's what I do. I like what I do. I was glad to help." He took the check, stuck it down in his shirt pocket, rose to leave, and handed her a sheet of paper defining the charges. "You know, I must ask you this. Did this thief...or thieves...get into your house?"

Here it came.

"No. No, they did not." Adam noticed the word *they* again. "Like I said before, I was awakened in the night and got up and turned the lights on. At that time I didn't know about the door, my bedroom being at the other end of the house. In fact, I really didn't even hear the noise. I just woke up and figured something had disturbed me. Annette told me about it the next morning. As far as I can see, nothing was disturbed inside or outside except for the door. I'm sure I scared them off."

"Hmmm. Well, I don't want to stick my nose in, but I must express my opinion that the police should be called."

He sat back down at the very front edge of the cushion.

"Are you...are you alone here?"

Sarah knew that he knew—bubbly Annette had spilled the beans—so what was the point of an evasive reply. She sighed.

"Yes. My husband died a year ago. That's why the security system is not complete. It was on his To Do list."

"I'm sorry. I really am." Adam was genuinely saddened by this news. He looked down at his shoes. "I'm not happy about this break-in. You know, bad guys know when women are living alone. They need to know that you have the police in your corner and besides, the cops really can provide protection just by driving by now and then."

"Adam, we both know that thousands of women have had to live alone. I am not up for a big deal. All I want is my quiet restored," Sarah admitted very slowly. "I don't think they will try it again."

"Why do you keep saying *they*, ma'am? You don't know who it is, do you?"

"No." she replied as convincingly as possible. "How could I know?" She hesitated. Adam was looking at her, his forehead wrinkled, earnestly inquisitive. Back and forth her mind went. She did not want to go on with this conversation and yet...was it possible that perhaps a friend was sitting across from her? She was tired. She closed her eyes for a moment. "Any inklings are just p—plain preposterous," she stuttered. Shaking her head slowly and slightly, she went on. "Couldn't it just be that any old thief did it? Couldn't it be that he knows the neighborhood is an upper class neighborhood? And isn't it possible that he's just...a thief! He wants what I have. Don't you think that this is what happened?"

"I guess it could be. I just kept hearing you use the plural and, well, that just threw me into thinking that maybe you might have a suspicion that whoever did this was...plural."

As the moments had ticked by since her first look at the bashed-in door, yes, a suspicion had been growing. She couldn't shake the fact that Annette and Tony had seen three men snooping around the house not all that long ago. Then there were the very uncomfortable encounters with the Payce boys the day of Mildred's funeral. Up until then, Sarah had absolutely no idea that there could possibly be something in her possession that they wanted from her—how could there be? There had been no contact with them for a year! What could it be that they were so desperate to lay their hands on—if, it was them?

Robert had been like a man with a mission rummaging through Chip's belongings and a very clear message had come from his lips: They would eventually get what they were looking for. Oh, it could not be! Such a suspicion was, yes, truly preposterous! Yet, Annette and Tony had witnessed the men—the prowlers. That image just wouldn't go away.

"Adam," Sarah said after a very heavy sigh, "I never laid eyes upon you until this week. You are a complete stranger to me. To tell you the deep secrets of my life does not hit me as smart. The only things I know about you are that you seem to be an excellent carpenter, you are honest—I know that because you didn't charge me for that second lock—and that you seem to be a nice guy."

"I **am** a nice guy," Adam said with a slight grin and a soft laugh. Passively, Sarah went on.

"A couple of months ago I was living a completely quiet life and oh, so content. Then came talkative Annette. Out of nowhere. She informs me that prowlers have been sneaking around my house in the night."

"Prowlers? When was that?"

"Way back in April."

"Prowlers?"

"Yes, but that was the end of it."

"That was the end of it until this, perhaps. Did you notify the police at that time?" When Sarah's answer was only a shake of her head, Adam wondered if she was holding back out of fear.

"Someone bashed in your door who knew the garage is not wired. That is a clue. Do you understand that? Who might that be?" he inquired solemnly.

How much did she really know for sure? How much should she tell Adam Cook who, in reality, was a perfect stranger?

"Here I sit with Adam Cook, the carpenter," she said, "Adam Cook, the carpenter, who I don't know from…Adam." A tiny smile touched her lips. The carpenter was amused. "Adam Cook wants to know if I know who broke into my house. What would Adam Cook do if he was me?"

"You know, it's true," Adam said after a slight hesitation. "You're right. You don't know me." Something about his demeanor as he spoke conveyed stability and wisdom. "You really don't. If you did, though, you'd know that I, too, am a very private person, and that I stay away from sticking my nose in the business of other people; but you would also know that I have an insatiable love for solving problems. Oh, I don't mean problems like marital or financial…I mean why things don't work and how to escape from a kidnapper…those kinds of things. My son calls me Mr. McGyver." He chuckled. "So, when you talk about a break-in and when you give even the slightest inference that you might know who it is, you have no idea what that does to me.

"I never laid eyes on you either until a couple of days ago," he said, "yet I'm not happy that someone is trying to get into your house, especially with no regard as to whether or not you are at home. Let me ask you this: Do you just want these guys to go away—whoever they are—or would you like to catch them?"

Now Adam's smile was broad. He sat back.

"I have the gadgets and the experience and Mrs. Finfield, I'm pretty smart. I'm smart because I'm careful and tenacious. Great combination. I know that I could help you figure this out. But, just tell me to take my check and to go home…and I'll go."

For Sarah, there was hardly a scrap of concern about anything. In that lifeless spirit, though, a very short wick of vengeance now flickered at the thought of catching the Payces red handed if, indeed, they were the perpetrators. Again, she felt herself going back and forth between two very opposite possibilities.

A little over a year before, life had been grand. Everything was wonderful. She and Chip had the world by the tail, as they say. Then, out of nowhere, in a split second, death painted Timber Lane and ice cream, mountain bikes, spring and fall, and even the white snow of winter…painted them all black. Death had also come to Sarah. She had not died slowly; death struck Sarah Finfield with haste. Finding Chip in his softly purring Jaguar sports car, lifeless, the car door open, was all she could remember—except that as the ambulance began its drive down Timber Lane, the siren mournfully sounding its death announcement, she had collapsed on the cement floor between the car and the new dry wall. She had decided to die, too.

A carpenter sat opposite her, one ankle crossed over the other knee. What did he know of such trauma? So, he loved to play Sherlock Holmes; so did she, once upon a time. But now the agony of life, the physical fatigue resulting just from the past few days and the overwhelming desire for peace could not be overruled.

"Please take your check and go, Adam," she said so very softly, using his words. "I'm sorry. I just can't take stress. When stress comes, my health suffers. I don't know why. Though there is a part of me that would love to catch him—or them—weariness, I must tell you, has won out."

He slapped his knee and stood up.

"You know, don't even feel bad. I didn't know whether to say anything or not. I do think you should inform the police, Mrs. Finfield. To not do so is asking for trouble,"—now he was at the door—"in my opinion," he added with his hand on the handle.

He said the regular things a carpenter would say…thanks a lot for calling me…you're all safe and secure…here's my business card…call me if I can do anything else for you…if you have any trouble with the door, let me know. Then he was gone.

For a moment or two, Sarah wondered if she had done the right thing. Of course, she had.

CHAPTER 5

On Saturday morning, Sarah stood before the long mirror at the end of the hallway, her arms folded, her mind elsewhere, but with a faint realization that the mirror was not lying. She looked haggard. Dark circles under her eyes stared back at her. The lines of her mouth fell downward. A hot shower took away some of the horror story the mirror had divulged; she felt refreshed—a little—and there was a measure of satisfaction from clean hair pulled back in a barrette at her neck. Beyond that, what did her appearance matter? Clothes and jewelry and especially, shoes, had ceased to matter to her. Chip used to love the way she dressed and wore her hair. Never did he fail to tell her that he thought she was elegant. Elegant. That was always his word for her. Now, *elegant* was the farthest thing from Sarah's mind. Chip was gone and she cared not at all how anyone else viewed her.

Nevertheless, with the unbidden rejuvenation that comes with a long shower, she stood before the mirror once again with a speck of energy required for the tasks at hand. The events of the previous two days had never left her mind. How could they? Great unpleasantness had invaded the stillness of Timber Lane.

With her regular fare of a peanut butter and jelly sandwich and glass of milk, she made her way to the love seat, making a valiant attempt to escape that unpleasantness within the pages of her book. Part of the time, she was successful, but such momentous happenings, not to be easily laid aside, seemed always to seep through the lines on the pages. Someone was disturbing her tranquility. Could it possibly be the Payce clan? Had it been the ill-famed Payce trio that Annette had seen—father and sons—and if so, could they be tied to the break in?

Sarah resolutely set her mind to unearth what it might be that the Payce family was hunting and convinced that she had—if indeed it was they who were sneaking around her house. Very soon, she would go through Chip's boxes with a fine toothed comb. It was all so odd. More than a year had passed since his death. What would they be looking for now?

Chip's death had brought on heightened involvement with the Payces simply because of what happens after someone dies…the funeral home and the graveside, lunch at the church, niceties by phone and an occasional unexpected visit. Then there was a very welcomed silence. Looking back—and Sarah at the time had not realized it— she had been relieved by that grand silence. How she despised all of them, except for Chip's mother. She loved Mrs. Finfield Payce! But even there, contact with her had been so limited. Sarah knew that this was greatly her own doing; her small corner of the world, hidden behind heavy draperies, protected by locked doors and unanswered phones, had shut everyone out—even her dear mother-in-law.

But on the day of her funeral they had barged in once again; why now? If there was something that Chip had of theirs from working alongside them at the office, why hadn't they come for it sooner? And why would they try to get in her house to get it? It could not possibly be them! If Raymond or Robert had wanted something, they were arrogant enough to approach her face to face. She could not imagine them ever breaking in. That was not their style. Surely, that was not their style!

On the way home from Shelton in the evening, her groceries, as always, set on the seat beside her, she could not help launching into a comprehensive deliberation as to the value of whatever it was the prowlers were after. Robert—if, indeed, he turned up on the guilty list—had searched feverishly for the prize and found nothing. His demeanor had then changed from seeking to threatening. Bend or break, he had thrown at her. Now, what was that all about?

There on the country road towards home, as Sarah dug through the limited information now hers, things began to come into focus. Evidently, something having to do with Chip's employment at Payce, and in particular, something to do with *The Street of Petetra*, was of value—clearly significant value. Could it be valuable enough to render the Payces desperate? It was not farfetched to assume they might stop at nothing to lay their hands on something that meant money in their pockets. Whatever it was, they were sure she knew about it and sure that she knew where it was. Sarah shook her head and smiled. She had no clue.

By nine-fifteen, the shopping trip had been completed. The songs of crickets filled the air as Sarah in her blue jeans and white cotton blouse stepped from her blue BMW into the dark, but their music was never heard by the young widow. With one fell swoop, she brushed aside all deliberation upon the episodes, conversations and musings of the last few days. She was glad to be home. A warm breeze touched her. It threatened to perform a ballad of happy days gone by; she, however, quickly scorned such a possibility, and ignoring the beauty of the evening, trudged up the stairs, the bag of groceries—and her heart—feeling exceptionally heavy.

She turned the key in the lock and entered the spacious front foyer. She gasped. There before her lay the scattered contents of the upper shelf of the front closet. Immediately, she deduced they had not fallen, for the closet was always orderly; besides, she recalled taking a moment to put things right after Robert's search. No, they had not fallen. Someone had been inside the house—someone who might still be in the house!

Tense and wide-eyed, her heart pounding beneath her blouse, she stood perfectly still, pressed against the wall between the foyer and the family room. Then, with imprudent courage, she inched along, her back to the wall, her hand reaching out for the next light switch. Gingerly, she turned the corner into the great room.

"No! Oh, no!" she whispered hoarsely, her knees giving way beneath her. The groceries fell first; Sarah followed. The spacious room had been ransacked. Every book, hundreds of them, lay scattered upon the floor. Chip's extensive collection of record albums, once neatly lining the bottom shelves, was pulled out, strewn everywhere. The chest was opened, its fine finish intentionally marred. The furniture cushions were slit, the chairs and couches overturned, the bottoms slashed. There was no need to check the dining room furniture; judging from the chairs scattered about, it was obvious that it had not been missed. Deliberately, she turned away from the shiny black Steinway. She could not bear to look.

Cross-legged and horrified, her eyes wide with unbelief, Sarah pressed her fingers to her open mouth. There on the area rug lay precious belongings that had been crushed beneath the feet of a ruthless person. Treasured photos and valuable Norman Rockwell prints—signed by the artist—torn from their frames, lay trampled upon the floor, the broken glass everywhere. The roll top desk had met with a massive blow.

Crawling a few feet to her right, Sarah peeked around the corner into the kitchen. Every cabinet was open and the shelves bare, the contents spread from one end of the large room to the other. The floor was impassable. Stiffly, she arose and investigated further, knowing full well that someone might still be present within her home. The door to the garage was secure. Locked. Halfway down the basement stairs, it became evident that the prowlers…or prowler…had done their dirty work there as well. Common sense told her that the whole house had been ravaged.

Once again in the family room, standing in the middle of the plush area rug at the south end, Sarah stood with her hands pressed against her hot flushed cheeks, her brow wrinkled downward above her closed eyes. Fiercely, her heart beat within her chest as she attempted to remain calm and think things through. Unknown to her, shock had set up a defense of emotional protection. There was strength enough to evaluate the situation.

How could they have gotten in? If the front door and the back door of the house, and the one leading from the kitchen to the garage, were all closed and locked, how could someone have gotten in? The only other entries to the ranch home were the two sets of patio doors that opened to the deck.

It was foolish to remain in the house and not call for help, she knew, but fury overruled fear. At the north end of the great room, she pulled back the drapes. The heavy board was still wedged in place to keep the sliders safely locked. Slightly panicked now, she edged her way through the house to her bedroom, assuming that she would soon discover the entry point of the culprits. There she gasped at the dreadful condition of her room but was relieved to find the patio doors were secure. She reached up and grasped a bedpost, resting her forehead against it, her arms quivering uncontrollably. Such destruction! It was not necessary to check the other three bedrooms and the office. Surely they were in shambles as well.

One fact was clear. Whoever had been inside this house tonight had gained entrance with a key. It was the only answer. But who? No one else had a key to any of the doors. Something was nagging at her about the garage door. What was it? Like a dream in slow motion, the truth dawned; hastily, she headed for the door leading from the kitchen to the garage.

Stepping carefully through the upheaval upon the stylish ceramic tile in the kitchen, she went to the door, unlocked it and pressed it open. Slowly, with trembling hands, she reached high above the door and felt for the spare key. The nail was empty! Somehow she knew it would be. At once, the whole matter became clear.

"Oh, God!" she cried in a whisper, sinking to a sitting position in the doorway. "They are the only ones who knew about the key!"

Sarah again pressed her fingers against her mouth as she stared blankly into the darkened garage. Her eyes widened. The three men that Annette had seen—it had indeed been the Payces! Why hadn't she been smart enough to think of the key when the garage door had been broken down? Both of the Payce brothers were well aware that Chip and she kept a spare key on that nail. The key—and only the key—had been their object the night of the bashed-in garage door. The ultimate conquest would come later, sometime when Sarah was out of the house. Tonight was the night.

Two facts emerged: they were after something big and they were not playing games in order to get it. It had something to do with *The Street of Petetra*. But what? And where was it? Surely not in her house!

Apprehension mounting, Sarah wandered through the torn-up house. Recollections entered her mind of the news story of a mysterious fire at the Wentworth Building. Though the building was owned by the Payces and used for Payce Publishing storage, there had been an apartment upstairs where lived the old and somewhat feeble author of *The Street of Petetra*. The old man—a wonderful old man—died in the flames. Sarah had met him once and liked him. Chip had been overcome with guilt and for some reason, felt that he could have kept the old man from dying. She had never before seen her husband shed a tear, but that night, she had watched him alternate between sobs and fury.

"I can't tell you anything right now, Sarah," he had said through clenched teeth in answer to her questions as to why he was so distraught.

"Was this an accident, Chip?" she had questioned him, anxiety intensifying.

"I don't know. I don't know. You must not ask questions."

"But you're not in danger, right?" she had asked, panic stricken.

"I'm family, Sarah," he had replied, enveloped in escalating emotion. "At least, I think I am. Don't worry about me. In a few days, I'll be out of there and on my own...gone! Away from all of them!"

Chip was implicating the Payces. Sarah asked no more questions.

Cautiously stepping over the clutter on the floor, she made her way to the family room once again. There she knelt, staring down upon a ruined wedding photo. Chip's tiny smile as he looked tenderly into her uplifted face, her long brown hair pulled back into a veil of Italian lace and pearls, tore at her heart. She had kidded him about that wonderful smile! Tears fell and splashed upon the wedding couple's silhouetted profiles. With broken heart, she tried to smooth away the creases put there by the footstep of a wicked man.

"I should call the police," she whispered, "right, Chip?" She scrunched her eyes shut and bowed her head. "I should but I can't.

I'm afraid. I'm angry. I won't let them do this to me! Oh, why is this happening? Oh, Chip," she cried, clutching the photo to her breast, "I can't go on without you!"

෧ ෧ ෧ ෧ ෧

At very close to four in the morning, a silver picture frame on the piano, having been left precariously positioned above the keys, finally fell. It ended up on the floor but not before striking several notes on the way down. The sound pierced the air. Startled to the core, Sarah awoke from where she had fallen asleep in a sitting position, leaning against the wall. She pressed her hand to her chest and sucked in a long, deep breath.

All was lost. Dismay crept in. Her tidy abode and hideaway—and her life—had been desecrated. No portion of the former Sarah Finfield was present to arise and attack the mess, a mess that would require professional attention, to be sure. Slowly she stood and walked to the kitchen, stepping over patches of shattered dinner plates, glasses and mugs. There she cleared off one of the solid wood chairs and sat. This room was like the rest. Why would Raymond and Robert—and perhaps, Richard—tear apart the kitchen? Was it retaliation or perhaps a means to frighten her...or was there really something to find in a kitchen which was so gravely important? Surely there was nothing in this room that would interest them unless they thought perhaps it was hidden down in the flour or behind the canned soup! The canisters had been carelessly opened and the contents spilled out on the floor. Why would they do that? Flour and sugar. Pine nuts. Raisin bran. A torn open bag of brown sugar. Cooking utensils, pots and pans, Tupperware. All was thrown about on the counters and on the floor. The cabinets were emptied. The refrigerator and freezer contents were thrown about and the stainless steel doors kicked in. The stove was pulled out as was the dishwasher, their front panels intentionally scratched. Could this really be all about *The Street of Petetra*? Why would this extremely successful tale of futuristic days be of such consequence? Sarah searched for clues in her head. None came. All she could muster were the memories of Chip being delighted that old Herman Lichten's book had been a huge triumph and would make it financially possible for him to finally move out of that awful upstairs apartment.

It was time for action, Sarah knew. This was ugly and criminal. This was hateful and desperate. Sarah was not slow to recognize that this was no small break in. Nearly everything in her home was broken, crushed, ripped—destroyed. The serenity of sleep tempted her, but she could not go to bed; the mattresses in every room had been recklessly slashed and searched.

Now it was four thirty in the morning. Back and forth she walked in the only clear area in the house—the long hallway. The abrupt entrance of trouble into her quiet life was threatening to undo her. Without warning and with great speed, discord had appeared, dealing a fatal blow to the silence and safety of grieving alone. And was there any satisfaction in knowing the identity of those who had done this? On the contrary, this knowledge heaped countless complications upon the whole situation. The missing key confirmed what had only been a sliver of suspicion! No one else knew it was there and the way it was hidden made it highly unlikely that a happenstance prowler would notice it. Yet, even though certainty had now replaced suspicion, how did that help? Did that not make it worse? A call to the police would be a whole lot easier if the identity was unknown. She entertained the thought of not calling, of getting to work to clean up the mess, of restoring things without the knowledge of another soul.

Heartsick and fatigued and surprisingly on the verge of tears, Sarah again made her way to the family room—the great room. If she could just get that back in shape, then the rest could be done a little at a time. At least if, of necessity, someone had to enter her house, a nicely restored family room would welcome them. Yes, this is what she would do! Then, she could take as long as she needed to get the rest of the job done.

A well-meaning plan this was, but one cultivated out of complete and overwhelming despair; a first step never even took place. How could one ever be sure that all the little slivers of glass were removed, no matter how painstakingly they tried? Nearly every item in the house would need to be replaced and the entire home restored. Reality set in. She would need the help of professionals. She would need new furniture. The floors would need to be refinished or replaced. Appliances would need to be repaired; no, they, too, would need to be replaced.

Leaning against the very same wall where she had fallen asleep earlier, and articulating the truth that was in her heart, she moaned, "I know I can't do this alone. I need to get help."

But, who could she call at this hour? And anyway, who was there to call? Alone and overwhelmed, she turned off all the lights in the house except for the little lamp on her nightstand, retrieved her comforter from the floor, threw it across the shredded mattress and fell upon the bed. Now she wept—it was only the second time since

Chip died. Her tears were for him, for her, from hopelessness, from confusion, from fear, from anger. She was not a weepy person. She had never been. Perhaps for that very reason, tonight's pent up flood of tears would not end soon.

When the tears did finally cease, sleep came. A two-hour escape into the wonder of slumber sheltered Sarah from the peak of the crisis. When she awoke, though her world was still a war-zone, a slight and strange sense of direction was hers. It was easier to think now. She washed her face. She stepped cautiously through the pieces of broken mirror and other items on the floor; the bathroom, too, had met with the intruders.

There were no new revelations, no astounding solutions...just a bit of strength for the journey. She found her car keys near the front door. Her groceries were still in the same place where they had fallen upon the first sight of the disaster. She picked up her keys and put them in her pocket. She felt other items there...her wallet, her receipt from the store, and a business card. Paying only slight attention, she glanced at it. Adam Cook, it said. Carpenter/Contractor. One after the other, words popped into her head...safe, strong, dependable, caring—and Adam's own words...careful and tenacious.

Could she call him for help, for advice? Instantly, she knew she could. She would.

CHAPTER 6

"Adam?"

"Yes, this is Adam."

Sarah looked at the clock, suddenly aware that she had no idea what time it was. Oh, how she hoped she had not awakened him! But the hands on the clock were kind to her; it was nine-fifteen. A short sigh of relief escaped her lips.

"Adam, this is Sarah Finfield."

"Mrs. Finfield?"

"Yes," she answered, surprisingly calm, given the events of her last twelve hours. "I wonder if you would be able to stop over here this morning. I know it's Sunday and I hate to disturb you and your family, but it's...it's important."

"Oh, no," he said very quietly. "More trouble?"

"I'm afraid so."

"I'll be there in twenty minutes."

"In twenty minutes?"

"Yep. Twenty."

There was no missing Sarah's tear stained face. Splashing cold water on it earlier had done little to lessen the red around her eyes. Adam, in his navy sport coat, blue jeans, white shirt and tie, took note of it at the first sight of her as she opened the door; he recalled that their last conversation had revealed a grieving, yet capable, woman. She had been weary, but not emotional. Her call had prepared him for something big; the tearful countenance confirmed that as he took his first steps into the house. She ushered him through the foyer and into the trashed family room. He raised his eyebrows and turned to look at her.

"This is pretty awful," he remarked as he made his way slowly through the room, stepping over the mess on the floor, "and pretty hard to believe." He stopped before Sarah, deep questions in his eyes, kindness on his face. "This is the work of more than one person, ma'am. You know that, don't you? How did they get in," he asked, almost like a big brother wondering who she had been out with, "and where were you?"

Sarah looked him straight in the eye, drew in a deep breath, and answered him with words even she could hardly believe.

"They—yes, they—came right in the front door...with a key. I was in Shelton. Grocery shopping. Like I do every Saturday night."

"With a key?" Adam was greatly perplexed.

"Yes, Adam, with a key."

"Who else has a key to your house?"

"I know who and I will tell you."

"What about the security code though."

Sarah stood and folded her arms. Adam read her expression.

"They knew the code?"

"Yes, they did, or I should say, they assumed they still did." Her answer was only just above a whisper.

"You're kidding. Then, it's true. You really do know who *they* is."

"Yes. I have been increasingly suspicious, but now, now I know."

Sarah closed the cover of the cedar chest, softly and gingerly, taking care not to harm it further, and then sat herself down on the love seat. Her countenance was filled with hope—and hopelessness. "Adam, there is much to tell, I'm afraid, and I am in a terrible mess. I don't think I would have thought to call you, but I accidentally found your business card in my pocket...and I couldn't help but remember what you said about trying to catch these guys. Can you see yourself as helping me in any way?"

"Mrs. Finfield, this is nasty. What about the rest of the house?"

"Feel free," Sarah said, motioning with a wave of her hand.

Adam was shaking his head in unbelief and repeating the word, "Wow," when he reappeared in the family room. "We must call the police, Mrs. Finfield, and you'll have to explain how these guys got into your house...with a key." Sarah made note of his use of the pronoun *we* and drew strength from it.

"I will call them. But first, I just need to talk. Do you have time? I hate to disturb family time so much, but as you can see, this is pretty awful. I need help. Asking for help is not something I do easily."

"There is no family, Mrs. Finfield. I live alone."

"I assumed that since you mentioned a son...."

Adam's lips tightened and he gave himself a moment to decide how much detail needed to be spoken at this moment.

"Daniel is in the Marines. And there is no wife. I had a wife. Like you, I have lost her to death. She is with Jesus."

"Oh, Adam," Sarah managed to whisper, her eyes touched with

sincere sympathy. "I am truly sorry. No one understands like some-one who has gone through it themselves. How long ago did she die?"

Adam knew that his wife had died the day before Chip, but it was not the time to make such a declaration. He simply answered that it had been the year before. Sarah asked no more questions.

"Well, I think I should tell you a story," she said expectantly, "and then, you can decide if you want to take on helping to get me through this." Her barely audible words were laced with anxiety. "I don't even know what to ask or expect from you, but for a start, I know I need a carpenter."

"We'll have to take this step by step," Adam replied with confidence. "I can help you. I will help you. Your insurance company will need to know. The police must be called. And I think I need to listen to your story. Is it a long one?"

"Yes. It's long."

Adam took a moment to strategize.

"Let's do those three things in reverse order. What do you say? Let's start at Square One. Let's talk and get you ready to answer a lot of questions. Where can we sit?" He looked around. "How about the kitchen?"

Sarah was tottering between great control and looming collapse. A stranger was in her house, taking charge, seeming sympathetic and sounding sure. Catastrophe had stricken, and in its wake, a young widow, known for her pluck, found herself without a first step. Where was Square One? Where was Start? She did not know. But Adam moved about with an air of *ready to conquer*, not only the house repairs, but solving the mystery. She followed him to the kitchen.

"And one more thing," he said, "do you think there is any way to produce a cup of coffee in this messy kitchen?" He chuckled. "Gotta have a cup of coffee on a Sunday morning! Come on, let's clear a place to sit and we'll talk right here. This is a very nice kitchen, Mrs. Finfield," he commented. "A very large nice kitchen." He brushed ground coffee from the chair seat and sat down. "Now why would a bad guy need to tear open this perfectly good bag of gourmet coffee like this?"

Slightly uplifted by conversation and somewhat surprised by that fact, Sarah took courage. Calling Adam had carried with it the possibility of *no* for an answer. Even if the answer was in the affirma-tive, there was no way to know how involved he would wish to be. She had leaned heavily on his apparent interest as expressed in their previous conversation. Adam had not been lying. There he sat, one ankle across his knee, anticipating the tale. Sarah began, pausing between each sentence.

"I know who has done this. I know who kicked in my garage door. And what's more, I know why they kicked in the garage door. All they wanted was the key to my house. Chip and I kept a key on a nail right outside this door—right there—that leads to the garage. It was hidden well. There are only a couple of people who knew about that key."

"And who...are *they*?"

"There are two—or three—who knew. They needed the key to get in the house and then disarm the alarm. The alarm system kept them from just breaking the door down, though no doubt they would have preferred to."

"And they knew your code, too?"

"They did. At least one of them did."

This perplexed Adam. He wanted to know how that could be.

"Let me tell you the story, Adam. Soon you'll know all the answers. I can only tell you what I know, though, and believe me, there are a lot of blank spots because I just don't know what they are after or what this is all about. Just a minute. Let me do this coffee thing."

Everything in place, she pushed the ON button and sat down across from Adam. How was it that she felt free to open up to him? He was basically an outsider. Yet...if nothing else, he was at least a carpenter and a carpenter would certainly be needed in her life in the days to come. Sure, he could help restore the damage, but why was she about to tell him the personal details surrounding this mess and get him involved?

She looked into his face for answers. He was waiting, leaning heavily against the back of the chair, his arms folded—and not showing any signs of disinterest. For some reason...she trusted him.

"Here goes," she said, sighing deeply. "Four years ago, well, now it's five, my mother-in-law remarried after being a widow for ten years. She married into the Payce Publishing Company. You've heard of them, I'm sure, out north of town. She married Richard Payce—sometimes the proud mogul, sometimes the simpleton—he being a very recent widower. Chip—my husband—was not happy. He did not like Richard but for his mother's sake, he...we...said very little—she seemed to be greatly in love with the man. Chip was offered a lucrative spot at Payce. It was an enormous move up for him...for us. Neither Chip...nor I...detected any red flags in the marriage.

"But, Mildred's life became a horror story. After one month of marriage, the Payces—namely, Richard, Robert, and Raymond—

Jan 18, 2015

Kim—

Thank you so much for sharing this book. What a treasure to read a story with the Lord in their daily lives.

I enjoyed this book soo much.

I enjoy Your friendship as well.

Your friend
Pat Samuelson

totally rejected her. Richard treated her despicably but she continued to be a caring and good wife. The family either ignored her at their celebrations or left her out of them completely; they did not talk nicely to her, even in front of us. Chip was so, so, so disturbed, but his mom kept saying that she was fine. She was an amazing woman."

"Was?"

"Yes, she died a couple of months ago and I was deeply saddened. I loved her. She died almost exactly one year after Chip. His untimely and unexpected death slowly undid her."

"What happened? I mean, how did he die?"

It had to come out. It was part of the story. But Sarah's ability to go on was instantly impeded. She folded her hands and pressed her thumbs to her lips and closed her eyes. Here came the anguish of death again. She could not articulate an answer to his question. The desire to die once again surfaced. How she hated thinking about it all over again! Thinking about it was bad enough, but now, to have to speak words and form sentences to tell the story to someone else nauseated her.

"I'm sorry," he said, great understanding in his voice. "I can see this is hard for you, Mrs. Finfield. It's okay," he said with a wave of his hand. "Let it go. Just go on with the story. I'm sorry."

"Please, call me Sarah," she said with little inflection. "Yes, I will go on with the story." She opened her eyes, folded her arms and leaned back in her chair. "No," she almost whispered, changing her mind, "I will tell you about Chip."

Staring across the room at nothing, she spoke words that she had never uttered before.

"It was...it was...." Sarah sucked in a deep breath. "It was ruled... they say he took his own life."

A masked question mark—or so it seemed to Adam—was present at the end of her statement, rather than a period. He wanted to ask, "Do I detect doubt?" but the word *inappropriate* came to mind. Instead, he waited for her to go on.

Sarah closed her eyes and continued her tale. "I found him in his car—the beautiful car you commented on out there in the garage—engine running."

Adam closed his eyes tightly, his brow wrinkled with sympathy.

"Why?" he asked softly.

"It was all about—at least this is all that I can figure—all about the old man who died in that fire. I don't know if you recall that awful fire a year ago. Chip was deeply grieved when that old man died and could not be consoled when it happened. Over and over again, he groaned, 'I should have had him come home with me for the night!'"

"Was there a note?"

"Yes...sort of."

"Sort of?"

"An unfinished note. It was enough, they say."

"And it said?"

"It was about the old man. Someday—perhaps—I will show it to you. I'm not sure I know where it is."

"Do I detect a question mark in your words?"

Sarah lifted her eyes to meet those of the carpenter. "Yes, and it will always be there. Knowing Chip as I did...it's so wrong. Knowing him at that time in his life and all that was ahead, it's just so wrong. What's more...it was his 29th birthday. Yet, considering the evidence, what can I say. The autopsy report...carbon monoxide."

Had Sarah been able to read Adam's thoughts, she would have missed neither the great depths of sympathy for her nor the burning questions beginning to gather in his mind. He sat across from her, his elbow resting on the table, a fist pressed against his lips, and the evidence of deep contemplation on his face. He would ask no questions—for now.

"My, my," he said, shaking his head with great compassion. "What a burden you have borne, Sarah. I'm sad for you." His words were quiet and full of sorrow. "I had no idea."

"I more or less died myself that day, Adam. Please understand— I wonder if you can—I really don't care whether I live...or die. The most I can say right now is that a desire to bring down the wicked Payce empire is poking its way up through the thick sod."

"Can you keep going with this?"

"I have to. You need to know."

"I'm fully engaged. This whole thing is not right. This is ruthless, Sarah. I want to hear the rest."

Pouring coffee as she spoke, she continued the tale. "Well, Chip went on with his job, making lots of money and allowing us to build this house and do a whole lot more. However, I noticed that he was increasingly unhappy, as I told you. Something going on at work. Adam...I can only tell you what I know.

"I told you a little about the old man, Herman Lichten. He lived in an old rundown upstairs apartment in a building that the Payces owned and used for storage. For years, he had been homeless, a sad story of a brilliant professor and a life gone awry. Chip's mother, you know, Mildred, struck up a friendship with him because she regularly saw him near the train station each time she went to have her hair done at some exclusive salon downtown. She felt sorry for him and valiantly arranged for him to move into Payce's building...uh...the Wentworth Building. I met him once. He was one of a kind with his bushy mustache and even bushier eyebrows, and a kind, raspy voice. I liked him. Anyway, after a while, out of nowhere—and a big surprise—he approached Payce about publishing his book, a fantasy he had written during the long days and nights in the apartment. The book was called *The Street of Petetra*. Maybe you've heard of it."

"Of course I've heard of it. It's a best seller...not that I have read it."

"Well, Chip was assigned to this man. He was the account executive. He worked closely with him all through the publishing process. Then one night the building burned down and Herman died in the explosion and intense fire.

"Like I said, Chip was distraught. He had been to see Herman just hours before. I can't help but think he was suspicious about the fire, and I think on top of that suspicion, Chip knew some things that perhaps no one else knew, and some things that no one else knew he knew. Unfortunately, I don't know what those things are. Several times he sounded like he wanted to tell me, but he would never do it, for my safety's sake.

"So, where does that lead to? At the graveside service for Mildred in May—a year after the fire and after Chip's death—both Raymond and Robert approached me to ask me to come to the office and help them with something to do with Chip. I know how Chip worked better than they do, and well, to be honest, I know my way around computers better than he did, although he was very bright. I told Robert I would not come. I basically said, 'For goodness sake, don't you have capable people around there to do these things?' He was not happy.

"Then, later in the day—the same day—Robert came by to talk again, threatening me nicely, telling me that it'd be better for me if I would bend rather than break, whatever that's supposed to mean."

"Better to do what?"

"Better to bend than to break—something like that."

"That was...a muted threat."

"Well, he asked to look through Chip's stuff. I didn't care. It was still in the same place where they had put all of it right after his death... and I might add, that was when I gave them the access code. Anyway, it sounds like it is more than just a piece of paper or a disk...more like a bundle of something."

"So," Adam interjected, "it must be that they have recently discovered something missing, new or old. Otherwise, they would have either had access to it right there after Chip was gone or they would have been bugging you for it long before now, don't you think?"

"I guess. It's a growing possibility. Robert also said something about a contract."

"My guess, Mrs. Finfield, is that the value of the prize is in direct ratio to the condition of your house. This is...dastardly."

"Well, I can only impress upon you, and hope that you understand, that I don't have the slightest inkling of what *The Prize* is or where it could be."

Adam's face was alit with eagerness. Each word that came softly from the lips of his new client spawned schemes and inspiration, and in his head, he placed himself—almost like a playing piece on a game board—on Start. Getting up and walking to the doorway between the kitchen and the family room, and scanning the vicious criminal destruction, he vowed in his heart to right this very malicious wrong.

"So, it was Richard, Robert and Raymond Payce that did this?"

"I have no doubts."

"I can tell. And it sounds right, even to me."

"What they want, I do not know."

"You'll either think of it or we'll stumble on it," he said with confidence.

"Robert went through everything here that day."

"Well, you said he went through Chip's things—not the rest of the house, right?"

"That's true."

"Now, though, it appears that they have gone through everything."

"I wonder if they found what they were looking for."

"I guess we won't know that, at least for now. We'll do our searching under the assumption that they didn't. We don't know what we're looking for. That's the hard part."

"Robert thinks I know. He basically told me that he knew that I know where it is, and that they would get it. I have no idea."

Sarah had finished—for now.

"So you actually gave them the code?"

"Yes. The Saturday when they were bringing the things from Chip's office and some other items, I just told Robert the code in case I was in Shelton. I had no reason to distrust him. I disliked him but I did not distrust him."

"But you would have changed your code by now."

"I haven't, but of course he didn't know that. Robert is a risk taker. He would take a chance."

"My, my, how stupid. He lucked out."

"Not really. They didn't know it, but I never arm the system."

"Ah, Mrs. Finfield, you are going to have change your ways. You are secluded here and you are alone. You must use that wonderful system that your husband installed. And I will finish it for you. I can tie your garage in. In fact, I'll do that right away."

"I guess you're right. I have never felt unsafe here."

"Maybe you weren't. Now you are."

"You have no idea how unhappy I am." She shook her head and scowled, "I despise the Payces. I always did. Yet, it's hard for me to believe they would do this. They are after something and I don't know what."

"Well, that's quite a story. I have a lot to think about."

"I'm sure I'm forgetting details. I'm sure I'll think of other points with time. I'll jot them down." A long pause followed. Sitting across from Adam was a woman who always prided herself in the philosophy, "If someone else can do it, so can I." Even as a child, her tenacity was noticed and spoken of by all around her—family, teachers, church leaders, yes, even her childhood peers who often verbalized their inability to keep up with her. What an asset she had been to Tom at Kerrigan, to say nothing of her stalwart loyalty to her husband and the strength she had been to him! But now, now she had been kicked in the stomach—for that is how she described it to herself many an early morning as she climbed out of bed. And now, piled upon the grief of losing Chip, here was an attack which never could have been anticipated. In her mind, she took a quick trip through the house, gazing upon the destruction inflicted upon her—Sarah Finfield, the widow.

"I'm...I'm helpless," she said, her eyes fixed upon Adam's kind face. "I never thought I would say such words."

Adam scratched his eyebrow.

"Helpless is not always a bad thing. Helpless gives others a chance to help."

"You will help me?" Sarah asked, her voice giving away a slight hint of the inner strength which for long months had been lying dormant.

"Yep, I will."

"I mean, will you help me with the house?"

"Yep."

"And with the Payce thing?"

"Yep. I will. I have two small jobs to finish up and in fact can do those in the evenings. Then I'm here to see you through."

Sarah drew in a quick breath of relief.

"This is like a bad dream. I wish I could wave a magic wand and it would go away. I really don't know what it's all about." She shook her head slowly. "I really have no idea. All I know is that it's something about that Petetra book."

Adam took a few gulps of coffee.

"You know, this coffee is not half bad for being brewed in such a messy kitchen!" he said with a mischievous grin. "Really."

He set down his mug with a thump and slapped his knee.

"It has something to do with the book," he softly declared with conviction, "and...or...something to do with a lot of money!"

CHAPTER 7

The Finfield house was in an area of prestigious homes known as Sharenne Woods, each on substantial rolling acreage. Behind it, a woodsy section of ten acres separated it from a wide creek, which people in the area called Pine Cone Creek, though its official name was Wolf Creek. On the other side of the creek was a meadow. Out the front windows of Sarah's house, the scene was a large cornfield, distinctly changing with each season. The closest house to the east was Annette's, nearly obscured by towering evergreens and lofty oaks. Looking west, cars on the state road could be seen a long way off past a grassy field, bronze and feathery and blowing in the wind. As a result of the seclusion, the police cars in Sarah's driveway went unnoticed. Her situation of privacy gave her a measure of peace knowing that the whole fiasco might go away before anyone else in the neighborhood knew it happened. Though Annette's house and the Dickerson's were the only homes beyond the Finfield house in this part of Sharenne Woods, Sarah realized that one of them could possibly drive by any moment on their way to the main road. She prayed that they would not.

Detective Franklin—for so read his badge—visibly disturbed with the magnitude of the invasion, approached Sarah who was now sitting in a wicker chair on the porch. Leaning against the railing, his arms folded, stood Adam, carefully observing the police activities. Sarah did not recognize this particular member of the police force, which was unusual; Timber Ridge, a town of about 5,000, was closely knit and everyone knew almost everyone else. This young man was a new face. When he asked if she had any idea who might have done this, she answered with a steady voice, "Who would do a thing like this?" She and Adam had agreed to avoid mentioning the Payces—for now—since they had no idea what they might be after.

"How did this person or persons—this had to be the work of more than one—how did they get in, Mr. Finfield?" the detective asked Adam. "There are no signs of forcible entry."

"Oh, I'm not Mr. Finfield. I'm a friend...actually a carpenter friend."

"I apologize. Then I redirect my question to you, Mrs. Finfield. How did they get in? There is no sign of forcible entry."

Sarah knew she had to tell the garage door story—and about the missing key. Why hadn't she reported that incident, he wanted to know? She had thought it might be kids. She just wanted it fixed and over with. And no, she had not noticed the missing key until last night's break in. Oh, so many questions! One by one, Sarah answered them as best she could.

"Surely you are well aware that this was not an everyday robbery. So, I'm thinking two possibilities," the detective said, his hands on his hips. "I can't help but think these people—as I said, it had to be more than one—were after something in particular, or else this is retaliation for something. Can you shed any light on either of those?"

How could she conceal what she did know and yet give an honest answer? She pondered carefully what to say.

"I really don't know. I'm just so tired of trying to figure it out," she said, "but you can be sure that I will have my eyes and ears open now, and if I come up with anything, I will contact you." She glanced at Adam who had retreated to the other wicker chair. He sat with his leg crossed over his knee, not looking, but listening. The sight of this man, an angel from the Yellow Pages, calmed her. She was not alone. Her demeanor was touched by this.

There were more inquiries about this and that and a great many people milling around, taking photos and fingerprints and checking the grounds! She handled herself with confidence, pulling that attribute out of a bag of fine abilities from her past life. Within, she was shedding tears. Over and over again, not able to muster even a speck of hope, she whispered woeful words to her heart that her quiet life had been irretrievably altered.

Hours passed—it was well past five before the whole law enforcement crew left the premises, but then at last, the hubbub began to die down. As they were departing, the police chief, Rod Taylor, stood in the kitchen doorway where Adam and Sarah were squatting on the floor inspecting the refrigerator. He was familiar with Mrs. Finfield; only a year before he had been at this same house investigating a suicide.

"You sure you don't know who did this?" he asked, looking for an answer in her upturned face. "Something...something about this whole thing is bothering me—I just can't put my finger on it."

"Rod," Sarah replied hopefully. "I count on you to figure it out."

"We'll be keeping in touch, Sarah," he said, still deep in thought. "Good day for now. Good day, Adam." He knew the carpenter. Rod Taylor knew everyone in town, it seemed. With a short greeting and a promise to "get to the bottom of this," he left.

Sarah sat herself down across from Adam in the kitchen. Beautiful Sarah! How haggard she looked! She did not care.

The front door was open. The last of the policemen were exiting. Sarah heard car doors closing. Then she heard the sound of their tires on the gravel road. At last they were gone. Quiet moments were almost in reach. Adam made a move to go close the door. More footsteps. Sarah's sixth sense told her that Annette was about to appear in the open doorway. She closed her eyes and announced the coming with a quietly whispered, "Oh, no. It's Annette." Adam understood.

"What...has...happened, Mrs. Finfield?" Annette wanted to know, her eyes opened very wide, her words slow and dramatic and matching her entrance into the foyer. "Mrs. Finfield!" Her mouth dropped open.

Annette was a noisy girl and full of animation but...she was not unkind. A good amount of sympathy was in her heart as she rounded the corner into the kitchen. There she stood, her hand clasped over her mouth. She just kept shaking her head.

Sarah stood.

"Hello, Annette."

"I'm shocked...and yet, I'm not shocked. Well, yes, I am shocked. I'm not shocked that it happened, but I'm shocked by how bad it is. You called the police. I'm soooo glad. Hello, Adam Cook."

Adam returned her greeting. Then, he stood, his entire bearing exhibiting confidence and kindness.

"Annette, you are a thoughtful girl, and yes, whoever did this had a pretty evil heart."

"Or hearts," Annette replied. "You know, Tony and I saw those three men that night. I can't seem to get that out of my mind. It could be them."

Sarah was undone with Annette's visit. At this point, the only option that sounded acceptable was going to her bedroom and flinging herself upon her comforter resting atop the ripped up mattress and going to sleep. Her mind had been moving in that direction. She had enough for one day. Tomorrow would be another day, a day for facing life anew. She could only find curt things in her heart to say to Annette. She would tell her thank you for stopping by, and that it would be a good while before she would feel like chatting again, and would she mind just not sticking around today.

Adam, on the other hand, and by nature, was composed. He spoke to Annette.

"That was a good thing you did, telling Mrs. Finfield about those men." Sarah wished that it would not be rude for her to roll her eyes. "A lot of people, especially young people, would have just let it go. That was good." He paused only briefly. The distraught widow wondered at his tact and composure. "You know, Annette, Mrs. Finfield and I were just about to go to get some dinner and start putting a plan together for attacking this place. She's going to need a good carpenter, you know." He smiled. There it was again, that mischievous grin. He started for the door.

"Mrs. Finfield, are you ready?"

She closed her eyes, cocked her head, and did an instant calculation as to what would be the most disagreeable...time with Annette in this horrid upheaval, carrying on trivial conversation, or going anywhere with Adam, let alone to a public place—a restaurant! A speck of sense helped her make the choice. They really did need to devise a very immense plan if ever her house would be restored again. Besides, she could not endure even five minutes with the chatterbox. Not today.

"I'll get my purse," she said, walking toward her bedroom. In the background she heard the friendly chat between Adam and Annette.

Somehow, Adam knew that Sarah would not want to go to a restaurant in Timber Ridge. So, he soon pointed his truck east. She had no idea where they were heading. She was only grateful that she did not have to form the words with her mouth, "Please, let's not go into town." When Adam pulled his truck into a parking spot, her whereabouts were unknown to her. The sign read, SILVER MOON CAFÉ. It was in the middle of nowhere. It was dusk. The air was filled with the smells of a lake on a hot summer night. She noticed, but she didn't care. After nearly a year of the absence of people in her life, the impending awkwardness at this moment obliterated the ability to be occupied with the beauty of the night. Adam held open the door. She walked in.

What Mrs. Finfield discovered quite quickly was that there was no end to the talent, ideas and skills of her new-found carpenter. He planned. She wrote. They talked—Sarah said little, but it was immeasurably more than during the previous months. Adam drew and scribbled and she agreed or disagreed. He could do almost anything and what he could not do, someone he knew, could. This was a preevaluation. Tomorrow—Monday—they would walk through the house, painstakingly assessing the damage. Sarah did not want to call her home insurance company. Adam argued. Sarah would not budge. Money was not an object.

After an hour of mentally going through each room, Adam grabbed up all the notes, folded them and stuck them in his pocket.

"Enough for one day, don't you think?"

Sarah agreed.

"You have not eaten much, Mrs. Finfield. That will not do for what lies ahead."

"I don't eat much anyway. Today, it is an impossibility."

"You know, I can't tell you what to do, but you had better take care of yourself."

"I do. I...I will."

"Well, ma'am, I'm thinking we should do your bathroom and bedroom first so you have a place to crash at night."

Sarah's chin rested on her open palm. She sighed, oh, so deeply.

"Whatever you think," she replied blandly, unintentionally showing no gratitude for Adam's sensible and considerate plan.

The ride home was quiet. Sarah had never ridden in such a truck and found it interesting to be up so high.

"Your truck is nice," she said, feeling like she needed to say something, "and big!"

"There's a story that goes with it. Someday maybe I'll tell you."

Sarah didn't care about a truck story. Not today. She stared out into the darkness, seeing a faint reflection of herself in her window.

"I wonder what those creeps are looking for?" she wondered aloud. Adam shot a quick glance at her. Her choice of words surprised and amused him. "If they found it," she went on, "perhaps this will be the end of it. If they didn't, I feel fairly certain that they'll be around again very soon, only this time it will be to try to pick my brain."

"I'm a little concerned for your safety," was Adam's response to that possibility.

"That has entered my mind though I guess I don't really think they would do harm to me personally. Then again, I would have never guessed they'd destroy my house. I guess I need to remember, too, that Robert did send a fairly clear message when he grabbed my arms the way he did. I actually had black and blue marks."

"He should not touch you again." The long silence that followed his adamantly spoken statement added to the fervor of it. "Do not stand for it," he said finally, emphasizing each word. Again, Adam paused, searching for proper words and suitable wisdom on this subject. "What they did to your house is pretty significant and it tells a nasty story. It is a story of criminals on the loose. You should take care, Sarah."

"If they are looking for a document and haven't found it at my house, the next step, might be to drag me to the office to scour the computers, but to me it sounds like whatever they're looking for is bigger than a breadbasket."

"Could it be that the *breadbasket* has been reduced down to fit on a disk?"

"That is a valid possibility, I suppose. Who knows?"

It was much later than Sarah ever thought to be out. She would be glad to get home. Yet, would she? She weighed the good and the bad. Life would never be the same. Thoughts of moving away crept in once again, more intense than ever. How could she stay in that house? Avoiding the garage had spared her from encountering Chip's car and the tempest of memories attached to it, yet the very fact that she was daily dealing with such dread by parking outside and hasting to the front door each time she came home—how was that better? And now, even if all were to be put back in place, there would always be a sense of having been victimized there. Her lovely house had lost its luster. It would never be the same!

"I'm really worn out, Adam. I have little fight left in me."

"I can tell."

"It seems pretty hopeless."

"I'm workin' on some things. I've got some thoughts mulling around in my head. Not ready to put them into words yet, but soon."

"I in no way can see how you would already have ideas based upon the scanty information I gave you."

Adam's response was tinted with fervency.

"I told you that day sitting in your family room that this is what I love to do. I'll need your help, but we're going to figure this out. My thinking apparatus is in high gear."

"I've taken up your whole day. Did I mess up plans for you? I notice you are not in your work clothes. I'm sorry."

"I was on my way to church."

"Oh. I'm sorry."

"It's okay. I think I've been there every Sunday for 37 years." He chuckled. "I think I'm okay." He laughed again. "I'm just glad," he went on kindly, "that you felt free to call me."

"I'm just glad you were available."

Where Adam should have turned right, he turned left. Sarah kept silent but hoped that she would soon be home. The destination finally became clear when he drove into the mall parking lot. He turned off the ignition and opened his door.

"Come on, let's get you a mattress."

How could two such opposite emotions reside inside a person at the same time? Mostly, Sarah was passively agitated. Nothing sounded pleasing to her but going home. Yet, it was true that she would need a new mattress and though she would have been grateful to flop on the severely damaged one at home, covered by a soft comforter, there was a bit of gratitude for Adam's initiative.

"Come on, come on!" he taunted as he headed toward the store.

Sarah climbed down and caught up with him.

"I'm not sure I'm going to be up to all of this," she said.

"Oh, sure you are. I'm a pretty good judge of character and I say you're a character!"

❧ ❧ ❧ ❧ ❧

A brief gust of relief blew into Sarah's spirit. Mentally, she put her finger on the two-fold source: A somewhat restored bedroom and the presence of a capable and clearly sympathetic carpenter. As much as she longed for solitude, which at this moment meant absence of Adam, common sense told her that restoration of her house could not be handled alone. Adam was businesslike, gentlemanly, and focused. Here, besides the acquiring of a mattress replacement, even before actually starting on the overall job, he had readily handled the handyman tasks in the master bedroom, securing the drapery rod that had been yanked down, and juggling the sliding closet door until it rode smoothly on its track once again. He carried Sarah's television—damaged beyond repair—to the garage. Together, he and Sarah swept up the glass on the hardwood floors and then vacuumed them, carefully moving the area rugs to the back deck.

They conversed little. Sarah, even though her familiarity with this man was so new, had a strong inkling that he was deep in thought. When all looked livable in the bedroom, he stood in the doorway leaning on the jamb and gave his approval.

"It looks good. Of course, I don't know how it looked before but at least you have a place to retreat. I like this flooring."

"It's Brazilian Cherry."

"I figured it was some kind of cherry. I really like it. This is an incredible house."

"How can you tell tonight?" Sarah asked cynically.

"I can tell. Well, what's next?"

Sarah's eyes widened.

"Do you mean tonight?"

Adam threw his head back and laughed.

"No, no. Just planning ahead. I'm assuming you want me back."

"Yes, Adam, I do. Tomorrow? We can go room by room in detail, I guess. Tonight, I am entirely drained. It's late."

"Yep. 9:05 to be exact." For Adam, 9:05 was not late. For Sarah, it was time to sleep away the pain just like every night for the past year. Now there was more to escape than just Chip's death; there was an unexpected ambush on her entire life and the dread of an impending battle.

Though grateful beyond words for his help and his spirit, Sarah could not wait for Adam to go. At the door, he checked with her on a time to arrive in the morning, secured a promise that she would change the code for the security system and set the alarm, and then made his way to his silver truck. Sarah had no reason to watch him leave or wave goodbye. She closed the door quickly, cleaned the coffee pot, and retreated to her bedroom—then remembered to set the alarm.

She prepared for bed. The huge room looked almost the same as it had a week ago—except for the paintings on the wall which now, with broken frames and absence of glass, stood stacked against the far wall. She ran her fingers along the deep scratches in one of the dressers. Her lovely master bedroom had met with the wicked Payces and the truth that it had been them should have undone her; but for Sarah, as she slipped between the pale green softly striped sheets, it was as though she was being transported to a faraway land. In reality, nothing was the same. A week ago, there had been safety in disappearing from the world, wonderful peace and quiet. Tonight there was crime and disorder, threats and fear, perplexing events— and Adam and Annette, and three men she despised. Physical exhaustion pulled rank on the subjects racing through her mind. Within minutes, she was asleep and all was well.

CHAPTER 8

Scribbles and doodles covered the yellow legal pad on the table before the new carpenter of Timber Lane. A night creature, his mind at midnight soared with logic and avenues of thought, answers and questions, all colored with intense irritation as he considered the evil that had befallen Mrs. Finfield. On and on he wrote, searching the internet, now and then taking some moments to get up and walk around—always ending up at a window, and finding solace in the fact that, even though darkness had set in, beautiful views surrounded his house on every side. His mental efforts alternated between two concerns—laying out a plan for renovation, and solving the mystery in which he was making a conscious choice to be embroiled. On his pad were lists; alongside them, there were points spelled out in chronological order. A diagram of the Timber Lane house had been put down on paper and was taped to the wall in clear view. It was very close to architecturally correct, for Adam was self-trained in the art of planning and design.

This little corner of the den had been Adam's workplace for years. Melanie had named it "Cook's Kitchen" simply because her husband was always concocting something, plans spread out on the drafting table, ideas and drawings of dream houses and dream cars, garages and additions, taped to the wall. Tonight, he worked with a peculiar mixture of anger and sympathy, confidence and perplexity—all of it in the shadow of his own grief. A black and white close-up photo of Melanie tacked to the corkboard in front of him watched over him like a guardian angel. Her smile stroked his troubled soul. In his white tee shirt and khaki shorts, he labored long over preliminary plans to make quick work of the Finfield restoration. The grandfather clock in the living room kept him informed of the time every fifteen minutes.

When at last he heard the chimes ring out announcing two o'clock in the morning, a fairly comprehensive strategy was in place for bringing order to her home, room by room, at least as far as he could remember. Tomorrow he would nail it down precisely and begin to track down pricing for the items needed to be purchased and the services required to repair the extensive damage. At last, at the sound of the Westminster chimes at two thirty, he shoved all of his paperwork aside, turned off the light, and went to bed, but not without kissing his finger and touching it to the lips of his lovely wife. Putting the renovation on hold till tomorrow was easy; not so the issue of ruthless men, priceless treasures, arson and maybe even murder. Unlike him, he churned in his bed, hoping for sleep, searching for clues and vowing justice.

When he awoke at seven o'clock, he nearly bounded out of his bed with anticipation, his brain full of new thoughts, hints and clues. Back to his drawing board and legal pad he went, writing feverishly, gulping down a cup of coffee and eating a slightly charred cinnamon bagel. Adam took note of the growing clutter around him and vowed to clean house in the evening. Except for the interruption of breakfast, he wrote without stopping until eight thirty. He must be at Sarah's house by nine precisely. Hating to quit in the middle of his brainstorms, he waited until the last possible moment to dash to the shower, throw on his work clothes and jump into his truck, his stack of papers, estimates and drawings tucked nicely into his leather folder.

Sarah had done her best to clear the kitchen, at least to the point of being able to walk through it, sit at the table and use the counters. Much of the debris was swept to the side, out of the way, but before she had the opportunity to do away with the black garbage bags, the doorbell rang. With the slight possibility that, rather than Adam, it could be Annette, she rounded the corner very slowly, peeking to look through the panes beside the double doors. The Home Depot hat relieved the anxiety.

The deep-seated weariness of the night before brought on by circumstances almost too bizarre to imagine had driven Sarah into a sleep of complete oblivion. She had slept for seven hours, hardly moving until five in the morning when her eyes opened slowly and her mind tried to process her somewhat changed surroundings. She groaned as she stretched to a sitting position, her legs over the edge of the bed.

"I feel like an old woman." Her lips barely moved as she whispered her words. With eyes closed, she felt around the top of the nightstand for her glasses. The time was 5:15 a.m.

Crushed with the grief of widowhood, and now overcome with an unbidden and unwelcome intrusion of the worst kind, Sarah stood up and decided to face the day. For a moment, she had toyed with the idea of crawling back into bed; her flesh was weak, but her spirit was intent enough to compel her to arise and get to work.

"Perhaps," she figured, "I can make some headway before the carpenter arrives."

So, showered and dressed in baggy jeans and a white, button-down summer shirt, her hair pulled up into a pony tail, Sarah, void of any trace of enthusiasm, had indeed commenced on the slow undertaking of doing what she could do in the midst of nearly insurmountable disruption.

At nine o'clock sharp, she opened the door for the carpenter, who instantly recognized that Sarah had been at work. He followed her into the kitchen, surveying the progress, but avoiding verbal accolades; Mrs. Finfield did not seem like the type—or in the state of mind—to appreciate such praise.

Many large bags were stacked at the back door. The mess on the counters was gone, the counters wiped clean. Things that had escaped destruction were setting in the cabinets, not in any order. The stove and dishwasher—both in need of new front panels—were back in place. Resolutely, she had attacked the front closet and the foyer, too, with the goal of giving her house an orderly appearance should someone come to the door. The rest of the house remained under the Payce devastation.

"You'll be proud of me, Sarah," Adam cheerfully said, placing his folder and keys on the table. "I have a plan all mapped out. Actually, I have more than one plan."

"I'm not really surprised. Have you eaten? I can only offer you coffee and cookies." She smiled. "They're in an unopened bag. No glass."

"I have. I had a bagel and coffee. But what about you?"

"I...I can't think of eating," she stammered under her breath. "Maybe in a while."

Adam had a response but it did not seem appropriate. He must refrain from trying to invade her personal life.

"Let's look at my notes, the ones about getting your house back in order. Then, Mrs. Finfield, I want to talk to you about the rest. Pull up a chair. We are going to work!"

For a little more than an hour, the two hovered over Adam's nocturnal notes, neatly written sheets outlining a projected schedule and an estimated cost and completion date—and a reminder to Sarah that work for current clients needed to be finished up. Then, a detailed inspection clarified the severity of evil inflicted upon the house at 12006 Timber Lane and its lovely occupant. What had started out as a search for a prize, Adam suspected, had progressed into a tantrum.

"There's no way you can link the search for anything…anything at all…to demolition of this magnitude," growled Adam, now standing in the doorway of Sarah's office at the end of the hall. "You know what I think, Mrs. Finfield? I think this is the work of the two boys on their own, without Daddy Payce, and what I think is that they are jealous of your husband, for some reason—still jealous—and angry at him for something significant! It's about a piece of paper or two—or a hundred—but it's about Chip and what he did or did not do with it. My guess is that Chip hoodwinked them!" Adam walked to the office window facing the front yard and leaned against the sill.

Sarah sat down on the office chair, laid the clipboard on the desk and turned her face toward Adam. Her mouth opened, ready to speak, three times before the words actually left her lips. With stern eyes upon him, she said, "Adam, you must listen to what I am going to say and it must be the foundation for every conversation we have from now on, every conclusion we make from now on and every step that is taken to solve this whole mystery. No matter how it may appear at any one moment in time, it will never be true that Chip was in the wrong. He was never dishonest, never disloyal and never did anything that could be considered illegal. His character was the most impeccable that I have ever known. So…as we work our way through all of this—and I'm pretty sure that this is just the beginning—the underlying rule of thumb must be this: Chip is in the clear."

Initially, after such a fine defense of the widow's husband, Adam stayed where he was, resting against the window frame. He did not know Chip. Chip, for all he knew, could have been a fine spouse but a crafty businessman. And, even in the word crafty, if the description fit, Adam calculated that Chip could have been a deplorable crafty person, or he might have been a successful and upstanding crafty person—all without Sarah's knowledge. A line from Hamlet came to mind: *One may smile, and smile, and be a villain.* Yet, there were other things to consider in this saga, here in its beginning stages. One of Adam's strengths was his ability to reason intelligently.

He pulled himself up from where he was perched, walked a few steps to where Sarah sat still peering into his face, and for the first time since he had met Sarah Finfield, reached over and gently touched her arm. As he did, his face, full of assurance, persuaded her that she had made her point; yet, he further satisfied her with a verbal reassurance, using convincing words, spoken in a low voice.

"Sarah." He paused. "You must remember that I have witnessed with my own eyes the deplorable character of the other actors in this movie. In all my days as a carpenter, in all my days as a person, reading and hearing the news, I have not ever seen such wicked and willful destruction." Gently, he squeezed her arm. "It's not hard for me to identify the bad guy and the good guy in this western."

"Well," she replied, rather wistfully, "I just wanted that out of the way."

"It is."

It was.

The two evaluated the rest of the rooms methodically and then faced the large task of doing the same in the lower level. They worked hard. The wrap-up took place in the family room. Adam situated himself on the piano bench and when at last he put his pencil behind his ear, a tentative day-by-day plot was in place. He promised an estimate by Friday. His enthusiasm was showing. "I will get to work," he said.

"And I will get to work," she added without emotion. Sarah sat cross legged on the floor, hovering over her books.

"Let's discuss the Payce thing over lunch," he called from the kitchen, setting his coffee cup in the sink. Then, politely he added, "Is that all right?"

Sarah did not want to have to think about lunch, and so she hadn't; but it was true, they would need to eat lunch.

"You know, I can just run home for lunch," Adam offered, taking note of her lack of response, "if that's better for you. That'd give you some relief from all of this—and from me—for a while."

Sarah saw his smile. She liked that plan better.

"I was only thinking," Adam continued, "it'd be a good time for us to talk about this whole Petetra thing. I have some interesting concepts in my mind and the beginnings of a plan to find out what we need to know. But, it's up to you. Maybe you'd rather just quit a little early and talk about it for a while before I go home tonight."

Sarah turned herself about on the floor where she was sitting cross legged to look toward Adam. She rested her elbow on the cedar chest and her chin on her fist.

"You really have a plan already?" she asked with a fully perplexed expression, not quite able to grasp such a thing.

"The beginnings of a plan."

"You really think that you've heard enough to actually have a starting point? Adam! I haven't the faintest idea where to begin, short of going along with their request to go to the office and dig through Chip's files at work, and hoping to stumble on something."

Adam removed his hat, ran his fingers through his hair, and then replaced the hat.

"You must promise me, here and now," he insisted, "that you will not ever go to the office with them by yourself. If you can't promise that, then I will be your carpenter only."

Such a statement caused Sarah to sit up straight and painted an expression of surprise upon her face. Should she be pleased with his protective attitude or should she be upset with an intrusion into her independence? He had been explicit in his words and as he deposited his work bucket and extension cord on the floor near the fireplace, his bearing concurred. She wished he would enlarge upon his statement, but he did not. The silence that followed was uncomfortable.

"Do you really think they mean me harm?" Sarah finally asked.

He thought through his answer.

"Yes. They will stop at nothing. Look around, Sarah. These guys did not egg your house!" Adam sat down in a recliner and looked down into her face. "Sarah, there is something going on here that has something to do with a lot of money. I haven't figured that out yet, but I know that human beings do not utterly destroy a house like they did yours except for one of three reasons: Revenge, greed, or desperation…and if my guess is right, we're dealing—or you're dealing, depending on your answer—with all three."

He was absolutely right, but why couldn't she agree to his terms? What she wanted to say was, "You cannot tell me what I can or can't do," but a great many things stood in the way. Sarah recognized the truth that she had been blessed with a treasure in the contractor she had picked from the Yellow Pages. Although another voice was whispering that she could always find another, that there were hundreds of carpenters out there, it was not hard to conclude that his interest in her plight was, for some reason, genuine, and his skills, noteworthy. Then why the hesitation on her part? He went on.

"Let me tell you what I think I see. I think I see a woman who was once strong and able to do just about anything, and I think I see a woman who has been devastated by the death of her husband whom she loved passionately and by the horrid details of that death, and I think I see a woman who is vulnerable because of hopelessness, and doesn't realize it."

She sat as still as a statue and did not utter a word.

"I'm still a stranger, Sarah," he said, shaking his head slightly. "You are at the wheel."

His last statement smoothed away the nagging resistance. He had left her with a wisp of self-determination.

"I will not go to the office without someone with me," she said, looking down at her hands. She stood up slowly, stiff from all her morning labors, physical and emotional, and looked directly at him. "And...I will go to lunch. But, Adam, after lunch, I need to call it a day. I've been at it since a little after five. Tomorrow I'll be better."

"You know, that will work for me. I've got that water heater job to finish up and I still have some stuff to get together before I embark on this hefty project. What do you say we do an hour right now on your bathroom and then do lunch?"

"That's good with me. I'm missing my bathroom. Can't use the other baths either. They're worse off than the master bath!"

"Well, I'll get that medicine cabinet out of there and fix the shower doors. We could take care of picking out another one right after lunch, if you want."

Sarah brushed by him and started toward the master bath. She stopped in front of the full length mirror and turned to look at him where he stood, fastening his utility belt around his waist.

"I don't know if you'll ever understand what I'm about to say, but I hope you do. I have to say it."

Why was everything an issue? Why all the hurdles? One thing after another presented itself as a snag. She drew in a long breath, folded her arms and closed her eyes, as if to gather inner strength.

"Adam, I don't want to go shopping." Almost frantically, Sarah spoke her wishes. "I don't want to go out and about. I would like to pick out my medicine chest from a catalog." Her voice and her passion increased. "I would like to replace everything in this house with as close to the same thing as was there before, and I am hoping that you can either provide catalogs so that I can do that or that you will take care of it yourself. You have said you see me as vulnerable and hopeless, and that I don't know that I am. In that you are not correct. My hopelessness makes itself known to me a thousand times a day. I need to tell you the truth about Sarah Finfield. Sarah Finfield is holding together through this whole thing only because she has to. Going to lunch with you in the middle of the day is so out of my realm of comfort that I cannot think of words to convince you of that fact."

Sarah closed her eyes for a long moment, choosing her words and gathering strength. Then, with her eyes fixed on her shoes and her arms folded, she finished her discourse.

"The driving force behind my entering a restaurant in broad

daylight with a carpenter, and anything heroic that I might do in the next weeks, Adam Cook, is that you have whetted my appetite for nabbing these hateful criminals who happen to be indirectly related to me. And the driving force behind my determination to work side by side with you to bring my house back to order is a little group of some of my favorite words like: solitude...peace...tranquility...and SOLD!"

These words she uttered with long silences in between, her voice choked up and tears threatening. "I have spoken more words to you in the last two days than all words spoken to anyone over the last year. I don't want to see people," she said woefully and emphatically, shaking her head very slowly, "and I don't want to walk through a store looking at furniture...or medicine cabinets."

Adam stood politely at attention, his electric drill in one hand, a box of screws in the other, both which he had quickly grabbed from the kitchen counter after the first few sentences, listening to her nearly eloquent paragraph. His heart was filled with sympathy for the broken widow standing at the end of the hall, her arms folded, her long frame slightly slouched. In her plain white blouse and blue jeans, there was an air about her of a teacher in a history book from days gone by. Her long brown hair, as almost always, in a leather barrette, was pulled to the front, long and straight and thick and shiny. Though Adam had no way to tell, he presumed that the very thin, tall pale woman looking back at him, one day not very long before, had not been so frail as she appeared today. He took a step or two and then stopped.

"I'm your handyman, Sarah," he spoke gently. "You are my customer. I do things the way the customer wants them. We'll talk about things but you will always have the last say. I told you a while back that I'm a nice guy. I am." He smiled as he walked toward her. "And you quoted me incorrectly," he said, brushing by her and into the spacious bedroom. "I only said that you are vulnerable and don't know it."

"Why would they break the shower doors if they were looking for documents or a disk?" Sarah asked, craftily changing the subject as she went around the corner into her room.

"Two reasons," Adam said, turning to look at her, "I think they were truly looking everywhere for their treasures but I also believe they were making a statement." His face darkened. "I don't like these guys. These are not nice people."

CHAPTER 9

An awkward lunch it was—at least at the start—even for Adam who was generally cool and collected; but Sarah, so ill at ease in this public place, only ate a few bites of food and talked little. Adam, nevertheless, fully cognizant of the fact that he must chart a course, articulated his ideas, asked many questions and jotted notes in his leather binder. So the planning commenced.

Because the exquisite family room was situated as the first room directly off the foyer, and because Sarah's restored haven would lie within its richly paneled walls, the widow and the carpenter decided the repairs there should be next, now that the master bedroom was greatly improved. It was a massive room, large enough and amply rustic, in fact, to have been the lodge at a northern woods hunt club. It reached from the front of the residence to the back wall of the house, with a 20-foot cathedral ceiling which peaked above a grand stone fireplace, roomy and inviting. Sarah's little sanctuary was snuggled around it and even in the heat of summer, though no fire burned inside, it warmed the soul of anyone fortunate enough to curl up with a book and read beside it or listen to the strains of brilliant classical music. A very impressive dining room was situated at the north end. The piano, resting on a thick and exquisite area rug of the colors of autumn, a roll-top desk and two straight-back brown leather chairs under the windows were the main pieces at the south end.

Adam could do much of the work; some of it would require a craftsman. The broken cedar chest, it was decided, would be lovingly mended and refinished by Sarah—it had been a wedding gift from Chip's father and mother. The piano top, with its long, deep scratches, intentional and nasty, would be sent away for refinishing. Some furniture items could be reupholstered; others, too badly damaged would need to be replaced. To avoid the presence of an unsightly dumpster, all discarded furnishings would be temporarily stashed in the garage; Adam would take it home in stages and burn much of it.

Secondly, the two came to the compelling conclusion that something of value—undoubtedly from a legal standpoint and of substantial worth, to someone—really did exist and was most likely concealed in Sarah's house. Adam Cook, new to the life and plight of Sarah Finfield, pledged his unwavering perseverance.

Though she gradually felt able to convey her thinking, and though a kind of fervency of spirit to bring the Payces to justice was coming to life, and too, though she appreciated the atmosphere of safety that Adam had brought with him, Sarah set up a guard around herself; she mentally maintained a safe distance from the carpenter. The whole endeavor—repairing her home and unraveling the mystery—must be nothing more than a business relationship. Emotionally, she spurned the idea of ever crossing the line into a friendship. Professional it must remain.

By the time the meatloaf special and salads were finished, and the paperwork neatly stacked and placed in the leather folder that Adam seemed to have with him at all times, Sarah's initial nearly lifeless involvement had moved over into more of an equal partner in the discussions on both subjects. Adam, observant as always, noticed it and derived satisfaction—and some humor—from her very valuable input. His common sense had been telling him that he could accomplish neither of these tasks without her contribution. He picked up the check, glad at the small spark of life he was seeing, and wished that she would have eaten more than a very small salad!

Sarah had nearly completed the climb into the silver truck when she heard her name. Someone was calling her. It was a woman. Quickly she pulled the door closed and murmured to Adam, "Please go." But Adam did not move. The voice was louder this time and Sarah, by her voice inflections, begged Adam to step on the gas and to do it quickly.

"Someone is calling your name."

"I know, Adam, and that's why I am asking you to please get going," she whispered unhappily.

"Sarah, that wouldn't be very nice. Whoever it is knows that you heard her."

Sarah scrunched her eyes closed. Now someone was knocking on the side of the truck, still calling her name. From that moment, all was unavoidable. Adam, from his side of the cab, pressed the button to roll down the window on Sarah's side.

"Sarah!" the woman cried with exuberance. "Oh, my goodness! Sarah, it's me, Charlene!"

There was no course to follow but to open the door and step down, though a strong current of resistance flowed in the veins of the widow and she did not move with any speed. When her feet hit the ground, she found herself pulled into a deep and loving embrace. Through the open door, Adam watched as Sarah responded. Her hug was guarded. Her arms did not seem to want to encircle her friend. Nevertheless, Charlene, obviously profoundly moved at encountering Mrs. Finfield, held her close.

"Sarah! I can't believe that we have run into each other out here in the middle of nowhere!" Tears flowed down her face. "Sarah," she cried in a whisper, "I'm so sorry about Chip. I'm so sorry."

Sarah stepped back, her attempt to form a sentence failing. The two looked strangely alike, Adam was thinking, except for their hair—unlike Sarah's dark brown hair, Charlene's hair was the color of wheat.

Poor Sarah! Now Adam was beginning to kick himself for not aiding and abetting in her escape. She was frozen and unable to talk. Charlene took her hands with fervor, her expression indicating that she was putting in place the things she would say next.

"Sarah, you have shut us out!" Adam wondered who *us* was. Charlene looked at the man behind the wheel, not so much puzzled as pleading. "Whoever you are," she was saying by her pained countenance, "help me out here."

Sarah looked down at the gravel, her hands still in the passionate grasp of her friend.

"I have shut everyone out," she replied blandly, her eyes still unable to meet those of Charlene.

"Yes, but Sarah, I am not everyone else."

An awkward moment of silence hung in the air, Adam, with his eyes fixed now on the passing cars, feeling the brunt of it. Then, Sarah's face lifted and she gazed at the woman before her.

"You must know that…that this is very difficult."

"I know. I just wish you would have acknowledged my letter. I hoped that the things I told you would somehow make it easier."

"Char, there is nothing that could make it easier. Your sympathy is appreciated but how does that help the situation between our two families? What could you say that would make it easier? We have not spoken for five years." Hesitating just a moment, Sarah let her eyes meet those of her friend. "I thought that maybe you still didn't know. How did you hear?"

"Very much by accident…and you must know how that hurt."

"That's unfair."

"It's not the time or the place to talk that through."

"Then you shouldn't bring up how much it hurt. You know full well why we are estranged."

"But…Chip…."

Sarah moved away slightly.

"I need to go. And just so you know, I didn't read your letter."

Char looked away, her forehead wrinkled and a heavy sigh coming from deep within.

"Do you still have it?"

"I guess I do. It's out of sight, out of mind, with all the rest."

"Oh, Sarah, you must read it! I have no time to talk. We had a flat tire on the interstate and someone told us this is a good place to eat. We must be in Chicago—downtown—by 4:00."

"Why are you all the way out here, Char?"

"Go home and read the letter. Then you'll know. I am very rushed and need to go."

The encounter was over, it was clear; Sarah turned her body just enough to necessitate the loosening of Char's grip on her hands. Char moved to where she could place her hands on Sarah's flushed cheeks.

"I love you. I think that soon we will be friends again."

There was a nearly imperceptible softening in Sarah's countenance, one that did not miss the eye of the carpenter. He watched keenly as the scene unfolded outside the truck. Slowly, she lifted her hands to place them on Char's. She closed her eyes, stood straight and still for a moment and then, leaned her forehead against Char's.

No more words would pass between the two women—not today, at least. As Adam drove slowly through the gravel parking lot, Char threw her friend a kiss. Adam did not see the gesture of love and kindness, but within the truck, he heard the deep breaths meant to dam a flow of tears.

Although he was not really sure he had done the right thing, Adam did not gush apologies for his course of action. Nevertheless, his heart ripped to shreds a bit more with each heaving breath from the widow. She would be angry, he assumed, when at last words came. She would declare that this is why she had become a recluse. What he did not know was that the *coincidence* of running into Char—whoever she might be—was far more amazing than he could imagine. It would take weeks before he, and even Sarah, would learn that this meeting was in no way, a twist of fate.

Adam's silver truck wound up and around the curving roads; it was void of conversation.

"Who was that?" he delicately asked at last, turning to look at the tense woman beside him.

It was a beautiful day, hot and dry, with a very blue, cloudless sky. On either side, July corn, bordered by Queen Anne's lace, was waving back and forth. Now and then, the truck made its way under a canopy of trees, only to break out once again onto the winding road that separated the fields of long green stalks.

"I took you as far away from Timber Ridge as I could without going to Iowa," he said, looking toward her again. "You know that there is no way I could possibly have known that we would run into someone you know. It was a coincidence—no, I don't believe in coincidences."

Sarah wanted to cry, he could tell, but he knew her well enough now to know that she would not. Her head was against the head rest, her eyes watching the road ahead. Adam ceased speaking.

Another hour passed before the truck pulled into Sarah's driveway. It had been an hour of decision for poor Mrs. Finfield. Could she go on or could she not? It was a simple reflection needing a simple reply—a *yes* or a *no*.

When Adam pulled at the door handle, ready to climb down, wanting to see Mrs. Finfield into her house, and call it a day, he was surprised to feel her hand on his arm, detaining him. Half in and half out, he turned his head to look at her.

"Wait, Adam," she said earnestly. "Can you wait?"

"Yep, I can."

Up he climbed into the truck, closed the door and stuck the key back into the ignition. There was a lengthy silence that filled the cab, one that caused no discomfort to the carpenter, and one most necessary for the widow. Adam turned his head to look at her, and waited.

"Why on earth I feel drawn to talk to you, I don't know," said the widow, slowly shaking her head, her eyes in a fixed stare upon her sandals. "For more than a year...for more than a year...I can count on these ten fingers the conversations I have had with anyone. I don't want to talk to anyone. Yet, something whispers in my ear that you are a friend...or perhaps...an angel. All of a sudden I am in the midst of total disruption and I know way down deep that I can't go it alone." Her eyes became wet with tears.

Adam said nothing, but he shifted his position so that he could look at her more easily. The setting sun cast its warm late afternoon glow upon her profile, highlighting the hint of red in her hair. Adam knew that the hurt taking place in the soul of this woman, this widow, his customer, was profound. He knew, too, the reason why she found it easy to talk to him.

"My heart has no life left in it. What little was left after the initial shock of Chip's death has slowly faded away to zero." The voice inflections gradually changed from listless to more fervent. "I do not care about anything. For two cents, I'd pack up and leave tomorrow just to eliminate the horror of these familiar surroundings. The one thing that kept me going this last year was my privacy and it has been craftily snatched away from me. Yes, I created a little tomb for myself—a crypt where I saw no one, I talked to no one, I turned off my phone and I adored my little safe corner of the world. It was...," Sarah hesitated, searching for a sufficient descriptive word to fill in the blank, "it was my own brand of suicide."

After some moments of indecision, Adam reached across the seat and laid his hand on Sarah's which was resting on the purse next to her. It was not meant to be a temporary act of sympathy; Sarah needed a strong, steady hand. Mrs. Finfield began to talk again, reverting to her quieter manner of speech.

"Then, in burst Annette," she exclaimed quietly. "Where in the world did she come from! She, then, introduces me to trouble...big trouble. Then came you. And then came the break-in. And then, here come the ugly-hearted Payces." Sarah closed her eyes, her head bowed. "And now, out of nowhere comes Char. I wonder if you have any idea of the pain and fear...and helplessness...in my heart today."

"Sarah...."

"Please, Adam, let me finish. How can I argue with the fact that you chose a restaurant more than an hour away and that I ran into Charlene? How can I? I mean, it's so preposterous that it has jarred me from head to toe, and in a very strange way, loosened my tongue." Gently she took her hand out from under Adam's and turned slightly towards him. Her face glistened with fallen tears.

"Char is my sister," she said shrugging her shoulders. "My little sister. She and her husband, Jeff, live in California. We have not spoken to each other for five years. And now, you will ask me why."

"I...I do wonder why."

"Adam, are you an angel?"

Adam chuckled and folded his arms.

"No, ma'am. I'm just a carpenter."

"No, really. I've heard stories about angels just popping into people's lives. I'm serious."

"Nope," Adam replied with a quick shake of his head. "Nope. I really am a carpenter from the Yellow Pages."

"Maybe," she said in a near whisper. "I'm quite certain, at least, that an angel guided my arrow."

Adam was puzzled.

"Never mind that. Let me tell you a long story in a short form. Before Chip started working for Payce, he and Jeff worked for another company. Actually, Chip was Jeff's boss. Jeff started gambling and it affected his work adversely. No amount of exhortation would make him wise up to the danger of losing his very nice job. Chip tried. He finally fired Jeff. Jeff sued Chip and the company. It was a long and ugly legal thing. Jeff did his best to slander Chip wherever and however he could. When all was said and done, Jeff lost; but it cost us and the company thousands of dollars in legal fees."

There was something more, Adam sensed. All was poignantly still. Seconds ticked by as Sarah's expression went through several visible changes. Her head bent low once again, her gaze upon nothing in particular, she spoke again. "It was a horrid experience. We suffered so deeply—together and separately...and I had a miscarriage."

Adam bowed his head. Sympathetic sighs broke the silence as he searched for words.

"That's really tough," he finally said ever so softly and kindly, closing his eyes as if to bear some of her pain. An ache in his own heart set in as the heartbreaking story continued.

"We were completely alienated. They moved to California. Like I said, we have not spoken for more than five years. Chip suffered a great deal from my utter anguish and from the legal battle, though he never wavered in believing that he had done what had to be done. They never tried to contact us and we did not try either. As far as I know, they never knew about our little Liselle Elena. It was a dreadful situation and bitterness toward them became the way of life. Since Chip died, Char has left messages a couple of times that I did not listen to, and yes, I did receive a letter, but I did not read it."

There were no more tears, but the words that flowed from the widow's lips were dipped in bitter sorrow.

"I stood there today, looking into the face of my wonderful sister, unable to think, unable to forget, frozen by grief and separation and shock and bitterness. Who could ever imagine that we would run into each other outside that restaurant out in the middle of nowhere? I could not get past the hurt they had caused Chip...and me. Both of us wrestled with untold grief at the loss of our child. So, today, I could not converse because of hurt that is the same today as it was five years ago coupled now with my grief at losing Chip. This year of seclusion had its effect on my response. I was frozen. I still don't know how to feel about seeing her. Growing up we were best of friends. With my whole heart I wanted to throw my arms around her and with my whole heart I wanted you to do what I asked you to do—drive away. I didn't want to see her...and yet, I did.

"So, now you know. Now you know who Char is and now you know why I wanted to leave quickly. And now you know another part of the sadness of my life. And I am completely talked out probably for another ten years. I'm done. I need to go in, Adam. I can't talk about this anymore tonight—maybe ever." Sarah wrapped her fingers around the door handle. "Thank you for listening when it really isn't in our contract. Thank you, Adam. You don't need to get out. I'm okay."

Adam thought to say, "Sarah, I will be praying for you," but he was stricken with the truth that the only thing that could help her at this moment was for him to pray, right then and there. He did not ask permission. Gently, he laid his hand on her shoulder.

"Father, Your precious Word tells us that You are the God of Peace...that You are the God of Comfort...and that You are the God of Hope. Please show Yourself to be all of these to Sarah Finfield."

Sarah climbed down from the truck. She looked up at Adam ready to close the door. She did not smile, but another *Thank You* glowed in her expression. "Good night, Adam Cook," she said softly.

Though she stepped even a bit sprightly up the stairs to her home, Sarah's spirit within was crawling. With a shudder, she glanced into the disheveled family room and then proceeded to the master bedroom. It was only six o'clock in the afternoon, but moving slowly and effortlessly, still in her clothes, she fell into her bed and pulled the sheet around her. Her body and spirit longed for sleep—*"the innocent sleep, sleep that knits up the raveled sleeve of care,"* as Macbeth had articulated so perfectly, *"the death of each day's life, sore labor's bath, balm of hurt minds, great nature's second course, chief nourisher in life's feast....'"*

"Ah, I long for sleep," she murmured. "I welcome the death of today; bring on the balm of hurt minds." Without another anxious thought, she drifted into the peace of slumber.

CHAPTER 10

On Tuesday morning, precisely at 9:00 a.m., Adam rang the bell. Sarah awoke and squinted at the clock. She was horrified at the thought of Adam finding her still asleep. What should she do? Devising a quick plan, she ran to the front door and hollered, "Would you mind coming around to the back?" Then she sprinted to the back door, unlocked it and dashed to her room. In a flash, her clothes were changed, her hair pulled back neatly and her pale face revived with a splash of cold water; looking very unruffled, she appeared in the doorway of the kitchen.

"Sorry, Adam, but maybe it will be better if you bring all your tools and materials in the back instead of the front. I don't know. Do you think that's a good idea?"

"Is there some way I can drive the truck around back?"

"Yes, there is a double gate on the east side of the house. You can use that and just leave it open while you're working here. How about coffee? Do you want coffee?"

"Sure, if you don't mind. I'm going out to bring the truck around. Be right back."

Off she hustled to finish putting herself together.

Sarah moved about, anticipating Adam's needs as he worked, all the while stricken with the incredulous thought that she had slept fifteen hours—and very unhappy to face the day without a shower. *"I must not let that happen again,"* she fervently resolved.

Adam threw open the drapes covering the rich casement windows at both ends of the family room, quietly stating that he would need the light. It was the first time in fourteen months the room had felt the glow of the outdoors. His manner in doing so—for he moved decisively and whistled a merry tune as he did—seemed to make a statement: It is high time to expel the darkness here! This did not miss Sarah's notice, though she could not for certain pass judgment on his motives. Nevertheless, sunshine flooded into what had been her self-made personal burial place. Today the light served, too, to further illuminate the incredible mutilation that had taken place. Mrs. Finfield looked upon the scene, her jaw set, her face marked with muted anger. Adam went to work.

Starting in on the mess on the floor, Sarah went at it and worked steadily at evaluating the condition of each book, deciding which ones were worth keeping. After a solid hour of handling them one by one, smoothing the pages and covers, sick at heart to see the literature that she and Chip had treasured, plainly ruined, and climbing up and down the ladder, putting them back on the shelves—and out of shape for any kind of manual labor, she was exhausted. The Payce matter, too, wearying her mentally, kept running through her mind, rewinding and playing again, each time stirring up bitter scorn; so also did little recollections of things race through her mind that Chip had said, and incidents which had seemed unimportant at the time.

The lower shelves, those where Chip's records had always been stored alphabetically by artist, were Adam's next project. With the heart of an assistant—as always—Sarah seemed to foresee the needs of the carpenter, stepping up to help where she could, and handing him what he needed even before he had the chance to ask. All morning, with commendable dedication, they did battle with the enormous mess. Adam kept a running list of things to buy, things to remember to do, and things to bring with him the next day.

At almost noon, very close to the time when Adam would leave for lunch, he informed Sarah that he was going to leave a bit early in order to stop at Home Depot to pick up a new bucket and paint brushes.

"I do have a couple of buckets," Sarah told him. "They're in that little room off the kitchen, in one of the cabinets. They're brand new. Is plastic okay?"

"Plastic is what I need."

Adam opened the cabinet door and saw the buckets on the bottom shelf. As he reached for them, he could not help but notice that one of them was overflowing with unopened mail. Most were cards, sympathy cards, he guessed, still sealed, never opened. For a moment he stopped to process such a thing in his mind, staring with wrinkled brow at the countertop; then, stooping once again to pull a bucket from its spot in the cabinet, he returned to the task at hand. In an hour, he left for home. The overflowing bucket of unopened mail told him a great deal more about the condition of his client than anything else he had seen or heard thus far. It told the story of grief greater than what was showing on the outside. Sarah was in deep hurt.

It was time for lunch. As the sound of Adam's truck died away,

Sarah prepared a half of a peanut butter and jelly sandwich and a glass of milk. She ate and continued to work at the same time.

At one, precisely, Adam knocked at the back door.

"Adam, you don't need to knock during these working hours. Just come in."

"Okay, I will. Thanks. Here, I brought the paint for the foyer and the basement stairway walls."

The pile of mail was still bothering Adam, but, no, he decided to say nothing. Instead, he went at the task again, and with the physical strength of an ox, he carried the furniture to the garage, piece by piece. The three-car garage, in which only one car was currently parked, was more than ample to hold the damaged contents of Sarah's house. For a few minutes, he stood looking at the Jaguar sports car parked in the spot farthest from the house, pondering the life of this widow for whom he was now working. Never did she smile. Until last night, there had been very little verbal interaction between them. No form of pleasant, happy talk ever left her lips. The contents of the high-end refrigerator told the story of a woman who, though obviously wealthy, had no desire for food. She rarely ventured out, by her own admission, and also borne out by how ill at ease she had been on both occasions of being with him away from the house.

His face illuminated by the sun shining through one of the skylights, Adam Cook breathed a prayer for this woman, Sarah Finfield, asking God to touch her life with a glimmer of hope.

"You must keep your eyes open, Mrs. Finfield," Adam said, as he packed up for the day. "I truly believe that your coattail relatives believe that whatever it is they are looking for is in this house. Be suspicious about everything. In a strange and curious way, your evil enemies have helped us."

"Helped us? How on earth?"

"Every inch of this 5,000 square foot house is in need of repair; that means we'll get a good look at every inch of it! That should make it easy to spot something out of the ordinary. Tomorrow morning, we'll both take some time to go room by room. And be searching your memory for something Chip may have said, something unusual or that you maybe didn't understand then. By the way...do you have a safe?"

"Yes. A safe was in his design plans, but he installed it long after we moved in."

"I suppose you've checked it out."

"I did."

"Where is that safe?"

Sarah made her way down the long hallway and stopped before the full-length mirror.

"It's odd that the thugs missed this. I'm glad. I like this mirror. Here look. Chip did a masterful job at camouflaging this safe."

Sarah's firm push on the upper right hand corner of the mirror frame activated a latch and the mirror and the whole panel opened slightly. As she opened it further, the safe came into view.

"That's pretty impressive!" Adam said, taking time to examine the setup. "I've never seen anything like this. The shelves for your towels on the other side are just not as deep as they appear to be, I guess. That's completely undetectable! Wow! This is really something. I guess you can understand how things like this intrigue me." He examined it closely, then said, "It is odd that the mirror itself escaped their wrath. They hit almost everything else."

"Even if the mirror is broken, though," Sarah said as she fiddled with the combination and opened the safe door, "Chip told me the security of the safe would not be breached. It would be pretty difficult to discover it."

The safe door swung open.

"See, there is nothing in here that we are looking for…just cash and other financial stuff."

"Well, good. That answers that question for me. It's quite innovative, Sarah. This really tells me a lot about your husband. He was an impressive guy! Really. I'm very impressed. I like things like this."

"There was no end to what he could do."

"Are you sure there's not more of this—another safe—in the house?" Adam said with a light laugh.

"I think not. I'd know, I think."

"Well, listen, I'll be on my way for tonight. Be on your guard, okay? Set the alarm, Sarah! And, use the double locks. I think this thing is far from being over!"

Sarah pressed her fingers against her forehead.

"Thank you, Adam."

"Good. Now, remember the locks…and the alarm." He received a slight look of annoyance in return. "Please."

"I will. I will."

Except for the lack of furnishings, the family room was amazingly improved. The woods floors were still scarred, but sanding them, they decided, would wait until the very end of the renovation. The floors in the entire house would need to be redone. Sarah had carefully returned the record collection, close to 2,000 albums, one LP at a time, to the lower shelves, not taking time to organize them in alphabetical order as Chip had always done. Even the ones that had been stepped on and bent were shoved side by side with the good ones. For now, she was thankful just to have them all back on the shelves. *"What would she ever do with them?"* she wondered. For now, she guessed, it really didn't matter. For now, they would stay right where they were.

Wednesday, with her Rip-Van-Winkle sleep of the night before still painfully fresh in her mind, she determined to work until eight o'clock and to be in bed for the night by nine—with the alarm clock set. The evening hours on Tuesday had been spent setting things in order, making sure that Adam would not be deterred in any way when he set to work in the morning. She swept. She shoved things out of the way. The Norman Rockwell paintings were carried to the lower level. She removed another load of black garbage bags to the deck. It was time to turn off the family room light.

The grand piano sat starkly alone in the middle of the huge empty room. She went to examine the gash that one of the depraved Payces had deliberately inflicted upon the lid, her eyes squinting with displeasure. It would never do for it to remain marred for any longer than necessary. Tomorrow, she would find someone to repair it. She ran her fingers along the keys as she started toward the door, not making any sounds, but remembering the days when Chip would lovingly request that she play for him.

"The music is gone, Chip," she said aloud. "My fingers have no desire to make music. I have died, and my blessed Christmas gift from you has been interred alongside me. I will never play again. Believe me, Chip, it is true."

కావ కావ కావ కావ కావ

The next two days—Thursday and Friday—found Adam and Sarah working feverishly, somewhat side by side, to restore the kitchen to a usable state. The refrigerator doors finally just broke off completely. Adam ordered a new one and it arrived on Friday. The cracked tiles presented a problem. It would not be an easy undertaking to replace them since finding tiles with the same lot number was most likely impossible. He would replace the whole floor, but not until everything else was done and at about the same time as the sanding of the wood floors.

Very little conversation outside of what was needed to accomplish the tasks took place. Occasionally, Adam broke out into short speeches about the cruelty of the Payces and his own personal vow to unravel the whole mystery. Sarah was silent, but within her heart, she, too, was pledging to find them out.

On Friday, the two of them sat down for a cup of coffee together at the wooden kitchen table in the much improved kitchen. They used the time to map out the coming week, noting that new furniture and other items were promised to arrive on Monday and Tuesday.

"I appreciate your work," Sarah stated simply. "You are **very** efficient and **very** skilled. I wouldn't have cared if you had been a novice. I only wanted a semblance of order; but you really are carrying this out remarkably."

"With a little help from my friends," Adam replied with a smile.

"You have been very respectful of my situation and that, too, has been appreciated. You have respected my silence."

"I am your carpenter, not your counselor," he said with another smile.

"Still, I'm sure you have plenty of questions."

"Not really. You must remember that losing my wife is just as fresh in my heart as your loss of Chip."

"I never asked you when she died."

Adam shifted in his chair; with his eyes fixed on his coffee cup, he said, "Melanie died the day before Chip."

This statement resulted in a quick change of expression on Sarah's face as she turned to look at him.

"May 14th? I hardly know what to say."

"Yep."

"The very day before?'

"Yep."

"How long have you known that?"

"Before I ever met you."

"What do you mean?" she asked, her face filled with questions.

"When I got the paper to read the obituary for Melanie, I saw the one for Chip."

This was an amazing coincidence to Sarah. For a few moments, she could not speak. Finally she said, "You seem to be doing well."

Adam shook his head slowly.

"I miss her so much. It's hard. I know what you're going through."

"Maybe it's different for a widow and...maybe it depends on the circumstances," Sarah said, standing up and walking to the sink. "I can only assume that this pain will never go away. My life...my life...there is no life."

The muted reference to Chip ending his own life when she used the word *circumstances* did not escape Adam; he knew that what she was saying was true, that suicide really did alter the definition of death.

"I can't imagine that part of it. That has to be hard for you."

"I don't want to talk about it anymore, okay? Not now. Not ever. I'm glad for you that you are moving on, getting along, going to church, doing your job. I really am. I am."

Was it the right time for Adam to share his faith in Christ, to tell Sarah that Melanie was with the Lord and that he would see her again someday? Something told him that it was not.

"I'm getting along as best as I can, God helping me. I'm glad to be doing this work for you. I feel good about it. It seems like it was meant to be."

"My feelings about God are not good right now."

"Are you angry with Him?"

"Yes...yes, I am. I don't like Him very well at all."

"Is it just Him or do you think there is some anger towards Chip?"

This time Sarah hesitated. Then she replied, "I don't like to think about it."

It was time to close up shop for the week. Adam interpreted the body language and he himself stood, took his cup to the sink and rinsed it out.

"Do you mind if I ask you a question?" he said, standing just a few feet away from her. "It may be personal and if you don't want to answer, don't."

"Asking me if you can ask me a question is in itself a little unsettling," she answered, looking squarely at him. "But...you know me by now. If I don't want to answer, I won't."

"A few days ago, when I went to get the pail from in there, I saw a bucket full of unopened mail."

"That is not a question. That is a statement," she retorted coolly.

Adam smiled politely.

"Okay. Why?"

"I'll answer that question. It's simple. I opened one and wept for four hours. It was the first and last time I cried over Chip's death, except a couple of weeks ago when all of this happened."

Adam looked back at her, reading her mood and her responses well. Sarah was edgy. He could see that plainly. Things to say came to mind, but he cautioned himself against taking on the role of a counselor.

"I am not a crier, Adam. I never was and I despise the thought of it now. I lose my perspective when I cry."

"Crying, though, is good, Sarah. Crying is healthy. Receiving sympathy and love from people who love you and care for you, even if initially it's painful, is healing."

"Well, I answered your question. I guess that's the end of it. Right?"

Her answer, tainted with a slight shade of rudeness, ended the conversation. Her face left no question about what she was thinking: It was time for Adam to go. She was exceedingly grateful that the weekend was before them.

With a sigh, she said, "Monday morning at nine?" With that, and with pursed lips, she opened the door and looked at the floor as Adam departed out onto the back deck.

Adam, in his own grieving heart, resolved to confine future conversation to the restoration of Sarah Finfield's house and the beautiful summer weather.

Sarah was fairly miffed, and she puttered around aimlessly for several minutes, dealing with her irritated spirit. She wished that **she** had gone for the bucket. Why had she stashed it away in such a conspicuous place? Better yet, why had she kept all of it, anyway? She scolded herself soundly. Char's letter came to mind, the one Char had begged her to *go home and read.*

"It's all going in the garbage, even her letter," she decided aloud after ten minutes of wandering here and there in the house. Every bit of it—sympathy card after sympathy card—was a year or more old now anyway. Why stir up grief?. She was past grief. She was on her feet again. It would not do to open any of the mail—not the cards, not the letters.

She yanked the cabinet door open, pulled the bucket from the lower shelf and angrily slammed it down on the kitchen table. Reaching in to grab the whole bunch all at once, the top piece of mail caught her attention. It was not a card. It was the letter she had received from Scott Dolan. Though she continued her determination and move to pick up the entire stack and toss it into the trash can, the thought of correspondence from this old friend—no, he was more than just a friend—checked her simmering exasperation with Adam's inquiry about the bucket of mail. She dropped the batch of mail onto the table and reached for Scott's letter. For several minutes she stood where she was, reading and re-reading the return address. Then, almost as though being moved along like a marionette, she glided into the family room and sat down on the long plaid couch.

Warily, Sarah opened the letter and began to read.

THE RESURRECTION OF SARAH FINFIELD

June 7, 2005.

Dear Sarah,

I have just now heard the news about Chip, just one hour ago, after a whole year. I ran into Bill and Nancy Getty and they told me. I cannot believe that it is true. I am so grieved for you. I have been shedding tears since I heard.

Did you know that Chloe died in February this year? We came home from Mexico hoping that the doctors in the states could help her, but they could not. She suffered so terribly that I was full of joy when she died. She is well now!

I wonder if it would be possible to stop to see you on my way home from dropping the kids to be with their cousins at a camp in Wisconsin. Their two weeks begin on August 7th which would mean I would stop by on August 8th. If I don't hear from you, I won't come. You may be away. There's no way to reach me by phone right now but there's plenty of time for you to send me a note.

Well, I am hoping that you are finding God's comfort to be sufficient in your sorrow. I will be praying for you. You will always be a dear friend. I hope you know that.

Yours truly,

Scottie

P.S. I might just stop by anyway and take a chance. I don't mean to stay at all. Just stop by to say hi.

As Sarah folded the letter, her countenance suddenly changed, and she jumped up and ran to the kitchen to look at the calendar. August 8th was only a week away!

"Next Monday is August 8th!" she half shouted. "I do not want to see Scott!" she firmly told herself. "I do not want to see Scott!" she repeated, her voice rising. "This is all too much! The Payces, Annette, Mother Finfield's death, the break in, Adam, and now Scott! I will not go down this pathway," she softly growled. "I will have my peace and serenity!"

There was nothing Sarah could do about the possibility of a visit by Scott short of telling Adam not to come that Monday and then leaving the premises for somewhere. She couldn't even hide away in the house and refrain from answering the door because her car would be in the drive. Never would she pull it into the garage! She went

111

back and forth with wishing that Adam had never brought up the mail and being grateful that he had. Oh, what should she do? Frustrated, she took Scott's letter, pushed it into the pail with the rest, snatched up the bucket, and angrily shoved it back into the cabinet.

For Sarah, the best place to think these days, now that her little haven had been destroyed, was pushed back in the soft comfy recliner in her bedroom. There she went, mulling over this new dilemma that was now facing her, and allowing herself to sort through things in a manner more like the old Sarah in the Kerrigan days. She concluded that there was nothing to be done today and that the likelihood of Scott appearing at the door at all was slim.

Yes, to fret about it today would be nothing less than anxiety!

An empty evening was ahead of her. She remembered the To-Do List that Adam had scribbled, the one with her name at the top. It was just what she needed. Line by line she went, working steadily, and one by one, she checked off the tasks. Nine o'clock came and went. Quitting was out of the question. She swept and scrubbed, loaded up more garbage bags, and washed every window in the house on the inside. Then she decided to look at Adam's list. "Paint the basement stairwell," was the very first item.

"I will paint!" she indignantly and smugly decided. *"I will drag that big old ladder in here and paint the lower level stairway walls."* Still peeved at the carpenter's step into her personal space, she taunted him in her mind: *"I can paint those walls, Adam Cook…and I will!"* The prospect of tackling a daring task invigorated her. Standing at the top of the stairs, she made her plans. "This," she said aloud, "will be good for me!"

Her watch was indicating that it was past her bedtime—and not just a little! She should go to bed; but, no, the momentum could not be assuaged. The intelligent side of Sarah Finfield told her that the wall to be painted was much too high and the task too precarious; the determined, tenacious side of her, however, though having been idle for such a long time, now sprang to life and assured her that this was something she could do.

"I will put on my grubbies and do this in a flash," she said, turning to run up the stairs.

Using extreme care and very little wisdom, she dragged a ladder from alongside the deck and into the house, banging nearly every wall as she went, and with great physical agony, carried it down the stairs. With each thump, Sarah uttered a groan and then, with a final effort and a final groan, she propped the aluminum ladder on a step and against the high wall ahead of her in the best spot for reaching the highest point. She got everything ready. She would do the cutting in at the ceiling first.

Up she went, moving very slowly, lifting the paint can one rung at a time. Finally, it appeared that she was in a perfect position to start the meticulous painting along the top of the walls, and she went to work. All went well—the painting on both sides of her and most of the section in front of her—but the corner to her left would be a bit of a problem, requiring a good reach even if she adjusted the position of the ladder. Situating herself carefully, she gingerly stretched to the side.

"Ah," she chuckled, "I can reach this."

It was not as though Sarah Finfield had never held a paintbrush in her hands. The finishing of their new house here at 12006 Timber Lane had entailed hours of painting and staining—and a whole lot more. Painting was not her favorite thing to do, but she could recall many long hours on this end of a paintbrush.

Things were going well, and the precarious part of this whole endeavor would have ended well had not the ladder jostled, only slightly, just enough to unsettle the widow.

"Ohhh, good grief!" she cried out as she slid down the ladder, oh, so quickly and smoothly. At last she landed, one of her legs between the very stout railing spindles, the other partially bent between two rungs of the ladder. Nervously she watched as the paint can swayed back and forth overhead. The can did not fall, but the wet brush slipped off the edge and tumbled to the carpet. She could not move. She attempted to break one of the spindles by pressing with great force against it with her leg, but Chip had not used less than the best when he built the house. The sturdy spindles did not budge.

Intensely exasperated, and fully grasping her predicament, she closed her eyes.

"Ohhhhh!" she snarled. "I can't believe this!" She pushed and pulled on the spindle again, but to no avail. "I must get out of this!" she whispered frantically. "I can't stay in this position very long."

Wiggling and squirming, she at last freed the leg on the ladder so that it was no longer bent, but instead, hung over the bottom rung. There was not another move for her to make. Of this she was sure. Sarah Finfield was inextricably stuck, and it was imperative that she get help.

She leaned her forehead against the rung before her, chastising herself sternly for landing in such a jam and not taking time to situate the ladder in a solid and stable position—and for not keeping her cell phone with her.

After a few minutes she breathed a sigh of resignation. How awful to have to call someone at this hour! It had to be after midnight.

"I cannot call someone at this hour!" she grunted. "I just can't."

But Sarah, lodged in two places that held her fast, came to grips with the truth. A telephone call...a call to someone...was her only alternative.

The rec room phone hung on the wall just next to where the railing began. It was her only hope other than staying put until Monday, an option to which Sarah had given honest thought. Carefully, feeling a twinge of pain in her left leg as it hung down through the wooden slats, she twisted around as far as she could and felt for the phone. She could not reach it—or, perhaps she was reaching too high. On the second try, her hand found first the cord and then the phone, and she moved the receiver to her right hand. With her left hand and with a shudder, and fumbling around to hit the right buttons, she dialed the only number that was even a consideration.

CHAPTER 11

Overhead, the sound of the ceiling fan did its best to lull Annette to sleep. A day at the dunes had done her in. Now, exhausted from a day of swimming and beach volleyball and suffering from sunburn—a slight one everywhere but on her bright red shoulders—she lay in her swimming suit upon her satin sheets, recalling the day's events. She had entered the house without a word and gone directly to her room. Her father was at home. His Mercedes was in the garage. Annette was not up for dialogue, especially if Father found a subject on which to launch an intellectual dissertation. Without question, Mr. Cappetti was an intelligent man, his speeches often making a great deal of sense. Annette tolerated the regular discourses of her father, partly because of a true love for him, but also as a result of the guilt he could inflict upon her if she showed any signs of disinterest. Mrs. Cappetti, hardly ever understanding the full sense of his Ph.D. language, always busied herself with some necessary facet of housekeeping. For the most part, the Cappetti household was not one of warm conversation and interested interchange. The three Cappettis still living under the same roof—Frank, Sophie and Annette—did not fight, simply because Mrs. Cappetti rarely had anything to say—and Annette was hardly ever home. Her two siblings, significantly older, had left the house and moved away.

Today as the moving air caused her somewhat baked body to shiver, she smiled with the remembrances of *an awesome day*, starting with a sunrise breakfast on the dunes. Life was fine for Annette. Now a high-school graduate, she felt no urge or need to locate employment. Her parents had money and since the subject had never arisen, it seemed that it was not expected. Annette realized in her heart that her father would settle for nothing less than a husband for her who could and would provide well for his baby girl. Tony was meeting all of the requirements: a car, wealth, looks, and a patient, listening ear for Mr. Cappetti…and Annette.

For an hour or more, Annette mused upon the pleasures of life,

115

concentrating her thoughts on the daily adventures. She had worried that graduating from high school would most certainly result in increasing boredom. The days as a senior had been unsurpassable where frolic was concerned. For her last year of school, twenty-four-year-old Tony had embellished her life with his 1958 Corvette. Now that he was part owner of his father's very exclusive clothing store, he had written a check for a new Porsche and Annette was ecstatic.

Mr. Cappetti had made it clear from junior high days that no daughter of his would have a car until she was twenty-one. She could drive one of the family cars but a personal vehicle was out. It was old fashioned to think that way, Annette argued. Her father simply and flatly told her that if Tony could not take her where she wanted to go, then he would. As owner of Cappetti Foreign Auto Sales—and of a highly opinionated personality—Frank Cappetti was free to do as he pleased.

The life of never needing, never waiting, always having, had yielded a spoiled young lady, yet not obnoxious. In their wealth, the Cappettis had not failed to impart a sense of love and belonging to their brunette princess. Laughter and joy resided with Annette. Enjoyment of life characterized this little rich girl, but her crowning attribute was how she wished the same for those around her.

"Annette!" Her father's voice sounded from the bottom of the stairs. "Do you want to snack with us?"

Annette looked at her clock. It was eleven fifteen. With a groan, she climbed out of bed and pulled one of Tony's long sleeved shirts over her swimming suit. Wearily, she trotted down the stairs. It was Friday night. Her parents would be having their regular late night goodies at the patio table.

"And how was your day?" her father asked as she sat down. "Oh, ho! I guess I need not ask! You're moving, what shall I say... gingerly? If the rest of you is as red as your cheeks and nose, I can understand why you're wearing that big shirt."

"Oh, I am sore, but mostly just my shoulders. They burn. But it was worth it. I haven't had such a day for...in my whole life!"

"Was it just you and Tony?" Mother asked, placing Annette's food before her.

"Six couples! What a blast! And no bickerers! Not one interpersonal squabble all day. Melissa and Davy weren't there, that's why."

"Where did you go?"

"The dunes. In Indiana."

"How does Tony do with the Red Flash?"

"Daddy, he hates when you call it that. It cheapens it, you know what I mean? Please don't say that when he comes tomorrow."

"A minute at a time, that's what I always say. Can't tell what I'll be saying in an hour, let alone tomorrow night! Well, how's he liking his new toy?"

"He loves it. I love it! We were moving 100 miles per hour today and it seemed like sixty."

Mrs. Cappetti shook her head and closed her eyes.

"That's too fast. If you're going to go that fast, I don't want to hear about it," she said.

"I agree," Mr. Cappetti added, his eyes and attention mostly upon the food before him.

"He's careful. He's an excellent driver! You know that. I'm not one bit scared when he goes that fast. It's a great car. Everyone just hung around it for a long time at the restaurant at lunch."

"Well, it's not a good thing to drive that fast. I can see it now because the car is new, but he should do it without you in the car. You tell him…no, I'll tell him…to keep his head on straight when you're in the car."

"You won't. You better not!"

"Why do you stand out in the sun so long?" Mrs. Cappetti said, masterfully changing the subject for her own sake.

Annette looked kindly at her mother who hardly ever ventured into a conversation with her and her father unless it was absolutely necessary.

"Are you worried about me, Mom?"

"You have beautiful skin. It's olive and deep without the rays of the sun. Someday you will look like a farm woman from the old country!"

"I didn't mean to get burned. In fact, I made up my mind to watch that I didn't. We just were having so much fun. We played volleyball until we all just dropped. And you know what else? Finally, somebody taught me how to throw a Frisbee! Ryan took the time to show me how to use my wrist, like this. I got to be pretty good by night. Oh, the night was so beautiful. I love the smell of the lake. I really, really love that smell! We lounged around on the blankets and watched the sunset in the west; then we watched the moon come up over the lake. I tell you, the moon is very big when it first comes up. I look at it and I think, 'What keeps it out there? What keeps that great big ball hanging out there in the same place?' Something about the moon affects me."

"There's something to that, you know." Annette looked down at her plate. Her father was going to expound. "Down through the ages, the moon has been suspected of affecting the moods of people. Actually, there are some who say that it affects people to the point of being responsible for their behavior. I'm not talking about sentimentalism here. I'm talking about actual, physiological changes in a person and their behavior."

"Like becoming a werewolf?" Annette smiled at her father.

"You think I'm kidding. Well, you talk to anyone in the hospitals, in the schools, everywhere. On a bizarre day, when they've had one weird incident after another, one weirdo at the counter after another, they'll always look at each other and say, 'Is there a full moon tonight?' It's true."

"That's not what I'm talking about though, Daddy. Oh, never mind. I can't explain it anyway. Tony thought I'd flipped out when I tried to explain it to him."

"It's not the *God* thing again, is it? Not the mashed potato cloud thing again?" Mr. Cappetti still did not lift his eyes as he spoke.

"Noooo, it's not that. I just look at the moon, I just look at it and...here, come here. You two, come right over here and look up there. See it? It's so tiny now compared to before, but look at it...it just hangs there. Gosh, I wish I could lean back. My muscles are getting sore just holding me up. I think I'll go to bed. It's not too bad when I lie on my stomach."

"You must take care of you, Annette," her mother pleaded.

"You must take care of your mind, Annette. The moon is a piece of rock, whirling through space much like the earth. Songwriters and authors have made it romantic. Theologians have dressed it up with spiritual meaning. If God indeed is responsible for the moon being out there, then indeed He has done better with the universe than with man. Make sure you use your head like I've taught you to do. Just take a look at the mess humans are in and it's clear that a god doesn't have anything to do with people."

"I know. But why does it all stay where it belongs? Why after all these millions of years does it revolve perfectly?"

Frank Cappetti looked up, his expression one of great knowledge...looking perhaps like one of Job's friends.

"You know, God could not have created man, man being the evil creature that he is; yet, look how time has perfected the human body. Everything is so intricate and structurally impeccable. Chance is not an arbitrary thing. Chance is beautiful and symmetrical and planned."

The moon was high in the sky, full and white, casting its shimmer upon the dark earth. Annette's olive skin glowed in its light as she leaned against the window, her head lifted to the heavens.

"You're smart, Daddy. You always make everything make sense …I think."

"You've got the same good sense. You just have a little of the Domenico side of the family that surfaces now and then."

He smiled, touched his wife's nose and walked to where Annette stood.

"You're okay. Eighteen is a hard year. I remember, believe it or not."

"What were you doing when you were eighteen, Daddy?"

"I was running away from home."

"He was running from the police!" Mrs. Cappetti said, divulging a secret to her daughter.

Both parents laughed.

"And asking your lovely mother to marry me! See what I mean? Eighteen is a hard year!"

"I'll be nineteen in two months. I wonder if Tony will ask me to marry him. I could marry him. I like him enough. Why were you running from the police? Why have I never heard that story before?"

"You'd better go to bed. You're getting nosey and you're beginning to sound sentimental."

With a kiss to her mother's forehead and one to her father's cheek, Annette left for her bedroom, promising to embark tomorrow on a life of taking better care of herself. After a few steps down the hall, she returned.

"Why don't you want me to go to college, Daddy?"

"Annette, you're forgetting something. You are the one that told me you don't want to go to college."

"I know, but you have always made it clear that you wanted me to marry and settle down. You never, ever talked about me and college."

"I know you, Annette. You're relieved to be out of school. You'd be there a year and want to come home and get married. I look at your mother and see such a fine wife. You will be a fine wife. It is a good thing to be married."

"Sometimes I really want to go to school. Sometimes. Maybe it's best to wait a year or so. And maybe you're right about me. I **would** like to be married."

Then she was gone. At the sound of her door closing, Mr. Cappetti got up and began to walk the length of the patio. Outside, there was a perfect night, the sky clear, the temperature mild and crisp.

"I worry about her. Joey and Tina never talked like she does. She loves everybody, loves everything, loves life! She's got the world by the tail and now out of nowhere, she starts dropping hints about college. And now all of a sudden, she's dropping those little mentions about God again." He shook his head. "I hope she'll be all right. I think she will be. She does seem to have her head on pretty straight."

"Maybe she remembers the old days when we went to church."

"She was only three or four."

"She remembers the priest."

"Then why not Joey and Tina?"

"They were gone by the time we started to church."

"Started. Only started. I doubt if a four-year-old can remember anything from a sour four-month association with the church!"

Mrs. Cappetti cleared the dishes as her husband, now sitting at the table and leaning forward, resting his elbows on his knees, talked freely about an ill-fated relationship with the church in their last city.

Upstairs, drenched with an Aloe Vera ointment and settled upon her bed, Annette took her cell phone and dialed Tony.

"Hi," she whispered.

"You're brave tonight. Your parents in bed?"

"No, they're downstairs. Friday night snack."

"It's past midnight."

"I know."

"I'm glad you called, girl."

"I had to."

"I'm just sitting here thinking about you. I meant what I said when I dropped you off."

Annette drew in a deep breath. She closed her eyes dreamily.

"I know, Tony. I was speechless."

"You just weren't expecting those three little words from someone like me," Tony responded with a laugh.

"I miss you."

"Annette, you're crazy. We just saw each other two hours ago! We spent the whole day together!"

"I know, but I don't like saying goodbye."

"You're such a little girl."

"Well, you're such an old man."

"I'm going to marry me a little girl to keep me young the rest of my life."

Like a shot, Annette sat up, grimacing with pain. Her eyes were opened wide. Marry? Had he said marry? A beep sounded in her phone. Someone was calling her. Who would call her at this hour?

"Tony, someone is calling me," she whispered hoarsely "I've got someone on call waiting. It's twenty past twelve!"

"Don't answer it. It's a wrong number. No one would be calling you at this hour."

"There's always the possibility that it could be something." The beep sounded again. "I'd better see who it is. Just hang on."

She pressed the button.

"Hello?"

"Oh, Annette," came a voice in an uneasy whisper, "I'm so glad that it's you. Are your parents nearby?"

"Mrs. Finfield?" Annette asked very slowly.

"Yes, Annette, it's me."

"Something's wrong, right?" A bewildering silence came as the reply. Annette did not wait. "Mrs. Finfield! What is it?"

In those few seconds, Annette concluded that a significantly traumatic event must have occurred for Mrs. Finfield to call her and to call at this hour of the night.

"What is wrong?"

There was another hesitation. Sarah was regretting her call.

"I should not have called you, Annette."

"What is going on? You would have never called me if it weren't something terrible. Are you all right?"

"I should not have called you. I'm sorry, Annette."

"Mrs. Finfield, I'm still up. I'm on the phone with Tony. Wait a minute. Let me get off with him."

For Tony, Annette's whispered "I've got to get off" sufficed and he willingly said goodbye, assuming that an angry father was outside the door. Annette took a deep breath and pushed the button to connect to Sarah.

"I'm back. What has happened?" The lack of an immediate answer resulted in a frantic Annette. "Mrs. Finfield! What is wrong?" she inquired, whispering loudly.

"Annette, this is so crazy. I was on a ladder and I slipped and well, I'm stuck." A nervous chuckle accompanied the word *stuck*. How hard it was for her to admit such a thing! She could not, however, bring herself to say, "I need help," though there was a prodding to do so somewhere deep within her character. "I'm inextricably stuck."

"I'm coming down there. I'm coming **right** now."

Mrs. Finfield, at first, did not answer. The old Sarah, sure and confident, was fighting with the new one, the grieving widow, the frazzled victim of recent crimes against her. She kept asking herself why she would pick up the phone and dial this girl that had pretty much done nothing but irritate her. In her heart she knew why. It would never do to call Adam! Personal pride and irritation kept her from dialing his number. He had crossed a line and had stuck his nose in her personal business! Anyway, there was something about Annette that told the story of a truly caring person and she was not five minutes away.

Even while fumbling around in her pretzel-like position for the right numbers to push, she had hoped that Annette would respond just as she had, though in her twenty-eight-year-old heart she realized that it was probably unreasonable for her to expect such a thing. But Annette had shot back in the affirmative. Sarah should protest. Annette should not be out in the dead of night. How would she explain such a thing to her parents? Were they up? Would they know?

"Annette, I can call someone else. I should not have called you. I can call 911."

"Give me five minutes."

"I have no right to ask you to come."

"You haven't asked me. I offered. I'm just glad you felt comfortable enough to call me."

"I...I," Sarah whispered.

"Sit tight. I'm coming."

Marveling at the brightness of the night, Annette sprinted across the field behind her home and out on to the gravel road. Freedom and benevolence flowed through her veins as she flew toward the gray ranch up Timber Lane. Her parents were in bed and if this escapade lasted into morning, their Saturday stay-in-bed-till-noon habit would give her all the time she needed. Nimble and agile, the spirited girl's feet made hardly a sound upon the dirt and gravel as she ran. The whole world glistened with the moon's brilliance. From its ordered place in the vast sky, it cast its beams upon the earth, lighting the darkness almost as though it were day. *"You could have a lovely picnic on a night like this,"* Annette thought.

For a moment she came to a halt and scanned the night sky. Moonbeams spread across her pensive face. Inside, her heart became strangely moved. What was keeping the big old moon in place? "It's a ball hanging in space," she whispered. "God, if you're out there, let me know, okay?" Something begged her to stay, to sit along the road for a moment, to not hurry on. Annette rejected the pleading and started her run again. Excitement and apprehension spurred her on. As she rounded the woods that bordered the Finfield house, Annette took note that every room was aglow. "That's a first," she said softly. "The *dark house* is bright tonight!"

She tried the front door. It was locked. She tried the garage service door to no avail. Around the back she ran, opening the gate, not taking time to close it again, and up the deck stairs. The back door was open. Annette was familiar with the house just enough to know right where to find Mrs. Finfield. Off she flew until she reached the door at the top of the stairs and flung it open.

"Yikes!" she spurted. "I knew you would not have called unless something pretty horrid happened. What were you doing up there! I'm surprised you remembered my number and well, I'm surprised you called me. I'm sure I have been a bit pesky, like a pesky fly. But I just try to be thoughtful and kind."

"Annette, there are tools in the shed on the back wall. The shed key is in the first kitchen drawer. Bring a hammer and I guess, bring a saw. There's not much room to work, but maybe the two of us can break one of these spindles."

Annette scurried away and returned with the requested tools and a few others.

"Do you leave the waterfall on all the time?"

"No, it should be off. The switch is next to the phone on the wall in that…. Oh, never mind that now! I'll get to it when I get out of here! Come down. Hand me the hammer. Wait! First can you get up the ladder and get the paint can? It's precarious."

"I'm sunburned," Annette said, carefully starting up the ladder and stepping around Sarah, "not terribly, but enough to make life rather uncomfortable."

"I'm sorry."

"Don't be. It was foolish on my part."

"So was this, Annette. So was this."

At twelve thirty five, the top of the spindle cracked after much pounding. With a long groan, Sarah pulled herself to a standing position, wondering if the Dickersons could have heard the noise. She was relieved the pain in her knee was minimal, though it was red and already slightly swollen. She looked at the young girl who had shown great enthusiasm at helping to free her, and was now sitting close to the top of the stairs. She put her hands on her hips and sighed.

"Thank you, Annette. I'm glad you made a big deal out of your phone number that day. Thank you."

"Oh, it was nothing. I love helping other people! I really do! You have green paint on your nose! Anyway, what's happening around here? I see the Adam Cook truck here all the time."

"Will you help me take this ladder outside?" Sarah asked, rubbing at the spot on her nose. "Then, I'll show you what we've done."

"Wow, Mrs. Finfield! You are being so nice to me. I've always sort of wondered if underneath it all, you were probably a really friendly person. I guess death can mess a lady up, more than I can imagine."

The two walked through the house carrying the long ladder out the back door—without a single bump to the wall—and onto the deck. A strange pleasure came upon Sarah as she pondered the unlikely friendship with this young, vivacious teen. Annette turned her face to the black sky, squinting at the stars and the silver moon, and then looked at Sarah.

"Mrs. Finfield, don't you sometimes just believe in God when you see something like that?"

Sarah folded her arms and looked down at the deck.

"It truly is a beautiful sight. Come, Annette, I'll give you a tour of the house."

The young girl went through the door being held open for her. Sarah lifted her face to the sky for just a moment. Then, she entered the house, locking the door behind her.

Deep in her soul, Mrs. Finfield knew that Annette would no longer be a bother.

CHAPTER 12

Monday, August 1st arrived, hot and muggy, a carryover from a night of sultry weather. Sarah heard the gate open and Adam's truck pull into the back yard at 8:45. The agitation over his gentle rebuke regarding her unopened mail was not the main thought occupying her mind today; no, today the story of the painting calamity would need to be told. Hobbling just a bit from her injured knee, now wrapped in an Ace bandage—mostly as a precautionary measure— she unlocked the back door and started a pot of coffee.

"Good morning," Adam said cheerfully as he walked through the door. "A hot one, eh?"

"It's 85 already. It's a good thing we're working in the AC."

"Your family room furniture, Sarah, should arrive tomorrow, I'm told. That's good."

"Tomorrow? That's pretty quick, isn't it?"

"Yep. I've got some connections. We'll see if they keep their word. How's the new frig working out?"

"Oh, I'm glad you talked me into the French-door model, though for just one person, it's far too big! For resale purposes, you are right."

"Hey, are you limping?"

Sarah sat down and rested her arms on the table.

"Coffee will be ready in five minutes…and yes, I'm limping."

Adam took note of the fact that his client seemed a little warmer than their acquaintance had evidenced thus far. Sarah was conversing in almost friendly tones. He smiled inside.

"What'd you do?"

"Well, it's a long story…another one. Sit down for a moment and let me tell you about it before you get started. Speaking of start- ing, what are we working on today?"

"Well, I'll be done in here today, except for this tile floor, of course. And I'd like to spend a little prep time in that fifth bedroom that you use as an office and fix those sliding doors and then start on the other three bedrooms. I'm assuming you want me to take care of new mattresses and anything else that needs replacing. The office is going to need a couple of days. Boy, you know, I took a longer look at that on Friday. They really did a number on that room."

"I guess if they're looking for something to do with Chip's job at Payce, they figure the office would be the most likely place to find such a thing...any papers, I guess...which is what I am assuming is their prize."

Adam shook his head, his lips drawn together in great disgust.

"I want to get those guys. I just wonder what they're up to now. You haven't heard anything from them for a couple of weeks. If they were desperate enough to trash this place like they did, doesn't it make you wonder why all is so still now?"

"It **is** such a puzzle. Perhaps they found what they wanted."

"That's a possibility, I suppose."

Sarah waited until Adam was comfortably seated across from her, coffee cup in hand before she started in. As she talked, a grin slowly spread across Adam's face.

"You're getting pleasure from my mishap, Mr. Cook."

"No, Mrs. Finfield...pleasure hearing you tell it."

"There's more."

"Fortunately, you were not hurt badly enough that you could not get up."

"Well...not really. That's the rest of the story."

The rest of the story brought on some gustier laughs from the carpenter. It was not easy to fathom Sarah calling annoying Annette in the middle of the night!

"There was a strange little bonding thing that went on between us, Adam. I'm still shaking my head about that. Anyway, the week-end was eventful and long. I'm glad I didn't get hurt worse than I did. I should never have taken that on at that hour of the night. I don't know what got into me. Well, I do, but it doesn't matter." A moment of stark silence followed this statement. Sarah fidgeted. "Well, yes, I guess it does. I need to apologize to you, Adam."

"For what?"

"On Friday, I was rude to you."

Adam questioned her with his puzzled expression.

"The bucket? The mail? I was curt and cold. I'm sorry."

"Hey, it's okay. I'm sorry for overstepping boundaries."

"I took it that way. I shouldn't have. I'm sorry."

"Apology accepted."

So began the new week. Adam, quite aware that he worked best from a list, prepared a project schedule, printed it, and taped it to a kitchen cabinet. Methodically, he tackled similar tasks throughout the house rather than sticking to a room-by-room approach. The perpetrators had created a horrible mess and Adam's efforts—temporarily—only worsened it. Sarah took on the task of cleaning up after him, sweeping and vacuuming, and carrying heavy items—far too heavy for her—to the garage. The dialogue between them was minimal. Sarah did her best to keep up with Adam who forged ahead with the plan, hardly ever stopping to rest. Plaguing him was bitter anger flowing through his veins, outright ire, a result of dealing with the malicious attack on Sarah and her home; frustrating him was the brick wall they found themselves facing as it had to do with the mystery surrounding the case. Adam stewed silently.

Sarah was pensive and agitated as well. Diligently she stayed at the task, sometimes working alone, sometimes assisting her carpenter. Truly they were seeing the fruit of their labor; that gave them satisfaction and motivated them to keep at it.

The pleasure and satisfaction, however, that Sarah Finfield experienced during each day faded as darkness rolled in each night. Still mostly in disarray, the house offered no friendly spot to spend the evenings. So, the evenings were spent in the best of the rooms—her bedroom. Now instead of curling up in the coziness of the plaid couch and loveseat and the soft leather chairs in the family room, she slowly became accustomed to reading in her grand master bedroom by the light of the tall nightstand lamp beside her bed and pushed back in the comfy recliner.

Once a house of joy and safety, and then, for the past year, a place of retreat and withdrawal, now the sprawling ranch home was just a dwelling-place, one tainted with danger and fear. When the lights were turned out and Sarah at last ended her day by climbing into bed, there were minutes of lying very still, hearing unfamiliar sounds, and yearning for days gone by, days with no thought of peril, days with her husband by her side. Fear had been far away when Chip was alive; in fact, until he died and until she learned what it meant to *live alone*, Sarah had been impervious to it. Now, sometimes fright came at the sound of the water softener clicking on or at the rattle of a screen. And then, chastising herself for succumbing to such worry, she would pull up into a little ball beneath the covers and talk herself into going to sleep. Nevertheless, often was the night when dread was her bedfellow. Never again would she be able to enjoy this house as a shelter, a safe retreat, a haven; plans to put it on the market began to take on flesh.

At the end of the week, Adam stayed away on Saturday and Sunday. Strangely, it resulted in a mix of relief and discontentment for Sarah, but talking herself into being strong, she spent those days organizing that which the Payces had undone in cabinets, drawers and closets. Saturday night, she left for Shelton after turning on the lights in nearly every room and setting the alarm. Not until finally deciding it was time to retire for the night did she turn them off. It had been a long, emotionally grueling week. Slumber would smooth it all away...for a night.

❧ ❧ ❧ ❧ ❧

Monday morning, the 8th of August—a gray day—arrived at last...and so did Adam. Promptly at nine, his truck pulled into the back yard, and within minutes, he was ready to work. In his head were the outcomes of his nearly constant deliberating and his own personal *sleuthing* throughout the weekend, conclusions and deductions that had come to him as he struggled to make sense of the mystery of Payce Publishing vs. Sarah Finfield. Sarah had little to offer; she was baffled and had no answers.

But Adam was in the mood to crack the case. As long as Sarah would listen, he would talk. He thought out loud for an hour, talking slowly, not stopping. Why such violence? Was the anger toward Sarah, or perhaps, was it still against Chip? What could have happened at this point in time, a year after Chip's death, that would be so important? It must be something critical. They were missing something, something that perhaps was right under their noses. Adam's gut feeling was that along with greed, the Payces, for some reason, were running scared.

"Now, Sarah, there's something important for you to know. Now bear with me on this. I think this is really important, just in case. I know I made you promise not to go to the office alone with them, but you and I both know that these guys could take you there against your will—by force. I totally believe that." Smoothing out a folded drawing, he went on. "Here's the scoop. I've gone over there a couple of times...."

"Over where!" she interrupted.

"Over near Payce headquarters. Several nights now I've parked in the lot of that freight company, you know, the next building around the curve—and have just kind of cased the joint."

"What?"

"I just sat over there and watched."

128

"But why, Adam? Why?"

"Just trying to get the lay of the land, so to speak."

"But why?"

"Okay, just think for a minute. What if they took you there and you discerned—and this isn't too farfetched in my mind—that they meant you harm. What if you had a chance to escape? I know, I know. This is preposterous, but one night in the middle of the night, I visualized you running for your life. That's what made me start going over there and taking some notes."

"I don't like to think about this. Besides, I've been there a hundred times and know how to get out of the building."

"At night?"

"I left there often with Chip at night."

"How, though?"

"He had his card. And besides, I can't picture them snatching me in the dead of night."

"Think Sarah, how did Chip get out of the building?"

"He had his.... Oh." Sarah got it. She yielded. "Okay. I'll listen."

"Good. Listen, when I see the damage done to your lovely home and I consider what might have happened had you walked through the door in the middle of the act, I am persuaded that they would have hurt you. Do you understand that, Sarah? They would have stopped at nothing if you were in their way. These men are not only angry and greedy—they're nuts! Just let me tell you a couple of things. Maybe someday we'll both be glad."

Fifteen minutes into his discourse on the subject of hasty flight from the Payce Publishing building, day or night, Adam set down his mug with a thud.

"Well, that's it...for what it's worth. I've watched them come and go, I know who comes early, who stays late, and just how they go in and out of that building. Maybe in the long run, you'll never need it; but just in case, keep it stored up in your head...especially the part of getting out of there at night. And one more thing: You should have your phone with you or nearby all the time—and...charged. Now I'm through. What do you say we get going?"

Sarah cleared the table and rinsed the dishes. From the sink, she good-naturedly said, "I do thank you, Adam, It's not everyone who has their own personal Yellow Pages angel."

He laughed and slapped his knee. "Okay, let's get going, eh? Let's work till three. Then, we'll start doing some *sleuthing*. The ideas that are rolling around in my brain are telling me that we need to put together a timeline showing what was going on around the time of the fire…everybody's movements, as much as possible. I'm sort of in the dark on that."

The day was spent installing the medicine chests and righting other bathroom damage, Sarah by Adam's side, doing what an assistant does. When her part was done, she stepped aside and leaned against the bathroom door, the palm of her hand against her forehead. Adam saw her in the mirror as she closed her eyes.

"How you doin'?" he asked.

Her answer would be a lengthy one, spoken without hurry.

"I know me." Taking long breaths in between sentences, she spoke her mind. "I know that I can go way up or way down right now. I have good moments and bad ones. We have such a long way to go. So much is happening and none of it is trivial…and all of this has crashed in on Sarah Finfield, the recluse. I admit it. Part of me, Adam, wants to tell you to go away, that my house is far enough along for me to live here now; yet, the confusion and anger I am experiencing makes me want to be sure that you keep coming back, that you stick by me until we bring the Payces down, and that you'll ignore me and my wavering, and finish the house. I hardly know you, Adam, and yet this, what is happening, is earth shattering, and far too much for me to handle! When you talk of the possibility of having to run for my life, I'm pretty sure that I don't want to pursue this any further. Yet, part of me is on fire with vengeance.

"I really don't know you and yet I think I need you. In a way, I do know you. I believe you when you say you are clever and careful and really good at solving problems, but…well, there are moments when all I want to do is hide away in my room. I'm a paradox, Adam," Sarah admitted faintly. "I'm exceptionally strong and exceedingly weak. You may come to wish you had not been so devoted to this whole mission."

Not expecting such a spewing of words, spoken seemingly without forethought, yet spoken quickly as though she was an actress in a play, Adam sucked in a deep breath. Using caution, he lightly placed his hand on her shoulder and just as cautiously, chose his timing and his words of reply. With his other hand on his hip, he replied with a reassuring smile, "Mrs. Finfield, I…am on board."

A tired widow, weary of body, soul and spirit, looked back at him, her countenance showing signs of that fatigue and weariness. She would tell Adam to go home for today so that she could lie down and rest. She would tell him, though, to be sure to come back tomorrow at nine, like always. She'd be better tomorrow. She would tell him that she was sure that she could not go on at all if he did not help her to bring the Payces to their knees.

Her words were on her lips, not yet uttered, when the doorbell rang. She was startled and her eyes grew wide.

"Annette?" Adam asked.

"Likely."

"Do you want me to go?"

"I'll go. I just need to take a few deep breaths."

"Sarah, wait," Adam said, taking her gently by the arm. "you'll never make it through this if you don't eat and if you don't sleep."

She folded her arms and sighed, deciding how to handle his obvious concerns. "I'll eat after you go, tonight. I'll go to bed early."

She slid past him and went down the long hall and turned toward the foyer. There was no way to know who stood outside the door.

As she opened the heavy wooden door, the humid summer air blew in first. Then, a figure appeared, one that Sarah recognized immediately though many years had created a chasm between them.

Scott Dolan put out his hand for a handshake, but in a moment, their meeting had turned into a warm embrace. What made him hold on to that embrace for what seemed like long minutes had to do, most likely, with grief and sympathy. There was no romance in the hug even though the two had been pledged to marry years before. Sarah, in shock, only now bringing up the recollection of Scott's letter, could hardly form a thought. She stood face to face with an unexpected visit from a man who was once her fiancé—unexpected because the reading of the letter a week before on Friday had completely left her consciousness.

With great gusto, he bestowed joyful greetings upon his long lost friend. With mock composure, Sarah responded. A thousand thoughts came at once. She could not invite him in; there was no furniture, her home was still in a terrible condition, there was no guest room available, and even if there was, Scott could certainly not stay with her! The kitchen was a mess with sawdust and tools everywhere, and Adam, the carpenter was just around the corner. Her life was caught up in mystery and intrigue, and here, standing before her was Scott, surely expecting to at least be invited in. Sarah was exasperated and trying desperately to mask that fact.

It was Adam who saved the day—kind, perceptive Adam—appearing around the corner and quickly and tactfully taking charge.

"A visitor, eh?" He sighed. "Well, there goes my helper! I don't suppose you could help me just a minute more?" he asked, with a drill in one hand and a piece of trim in the other. He set down the wood and extended his hand to Scott.

"Hi, I'm Adam, the carpenter."

"And I'm Scott, an old friend of Sarah's from college."

"We're just finishing up with a medicine chest and I need her just a minute or two more. Why don't I take a couple of kitchen chairs into the family room, Sarah? The kitchen is still in process," he hollered to Scott from the kitchen, "if you know what I mean. And the family room furniture comes tomorrow. Finally!" He laughed as he went for the chairs.

Sarah retreated to her room, profoundly grateful for a moment to settle down. Adam found her plopped down in her recliner, her head leaned back and her eyes closed.

"Take some deep breaths," Adam said lightly, chuckling as he handed her a glass of water. "Did you expect him?"

"Sort of. Thanks to you." Now it was Adam's turn to be in the dark. "A letter in the pail," she said with a tempered scowl.

"Oh. But what? You forgot?"

"Yes. I read it but…."

"You read it but it slipped your mind?"

She nodded.

"You gonna be okay?"

She arose from the chair, and then exited the room. A slight smile was on her face as she walked by him. Adam felt good about that.

Sarah and Scott visited in the nearly empty great room, sitting in the chairs that Adam had retrieved from the kitchen. Adam put himself to work in the office.

"You got my letter, right?" Scott asked.

"Yesss…yes, I did. You did say you might stop by on a chance I'd be here."

"Is this awkward?"

"No."

"I'm really sorry about Chip. Really, Sarah. He was so young."

Hoping that perhaps Scott had not heard all the details, and hoping that by not responding, the subject would change, Sarah only uttered a quiet "thank you." There was a short silence. The subject changed. Sarah was grateful.

"You're working on your house, huh?"

"Yes, we're doing an extensive remodeling job on it. Adam is my carpenter."

"Yes, he said that. Hey, is it awkward seeing me again?"

"In a way, yes, though I can honestly say you have long disappeared from my daily thoughts."

"Sarah, I've wished so often, especially at the beginning, that I could tell you I'm sorry." Tall, lanky Scott, looking older than Sarah thought he would, and somewhat weathered from exposure to the sun, reached over and put his hand on hers. "I'm sorry."

Politely, Sarah withdrew her hand. For a moment, she could not speak. No, it wasn't that she could not think of words to say, but rather that she felt paralyzed. Life was happening so fast and her spirit, heavy laden and drooping, could no longer keep up. Her silence was making Scott noticeably uncomfortable.

"Sarah, I just...just wanted to greet you, to see you, to touch base. That's why I came, although it is true that I have felt strongly that you deserve an apology."

When no response came, Scott repeated his apology.

"I am...really very sorry."

With a slightly uplifted chin, and starting unhurriedly, she retrieved strength from somewhere and dully told him a story.

"You left me, as the saying goes, standing at the altar...almost literally. I was an hour away from leaving for the church. An hour away from being Mrs. Dolan." Sarah's voice was low and somber. "Everything joyful turned to ashes...the dress, the ring, the letters, the flowers. It turned into a day of mourning with Char and Brenda and Carole hardly knowing what to say...you, my strong tower, gone; your parents and your brothers, whom I had grown to love—having no parents and hardly any family of my own—snatched from my life. What I remember the most is crying in my car and saying, 'Oh, my goodness! What do I do now?' That first month...I was devastated."

Bravely, Scott did not look away.

"Then, after a month of, well, grieving, I wrapped up everything—as you know—ring and all, and sent it all back to you. Then I worked hard to get on with my life and figure out how to deal with the demoralizing pain of rejection. Six months later, I met Chip—wise and encouraging Chip." There was a slight lilt in her voice as she spoke those words. She lifted her head just a bit and went on. "Though he had no degree in counseling, he walked through it with me and convinced me that I was a woman of great worth, and in the process, fell in love with me. Six months after we met, we were married right here in Timber Ridge. That's the long and the short of the story of Sarah Yost."

He said it again. "I'm sorry. I got cold feet. I guess that's what they call it. We were young."

"You were twenty-two. You were old enough."

"Okay, then, I was immature." Scott rested his elbows on his knees, clasped his hands, and rested his chin on them. He stared at the floor. "You were only twenty. A young twenty. I hurt you and I'm sorry."

Sarah kept silence.

"Hey," Scott said suddenly, looking up at Sarah. "Isn't today your birthday? It's the 8th today. Yes, it's your birthday. Yes! It's your birthday! Happy birthday, Sarah!"

Her birthday was not something that she wanted broadcasted. With her next words, she put the subject to rest.

"Thank you, but returning to the previous subject, you were immature, Scott. But then again, I was too."

"You were committed to me. I know that."

"Scottie, I would have gone to the ends of the earth with you—which I guess turns out to be Mexico." Sarah grimaced inwardly at her unintended use of her pet name for him at college. No one, no one else, called him Scottie. It did not go unnoticed by her visitor.

"I know. Yet, Sarah, looking at the whole picture, can you not see God's hand and guiding through all of it?"

Sarah glowered. She did not want to talk about God. Besides, God could not be held to blame for such a cowardly act! She bit her lower lip and did not reply. At that moment, any words from her lips would not have been pleasant.

"We don't have to talk about it any further. I desired to tell you that I am sorry for my disrespectful and self-centered actions, which, by the way, have been replaced with a better spirit...with the fruit of the Spirit, I guess you'd say. Now I've said it. Let's talk about something else."

Adam had heard a good deal of the conversation thus far, even though the office was at the end of the long hall in this spacious home. To be truthful, he really did not want to hear anymore. He continued his tasks with deliberate noise—considerably more than before—noisily pulling items out into the hall, shoving office furniture around so that he could repair door jambs and window sills. He had obtained the answer to the crucial question, "Just who is Scott?"

As he pulled on the tall bookcase in the corner, it began to rock a bit. It cantilevered, and within a few short moments, books started tumbling down. Adam fell to his knees and shielded his head with his arms. Books bounced off his arms and back and landed with a clatter on the hardwood floor. The clamor brought a hearty yell all the way from the family room.

"Is everything all right in there?"

"Yep," he replied loudly.

"Do you need me?"

"Nope."

Adam picked up the books and piled them on the corner desk. A Bible had fallen, too, open and face down. The contents that had been tucked in the front cover scattered here and there. He scooped up the blue Bible, laid it on the desk. *Sarah Liselle Finfield*, the gold letters on the front read.

"Nice name," he said softly, slowly and emphatically. "Very nice name. Nice Bible. Dusty Bible."

It was as he gathered up the little pieces of paper to replace them inside the front cover, that Adam saw a short note, written on a torn off piece of paper in a bold handwriting.

> *Sarah,*
> *This is the key: The Eye of the Eagle. If you remember that,*
> *the rest will be easy. Memorize this sequence. 369152748.*

That was all it said except for a "2" in the upper right-hand corner and Chip's name at the bottom and a date—May 14th. Adam winced as he realized that it was the very day Melanie had died. How strange all of this was turning out to be!

Understandably, Adam was bewildered. Had Sarah ever seen this note or...was it possible instead that the dusty Bible had never left the top shelf for a whole year? What was the story here? A dozen questions swirled through the carpenter's mind. Could it be that Sarah, perhaps, was a Christian? He opened the Bible with its dark blue soft leather cover and looked inside.

> *August 20, 1997*
>
> *My darling Sarah~ Our first anniversary! I bless you*
> *for the most wonderful year of my life! I live each day in*
> *wonder and pure joy! How can it be that we are so perfect*
> *for each other? God is the best matchmaker ever! I pray*
> *every day that God will bless you and use you and draw*
> *you closer to Him.*
>
> *Such a helper you are! I'd rather have you working by my*
> *side than anybody I have ever known. Your spirit is like that*
> *gentle breeze that blew across the deck last night after the*

blistering heat of the day. I will always remember sitting in the deck chairs with you, looking at the moon, loving each other and loving our great God!

You know that I will always love you.

Love in Christ,
Chip

Adam closed the Bible and closed his eyes simultaneously, attempting to process the reality of what he had just read. Very slowly, he sat down on the office chair. *"Sarah Finfield is a Christian?"*

Adam looked out the window, amazed, his lips slowly breaking into a smile of realization.

"Sarah Finfield is a Christian!" he exclaimed in a whisper. Could it be? Yes, evidently it could be! In fact, yes, it was true.

"Sarah Finfield is a Christian, but angry at God and miserable," he concluded. As he tried to piece the whole thing together, in the distance he could hear Scott saying something about wondering if Sarah would ever consider the missionfield—off to Mexico—and he made note of the silence that followed.

"Well, well," Adam declared, "you just never know what might happen when you get hit in the head with a Bible!"

Now Scott was talking about Chloe's home-going and Chip's death. Adam could not say that Scott, with his somewhat booming voice, was being distasteful or out of line; actually, he sounded like a nice guy. But it was enough. Adam did not want to hear anymore. He began to work vigorously, making more noise than even before, and at the first possible opportunity, after the desk was out in the hallway, he shut the door, working with diligence, without interruption, in the quiet room; but it was not without a great deal more pondering.

So...Chip and Sarah were both Christians, most probably for a good long time, judging from the wording in Chip's inscription. And Chip and Sarah were crazy in love with each other. This truth cast a slightly different light on the plight of the widow for whom he was working. What nasty business to find that your lover had ended his own life!—and to be the one who came upon the scene first. Was it any wonder that Sarah had withdrawn? Losing Melanie had been painful but there had been time to talk and pray before she passed away. For Sarah, one moment had been bliss; the next was grisly.

Adam decided to say nothing. He felt a twinge of guilt—only a twinge—for having read the message from Chip. Stopping to look out the front window, he viewed the sky, now peppered with patches of light gray, the remains of an earlier shower, floating eastward. The sun, though he could not see it from where he was standing, was off to the west, creating long silver rays high above the world.

"Almighty God, my Father," he fervently prayed, "sometimes I just don't know what to do. This is one of those times. I have to leave this whole thing, all of it, with You. I do ask You to revive the heart of this weary widow. It turns out, evidently, that she is Your child...so she is in the best hands. And Father, just one more thing: This Payce mystery...will You help us with it?"

A flock of geese flew across the tranquil scene outside the office window of the Finfield house. Adam, the carpenter, smiled. He wished he could paint.

At three o'clock, the hour that he and Sarah had designated to get down to serious business on the missing sought-after treasure, Adam opened the door, ready to leave for home, if need be. He wondered if he should take Chip's note with the number sequence and give it to Sarah or put it back in the Bible. He wished he could show it to her, but absent mindedly, he slid it into his leather binder. If Scott was still there and they were still talking, he needed to exit quickly—just sneak out the back. Purposely making some noise as he walked the hallway, he came to the foyer where it appeared Scott was about to leave. Just as Adam walked by, Scott put his arms around Sarah in a somewhat surprising embrace. Adam could not see how she responded. He was walking out the back door.

The Timber Ridge carpenter hardly ever felt uncomfortable. He was the kind of guy that people described as able to *go with the flow*. He adapted easily. Out at the truck, he undid his carpenter's belt, straightened things up in the back, jerked the tailgate into place, kicked his tire and climbed up into the cab.

"Now why did I kick that tire?" he asked himself. "It's not like me."

He started the engine and heard Sarah's voice at the same time.

"Where are you going?" she hollered. He turned off the key and turned to look in her direction. "It's three o'clock! Time for *sleuthing*, remember?"

With an almost imperceptible chuckle, Adam climbed down and walked slowly to the deck, his eyes on her face. It was her *always* face, except that Adam noted a tiny trace of kindness in the tilt of her head.

"I thought I'd knock off early, if you don't mind. I've been working on some things that just may help us."

"You mean, like plans? Or do you mean, like gadgets?"

"Plans **and** gadgets," he said. Adam watched as Sarah leaned against the deck railing. Her eyes went toward the woods and then to the sky above them. He found himself unable to describe his thoughts—internally, of course—about her beauty. He shielded his eyes from the sun and looked into her face. Her profile was truly very beautiful. *"She's just a really nice looking kid,"* he concluded.

"I guess that's fine," she said, now turned to look down where he was standing. "Honestly, though, I was looking forward to, well, *sleuthing*, as you call it." It was in Sarah's mind—and the words almost spoken—to ask the fleeing Adam if he was leaving because he felt uncomfortable; but she let it go. "Go on, then, but it's like Holmes without Watson or Lois without Clark!"

This brought a hearty laugh from the carpenter, but still, he turned toward his truck. She watched as he climbed up into the seat, shut the door, and put the window down. The sun was still hot and the air muggy.

"I'll be here in the morning. Nine o'clock sharp."

Adam started the engine and still Sarah did not move from where she stood leaning against the deck rail, her arms folded. The carpenter drove in a big circle and stopped directly below her.

"Sarah Liselle Finfield, I have something to show you!" he said in a taunting tone. "Tomorrow," he called out above the engine's roar, and with that he slowly headed out of the yard.

Sarah, who had already made a slight move toward the door, stopped in her tracks and spun around on the spot. She processed his words quickly and without effort. He had been working in the office. The books had fallen. She had heard them. Her Bible was on the top shelf.

"Nice name, Sarah," he called, looking back at her.

"Never mind my name, Adam Cook!" she shouted. "What do you have to show me?"

Adam made his getaway, but he left behind a whimsical expression of disgust on the face of the lovely widow.

It was Monday, the 8th of August.

CHAPTER 13

Where River Road intersected Pittman Road, partly hidden by a grove of oak trees and honey locusts, there was a picturesque two-story farmhouse, one that evidenced the talent and skill of a fine carpenter. The house, though it appeared small, was not. Adam Cook had added a sizable family room to the back, blending the layout into the kitchen and creating what his son, Daniel, had called *wide open spaces*. It was where the family had spent most of their time. Home...was the family room.

Lilac bushes lined the immediate back yard mostly obscuring the fine pond beyond them; beside the pond stood a weeping willow, graceful and tall, nearly always swaying in the breeze, its long, swooping branches now and then brushing the top of water. And there was the unkempt garden, untouched for two summers now, parts of it bordered by chicken wire to keep the rabbits from the radishes. Beyond the yard and a good ways away at the south end of the Cook's ten acres was a picturesque fence, up a sloping meadow. There, a small gate gave entrance to the Nielsen's acreage.

Stillness had replaced the happy life of recent years here on River Road. Daniel had gone first. Off to the Marines he went, barely giving his mother and father two weeks of warning. Strong of spirit and body, he chose to serve his country rather than take on more schooling. Even though he was a B+ student, he did not like school; graduation day was a day of personal exhilaration and bright hope for something new and exciting. When he turned eighteen, he casually asked his dad what he thought of joining the Marines; two weeks later, Melanie and Adam drove him to O'Hare Airport.

Then, almost a year later—eleven months, to be exact—Melanie died after a short battle with cancer. Alone became the way things were for Adam.

Though he had often found refuge in his workshop behind the garage, working long hours on projects—personal and for clients— the real Adam Cook had most definitely preferred the company of his family. He and his son were close friends. He and his wife had been friends and lovers. Now the nights were long and very quiet.

Most of the time, he made it just fine, trying to keep up with the dishes and the garbage and the rest of housekeeping, while steady carpentry work kept him on the run. Routinely, he set aside the first Monday night of the month to pay all the bills. A scribbled calendar above the computer desk reminded him when the big ones came due, like property taxes and insurance payments. Saturday evenings were reserved for cleaning house—at least that was the plan.

It was just about five o'clock on Monday, August 8th. The hot and humid air when talking with Sarah in her yard had helped him decide, as he parked his truck next to Melanie's Jeep in the large garage, to turn on the air conditioning in the house tonight. Most of the time, he preferred the open windows and fresh air.

Just like every other night, he took care of the regular chores in the garage and in his truck. The overhead garage door shut slowly with an eerie groan at the end as he made his way toward the back door. It was life as usual: Dinner, a ham and cheese sandwich tonight; daily Bible reading, some about King Hezekiah in Isaiah and some from Romans; phone calls to clients; lots of dishes in the sink. One look at the overflowing trash can and several white plastic garbage bags sitting next to the door told him it was time to deal with them. "Hmm," he said, "tomorrow."

By seven o'clock, the sun was slowly making its descent, without taking with it the temperatures in the mid-90s. Adam sat in his recliner, watching the departing ball of fire slowly paint the sky with a stunning sunset. "I'm glad I stuck with the first set of drawings," he said. "I love all these windows!" The cool air coming from the vent above soothed his tired body.

The room, like all the others, was in mild disarray. Melanie had been the one to keep the house spotless, to pick up after him—she always said that she loved serving him—but now, what did housework matter? *It's pretty bad this time,* he thought. With a sigh, he resolved to get at it on the weekend. Not tonight.

In his lap lay his leather folder and laptop. It was a night for working on *The Case.* His demeanor told the tale of a man who would soon be doing what he loved to do, solving a mystery—in particular, solving the dreadful and mysterious invasion of Mrs. Finfield's home! Something was telling him that it was time to get serious about it. Something was telling him that the bad guys would show up again soon. Tonight he was dedicated to the task. He'd do some work on paper and then go do some inventing in the shop!

He opened the folder. Chip's note was the first thing he saw. He groaned. He had most certainly not planned to bring it home! After a verbal chastising about not keeping his head on straight, he stuffed it in one of the folder pockets, and yanked on the yellow legal pad. The sound of a car on the gravel went unheard as he delved into the timeline; but, a moment later, he heard steps on the front porch.

With the sound of the bell, he was up. People stopped by now and then. His closest buddies from church often came by just to chat, though not so much now as right after Melanie's death. He had known them his whole life. They had been his lifeline.

When Adam undid the lock and pulled open the door, there was no possible way to mask his surprise.

"Well, Mrs. Finfield! You could knock me over with a feather!"

Embarrassed, she smiled.

"Do come in!" he exclaimed.

She swallowed hard, thinking of a hundred reasons why this had been a bad idea.

"I was in the neighborhood and...."

Adam laughed.

"No, I really was."

"And why was that?"

Sarah stood perfectly still and straight, any nervousness being hidden where it could not possibly be detected. It was one of those traits you keep in your *back pocket*, so to speak, that stick with you through life. When it took her a while to answer, Adam again invited her in.

"N...no, really, I only stopped by for a moment." She hesitated. "Did you know that Chip's parents lived not even five minutes from here?"

"Really? Which direction?"

Sarah squinted in the sun, which would soon disappear, and pointed to the northwest. "Do you know where Crimson Creek is?"

"Yep."

"Where it crosses Simpson Bell Road?"

"Yes, I know exactly where that is."

"There is a tiny brick house on the east side of the road. That was...well, still is...their house."

"No kidding. We used to fish very near there. Why'd you head up that way?"

In his mind, Adam was fully astonished that Sarah had ventured out anywhere. He could hardly believe it, but it would not do to say so. With her chin lifted slightly, she allowed her eyes to pan the area around Adam's house. A muted smile of approval was on her face. He waited, using the time to enjoy her beauty. Her long brown hair lay in front of her left shoulder, her cheeks slightly flushed. She had changed into white slacks and a summer tee of moss green—the color of her eyes—and on her head was a white casual summer hat.

"Well, Adam, you'll be proud of me. I went through some of my mail and pulled out anything official looking."

He laughed again, such a kind and cheerful laugh.

"Yes, and lo, and behold, a notice from the Chippewa County powers-that-be saying that if the property taxes on that house were not paid, it would be confiscated—or something like that. I had to go see what was going on."

"Hey, you sure you don't want to come in, just for a minute?" he asked, recalling the lack of housekeeping and half hoping she'd say "no."

"No. I really do want to get back. You know how I just love being out and about. To be honest, Adam, I came this close to asking you to do this for me. But...it's just not in a carpenter's job description," she said, finally turning her face toward him.

"I would have done it. You know that. What'd you find out about the house?"

"There was a notice stapled to the door. I'll call the number tomorrow." Sarah's body language was saying that she was about to leave. "I like this place, Adam. It's...it's like...well, it's like home." In Adam's mind, no nicer compliment could have come from her lips. He had worked hard to make it be just that.

She started down the stairs, Adam following behind, and when she got into her car, she rolled down the window. He put his hands above the door and leaned against the car.

"You really should come in. Have some lemonade or something. Did you eat? We could go get something?"

"I ate."

"Okay. Well, I guess I'll see you early tomorrow. Hey," he said with a cheerful laugh, "I'm glad you stopped by. That was nice."

Now Sarah turned her face toward him, again shielding her eyes from the setting sun. He moved to where his body would block it. She wanted to say something. She was vacillating.

"You don't know this about me," she said at last, struggling with shyness unlike her, "but one of my strongest motivations (as borne out in the many personality tests I have taken) is curiosity. Challenge always comes first; then curiosity—a good trait, I've been told, for someone working with computers." Now she looked at her hands in her lap. "I need to come clean, Adam," she said.

With a wrinkled brow, Adam leaned in a bit to listen.

"You did absolutely the worst thing you could possibly do to a person whose tested motivation—second place—is curiosity. When you used my full name and said you had something to show me, I knew then and there I'd have to figure a way to find out tonight!"

Adam stood up, his laughter carrying with it a bit of pleasure and a dash of amazement. He slapped his thigh and said, "Why, Mrs. Finfield! Did you make up the story of the old brick house on Simpson Bell Road?"

"Now, Adam."

"Come clean, Sarah!"

Sarah shoved the official looking paper into his hand. "Here. Look. This is the paper that was tacked to the door. I just thought I'd kill two birds with one stone. Truly though, I just couldn't get it out of my mind!"

"You want to come in?"

"Can't you just tell me what you have to show me? I'm tired and you should be, too."

"Well, you'll have to wait. I'll run in and get it."

"Well, okay. I'll come in, but just for a minute."

"*Uh, oh,*" he whispered to himself.

Once inside, Adam pointed her to the family room, kicking himself sternly for the messy house. He did not miss her slow scan of the room as she sat down on the couch.

"I was not expecting visitors," he said, duly embarrassed.

"I'm surprised. You are the personification of neatness when you work."

"You've seen the inside of my truck, however."

"It wasn't that bad."

Adam rubbed his eyes with his fingertips and then ran them through his thick blond hair, and when he opened his eyes and looked across at the unexpected Sarah, she was smiling. What was this...the third time he had seen her smile? Kindly, she spoke.

"No one knows better than I that not much matters when your spouse dies. Either you become fastidious or you become indifferent. I understand. Your house is nice, Adam. The setting is very nice. You really are out in the country."

"It's good for a carpentry business. You didn't see what lies beyond the garage! I could never get away with that in town."

"Melanie?" she asked, gazing at the 8x10 black and white photo hanging in a silver frame behind Adam.

"It is."

"Hmm, how beautiful! And, I take it that's Daniel," she said pointing to a picture on the wall near the front door.

"Yep."

"I suppose you miss him...and her."

"I do."

"When will you see Daniel next?"

"Actually, he called yesterday to tell me he'll be here in two weeks. I've been figuring out the details and what I would need to tell you. I—we—should be done by that time, but if not, we'll be close enough for me to take some time with him. He wants to go fishing. There's a place near the Mississippi we always go...the Cook clan...camping, cooking out, you know."

"Why, of course. We're really in a good spot now. I did a walk through after you exited the premises today—and left me hanging, I might add." Again she smiled. Adam decided against an explanation. "We really are in good shape."

"We are, and...oh, I meant to tell you that when Daniel is here—that second week—we will re-do your deck. That's an awesome deck and it breaks my heart seeing it suffering like it is. I just want to do it. No charge."

"That would be nice."

"Good. Glad you like the idea."

"But not without pay."

"We'll see."

"Yes, we'll see."

"We're in pretty good shape now, if that family room furniture would ever come!"

"Please don't worry about it. What's a few more days?"

"Well, in these next few days, let's change the ratio a little and do a little more *sleuthing* for a while and a little less re-vamping. We really do have to somehow make some progress. It's frustrating that we haven't run across a single clue in that whole great big house. Not a single clue. We're as much in the dark now as on the first day. The Payces will be comin' around again, I feel sure. Hey, can I offer you a Coke or lemonade or water?"

"No, really, I'm fine."

"Did you eat? Oh, I asked you that already."

"Adam! What do you have to show me? I drove twenty one miles to find out. And yes, I ate."

Adam pulled the handle on the recliner and sat up.

"It's a funny thing. If things had gone like I thought they had, you would have come here for nothing. The reality is that what I found, I intended to leave at your house, but instead, I absentmindedly stuck it in here. Here."

He got up, walked to where Sarah, still feeling awkward, was sitting at the front edge of the couch. He handed the note to her. Then he sat beside her.

"What is this?" she asked, not grasping the significance of it, "and what does it mean?"

Now he got up and settled into his recliner once again.

"It was in your Bible. It fell out when your Bible, along with all the other books, hit me in the head!"

"You made a lot of noise. It was quite interesting sitting there in the family room trying to visualize the scene." A slight smile arose in Sarah's eyes.

"Technically, Mrs. Finfield, it was the books that made a lot of noise," Adam clarified, returning her smile.

"Well, that's true. Anyway, about this note...do you think Chip deliberately put this in the Bible, Adam?"

"Don't you?"

Sarah's face bore signs of confusion. "What do you think it means?"

"I have not the slightest. I figured you'd know. I don't have the slightest idea why he says to memorize those numbers...that sequence...but you'll have to be sure to do it. I have a feeling it's going to pop up somewhere."

"I already have."

"Ah, Sarah! Amazing woman! If I had to choose someone to be my fellow private eye, I would choose you! You are very bright and you are the key here. You knew him well. Do you not recognize the note?"

"I've never seen this note. It's dated May 14th. That's the day before...he... died."

"Why would he put a note like this one in your Bible? Was he purposely hiding it?"

"Why would he write the note at all? It almost sounds like he...."

"I don't know. It just doesn't add up. I can't make myself believe that your husband was setting all this up way ahead because he knew... well...because he knew that he would take his life."

"You know, Adam," she said, staring down at Chip's handwritten note, "the Payces are capable of great evil. Questions are beginning to swirl in my head. He wrote this in a hurry. I can see that this is his handwriting, but it's not his regular handwriting."

"I wonder if he feared for his life. Why would he write—actually, scribble—such a note? This seems to say that he was expecting trouble. If you had found this note a year ago, what do you think you would have done?"

"I would have been baffled like I am now. This must have something to do with something that I'm supposed to figure out," she said. "Hmm, 'the eye of the eagle'. It sounds like the name of a book, though, doesn't it?"

"I wonder," Adam thought out loud, "could it be…the name of Herman Lichten's second book perhaps?"

"Could be."

"I don't get it at all. It really does seem that your husband might have suspected trouble. Is it possible, I mean, what do you think? Do you think that he feared for his life? Maybe, just maybe, he knew something that they didn't want him to know, and it was damning enough for possible retaliation."

"That popped into my head more than once in the last few days. I think I can safely say that he was sure they set the fire."

"I never asked you this…although it has crossed my mind…but is everyone sure…I mean, are you sure that he ended his own life?"

"Autopsy: Carbon monoxide poisoning, no signs of struggle."

"Hmmm. I have lots of questions and an equal amount of suspicions. From what you have told me about Chip, and everything that has been happening, I am really wondering about it all." Adam stared out the window, silent and thinking. "But the note you found the day he died. Where is that note?"

"I have no idea. Who gets to keep such a thing? Except for the note, though, tiny misgivings have been creeping into my head, too; I put them out of my mind; I cannot process the alternative."

Letting it go for the time being, Adam brought the discussion back to the note in Sarah's hand, and knowing exactly what he was doing, he put the question to her again.

"Why would he put that note in your Bible?"

An answer could have come right away, but instead, Mrs. Finfield, still not completely at ease with barging into Adam's quiet life, chose to put together thoughts and words in her mind rather than articulate them. Why was today seeming different? Was it the reunion with Scott, hearing him talk of how the Lord had carried him through the awful death of his wife, listening to him share the stories of bringing the gospel to the villages near his, being reminded that once she had been like him? Or could it be the presence of another person in her house—a nice guy—day after day, making it necessary to talk, to interact, to decide…to fix coffee for another human being? Was it the totally unexpected encounter with Char? She thought about Annette and her questions about God and how inwardly guilt stricken she had felt for not touching her life for good. Which one was it? Or had it all been a craftily laid out plan by Almighty God?

Yet, Sarah was not ready to verbalize her story, to sit in this living room with her carpenter and own up to being a Christian. Even now, the talk of Chip's death stirred within her that resident desire to hurry home, to shut herself in her house. Yet, it was true: Everything was a little different than three months before. Though she could not really put her finger on it, the ache did not seem quite so severe.

She sighed. Yes, she knew well why Chip would put an important note in her Bible, but tonight, the answer would be, "I really am not sure."

The arrangement of furniture in Adam's family room put him and Sarah facing each other and she could feel his gaze upon her as she stared at the western coasters on the coffee table. *Cheyenne, Wyoming* they read.

"I take it you've been to Cheyenne?"

"I have. Often. It's a favorite spot. Great fishing."

"And you love fishing, I take it." Hesitating and sighing several times, Sarah attempted an answer to Adam's question. "Well, Adam, to answer your question, I'm really not sure," she said pensively. "I'm not even sure why he wrote it in the first place. Why would he write such a thing one day, and the next, take his own life? It makes no sense. I am in the dark."

Somewhere in another room, the ticking of a grandfather clock could be heard in the silence, and off in the distance, out in the oppressive summer air, Sarah heard a train going somewhere. She loved trains. Wouldn't it be just so cool to go away, to take a train, away, away, away somewhere? It was time to go, she could tell. She gathered up her purse and stood.

"Time to go. I have no answers. Maybe when we get things all mapped out on a timeline, it will start to make sense. This note,"— and she handed it back to Adam—"makes no sense to me. I'm going to have to put my thinking cap on."

She went to the door.

"Wait a minute, Sarah. Wait here," Adam said as he hurried into the kitchen, leaving Sarah at the door, anxious to head for home. The many photos on the wall captured her attention. What a handsome family! Melanie truly was strikingly beautiful; and who was the little blond girl in this picture with Daniel?

She heard Adam's footsteps and turned. There he was, smiling, walking toward her with a chocolate cupcake with white icing, complete with a burning green candle.

"Happy birthday, Sarah."

Such a smile on her face! Her eyes sparkled with a touch of tears as she took the little birthday treat. "You were listening."

"Yes and no," Adam said. "But mostly no. What is it, Sarah? Twenty-eight?"

"Twenty-nine. Yes, it's twenty-nine. I can't quite grasp such a thing," she said lightheartedly. "So, Adam, aren't you going to sing?"

This question brought on a laugh.

"No, not this time."

"Then I shall take my birthday cake and go home...home where I will put my thinking cap on once again and try to figure this note thing out."

"Wait. You have to make a wish and blow out your candle."

"I'll blow out the candle but I'll have to think of a wish later. You know me."

"Not acceptable. Wishes don't work that way!" he informed her.

"Then, hmmm." Sarah stared at the floor. "Okay, I think I thought of a safe one."

"Safe?" Adam softly bellowed. "Who ever heard of making a safe wish!"

"It doesn't say anywhere that it has to be a fairy tale wish, now does it? And, actually, it doesn't say it has to be personal."

"Okay. It's your loss, you know," the carpenter jested.

Sarah blew out the candle and said, "It's time to go, Adam," and then, she walked out the door. He followed.

Adam always walked everyone to their car, chatting and joking as he went. Tonight he followed Sarah to her blue BMW, but he was silent and pensive. He closed her door. She started the engine and rolled down the window. Adam was still somewhat astonished with the fact that Sarah had ventured out at all, let alone stopping by his house. It was a big step—no, a huge step! He leaned his arms against the car above her window, resting his forehead upon them.

Sarah sighed and said, "You know, I really did have to take care of that Chippewa County matter...but, I really did want to stop by. Little did you know how inquisitive I am!"

"I know now," he stated with some enthusiasm, "and you know, it might come in handy some day!"

"Boggles my mind, that note. Knowing Chip, this was all meticulously orchestrated. Something was going on. But do I know what was going on in his head? No."

The evening was filled with the sights and sounds of a hot, muggy summer evening. Crickets started up and a chorus of frogs sang from the pond and the marshy area on the other side of the fence. Against the metallic blue sky that shows up right before dark, fireflies by the hundreds flitted here and there. Adam did not budge. Sarah really could not leave with him propped against her door.

"Who would have ever dreamed that you'd be faced with such a thing," Adam said with heartfelt sympathy. "I wish you could just let it go, but I'm thinking that it's not over."

"No, I know it's not over. Those Payce boys are downright mean." Sarah glanced in the rearview mirror and adjusted her hat. "And lest I give the wrong impression, they are only the pawns of their father. They're all incredibly arrogant and malicious, but he is vicious. Someday I'll tell you some stories of how they treated Mildred. If I didn't know better, I'd be suspicious that they did her in."

"You must be careful, Sarah," he pled. She turned her face toward him, reflecting on his words.

"I will. I think you've convinced me."

Now Adam stood up, though he did not move away from the car. He looked off into the oncoming night.

"I'm going to take off, Adam. Tomorrow at nine?"

"Yep, nine." He stepped back. The car slowly moved away.

"Goodbye, Adam."

"Sarah Liselle Finfield," he said just loud enough so he knew she could hear him, "are you a Christian?"

The car stopped at the entrance to the yard, picket fence on each side, and Adam ambled very slowly to stand beside it, his hands in his jeans pockets. He bent over just a bit in order to see her face which was now turned upward towards him. Even in the darkening evening, her green eyes glistened back at him.

"Why?" she said cynically, "because I have a Bible with my name on it?" His question exasperated her, yet coming through the tone of voice and the toss of her head was an almost spritely air. In the weeks that Adam Cook had been in the employ of Mrs. Finfield, the widow, he had not heard one sentence from her that carried the spunk oozing from this quick retort. He waited for her answer with a welcomed measure of satisfaction.

"Are you?" he asked again when she withheld her response.

"Yes, Adam, I am. Yes, I am, Adam," she said a second time with slightly different emphasis. "And just so you know, there was a day when you would not have had to ask me."

"I didn't have to ask. I read Chip's inscription on the fly leaf of your Bible. I knew you were both guilty." Adam squatted next to the car. "Well, well, Sarah Finfield," he said, expressing amusement, "I do declare. Look at the two of us...both incognito Christians!"

Sarah folded her arms, stared at the steering wheel for a few moments, and then looked out at Adam.

"If you are the nice guy you say you are—and, you are—please don't press this tonight. The fact that I am sitting in my car in your driveway late at night, twenty-one miles from home, chatting with you about the unpleasant details of a significantly distressing attack on my *hermitude*—I just made that word up—should signal progress on my part. I'm spent, Adam. Nevertheless, today I experienced a flicker of revival of my old self and decided to take one baby step for mankind. I promise to tell you everything you want to know... someday."

"I *am* a nice guy," he said with a broad smile. "I was telling you the truth that first day! And, hey, it's enough just to know that you're a real live Christian!"

"Let me say this: A lot has been going on in my mind, back where you could not see it, and when you told me that Melanie had gone to be with Jesus, I was pretty sure you must be a Christian. But if you remember, I made it clear that day that God and I were not hitting it off that well."

"I remember, and I remember that the day I said that, I kicked around telling you about the Lord, but something—I think it was Him—told me to wait. You were in a world of hurt. I felt like you were going to be something like a butterfly, you know how they say it's no good to try to help them out of their cocoon when you see them struggling? I haven't liked watching you in such pain. Maybe this will make it a little easier."

"Maybe...but, I've dreaded this day, Adam."

"What? Why?"

"I knew it would mean surrender...humility. I knew it would mean tears...probably weeping. I know myself. If I shed one tear on the way home, it won't shut off for a long time."

"I'm not sure what to tell you," Adam said, still stooping beside her car. "Part of me wants to tell you not to cry because this is a day of great triumph, yet, I know that everyone says that crying is good."

"Mr. Carpenter," scorned Sarah lightheartedly, "you may recall that once upon a time, long ago, sitting at my kitchen table, you told me that crying is healthy. Remember?"

"Yep, I do. So, I stick with my first answer. I think it's good."

"I'd better go. Thank you for the cupcake and the candle. That really was very sweet."

"You're welcome and happy birthday."

"I'm off. That's enough warm and fuzzy for one day."

"You're right," he said, stiffly standing up. He placed his hands on her open window. "Go. Don't forget the double locks and the alarm."

"It's not my favorite thing."

"What? Locking the doors and setting the alarm?"

"No. Getting home after dark."

Adam subdued the idea of offering to follow her home, though he pretty much wished he could.

A car drove up and stopped in the road, and when it was obvious that Sarah's car was blocking the driveway, the driver pulled off to the side. Adam watched with interest and Sarah squinted out into the dark road. A passenger got out, a duffle bag slung on his back, and made his way quickly toward where Adam stood.

"Hey, Dad! Is that any way to greet a Marine returning from a far country?"

In the light from the yard lantern, Sarah saw Adam's handsome son, decked out in his Dress Blues, his face filled with joy at the sight of his father. She felt awkward and sincerely wished she would have left just a few minutes earlier. Now there seemed to be no easy way to escape.

Daniel stopped for a moment, squatted a bit to see who was in the car blocking the drive, the glow from the same lantern shedding enough light for him to see the woman behind the wheel; then he proceeded toward his dad. A puzzled expression covered his face as he looked back and forth between the two.

"Wait, wait, Sarah." Sarah heard Adam, and in her side mirror, she saw him take a few steps as though to catch her, but she stepped lightly on the gas. The BMW slowly glided towards home.

Adam watched the car for a moment and then turned his attention to his son. He displayed a smile that got bigger as he came to grips with the fact that his son had come home—a good deal earlier than expected. He grabbed Daniel around the neck and pulled him into a loving embrace.

"Son, son. You're home!" he exclaimed, relieving Daniel of his duffel bag.

"Sorry, Dad. My orders were changed and I had to take the ride when I could. Let me send Lyle off."

"Send him off? He can stay here. It's late."

"He's got someone to see," Daniel called out as he trotted to the waiting car. "A girlfriend, you know."

"You'll never know how delighted I am to have you home, son," Adam said as they walked slowly to the house.

"And you'll never know how glad I am to **be** home. I love this place."

"You've never heard such silence in your life."

"I bet. When I signed on, we never knew that Mom would leave you here by yourself."

"Well, I've made it through the first year and a little more. And I'm deeply involved in a major repair job—a whole house repair—which really takes my mind off of things. I'll have to make some quick adjustments, schedule-wise, since you're home early. We'll take off for the lake in a few days, okay? It'll work out just fine." The two climbed the front stairs together. "Let's not even think about it to-night. Man, it's so good to have you home!"

"It's great to see you, too, Dad!"

"It gets quiet around here sometimes."

Adam's son, tall and handsome, with a California tan and a near-ly shaved head, did not respond to his father's sentimental statement. Daniel favored his mother's side of the family in appearance, but was very much like his dad in personality. He was reserved, but congen-ial; wise, but humble; and he was very perceptive. The Marine had something to say, but it would wait.

"You look good, son. They must be working you hard out there!"

"Believe me, they are! Yet, it's been really good for me...in every way. I was thinking the same thing about you, though. You look great! I wondered how you'd do with mom gone."

"God has been good to me. I'm doin' okay. I'd be lying, though, if I didn't say it's just not as much fun without Mom."

"Work been busy?" Daniel wanted to know.

"Yep. One job after another. Got that big one right now."

"That's great! Still inventing, Mr. McGyver?" Daniel joked.

"I work on stuff in the shop," Adam retorted, sensing Daniel's meaning.

"Like what? Anything specific?"

"I wouldn't tell you if there was! You'd just laugh!"

"I promise. I won't laugh. You have to admit that some of them have been humorous!"

"You laugh, but someday you'll be sorry you laughed."

"I'm just remembering some of them, that's all...like the battery operated under-the-bed sweeper!"

Memories and a spark of life filled the kitchen at the Cook house. Adam and Daniel had always been close. Tonight it was heartwarming to once again chat and laugh together.

"I can't believe you're really home! I'm glad you got here early. Here, sit," Adam invited Daniel as he sat down at the kitchen table. "I'm really doing very well, but life gets pretty lonely out here in the country."

Daniel ignored his dad's invitation—for the moment—grabbed an orange from the basket on top of the refrigerator and proceeded to peel it as he went to lean against the sink.

"Yeah, well," he said, hemming and hawing a little over the words about to come out of his mouth, "yeah, well, who was that very gorgeous woman in the Beamer?"

"That's Sarah. Her name is Sarah Finfield. She's a customer. In fact, her house is the big job I'm working on...on the east side. Do you know where Sharenne Woods is?"

"That's those three or four great big houses over by Pine Cone Creek, right?"

"Yep. That's where I'm working right now."

"Wow! That neighborhood is so classy I never felt like I was quite good enough to even drive by there!"

"It's really a nice part of this area, not just the houses, but the lush, rolling acreage, too. Sarah ran into big trouble, looked in the Yellow Pages and called me."

Daniel took a bite of his orange.

"Do all your customers stop by to see you?" he asked with a twinkle in his eye.

"No, not all." Adam detected Daniel's meaning and sent him a comical sidelong glance. "When you hear what's going on in her life, you'll understand what brought her out our way."

"Is she married?"

Daniel's blunt question resulted in a long, hearty laugh from his father.

"No, Daniel, she's not. She is a widow."

"Christian?"

"Yes, Danny Boy...and she is a client and only a client! Are you listening? Sarah Finfield, unlike my other customers, is a client who's in a peck of trouble."

Daniel's eyebrows raised and a smile appeared on his face.

"Well, okay. I guess I'll have to believe you."

"Good, because that's who she is. Nothin' more."

"Hey, okay, Dad. I'll be right back. Okay? I'm going upstairs to dump my duffel bag in the bedroom. I have something to give you. Be right back."

"I'm going to make a quick call."

All that Daniel heard of that call as he walked back into the kitchen was, "Just wanted to be sure you made it home okay."

Daniel handed a USMC sweatshirt to his dad.

"Client, eh?" he kidded.

"Client."

"Dad," said Daniel, leaning in close toward his father, "let me give you a piece of advice: Don't let that beautiful woman slip through your fingers!"

CHAPTER 14

At promptly nine o'clock the next day, the Adam Cook Carpentry truck pulled up to the gate. Behind Adam, in his mother's Jeep Cherokee, was Daniel. Adam drove into the yard; Daniel stopped in the drive. The truck made a circle and stopped next to the deck, facing the house.

"I have to get going pretty quick, Dad," Daniel called.

"Just come in and meet Sarah and then be on your way," Adam hollered, beckoning warmly with his hand.

Out on the deck at the Cook house on River Road the night before, the young Marine had heard the story of Mrs. Finfield and her plight, and wishing to please his dad, he had promised to stop in, though his schedule for the day—catching up with his old friends— was a busy one.

Sarah was not in the kitchen when the two walked in the back door. Adam started through the house, calling her name. He hesitated at the counter beneath the phone, but only for a moment, as he came upon two letters—one from Scott Dolan, and one, stamped and sealed, ready to be mailed to Mexico. An email address and phone number, obviously Scott's, were written neatly on the pad of paper hanging next to the phone. Adam deliberated but for a moment, and then went on his way.

Daniel did some limited exploring, somewhat dumbfounded by the beauty and grandeur of the house, especially the family room— The Lodge, as he called it. He looked out this window and that until he stumbled on a view of the front porch. He heard his dad enter the room.

"You didn't tell me she had a gorgeous daughter!" he said, secluding himself a bit behind the drapery. Adam walked to the window.

"That's not her daughter, Daniel, my boy," Adam explained as he situated himself to see the porch and the stairs. Annette had not visited for several days, but today she stood at the bottom of the

155

stairs, dressed in a white jogging outfit, in happy conversation with Sarah, who was sitting on the top step. The bright white clothing accentuated her tan and her shiny dark hair.

"Niece, sister, next-door neighbor, whatever. Look at the two of them. Did you ever see such a pretty sight?"

"You've been with the guys too long, son!"

"No, Dad, it's just that you taught me by example how to pick out the prettiest girl at the party."

"Well, never mind that. Let's go out. You may as well meet both of them at the same time. And Daniel…down boy. Annette has a boyfriend."

For a long hour, entirely too much time for two people facing a duo of colossal tasks, Adam and Sarah, together with Daniel and Annette, talked and became acquainted over coffee and scones—iced tea for Annette. For Sarah's part, she was content to be a listener, finding pleasure in getting to know Adam's impressive son. She marveled at the amount of words that could pour forth from Annette in short bursts; yet, too, she was stricken with the fact that Annette was not shallow—youthful, yes, but definitely not small minded. All three—Sarah, Adam and Annette—were happily entertained with Daniel's animated and often hilarious stories of military life, but it was he who finally broke up the party.

"Gotta go," he said, shoving back from the table and slapping his knees.

"I'm sorry to see you go," said Sarah. "I've enjoyed listening to you."

"Me, too. And now, where are you off to?" Annette wanted to know.

"I've got some buddies waiting to see me. I've got to fit them in before the fishing trip. I must run. Mrs. Finfield," he said, standing and extending his hand politely, "I'm pleased to meet you. Dad told me all about you last night and your predicament." Daniel shook his head sympathetically. "You're in good hands with my dad, that's for sure." He turned to Annette. "And Annette, it was nice to meet you, too."

Adam walked out on the deck with his son. Through the kitchen window, Sarah and Annette witnessed their meaningful embrace.

"Wow!" Annette said melodramatically, as was often her way. "You don't see that every day. I know that I have never seen such a thing!"

After several minutes, Adam returned to the kitchen, expressing his delight that Daniel and Sarah had met.

"And you, too, Annette," Adam said looking around for the teen. "Did she go home?"

"She didn't say goodbye or anything. Annette?" Sarah called toward the bathroom.

"Sarah, come look." From where Adam was standing in the family room, he had a perfect view of the front yard and driveway. He motioned for Sarah to come.

Annette had sprinted from the house, as quietly as a mouse and with the grace and speed of a gazelle, evidently in an effort—a successful one—to catch Daniel before he pulled out on the gravel road. There she stood, talking with all her exuberance, communicating with her hands, her hair twirling about with each gust of wind. All that was visible of Daniel was his arm resting on the open window.

"He's had two unsaved girlfriends. Neither one good," Adam said, making his way toward the kitchen.

"I'm sure this means nothing."

"She is a captivating teenager and Daniel likes nice things."

"You were not expecting him so soon, right?"

"Nope."

"He seemed glad to see you last night."

"Oh, he was. I was glad to see him, too. Surprised, but glad."

The sound of a car door followed by tires on the gravel road indicated a finish to the conversation at the end of the drive, and sent Adam to the front window once again. Sarah broke into his thoughts.

"Where's Annette?"

"Either she's very persuasive or he is easy."

"She went with him?"

"Yep."

"If it helps, she is at the very least, a seeker. She has asked lots of questions about God. This morning I finally took the time to talk a bit with her."

"Well, that's great, but you know, you want your kid to end up with someone that's grounded. At least, that's my hope for him. We'll need to talk. We have a good relationship."

"It probably would have been better if I had been gone before he drove up last night. He probably wondered who in the world I was."

"He asked."

"Who I was?"

"Yes. It was an easy explain. I'm your carpenter. You're my customer."

"Yes, of course. He is a handsome, handsome boy."

"Well, I won't tell you what he said about you. Here. Take a look at this list I wrote up last night. Mrs. Finfield, I am announcing that another day of work up here and I'll have to start downstairs."

"What's the plan for today? My To-Do list is all checked off. Any word on the furniture?"

"I called Bud last night again. Maybe today. Maybe not. He's very apologetic, but it's the factory where the problem lies."

"I'll be glad to get it. You will, too, I guess."

"It's a good thing there was no real rush, that's all I've got to say!"

"Was Daniel going to be gone all day?"

"He's got three buddies from high school and church that he is meeting up with."

"All together?"

"No, one at a time, I think."

"It seems odd that he would want Annette along."

"Well, either he wanted her to go along, or he didn't, and couldn't say *no*. I'm uneasy about it. Doesn't anybody want to know where she is?"

"Her parents don't seem to care where she is or what she does. I know she's got a boyfriend, and I think they are rather serious."

"Well, I've got to let it go. Daniel's no kid anymore. And we're close. That's good. He'll listen to me. It's good that we're going to have a few days together. Well, we've got work to do if I'm going to be gone next week."

"Adam," Sarah said, nonchalantly, she hoped. "What did he say?"

It was the curiosity thing flaring up, he figured. He smiled inwardly. Her question did not go unheard; but it did go unanswered.

At just about eleven o'clock, the carpenter and the widow participated in a *walkthrough* of sorts, carefully reviewing each room and adding to Adam's list. They were little tasks; nevertheless, they had been missed and needed to be completed—from replacing light bulbs to painting the walls in the closet in the second bedroom. The guest bath, for some reason, needed a complete makeover. The office—most certainly the hardest hit—received a final okay. The large desk, though, remained in the hallway, waiting until the paint and stain were dry.

"I can do most of these things while you are away. I think you are good to go. You're almost entirely done."

"Except for the floors and the rooms downstairs...and the deck...don't forget the deck."

Sarah glanced at Adam, muttered an "uh huh," and then moved past him down the hall and toward the kitchen.

Not but a second or two after Adam griped once again about the delinquent furniture delivery did the doorbell ring! Sarah, already near to the front door, swung it open to see the Gleason Furnishings driver standing there. She was very pleased, yet her basically taciturn personality held her back from announcing his arrival with a holler. Besides, Adam, it turned out, was close behind. The sound of the door chimes had raised hopes that Daniel and Annette had returned.

It would be difficult to say who was more delighted. Pushing and shoving the pieces around here and there, the widow and the carpenter arranged all of it as it had been before—the Sarah haven, the repaired dining room chairs and the roll top desk. She walked to the love seat and sat down on the edge of one of the cushions, folding her hands in her lap, content. Adam watched her unobtrusively, not missing the serene countenance. This was why he had been worked up over the lateness of the delivery. He had placed a rush order two weeks before with only one thought in mind: Restore the tranquil haven of the suffering Sarah Finfield.

Sarah settled in, turning this way and that, looking at a scene which, a very short time before, had seemed beyond repair. Everything was in place, except for the piano lid. It was unknown when to expect its return. At last, she looked toward Adam, who by now had found a place to lean against the wall.

"Adam, sit," she said.

"No, no! I've got sawdust on my jeans. Besides, I'm taking it all in from over here."

"It doesn't matter. Just sit. Please."

Adam sat. He made himself comfortable in one of the elegant navy leather chairs, and sat as he often did, leaning to one side, one ankle crossed over the other knee. Sarah was happy with the room, it was evident. Adam remembered their first meeting in this room. He could see that Mrs. Finfield had come a long way; he wondered if she could.

"I can never thank you enough," Sarah said, not able at first to look at him; but then, slowly, with squinted eyes and wrinkled forehead—and her head leaning slightly to one side—she raised her face toward him and repeated her words. "I can never thank you enough."

Adam was silent and pleased. He waited for her to go on.

"I don't mean just the fact that you are a skilled craftsman and a perfectionist; I mean, thank you for your kindness. I am fully aware that throwing a dart at the phonebook is not a sensible way to decide upon a carpenter, but in this case, it worked."

"You didn't," Adam said, understanding for the first time her comment about an angel guiding her arrow.

"No, but close." Sarah sat back more comfortably into the loveseat. There was a sigh, then another. It would not do to launch into a lengthy speech, though in her current state—very pleased, but very tired—it could certainly happen if she was not cautious. A good deal of sentiment was in her heart, but she was aware that Sarah Finfield was still a long way from getting back into the race. She sighed again, her heart torn between a desire to be alone—alone in her renovated room, her haven—and gratitude at having another human being, one you could almost call a friend, sitting across from her.

How uncanny in its unpredictability life could be!

"What do you think, Mrs. Finfield?" With a shake of his head, he emphatically said, "This is an unusually nice place, Sarah. Things are beginning to take shape. Does it feel like home again?"

Sarah shrugged.

"What is home? It's not home, Adam. You would know what I mean. No, it'll never be home and I guess that's why I know I'll eventually move. I've thought of it a thousand times this year, especially every time I have to walk by the garage. However, if you mean, does it feel like it did three months ago, I guess the answer is yes. Yes and no. I'm different...a little. This room was, well, sort of like solitary confinement for me, a self-imposed solitary confinement. That's different now." It would be a perfect time and place to say more, but Sarah feared what she had always called *gushing*. Yes, there was a speck of life peeking up through the thick sod of her spirit; but Sarah, always good at evaluating herself, knew she had a long way to go. At last there was a pulse, but it was faint.

"All I can say, Adam, is that the abrasiveness of having people around is not as rough as it was."

"That's good to hear. You know what? I can tell."

"Sometimes, though, as I'm going to sleep, I still have real fear and my mind whirls thinking about my life since the day Annette and Tony told me about the three men creeping around my house." Her words gathered energy as she went on. "Annette and Tony, Robert and Raymond, Richard, Mildred, busted garage doors, Adam Cook Carpentry, Silver Moon Café, Herman and Petetra, Charlene and Jeff! Is it any wonder my mind whirls?"

"Even for me," Adam said, "it's hard to believe! Maybe someday you can put it all into a great novel!" He leaned forward. "Sarah, I'm really happy with this room, except, of course, the floor. My buddy, Rico, and I'll take care of it—and the kitchen floor—when I come back. Daniel coming home early sort of threw me off, but we'll get it done, and we'll get the downstairs done, and we'll do the deck."

Adam's phone rang, the ringtone playing, "If I Had a Hammer." He looked at his watch, excused himself and then answered the phone. Daniel was on the other end. Amidst the "uh huhs" and "hmms," Sarah pieced together a change in Daniel's orders.

"Now he's only got till Sunday," Adam told her, shoving his phone into his shirt pocket. "Oh, brother. This changes things. My, my, this changes things."

"And where is he right now? Is Annette still with him?"

"They are at his friend Mickey's house, and yes, Annette is still with him." Adam sighed heavily. "He didn't get to see the other guys, for some reason. You heard me tell him he needs to get Annette home. He said not to worry."

He paced back and forth in front of the windows.

"Would you be okay with my being gone the rest of this week? This messes up the plan. I had it pretty well nailed down to the point of finishing the upstairs by Friday."

There was little emotion in her reply. It did not matter, she said.

"We'll be gone till Sunday—well, through Sunday. I'll be back on Monday."

"Adam, that's fine. While you are gone, I'll give each room a once over. You must remind me to give you your check before you go. Why don't I give it to you now?"

"Later. I'll remember." He hesitated. "Mrs. Finfield, I say let's wrap this up. Let's attack this list of things to do, and then, let's go for a ride. I need to get out on the road," he said decisively. "I do my best thinking there and I don't know why, but it's got sort of a healing effect on this old guy. What do you say?"

Sarah stuttered her approval. Life was moving fast.

"And you know what else, Sarah, we can go to Carlson's and pick up the piano lid."

"I thought it wasn't ready till next week. Clint said he'd deliver it Monday or Tuesday."

"That's the earliest he could deliver, but it's ready now."

"That's a long trip. I don't mind waiting until next week."

"I know, but look how naked that piano looks over there. It's like a handsome gent without his toupee! I'd like to leave for my trip with this room done, finished, complete!"

"Well, I'd love to have the piano intact again, too. I just figured I'd have to wait till Monday or Tuesday. And I guess you can talk me into lunch. I'm just curious to see another one of the restaurants on the Adam Cook culinary recommendation list!"

"Oh, it's the old *curious* thing rearing its ugly head again, eh?"

She stood and straightened the books on top of the cedar chest.

"Before we go, should we take out all the trash and garbage bags first, and do a couple of things on the To-Do list?"

"Good idea."

"On that same subject…," Sarah said, checking for dust on the mantel.

"What subject?"

"My curiosity."

"What about it?"

"What did he say?"

"What did who say?"

"Adam…you know."

Adam removed his cap, smoothed his hair, settled the cap comfortably on his head once again, grinned and started down the hall.

He sighed and with a trace of embarrassment, smiled. "Maybe I'll tell you someday. Not today." Again he took his hat in one hand and pushed his fingers through his hair. "Here," he said, looking away from Sarah, "listen to this list and tell me if you think we have time to do all of this: Hang the wood blinds in the middle bedroom; move the stuff in the hall back into the office; hang that new mirror—that was a nice mirror they broke in the middle bedroom; vacuum the sawdust downstairs; and carry up that damaged furniture."

"I guess. Some of that stuff, I can do. I'll vacuum."

"I'd rather have you stick close and help me. I'll get done faster with four hands."

"Fine."

As a team they worked diligently at marking off the items on the list. At 2:15 p.m., while Adam was in the garage, the doorbell rang. Without much thought—except that it was odd to have two visitors in one day—Sarah walked to the door where she encountered a stranger. He was in his mid-fifties, she supposed, dressed in a suit and string tie, cowboy hat and cowboy boots, and very flamboyant sun glasses.

"You don't know me, ma'am. Let me introduce myself. I am Glen Lichten. I am Herman Lichten's nephew."

"Herman Lichten's nephew?" Sarah did her best to hide her extreme surprise.

"Yes, ma'am. Do you know of the book, *The Street of Petetra*?"

"Of course I do. Everyone does."

"Well, I am the nephew of the man who wrote that book. As I

said, my name is Glen Lichten. And you are?"

"I'm...Sarah Finfield," she replied guardedly and very slowly.

Adam appeared at the door and stood behind Sarah.

"And you must be Chester," Glen said, making his hand available for a handshake.

"No, sir. I am not. My name is Adam Cook and I am a carpenter."

"Oh, ho!" Glen laughed. "I'm so sorry! I just assumed. Is Chester around? No, he's probably at work. He might be home soon, I suppose," he went on, looking at his watch.

Sarah was not about to ask him in. She made an immediate decision that anything that needed to be said would be said right there, standing under the door frame. In fact, out on the porch would be even better. She stepped outside. Adam stood in the doorway.

"What is it that you need, Mr. Lichten?" Sarah asked.

"Oh, call me Glen!"

"All right, Glen, can I help you with something?"

Glen, taking the cue, moved to where he could lean against the railing.

"Well, I think I have to talk to Chester."

This unsettled Sarah. Adam saw that and moved out where his presence was a little more prominent.

"Why do you need him?" Sarah inquired, still responding carefully.

"Wellll...it's a long story, but I think I can make it short. I live in Idaho. I'm a banker in Boise. Herman was my father's brother and he was my only living blood relative. We—he and I—kept in, oh, infrequent contact, but enough so that I knew where he was and what he was up to—of course, not when he was, well, homeless. I know about his book and its success. It doesn't surprise me. My dad was an excellent writer, too, and I am somewhat of a writer myself, though not in the way of books. I write for magazines.

"Well, anyway, just a few months ago, last May or so, someone at his bank called me—couldn't find me real easy because I've moved a lot this year...well, never mind that—to tell me he had a security box that had my name on it as well as Uncle Herman's, and since they knew he was now deceased, I would need to open it. I made the trip here, looked through the contents, and along with a copy of *The Street of Petetra*, handwritten in Uncle Herman's remarkable penmanship, found a hastily scribbled list of eleven more books that he had written."

At this revelation, spoken so nonchalantly, Sarah stopped

breathing for a moment. Adam lowered himself slowly into a wicker chair. Their reactions went unnoticed by the visitor, but neither Sarah nor Adam missed the total astonishment hidden in the expression of the other. Glen went on.

"It took me a few moments to process that. Eleven unpublished books? Eleven unpublished books! Oh, there was, let's see, *Silver Cobblestones* and let's see, *Brave Bonnie Augustine*, and uh, *The Invisible Needle*—or something like that. The other titles were quite interesting as well. But where, I wanted to know, were those books? What could I assume but that they had gone up in the flames; yet, I knew I would eventually have to do some investigating. Best to get it done while I was already here, right? So, I went to Payce Publishing on that same trip. I had two hours to spare.

"Richard Payce was surprised—I believe a better word would be dumbfounded, although it seemed that after his initial show of shock, he attempted to mask it. That's my take on it. He shook his head and said he knew nothing of eleven other books. He knew of one other but not eleven. He said that almost for certain they went up in flames with the rest of my uncle's belongings—of which he had very little, I assume. My visit with Mr. Payce was three months ago. May. May 17th, I believe."

Swiftly, like a computer, Mrs. Finfield's brain processed the date. It was the day before Mildred's death. Raymond and Robert had preyed upon Sarah immediately after the funeral! Now it all made sense. Until May 17th—a whole year after Chip's death—they had known nothing of the additional writings!

Adam arrived at the same conclusion, but he immediately wondered why it took until mid-July for them to kick the door in and then ransack the house. What were they doing for two months?

Glen was continuing.

"Mr. Payce dismissed me abruptly. I then investigated further and got Chester's name. Well, I have not had time since that day to do a thing about it. Today, I am once again on business in the Midwest, and again, my time is very limited. I thought I'd come by and see if Chester can shed any light on the subject."

He adjusted his tie and removed his sunglasses. Sarah noted that he looked better with them on.

"I flew out here today pretty sure that those wonderful manuscripts went up in smoke. What a disappointing development! Oh, I don't care anything about money, royalties, that sort of thing. I just am heartsick that such works of art are gone…that is, unless Chester knows of their whereabouts."

Adam moved to where he could stand and put his hand against the post. His eyes moved slowly to the widow's face. Mentally, he stepped aside from the scene playing out before him, and studied Sarah's expression and manner. Had he missed it? There was something different about her. The lines of pain in her face, always there, seemed to be lessened—no, they were gone! Was that serenity he was beholding? He scrutinized her whole demeanor as she spoke. Yes, something was different.

"I'm sorry you came all this way…for nothing," she calmly said. "My husband died a little more than a year ago. I know very little of anything to do with his work."

The awkwardness this inflicted upon Glen Lichten was obvious.

"Oh, my," he groaned, "I am so sorry to have bothered you. Here I told you this whole story which you didn't need to hear at all! I am so sorry about your husband. I cannot understand why the young woman at Payce—was it Gina? I think it was Gina—would not share that information with me. You can understand, though, why I would pursue this checking into this whole thing. Such a book, *The Street of Petetra!* Without a doubt, there were eleven more outstanding pieces of literature!"

Almost as quickly as he had blown into Mrs. Finfield's life, he was on his way down the steps and into his car, with the humblest of apologies for needlessly bombarding into her day. Holding their breath, the widow and the carpenter stood at the railing and watched his rental car back out into the road and then towards the state road; then, they turned to look at each other with nearly identical expressions of astonishment.

"I'm speechless," said Adam, emphasizing the fact with wide eyes and a broad smile.

Sarah sank slowly into one of the porch chairs. "Eleven more?"

"Yep, he said eleven."

"I can't believe it!"

"Well, now, doesn't this just explain a lot!" Adam said looking down at Sarah.

"Greed and desperation. Adam Cook, you hit the nail on the head!"

"You could almost say that this justifies—well, not justifies, but for sure explains—the magnitude of their evil. Sarah, eleven manuscripts—eleven Herman Lichten manuscripts—equals enormous amounts of money for the winner."

"I can't believe this," Sarah said, her eyes upon his bewildered face. "But, Adam, where are they? Where could eleven manuscripts be? Not in **my** house, that's for sure."

"You know, Mrs. Finfield, don't you, that the odds are that they were destroyed in the fire."

"I'm afraid I think you're right. Perhaps, finally, this can be the end of it all."

Leaning over and resting his hands on the railing, Adam set his gaze upon the front yard and the cornfield beyond. "No, not for me."

"Adam, we're back at Square One."

"We really never left Square One," said the elated, but pensive, Adam Cook, "because we had no clues. Now we have clues. I think this actually means that we are on Square Two. **Everything** has changed," he went on evidencing notable enthusiasm. "The Prize has been identified and as long as there is a chance that the books still exist, I think we should keep looking." He turned and held out his hand. "Come on," he coaxed, pulling her to her feet. "We have work to do. Are you up to it, Mrs. Finfield?"

"Yes, I think I'm up to it." Sarah stood, determination upon her face, and with her hands on her hips, she said, "I guess I'm up to anything that will keep the Payces from finding them first."

CHAPTER 15

"Eleven manuscripts," Sarah murmured, her bright mind stirring. "Eleven manuscripts, Adam! Now we know what the Payces are so frenzied about!" She rounded the corner with a pot of coffee and two mugs.

"I'd say so!"

"But," Sarah mused, "I still have to ask why? Just because they published one book, that wouldn't mean an automatic deal with the others."

"Not unless Herman and Payce had one of those deals that include subsequent manuscripts."

"That's called an Option Clause. Maybe there was a contract like that. Or maybe there was supposed to be after Chip's meeting with him that night. Maybe they're looking for the manuscripts but they're looking for such a contract as well. Maybe Chip's meeting with Herman included the signing of such a contract."

"Would you tear a place apart for a contract?" Adam asked, thinking aloud. "I suppose you would if you thought a contract was floating around somewhere that would give you the exclusive publishing rights for eleven golden eggs...or, I suppose, one that kept you from them, one you didn't want to come to light."

"That is true. That would be what you termed *desperation.* I hadn't thought of either one of those possibilities. Yet, on the greed side of things, I can't help but believe that it was the quest to own those golden eggs that drove them to destroy my house. I believe they were looking for those manuscripts and at the same time, posting a warning to me: This is what happens when you don't bend! If there are eleven manuscripts in existence, you can bet on this: Payce sees them as theirs, contract or no contract. This is the gospel truth."

"The question in my mind is whether or not they were ever in the hands of your husband. The Payces think so, evidently. But why, even if Herman had told Chip about them, why would Chip have them in his possession?" Adam sighed. "I don't like to say it, but it's very possible—possible, I'm saying—that those books went up in smoke, sad as that is."

The atmosphere in the family room was warm and inviting as Sarah and Adam mused upon Glen Lichten's unexpected appearance. Having been diverted from their earlier plan and in the mood for making serious headway into the whole mystifying story of the Lichten books, the Payces, and the fire of a year ago, the two settled into Sarah's restored little haven, gathering their papers and pencils, spreading everything out on the cedar chest, the couch, and the empty chairs. Glen Lichten had added a clue—in reality, the key clue—to what little they already knew. They were eager to solve the mystery. The time was right. The place was perfect.

"Hey, are you doin' okay?" Adam said with a pencil in his mouth and a stack of papers in his hands.

Sarah squinted at him, and at the same time reached for her glasses.

"I am. Why?"

"I don't know, you seem a little, well, stronger today."

"I actually feel strong—more than I have for a long time. So, let's get to it!"

"Okay, okay!" Adam laughed. "It's obvious we're not going to get any other momentous clues dropping into our laps today! So I'm with ya'…let's work on the timeline. What do you say? You may have things pretty much sorted out in your head, but I sure don't."

"Really, I don't either. The truth is that I lost some of those days, days that I can hardly remember. I think your idea of a timeline is quite practical." There was a hint of the businesswoman in her statement. Her demeanor concurred.

Determinedly, they went to work on a chronological outline, filling in the empty spots on the legal pad. They talked and wrote, drew up sketchy calendars, erased and re-wrote, and crumpled up many of the long yellow sheets, tossing them on the floor. Their efforts were not in vain. Awareness that they were getting somewhere could be seen in their expressions of enthusiasm.

The Wentworth Building fire, as the two of them confirmed after verifying the information on the internet, occurred on the night of May 12, 2004. It was more than a fire; there had been an explosion. Mr. Lichten, it was reported had left the gas on while out to get an ice cream cone at Smitty's. Who could know what happened when he returned?

"Adam," Sarah broke in. Adam looked over at her. He could tell that she was very deep in thought. "Adam, something has just come to me, something that Chip said."

"Good, Sarah! About the books?"

"No, about Herman. When Chip was pacing back and forth, he said that Herman very clearly told him that he never used the stove. That just came to me for the first time. It's so odd."

"What are you saying?"

"This article says the explosion was because Herman left the gas on accidentally. The news that night said the same thing. Chip was saying that Herman would not have left it on!"

"Wow. No kidding?"

"And you know what else? I'm remembering now that Chip said that Herman was moving out the next morning, that he had been notified to be out by the 13th! That is what upset Chip. He kept saying that he should have brought him home with him."

"How could he have known there'd be a fire?"

Sarah sighed. "I don't know what this all means. If the Payces set the fire, did they mean to do away with Herman, or...we know that he went for ice cream...did they maybe set the fire—if it was them—thinking he was out of the building?"

"An arson fire, you mean. Could be. How will we ever know?"

"Well," Sarah concluded "I think we can be pretty sure about two things. It appears that it was not Herman's recklessness that caused the fire, and for sure we know they would not have burned the building down if they knew about the other books, and we know they didn't."

"Sarah, keep this all in that computer in your head. It may come up in a courtroom someday. Keep at it. I've told you before, you're the key. I think more things are going to surface as we go along."

On they worked at the timeline, adding dates, jotting down anything at all about the situation, drawing arrows and callouts. Then Sarah had an idea.

"I know what will help me here! My day timer pages from those days! I kept such a detailed schedule because I was working then. And I even kept track of Chip's whereabouts, too, to a certain extent. Now, if I can just think where my book might be."

She found it easily. It was in the desk still sitting in the hallway.

"My mind is strangely blank," she groaned. "I'm afraid I'm somewhat overwhelmed. My only hope is in these pages."

"You're remembering a lot. Keep going."

"Okay, here. On the 12th, I worked a regular day. Oh, Adam, this is going to help me! Those days are such a blur that I have not been able to fit the pieces together. Let's see...Chip and I met for an early dinner—5:30 p.m.—at Stonegate downtown. We had a celebration, so to speak, because Finfield Publishing was finally in place and legal. But, I could tell he was edgy about resigning on Monday and he was not the edgy type. I struggled seeing him like that, but there was nothing I could do. It was getting him down. That's all I remember."

"That was the night of the fire, Sarah. Did you guys see the news that night?"

"Yes! That's right. Yes, we did. When we got home, we got in bed and watched the news. No. No, that's not right. No, that was the night he went to talk to Mr. Lichten; I went home; he went to pick up his new business cards first, then to Herman's. I'd say he came home around 9:45. **Then** we went to bed and watched the news. Oh, this calendar is going to help me so much! See what I mean? It helps me to see things in black and white.

"He took the news very badly. Extremely so. I've I told you about his reaction. He paced the floor, back and forth, wiping tears from his face and using up a box of tissues—and he was throwing things. This was not Chip's normal self," Sarah explained. "I was apprehensive. Hours later, as we talked together in bed, he earnestly blamed himself for the old man's death. I had questions. 'Would they stoop low enough to hurt someone?' I asked him, 'Chip! Are you saying they might actually…kill someone?' He wouldn't answer my questions. Though I despised the Payces, I had no inkling that they could be responsible for such a thing, not until he said, 'I know things and they know that I know.' Something like that. I asked if he was in some kind of danger. 'No,' he said, 'I'm family. I'll be okay.' I'm pretty sure he believed that they meant to do away with Herman."

Adam arose and walked to the front windows where he looked out upon the summer day. The sky was August blue…and cloudless. He was processing, not only the latest document and Sarah's reminiscing, but the whole story from beginning to end. His mind worked through the stages, one by one, putting down piece by piece, almost like a chronological jigsaw puzzle.

"Did he go to work the next day?"

"My book says he did, but I know he did not. He was awake the whole night. I know that to be true because I kept waking up and finding him in here, working on something in his computer, and then he stayed home the next day, uh, Thursday, and on Friday—the 13th and 14th. He called in sick. I left Thursday morning for Boston to train employees at the new Kerrigan facility. There had been a merger. I was gone till the morning of the 15th—Saturday. His birthday. My flight got in at 9:10 a.m."

"I'm assuming you communicated with each other during those two days."

Sarah groaned. "I've only had to do those training things a few times, but when I did, I was training from eight in the morning until ten at night. I called him at lunch and dinner—it was always easier for me to call him than for him to reach me—and we both emailed each other once each night."

"How did he sound, Sarah? Could you tell?"

"He seemed like he was on a mission. He said he couldn't talk long, that he had some stuff to do."

"How about his emails?"

Sarah sighed. She could remember them well.

"I can show them to you. I'm sure I kept them. Basically, he told me that he couldn't wait until I was home and that he didn't want me ever to go away again. They were both short. In one, he happily reminded me that I could quit Kerrigan and we could work together now on the new venture. In the Friday night email, he gave himself a pat on the back for finally getting the dry wall up in the garage."

"Did he say anything at all about Herman or Payce or the fire...or better yet, the manuscripts?"

"Not one mention of any further writings," she replied, shaking her head dolefully. "He told me that resigning was going to be a rougher road than he first thought, that Richard had been in a foul mood lately. I actually asked him how he was handling the fire and Herman."

"What did he say?"

"I can tell you exactly what he said. He said: 'Sarah, do you remember that Charles Bronson movie called *The Evil that Men Do*? That's all I'm going to say on the phone. When you get home I'll tell you all about it.' Right before we hung up, he told me that he had some very important things to show me when I got home, some of them pleasant surprises."

"Pleasant surprises could have meant manuscripts."

"He didn't tell me. He loved to keep me curious. Imagine that!"

Such contemplation stirred in Adam's mind; it was not the time to say so, but with Sarah's last words, a suspicion was replaced with a certainty—Chip's demeanor, as being reported by Sarah, did not coincide with someone taking his own life! The full ramification of such a belief was still cloudy; Adam tucked away his conviction for now.

"Go on, Sarah. Tell me the rest."

Sarah's face bore signs of heartache. Adam knew full well where this discourse would lead. Moving not a muscle, he listened as she recounted the story, speaking without emotion, her eyes fixed upon the neatly handwritten timeline in her lap.

"I got back from Boston on Saturday morning, so ecstatic to be back. Very few trips such as that one fell into my lap. It was not part of the plan when I was hired on, but now and then, what I knew, no one else knew. I went but I couldn't wait to be with Chip again. We were never apart, Adam. Never. I remember pressing the garage door opener as soon as I thought I was close enough for it to work.

"I remember grabbing my purse and my briefcase and jumping out of the car, and that I headed through the garage toward the kitchen door. Then I heard the engine." Sarah's voice was now a near whisper. "I wondered why but even when I saw him in the car, I had no suspicion of trouble. I was still anticipating a happy reunion. I pulled open the door of that steel gray Jaguar and called his name. I was so happy."

Adam could not bear to turn towards her. He stared at his wedding ring. A flood of intertwined emotions seemed to tell him to be still, not to speak, not to stir. He was strangely moved by the turn their conversation had taken and deeply pleased that Sarah was, at last, mouthing the words that told the story of that horrid day. She stood and walked to the piano, sitting down on the black bench. She was facing him. Now his eyes moved from his hands to her face. A long deep sigh came from the widow's heart.

"The note...the note, which had been in his lap floated to the floor, I guess with the pull of the door. He always wrote with a favorite pen, one with black ink. It was easy to recognize his bold writing...and, to read the words, words I will never forget. 'Sarah, you know I will always love you. I could have saved that old man, but I missed the warning signs....' I think I read more—something about not being able to go on with such guilt—but it's very fuzzy. I can't explain it, but the truth dawned like a dream in slow motion. I reached for the key and turned off the engine."

She pulled herself up into a cross-legged position and folded her arms in her lap. With her eyes closed, she finished the grim tale, her voice and each word embedded with what should have been actual tears. Adam strained to hear her.

"I shook him gently and softly said his name. He slumped to the side and then I screamed his name. I felt for a pulse but there was none. I dialed 911 and collapsed in a heap next to his car. I can still hear the wail of the siren. I wish I could erase it." She waited briefly before relating what would be the end of the story, then bravely opened her eyes and gazed at Adam. "The last thing I remember is that I decided that I would die, too." Deep in thought, she hesitated once again, and then, very slowly shook her head as she went on. "I have no recollection of making funeral plans and for that matter, only faint recollection of being at the funeral. I remember nothing about the graveside service. I remember nothing. It's all gone."

Adam heard the tick tock of the mantel clock and he heard the lovely chiming of the twirling golden bell as it heralded the hour. He listened to the little tune that followed. All was quiet and still. He laid his fistful of papers on the cedar chest.

Sarah leaned against the keys and sighed again. Like an exquisite ivory statue, she sat perfectly still, rigid and tense, her face blank. Adam walked to the fireplace. He swallowed hard and blinked back the threatening tears. All was quiet for hours—or was it only a few moments?

"Sarah," he said at last, slowly ambling to where she was sitting, "let's get out of here for a while. Will you come? We can talk with the good summer around us."

"I will go."

"Are you sure?"

"I am sure," she replied, nodding her head decisively.

Gracefully, she arose and walked to where the evidences of an hour of deep deliberation lay all about. There she reached for her pen and glasses, told Adam she would get her purse, and when she returned, she waited in the doorway, her eyes resting upon the eyes of her carpenter. There was no smile on her lips, but her face was aglow with peace. Her words were like those on the last page of a good book.

"I just caught a faint glimpse," she said tenderly, "of how Lazarus must have felt when Jesus called his name."

Sarah's face smiled.

Her words drifted through the room like beautiful music. It was a moment of great triumph and joy, and Adam, with a kind and contented smile, spoke without words to Sarah: "*You're going to be all right, Sarah Finfield.*"

It pleased him that she agreed so readily to get out of the house. Driving his truck was his therapy. It did him good to get on the road and as they drove out the west hardtop, out of town, the windows open—after a stop at Sarah's mailbox at the end of the driveway—it seemed there was the triumphant sounding of a bell tolling, ringing out the words, "All is well! All is well!" Adam glanced over at Sarah who was depositing her pile of mail into the side pocket of her purse.

"How strange this all is!" Sarah mused. "How odd that you would be the one to rescue this poor widow in her hour of need...not just digging me out of the massive operation to restore my house, but...well, I guess I'm not so blind that I can't see that a hundred other carpenters that I could have called would not have been interested in my personal plight. You have no idea how resolute I have been in a determination to never speak of Chip's death and the whole story—ground-in, deep-down, etched-in-stone resolve. Even now, Adam, I would not relate it to another person on this earth."

Her words were playing in his heart like the song of a robin after a long, cold winter. Such beautiful music!—not such that it set off wild thoughts of romance, but rather a deep and pleasant realization that God was brushing away the thorns and thistles.

He said nothing.

"I feel unlocked. Your presence and patience has unlocked me. Did you notice that the drapes were open this morning?"

"Yep, I did."

"I even called Pastor Samuelson. That was a huge step for me."

"No kidding. What did he say?"

"Basically, he said, 'God answers prayer.'"

"Meaning, I guess, that they've been praying for you."

"Oh, yes. You can count on that. He and Patty will no doubt stop by. How could I have shut everyone out, people who care about me?"

"I've always appreciated the fact that the Bible includes stories of great people of God who went through times of distress and utter discouragement. I've felt like Elijah in the cave more than once in my lifetime."

"Adam, I read my Bible for the first time in 14 months last night."

"The Sarah Liselle Bible?" Adam asked with a smile.

"Yes, the Sarah Liselle Bible," she replied, with mock aggravation. "I only read one chapter. It was all I needed. Then, I wanted to pray but I couldn't bring myself to kneel. I tried to pray stretched out on my bed, but I knew I needed to bow before the Lord. I had a suspicion as to why I was having a hard time and it turned out that I was right. I finally knelt and started to pray and I got as far as 'Heavenly Father' and I began to weep. I couldn't speak any other words out loud. In my heart, though, I humbly admitted how wrong I've been to shut Him out, to see Him as the enemy. I cried for help. I ended up lying on the long rug at the end of my bed and woke up four hours later. I was filled with peace and light. The pall of death was gone." She turned slightly toward the carpenter. "Really, Adam, there has been a real...pall of death... hanging like a black cloud in every room, shrouding me, following me as I moved about. It was gone.

"I stood up and went to look in the mirror at the end of the hall and—now don't laugh, don't even smirk—I hardly recognized me."

"Hey, I'm not smirking. I hardly recognized you today when you were talking to the cowboy!"

"I've had such a warm relationship with the Lord for many years, and I just threw it out the window! I'm not happy with myself that I turned on Him so fiercely."

"I'm glad you're back, Sarah. I'm sure He is, too. And what was the chapter you read?"

"Psalm thirty-four. I can only remember one verse though. 'The Lord is near to the brokenhearted and saves the crushed in spirit.' Oh, one more: 'Oh, taste and see that the Lord is good! Blessed is the man—or woman—who takes refuge in him!'"

Adam began to whistle. *"Oh, Jesus is the Rock in a weary land, a weary land, a weary land; Oh, Jesus is the Rock in a weary land, a shelter in the time of storm."*

The miles passed by, one by one, accompanied by the rumble of the engine and the whir of the tires as they thumped down the poorly kept highway. The quiet, the silence, the absence of conversation filled the cab of the truck with safety and tranquility. Sarah, with her head leaned back against the headrest, now closed her eyes as they drove, something she had not been able to do for a long time.

"Eleven books, Adam," she said, finally breaking the silence. "So amazing, isn't it? It boggles the mind. I've been thinking and cogitating over here. Such titles! Didn't it just make you want to run out and buy a copy of *Brave...Bonnie...Augustine?*"

"The one that caught my attention was *The Invisible Needle.*"

"That's probably the McGyver in you!"

"No doubt."

"I'm sure the rest of his books were as excellent as *The Street of Petetra.*"

"Listen to you. You're using the past tense," noted Adam light-heartedly.

"It seems pretty likely, Adam, that they perished in the flames," Sarah said using her hands to accentuate her point.

"I'd agree except for one thing."

"What's that?"

"I'm wondering what Chip was doing all night on the computer and during those days you were away. Am I not hearing from you that you're suspicious that he was up to something?"

"Yes, you are."

"Would he—though it doesn't seem likely—would he, could he have had the manuscripts right there in your house? Why exactly did Chip go to see Herman that night?"

"I think...I think it was to get a signed contract on a second book."

"So it seems that we'll never know if Chip even knew about those other books, not unless we stumble on them somewhere... which doesn't look too promising since we have been over every inch of your house."

"Adam, we may as well face up to it; we'll probably never know the truth about those books."

"Nor the truth about the fire, although if they knew Herman was not going to go with Payce for the second book—and chances are they knew—the fire very well could have been retaliation."

"Perhaps they told him, too, like they did me, that it's better to bend than to break...and he didn't bend. Yet, as we were saying before, they could have just been doing the insurance thing."

"I go back and forth. I'm not sure what to think."

"Well, like I said, we at least know that they didn't do it because of the manuscripts. They didn't know about them. And we may never know if Chip was aware of them...except, as you say, what was he doing all night and why did he go to the office? The measure of activity on his part during those two days does stir up a trace of suspicion that maybe he had them."

"Maybe he did."

"But I've gone over the house. We've gone over the house. I've scoured the computers with a fine toothed comb! There is nothing at my house. If there is something, it has to be at his office."

"If he had the manuscripts why did he need to go to the office?"

"I don't know, I don't know. I'm clueless and tired of it all," she announced, reaching for her mail. "Aren't you? Hmmm, here is something from Scott. It doesn't even have my address on it," she noted, her forehead drawn into deep wrinkles. Adam said nothing. "It has no postmark! He must have stopped by...maybe last night while I was out gallivanting." Her glance toward Adam was not returned. She put all the mail next to her on the seat. "I thought he was not to come back until next week."

"My biggest question is where have the Payces been since they tore your place apart," Adam said, steering things back to the manuscripts—and away from Scott's letter. "Do you think they found what they were looking for? The silence makes me nervous."

"I hope they did. Really, Adam, you and I both know there is not a nook or cranny where eleven manuscripts could be hiding."

"Could he have entered all eleven books into his computer or scanned them in? There is nothing on his laptop? You're sure?"

"Not a thing! I searched both computers, and I know how to search. There's nothing. Besides, although that would tell us that he had them, it wouldn't tell us where they are now. Really, I see nothing of magnitude on his computer. I'll look again for documents, but I really feel like we're at a dead end."

Adam thought on that a moment, then taking Sarah completely off guard, he changed the subject. It was not a big deal, but he had a question nagging him.

"How'd it go with Scott last Monday?" he inquired, not looking her way.

Hardly ever did Sarah look at him when they talked in the truck. She pretty much kept her eyes looking at what was ahead; but this question caused her to turn towards him.

"I'm just wondering," he added, interpreting her reaction.

Actually looking past Adam through the window and out upon the scenery whizzing by, in a melancholy tone she answered, "It was just another thing to struggle through. Like all the rest."

"He seemed like a nice guy. I like when a guy gives a hearty handshake. It tells a lot about him."

"Well, it's because he is a missionary to small villages in the mountains. He builds churches and schools, chops trees, walks everywhere, climbs his way from town to town. He's pretty tough, even though it doesn't really look like it. He's lanky, but strong."

"Do I have it right that his wife died?"

"She died in February."

"What happened?"

"She was bitten by a snake and he couldn't transport her quick enough for the medical attention she needed. By the time he got her to help, she was not doing well. She actually died here in the states. In Arizona."

"Boy, that's tough. Is he going back?"

"He has already gone back and is going again."

Sarah was talkative. Adam was pleased.

"Did you meet at college?"

"We met at college; we dated in college; we fell in love in college; we got engaged at college."

"Did you get an education in college?" Adam jested.

"Yes, as a matter of fact, I did—a B.A. in English Lit.," she retorted, "and…I almost got an M.R.S."

Adam found that amusing.

"I think I must have the gift—or perhaps, the flaw—of quickly falling head over heels. I was immeasurably in love with Scott. I would have gone to the ends of the earth with him. We were headed somewhere, wherever the mission board thought to send us. He backed out—cold feet, he calls it now—one hour before the wedding."

"One hour!" Adam bellowed.

"One hour. I was a needy girl. I had attached to his family as though they were my own. In a moment, I lost him, his wonderful folks and siblings, and direction for my life. Basically, I fell apart. Chip put me back together again."

"Why exactly did he stop to see you the other day?"

Sarah's eyes closed and she scratched her forehead as she contemplated an answer.

"Mostly?"

"I guess."

"Mostly to apologize. Upon the news of Chip's death, and the death of Chloe, I guess he felt it showed no impropriety to make an effort to stop by. He was, you know, in the neighborhood."

There was more, Adam safely assumed, after seeing the correspondence by the phone, and especially now that he knew that Scott had actually come by the house again…and left another letter; but he felt little unrest. The entry of Scott into Mrs. Finfield's life had stirred the widow's heart and helped to create a healthy diversion.

They drove for two hours, sharing long comfortable silences. Along the way they succumbed to the heat and switched on the air conditioning.

"Should we get something to eat," Adam asked, "now that we've got the piano toupee taken care of? We're two hours away from Timber Ridge and neither of us has really had much to eat so far today."

"Amazingly, I'm sort of hungry."

Adam knew all the spots. He drove a little farther and then pulled into the parking lot of an old gas station, now a restaurant called Jerry's Corner.

It had been a good idea, taking a drive. Over lunch, driving to nowhere in particular, sitting at a picnic table by the lake, and on the long ride home, the mystery at hand was the main topic of conversation. When they returned home, the sun had disappeared leaving a lightly illuminated western sky. Adam ran around to the other side and assisted the very exhausted Sarah from the truck. He walked her to the door, opened it, disarmed the alarm and went in ahead of her. She knew he was making sure that all was well and safe.

"Time to turn off our minds, Sarah. Please get some sleep tonight. I'll come at ten tomorrow, okay? Get an extra hour. And no sleuthing!"

"Wait. I'll make a copy of the timeline for you. Take it. You get up earlier than I do."

Adam went to the door and waited. Sarah returned, but she did not walk toward the door. Instead, she stood in the doorway to the family room, the timeline in her hand, a question mark on her face.

"Will you stay for a little while? Please?" Taken off guard, Adam squirmed deep down inside where Sarah would never see, and taken off guard, a million answers came to mind, many of which made no sense at all. His discomfort, however, went undetected. "I'd like to talk to you about something."

"I guess I can," he replied, looking at his watch. It was 9:30.

"Just a few minutes. I'll get some of my tasty lemonade. Have a seat in there. I'll be right back."

There was something on Sarah's mind, Adam could tell, but she skillfully kept the conversation on a casual plane. He waited, but he knew that if she did not speak up soon, he would have to ask. It was getting very late. They chatted about the style of the great room, both very glad to have it back in order.

"Who did the fireplace?"

"A friend of Chip's. Warmth and Beauty, that's the name of his company."

"I've heard of them. That's Brian Thomas, right?"

"Yes, you know him?"

"I do. Not well, but I know of him."

"He's the one that suggested the eagle heads on either side. Chip actually designed them. I never showed you this, but watch."

Sarah went to the fireplace and stood to the side so that Adam could see what she was doing. She pressed the left glass eye of the bronze eagle. A drawer, skillfully camouflaged, opened in the rich wood panel that separated the record albums from the books above. There sat Chip's turntable.

"Cool, eh? He was very proud of that and well he should be! He did the whole thing himself."

"That is cool! More of Chip's innovative tendencies...and electronic proficiency! I didn't know about the techie side of him."

"Well, as far as artistic skill is concerned, he designed this house, inside and out, and that includes most of the interior design. Electronic? Now that's a little different. I won't tell you how long it took him to get this thing to work or his frame of mind during those hours! I was happy for him—and me—when he tried it the last time and it worked."

"What happens when you press the other eye?" joked Adam.

"I asked Chip the same thing and I tried it. Nothing. He said, 'Not yet.'"

"Can you play a record right now?" Adam asked, fascinated with this gadget.

"I haven't touched this in over a year. In fact, I rarely played the records. It was Chip's way of relaxing."

"Are you up to it? I'd just like to hear something."

"I guess I could."

"Just anything. Something you like. What do you like?"

"I like piano. Chopin."

"Like what?"

"Chopin's Second Piano Concerto is really a favorite."

"Good. Let's hear that."

"Oh, I could never find it in a hurry. When I put them back on the shelves, I just shoved them in, any old way," she reminded him. "Chip had them alphabetized by artist."

"Well, then, just pull one out—anything—and play it."

Sarah complied, experiencing the unlocking of yet another little room in her heart. In all probability, the records would have forever remained on the shelves, silenced by the loss of their friend.

"Hmm…not Chopin…but Rachmaninoff. Okay?"

The magnificent strains of Rachmaninoff's 2nd Piano Concerto flooded the room; Adam was deeply moved and somewhat overwhelmed in his soul. He loved classical music, but he had never heard it like this before! Chip had invested in nothing but the best in a sound system.

There was light conversation as Rachmaninoff's masterpiece played in the background. Now and then, they ceased talking in order to listen to a particularly awesome part of the performance, and when at last it was done, Adam simply said, "I'm sure I never heard that before. That was amazing and I'm sure that a lesser sound setup would not do it justice like this one does."

"I guess you can't understand the emotion of this. Chip loved his records. I loved my books. We both learned to love the love of each other. I'm glad you asked me to do that."

"Hey, that was excellent. I hope you start in on the rest of those albums!"

Adam got up slowly, stretching as he did, and sauntered toward the door. "Wow! I'm tired! What time is it anyway? Eleven thirty! Eleven thirty! How did it get to be eleven thirty? And where, I'd like to know, is my son."

He pulled his phone from his shirt pocket and dialed. Sarah heard it ring only once before Daniel answered.

"Hey, son, you do know we're getting' up at the crack of dawn tomorrow...you are? When did you get home?...You did?...Well, I guess I'm the one that needs to hustle home!...Yep...We'll talk to-morrow."

Sarah smiled. "He's home, right?"

"Yep. And I'm not. Time just slipped away. I'll be okay. I operate on very little sleep."

Adam stopped just inside the door.

"You'll be back on Monday morning?" Sarah wanted to know.

"Yep. Let's say ten. You keep your eyes open and be careful. I'm not kidding, Sarah. Be careful."

"I will, you can be sure of that!"

"It's time to go. See you Monday. Hey, didn't you have some-thing you wanted to tell me? I forgot about that."

"Yes. Yes, I do." Taking in a deep breath, and looking at the floor, Sarah began. "Adam, I am going to Mexico on August 24th, two weeks from tomorrow. Scott has begged me to come for two weeks, just to visit, just to see his work—well, mostly for that. I just wanted you to know."

Even though Adam was very aware of significant communica-tion between Timber Lane and Mexico, this news took him off guard. Different responses came to mind but only one made it past his lips: "That's good, Sarah. That will be a good trip for you."

For the very first time since Adam Cook had knocked on Mrs. Finfield's heavy rustic door, everything seemed awkward. Sarah fi-nally looked up. Her eyes met his.

"I need to go. I don't know if you understand, but I need to go."

"I told you that it's good and I meant it."

Sarah opened the door and stood to the side. Adam stopped long enough to say, "Smells and feels like rain. I feel a storm coming." Then he started down the steps.

"It's supposed to storm tonight," she said.

"Both locks, okay? I checked all the other ones. Set the alarm and go to bed."

"Yes, Adam, I will. You are like the big brother to me that I never had! Thank you for that. Now go home."

"Promise you'll set the alarm."

"I promise."

"We're going to lick this Payce thing! You can always call me, you know, fishing or not," he said, not turning around.

"Okay. Now go home. Please, Adam, enjoy your time fishing. Have a good time with your son."

"I will. Looking forward to it."

At the bottom of the stairs, he turned and looked towards the front door. Uncharacteristically, Sarah was still standing with the door open, watching him go.

"You really ought to read that letter from your sister."

"Go home. Go fishing."

"Both locks," Adam said.

Sarah saw Adam's company name—Adam Cook Carpentry— shimmer on the driver's side of the truck as he drove by the yard light. The silver Dodge Ram began its turn onto Timber Lane. He glanced into his rear view mirror. Sarah was still standing in the doorway. *"Maybe she finally noticed the tailgate. Someday I'll tell her that story."*

❧ ❧ ❧ ❧ ❧

At two o'clock, in the pitch black of night, tornado sirens pierced the air, reverberating through the countryside. There was little, however, that could have jostled the carpenter's mood and focus, not even the evident thrashing of the wind and the quivering and shuddering of his work shop. The rain pelted its metal roof, sounding much like he had imagined as a child how reindeer would sound on Christmas Eve. Well into the three o'clock hour, one storm front after another blew through the area, each one setting off the ominous Timber Ridge warnings; but on River Road, the work lights burning in the secluded work shop set back from the road and behind the four-car garage, stayed on through the night. Within the carpenter's heart, his own storm raged, one nearly identical to the one sweeping through Chippewa County. Adam, however, had work to do. It had to be done by four o'clock. There was no time for Mrs. Finfield's big brother to give heed to the tempest within his soul.

CHAPTER 16

At 4:15 a.m. on the 10th day of August, Adam's silver truck left his driveway, stars spread across the sky that had so recently been blackened by thick clouds. The startling claps of thunder and nearly continuous lightning had ended at last. Fishing gear was meticulously loaded into the side compartments in back, suitcases stashed behind the truck seats, and the bass boat on the trailer behind.

"There is no other circumstance on God's green earth more magnificent than what is occurring at this moment," Adam cheerfully said. "Ducking out in the middle of a starry night to go fishing…with my son…and sort of sneaking down the road, heading west."

"I was thinking the same thing, except, I have to insert *dad* where you said *son.*" Daniel lightly punched his dad on the arm. "You love this even more than I do," he said with kindness.

"All my life I have loved getting up when it's dark and gettin' on the road."

"Well, you didn't exactly *get up* now did you, Dad? I looked out three or four times last night and the lights in your workshop were shining brightly. You never went to bed."

"Never mind that. We're on the road now. We've got two stops to make: One, the Coffee Hut, and two, Mrs. Finfield's house."

"Why on earth her house?"

"I'm just sticking something in the mailbox. Look in that little box on the floor. Open it and read the note."

Daniel complied.

"Okay, Mr. McGyver! What are these? These are Mom's! Why are you giving Mom's earrings to Sarah? In a little Ziploc bag?"

"Read the note. It'll explain everything. And tell me what you think. Read it out loud."

"*Mrs. Finfield….*"

Daniel stopped abruptly.

"Mrs. Finfield? That's a little formal, wouldn't you say?"

"Maybe. Maybe not. Lately it seems like it might be better that way. Anyway, I asked you to read the note, not critique it!"

"Ooookay," replied his son.

Mrs. Finfield, in this little bag is a pair of earrings.

"Dad, she can see it's earrings! You don't have to tell her! Here. I'll write the note, and I'll just leave off the *Mrs. Finfield!*"

"Okay, make it *Sarah.*"

Sarah...Dad worked on these earrings last night so you'd have them while we are gone. One of them has a transmitter embedded in it. He wants you to wear these all the time, night and day. He doesn't know if it's a sixth sense, Murphy's Law, or God, but something is telling him that trouble is around the corner. As long as you have these on, he will be able to track you wherever someone might take you. Please put them on immediately. We should be back on Sunday night and he will see you at ten on Monday, God willing. You are close to being done with the house, he says, and making good progress with the Payce thing. We are praying for you and for your safety.

"How'd I do?" he asked as he folded the note.

"It's fine."

"It sounds like you're pretty worried."

"The reality," Adam said "is that now, more than ever since I first heard of this Payce Publishing thing, now that I know the prize, I believe they are capable of brutish means to get what they want, and that includes Mrs. Finfield. I wouldn't be surprised if they would break in while she's in the house, abduct her and take her to that office. What she thinks is that they'll come and get her in style, as she puts it: They'll knock at the door, ask her to go with them, and then take a friendly little ride. Either way, Danny boy, I would not be happy."

"But Dad, let's just say we're at our destination, four hours away; the Payces whisk her off to the office and she's in danger. So, she has the earrings on. How does that help? Do you have a time machine or space capsule gadget that will get you back there in time to save the widow in distress?"

"Don't think that I haven't thought about that. Remember,

though, I can call the police and tell them where she is. That's the only thing that gives me peace about being gone. Of course, I pray that nothing happens while we're gone. Two things: First of all, we'll only be gone four days, and secondly, though I'm uneasy, the Payces truly have been very quiet. In fact, it hit me in the middle of the night that perhaps they found what they are looking for, at least part of it." Adam sighed. "Now, is the note done?"

"Yeah, I think so."

"How about the P.S.?"

"I didn't write that yet."

"Read it to me."

P.S. Give your little spy gadget a try. Put the earrings on and go for a short ride. Be sure to have your cell phone (I hope it's charged…if not, charge it now). Then call me and I'll tell you where you are.

The burst of laughter that came from the passenger side of Adam's truck made him smirk.

"You laugh," Adam said, "but Adam Cook Private Eye may just save her life!"

Daniel's laughter erupted with even more gusto.

"I remember that chain thing you made for Mom because stuff kept falling behind the washer and dryer, the thing with the claw on the end!"

"It worked, didn't it? You always laugh at that one, but how about when someone kept letting the air out of your tires wherever you went. Huh? Huh? Now, son, do you know of another dad who would—or could—rig up a camera in their son's hubcap?"

"Well, that one was pretty clever. Most of your inventions, I have to say…have been pretty clever."

"Just add the P.S., please."

It was still dark when Adam pulled up to Sarah's mailbox.

"Here we are," he said in low tones. "Would you put that stuff back into the little bag and stick it in the mailbox? Do it quietly. We don't want to wake anyone up."

"Like Sarah? There's no one else around here."

"Yes, like Sarah. Just put the bag in the mailbox, okay?"

Adam and Daniel had completed task No. 1; stealthily, they drove the loop past Annette's house and back to the state road, headed towards task No 2; two large coffees and a box of donut holes, a little pre-breakfast snack—and they were off.

The back roads going west were closed and impassable, due to flooding. This meant detours. Though they had no schedule, a nagging sense of hurry was in the air; Daniel had to be back to his base by Sunday night. This was Thursday. Once out of the county, though, they were able to take off with speed down their favorite country roads toward their special fishing spot.

Conversation in the truck never lagged. The two chattered on with memories of days gone by, stories that included much of Melanie. Daniel's tales about military life were interesting and full of humor, but they stirred concern in Adam's heart as he realized the hazards of spending 24 hours a day with guys, some of whom boasted little moral character. Yet, Daniel reassured his dad with reports of finding a Sunday church service, a friendly couple with the gift of hospitality, and a couple of Christian buddies.

Such a relationship it was between the two! When as a younger teen, Daniel's life veered to the left or right, there was a great combination of love and wisdom on Adam's part, and an unusual respect for his dad on Daniel's.

As Adam drove along today, listening, talking, thinking, his arm resting on his open window, he repeatedly breathed a prayer of thanksgiving for this warm love between him and his son. A short way before time to stop for breakfast, Daniel brought up the subject of Annette.

"Do you know Annette very well, Dad?"

"Mostly just from what Sarah has told me, but I have picked up some signs of good character and sensitivity in her. I'm quite sure she is not a Christian."

"I think she wants to be—at least that's how it sounded to me."

Adam looked at his son, far too long to have his eyes off the road.

"She was full of questions, Dad," Daniel explained, "and that's why she hitched a ride with me."

"What do you mean?"

"It's a long story."

"Danny, it can't be too long. You've only known her for one day!"

"Well, Dad, you know a good author can write a whole fascinating book about the happenings of just one day! I'm telling you that it's a long story, but I'll make it short."

"I'm all ears! We've got a half an hour till we get to the Log Cabin. If you aren't done by then, you can continue the story while we're eating. You must know that I'm very interested. Go ahead."

"Did you see her out by the car before I drove away?"

"Yep."

"She stood right there, talking a mile a minute, her hair blowing every which way, and asked me point blank: 'Do you believe in God?' First she asked me, 'Where are you off to?' Then, just like that, she looked me straight in the eye and said, 'Do you believe in God?'"

"You're kidding."

"No, Dad," Daniel chuckled, "I'm not. Incredible, huh?"

"And you said?"

"Well, what do you think I said?" Daniel replied with a quiet laugh. "I said, 'Yes, I do.' But first, being very puzzled, I asked, 'Why do you ask?'"

"And she said?"

"'I saw a Bible in your dad's truck once and I figure if he believes in God, then you must, too.'"

"Wow. I can only remember one day when I had my Bible with me and that was early on in this whole thing. It was actually the day I met with the high school guys, you know, the Troopers, right after we got back from the missions trip to Honduras. That was at the beginning of summer. I can't even remember when I actually met her for the first time, but it had to be that day."

"Funny, isn't it? Anyway, she says to me, 'Will you talk to me about the Bible? I want to know more about God. No one seems to want to talk to me about it!' Then she sort of looked off to the cornfield and asked me if I'd mind having a passenger. 'I won't get in your way,' she said. 'Just talk to me while we're driving and I'll stay in the car or go for a walk while you visit your friends.' Then she looked back at me and said, 'It would mean a lot to me.'"

"So **that's** how it went down. We were very puzzled! So, you had an unexpected tagalong for the whole day, your day to see your buddies."

"She just popped into my day!"

"How very much like Annette! She just pops into your life and seems to stay. Ask Mrs. Finfield." Adam chuckled. "She notices everything—like a Bible on the front seat—and is not afraid to talk about it. What on earth did you do about visiting Chuck and Larry and whoever the third one was?"

"Mickey. I never made it to see Chuck and Larry. Annette and I had breakfast at Jerry's Corner...."

"Jerry's Corner! That's quite a trek!"

"Well, we talked on the way and talked while eating breakfast and talked on the way to Mickey's—but I only stayed there for a half an hour or so. She was home by two. When I went by Chuck and Larry's, their mom said they had to go somewhere. So I went home."

The Log Cabin had always been the only place to stop for breakfast when heading west. The rising sun and the familiar roadside billboard announcing that it was just five miles ahead, prepared Adam's taste buds for the famous blueberry pancakes and his favorite coffee anywhere. The Log Cabin was a tradition.

As the next five miles went by, he listened intently as Daniel told how he sacrificed his only day of catching up with his best friends to tell young Annette everything he could about his God. Adam listened, all the while weighing his son's narrative, thanking God for such a story, taking note of little phrases and explanations, seeking to be sure that what he was hearing was an account of a genuine encounter. The Log Cabin sign came into view.

"Hey, Son, look! I like that sight!" Adam interrupted.

"I love that it's a family tradition. We didn't have many but the ones we did are special to me."

It was time to eat. They sat down at a table near the window. Daniel picked up where he had left off in the Annette story.

"By the time we got to her house, she had fatigued me with questions." With a hearty laugh he said, "Each thing I told her just brought new questions! Somebody needs to talk more to her! She's definitely searching."

Adam held his coffee cup in both hands, his elbows resting on the rustic table. Closely, he watched his son's face as he finished up the story.

"We'll tell Sarah," he said. "She'll take care of the rest. She and Annette are bonding these days, you know."

When the two fishermen boarded the truck and once again started on their journey, Adam had two things on his mind. Was the transmitter working? That was the first question.

"Let's see where Mrs. Finfield is. Hmmm," he said, viewing the screen. "The earrings have not moved. Well, it's 9:15 only. She would not have gotten her mail by now, I guess. Let's just keep an eye on that thing. Now...let me ask you one question about Annette. Is it at all possible that she was an avid *seeker*, as you called her, because a handsome Marine was driving her around and was the one doing the explaining?"

Daniel rubbed his hand back and forth on his nearly bald head.

"To tell the truth, that thought crossed my mind, but, you know, as the day went on, I had no doubts that she was truly interested."

"Well, it crossed my mind, too, when I saw the two of you drive off. I worried a little. I was remembering Lori and Mary Beth and I sent up a quick prayer on your behalf. Annette is an attractive girl. You are a handsome boy. Sometimes that messes things up a bit."

Daniel shook his head, with enough emphasis to make his point.

"I'm 99% convinced that her interest is genuine. I can't say that I wasn't aware of the fact that she is attractive, but, I'll tell you, when I was talking to her, I had to work hard...and pray hard...to say the right things. She had a lot of questions; I had to dig deep into the knowledge base of all my years in church! No, I really didn't sense any amorous things going on. Besides, when she got out of the car, her last words were, 'I can't wait to tell Tony.'"

"Well, that's quite cool. When I next talk to Sarah, I'll let her know. I wonder what else is going to come from this whole Finfield thing!"

"You got your eye on...Mrs. Finfield, Dad?" Daniel asked with raised eyebrows.

"Daniel, that's not funny."

A long quiet intermission in the father-son conversation moved into the truck. A nearly imperceptible smile was on Daniel's lips; Adam's expression was stern.

"Dad, you just missed the turn to the lodge," Daniel smirked.

"Never mind that. Check the whereabouts of Mrs. Finfield again."

"No movement. Besides, she's supposed to call you after she does a test run, right?"

Adam found a spot to turn around and went back to Tamarack Trail feeling a smidgeon of embarrassment at having missed the road that he knew like the back of his hand. The truck wound its way down the meandering road and came to rest in front of Cabin 8 which overlooked Lake Loon from a low ridge. Adam looked out the window, unnerved by his son's question and firmly resolving to redirect the foolish conversation as quickly as possible. Daniel, however, was not through.

"Why not, Dad?"

"Let it go, son."

"Now listen, Dad. There are some things I want to say."

"Daniel, we are not going to talk about this. Let's get our stuff into the cabin."

"Just one thing, okay? I would be absolutely in favor of you marrying again. And so, too, I'm pretty certain, would Mom. And I told you what I thought of Mrs. Finfield the night I came home by surprise and found her in our driveway."

"That's enough."

"Just wanted you to know that I wouldn't stand in the way. I'd be for it. You think I like thinking of you being alone all the time?"

"I'm not alone all the time. Right now I have had steady work at Sarah's house and more yet to do."

"Well, that's sort of what I mean. You'll never know how glad I was to come home and find you *not at home all the time*—but with Mrs. Finfield, the widow!"

"Daniel," Adam said with a very persuasive inflection, "Mrs. Finfield is a client and I am ten years older than she is. There is nothing for you to get excited about."

"You told me she's a Christian! A good one! And what's ten years! So, what would keep you from finding her attractive?"

"I didn't say that I don't find her attractive. I said we're not going to talk about this."

"Just one more thing."

"You had your *one more thing*," Adam said with a faint grin, his hand on the door handle. "Now, did we come here for a counseling session or to fish? Let's go."

He got out and began to work with obvious fervor to transfer the fishing gear and suitcases to the cabin. In the spirit of things, Daniel joined in on the operation. When all was finished, he caught his dad by the arm as he began to climb the steps.

"I'm sorry, Dad. It's your life...and you certainly don't need my help."

Adam grabbed him and hugged him.

"I'm content the way things are, son. I kind of like my solitude. Besides, I took on a carpentry job and it turned out that God used me in a couple of different ways. Sarah was what you might call... lifeless...when I first encountered her; now I see signs of crocuses and tulips and...and hyacinths—so to speak—poking up through her difficult life. And now, besides the huge restoration thing, we've been thrown together to try to unravel this strange mystery and really, I'm convinced, to save her life. Besides," Adam said giving his son a light shove up the stairs, "her widower fiancé from college days has entered the scene. I don't know where that's going but I'm happy for her. She's off to spend time with Missionary Scott somewhere in the mountains of Mexico in a week or so. That's where things stand. I still love your mother. So, the answer is *no*, I don't have my eye on Mrs. Finfield."

That was not to be the final dialogue on the subject, but anticipation for a day of fishing on Lake Loon moved Adam and Daniel to an understandable mode of hurry. Within a half an hour, the groceries were in the refrigerator, sleeping bags on the beds and everything having to do with catching fish all situated in the boat. Both working together, Daniel very accustomed to his part in the operation, the boat was lowered into the water at the only ramp—rocky and uneven—at this almost secret spot near the Mississippi. Eight cabins—that was all there were—and they were hidden from each other by the dense foliage. For 20 years, the Cooks had reserved Cabin 8. It, too, was a tradition.

In the silence of the morning, the sun peeking through clouds that might possibly muster up another storm, father and son chatted in low tones, discussing lures and what spot to try next, struggling now and then with snagged lines, but successfully catching fish! Daniel could not help but take note of how often his dad checked the screen for signs of movement back on Timber Lane.

At 11:10, Adam snapped his fingers and pointed at the screen.

"Movement," he said quietly. For fifteen minutes, in between casts, he followed her route on the screen.

Finally, his cell phone rang.

"Well, well! There you are sitting at Pittman and River Roads!"

"Now that's scary! I'm not sure I'm going to like this!" Sarah soundly declared.

"But Sarah, it puts your big brother at ease." A question mark showed itself on Daniel's face. "What," Adam asked, "are you doing at Pittman and River Roads?"

"I'm good with the county now and so I took the opportunity to drive out and get inside the house. It's pretty awful inside. It looks like Mildred had not been back there since she married Richard. It's musty and dusty—everything just sitting there like a museum. So, I'm just now heading home."

"Well, while you're in the neighborhood, would you pull my garbage cans out to the road? I forgot to do that this morning!" Adam laughed. Daniel smiled, feeling very sure that he knew exactly what was going on. "I'm only kidding," Adam joked.

"I don't mind doing that," Sarah responded. "Are you serious?"

"No, I'm just kidding you."

"How is it going out there?"

"You know, we couldn't ask for anything better. We got here safe. We got settled in. We caught fish. We'll make a fire tonight and have a feast."

"Well, Adam—Mr. McGyver—are you satisfied that this very nice pair of earrings is working?"

"I am."

"Okay, then. I'm off to Timber Lane. I have a long list of things to do. I must get my passport today, along with a bunch of other things. Have fun."

"When are you leaving? I forgot."

"August 24th."

"You gonna need a ride to the airport?"

"I...I...uh, I think I'll just drive and park. I can't believe I'm saying that...but I used to do it all the time."

"Well, you can always look up Adam Cook Taxi Service in the Yellow Pages."

Sarah understood his meaning and was amused at his lightheartedness.

"It's going to be a stretch for me." She sighed. "I'm sure I'll do just fine. It's the single-engine airplane ride when I get there that has me biting my nails!"

"Where's your final destination?"

"I fly to Mexico City. That's where I board the *little* plane, as Scott calls it, and fly to Villa de Tututepec. I'm sure I'm not pronouncing it correctly. Then there's a long drive. We drive for most of a day to get to where he lives."

The inner thoughts of Adam Cook could not be detected by his voice, but Daniel, his perceptive and caring son, watched as the expressions on his father's face changed as he talked cheerfully with Mrs. Finfield—and changed again and again.

"You getting excited?"

"Yes...and no. You will never know how I have gone back and forth on this. It took much persuasion on Scott's part...by letter and by phone. I will go. I must trust God for the rest."

"You'll do fine. You're back on your feet...or very close to it. Hey, one more thing before I go: Has Annette been by?"

"I haven't seen her. Why?"

"We were talking about her before and I just wondered. Daniel tells me she's asking lots of questions about the Bible."

"I know she is. I must make time to talk with her. Maybe this afternoon."

"Well, okay. Let's sign off. Be cautious, Sarah. We're praying that things will remain quiet back there. I'll be watching."

"I have mixed emotions about that!" she declared, her words thick with sarcasm. "Bye for now."

"Yep. Bye."

Daniel squinted at his dad and smiled. His father's expression resounded with the message: "Let it go."

Adam napped in the afternoon, dead tired from his all-night inventing, pacing, packing and praying. For Daniel, it was a perfect opportunity to walk around the whole lake, fishing now and then from the shore. Shortly after five, the two met up at the water's edge.

"Man! I'm ready to eat," called Daniel.

"Well, come on! Mr. Cook is ready to cook!"

Now it was time to talk again and when they finally sat down at the picnic table and gave thanks for the food, they journeyed deep into talk of Timber Ridge, of Annette and Sarah, and of the Herman Lichten books. Just like his father, Daniel's thinking began to fire up, devising ways to outsmart the Payces, and his ability to think things through logically took him chapter by chapter since the day of the fire.

Lake Loon was now a tradition. Adam and Melanie had started it way back when they were expecting Daniel. And a meal on the shores of Lake Loon, cooked in Adam's heavy cast iron pans and over an open fire, had always been a favorite part of the yearly vacation.

"In a way, son, you've been coming here for twenty years," Adam said, finishing off his coffee, "if you count the year that Mom was pregnant with you."

"This is almost like home to me. I love this place. I always liked this cabin because you can see the sun rise to the left and see it set on the right." Daniel sighed a sigh of contentment. "We did okay today, don't you think?"

"Yep. We'll get up early tomorrow and get out there. You through eating? Want more coleslaw?"

"No, sir! I ate a lot!"

"Let's clean up. I'll take care of the food and the dishes. You take care of the fire and the garbage. Here. Here's the garbage bag. And then, how about Scrabble?"

"Oh, Dad, you want to get beat again?"

An even match they were, their scores staying extremely close as they played and joked, drinking Shasta soda from a little store down the road. It, too, was a tradition. Adam checked on Sarah's whereabouts repeatedly; he was relieved when her errands were apparently completed and her car pulled into the driveway at 5:35 in the afternoon. He settled back comfortably into his chair. It was the first time since the game had started.

"Well, she's home. That's good. I hope she remembers to set the alarm."

Daniel got up slowly, aching a bit from sitting so long. He rummaged around in "The Goodie Box" and found peanut butter cookies.

"Want one?" he asked, leaning up against the bedroom door frame.

"Yes and no," his dad said, with a chuckle. "Maybe later."

"Dad, let's talk."

"Haven't we been?"

"I mean, let's have a heart-to-heart talk."

Adam's eyes locked on the word *contentment* on the board. It would come in handy, he surmised. Daniel was standing directly behind him now, and after brushing off the cookie crumbs, came and put his hands on his dad's shoulders. He massaged them for a moment and then set the heart-to-heart talk in motion.

"Dad, you have not really stopped thinking about Mrs. Finfield for one moment since we got here. Do you know that?"

"That…is not true," Adam retorted firmly, yet kindly, in his defense.

"It is true. That little gadget has not left your sight and you have not left off scanning it."

"Daniel, Daniel," his dad said in a near pleading tone, stretching his neck back so that he could almost see his son, "surely you know the difference between loving and protecting. Mrs. Finfield is my client. A customer. I am like her big brother," he continued, leaving out the fact that he was quoting Sarah verbatim. "She is in trouble. I love getting people out of trouble. You know that. And now I am making sure she stays out of trouble."

"You know, I partly believe that. In fact, I believe that; but, Dad, I'm no dummy and I see your face light up when you talk to her or when you talk about her."

"That's nonsense, Daniel. I've only known Mrs. Finfield for…27 days! My goodness!"

"It's not nonsense. It's true. And you know what? I like seeing it. You're so young, Dad, and it's going to be a long, lonely life all by yourself."

"I don't count out the possibility of marriage someday. I'm not interested now, though. I'm really not interested now, son. It's only a little more than a year since Mom died."

He turned in his chair so that he could look at the handsome Marine.

"Sit, son. Let me talk to you."

Daniel relinquished his position where he had been *mentoring* his father, and sat once again in his chair at the little wood table in the center of the cabin. Adam pointed at the Scrabble board.

"You see that word? Contentment? That describes Adam Cook." He shook his head. "I don't mind this life. I have lots to do. I have lots of work and lots of clients. I have friends—good ones—who keep after me. We spend time together and that's good. I've got church. I've got Pastor Pruitt. You should not worry about me."

"I'm not exactly worried," Daniel said, trying to put his finger on what exactly was bothering him. "I'm thinking that you shouldn't pass up the prettiest girl at the party. I want to ask you if you are blind, but then, as I said a few minutes ago, I think you're seeing the truth, but...what, Dad? Scared? Giving up? Not sure? Too soon? Love for Mom? Dad," Daniel said with facial expressions showing his unmistakable deep conviction on the subject, "I think you're in love! You know, Dad, just like that!"—Daniel snapped his fingers—"you told me how many days it has been since you met! Why would you be counting?"

Adam threw back his head and laughed heartily.

"Are we done?"

"No."

"I mean, are we done with the game?"

"Yes, except for one thing...well, two."

Adam laughed quietly.

"You're good at getting two for one!"

"First, do you realize that Mom and Chip probably know each other up there in heaven, and they don't care if you marry Mrs. Finfield? Oh, I know, that's conjecture, but you know, realistically, it's true. So, that restraint has to go. And secondly, look at this Scrabble word of yours—contentment. Actually, you just took my word—content—and made it longer. And then what did you put down over here? You put down...alone!"

"It's a game, Daniel! All I had was a **Z** and a **Q** and a **J** and an **A**, an **L**, an **O**, and an **N**!"

Adam jumped up, pulled his son from his chair and began a father-son wrestling match, one like so many in the past.

"Come on, buddy! Your dad can still take you, Marine or not!" He maneuvered Daniel into a headlock. "I'll let you go if you promise to put an end to this Daniel Cook Dating Service thing!" He rubbed his knuckles on Daniel's tanned scalp.

"I could take you, Dad, but I don't want to hurt you."

"Oh, ho, ho! Who's got who in a headlock? Give me your word: No more Sarah talk!"

"I've said all I need to say, except for one thing."

"You've had your *one thing*."

"If I were you—I know, I know, I've said this before—I'd go after that prettiest girl at the party. I can see she's pretty special—a good catch. And, Dad, I'd do it pretty quick. Sounds like there's a missionary waiting in the wings."

Adam released his hold and put his arms around Daniel's neck, pulling him close.

"Let it go, son," he said. "I am content."

"And alone."

"I'm not alone. We have a great God. He and I walk together. He says He'll never leave me."

"He also says, 'He that finds a wife, finds a good thing.'"

"I've had a wife—the best a man could ask for."

"Have another one, the lovely lady of Timber Lane."

"You're a pain in the neck."

"Remember...the apple doesn't fall too far from the tree!"

"Come on, my boy, let's get some sleep. It's almost ten. We'll get out on the lake by five tomorrow morning, okay?"

CHAPTER 17

The red digital numbers told Sarah it was exactly 5:00 a.m., a fact which registered with her the moment she suddenly sat up in bed. Something had awakened her. She swung her legs over the edge of the bed, puzzled and to some degree, apprehensive. She reached for her glasses, and after throwing her light terry cloth robe around her, parted the drapes covering the sliders in her room. There, she heard it again. Was it the garbage truck? No, this was Friday. She sat back down on the bed. It was disturbing that the sound seemed to be coming from the back door. Was someone trying to get into the house? It was not a ridiculous idea, given the incidents of the past months. Could it be Adam? No, Adam was off fishing.

"I am going to walk through my house and go to the back door, turn on the light and look outside," she said with raw determination. Halfway down the long hall, she heard the noise again—a rattling definitely coming from the kitchen door leading to the deck. Quite startled, instinct sent her dashing to her room, her robe trailing behind. Hurriedly, she shut the door and locked it. *"At least in here, if necessary, I've got the patio doors as an escape route,"* she thought.

She stared at the clock. From 5:04 to 5:15, she heard no more sounds. Mustering courage, she ventured out into the hall again, stopping to look out of the windows in the second bedroom. The sky was losing its blackness. There were no hints of trouble or activity. "My heart is beating like a kettle drum," she whispered, slowly inching her way toward the kitchen. She peeked around the corner, cautiously, where she could view the back door. She saw nothing and no one. Her level of bravery increased. Trembling, she took six long strides, reached for the door knob and unlocked the door, simultaneously, yanking it open.

The suction her strong pull created rattled the screen door. It rattled again with the wind. Angrily, Sarah grabbed the door handle and jerked it shut, and then firmly shut the kitchen door.

"Ohhhh!" she scowled, looking at the ceiling, "I will not let this happen to me! I will not let this happen to me!"

Up and down the hall she marched, back and forth; into the family room she went, with long strides, circling the furniture, and going from one end of the room to the other; in and out of each bedroom, into each bathroom, into every corner of the house, she stalked, speaking with a loud voice that steadily increased in volume with each step: "All right! That's enough!" she barked, shaking her finger at her invisible foe. "You've had your day! Now it's my turn! You will not do this to me! You cannot frighten me anymore! That's enough, Payce brothers! It's enough, it's enough, it's enough! It's over! I will not run scared anymore! Watch out for me, ohhhh, watch out for me! You cannot mess with me anymore!"

When she returned to her room, the clock read 5:54. She plunked down in the recliner.

"Ohhhhh!" she exclaimed, her face twisted with resolve and fury. "I will not let this happen to me again! I...will...not...live in fear!"

Going back to bed was out of the question. Into the shower she went with haste, still grumbling, though now in more subdued normal *Sarah tones*. Quietness gradually seeped into her spirit and gradually she became still. As the water soothed her body, she let God's peace soothe Sarah Finfield.

"Be of good cheer; it is I; don't be afraid." The words of Jesus to His disciples on the tumultuous sea came whispering to her listening heart. She began to hum. It was a favorite song that popped into her head, one from long ago, almost forgotten: *"I heard the voice of Jesus say, 'Come unto Me and rest. Lay down, thou weary one, lay down thy head upon My breast.'"* Water, like rain, fell gently from the shower head, blending with the tears, and bringing hope and comfort to a revived, renewed widow.

ชชชชช

Annette appeared shortly after six o'clock in the afternoon, and when Sarah opened the door, the neighbor girl bounced into the house, and dragged Sarah by the hand into the kitchen.

"Annette, I need to shut the front door!" she exclaimed.

"Leave it open! I've got something to tell you!"

"I'll be right back. Hold on for a minute."

The bouncing girl came to rest at the kitchen table, flopping down into one of the chairs. Sarah returned and stood in front of her.

"No, no. You must sit down."

Sarah sat down. Annette took both of Mrs. Finfield's hands in

198

hers, leaned forward over the table, and smiled broadly.

"I would have come earlier," she said with pronounced sincerity, "but I have been with Tony, talking and talking and talking. All afternoon. Well, not all afternoon. I didn't get up until one. But since then, we've been talking. He just went home and I ran down here as fast as I could. I ran like a deer! That's how it felt! Look at me—I'm barefoot, and yet I ran down the gravel road and felt no pain! Oh, it did hurt a little. Well, anyway, are you ready for news?"

"Yes, Annette, you have made me very curious! Let me see your left hand."

Annette laughed jovially. "Oh, no! It's way better than that! Well, I may as well just come right out and say it. Mrs. Finfield, I am now a Christian! I think. A believer, as Daniel puts it."

"What?"

"I am a brand new Christian!" Annette repeated. "I think," she added slowly.

"What on earth are you talking about?"

"You know how I kept asking you about God? Well, I asked everybody about Him." Her eyes widened and she shook her head slowly. "Whenever I was out at night especially, I just knew there must be a God with the beauty of the sky, the stars…and especially the moon. You remember, right?"

"Yes, I remember."

"I asked a lot of people but everyone either thought I was crazy or too young…or something."

"So, you are now a Christian?" Sarah asked, not able to steer clear completely of the skepticism that was troubling her.

"I am! I think. I finally found someone who would listen to my questions and knew the answers!"

Sarah gave the teenager a sidelong glance.

"And who was that, Annette?"

"I told you. It was Daniel."

"Daniel? Adam's son, Daniel?"

"Yes. Remember that I went with him yesterday?"

"Yes?"

"He and I talked as we drove and while we ate breakfast. He told me all about the cross and about Jesus and when we got to my house, he said that someday I would have to make a decision about everything, you know, about Jesus dying for me. He said I needed to stop and pray at some point along life's way and tell Jesus I believed in Him, who He is, you know, the Son of God, and that He died for me." Annette leaned in closer to Sarah and expressively said, "You know, I always believed He died for the sins of the world, and I always kind of felt like it was my fault, and it turns out, it was! So, last night, I prayed to the Lord—I think my prayer was probably very long—but that probably doesn't surprise you—but when I was done, I think...I was saved! I'm a believer, Mrs. Finfield! I'm pretty sure I'm a Christian!"

Sarah watched in total surprise as Annette, in her animated, cheerful and talkative way, told the story of her encounter with God the night before.

"I'm 18 years old and I'm old enough to decide, and I'm telling you the truth. Mrs. Finfield, something happened in here." Suddenly, Annette's expression changed and she became very serious. "Mrs. Finfield, are **you**...a Christian? If you're not, you should be."

Pulling her left hand from Annette's gentle grip, Sarah placed her hand over her mouth and shut her eyes. Her forehead scrunched into a symmetrical series of wrinkles.

"Dear, dear Annette," she began woefully, "I am, and I have been almost my whole life." She opened her eyes. "But I have been, what you might say, living in a coffin for the last year or so. I climbed in and pulled the lid down tight. I'm not proud of it, for I sensed your yearning for God and I failed you."

"Ohhh, Mrs. Finfield!" the teenager wailed melodiously.

"Please, let me say more. I have been angry with God, if you can believe such a thing, as though He, in meanness, snatched my husband from me. I lost my trust in Him. I crawled into a dark chasm and died. How many times did you bring up your questions? And I ignored you. I'm sorry, Annette. I'm sorry, but I'm thrilled that now you have put your faith in Christ."

"Well...and I'm thrilled that you crawled out of the dark chasm! You know, I could see it happening, not that I see you that much, but I thought, 'She's nicer than she used to be.' I said that to you one night, remember?"

"I do. I do. How odd life is! Daniel comes home for a few days, you climb into his car, and he pays attention to your question marks!"

"Do you think I did it right...praying, I mean?"

"The Bible says that if you confess with your mouth that Jesus is Lord, and believe in your heart that God has raised Him from the dead, you will be saved. It sounds to me like you prayed a prayer of faith and understanding. We can pray together right here, right now, you and I. It's one of the very best things about being a Christian... praying together. I'd like that."

"Really? You mean…just pray out loud right here?"

"Yes, Annette. Right here."

"I wonder if I'd be embarrassed."

"After hearing your story, I doubt it! I'll pray first; then you can pray. Okay?"

"Okaaay."

The two joined hands once again and Sarah began to pray. Though she did not weep, tears rolled down her cheeks as she unhurriedly talked to God.

"Heavenly Father, Almighty God, how loving You are! In Your wisdom and love, You have brought Annette and me together. We just want to thank You for Your amazing love and for salvation. Thank You that our sins are forgiven because Jesus shed his blood to pay the price of our sins. Thank You for the cross. Thank You for Your promise of eternal life to all who believe. Father, how I thank You that Annette has put her faith in Your Son! I pray for her. I pray that she will make You Lord of her life. I pray that she will walk with You from now on and learn more of You every day. I pray that You will guide her future and that she will live for You. Thank You for Daniel and that he cared enough to share the truth with her. And thank You that You have revived me and put me back on my feet…and thank You for Your forgiveness for long months of turning away from You. We love You. We pray in Jesus' name, Amen."

Annette opened her eyes wide and looked at Sarah. "I could never pray like that!"

Sarah smiled. "Just talk to Him like you talk to me."

"Okaaay. Our Father who art in heaven—well, that's not how I talk to you, Mrs. Finfield—anyway, God and Father, I am the one who prayed to You last night. Remember? I know I am saved because…well, because You said so…and because I feel it, right here. In a way, I thank You for the three prowlers. I'm sure it was no accident that I met Mrs. Finfield because then I met Adam and then I met Daniel and he told me about You. I'm going to tell my dad and mom. You know Dad; he does not believe in You. And Father, I guess I'll need help with Tony, too. I think that's all except to thank you for Daniel. Amen."

Embarrassment was not something that Annette experienced often. Her bubbly personality made it so that even at times she should have experienced it, a simple kind of confidence and enthusiasm snuffed it out. Today, however, her expression at the end of her prayer, as she looked into Sarah's face, was one of uncertainty and awkwardness. Sarah encouraged her.

"How God must love the prayers of new Christians!"

"Really?"

"Really. And you must tell Daniel as soon as you can what has happened. Adam and he are fishing today, you know."

"Oh, that's right. Fishing. I'd love to try that sometime. Doesn't that just sound heavenly? Oh, how I wish I was there right now!"

"I'm sure they are enjoying the peace and quiet...of the lake, I mean. You said you were talking to Tony. I'm assuming you were talking about all of this?"

"We were. He says he believes but that he never wants to be wrapped up in all of it. I think you could call it sort of a Sunday religion...and not really even that because he doesn't even go to church except on Easter...not even Christmas. But he says he loves me with his whole heart and anything I want to believe is all right with him."

"Well, you and I can talk about that. Keep talking to him, though. Most often, it takes time."

"I will because I think that I love him as much as he loves me. Yet, just knowing that someone like Daniel exists sort of casts a different light on the whole issue of love and marriage. Wouldn't it be nice to be married to someone who knew all that stuff? Was Mr. Finfield a Christian? I can only imagine that the answer is *yes*.'"

"He was. A fine Christian."

"I knew it! What a day! What a wonderful day! I'd give anything to be able to tell Daniel right now!"

CHAPTER 18

A soft mist hung over the lake Friday morning. All was still. The soul of a fisherman carries within it a deep affection for that stillness; it is equal to the catching of fish. The beauty of nature and the joy of the sport could not, however, surpass the companionship of this father and son. Adam had missed his son; he just hadn't known how much. And Daniel who had, for the most part, spent his days and years knowing that life was not all about him, detected that loneliness in his dad—after all, it had only been a little more than a year since Mom had died.

Thursday had been a perfect day for fishing, but also for meaningful conversation; the subject of the Payce Publishing mystery became the topic of choice. As Adam and Daniel had taken turns keeping a nearly constant watch on Sarah's whereabouts, the two had pried into the facts, hoping to have a brainstorm. None came—that is, not until after lunch on Friday.

Daniel wanted to nap. Adam needed a therapeutic jaunt. Since Daniel understood his father's fondness for driving and his custom of taking a drive when he needed to think, and Adam understood that when his son said he needed a nap, he needed a nap, when the silver truck left its parking spot beside the cabin, father and son were equally content. Adam had a route in mind: A familiar stretch of winding, hilly road along the river.

The truck, moving casually along at fifty miles per hour or so, was the perfect place to think. It always was. There, as each mile showed off its particular late summer scenes, Adam's brain, at first, jumped from subject to subject. Then, as he himself settled down, so did his thought patterns. Specific spots along the road reminded him of Melanie, for they had often driven this very path together. Very few tears had been shed since her death; but today, Adam had an unknown sentiment surfacing in his spirit, and he did not hold back the ones rolling down his cheeks. How he missed her! Years of such closeness somehow made death harder. In a way, losing a spouse

203

would be easier if a marriage had been only casual. For Adam, however, every red barn, every country-road antique shop, every small town restaurant, all the town squares and local IGAs, a thousand songs, each sunset and sunrise...even the towering green and white interstate signs...everything reminded Adam of his beautiful wife. He remembered how she often rode with her hand on his back, gazing at him, listening and chatting and laughing.

"I could never forget that," he told himself. "I could never let go of all of that. Ah, I needed this drive to straighten me out! I'm going to have to put this Mrs. Finfield thing to rest with Daniel," he concluded out loud, "and I'm going to have to put it to rest in my own heart, if indeed there is even a speck of such a thought." He argued with himself as to whether there was such a speck! Mrs. Finfield was a client, one that God evidently had arranged to be so. He liked her. He liked working for her, and in reality, working with her, for she labored persistently alongside him—an impressive sidekick. He had seen her change, taking tiny baby steps toward healing, and that gave him pleasure. But, today as his truck smoothly moved along down this much loved country road, he reinforced in his own mind that Sarah Finfield was a client, and only a client. Tears dry now, Adam chuckled, remembering her asking him if he was an angel.

"First an angel...now a big brother!" he said with a smile. "That's me!"

These thoughts could not but take him to ones of the terrible home invasion and demolition. Nearly 24/7, mulling over the facts, dealing with his own anger, and searching for a key to the whole thing occupied his attention. "A key, a key," he had always said about every puzzling situation, "there has to be a key." But it had eluded him in this case. As he drove, he decided to think through what he did know for sure and then, he'd go over the things that perhaps he could do to get this thing resolved.

"I'm 99% sure Chip did not take his own life. That's first. What does that leave for an explanation then? Does it mean that someone else was responsible? What other alternative is there? I don't know. I don't even know what it would take to find out. But I'm feeling mighty sure about that.

"And then, there is the fire," he went on, his thoughts very deep. *"The fire took place very soon after Herman and Chip met that night. What does that mean? Was there anyone who might have seen something that night? Did anyone investigate or was it a foregone conclusion that it was just a gas explosion? Had Herman left the building after Chip went home? Yes, Sarah had filled him on all of that."*

Just moseying along now, Adam thought upon the possibilities regarding that fire. Could it have been an accident, or was it arson or worse yet, murder? Would anyone ever know for sure? Probably not.

Now that Adam and Sarah were aware of the additional eleven manuscripts and that the Payces were also aware of them, it seemed to Adam that their wicked rules of the game would most certainly have upped for the worse. He shook his head, acknowledging to himself that nothing—absolutely nothing—was out of the realm of possibility for the Payces' definition of *ethical*. Deviously, they would do whatever it took to obtain the books, and being masters at appearing to be honest and principled, they could very possibly pull it off. Adam groaned. He wanted to be a one-man army, if necessary, to put a halt to their crusade.

Why, he wondered, was he so incited by this? *"Well, this is why,"* he reasoned within himself, *"I hate violence and I hate when people bully others!"* There was something else though. It was the widow. Mrs. Finfield, was in danger. That, he admitted, was the real issue.

He pulled his truck to a spot high above the Mississippi River where he could sit for a while and look down on the little town on the other side and at the barges going their way, north or south. For a while, he left off his deliberations regarding the Timber Lane mystery. He had always loved the river. *"One day,"* he had once thought, *"I will live on the Mississippi."* But that was a long time ago. Though the sight of this beautiful river gently dividing the United States into two stirred him, he was content now in Timber Ridge. Contentment had become a permanent part of him. He was glad.

"Something else," he mentally journeyed on, *"I am significantly suspicious that those manuscripts are at the house. Now, I know they could have gone up in the fire,"* Adam intelligently surmised. *"That is a strong possibility. In fact, I can think of no reason why Chip would have brought them home with him except...except that a fully operating Finfield Publishing was just around the corner. Chip and Herman could have come to an agreement about publishing those books...not right away, but when Chip was free to do so! That is a possibility! A strong one!"*

Adam wished he could just dial Sarah and talk over this idea with her, but things were different now. Uneasiness checked him. Besides, what good was such news without an idea as to where those manuscripts could be? Even if Herman and Chip had discussed the possibility of Chip's new company publishing the books, it did not necessarily follow that Chip would bring all eleven home—or any, for that matter.

A barge with the name **BROCK TRANSPORTS** made its way into view with its monotone engine becoming louder as it came closer.

Adam watched as it pushed south and wondered if the owner was somehow related to Melanie since her maiden name had been Brock. The drone of the engine brought pleasure to him. He had always loved that sound. He still did.

"Eleven manuscripts nowhere to be found," he continued in his solving mode. *"I don't know. It just can't be that there are eleven handwritten manuscripts hidden in that house!"* Adam stopped to consider the shed, the well-built shed in the yard, constructed by Chip and as solid as First National Bank. Could they be out there? Why would he put them out there?—unless, of course, to hide them in a place where no one would think of looking! *"I don't think anyone looked out there. I know I didn't. Well, that's a possibility...you might say, the last one. I've checked the garage out. There's nothing in the garage except the rake and hoe and those tools, and that cabinet with paint in it. There's nothing in Chip's trunk. The shed is the only place left to look as far as I can figure!"*

For just a few minutes, Adam got out of his truck and sat on a tree stump where he could watch the barge and the rest of the refreshing scene below. He turned his hat around so his cheeks could feel the heat of the afternoon sun. He allowed his mind to think forward to what might occur if answers didn't come soon. What could the Payces do further to get what they wanted?

He looked at his watch. Two-thirty. Time to head back to the lake. He stuck his fingers into his back pockets and with his eye, followed the river to the south, and then to the north. It was a beautiful sight and he could gladly live here; but no, home at Pitman and River Roads was all that a man could want.

Hardly ever did Adam have the radio on in his truck; he just liked it quiet most of the time. Today, he pushed the button and found a country music station. A couple of minutes later, he turned it off. The majestic sounds of the classical music he had heard at Sarah's on Tuesday evening came to mind. Such music! He hoped that he would soon hear the Chopin composition that Sarah liked. He could visualize Chip and Sarah together, now that he was learning a little more about them each day. How loving! How talented! What a team! Chip's hidden turntable had genuinely impressed Adam and had given him some ideas for his own house.

"That really is pretty cool," he mused. *"No one would ever suspect such a thing. No one would ever just think, 'I think I'll just go press the eye of the eagle and see what happens!'"*

In an instant, he strongly suspected that he had stumbled upon a key—a key to the whole case! Why had he not thought of this before? He forgot his qualms about calling Sarah and reached for his phone. After fighting to get it out of his front jeans pocket and past the seatbelt, he speed dialed her. Sarah answered after a few rings with a cheerful, "Hi!"

"Hi," Adam said, doing his best to sound like a big brother. "How you doin'?"

"I'm actually pretty good," she replied. "Why are you calling? You're supposed to be fishing."

"Hey, I just had a couple of ideas come to mind. Maybe you can check them out."

"Where are you? It sounds like you're driving."

"I am. I went for one of my think tank drives. You know."

"I do. I take it you're by yourself?"

"Yep, Daniel's taking a nap."

"So what are your ideas?"

"One of them could be a solid one; the other is a shot in the dark. First of all, we didn't check the shed. I didn't, at least. Did you?"

"No. I never thought of it. I wonder if the brothers did."

"You should be able to tell if they were out there when you go out to look."

"I'll go and look around and I should probably check above the dropped ceiling. I'll stand on the tractor and take a look."

"That's a great thought, but don't take chances. Maybe get the ladder and Sarah, maybe get Annette to help you!"

"Very funny," Sarah moaned. "I'll be careful."

"Okay. Well, that's one. The second one is…go get the note Chip wrote, the one in your Bible."

"Well, it's not in my Bible anymore, but I'll get it."

"Read it to me."

"Well, here. It says, *'Sarah, this is the key: The Eye of the Eagle. If you remember that, the rest will be easy.'* Then it gives all those numbers."

"Sarah, Sarah. Think for a minute. The Eye of the Eagle. What could that mean?"

"I don't know. I've tried to figure it out, but I don't know. It's the name of a book, I think."

"Keep talking to me, but go to the family room." He waited a moment. "What do you see?"

Immediately, the light dawned. Sarah gasped.

"The eye of the eagle!"

"Do you think it could tie in somehow?" Adam asked.

"It certainly seems like it should. It sounds feasible. But how? I don't see how it ties in with what we're looking for."

"I'm wondering…could it be that there's more to that turntable apparatus? Check it out and see if there's some hidden opening or latch or something. But, then, too, could it have something to do with the albums? Could he have hidden the manuscripts page by page in the covers? It's a highly unlikely possibility, I know, but you could at least just look in some of them. I could see him hiding three or four pages in each one."

"What other *eye of the eagle* do we have as a clue? I was sure it was the name of a book. You may be on to something, Adam. We know that Chip was a master at hiding things!" Sarah shook her head. "Anything is worth a try. I've got some things on my list to do before I leave but this is a priority. I'll get it done. Annette is here. She'll help, I know."

"Good….and Sarah, I think you're going to have to check the sleeves inside, too. We've got to be sure."

"Why are you thinking about this when you're supposed to be vacationing? Stop it!"

"Sarah, at this stage in the game the whole thing is churning, churning, churning inside. It gets in my blood. I told you that right from the start, on Day One, right?"

"You did. But go now and catch some more fish and eat some more fish and have fun with Daniel. And I will find a way to buzz through the albums and I'll check around the turntable. Part of me is encouraged with hope; part of me says that this is a long shot."

"No way to tell without trying. I'm on my way back to the cabin. It was a good diversion for me. But one more thing. I can't get it out of my head that Chip may very well have brought those manuscripts home with him. This is another thing that just came to me a little while ago. Isn't it a very strong possibility that Chip and Herman ended up with some kind of arrangement to have Finfield Publishing do the books? If there was bad blood between the old man and Payce—which it sounds like there was from the fact that Chip told you Herman would not sign a contract for the second book—then perhaps Chip told him about his new company, either on purpose or by accident. Even at that, I guess it doesn't prove anything, but…Chip could have ended up bringing them home."

"There would be a clause in Chip's arrangement with Payce, though, regarding current clients and freedom to publish…can't re-member what they call that."

"Well, I have a gut feeling about this, Sarah. I'm thinking those manuscripts are at your house. We just haven't found them."

"Well, they're in some secret compartment somewhere then. Or up by the rafters. Or, buried in a secret box in the garden. Or…well, I guess if Chip could so successfully hide the safe behind the mirror and his turntable in a conspicuous wall, then he could have certainly hidden the books."

"Hey, those are good thoughts! Not too farfetched!"

"I'll tell you what, while I'm gone, have at it! I'll be gone two weeks. While you're doing the floors—or afterwards—just go step by step, inch by inch, and see what you can find. For now, I've got to go, especially if I'm going to get at the records!"

"Are you doin' okay?"

Sarah responded with a quiet laugh and proceeded to tell Adam of her frightening morning and the subsequent calm.

"I'm sort of a different person than I was this morning. If you would have been a fly on the wall you would not have recognized the Sarah Finfield of five o'clock a.m.! I'm okay now and I'm not afraid anymore. Really, the fear is gone. But, Adam, I have to go. I'll call you for sure if I find something. You know I will."

"Okay. You sound perky. It's good to hear your voice…I mean that you're safe and okay. That's good. I'll be anxious to hear what you find. But Sarah, be on the watch!"

"I will. Bye for now, Adam."

"See you later."

Adam turned on to Tamarack Trail. His Dodge Ram 3500 therapy session was over.

"Well, so far, so good," Adam concluded as he set the tracking screen on the kitchen table. "I'll go out and get the fire going. How was your nap? You slept a little more than two hours!"

"I know! It was great! Where were you, Dad?"

"I drove south along the big river. Had a really good time."

"I knew you would. You and your truck!"

"Can you believe it's Friday evening already, son? Two days to go. Wish you didn't have to go back quite yet."

"I have mixed emotions, and that's no reflection on you. You know how much I love being here and back in Timber Ridge, but— and it's hard to explain—where I'm stationed now seems like home. Weird, eh?"

With a deep sigh, Adam stopped on his way out the door, looked down at the floor, thinking. No, he did not think it weird. Moving away is what young men do—out of the house, down the street, on the other side of town, across the country; but Adam knew that it was more than just a physical move. Daniel had moved away emotionally. As he looked back toward his son, standing in front of the kitchen sink, tall, broad shouldered, handsome, physically fit and so grown up, the truth was clear that his son had become a man, able to live apart from parents and do it very well.

"It's not weird," he said, slowly shaking his head. "It's right."

"I do wish I could stay a little longer just to help in the fight! I know you'll figure it all out, though. You're a thinker and I bet all our talking about Mrs. Finfield and the Payces has jarred your brain. You've already got a lot of the pieces to the puzzle. The rest is gonna pop into your head, just like that. I know you."

"Some of it just popped! I had a couple of inspirations while on the road."

Adam disclosed his brainstorms to his son.

"You're a genius, Dad. I know you're going to figure it all out. You'll get those guys. I know you will!"

"The bottom-line crux of the matter is the huge profit on Lichten's first book. That's a pretty compelling motive to find the other eleven and claim possession! Big, big bucks," Adam lamented, "and quite possibly enough to snuff out—without conscience—anyone who gets in the way. You know," he added, "I can't for the life of me figure out why those Payces have not come around any-more. I'm totally wary."

"Well, from what you've told me, you have reason to be."

Adam shook his head, his eyes squinted.

"It's not good. It's just not good. But, son, right now, we need to eat."

Adam went down the steps and then back up. He peered through the screen door.

"Hey, keep your eye on Mrs. Finfield."

CHAPTER 19

"Annette, I have an idea. Do you want to stay and help me with some things? I'm trying to get ready to take a trip to Mexico and now I have a new project!"

"You really want me to help you? What do you think I'm going to say?"

"I think you'll say *yes.*"

"Why are you going to Mexico? What's in Mexico? Is it a vacation?"

"No, it's not a vacation."

"Sooo...if it's not a vacation, what might it be? That baffles me, unless.... You're not going for an interview or something, are you? Are you moving away?"

Sarah sighed and smiled. "No, I don't know exactly what to call it. It's not a vacation, although I'm sure it'll do me good. It should be interesting...I don't even know how to say, 'Good afternoon' in Spanish!"

"Hmmm. I give up."

"This is the story. I have a friend who is a missionary and he has invited me to visit him and his children and take a look at the work he is doing there."

"A friend?"

"Yes. He is a friend that I have known for a long time. He and his wife and I were friends in college."

"Are you going to see a *he* or a *he* and a *she?*"

"Why would you ask that?" Sarah asked, busying herself with setting up.

"Oh, just because I heard you say that your friend invited you to visit *him.*"

"Yes, it's a *he.*"

"Oh." Annette squinted at Sarah. "Oh," she said again.

"Yes, Annette, it is a *he* whose wife died a short time ago, and *he* has been a good friend for many years. I'll be glad to see what it is that he actually does in his mission work there."

"Well, it sounds adventurous and you will do well with that, now that you are out of the crypt!" Annette's smile said that she understood more than one might think. "What is your friend's name?"

"His name is Scott Dolan."

"Hmm. Is he anything like Mr. Cook?"

A flow of changing expressions moved across Sarah's face. When she at last spoke words to Annette, they were accompanied by a countenance of insight and perception. "Actually," she said, her face bright, "they are quite different in every way. Now, young lady, let's talk about what needs to get done around here before I go on that exciting trip south of the border."

"Okay, but first let me say this: There's something about you that I really like. I sensed it immediately the first time I met you. Remember the day I told you about the three men outside your house?"

"How could I forget?"

"I'm interested in what happens to you. I don't know why. I'm interested in this Adam/Scott thing." Annette drew in a long breath and then sighed deeply.

Sarah looked curiously at her.

"What exactly...is an Adam/Scott thing?"

"You know. Just keepin' up on things. Just watchin' out for you."

Sarah hid her smile as she turned toward the kitchen.

Annette jumped in on a new subject. "It's cool that you and I can hang out together, don't you think? I'm interested in your welfare and you're interested in mine." Again, she took a deep breath. "Well, anyway, I guess we should get going. I'm here to help. Nothing would make me happier."

"Well, okay then. It's a little after six. My goal has been to paint the two guest rooms in the lower level before I go to bed tonight, but now I have something more important to do. It will seem like a mindless task, I'm sure, but it's very important."

"I'm good at just keeping at something until it's done. I don't know why I'm that way because I've never had to do much work my whole life; but when I do, like at school or when the car gets stuck in the snow, I just love being involved in the solution. I probably don't seem that way to you."

"Ohhh, yes, you do. No one knows that better than I do!"

Annette understood the meaning of Sarah's remark and had a hearty laugh at herself.

"So, what's the big assignment?"

"There are 2,000 plus records over here. We need to pull some of them out and look to see if there is anything other than a record inside."

"Really? Are you kidding?"

"No, unfortunately not. Actually, after a couple of hundred or so, we'll know if we need to keep going or not."

"Well, I'm good with that. What? We just take one, look inside and then go on to the next one? You know, some of my friends don't even know what records are. We're the CD generation. And now, the new generation is the IPod generation! I wonder what's next."

"You can count on there being something."

"What are we looking for?"

"You know, let me think about answering that. I'm not sure how much is good for you to know."

"Really?"

"Yes. Just let me think that through. Now, Annette, before we start, let me ask this: Have you eaten supper?"

"No."

"Let's put a frozen pizza in the oven. I bought the Cadillac of frozen pizzas today! It's supposed to taste like Papa Luigi's, whoever that is!"

"Papa Luigi is a chef in Italy! Everybody knows about Papa Luigi over there. He is the Colonel Sanders of Italy!"

"Well, I don't suppose many people over here know how his pizza tastes. This is the first time for me. I guess if they love his pizza over there, it must be tasty for people everywhere, right?"

Soon the pizza, hot and bubbly, was out of the oven and the two sat down to dinner. Laughing and chatting could be heard at the kitchen table. Only two months before, Sarah had been in a nearly constant state of hiding from this pesky neighbor girl—emotionally, mentally and physically! Sarah, like Annette, wondered how it could be that they were now, in a strange but real way, good friends.

"Such a day this has been!" she mused. *"Here I am moving about with incredible peace filling my heart."* How was it that she was experiencing such freedom from strife now after such an episode of fright and ranting and raving as she had experienced at five in the morning? She knew the answer: God had been a very present help in the time of trouble!

Thus began an early evening of enjoyment and hard work for the two unlikely friends. Chip's albums soon covered the floor of the great room, each one being checked in hopes of finding even one jacket with more than a record in it.

After a good while, Annette looked up from where she sat in the middle of the floor and asked, "Can you tell me now what we're looking for?"

Sarah had been considering the possibility, and even the need, to fill the teenager in on at least some of the latest developments. After all, her sighting of the three men had turned out to be a crucial clue. Then, too, she had walked in on the break-in mess and had put two and two together in her own mind as to the culprits. Yes, Annette was involved. Sarah should fill her in.

"Okay, Annette, I guess I really should let you know at least some of what is going on, but let me say two things before I do. What I tell you is top secret—highly confidential—and for your safety not to be shared with anyone. Secondly, also for your safety, I will tell you only what I think you need to know."

"You know, Mrs. Finfield, I am so involved in this, more than you know. I think about it night and day." Annette declared, leaning back on her arms. "I understand that it's an ugly situation and I worry so much about you." Annette's concern was genuine; that fact evidenced itself in her expressive face and in her voice inflections. "I'm smart enough to know that people who would wreck your house like they did must be after something huge. I also know that they have an evil heart. And evil hearts have no boundaries. From the moment Tony and I saw those three figures—those three men—in the shadows, I became Annette Cappetti, P.I.," she somberly proclaimed. "That's just the way I am."

Sarah lowered her eyes and slowly shook her head. "I'm sorry to hear that you have this on your mind all the time."

"Oh, don't worry about that! I have to be thinking about something so I may as well be trying to solve a mystery."

"Well, Annette, for now, at least, let me answer your question. We are looking for some manuscripts."

"Manuscripts? In these record albums?"

"Yes. We're looking for eleven manuscripts, to be exact. Eleven handwritten manuscripts."

"Handwritten? Who wrote them?"

"The man who wrote *The Street of Petetra.*"

"Herman Lichten?"

"Yes, Annette, and since the Petetra manuscript was handwritten, we're assuming the other eleven are also."

"So that's what this is all about!"

"It is, and we are running out of ideas. So, we'll look in these record albums, and in just a minute or so, I will go out to go check the shed. We forgot to look out there."

"Wait. Are you telling me that you think the manuscripts could actually be in these records? How could you hide them in here? And who would do that?"

"Maybe my husband. There are 2,000 albums here. I suppose you could hide three or four pages in each...or maybe a note or something telling where else they could be. It's a long shot, but it's worth a try. We only need to look at a hundred or so, I think. The Payces are looking for these manuscripts, too. If we find them here, that means they missed them in their tirade a couple of weeks ago. That will not make them real happy."

"That's why they destroyed your house?"

"That's a big part of it, we think. That may be all of it for all I know."

"That's what we're looking for?"

"Yes."

"Why do you really think they could be in the record albums?"

"That's a long story. Like I said, it's a shot in the dark. It's Adam's—Mr. Cook's—idea. We've looked everywhere else. You can imagine how extremely important it would be to have them. The Payces, it appears, will stop at nothing to obtain them."

"I think that *stopping at nothing* includes the possibility of bodily harm, if you ask me. If they would trash your house like they did, then...." Annette stopped to take a breath. "Anyway, I'm assuming, then, that you believe they didn't find them when they searched your house."

"I don't know. I have heard nothing from them since the break-in. Maybe they did and maybe they didn't. We—Adam and I—are working off the sense that they did not. Therefore, we are on a mission to find the books first—or perhaps a disk with the manuscripts saved on it—or something. Keep going, okay? I'm going to take a trip to the back."

"Do you ever feel like you're in danger?" Annette called after Sarah as she went toward the back door. "I'd be pretty nervous if I were in your shoes, I think."

"I might be. Mr. Cook sincerely believes that I am," Sarah hollered back.

At 7:30 p.m. the prospect of finding the manuscripts in the albums was dim, and Sarah made the decision to shut down the operation. From the front porch, a little after 7:45, Sarah made a call to the carpenter.

"Nothing," she simply said. "Not in the albums and not in the shed."

"Hmph. I'm surprised. I really am. I had high hopes."

Sarah could only sigh. She was getting close to not caring anymore.

"I'm wondering," she said wearily, "if they have put this to rest, at least the books, since I have heard nothing at all from them. Maybe they've concluded the manuscripts really did go up in smoke, and maybe the threat is over."

"I'd like to think that, but I don't, Sarah. Keep thinking about it like 9/11. Always keep a picture in your mind of the devastation or else you will go soft. I told you, as long as that much money is involved, Richard will not retreat."

"I'm sick of it all. Just plain sick of it. Strangely, it has been a comfort to have Annette with me."

"Where is she?"

"Cleaning up the kitchen after our pizza party."

"How much does she know?"

"She's smart. She has put two and two together, especially now that she knows about the manuscripts. I'll keep tabs on her. I don't want her mixed up in this. I **don't** want her hurt by this in any way."

"I'm praying for **your** safety. That's all that really matters. It's true, Sarah. There's nothing that comes close, not even manuscripts worth what?...possibly millions? Don't take any chances. My rule in these things is *People first; Things second.*"

"That sounds like you and I know it's right. I just want it to be over."

"Me, too."

"Adam, where are you? Are you fishing? Is Daniel with you?"

"He's right here. We're actually out on the water."

"Put him on the phone a minute. I think Annette would like to talk to him."

Sarah stood, stretching a bit, and went in the house. Cautioning her to only talk for a minute or two, Sarah handed the phone to Annette who held it far away from her mouth and sheepishly said, "You want me to tell him?"

"Don't you want to?"

"Yes, but I guess I need a little time to plan what I'm going to say!"

"Annette, I know you better than that!"

With a smile, the young girl put the phone to ear.

"Daniel? Are you there?"

"Hey, I'm here. How you doing?"

"I'm so good that I'm bursting at the seams!"

"Wow! And why is that?"

"Well, you know that day we talked?"

"Yeah?"

"That night, I did what you said. I stopped on the pathway of life and prayed to God the Father. I did exactly what you said and prayed just like you said—I think it was a fairly lengthy prayer and I apologized to God for that because I know that when I get going, I can talk up a storm. Anyway, Daniel, I am a Christian now!"

Daniel hesitated before he answered, a thousand thoughts running through his head. He had never told anyone about Christ before. Could it be true that this neighbor friend of Mrs. Finfield had really decided to become a true Christian because of his words? A sense of satisfaction and joy came to him.

"Annette," he responded, laughing quietly, "that is very cool!"

"I just wanted to tell you that and tell you thanks for taking time with me...and for not being afraid or ashamed to tell me what you believe! I just knew there was a God, no matter what my father says! And I knew down in my heart that everything I had heard and read about Jesus just had to be true. I just thought that if I was good and honest, I would go to heaven. Now I know. You made it really clear."

"I'm really glad. That's awesome news."

"Daniel, have you ever thought of being a preacher?"

Daniel laughed heartily.

"No, never."

"You should. You did a good job with me."

"Hey, maybe I'll see you when we get back. I go back to California on Sunday."

"I'm sure our paths will cross over the weekend," Annette said quietly. "Bye...and thank you again."

"You're welcome."

Sarah took the phone.

"Sarah? You there?"

"It's me, Adam. I'm here."

"How are you doing?"

"Can't say I'm not a little weary, though I am much better than this morning."

"We are on our way to victory. Don't be afraid. God has His eye on you. That's what He says."

"I need to run," Sarah said with a sigh. "I have so much to do and My To Do List always seems to get longer every time I talk to you!

I'm glad you're praying for me. I'm counting on it."

"Just call me if there are any further developments."

"Bye."

"Bye...no...wait, wait, wait! Sarah?"

"I'm still here."

Adam did not speak.

"Adam?"

"I'm here. Just want to tell you once more to be careful. This plot is very perilous for the main character, and that's you. Don't let anything happen to you, Mrs. Finfield. I'll talk to you later."

"Thank you, Adam," Sarah said with warm gratitude. "I'll be careful."

"Well, Annette, we've done our private eye duty. Now it's time to put on our painter's hats! Are you ready?"

"I am, and just so you know, I'm praying about this Adam/Scott thing."

Sarah, who had already taken steps towards the stairway, stopped, turned her head, scrutinized Annette's face and then stared for a moment at the floor.

"Come, Annette," she said, wrapping her arm around the shoulder of the teen. "We have work to do, my friend."

They retreated to the basement—a lower level of beautiful rooms and exquisite décor. It was time to paint and with the strains of Rachmaninoff's 2nd Piano Concerto resounding through the full-house speaker system, they began the transformation of the sprawling lower level guest rooms, changing them from Thistle to Sea Green.

CHAPTER 20

Evil of the worst kind hung in the air of the posh penthouse office of Payce Publishing: Greed without conscience. Greed was no stranger here in the CEO's enormous suite; tonight, though, it was being wined and dined without pang of conscience. Like suffocating smog, it permeated Richard Payce's ritzy office—and his heart—eliminating all that was honorable or ethical.

Out of the huge glass panes on the north, had it been daytime, one could have looked across fields of corn and soybeans; and if someone were to stand at that same window—during the day—and look directly downward, the loveliness of the White Rock River and railroad tracks running alongside could not help but inspire them; but it was night, and the glass only served to act as a mirror, reflecting the luxurious trappings of the office and the figures of three wicked, greedy businessmen.

The view to the south, however, was the town, the small city of Timber Ridge. In the distance, the lights of the downtown area of this small city sparkled in the night. It was an August Friday night. The newly refashioned central part of town—the black wrought iron railings, fancy streetlamps, new shops and cobblestone streets—drew people from surrounding neighborhood towns and villages, by the hundreds, into the glittering clothing stores and chic coffee shops.

Richard Payce, red faced and breathing heavily, walked back and forth from the windows on the north to those overlooking the city. He seethed with displeasure.

"Do not talk spineless and weak to me! What happens tonight is more important than any other incident in the history of Payce! I have given you the plan and it needs to be carried out exactly as you have heard it. Raymond, if you fold, do you know what that will mean?" He coughed uncontrollably, swearing as he did. Alarmed, Robert sat forward in his chair. It always seemed that his father was about to die with every coughing spell. "We have given her all the opportunity she is going to get," he said, gasping for air. After a few

219

deep breaths, he went on. "We asked nicely," he said in a silly sing-song voice, "but the widow does not play well with others."

Robert, the older Payce son and Vice President and COO of Payce Publishing, smiled at his father's performance. To describe Robert Payce, tonight still clad from head to toe in his expensive and fashionable clothing, one would have to include that the dark-haired man was a somewhat well-known and brilliant attorney, marked with a clever business mind; but it was his crafty character that should not be overlooked, often concealed behind his handsome appearance. His good looks and suave demeanor had carried him a long way in the business, in particular, the legal end of things. There really was no need, however, for him to prove himself; he was a Payce and that was his ticket to wealth and prestige. Looking determined and cocky, he sat in one of the two very rich leather chairs that faced each other before Richard's desk, a low marble table separating them.

On the other hand, there was his younger brother—Vice President of Marketing—popping one chocolate kiss into his mouth after another, crinkling the silver wrappers and tossing them back into the candy dish with an impressive level of accuracy. Now and then he offered a suggestion, but mostly, his part in the conversation was the uttering of "uh huh" to nearly every thought and idea. Raymond did what he was told; he had done so his whole life, emulating somewhat, his older brother's personality and image, without the polish. Tonight, the explosive response of his father had come after Raymond voiced his thoughts about the futility of *doing away with the Widow Finfield.*

"It's risky and unnecessary, in my book," he had said. "What good will it do if, well, you know?"

"Raymond, Raymond," Mr. Payce had replied, turning toward his second son, his arms folded over his round middle, "there is no *if* in this mission. Actually, Raymond, the truth is that she **must** do what we ask. You know there are ways to make that happen, right? You've seen this in action before, right?" he had continued, his voice rising as he stood and walked to the window. "You know this is crucial, right? Raymond, for the first time in 35 years, I'm edgy. Not a lot, but enough for me to refuse to play games with this woman who could possibly stand in the way of our acquiring the golden goose! Do not even breathe a breath that tells me you could possibly weaken at the wrong moment!"

Now Father Payce walked to his desk with a bit of huffing and puffing, and sat down. "Call it a hunch—a healthy hunch—but Mr. Chip Finfield had those manuscripts here the night before he died and he made copies."

"You could be right, Father," Robert suggested, "but still, we just might not find anything,"

"But...Robert Stanfield Payce, we...will...try. As for the originals, they are somewhere in the widow's house, I am very certain! You...you two missed them," Richard nearly shouted with great aggravation, holding up his hand to ward off any contending of his statement.

Robert shook his head, clearly showing his disagreement.

"I told you, we literally tore the place apart, inch by inch. If they indeed still exist, they are somewhere else. We are missing something."

"I'll tell you what we're missing," Raymond said, taking a short break from his consumption of the candy. "I don't like to say it, but we're missing Mrs. Finfield."

"We know that, Raymond," said Mr. Payce with disgust. "We know that. What do you think we're talking about? We are at this moment working on the plans to bring her here tonight. However, my guess is that she is not going to come willingly."

"She might," Robert said with a haughty lilt in his voice. "I can be persuasive."

"Robert, Robert," Mr. Payce growled in low tones. "You think you can do everything by slicking back your hair and wearing expensive aftershave." He allowed a light laugh to escape his lips. "This time, though, we are up against a formidable foe."

"And what is that?"

"Sarah Finfield!"

Abruptly, Robert stood, his hands on his hips, near unbelief on his fine face.

"Look around, Father!" the elder Payce son declared vehemently. "What do you see? There sits you—president and CEO of a multi-million dollar enterprise and a man with a history of letting **nothing** and **nobody** stand in your way. Then, here we are, your very successful, big and strong, capable sons. And you call her a formidable foe?"

Richard laughed through his teeth.

"She met both of you, eye to eye, and you both came back with your tail between your legs," he scorned.

Bristling—respectfully, of course—Robert responded to his father's sarcasm.

"I will have her here at precisely ten o'clock, according to your plan, Father. We'll see about formidable!"

"I suggest not knocking on the door, if you know what I mean." Richard paused. "Just get her over here. I don't care how you do it. You've got two hours until ten. Andrew will be here—I worry about his allegiance but I think his job carries more weight than his moral fiber. He's not all that he's cracked up to be, but maybe he can help the widow help us. Those manuscripts are locked up in Chip's computer!"

"Father, I just hope—now hear me out, Father—I just hope that this whole thing goes down, you know, without a problem. I hope she cooperates," Raymond said with a look of importance on his face.

"Listen, you two! Both of you! Are you listening? I mean are you listening with your brains? The amount of money we are talking about here is staggering. I'm in pain," Richard whined melodramatically, "here, right here in my stomach, just thinking about it. Widow Finfield needs to cooperate, if you understand what I'm saying. Keep that right here," he said, poking his finger against his forehead. "She is nobody. Let me hear you say that."

"She is nobody," they repeated like robots dressed in professional business attire.

"No! The Widow Finfield is nobody!"

"The Widow Finfield is nobody."

"With fervor!"

"The Widow Finfield is nobody!" the two sons dutifully—and ridiculously— shouted.

"You both told me," Mr. Payce scowled, "that she wishes she was dead—or something along those lines. She's despondent. It's a well-known fact. She goes nowhere. She sees herself as dead already. If she refuses to cooperate and if something just happens to happen to her, if you do it right, not a person alive would doubt that…she just took her own life."

Richard sat for a long time without speaking, tapping his pencil eraser on his desk. He stared at the little silver clock staring back at him. Over and over again, he drew in deep breaths. His sons, knowing their father's method of spouting, waited for him to give his closing thoughts.

"Some of the things I've done to get where I am, you know," he finally snarled. "Some of them, you do not. If I had not done them, you would not be driving those fancy cars and living in three or four houses around the globe. Your wives would not be wearing the jewelry they so love nor would they be living disgustingly gaudy and easy lives. Listen," he hissed like a snake, "if you like your lucrative spots here, you'd better grasp the importance of this whole thing.

Sarah Finfield is no dummy," he sneered. "Sarah Finfield will not give up those manuscripts without a fight." Richard stood up and stuck his thumbs into his belt. "You know, I never really liked Chip. I'm not crazy about his wife either. Let's get to it."

"I guess you're right," Raymond said, having not the slightest inkling that his conscience had gone silent.

☙ ☙ ☙ ☙ ☙

Annette heard a car door. Sarah, heard it, too, and something warned her exactly what to expect. She sprang into action.

"Annette, stay here! Do not make a single noise!" she whispered firmly. "If it's trouble, I don't want them to know you are here. Do you understand me? Promise me."

With that, she ascended the stairs and stood for a moment, listening for more clues. Surely they would come to the front door, no matter who it was. But no, she heard footsteps on the deck. Like a cat on the attack, she sprang toward the back door, unlocked it and yanked it open.

There stood the Payce brothers—Robert and Raymond—stunned to the full extent judging from the looks on their faces. Robert's foot was slightly raised, ready to kick in the door, but Sarah had beaten him to the draw, leaving him staggering and bewildered.

"So, you have come back," she snapped. "And how very childish, Robert! Bash in the widow's door! You're so good at that! Why have you come?" Words from Sarah's lips came with great force, surprising even her. "What...do... you...want!"

"Feisty little thing you are tonight! Well, my dear Sarah, you are going to spend some time at Payce Publishing...but without pay," Robert informed her, rudely taking her by the arm.

Raymond snickered.

"I am not going with you!" she spoke with unmistakable firmness. "Take your hands off of me!"

Robert, however, was robust and strong and was operating under a powerful impetus—the threats of an angry father.

"I told you, Mrs. Finfield, that you should bend. Bend, Sarah, bend, I told you, but you are stubborn and foolish. Now, you have no choice but to come with us and you will scour Chip's files—all the files, for that matter. You will do this, Sarah! One way or another...or break!"

"Take your hands off of me," Sarah loudly whispered without flinching. She swung and twisted her arm until she was free from his grasp. He grabbed her again, chagrined at her momentary escape.

"You just come with me! You and I have a date. Raymond is going in his car, and you and I are going in yours."

"I thought we were all going back in the Escalade," Raymond complained.

Robert glared at his brother.

"Follow the plan, Raymond. Get going."

Robert was upset with his brother and he took it out on Mrs. Finfield, half dragging her down the deck steps and out toward the front. Raymond followed behind, like a puppet.

Halfway up the carpeted steps from the lower level sat Annette, her forehead smudged with blotches of Sea Green. She listened for the kitchen door to close, but evidently it had been left open. Like a mouse, she crept up the stairs and slowly rounded the corner. What was that? Sarah's voice?...sounding like it was getting closer?

Annette, with wide eyes and a heart of panic, took a step back and pressed against the wall as though, like a cartoon character, she would disappear into the paneling. She could not chance returning to the stairs.

"I will be of no use to you without them," Sarah was saying very firmly as she appeared suddenly in the doorway.

"Let's go, Sarah!" Robert's voice boomed. "We must be at our destination at 10:00 sharp!"

"I'm not sure where they are."

"There! There on the counter by the coffee pot. Your glasses. Get them and let's go!"

Now they were gone, most surely. Annette ran to the front window and through a tiny crack, watched the kidnapping.

"It **is** a kidnapping!" she whispered as she witnessed the getaway. Robert shoved Sarah into the passenger seat of her own car and then quickly ran around to the driver's side. Raymond climbed into the Escalade. The two vehicles hastily drove out onto the gravel road. There they left behind a trail of dust. Annette watched to see which way they would turn at the state road. They went north.

Annette, alert and astute, made haste to find Sarah's cell phone.

CHAPTER 21

Friday night supper was over as was the Scrabble game—Daniel won this match. Plans were made to be up even earlier on Saturday and preparations for bed began. Adam started to place the tracking screen on the sink while he brushed his teeth, but glancing to see if Daniel was watching—and wishing to avoid more Sarah talk—he walked to the knotty pine nightstand and set it there. Then he went to brush his teeth.

"You'd better come here, Dad," called Daniel after just a few minutes. "I think something is going on back home!"

Wiping his mouth as he hurried into the bedroom, Adam flopped onto the bed and watched as Sarah Finfield, for some reason, left her house 9:55 and started north on the state road.

"Let's go!" Adam half shouted, going for his clothes. "We'll leave everything here."

Daniel was still dressed. He was ready to go. Grabbing up all of his belongings, he said, "I'll drive, Dad. You know I'll get you there faster."

"Okay, turn the truck around. I'll lock things up."

"What about the boat?"

"Not worried. Let's go."

The sound of the wheels spinning on the gravel went unnoticed by Adam Cook. He prayed aloud. "Keep her safe, Lord. Just keep her safe."

The Adam Cook Carpentry truck raced down the interstate, its two occupants in a state of alarm. Knowing that Daniel's speed was just asking for a ticket, Adam periodically reminded him that if they got stopped, all the speeding would be for naught. They were just words, however; Adam secretly approved, glad to see the cornfields and barns and an occasional gas station flying by. Subconsciously, he developed a response to the policeman who might pull them over.

Except for an occasional glance at the clock where the white digital numbers seemed to change so slowly, he fixed his eyes on the screen with the little blue dot bleeping back at him.

"They're entering the parking lot at Payce. It's 10:10. I'm calling the police."

The call to the Timber Ridge police department was not reassuring. How could they take action on the word of someone miles away claiming to have tracked a woman to a legitimate place of business—with an earring? They agreed to cruise around the area and check it out.

"Give this info to Rod," Adam commanded.

"He's not here."

"Well, find him! And tell him what I just told you!" Adam again commanded.

He slowly closed his phone, bit his upper lip and closed his eyes.

"This is not good."

"I know it sounds trite, Dad, but you've got to trust God about this. There's nothing you can do. Maybe that's good."

"If I was there, I could do something."

"But you're not. We're making good time. They're not going to harm her given all the other people involved."

"Like who? As far they're concerned, she's in it alone. All they know about me is that I'm a carpenter. They don't know how involved I am in this situation. Daniel, with her emotional condition this past year, they could do her in and make it look like suicide very easily. I'm already suspicious about her husband's suicide and if they are responsible for that one, then what's...one more? And then, maybe you don't know this, but Chip sounded pretty sure that they had done away with Herman Lichten."

"No way! I didn't know that. I guess you have legitimate reason to worry! Do you think that if she gives them what they want, she'll be okay?"

"No," Adam replied, "I don't."

"On a scale of 1 to 10, what's the level of danger?"

"It's a 10. Whether or not she cooperates or whether or not she is successful, they cannot have her walking around knowing what she knows. The destruction on her house was extreme and malicious. They are wicked people and they have gotten away with a whole lot more than we know."

"What do they want from her?"

"All I know is that they desperately want to get their greedy little hands on eleven golden eggs—Herman's manuscripts. If they have those things, they are in a position to wheel and deal with the Texan from Idaho...you know, his nephew...or better yet, outright falsify documents to appear that a deal was sealed before the fire. I think they're convinced that Chip's files will divulge the location of those eleven Lichten books or that they could even reside on his computer. Their people have tried to dig it out, but they can't seem to find anything. I think they see evidence of Chip's visit to the office the night before he died and want to know what he was up to."

Adam's phone rang and he stretched out to be able to retrieve it from his front jeans pocket. Annette did not give him the opportunity to say "hello."

"Mr. Cook! They have kidnapped, yes, kidnapped, Mrs. Finfield!"

"Annette?"

"Yes, Adam Cook, it's Annette! The men have captured her!"

"We already know, but how do you know?"

"I was still in the house. We were painting. I was on the basement stairs and I heard it all and then, I saw it all. The one with the brown hair, the big guy, you know, the one that looks like Cary Grant, shoved her into the passenger seat of her car and then got in to drive. The other guy, Raymond...that's what Cary Grant called him...the one with the reddish hair, he took that great big Escalade like my uncle's got...but my uncle's is black...this one is white. And I watched and they went north."

"Why were you still at the house?"

"We were still having our evening. After we did the records, I stayed. I didn't go home. We went downstairs to paint those two rooms."

Adam looked at Daniel and nodded.

"It's Annette and she witnessed the whole thing. Annette, you must go home. Right now! Do you hear what I am saying?"

"But, Mr. Cook, I've got to do something to help her."

"Annette, there is something you can do. Go home and wait for the police. I will call them and tell them what you saw and send them to your house. I need for you to talk to the police. Tell them everything. Go home and I'll direct them to your house. What's your address?"

"12509 Pine Cone Creek Trail."

"Go home right now. I need to know that you are safe at home with your folks."

"Oookaay, but I think I could come up with a plan. Where are you guys?"

"We've got another three plus hours."

"Hurry home! I'm praying! I really am." she gasped.

Adam detected fear in the teenager's voice and he did his best to calm her down with a new subject.

"Annette, what is this news I've heard about you?"

"You mean from yesterday?"

"Yes."

"Daniel must have told you. I became a Christian, Mr. Cook. I prayed to Jesus Christ to be my Savior."

Annette could not see Adam's smile, but she heard it in his voice.

"That's awesome news, Annette. I'm really glad. Do you know that Mrs. Finfield is a Christian, too?"

"I didn't, but I found out tonight. We had a long talk. We were having such a good evening together and then this! I could maybe do something—like create a diversion or something. We've got to help her!"

"She's in God's hands. That's not just a trite saying," Adam said, glancing toward his son. "It's truth. Keep praying and trusting, okay? And get out of there now. Take Sarah's phone with you, but leave the house just like it is."

No response came from Annette.

"Annette, did you hear what I said. Go home. Leave the house as it is and go home."

Another short silence followed and then Annette very calmly said, "I think I should set the alarm. We can't have those rats getting in here again!"

There was wisdom in her suggestion, Adam knew.

"Good thinking. Do you know how?"

"Well, we have one. It can't be that much different."

"Annette, are there any doors open?"

"The back door."

"Close and lock it. Go out the front. Press the star and then the zero and then get out. Pull the door shut firmly. Can you do that?"

"Of course. Worry not."

"Then go home."

"I will although my heart is telling me I should do something to help Mrs. Finfield."

"The best way to help her now is for you to go home and when the police arrive, tell them everything you saw."

"Okay. I will."

The interstate was dark and the miles flew by; yet, to Adam, it was a nightmare in slow motion.

"Where are we, son?" he asked after a lengthy spell of silence.

"We're two hours from Mrs. Finfield."

CHAPTER 22

The normal twenty minute trip to Payce Publishing happened in exactly twelve instead; Robert, like a maniac, drove at speeds sometimes exceeding 100 mph. To be sure, Robert was risking his life and Sarah's at such speeds, but Sarah, doing her best to ignore that fact, used the twelve minutes to hurriedly prepare for what might lie ahead. Now and then Robert gave short speeches about *bending* and *breaking* and the importance of cooperation on Sarah's part, but her mind was not on his ramblings; instead, she was methodically going through the events that likely were taking place elsewhere as they drove toward the corporate office.

She took comfort in the thought that surely Annette would call someone and tell them what had happened. She would call the police, Sarah figured. Would she think to call Adam? She could not call Adam; she did not have his cell phone number.

It was okay. Presumably, Adam's earring gadget was operational; he surely knew that she was on the two-lane road that, after taking any driver on a winding trip through the city streets of Timber Ridge, headed directly north from the middle of town. He would call the police; perhaps they were already on their way. Sarah glanced at the time showing on her dashboard. What if Adam was sleeping? She told herself that she must keep that in mind as a possibility; he might not know; she could be in this thing alone. Who would have thought that they would accost her at 10:00 at night! However, if he saw that she was moving—and something inside assured her that trusty Adam would be fairly glued to the little screen—then the police might already be informed, and yes, even on their way. A silent prayer of thanks went heavenward that Annette had not been discovered. She was either still at the house or safe at home.

It was a dark night, even with heaven's shimmering night lights aglow. It was summer, hot and humid. A slight breeze played with the smells of the country but brought no relief from the muggy temperatures. No fanfare took place upon the arrival of the two Payce

brothers and their captive on this night of August 12th. The building, as they walked toward it, was shrouded with shadows except
where the fountain lights illuminated the entry. In only one office
were the lights burning—Chip's old office.

With one swipe of Robert's card, they were inside. He held Sarah
tightly by the arm and escorted her to the elevators. A door opened,
they entered the car, and the door closed. A smile of conquest illuminated Robert's face; Sarah straightened, pulled her cotton sweater
around her, and glared at him with defiance that could not be misin-
terpreted. She prayed a desperate prayer: *"Lord, please watch over me!"*

When they exited at the third floor and turned to the left, they
walked towards Chip's old office. How familiar this all was! The
sounds and even faint smells brought it all back to her. Though the
stillness and after-hours dimness cast an almost eerie spell upon her,
a flood of pleasant memories rolled in upon Sarah. Payce Publishing
had been an enormous part of Chip's life—and hers. Even though
those years had been bittersweet, tonight as the three made their
way down the darkened hallways, only the good came to mind.

She was not surprised at what awaited her when once the door
was opened. There sat Richard, leaned back in Chip's chair, his collar
open, his tie loosened, a cynical and arrogant expression spread over
his bulging, red face. He laughed heartily upon seeing Sarah.

"Ho, ho, ho!" he laughed with gusto, his guffaws quickly changing into a violent coughing fit. Sarah's pursed lips and narrowed eyes
displayed her disgust. "Sarah Finfield! The widow!!"

"I told you I'd have her here by ten," Robert boasted.

"It's ten after, Robert," Richard replied derisively.

"Yes, but Mrs. Finfield was not quite ready to walk out the door.
It took a little doing."

Raymond entered. He had confiscated the candy dish from the
library. Into a corner chair he went. He was content.

"Well, Mrs. Finfield, as soon as Andrew arrives, we'll get started," Richard informed the waiting widow. Robert released his grip on
Sarah's arm.

"Sit down—over there in that chair—over there next to the table," he ordered, motioning with a quick jerk of his head. "Let me talk
to you for a minute."

Robert was cocky—as always—basking in the pride of having
the upper hand here. He shook his head with great drama and walked
back and forth in front of her. How handsome he was! Sarah had a
recollection of trying to convince Chip that his new stepbrother
looked very much like Cary Grant; Chip could not see it. The fine-

looking features of the man now strutting before her held no appeal, however, for the ugliness of conceit and coldblooded greed were veiled beneath. She shuddered and glared at him.

"You could have made this easy, Sarah. But, no, you chose to hold out, claiming that you had, well, how did you put it?— died along with Chip. Okay, so you're dead. You're dead, you're dead. Hear ye, hear ye!" he mocked in a town crier's voice, "Sarah Finfield is dead! Sarah Finfield is dead!"

Totally acting the part of a fool, as was his manner occasionally, publishing mogul Richard Payce arose and began to dance in a circle, chanting, "Mrs. Finfield's dead, you know, dead you know, dead you know, Mrs. Finfield's dead you know, Never to rise no more!" He motioned for Raymond to join him. "Come on, we're having a funeral!" Once more, this time, with father and son performing, the dance in the center of Chip's office proceeded until a coughing spasm sent Richard to the closest chair. Robert did not join in the dance, but he slapped his hand on his thigh, keeping time with the song. Sarah watched with incredulity and disdain.

"How idiotic! Someday you will pay for such foolishness and stupidity," she promised almost inaudibly.

"Yes, yes, perhaps we will," laughed Raymond, now stretched out in a chair, a People Magazine laid across his lap. Richard returned to his spot at Chip's desk. Robert returned to his speech.

"I think you're just ignorant enough to live out the rest of your days under that black shroud. I honestly believe there is no hope of resurrection for you because you're a foolish, stupid woman. But let me tell you this, one way or another, my dear sister-in-law, you will need to be successful tonight; the future of Payce rides heavily upon it. And I believe, waaay down here, that you know exactly what we are looking for."

"No, Robert, I do not."

Sarah could hardly bear to look at any of them. As Richard took command of the conversation, she allowed her eyes to fix on the painting on the wall between two of the enormous windows—an oil of an Amish hillside in autumn. Richard now took his turn, prattling on about the futility of Sarah opposing them and how his publishing firm would undo her should she choose to do so. Now Sarah glared at him, moving not a muscle.

After enduring as long as he could, Robert looked toward his father and spoke to him in a forceful tone— risky, in Sarah's opinion. Not only were his words cold and hard, but Robert's agitated demeanor left no doubts as to his dissatisfaction with the way Father

Payce was conducting his business.

"Why don't you stop beating around the bush with her, Father? You are getting nowhere and completely missing the point. Why don't you just get on with it and tell her why she is here."

Richard Payce slapped the leather top of Chip's desk and glared at his son.

"You dare speak to me in such tones? Sit down. I am in charge here."

Still Robert stood, and with a nearly equal evilness in his eyes as that of his father's, he shot back, "It is now almost ten-thirty and you've gotten nowhere! Get on with it. Tell her what she has to do and let her get to it!"

Slowly, Richard adjusted in his chair.

"Sit down, Robert," he said gruffly. "When I need your help, I'll ask for it."

It **was** ten-thirty, or would be in five minutes. Andrew had not arrived, much to the dismay of Sarah and the aggravation of Richard. In the meantime, Sarah had been listening to the drone long enough and she wished she could *get on with it*, as Robert had put it. There was no hurrying of Mr. Payce, though. Once again, he sank into a mental mire that would not allow him to ascertain where he had left off and where he should pick it up again.

"For heaven's sake, Richard," Sarah exclaimed at last, "why am I here?" Again she waited. Robert stood with the air of taking over, and as he did, Richard cleared his throat and took charge.

"Listen carefully, Mrs. Finfield, for I wish to give you some re-markable news," he said, tapping a pencil eraser like a drum on the arm of the chair. "I planned to do this with Andrew here, but he is late. Let's move ahead. This news is about Chip and Herman Lichten...you know, Herman Lichten, the author. Now," Richard went on in a parentheses, "this news may or may not be news to you. We'll see."

Richard Payce always delighted in dragging things out, but Robert was still standing, glaring the message, "Get on with it," to his father. Richard continued.

"We have received information that *The Street of Petetra* was not old man Lichten's only book. Imagine that! And...we have learned that he wrote more than just a **second** book. Imagine that! No, Mrs. Finfield, Mr. Lichten did not only write two amazing fantasies, but in total, twelve books! Twelve manuscripts, Mrs. Finfield, and your husband was the last person to see the old man alive!"

Richard adjusted in his leather chair in order to place his folded arms on the desk. "Now what does that tell you, Mrs. Finfield?"

"What do you think it tells me? It tells me that Chip was the last to see Herman Lichten, a great literary gift to mankind, and that along with the loss of that great man, if it is true what you say, the world lost a collection of fine writings...a great treasure. Sadly, Richard, but most likely, those manuscripts went up in smoke in that awful fire, as you are no doubt aware."

"Chip had them!" Richard exploded without warning. "I know that he had them! I know that I know that I know!"

Not willing to offer any help to Richard's mania, Sarah sat quietly, her hands folded in her lap, her eyes squinting at her captor. He pushed his chair to where he could stand and painfully arose. He leaned over, placed his palms upon the blotter on the desk, and took on an expression that left no doubts as to its meaning.

"Your husband was a conniving, underhanded employee—and son—though I will never refer to him again as so. Chip was out to get me because he was sure that I had deliberately manipulated Lichten's contract over a mere pittance in the royalties.

"This is what I think happened. Lichten, feeble old man that he was, didn't like the first contract...said we had cheated him out of royalties. Chip took another one to him—a corrected one—for him to sign. Indeed, he did; I have that contract. But, the old man would not do business for the second book, like I said, over an understandable error. So what do you think they talked about that night when Chip went to see him? Before you answer, keep in mind that by now Chip and Herman were buddy-buddy. Without a doubt the old man shared the news that ten more stories existed. Now, Widow Finfield, what do you think Chip did? What would you do if you were in that spot?"

Sarah was expressionless as old man Payce walked toward her. She offered no response. How old and haggard he looked at sixty-five! His face always bore lines of meanness and greed; but, in his current state of unrest, they were greatly exaggerated. He waddled this way and that as he approached her, each breath difficult. As he came closer, his scowl intensified.

"Chip was at an end here at Payce. As you are no doubt aware, his resignation—and the paperwork—were on my desk the Monday morning after he, uh...passed on."

It was news to Sarah that Chip had submitted his resignation. She said nothing.

"Chip did the right thing and left the three contracts on my desk as well. So, put it all together. With his mind set on leaving this company, and leaving it out of extreme displeasure, do you not think that such evil intent would inspire you to partner up with Lichten—who was also displeased with Payce Publishing—and grab up those manuscripts? Ah, Sarah, if you are honest, you will agree! Your husband took those manuscripts home with him!

"Now, I will give you this," old man Payce went on more calmly, "he may not have shared that information with you at that time. You may have no knowledge of them. And, let me add right here, that there is a slim, very slim possibility that they never made it to your house. We, however, do know—well, we are quite certain—that he brought them here on the night of the 13th. He was on the scanner for close to three hours. What else would he be scanning?"

"Why are you asking me? Why don't you look at the scans?"

"There are no scan files!"

Sarah was immensely puzzled by this declaration.

"If there is nothing in the scan log during those hours, then it seems to me that he must not have used the scanner. I know very little about your operations here, but I know one thing, only one person has clearance to delete scan files without your authorization...and that's an excellent rule, this being a publishing company."

"You are absolutely correct—and he was not that person!"

"Hmm, seems to me then that Chip did not use the scanner. Or that he did, and your one authorized person deleted them. This makes no sense whatsoever. What makes you think Chip was scanning anything at all?"

"I told you. He was here three hours and there is nothing to show for it except that the counter indicates an inordinate amount of copies were made. You listen to me, you sneaky little corpse, your husband and that old man connived! I'll bet my life on it! Chip knew about those books and he did what we always do with handwritten manuscripts—scanned them in! Then,—and I don't know how he did it—he deleted those files!"

"Why would he scan the documents and then delete the files? Weak, Richard, weak. If you have no more proof than this nonsense, there is no reason for me to be here. And, Richard, you keep glossing over the significant fact that Chip could not possibly have deleted the files!"

Slowly Richard returned to Chip's chair and with dramatic flair, he tapped his fingers on the arm of it. "He did it. Somehow, he did it. Chip was an emerging star. His computer expertise was surprising all of us. I have no problem with believing he figured out a way to override the system and delete those scans!"

"I wonder if that's even possible."

"He was smart, Sarah, but such a human failure! And **he** claimed to be religious! Hah! Why did he turn on me, Sarah? I was good to him! He got it in his head that we cheated old man Lichten and he just went soft. We made an honest mistake in dealing with Herman, right boys? Right? It was an honest mistake." Richard called on his sons to confirm his phony assertions. They concurred. "He was trying to get *the goods* on us, as they say...noooo, no, no...that's not how families work and it's not how corporations work!

"He hoodwinked the Payces"—Ah! There was the very word that Adam had used! "He did something undetectable to cover his tracks, right here in this computer, right here," he said, tapping his finger on the monitor. "I'm sure he meant to come and finish things up. But guess what? He didn't. Instead, he killed himself!" He turned slightly in his chair, desiring to speak directly to his two sons who were sitting in one corner of the room. "Tell me, boys, do you go to heaven when you commit suicide?"

Richard's words ripped at Sarah's attempt at composure, and the callous chuckle that came from the corner stirred up the anger already simmering in her spirit. She had resolutely vowed to avoid any sign of distress or weakening; yet, Richard's last sentence and the malicious inflections tore her spirit to shreds.

The room fell silent, the foul stench of Richard's last words pervading the atmosphere in the finely furnished office. Sarah relished the silence. The pain on her face slowly disappeared, replaced by repugnance.

"You are a wicked man," she sneered, each word coated with scathing bitterness.

"Yes. Yes, that may be. The difference is that I admit that I am. Your husband was a wicked man and pretended to be a righteous and moral man."

Sarah stared blankly at him, not masking her dislike. "Andrew or no Andrew, I want to get going."

"Yes, I suppose you do. I think you have a long night ahead of you."

"Perhaps." She leaned back in her chair. She stewed. It would be a long night, she was pretty sure. She looked Richard squarely in the eye, ready to ask the extremely pertinent question that was bothering her the most, given his lack of integrity.

"Let's say I find what you're looking for." Sarah's expression left no doubt as to her thoughts on the coming subject. Like an attorney in court, in a stable and firm voice, she asked, "How does that make the manuscripts yours? You cannot publish them," she grimly reminded him. "You have no contracts for anything but the first book."

With a twisted face and a sinister grin, Richard responded, his words coming slowly, "Don't...trouble....your little deceased self about that." His evil stare spawned her first hint of fear. "That...is not your concern."

Sarah shuddered.

"You know, Mrs. Finfield," a slightly calmer Richard Payce said, pushing way back in his chair, and closing his eyes as though experiencing a wonderful dream, "I like to think of this room as Fort Knox. You know what Fort Knox is?" He looked at his captive, expecting a response. Sarah nodded, but only very slightly, just enough to hurry him on. "In this room, there is mon...ey," he said, over-emphasizing the word, "lots and lots of it! Your husband stashed it away where the Payces cannot find it or get to it. That, my dear, is the bottom line why you are here."

"Money?"

"Essentially."

"Why have you waited this long?" Sarah asked matter-of-factly. "Why not right after Chip's death? Why more than a year later?" She knew the answer to her question, but she pressed to hear the story from Richard.

"This situation unfolded slowly. We did not know about the remaining manuscripts last May. Things were not real clear at the time Chip left us, you know...died. Those are things you don't need to know. What you need to know is that you will be searching and finding the files Chip hid away, obviously hoping to do something with them later. Now, you, come sit here."

If Mrs. Finfield had not been saturated with disgust and anger, she would have wept. Chip was everywhere. How many days had she lunched with him here? She remembered sitting in this very chair, flirting with her dear husband as he finished up a phone call! Although his personal touches had been removed at the time of his death, still, much of what was left overwhelmed her with memories. Slowly she arose and went to sit behind Chip's desk. Seeking to escape the babble, she pulled the desk calendar closer and turned the pages until the correct date was visible—August 12, 2005.

"Oh, Sarah," whined Richard, pacing back and forth in front of her, "your husband was a crook...a bona fide religious crook! I'm glad he was not my real son. How ashamed I would be!"

Sarah's lips tightened. She took quick, short breaths to keep from extreme emotion of one kind or another. Here was Richard, casting aspersions on the most decent man she had ever known; and, saddest of all, Chip was not here to defend himself. She squinted back at him and then checked her watch. It was agitating that Andrew was not here, ready to move ahead.

She tuned out the ravings of Richard and switched once again to Adam and Daniel. If they indeed had seen her exit from the house, it would be close to four hours before they would reach Timber Ridge. That would mean 2:00 in the morning! Adam, she realized, most likely would not be rescuing her; but he would call the cops. Perhaps the TRPD would soon make an appearance!

"This, Sarah, is why corporations with sensitive information walk their dismissed employees out of the building upon informing them of their dismissal. Who would figure, however, that Chip, my own son, would do such a thing—after all that I did for him? And who would figure that he would die so unexpectedly? But then again, who wouldn't...kill themselves...caught up in such deceit and thievery, a traitor, conspiring against his family and his company! You must be ashamed, too!"

Mr. Payce was about to address Sarah once again, his expression divulging the intents of his heart. Why not enlighten her as to the grim consequences that defiance would bring? He leaned over the desk, about to tell all. A knock at the door, however, drew the attention away from the center stage. It was Andrew in his usual attire—a dark plaid button down shirt and black pants. Sarah, grateful for deliverance from Richard Payce's ranting, smiled at the young computer expert; she remembered that Chip liked him and had felt sorry for him. She wondered if she could count on him as a friend.

"Hi, Sarah," he mumbled, glancing at her with some kindness, and then, looking at Mr. Payce, he added, "I'm here."

"Late."

"Car trouble."

"You have not heard of phones, evidently."

"Sorry, Richard. Where do we stand?"

"We...are about to go treasure hunting, Andrew. Sit in this chair, right next to Mrs. Finfield. I'm going to join the boys for a bit. And Andrew, I don't need to remind you of the little matter of, well, let's just say..." and he turned to Robert and said, "What are the latest government unemployment figures?" Turning back to Andrew with a foul grin, he stated forcefully, "Do not, young man, take your eyes off of that screen!"

The explanation commenced. With his dry, dull voice, Andrew showed Sarah around Chip's computer and offered a quick education on the subject of Payce's overall file system.

"How much am I telling her at this point, Mr. Payce? Am I telling her what we're looking for?"

"She's ready to go. She knows. Turn her loose."

The young Payce employee in charge of all technological issues for the publisher started in, his manner and his words listless. Leaning in close to Sarah, he told the story of Chip's night at the office.

"Mr. Payce feels certain that Chip used the scanner for hours on the night of the 13th. Scans get saved automatically to the S: drive, but there are no scan files for the period of time Chip was here. The scanner registered high usage that day, but I keep reminding him that the scanner is used as a copier, too."

"Andrew, it's nonsense to assume that Chip used the scanner. If there is no trail, then why are they so sure he scanned anything?"

"He was here. I guess they figure, what else would he be doing?" Andrew replied very softly.

"Andrew," she murmured, "this is foolishness." She shook her head impatiently.

Andrew leaned closer to Sarah and whispered, "I can tell you this, something odd did occur that night, but I can't put my finger on it. It is all very strange."

Sarah shook her head very slightly. "And you are the head of IT around here? Andrew, what do you mean by *strange?*"

"What I just told you. The counter on the scanner shows heavy usage; there is nothing on the S drive; and Chip could not have deleted the scans if he wanted to. Robert is the only one."

"Robert! Well, well. Has anyone asked Robert about that?"

"He laughs it off as ridiculous. Besides, the log does not indicate he was here. Only Chip."

"He could log in from home, right?"

"Yes, but he didn't…at least, there is no record of it."

Sarah suspected Robert immediately for something, though she did not know what. She constructed a scenario. Perhaps Chip had been scanning. What? Not known. So Robert enters the scene. How, without using his pass? No doubt every door—even the utility door—is electronically monitored. Yet, Robert, of all people, would have the savvy to circumvent a system, she was sure. Okay, then. Something tells him that Chip has been there. What? Chip's car? Was Chip already gone or perhaps had Robert and he nearly crossed paths? So, why would Robert check the scanner? Ah! Maybe he suspected that Chip was on to something. Sarah sighed. But what?

Looking at Andrew, she held up her finger and very, very quietly said, "Andrew, is it true that absolutely no one else can delete the files from the scan folder?"

"It's true. A disclaimer, though, I don't run this company. I'm pretty sure a lot goes on that I'll never know."

"Why aren't you all badgering Robert?"

"Yeah, sure. The Vice President. The boss's son." Andrew snickered. "Why don't you?"

"I'm not afraid to and in time, I will. But I need the time to snoop right now. If you ask me though, I say it's circumstantial evidence to say that Chip was here scanning and somehow knew how to delete the files. Don't you?" With a sigh and an aggravated shake of her head, she began to type. "Show me everything you can, Andrew. Let me look around."

Staring into the air, Sarah had begun the task of unraveling the mystery before her fingers touched the keyboard. She was actually glad when the task began. They were a boring lot—the Payces—and inherently bad. In a steady stream, her earnest prayers that God would control her discernment and reason—and her fingers—made their way to heaven. The adeptness of past days at The Kerrigan Corporation surged into her spirit.

Mentally, she blocked out every possible distraction—the emotional strain of sitting at Chip's desk and visualizing him in this setting; the voices of three men she despised, voices that increasingly became mindless chatter; the odor of Andrew's long greasy hair so close to her face; a cautious, yet ardent, letter from Scott sitting at home on the counter and a trip to Mexico close at hand; and Adam— did he know where she was—or was he asleep? Would Adam have thought that they would strike at night?

The click, click, click of her fingers on the keyboard was music in the ears of her captors. Raymond got up from where he had devoured the rest of the chocolate kisses, and went to stand behind Sarah. This did not please her. Then he sat down on the ledge beneath the window, squinting, watching, as though he knew anything at all. It was his turn, she guessed, to keep an eye on things.

Admitting that there was a slight possibility that Chip had the Lichten books and that he—for whatever reason—had scanned them, Sarah took another path other than the one that seemed to lead to Robert as a villain, and prepared to scour every nook and cranny for them. If she should find them and they should suddenly appear on the screen, she must have a plan. The two watchdogs hovering nearby must never catch even a quick glimpse of them. One of her rules for years had been, "Always keep some tricks in your back pocket."

She had some; she would use them if, and when, the time came.

With Andrew leaning in close, his face uncomfortably near to hers, and Raymond playing IT Guru behind her, she stalled, not wishing to let them in on her way of working. Methodically, she followed a rabbit trail through the files already accessed by Andrew, searching for traces of folders in strange places.

As she rapidly typed away, at a pace that neither of the nearby snoops could hope to follow, she talked to herself. *"Where is Mr. Cook? Has he contacted the police? Was he even awake? I hope Annette went home. And why did I have to take my car tonight? Is that a red flag? I must be smart...Adam was so right. I've got to keep my head on straight."*

Talented and skilled, Sarah typed and maneuvered through the file system—finding nothing interesting. She ran a search on all drives that would identify all files from a year before, created or accessed during the hours in question. An extensive list appeared on her screen, one screen after another of single files and regular automated computer activity. She was looking for a stray. In her heart, Sarah was confident that she would find it, but she must do it without calling attention to it. She would need to speed save it in a covert spot where she could intermittently examine the file or files. She would have to stall. She needed a diversion.

"Father, I need help here," she prayed. *"I need a diversion."*

CHAPTER 23

Figuratively speaking, Sarah darted in and out of the file structure of the company, going nowhere in particular and leaving Andrew in the dust. Her mind ran ahead of her, paving the way for an attack plan. She did another rush, a long stream of keystrokes that meant nothing; they were a temporary diversion.

Chip's lovely wife was increasingly weary and entirely provoked, but suddenly she knew exactly where to look. A recollection of a conversation with Chip more than a year before now guided her thinking. They had talked about how to hide data; she understood now why he had asked for her input. Sarah had told him that data could be hidden within an executable file, but that creating a hidden partition using special software was safer. With more misleading actions and sufficiently throwing Andrew and Raymond off, Sarah took a trip to Chip's hard drive. *"Ah, ha!"* she exclaimed to herself. *"It is as I thought! He did indeed create a hidden partition. Andrew, Andrew,"* she silently scolded the Director of Technology, *"you should have gotten this! It's basic, Andrew, basic."*

Her next steps would be perfectly clear. Trying Chip's favorite passwords that she knew, she easily accessed the hidden partition. There, three folders were staring back at her. She backed out quickly, hoping that neither Raymond nor Andrew had seen the screen. She mulled over the names of the three folders that had popped up: RICHARD; ROBERT; and DRYWALL ESTIMATES. Attempting to appear casual, she made a misleading move to view a bogus folder, but before she had a chance to do so, Raymond suddenly stood up and sputtered an "Uh oh."

"Uh, oh, what?" Richard asked, sounding peeved at being interrupted as he murmured in low tones about Chip and Mildred.

"Uh, oh, look at the parking lot."

Richard and Robert scurried to the window. Andrew twirled around to look. Police car lights blazed in the darkness, illuminating the fountain and the woods across the road with red, white and blue flashes. Timber Ridge, being a small community, did not boast a large police force, but it appeared that most of its cars were situated strategically below. Sarah heard the news. So Adam was not asleep! She drew in a long, quiet breath, settling her nerves. Taking advantage of the ruckus, she accessed the hidden partition once again.

Chaos was afoot. She could have turned to view the spectacle, but at that very moment, as Richard and his two sons, as well as the computer watchdog, were dealing with an unexpected jolt to their plan—and verbalizing with curses and protests—she stealthily went to the folder entitled **RICHARD**. A long list of files with dates as their titles, rolled down her screen.

"We'd better go down, Father, or they're likely to break down the door," offered Raymond.

"Blasted! What do they want? How would they know? Tell me, boys, how would they know?" A shouting match had begun!

"I have no idea!"

"What about neighbors? Did you rough her up in sight of the neighbors?"

"We didn't rough her up! And besides, there are no neighbors, Father. The next house...you can't even see the next house!"

"Then, was someone else in the house?"

"She lives alone! It was ten at night. There were no other vehicles in the drive. No, there was no one else there!"

"Go down and open the door while I talk to Sarah...alone. Both of you. All three of you...out!"

Sarah knew well that he would threaten her with harm should she divulge the fine points of this situation, and she briskly held up her hand as if to say, "Do not threaten me!" Then she defiantly pointed her finger at him and audaciously told him to sit down! He began to speak; Sarah commanded him to be quiet.

There was no time for significant words to come between them before the room became occupied with five officers, Timber Ridge's finest. The police chief himself, red-headed Rod Taylor, entered the office last. Richard had tried to *buy* him now and then, but he was not to be bought. He looked around the room, looked at Sarah, who had now stopped typing and sat with her hands in her lap, and spoke directly to her.

"Sarah?"

"Officer Taylor."

"What do you mean by this intrusion?" Richard barked. "Don't you have something better to do than drive around at night and visit legitimate businesses in the process of making a go of it? Look out that window over there. Take a look at the center of town, still teeming with twice as many people than who live here, carousing and wild. Why aren't you driving the streets down there, or better yet, walking them? What is it you could possibly want here?"

Rod answered coolly. "We have been informed that Mrs. Finfield has been taken against her will from her house and brought here."

Richard snorted. He stuck his thumbs behind his belt and walked to face the chief.

"Your information is in-cor-rect!"

"There are two witnesses."

"Oh, ho, ho! Two witnesses, boys. Andrew, did you hear that? They have two witnesses," he exclaimed, sounding much like Ralph Cramden. "And who might that be?"

The chief shook his head just slightly, but pointedly enough, to say, "Oh, no you don't." He walked to the large mahogany desk, ignoring other somewhat foolish remarks by Raymond and Robert, and talked to Sarah directly.

"Hello, Sarah," he said, recalling the tragedy and trauma of this woman hardly more than a year before. He nodded. "Come with me."

Taking a quick glance at the monitor, she hesitated, taking all the time she needed to form a course of action. She dared not leave the computer and she really did not want to. She was on to something. There had to be a way out of this situation.

"So the word on the street is that I've been kidnapped, eh?" she asked, leaning back in her chair and folding her arms.

Officer Taylor looked down into her face, studying it intensely.

"Come with me, Sarah. Let's talk in the hall for a moment."

What to do? A couple of options came to mind. Sarah looked calmly into the police chief's face and said, "I drove here, Rod. Didn't you my car in the drive?"

"Then…you're saying that you are here of your own accord?" he asked.

"I…I," she sputtered, "I'm here to unravel some computer issues dating back to Chip's employment here."

The three Payce executives fell silent. Wisely.

Sarah, taking advantage of the confusion permeating the office, under pretense of nonchalance, flitted back to the place where Chip had craftily hidden something away—evidently, something important—and opened the **ROBERT** folder.

"We have two reliable reports of you being removed from your home against your will," the police chief said, scanning faces of all in the room.

It was all she could do to fix her eyes on Rod in order to answer him. No one was watching over her shoulder. She must take a chance. She tilted her head, sat back in her chair, looked the police chief in the eye, and casually resumed typing as she answered him. She chuckled.

"No, really. I am here of my own accord," she said, realizing that it was not true, "and though it takes me into the night, I am resolved to be done with their pleas for assistance. Do I want to be here? No. But do I want closure on all of this? Yes."

The eyebrows of each of the Payce executives lifted simultaneously and their eyes widened; then lest they give themselves away, the spirit of smugness once again spread across their faces.

Sarah acted instantly, taking advantage of the moment. Her fingers flew. She chose one file on the list and opened it. A memo appeared. A memo to Joel Cassidine it was. Sarah recognized the name, something to do with a failed hostile takeover and the unsolved murder of Joel's father. It would not do to linger here. She backed out.

Still, the people present in the room, griped and groaned, throwing out questions of mistrust to each other and to the police chief...and Sarah, in between the steps she was taking on the computer, answered Police Chief Rod Taylor's inquiries. She had found the scans, the Fort Knox treasure—not a treasure at all! *This was evidence for something! This is not Fort Knox! This is Sing Sing!*"

There was nothing that could be done on the part of the Timber Ridge handsomely dressed law officers, their light tan uniforms looking impressively wrinkle free and spotless. Rod turned to go. With squinty, piercing eyes, he looked long and hard at the three Payce executives; then, with one last look at Sarah, searching for a hint of fear or a veiled message, and finding none, he motioned for his men to follow him. Out the door they went, Raymond escorting them all the way out the front door.

Richard, upon the shutting of the heavy door, did his best to strut to the desk and shook his finger at Sarah.

"I would be pleasantly surprised by your performance apart from the fact"—and here the volume rose—"that two people somewhere out there know the truth. That cramps my style! Who are they?"

Sarah answered him with pronounced assertiveness.

"That is not my problem," she spouted. "Do you want technical help or do you want me to play Private Eye?"

"A loose end charts my course, Mrs. Finfield. Do you understand what I am saying?" His inflections were gruff and his implication, clear. His intentions for the widow were not pleasant. "Do you understand that it is not a good thing, one way or the other, that two unknown people are now entwined in this whole business? Do you understand that it is not good for you, and it is not good for them? And Sarah," he barked, "it is not good for me! I do not do well when people try to outsmart me!"

"I am doing what you have asked. If you want answers, then leave me alone and let me get it done. Andrew," she called across the room, her body tense, her nerves shattered, "come, sit down, and let's get this over with."

Her plausible defense won the debate—for now, at least. Andrew settled in again; Raymond, Robert and Richard gathered around Chip's round coffee table, teeming with incessant conversation rising and falling in volume, and offering possible solutions to the mystery witnesses. This bedlam—for the Payce clan—was a highly unwelcomed incident and very possibly, damaging.

One last folder to view. Operating within a smaller screen and less conspicuous, Sarah opened the **DRYWALL ESTIMATES** folder, shoving a pad of paper and a pencil toward Andrew simply as a diversion. He took it with a puzzled look. The screen was showing a list of twelve files, named with the first 12 letters of the alphabet. Sarah suppressed a gasp. Could it be the twelve manuscripts? Yes, it could be! She knew she could not safely open them, not with the techie sitting next to her.

Sarah had a plan, a daring one—but could she pull it off?

"Andrew," she said, her voice just over a whisper, "do not say a word."

Andrew squirmed in his chair, but as Mrs. Finfield accessed the internet and her own Yahoo email account, there was no verbal outcry from the Payce employee beside her. As she addressed an email to herself and attached the unknown file, **DRYWALL ESTIMATES**, Andrew was jumpy.

He leaned in closer and mumbled, "Drywall Estimates?"

Impatiently, Sarah put the monitor between her face and the threesome in the corner.

"Um, yes," she said in very low tone, "Chip wanted so much to drywall the garage after putting it off for so long."

"And did he?"

"Yes, he did, but, Andrew...that's inconsequential at this moment, for goodness sake! I just want this file. It's a personal thing."

"You're makin' me nervous, Sarah."

Sarah, too, was nervous—nervous that Andrew's growing panic would be detected—and that the abrupt absence of keyboard activity would draw some attention. At last, the attachment was in place. With a wave of her hand meant to have a calming effect, and the words, "Worry not," she hit Send. The email was on its way. Andrew scribbled a note. *"I can die for this!"* With one brisk move, Sarah tore it off his pad, crinkled it and stuffed it in her pocket. She must act quickly. She must remove the drywall file permanently; she knew how; she had done it before. Adroitly, she maneuvered to software online which would accomplish the deed and soon the file was gone. Her hands trembled. She clasped them together for a moment; then, drawing in a deep breath, she returned to the other two folders containing the long-lost scans. *"I must take a quick look at some of these,"* she told herself. *"I must send these home, too!"* She glanced at Andrew. Beads of sweat glistened on his forehead.

"Chip created a hidden partition on his hard drive," she whispered to Andrew.

"What? No!" he mumbled leaning forward in unbelief.

Taking a chance on Andrew's allegiance, she clicked on the **RICHARD** folder and started through the files one at a time, analyzing them quickly—and listening carefully for any indication that one of the Payce men would be coming her way. There were copies of handwritten notes that had gone back and forth between father and sons. One directed Raymond to "exchange the contract at just the right time." "I trust your instincts," was an added scribbled note at the bottom. Financial documents were many, ones that had Chip's late-night scribbled notes in red in the margins. Sarah understood that if indeed Chip had copied them, he had not done so without reason. She opened yet another file and had a glimpse of a note written by Richard, "Mildred will be home alone tonight," the note read. What did that mean?

Astonished and infuriated, Sarah closed that document. Feeling justifiably devious, she went back to the screen with the two remaining folders. Making a mad dash to view at least another of the files in the **ROBERT** folder, she clicked on one randomly. Its subject was not familiar. *"One more,"* she decided. As she poised to open another, Robert got up and, after a brief hesitation in the center of the room, started toward the desk. The two folders named for the father and son of Payce Publishing were on her screen, unopened. Robert now stood beside her. She knew his perception of the situation would be instant. She chose to beat him to it.

"Well, well," she said, flopping against the back of her chair, "you're just in time, Robert." With a dramatic wave of her hand, she motioned for him to look. "Here...here are your scans! Not a trace of Lichten. Just two folders...one called **ROBERT** and another one called **RICHARD**...and a whole heap of files with dates for names."

Indeed, there upon the screen for him to see were the two folders, each with no indication as to what lay beyond.

"These are your scanned documents, Richard—and sons!"

A blanched face would have immediately given Robert away as he looked at the screen had Sarah seen it; but she did not. His nearly inaudible curse, however, did not go unheard. He rudely shoved her out of the chair. With impressive speed he went through several files within the **ROBERT** folder. And then, as Mrs. Finfield inconspicuously watched from behind, pretending not to see or care, Robert deftly rid the computer of all traces of the folder bearing his name. Sarah turned to face the window. Robert looked around and was satisfied that his devious deed had not been seen.

"Father," exclaimed Robert Payce, shady character that he was, "she's found the scanned documents and they're not what you thought!"

All was plain. At the speed of light, Robert had expunged Payce Publishing of all traces of a file meant to incriminate him for something or perhaps a multitude of things! The things that Chip had discovered! There was more to this story, she was sure. Unraveling it would have to wait, for Richard was charging like a bull toward Chip's desk.

Raymond flew to his perch on the window sill, joining the other onlookers. All three Payce men revealed their inner thoughts with outbursts of swear words. "Move," Richard commanded, roughly moving his son from the chair before the computer. He sat down and stared at the folder on the screen.

"Richard?" he mumbled in confusion. "What is this?"

He began to open the files, one by one, and as he did, his words reflected his boiling ire.

"Did she see these, Andrew?"

"I don't know."

"What do you mean, you don't know! Did she see this one?"

"I'm not sure," he answered, himself mystified by the happenings of the last five minutes.

He opened another one.

"And this one? Come on, Andrew! You were sitting here! This was your duty! Did she see this one?"

"She does what she does at lightning speeds! If you ask me, she didn't see any of it, I'm sure."

The handwriting was on the wall; devising a plan of some kind—a flawless one—became a necessity.

"Why badger him?" Sarah broke in, her voice assertive and bold. "Why don't you ask me?"

She surveyed the room. There were her car keys. She assumed that the keys sitting next to them were for the Escalade. Where was her purse? A valet key was in her purse, but it mattered not; all of it was on the side of the room away from the door.

Richard's voice boomed. Sarah desired so much to avoid any appearance of being rattled, but when he shouted his next words, she flinched.

"How much of this did you see? I see it in your eyes that you saw enough!"

"Richard! Use your head! I looked at a thousand files tonight. When I finally opened this file, I had to see if it could possibly be what you were looking for! Of course I saw some of it. Do I know what any of it means? How could you think such a thing?"

Her purse was irretrievable if she were to make a dash for the door. It was leaning against the lamp on the side table, exactly where she had put it when she first arrived.

"If there is one thing I know about you, Sarah Finfield, it is that you are no dummy. I don't need to explain that. You and I both know that you have a reputation, not only of extreme computer expertise, but also of keen and quick insight; and your marriage to Chip undoubtedly has entitled you to enough familiarity with the goings-on of this company to view what I just viewed and condemn me. You are a hazard to me now!"

"I wish I could say that you are no dummy!" she snapped. "You are the fool for ever hanging on to such incriminating evidence against you! Why would you keep such information? In the second place, why are you worried? These files were only a hazard to you with Chip alive. He was on to something and was planning action, but he is gone now. And Richard...there is something you can do to make sure they will be gone forever!"

Richard looked at Andrew as if to ask, "Is that true?" Andrew nodded unconvincingly.

It was very close to one thirty in the morning. Sarah needed to create a believable distraction to turn the tide. She wanted no more talk. Silence was safer. In a sort of collapse—genuine, but tainted with the theatrical—she crumpled into a chair in front of the book-cases—the chair closest to the door.

"I'm worn out!" she groaned, rubbing the back of her neck. "I've searched everywhere for your missing files. There is nothing more than what you see on this computer and I found nothing in the company files. I am going home."

Robert made his way to a spot behind Sarah.

"Here, let me take those kinks out of your neck," he said, his hands lightly wrapped around her neck. His message could not be misunderstood.

Like a shot, and miraculously healed from her exhaustion, Sarah bounded up and pushed him to a sitting position on the ledge.

"Do...not...touch...me!" she yelled, pointing her finger very close to his nose with each word. She moved away from him. "I...am... through, not just for the night, but for good. I don't know what you are seeking, but I found nothing that could be called *hidden treasure!* You had better put a new brass plate on the door. Take down the **FORT KNOX** sign and put something else in its place—like **THE BRIG!**"

A confab convened around the desk, Robert joining the other two and glaring at Sarah as he walked. The three men leaned in close, their faces just inches away from each other's; Andrew sat hunched over with great weariness and legitimate fear, a silent member of the discussion. With muted voices, the three evil-hearted men of Payce Publishing discussed the situation. Mrs. Finfield, truly drained, perched on the edge of Chip's credenza at the farthest point away from the Payce chatter as possible. Finally, Robert addressed Andrew in somber and serious tones.

"Tell me, Andrew, is there a way to retrace Mrs. Finfield's history on Chip's hard drive tonight? I'm asking if there is a way to see exactly where she has gone on this computer and what she has seen, step by step."

Sarah—and perhaps Andrew—knew Robert's motives of self-preservation for such a question, but there was no way they could be known by the other Payces in the room. His keen eye and his sharp brain had saved his skin! His question for Andrew was not meant to be answered; it was a diversion. Robert Payce knew that the other two did not have a single idea how to go about such a thing.

For Andrew, an affirmative answer would result in a death sentence on him, for he had witnessed Sarah's hasty transfer of a folder containing twelve separate files to somewhere else in the world. He had no possible defense except to suggest that perhaps she had done so during the bedlam that occurred with the police visit. So, somewhat unwillingly, he articulated his answer and in so doing, pronounced a probable edict of unemployment on himself and possible harm to Mrs. Finfield. Sarah pondered her options. *"It doesn't take a rocket scientist to figure why they had me come in my own car,"* she had already deduced. *"Yet, would they be so stupid as to harm me now that the police have become involved? The Payces are a clever and cunning lot. I do not trust them. I cannot take a chance."* She visualized the headlines: **GRIEVING WIDOW TAKES HER LIFE!** The Payces could pull it off!

Another huddle formed. Sarah knew it was now or never. With renewed vigor and catching her captors off guard with her split-second decision, she bolted, leaving her keys and purse where they were—definitely not on her escape route. Out the door she ran, slamming it behind her, down the hall—she knew this building well—down two flights of stairs.

Like a fine architectural drawing, Adam's escape plan spread itself out in her mind.

CHAPTER 24

A simple prayer escaped her lips as she descended the steps of the sweeping marble staircase and out into the luxurious lobby: "O God! O God! O God!" was her unbroken cry. "Adam, Adam, where is that big gray emergency button you told me about?" He had pinpointed it: "On the wall above the awards." Her eyes searched the entry way. There. There it was, just above the awards, like he had said. At the glass sliding doors, she smacked the emergency exit pad as she flew by and the inner and outer doors slid open. Not out into the night did she flee, however; no, grateful for her carpenter's premonition and preparation, she turned back toward the stairs, opened the janitor's closet and slipped in, closing the door almost all the way. She shivered and tightly clutched her sweater. The massive glass doors lingered open.

She heard the slide of elevator doors; Raymond's words—"Look! She hit the emergency button!"—were shouted not three feet away from her hiding place as the two men dashed by; she saw them slip through the now slowly shutting glass doors and out into the night. Warily, she inched the closet door open a little further, straining to see which way they went. She saw them look both ways; one went to the left; one went to the right.

"Be patient," Adam had said. "Stay concealed. One of two things will happen: They will get in their car or they will come back in. In either case, you will have a block of time to push that button again, only then you must get out and go quickly."

Minutes later, Sarah watched as the Escalade drove slowly down the driveway and off to the west. Cautiously slithering toward the sliding doors, she firmly smacked the button once again and exited out into the night.

"Oh, if I just had my keys! Or my purse! It has an extra valet key inside!"

"Go to the left into the shadows," Adam had carefully instructed her. "Hide first behind the patch of tall grass by the light pole. Then, when it seems safe, run to the freight yard where the trucks are parked, but stay as far away from the streetlight as possible. In the freight yard there is a fire alarm on the north side of the building, under a canopy next to the gas pumps. Pull it down. Help will come."

Running with haste, she made her way east, her target, a large area of tall Japanese grass, right where her carpenter had said it was. As she ran, the light from the brightly lit fountain in front of the building cast her long, thin shadow before her. Her breathing was shallow; her pulse rate high; her confidence level strong.

Her first line of defense, she was aware, unless she made it to the freight yard, would be the darkness. Her second hope—a slim one at this hour, she knew—would be an oncoming car. She would flag them down and surely they would stop to help!

The light brown stalks were waving in the wind as Sarah ran to hide in their shadow. Peering through them, she saw no further activity and no headlights or taillights, at least not yet. Her hiding place was a perfect spot to watch for any activity in the spacious lobby; but just how long would it be before she was discovered? Was it safe to head for the fire alarm?

"Mrs. Finfield! Mrs. Finfield! Over here!"

Out of nowhere, a voice just above a whisper came from the shadow of the trees across the road. It was the faint voice of a female. Sarah looked about, scanning the obscure scene. There. There, in the shadow of the trees, barely visible, was a car, a small car. Was it a Jaguar? She squinted. Could it possibly be Chip's?

"Mrs. Finfield! Over here! Run, Mrs. Finfield! Over here!"

Not believing her eyes—or her ears—Mrs. Finfield did run and as she did, she stole a look back. There in the window of Chip's office stood the silhouetted form of Richard Payce. That was unfortunate. His sons would soon know the details of her daring escape—at least as much as he had witnessed. She turned to concentrate on her getaway.

The door on the driver's side of the Jaguar slammed shut and the engine started; the car began to move before Sarah was situated in her seat. A pile of papers that had been on the passenger seat fell to the floor; they distracted her; Chip always kept his car neat and clean. She kicked them aside.

"Annette, I can't believe it! Go, go, go!" she shouted, trying to catch her breath.

Lurch. Squeal. The sports car screeched to a stop. Annette turned the key and started the engine again. Lurch. Lurch. Dead stop. Sarah quickly calculated what was best—change drivers or give the current arrangement a chance. Annette started the engine once again. This time, the car lurched and jerked. The escape was in motion.

"Ohhh, Mrs. Finfield!" Sarah's teenaged friend lamented, barely over a whisper. "Tony gave me four lessons in driving his Porsche, but I'm still having a lot of trouble with this stick shift!"

"Let the clutch out very slowly," Sarah said in a soft, firm voice as they drove past the Payce building. Headlights appeared far ahead of them. The car turned north. "Go, Annette, go!"

This time, following Sarah's instructions, Annette successfully went from second to third.

"All the way here I haven't been able to get into fourth gear!"

"Drive in third! Don't talk. Go, Annette. Step on it!"

Sarah, her heart thumping, pressed her hand against her chest as she watched out the back window for headlights. None appeared. With a sense of a small measure of safety—though perhaps temporary—they drove out into the countryside.

"Now there's something!" she said after several minutes. "Someone is behind us—pretty far, but out here speed outweighs distance. You must listen to my directions. Go to the stop sign and turn right. Don't stop. Just keep going in third. We're not going to run into other cars at this time of night. Watch, but just go through it. Then in about a mile, you're going to turn left. I'll tell you when. God has blessed us with a good tall corn crop this year! It will be hard for them to track us!"

"Yes...but we won't know where they are either!"

"That's true and that's why we must get three turns ahead of them. We don't want to be on any long stretch of road. We're going to head for town."

Annette made the first turn, almost going off the road into the ditch. After the next turn, the car went into a nearly irretrievable zigzag; with Sarah's help, they were soon under control.

"Turn left and go to the red barn with the big light in front and turn right."

Again Annette capably followed her orders. Sarah watched for the headlights of the white Escalade.

"We lost them in the turns, but they are not going to give up, of that I am sure. Annette, listen. Right over the river is a narrow dirt road that runs along the railroad tracks. I'll tell you when, but pull in there and turn off the lights. We need to switch places."

"Okay."

"When I give the word, run around over here as fast as you can.

If they drive by while we're switching, they will see the inside lights—so, hustle!"

The transfer took place swiftly, but before cautiously sticking the nose of the Jaguar out on the road far enough to look for oncoming cars, Sarah waited several minutes in the shadow of the trees. Then she nosed up.

"Look that way, Annette. Anything?"

"Nothing that I can see!"

"Good. Here we go! Hang on!"

Oh, how the love for driving—and driving fast—revived in the heart of Sarah, the widow of Timber Lane! Shifting seamlessly, she took the car into 5th gear, the beautiful sound of a Jaguar engine purring in the night.

"Do you know where you're going or are you just trying to leave them in the dust?" Annette asked, her voice quivering, her hands clutching the sides of her bucket seat.

"We were heading to town, but look. Look at the gas level."

Annette leaned slightly to look and groaned.

"We're almost out of gas. We would never make it to town."

"So, do you have a plan? Do you really know where we're going?"

"Exactly."

The territory was not unfamiliar to Sarah. Each turn was carefully calculated. Skilled at driving and an expert at outwitting—and driven with a compelling refusal to meet defeat, she fled from the presumed enemy at speeds exceeding 100 mph. Finally, she crossed Crimson Creek on Simpson Bell Road.

"Here, look in the glove compartment for a garage door opener," she said, still speeding down the country road.

"It's above your head!"

"In the glove box, Annette! The one I need is in the glove box!"

At a little red brick house, dark and overgrown, she pressed the button. Creaking and squealing as it went, the door crept up and Sarah, after skidding to a stop on the gravel road, inched the Jaguar into the small, crowded one-car garage of Mildred and Chester Finfield. The noisy door slowly closed them in.

Hardly daring to breathe, and nearly unable to speak, Sarah and Annette sat motionless in their seats. Annette's muffled sobs were nearly silent, but the magnitude of them touched Mrs. Finfield's heart. Still afraid to move for fear that someone could have followed them and could be creeping around outside the walls of the garage, she reached over very slowly and took Annette's sweaty hand.

"You probably saved my life or at least kept me from harm, dear girl," she whispered, so aware of the evil intent in the heart of Richard Payce. Sarah's declaration brought on a new flow of tears.

"But my driving nearly got us caught!"

"Shhh! Lights."

Through the side window, partially covered by a drooping curtain, headlights were visible. The car was stopped where the two roads met. The driver was deciding which way to go. Had they seen the Jaguar virtually disappear into the darkness?

"Lights where?"

"Shhh."

The car inched its way across the intersection, out of Sarah's view. There would be no way to tell if it went on or if it stopped outside the Finfield's house. Wracking her brain, Sarah tried desperately to recall if there had ever been any occasion that the brothers had laid eyes on this little red brick house. Did they know that this had been Mildred's house? If they did, and if they had been close behind the Jaguar, the outlook was not good.

"Oh, how I wish I had my phone! Annette, by any chance...do you have your cell phone?"

"I don't."

"Nuts."

"But...I have yours! I totally forgot. It's in my pocket. Just a second. When those criminals took you away, that's the first thing I did...grabbed your phone and called Adam. He told me go home and he told me to take your phone. So, I just stuck it in my pocket!"

"Ah, Annette! You amaze me!"

"I looked at your calls and found his number. Besides, it's all over his truck!"

"You're amazing." Sarah smiled, now absolutely sure that her carpenter **had** been clued in on the whole story from animated Annette. She tried a call to the police but even though it showed a connection, no one was on the other end. It was a one-sided conversation. She tried again...and again. Was it because they were in the garage or was it the fact that her battery level was low? She tried again. The call did not go through.

"I'm thinking we are okay," she whispered, still trying to stir her memory for recollections of Robert or Raymond being at the house, "but I'm going to get out and see if I can squeeze through all this stuff and look through the cracks."

As Sarah climbed back into the car, she whispered, "I can't say yes or no. It's dark. There are no lights that I can see through that little crack, parking or otherwise. I don't see anyone, and I think we should get out of here." She sighed. "It's impossible to be sure."

"Where are we?" Annette asked, still wiping her tears away with her sleeve.

"This is the house where Chip grew up. It's his parents' house and oh, I at this very moment…oh, my goodness…I recall that Robert and Raymond have both been here. How could I forget such an awful Christmas?"

"It is? They have?"

"Yes. It's all so strange."

"Are we just going to stay here? What are we going to do?"

"I don't know. My attempts to reach the police were in vain. If that was the Escalade that I saw through the window…Annette, I think we need to get out of here."

Waiting in the darkness, without any good way to peer into the night, was unsettling. The knowledge that the Payce boys were aware of the existence of the Finfield house gave her reason to conclude—or at least suspect—that she and Annette were sitting ducks. A sinking feeling overcame her. Holding her phone in the folds of her skirt, Sarah checked the time. Two fifteen. Her phone announced its near death with a single beep. She grasped Annette's arm and gave a short word of warning. "This is not a pretty picture. We could be in trouble."

"What do they want from me? Why didn't they just go straight to the house? Perhaps Richard wants to do away with me. He's good enough at such a thing that he could pull it off and make it look like an accident. The anger that I witnessed in that office made that clear. Still," she thought, *"with the police involved, how risky it would be to harm us!"*

"It'd be nice if a knight in shining armor would barge into this scene right about now," she whispered, "like the cops or Adam…or somebody! But I'm not holding my breath for that, Annette. I think we need to go. We're going."

After what had seemed like hours of dark and haunting confinement, with her hushed announcement that they were going to make a run for it, Sarah pushed the remote button to open the garage door. Creaking and groaning, it went up. She began to back out, ever so slowly, not turning on the headlights, hoping to just slip away—slip away to freedom. It was the brake lights of the Jaguar XK8 that broke the news, their glow illuminating the side of the white SUV towering like an army tank across the end of the short driveway. Robert had won the cat and mouse game!

CHAPTER 25

Without a word, Robert dragged Sarah from the car—after ripping open the door with startling force. Sarah could tell by his extreme brusqueness that he fully comprehended his race with time. Bending down, he eyed the girl in the passenger seat.

"Who's the girl?" he growled.

His question was met with silence.

"Ray, get her out! Who's the girl?" he again asked, this time thrusting his face near to Sarah's.

Raymond roughly removed Annette and held her upper arm in a tight grip.

"Likely one of the police chief's mysterious *witnesses*," he cleverly deduced, using his head quite nicely. As for Robert, his cognitive powers had been disabled by his rage and avarice, a not-unknown condition in people with tempers. Under less frenzied circumstances, he would have cracked the case of the identity of Annette himself and quickly. As it was, however, his normally puppet-like brother was one up on him.

"Who are you?" Robert yelled across the top of the car. "Who is this girl?" he haughtily inquired of Sarah once again. He received only an icy glare from the widow.

"No matter now, Robert, let's get out of here! The prize is ours if we don't stop to chat!"

"No, no," the elder Payce responded to his brother, making his way to the other side of the car, and dragging his captive behind him. "This is a loose end. I totally understand the uneasiness of Father in this matter. Raymond! This girl somehow witnessed the whisking away of Sarah Finfield. She is...our ticket to Chateau D'if!"

"Huh?"

"Prison, the slammer, the pen! Get it? This is trouble, Raymond, these two!"

Raymond's response was brimming with simplistic logic and

257

spoken in a loud convincing whisper. "Listen to me. Sarah herself put to rest any idea of kidnapping when Rod questioned her. What's important is possession of the books! If we have the books, the ownership part is easy. Let's go, Robert! Let's go!"

"One little glitch could undo us. This girl is a witness and not just a witness to a candy store theft. She's trouble."

"And Sarah is not? I say, take the keys and leave them both here…and let's go."

"No, I say, let's go, but take them with us. I need Sarah. I think there is a safe in that house and we missed it! Ray, you know there has to be one."

In moments, the Escalade began its treacherous journey toward the house on Timber Lane. Annette, with her hand clenched on Sarah's arm, scrunched her eyes closed, frightened at the speed at which the car was swerving on the country roads. There was no doubt in Sarah's mind that this was a perilous situation, especially since it appeared that Robert had a jump on the time element, and being honest within her spirit, she sported a growing sense of fear for her life—and Annette's. Being Sarah, however, she went to work, devising, plotting and searching for a Nancy Drew escape.

"Robert!" she demanded, "you are driving like a maniac! You will kill us all! Including you!"

He did not answer, nor did he alter his driving technique. They came to the north state road. He ignored the stop sign and made a frightful right turn.

"Let us out! Pull over and let us out!"

"No, Sarah, we need you at your house."

Robert's cell phone rang.

"Richard, no doubt," Sarah instantly deduced. *"Who else would be calling at this hour of the morning!"*

Driving one handed—adding to the already high-level anxiety—he grabbed it and answered it gruffly. His tone, however, became immediately and disgustingly respectful at the sound of Richard's voice, no doubt. Sarah strained for clues. Richard was not calling to say *hello*. Something was going on. The conversation as heard in the Cadillac was one of furtive "Uh huhs" ending with a highly dramatic and transparent "Well, well," from the elder Payce son.

"You cannot outfox the Payces!" he sneered, shoving his phone into his pocket.

"What's going on?" Raymond asked, looking at his brother questioningly.

"It appears that Andrew will enjoy a long, illustrious career with

Payce Publishing! You know," Robert continued with stabbing sarcasm, "I always liked Andrew, and apparently, he likes his job!"

"Andrew, eh? That's not too hard to figure out. I figured he'd come around with a little coaxing."

Sarah scorned Robert's arrogant smugness but she shoved it aside to focus on Andrew's disclosure. Andrew had nothing to tell! Either he had outright lied or else he fancied himself as seeing some golden nugget of information of value to the Payces.

Raymond went on. "What's the scoop?"

"The scoop is that Andrew—thanks to the dear departed widow in the back seat—has pinpointed the location of...the Herman Lichten manuscripts!"

"No kidding? And where does Andrew say they are?"

"When I tell you, you'll be kicking yourself like I am. You know we went through that house, every inch..."—it was a confession, and admission of guilt, outright and spoken in not only her hearing, but in Annette's! Was it carelessness on Robert's part or was it a subtle warning for Sarah. Perhaps she would never get the chance to testify to such a confession in court—"and did not find those books," Robert was continuing. As he divulged the secret, his voice progressively rose to a dramatic exclamation. "Well, you and I, we missed it...right under our noses. Listen to this my dear brother, the illusive manuscripts are after all, truly at Timber Lane entombed behind...the garage dry wall! What a clever man your husband was, Sarah! I have to admit that, though I disdained him. Be that as it may, soon what belongs to Payce Publishing will be in our hands."

Raymond tapped his brother's shoulder and asked, "Behind the dry wall? Do you really believe that?"

"It makes sense. Chip put that drywall up that week! And you and I, we looked everywhere else, right?"

"I guess it does make sense. How did Andrew conclude such a thing?"

"Father had a heart-to-heart talk with the boy. You know. Turns out he saw Sarah send a file with the word *Drywall* in the filename and he got to thinking, *"Drywall, hmmm."* Drywall, Raymond. Do you get it?"

Sarah squeezed her eyes shut and pulled her lips tightly together. Her brain went into deep thinking mode as she considered such a prospect. What could Andrew have seen? He had seen a file with the word *Drywall* and was making a case out of it! But, had he seen the twelve files listed and made a conclusion from that? No, he had not. She remembered the moment and she was sure he had not. Andrew was inventing to save his skin!

But, wait…could he have innocently put the X on the map? Was there even the slightest chance that Chip might have hidden the manuscripts between the studs while completing the garage? Sarah leaned her head back, intensely agitated. Of course he could have! It sounded just like him. It was the only place left with enough room to hide eleven manuscripts away!

"Soooo, my dear helpless widow, you sent the file off thinking we would never know, eh? Well, well, well. Andrew is to be trusted and you are not." Robert paused, shaking his head emphatically. "I have always mistrusted you" he went on. "You are just too smart, too intelligent to be authentic and upright. But, Sarah, it didn't pay off for you. Not this time. With a little bit of pressure, Andrew—brighter than we thought—has sung like a bird!

"My dear, you have unveiled the whereabouts of the manuscripts with a slip of false confidence. You underestimated the talent of our chief technology guy. He saw a whole lot more than you suspected. Foolish girl! You trusted foolishly. You took a chance and lost. Yet, Sarah, your lack of care threw the answer right into our laps, and I might add, right where it should be."

In the darkness, sitting just as she had been thrown onto the plush leather back seat, an expression of sheer unbelief passed over Sarah's lovely face. Muffling a gasp that was threatening to escape her lips, she grappled with this news which now was appearing to be surely more than a possibility. The manuscripts hidden behind the dry wall? Why, of course! Why had she never thought of that? It all made sense. Chip strangely driven to quickly finish the walls inside the garage? Eleven manuscripts missing? No trace of them in the thorough searches of the entire house?

"Oh, but if it is true, how could I—and Adam—have missed such a viable possibility. Ohh, it is more than a possibility!" Sarah groaned silently. *"It makes perfect sense! The drywall! The drywall! Oh my goodness! How did we miss it!"*

It took her but a moment to identify her course of action and to understand that she must act without hesitation. Stealthily, she took her phone from her pocket, and hiding it in the folds of the skirt to muffle the sound and veil the light, Sarah sent a desperate text to her friend, the carpenter. She must hurry for her phone would very soon be breathing its final breath. Would it have life for one more message? Sarah sent a prayer upward, and sent three words through the humid night: *Drywall. Manuscripts. Hurry!*

Suddenly, the car screeched to a stop. The dark cornfields

formed black walls on either side, closing them in. Sarah held her breath. Had Robert...or Raymond, for that matter...heard the beeps or gotten a glimpse of the light from her phone? Gruffly, Robert opened his door and yanked Sarah from the car.

"Get the girl, Ray."

For the first time since being extricated from her kitchen, fear welled up in Sarah's heart. The Payces were capable of anything in their quests for dominance—and wealth. Every telltale fact and innuendo regarding the haughty family that had left the lips of her husband rushed in upon her. Had he not suspected them of arson and murder? For Richard, Robert and Raymond it was Payce law— nothing else.

Her fear was not only for herself but also for the innocent teen who was at that moment being manhandled by a male with Payce for a last name. She shuddered. If the Payce intent was to harm them, this would be a perfect situation—inky darkness, fields of tall corn, higher than she could remember, wee hours of the morning, and seclusion. Raymond, not much more than a puppet, would be adverse to violence against a human, Sarah reckoned; but not Robert. She evaluated his every move; she snapped at him regarding the girl.

Adrenaline, no doubt, was accelerating this step in Robert's quest to take possession of the Lichten books, for he accomplished it in mere moments. With a quick shove and a final declaration, his body and face placed disgustingly close to Sarah's, he prepared to deliver a short sermon. The widow tore her arm from his vice-like grip and stepped away as he spoke.

"We no longer need you, Sarah. We know where they are and apart from the intervention of angels or God Himself, you are now blocked from interfering...and Sarah," he growled, evidently not satisfied with an apparent impending victory, "admit to the powers that be that these manuscripts are rightfully ours and you will not have to look over your shoulder for the rest of your life!"

Sarah discerned halfway through his speech—with the words "now blocked"—that physical harm was not part of his plan. He had, she was sure, weighed the acquiring of the manuscripts *with* violence against acquiring them *without*. His intent was discernible. He was working toward a clean theft with minimal aftermath. Stranding them by the side of County Road B would do the trick.

With one thoughtless shove by her captor, Sarah lost her balance on the uneven terrain and crumpled to the ground by the side of the road. A flower brushed up against her cheek—a Queen Anne's lace. As she moved to push it aside, she became conscious of stinging pain in her ankle. She swallowed the cry of agony about to leave her lips. Was she to be left alone in a ditch, alone with an injury of some magnitude to her foot, twenty miles from anywhere? Yes. Yes, the Payces would do that. They would abandon her and Annette without a sliver of shame. Yet, the God of heaven heard a prayer of thanksgiving at that moment, words of thanks for the sparing of lives.

There at the rear of the car, the shadows of disgust and the facial lines of pain on Sarah's weary countenance were only slightly illuminated by the faint, indirect glow of the headlights. In the shadowy wee hours of the morning, the intended receiver totally missed both. The two men turned toward the car.

"I'd tell you to not try anything," Robert called over his shoulder with a laugh, "but you'd have to run pretty fast to get to those manuscripts—our manuscripts—before we do!"

"They are not yours," she retorted defiantly. "You know it and I know it. You may put me out of commission by leaving us here, but you are too stupid to pull this off! Legally, you're a dead duck!"

Her remark turned Robert on his heels and he moved as if to deal unkindly right there with the widow; Brother Raymond, however, spoke wisdom.

"Robert, it's all within our reach! Why spend precious moments on such foolishness? Leave her here!" he protested. "Can't you smell success?"

For someone whose words rarely merited attention, Raymond's remarks resulted in a hesitation, a turn, an angry frown, and a brusque exit from the scene. He smiled inwardly realizing that his thoughts had been viewed worthy—again. It was a rarity; he knew it and said no more. Smugly, he settled down into the comfort of the fine car as his brother charged toward Timber Lane.

Sarah repositioned the barrette in her hair, and took a long look at her phone.

"My phone is completely dead!" she wailed, "and I have injured my ankle."

"What do you mean? How?"

"When he shoved me, I lost my balance and was heading for the ditch. I kept myself from going into the ditch but unfortunately, I twisted my ankle."

With genuine sincerity, Annette asked, "What can I do to help you?"

"Help me up. Let's see how bad it is."

It was bad. Sarah sat back down, grimacing. "I won't be walking anywhere tonight, that's for sure."

"What do we do? Do we just sit here till we're rescued? Surely that won't be until daylight! It must be around 3:30 right now, don't you think?"

Looking up into the teen's face, she said, "That's about right and I think we're just plain stranded. I think that this whole ugly mess is about to end. Those guys will soon have their hands on what does not belong to them and in a matter of hours, make it all look legal. We have lost. No, I have lost." Sarah squirmed trying to be comfortable. "I need to get to a tree or a stump, something that I can lean against. I can't sit like this."

"You can't walk, but I can. I can walk until I see a house and find someone to help."

"No. I thought about that, but I want you to stay with me where I know you're safe. I wonder about your folks. They must be worried."

"They're not. They're used to it. I often don't come back for a couple of days."

"Are you kidding? Where are you when you're gone?"

"I have a girlfriend who lives on the lake. She has a dreamy apartment attached to her parents' palatial home. (I only know that word because that's what her parents tell everyone.) Don't worry about Mr. and Mrs. Cappetti! They are quite lenient with me!"

"Well, it wouldn't be so if you were my daughter!"

"I think I figured that out!"

"I am so uncomfortable."

"What can I do?"

"Oh! I am really in pain."

"Oh, my goodness, Mrs. Finfield! What can I do for you?"

"I'm actually having more pain coming to grips with the fact that I completely missed the drywall thing than I am with my foot. Ohh! Just to think of Mr. Lichten's books—those wonderful treasures—in the hands of those despicable men. But it's over." Annette helped her injured friend to a large rock at the access road to the farmer's field. "My focus must now be on our predicament here."

"But at least you got a message off, right?"

"Yes, but if I had kept my phone charged, we'd still have a chance. As it is," she groaned, "those two—no three—ugly creatures will have their greedy, corrupt hands on those manuscripts in the next half an hour because I can't make a call!" She sighed and shook her head. "How stupid could I be!" she moaned, looking up into the starry sky.

"Stupid because your phone is dead?"

263

"For more than one thing, I'm afraid…at this moment, stupid because I didn't solve the mystery when the answer was right… under…my…nose! Oh, Annette, those books do not belong to Payce and it will break my heart—no, I take that back—it will infuriate me if they falsify things to look like they do…and they can do it. They have the means."

"Do you really think the stuff, you know, the manuscripts, really are behind the walls of your garage?"

"Yes," Sarah replied with another morbid shake of her head, "What a perfect hiding place for that much material!"

"How very strange all of this is. Your husband must have had reason to devise such a plan."

"Evidently he was the only one that knew about the other books by Herman, at least at that time. I don't know why he had them. It's all very strange, but those manuscripts are like a carload of gold. He knew that, and I guess he knew the Payces and their character—or lack thereof—better than anyone. It was such a good idea hiding them where he did, but the one who should have figured it out, did not. Me."

"I don't know…I don't think you should be so hard on yourself. I think you did everything you could. It seems to me that this is a **big** issue! If *The Street of Petetra* was so successful, I can see why all the uproar over the rest. The text message…was it to Mr. Cook?"

"Yes."

"Can I ask what it said?"

"All it said was, Manuscripts, Drywall, and Hurry."

"Oh! That was perfect! Good choice! I bet he's on his way. I bet any money he and Daniel will get there first!"

Sarah did not share the teenager's optimism. After all, where was Adam? He could be yet 100 miles away for all she knew. "At this point, I hold out no hope for Adam arriving in time. We have not heard from him at all. It's strange. There must be a reason."

"Was your phone on *Mute* maybe?"

"I don't know. I won't know now. It's dead…and so am I. Oh, Annette, I feel pretty certain that by now, or very, very soon, the crow bar has landed its first blow."

"Is that what they'll have to do? Isn't there a way to remove it carefully?"

First a short chuckle came, then a laugh of amusement, then a cry of pain.

"Oh, when I move, that ankle hurts. As for removing anything carefully, dear Annette, let me say this: This will be a special treat for the Payce boys with their villainous destructive instincts! Yes, there is a way, but do not plan to see my garage looking disbanded in an orderly, neat fashion!"

"This is really awful. And here we are with our hands tied. There's really not anything we can do."

"You have no idea how unhappy this makes me! My hands are, as you said, completely tied and I don't like when my hands are tied!"

"Oh, I totally see you that way! You are spunky, Mrs. Finfield! And I can't help but think that even now, even if Cary Grant and his brother get the manuscripts, that you will get them back—somehow."

"It irks me no end that no one knows where we are, sitting by the side of the road in the middle of the night. Who knows where the police are now! And who knows where we are! No one knows."

"Well, someone knows."

"Well, yes, of course, God knows. And I shouldn't underestimate that."

"I didn't mean God. I meant Adam. What about the earrings?"

"That's true, Annette, but when I sent that text, I sent him on a race to Timber Lane. If he's going anywhere, he's racing against time—and Robert—toward those manuscripts."

A soft breeze made its way down the road between the cornfields and blessed the two women with a touch of coolness to their cheeks. Annette, enraptured as always with the moon, looked into its face and pondered all the events of the day.

"Do people pray about stuff like this, Mrs. Finfield? I mean, would a Christian person just stop in the middle of a gravel road in the dead of night—in big trouble—and just, I mean, just stop and pray? I don't know enough about it all to know if God even would be concerned with such a thing if it's not a global crisis or something."

Another comforting breath of wind came and brought with it a trace of encouragement for Sarah, the young widow with injury to body and spirit. It seemed to carry a message to her—like a divine text message. Yes, God was truly whispering to her, "Trust Me." She scanned the heavens, her eyes wet with tears.

"Are you gazing at the moon?" Annette asked. "Don't you just know for sure there was Creator in all of this? Oh, it's a beautiful thing, the moon!"

It was the moon, the stars, the thick black background behind them, the aroma of the August corn stalks and the wet ground; but it was more, much more. Sarah had sensed the presence of Almighty God, interrupting her life with a simple message from the courts of heaven. She closed her eyes, her face still upward, and softly and slowly spoke to the girl beside her.

"Yes, Annette, people...Christians...do stop in the middle of a gravel road and pray about anything—anything at all! That's what we're supposed to do. God's Word is full from cover to cover with stories and, well, reminders, to do just that. God is a personal God. He knows me well," she said, not hurrying, "and He knows you well, and He wants to walk with us, closely, intimately. He shouts His love to us in whispers as we go step by step through life."

"I want to say, 'He does?' but I can hear it in your voice that there is no reason to doubt you."

Sarah paused, a deep sigh coming from within her heart.

"I've stopped in the middle of many...*gravel roads*...in my life to pray, and when I didn't and should have, I was the one who lost out. This whole thing—this thing that started with you and Tony seeing three men outside my window—has been hard. I went through a lot of it without praying, I'm afraid—and without trusting. Now, because of this and that, He is teaching me once again to take my troubles to Him. I'm amazed at God, Annette, more right now than ever before. Yes, Christians do pray in any kind of trouble."

"I don't have the slightest idea how to go about such a thing."

"Yes, Annette, you would," Sarah said with a small cheerful laugh. "You know how to pray because you know how to talk."

Annette laughed. "Perhaps, but I'm pretty new at this and just thinking about the One who made that awesome moon up there—do you see it?—and everything else, unnerves me a lot!"

"Yet, Annette, we can actually come before the throne of Almighty God through Jesus. You can do that now! You have become a Christian, a believer in Jesus Christ!"

"Well, if you don't mind, I'd still rather have you start."

Annette thrust her arm through Sarah's as they sat side by side, happier than she ever remembered, and the two friends prayed before the throne of God with His spotlight glistening atop their heads.

It was a simple prayer, from Sarah's newly warmed heart. "And we plead, Lord," she said, closing her prayer, "for protection and safety. You know that the Payces are evil and have evil intentions, but You have said that your angels will be about us. Help me...help me, Lord, to leave it all with You. It won't be easy. There's so much at stake, but I will try. Thank you for my dear friend, Annette. How good of You to bless me with her friendship. In the name of Jesus I pray. Amen."

"Our Father who art in heaven," Annette began, oh, so much

more softly than usual, her eyes fixed upon the starry sky, "I don't know what to say except for this: You know who is right and who is wrong. I know that You do. So, I just ask that You would stop the bad guys and help the good ones. I just know that You are looking down right now and that You see us and hear us. Please send us help. Mrs. Finfield needs help about her ankle. Thank You. Amen. Oh, I mean, in Jesus' name, Amen."

It was the wee hours of the morning. It was August 13th. It was a beautiful night. Annette rested her head against Sarah's shoulder.

"Did God ever answer one of your prayers? I mean, did you ever actually pray for something specific and then get it?"

For a few moments, Sarah said nothing; then as though she had not heard Annette's question at all, she began to think aloud.

"I wonder what's happening at this very moment," she said, her mind obviously not quite ready to wander too far from the crisis at hand. "Where are the police? Where is Adam? Is anyone going to get to that garage while the Payces are still there? Ohhh, I can't believe that I didn't figure that out! I can't tell you how many times I said the word *drywall* in the past few weeks! Oh, how stupid of me!"

"Is it the manuscripts," inquired Annette, willing to change subjects along with her friend, "or is it the Payces that upset you? Or it is both?"

Sarah sighed, truly irritated.

"This is what it is: It is the wickedness of the whole Payce clan and the thought that they could get away with this and with murder and more!"

"Well, Mrs. Finfield, maybe not! I did pray that those who are in the right would win, and those who are the bad guys would not. Hmm, maybe this will be my first chance to see a real answer to prayer."

"Oh, Annette, I'm sorry. You asked me about that and I went off on a tangent. Yes. In answer to your question, yes, I have asked for specific things and received a specific answer."

"Tell me one. Okay?"

"Okay."

But Sarah, exhausted and spent, more that she knew, gave no answer. Instead, her thoughts elsewhere, and her foot aching, she allowed memories of Chip to drift in. Thoughts of Chip would be expected on a night like this. How nice it would be to have a strong man nearby right now! How painful to have to face such a night as this all alone!

Annette periodically looked over into the face of her friend, wondering if she was thinking of an answer to prayer that she could share with her, but Sarah was far away.

With a sigh, Annette said, "Well, I guess I'll get a chance to see for myself. I just prayed all by myself that God would bring us help right now."

Even before Annette's sentence had truly trailed off, far down County Road B, a vehicle rounded the corner and flew toward them, stones skipping in every direction. Like an ominous monster it drew closer and closer. Sarah turned abruptly, letting out a howl of pain, her spirit ready for a fight. The vehicle stopped abruptly, raising a cloud of white dust all around. The glare of the headlights, blinding and bright, could not mask the shape of the vehicle; it was a truck. It was a silver truck, Sarah was sure.

Adam and Daniel were on the ground instantly and with a few long strides reached the women. Adam reached down to pull Sarah up, but she raised her hand to stop him.

"My ankle, Adam. My ankle" she groaned. "It's sprained or broken or something. Probably sprained."

Quickly and smoothly adjusting his approach, Adam stooped down and effortlessly lifted her into his arms; his tears could not be seen as he left the illumination of the headlights, but they could be heard in his voice and in the depth of his sighs. With Sarah's arms wrapped tightly around him and her face cradled against his neck, Adam took careful steps on the uneven ground.

Great gratitude and relief could be heard as he sighed and murmured, "You...you are all right, Sarah." Holding her close, he carried her towards the truck. Annette, privately awed that God had directly answered her prayer, kept watch as Adam moved her friend, Sarah Finfield, to safety. As the tender scene unfolded, teenager perceptively drank it in.

"Yes. Sort of," Sarah replied.

Daniel ran ahead and opened the door, standing aside to allow his dad to place Sarah safely inside. With care, Adam positioned her comfortably and gently turned her to sit so he could close the door. He grasped her arm and squeezed his eyes shut; then, not able to mask his emotion, he stammered, "I...I...I've been thinking the worst. The transmitter hasn't moved for 45 minutes."

He gave Sarah's door a quiet shove and then made his way to the other side, rubbing his furrowed forehead with the tips of his fingers as he went. At his door, he took off his hat, ran his fingers through his hair, and gazed into the star-filled heavens. His lips moved. A prayer of thanks was in order. It could not wait and it could not be rushed. His words of gratitude took wing through the black night and fell upon the ears of Almighty God. Then, he returned the cap to his head and with a long deep breath, settled into the driver's seat.

Sarah, regardless of suffering painful throbbing in her foot, had absolutely no room for *warm and fuzzy*. All she could think was why it was that Adam was here and not at Timber Lane. Had he not received her urgent text?

"Did you get my text message?" she asked, her voice inflections revealing her intent. The silver truck rumbled on toward her house.

"I got it," he replied, sensing correctly that Sarah was perturbed, or at least perplexed. "I got it, but the manuscripts had to come second, Sarah, you must know. There is no way I would go there without knowing that you...were...okay. The transmitter was telling me that evil had befallen you. You have not moved for more than a half an hour...forty-five minutes!" he softly exclaimed. "We could only imagine...well, you know what we would be thinking, right?"

That was something that Sarah had not thought of. That would have been disconcerting for the returning fishermen. Yet, she stared wide-eyed into the night, her irritation evident, a vision of Robert Payce escaping her garage with the manuscripts in his hands ruling her thinking. She could hear Daniel and Annette telling their stories in the back seat of the cab. They were not listening to the front-seat conversation.

"But, Adam...."

"Sorry, Sarah," he replied in such a low whisper, shaking his head. "People first."

"Fine, but let's fly to my house now!"

"What about your ankle?"

"Adam! Do you not know me well enough to know that this ankle thing means nothing compared to triumph over those Payces? Please listen to me...go to the house! My foot can wait! Please remember what they did to my house. Please remember what they have done to me. Please remember the fear I've had to deal with." Agitated, she bit her lower lip and thought for a moment. "I guess, in reality, you don't know me very well."

There was no doubt as to the relief that the arrival of Adam and Daniel had brought. Sarah was tired, beaten in spirit and in body, not even taking into account the overall damage done to her by the night encounter at Payce corporate office. How thankful she was for the rescue, but grave disappointment played with her spirit. Adam evidently had not detected the urgency in her text; more than that, he seemingly was missing the magnitude of the race for time. Of course she was all right! One does not send a text that says *Manuscripts, Drywall and Hurry* if one is in danger! Wouldn't she have texted, *Help and Hurry?*"

"Please, Adam, you have no idea right now of what I have been through since I saw you last. They must not win! Let's not let them win, if we can help it! Robert and Raymond left a long time ago for my house. We're behind."

"I know."

"I'm sure we have missed our last hope." She plopped her hands into her lap. Woefully, she went on, her head leaned back against the headrest and her eyes away from Adam's direction and fixed on the cornstalks whizzing by. "I don't care about the manuscripts, Adam. I don't care about the money they represent. I just don't like the Payces. I don't like what they've done to me and my life and I don't like that it looks very much like they have won."

Adam gave her a long sidelong glance. He had taken over from Daniel the task of driving and fairly flew toward Sarah's exquisite home. She sat beside him, a thousand notions running through her head, her foot in pain, and watched the speedometer climb to 100. Daniel and Annette's nearly inaudible conversation in the back continued, chapter by chapter.

A mile or so from the house, Adam spoke, without turning toward the widow beside him.

"I guess…you really don't know me well either. It's people first, Sarah, then things. Always."

CHAPTER 26

As though it were an international crisis, the situation in this little corner of the world, Timber Ridge—a mere dot on the map—escalated into a near life and death calamity; or so it seemed to everyone in the story. The stakes were not insignificant for any of them. From Richard Payce down to Annette Cappetti, the outcome of the events of the next half hour would most certainly chart their course for years to come. Greed and deceit, hope and justice, fondness and friendship, and yes, even love, motivated the characters in this tale.

The whole of Cherokee County and beyond—the town of Timber Ridge, the outlying countryside, an interstate running from the Mississippi River to a place unknown to most of the world, and the exquisite sprawling ranch home at 12006 Timber Lane—was teeming with mystery and urgency, but not over secret plans for a missile or the whereabouts of a kidnapped scientist; no, it was eleven manuscripts of inestimable value, the artistry of master author, the late Herman Lichten. His name was a household word now, but only a handful of people on the face of the globe were aware of the transpiring battle to take possession, as it were, of the old man. Realistically, when all was said and done, the end of the story depended on the chronological order of the imminent events. It was all in motion. What would be—it appeared—would be.

An aerial view, had there been one, would have told all: Timber Ridge police cars, their sirens reverberating in the night, their lights illuminating the dark and tranquil countryside, racing first here, then there; a silver Dodge Ram closing in on the Finfield house, transporting an anxious widow, her teenaged neighbor, a grateful carpenter and his son; in his posh office at Payce Publishing, the greed-driven president and CEO, purposely avoiding the actual action, sitting impatiently waiting for word; and an Escalade heading toward the prize at top speeds, its driver and front seat passenger, smug. Each person or persons was acting for their purposes alone and, for the most part, devoid of knowledge about the movements of the rest.

The Cadillac arrived at the widow's house first, the only light inside, the one in the kitchen. Except for the illumination being freely provided by the lights in the heavens, the surroundings were exceedingly obscure. Like a shot, fully aware that time was not on his side, Robert jumped from the car, retrieved the tire iron, and tore to the garage. With one kick, the side door was down just as it had been at the start of the whole tale, lying in splinters on the cement floor. This time though, the still night was pierced with the widow's blaring security alarm! Stunned, Robert growled a loud curse under his breath. Only momentarily deterred, however, he hasted to carry out the plan, counting on a twenty-minute travel time for the police responding to the alarm. The piercing siren undid Raymond. He slapped his hand to his chest and then covered his ears with the palms of his hands. A sharp command and a scowl from his older brother jolted him into action.

After dealing with a flat tire, the two fishermen had made their way exactly as the transmitter guided them. The text from Sarah, and the precious Lichten books, took a back seat to Adam's first concern—the safety of the widow; instead, the instructions to Daniel, had taken them away from her house and no doubt, first dibs on the coveted manuscripts. Now, with the rescue effort complete, the silver truck was flying toward Sharenne Woods.

The Simpson Bell house—the little red brick home—had been the initial target of the police because an odd call had come from within the confines of the one-car garage. When they converged on the place, they found the Jaguar sitting exactly as it had been left, doors open, lights on, and a steady, aggravating bell drawing attention to the keys in the ignition. Had Sarah been abducted again? Or did they need to comb the area for her?

Rod hurriedly left for Sarah's house, taking a team with him, but leaving some behind to look for the widow. The quiet Cherokee County night enveloped the searchers. The time was somewhere between three and three thirty; stars nearly covered the black sky and a slight breeze tempered the humidity. For twenty excruciatingly long minutes, they searched...for a body...the light of their flashlights moving about, looking like giant fireflies. Then they, too, headed for the widow's home.

At last, the final page of the story burst into action. The Dodge Ram was second to arrive. There was no detaining of Adam once his silver truck fishtailed to a stop on the grass. Out of the truck he bounded, taking a quick look around as he ran to the garage. Behind him came three officers—Rod Taylor being one of them—and as they entered, Adam was already confronting the elder Payce son.

"Stay away, carpenter!" Robert scowled over the screech of the alarm. He rammed the tire iron into yet another section of drywall. Adam was unmoved; he slowly and without fear walked toward Robert, stepping over the mess on the floor.

"You wrecked my door," he shouted in order to be heard over the deafening alarm, his angry expression not to be misunderstood, "and Bob, this is not the first time. This...is the second time."

He inched his way closer, not flinching. The police chief sternly commanded him to step back.

"And I don't like the way you treat widows, either," the carpenter continued, ignoring the command.

"Listen, carpenter, I am only looking for what is mine. It is mine...ours, and we have come to take it! Move away. Don't involve yourself in this; it's way bigger than you."

Adam took another step. Robert shoved him with his free hand.

"I'm telling you, get out of here!" Robert warned, his voice booming. "This does not concern you!"

"Adam Cook!" Raymond hollered. "Get out of here!"

The police chief moved in closer to the impending confrontation. The earsplitting alarm ceased, causing Raymond's next ridiculous words to reverberate within the garage walls.

"Taylor! Back off!" he warned Rod as he watched the police chief step closer.

Rod looked toward the younger Payce, not believing his ears.

"Shut him up and read him his rights," he growled to one of his deputies. Without delay, Raymond was subdued, handcuffed, and escorted out.

The scene with Adam and Robert as the main characters was not deterred and seemed to be happening in slow motion, Sarah was thinking, as she clung to the broken door frame and watched from around the corner. Police officers moved into strategic positions. Daniel brushed past two of them to be near his dad, his hands on his hips, ready to leap into action as needed.

Rod made his decisions based on the possibility that Robert might have a firearm; but he was not armed, except with a powerful physique and a tire iron which Rod repeatedly commanded him to drop. Robert ignored the command. Payces did not abide by any rules outside of theirs. He did not comply.

But Rod likewise firmly ordered Adam to stand down, also with no response. The broad shouldered carpenter ignored the chief's directive. He was in motion and not to be easily stopped. The situation sizzled with unpredictable grave outcomes.

Adam took another step. Robert raised the tire iron, intending to stop him in his tracks, evidently shunning common sense that no matter how this scene ended, his dismal future was cast in stone. Richard Payce's brawny eldest son left no question as to his intentions. High above his head, in his large muscular hands, he gave the tire iron one last jerk before bringing it downward. A dismal cry in the night rang out. "Nooo!" The female cry came from the area of the service door in the corner of the garage. It was Mrs. Finfield.

As though someone had turned on the switch under a mechanical winter scene under the Christmas tree, the figures inside and outside the garage came to life, moving here and there, doing exactly what they had been trained to do.

"Halt, police!" came the steely command from the chief as he shifted closer to the two men. "Lose the tire iron, Robert!" Rod shouted again, his gun drawn. "Stand back, Adam! Stand back!"

Adam, however, had already initiated his next action, moving his arm back into position, not caring about consequences, clenching his fist and uttering his own thoughts for all to hear. With a right to the stomach and a left to the nose, Adam pronounced his judgment upon the despicable man standing threateningly before him: "This...is for the widow, you creep!"

The tire iron hit the floor with a deafening clang before Robert's well-built frame, which left him more angry than stunned. He tried to get up—unsuccessfully. Adam's blows had finished him.

"Cuff him," Rod ordered. Face down on the cement garage floor of the lovely widow of Timber Lane, quickly and without fanfare, Robert Payce, clothed in the finest of men's wear, was shackled. The rustling of human life stilled; cops and citizens were glad it was over.

"You'll pay for this, Rod!" Robert growled. "Sarah has stolen what is ours! This is the only way! She will not turn over to us what is legally ours!"

"Tell it to the judge," Rod responded, punching the button to open the overhead garage door.

"You know we've got big gun lawyers," Robert shouted proudly.

"Those aren't big gun lawyers, Robert," the chief scoffed. "You're looking through the wrong end of the telescope. Those are little gun lawyers. Here you go, Detective Kinzie...Banks...do your thing; then get him up and outta here. We're done here. Let's wrap this up. Where's his brother?"

"He's waiting for Brother Robert in a police limo."

Adam walked slowly to where Sarah stood, her arm around Annette's shoulder for support. She watched him come, her face bearing shades of admiration and relief. He took over, his strong arms bearing her up as they walked to his truck and then he carefully lifted her into the passenger seat. He was tired; Sarah was drained; but the battle was over and the triumph obliterated the fear and anxiety. The Payce regime had been brought to a halt—at least as it had to do with Sarah Finfield.

Gradually, the Timber Lane property returned to its normal serenity, police cars and other emergency vehicles turning around on the grass and exiting down the noisy gravel road toward the state highway. In her spot in the truck, Sarah twisted around so that she could watch the taking away of the two men who had shattered her life for the sake of greed. The departing police vehicles moved stealthily away transporting Robert and Raymond Payce, high level, wealthy businessmen, still in their professional finery after a hard day's work, taking them to the Timber Ridge police station...each in their own personal squad car.

"Sarah Finfield's alive and well, alive and well, alive and well..." Sarah murmured.

"What? What's that you're saying over there?"

"I'm singing 'Sarah Finfield's alive and well, alive and well...,'" she repeated dryly.

"I'm missing something, I guess."

"Oh, how I wanted to just belt it out when they were walking by...in cuffs! Richard and Raymond sang a little song about me up in Chip's office—in the dead of night, I might add—a stupid, ridiculous little ditty, dancing around the room as they did." She shook her head, still finding it hard to believe such a thing.

"That's what they were saying?"

"Yes...well, no. They were singing, 'Mrs. Finfield's dead, you know, etc., etc., never to rise no more.'"

"Oh, Sarah, you should have done it! That would have been a perfect ending to the mayhem!"

"Maybe someday in court," she said laughing.

Rod, the last to leave the scene, ambled over to where Sarah was resting in the truck and Adam was standing beside her. "We'll talk more tomorrow...well, actually later today," he joked. "Sarah, did you try to call from out north and west?"

"Yes, but even though it looked like it went through, I heard nothing on your end."

"You were breaking up but we at least could make out the general idea of what you were telling us."

"Did you go out there?"

"You bet. Like lightning. It was disconcerting, to say the least. The car was there, doors open, the key in the ignition, but no Sarah. You can imagine what we thought."

"I can see where that would be disconcerting. You thought... well, I know what you must have thought. I'll have to get out there and retrieve the car and make sure things are closed up. Anyway, Annette and I got whisked away again by the Paces, but left by the side of the road later. It's a long story. I know you and I will be talking. Later, okay?"

Rod was not quite ready to leave the premises. There was something on his mind. It was obvious that he had more to say and that he was choosing his words carefully.

"The break-in, Sarah. It was them, wasn't it."

"Yes."

"And you knew, didn't you."

"By the time you talked to Adam and me by the refrigerator, yes."

"And your kicked-in garage door?"

"It was them."

"Of course it was. Do you recall that that day, talking by the frig, I said something was bothering me?"

"Yes?"

"It came to me tonight. Funny thing, one day I ran into Chip and Robert at the donut shop and we got to talking about alarm systems. Chip was telling the two of us about your new security system and how he still had to tie in the garage. Funny thing, that was the day before he died. Of course, you never called us about the garage break-in. I only found out about it the day they trashed your house."

"I didn't figure it out either until that day. Then I knew it was them."

"All this time."

"Yes."

"We might have avoided all of this if you had told us."

"Rod," Adam interjected, "we felt sure that we had to keep it to ourselves until we found out what they were after. At that point we didn't know. A police investigation would have tipped our hand. That's why we didn't say anything."

"Well, we'll go from here. So, Adam, it was the manuscripts, huh?"

"It was, but when they trashed her house, we had no idea about any manuscripts and that there were eleven more Herman Lichten books. We found that out along the way."

"Who do the manuscripts belong to?"

Adam waited for Sarah to answer. She took her time and Adam was glad because the subject was indeed a touchy one.

"Not the Payces," she stated decisively. "Absolutely not the Payces. That I know for sure. After that, I think it'll take some time before we know the answer to your question."

"Well, I'm sure we'll be seeing a lot of the two of you in the next weeks. Right now, though, before I go, I have one nagging question."

"That's not hard to guess," Adam said.

"Are the manuscripts really behind the drywall?"

For Sarah, such a question seemed perfectly acceptable, and she would have answered him, at least briefly, "Yes, I am nearly certain of it"—but Adam's body language revealed that he wished to protect his friend from further interrogation. The widow's face bore the signs of twenty-four hours of harassment and torment. Lichten manuscript talk could wait...Adam's wish was to drive post-haste to the hospital in town and see Sarah's ankle taken care of. He gave her legs a gentle shove and closed the door.

"Let's wait until tomorrow. I know I've had enough for one night and looking at Sarah, I can see that she feels the same. She needs to get to the ER. Tomorrow. Okay?"

"Later today, you mean," the police chief agreed, grinning. The two watched as he headed toward his car, carrying on a two-way conversation with someone somewhere. It had been a night of chaos and too many hours of madness for the chief; Rod was glad to be heading back.

"Is he gone?" Sarah asked.

"Yep."

She drew in a grateful breath. "He's a nice guy but I'm glad he's gone."

"Why?"

"I just want an end to this August nightmare."

"What a terrible night and if it was terrible for me, I can't imagine what it has been like for you. We need to get going."

"Do me a favor and let's not talk about all of this tonight. I'm in a Sarah-Finfield danger zone." Sarah could not help but smile at Adam's chuckle.

"Tonight is over," he said. It's morning. Look at the awesome horizon. That row of clouds has a silver border. It's morning. Anyway, you don't have to explain about Sarah Finfield. Got a mirror?"

"I'm sure it's not a pretty sight."

"You're pretty done in, Mrs. Finfield. I'll take you to get that ankle fixed and then drop you off so you can sleep. Tomorrow... later, I mean...we'll talk. We'll have to. We're still in this thing up to our noses, you know. Maybe later we can get together for a bit with Daniel and Annette. Daniel leaves on Sunday."

"He came and said goodbye before he walked Annette back to her house. Such a polite young man he is. I'm assuming she is tucked safely away by now."

"Yeah, he was taking her home when the hubbub was beginning to quiet down and I was glad for that. I told him I'd be taking you to the hospital so he should just come back to your place and wait. I'm pretty uncomfortable with her out all night like she often is. I don't understand that kind of parenting."

"Me either! I told her it would be different if I was her mom!"

"She was pretty well done in. I could tell by the lack of chatter! I'm interested to hear the story of how it came about that she ended up with you."

"It's quite a story. Really, she saved my life, I'm pretty sure."

"I don't doubt it. She's an unusual girl," Adam said, smiling and shaking his head. "She really didn't want to go home tonight. I guess she thought we'd be hanging around—you and Daniel and me—telling stories and she'd miss out on it."

"I'm sure we'll be talking about it for a long time to come whether I like it or not. I hate courtrooms and gavels. You and I both know there's a lot more to come on the legal scene."

"Yep. I'm pretty sure it'll all drag on for a good long time. For now, though, let's be off to the hospital."

"Well, okay. Rod wanted to send me off in an ambulance, but I declined."

"You would have missed the fun."

With her head pressed against the head rest, the widow of Sharenne Woods articulated her thoughts on the subject.

"It was not fun, Mr. Cook. You freaked me out going after Robert like that, him with the tire iron in his grip."

"You mean, Bob?" Adam said, his humor not missed by Sarah.

"Hilarious! That was the best part of the whole thing! No one would dare call him Bob!"

"I did."

"You did and then you decked him! You decked him good! That helped. I was all sorts of things at that moment—scared to death, dreadfully sorry for ever calling you to fix my door, and...and, overjoyed that you really got him good! You took down a proud man who sees himself as Hercules!"

Adam snickered. "Hercules."

"Were you afraid out there?"

"Nope."

"Not at all?"

"No. You've got to take into account my frame of mind when I got here and walked into the garage. Besides, he's mostly talk."

Adam started the engine at 5:56 a.m. That, at least, was the time in the Sharenne Woods community of Timber Ridge. A rim of white and pink now lined the horizon over Annette's way. They were heading into a perfect summer day.

"How's the ankle," Adam wanted to know before heading out of the driveway.

"It hurts, and look, it's pretty swollen, but Adam, wait." Reaching over to tightly grasp his arm she spoke words that took Adam off guard. "Please don't argue with me."

This statement brought about a quick perplexed look, tempered with an inquisitive smile. "Argue?" he asked somewhat dumbfounded. "About what? Am I arguing with you?"

"I can't go yet, Adam. Before I go anywhere, I just have to check the rest of the drywall."

"I'm not surprised," was his calm reply, "but what happened to the Sarah Finfield danger zone?"

"I know. It's still true. I'm wiped out but it seems so ridiculous to be this close to victory and put it off till tomorrow…I mean, later. I want to get it done right now!" she said enthusiastically. "Don't you? After all that we've been through, don't you want to get your hands on those manuscripts?"

"What do you think?"

"I think you do."

"I do, but I'm worried about your foot."

"Oh, I don't care about my foot right now! You must know that I could never, ever just drive away like this! I can't imagine that you aren't dying to get at that dry wall."

"I am."

He turned off the engine.

"Let's stay, Adam. It can't take that long."

"I'm thinking it'll take longer than we think. The boys didn't get too far, you know. I'm thinking that it's all behind one section, but we don't know which section it is."

"Tell me you aren't dying to do this."

"I can't," he said, looking at her. "But, Sarah, good sense tells me that we need to get that ankle looked at. I'm surprised the pain is not killing you. That's a pretty swollen ankle, kid. We can come back after you get it taken care of."

"Think of it this way: I could still be sitting by the side of the road. Let's go, Adam. I'm crazy with the scent of victory!"

"You...are in the driver's seat, Mrs. Finfield," he said, displaying a lesser version of his famous grin. "You are the customer. I do what you want. Remember?"

Sarah smiled and retorted kindheartedly—but dogmatically, "We are friends, Adam. I think we've gone through enough together to do away with the carpenter/customer thing, don't you?"

Responses lined up in Adam's head and wisely, as usual, he took his time choosing one. Change was in the wind. Of that he was sure. One way or another, friends or not, forks in the road were ahead.

"Let's go treasure hunting, Sarah Finfield, my friend," he said, climbing down from the truck.

With Sarah's arm around his shoulder, the two friends walked through the battered doorframe in high spirits, ready to go to work. Herman Lichten's chronicles of adventure and intrigue—eleven handwritten manuscripts—were within their reach!

CHAPTER 27

In between the clouds, patches of blue permitted the sun to shine down on the valley, decked out in its August beauty. A lovely day it was, and Sarah and Adam sat in the truck discussing the absence of wear and tear around her house in light of the fact that it had been the stage for a calamity in the dark morning hours. Apart from the faint tire marks of many police cars in the grassy front yard and a more noticeable one from Adam's skid, the scene was not altered. All was serene.

"Well, here you are again, Mrs. Finfield," said Adam, rolling down the windows and sensing a short chat might be a good thing, "back home."

"Funny it is," she said as she gathered up the hospital paperwork and placed it in her lap, "no one would know what went on here last night."

"They might get an idea from the side door," Adam said.

Sarah laughed. "Your expression is a strange blend of jest and disgust."

"If you look closely, you'll see it's 51/49 in favor of disgust."

"Yes, yes, I can see that. Well, apart from the door, it looks the same as a day ago—actually it looks the same as a year ago. Even two."

"By the way, I'll fix that door—again—while you're in Mexico." he said. "You know, Sarah, except for your floors—the tile in the kitchen and sanding the wood floors in the rest of the house—it appears that I am just about done here. Well, we must not forget the garage door, too."

"I know. I guess it'll seem a little strange not having you around. You're like a fixture. I guess that isn't too flattering…but, really, I mean it as a compliment."

Adam spoke not a word of what was in his mind: *"That's me! Carpenter. Brother. Friend. Angel. And now…Fixture!"*

"I'll take it as one. Hey, I wonder if Daniel's here," Adam said.

"I'd think he'd be out to greet us. Maybe, though, he's sleeping. I totally forgot that I told him to wait here."

"Oh, me too! That could have given me a scare had I run across him sleeping on the couch!"

"Well, I hope he's here. He must be. Where else would he be? He can help me with the door, and then we'll get out of here."

"Do you have work lined up now that this whole thing is over?"

"Some. It always comes along in time."

"Would you like another big job—minus the grieving widow and prowlers?"

Adam laughed. "How boring!"

"I need to get the in-law's house—the musty in-law's house—ready to sell and I think I could probably create another whodunit, if necessary. Either way," she said with a mischievous smile, "are you interested in doing that? I tell you, there's a lot of work there, I think. Pretty much the whole house needs not so much remodeling as redecorating. And it's not very big, Adam, yet I would think it would be work for a couple of months. Interested?"

Wisdom held back a hasty answer. For some reason, Adam had been sensing a forthcoming relief at finishing up at his *little sister's* house. The thought that it might be time to move on kept appearing on the screen as he considered what was next for Adam Cook Carpentry. Should he take on this new job knowing that it would mean continued interaction—a fair amount, no doubt—with Sarah? Should that bother him, or should he take this as God's providing work for him?

"When are you wanting it done?"

"Soon. I don't know what lies ahead and I don't want it weighing me down at the wrong time."

"Soon...as in?"

"I'd like to get it going in about a week or two."

Wisdom again whispered in Adam's ear, this time Sarah's exact meaning: She was on course to go one direction and he, another. The possibility of her closing down her existence in Timber Ridge, and closing it down almost immediately, was strong. He was well aware that she would need help to make that happen. He would help her and then, at the fork in the road, he would go his own way.

"I'm thinking yes, but can I have a few days to let you know?"

"Sure. Of course."

"And Sarah, one more thing...I told you Daniel and I would get your deck in shape. He'll be leaving for California tomorrow, but I still intend to take care of that. I'll be able to get that done while you're gone, too."

Yes, soon she would be off to Mexico, off to see Scott, and after that, who knew? Perhaps she would not see Adam anymore—unless, of course, he agreed to do whatever needed to be done at the little red brick house on Simpson Bell Road.

"That would be great if you would take a look at that forgotten house and see what can be done. Going through everything inside will be an enormous task. I may just go through and grab the sentimental and let an auction company do the rest."

"When are you going to be able to do that with your foot like it is and a trip to Mexico around the corner?"

"Maybe Annette can help. I'll sit and direct; she can be the hands and feet. I'll do it somehow and I'll start soon if you tell me you'll take on the job. Otherwise, I'll wait till I get back. I'll get it emptied so that you can get going on it, if you say yes. You are a master carpenter; I'm sure you can do wonders. You will not believe the surrounding property. It is incredibly beautiful."

"You think you'll be okay for the trip?" Adam questioned her.

"I'd rather be going with a good foot," she answered, "but I'll be okay. I'm glad it's not broken. That doctor has no idea what good news that was!"

"Yep, that was good news. The Simpson Bell house...what if I let you know by Monday?"

"That's good. I hope you know how grateful I am to you for all you've done, Adam, especially in the last 24 hours, and thanks for taking me to the hospital. I don't think *ambulance driver* is in your contract, is it?" she quipped.

"It falls under the *etc.* at the bottom of my contract, though," he joked. "Sarah, you know it was my pleasure."

Always kind, Adam was. *"He is really more than just a friend—he is like a brother,"* Sarah mused. From the start, since he enthusiastically, though guardedly, expressed interest in solving the break-in case, Adam had been superbly courteous and gentlemanly, never creating any awkwardness, all with a seemingly genuine care about her welfare.

"Let's get you inside so you can get some sleep," he said with a tone of kind command. "I think you've been up for more than 24 hours, and not just up, but the main character in a nasty nightmare."

"Oh, my goodness," she exclaimed with a groan. "Main character in a nasty nightmare—you are quite good with words! I suppose no one will ever know the full story." She sighed. "I really do need to get some sleep," she said very slowly. "I hate to admit it but it's true what I said before—I really am in a Sarah-Finfield danger zone. I know myself."

(Later that day, after a nap, while sitting in her family room with her foot propped up on the cedar chest and a pillow behind her head, she couldn't help but roll her eyes at inventing such an idiom as a *Sarah-Finfield danger zone!*)

Sarah put her hand on the door handle, ready to take steps that would thankfully lead to some hours of sleep. Looking at the carpenter through battle-weary eyes, she spelled things out a little better: "I don't know if you can understand this, but I'm pretty sick and tired of this whole thing. I suppose a part of me can rest now knowing that the Payces have been stopped. Other than that, I'm going to try real hard to stop thinking about Herman Lichten."

Adam showed no signs of surprise at her words. Why should he? If anyone understood her disappointment, it was he. Their last crusade had ended in defeat.

There were no literary treasures concealed in the walls of the garage, though the two searchers had held out hope to the very last drywall section. Adam had been the laborer; Sarah had parked herself on one of the steps leading to the kitchen. Their conversation had been lively and spirited as they discussed the bizarre events of the previous 24 hours. Expectations were high; they had both been downright certain that they would soon hold the cherished manuscripts in their hands. Nevertheless, they had left empty handed; perfect hiding place or not, Herman Lichten's books were not there. Sarah was dumbfounded and quite agitated and would have liked to have ranted and raved and paced the cement floor, but she was sidelined. Displaying a mood of resignation, Adam had pulled her to her feet from the step where she had been sitting. "ER," was all he had said; "Not yet. One more thing," had been her response.

The *one more thing*, Chip's **DRYWALL ESTIMATES** folder which Sarah had covertly and at the speed of lightning sent to her private email account in the middle of the night from Payce Publishing, turned out to be exactly that! There in her newly renovated home office, with Adam sitting beside her, looking over her shoulder, and thoroughly absorbed, Sarah stared at her monitor in unbelief as they viewed each of Chip's twelve files.

"These...are actual quotes!" Sarah had fumed in a gruff whisper, exasperated and throwing up her hands. "These are quotes!" And when the last file—No. 12—proved to be a genuine estimate from Home Depot, Sarah had resolutely announced she was raising a white flag. "I am done," she had unambiguously informed Adam, "done forever. Seriously, Adam, are you listening? I don't want to talk about this anymore!"

The disillusioned widow of Timber Lane had then succumbed to Adam's insistence that her ankle needed attention, closed the office door with a semblance of a slam, and hopped on one foot to the front door.

"I wish I would have gone to the hospital! Why on earth did you listen to me?" she had asked him as they drove toward town. Adam had not looked at Sarah after her remark. Instead, looking straight ahead as he took the truck toward the hospital, he had smiled. Sometimes Sarah just plain amused him.

Now it was close to ten o'clock in the morning. Sarah's ankle had been tended to. The whole story, starting with a neighbor girl's announcement of prowlers, all the way to the arrest of those very prowlers, had come to an end. Oh, perhaps an epilogue would follow, when all was said and done, in the courtroom, but for right now, the saga had ended.

"Here. Stay there. I'll come around," Adam said, noticing her reach for the door handle and move to climb down from the truck on her own.

Carefully, he lifted her down from the cab and wrapped Sarah's arm around his neck; then with his strong right arm around her waist, he walked her towards the house. "Are you okay? Do you need help getting in?" he asked. "You know I can just carry you like I did out on the road."

Yes, indeed he had picked her up rather effortlessly and at that moment, she was supremely grateful. Besides, he had not given her a choice; in a moment he had her up and on her way to safety in the truck. But that was then and this was now. She thought better of it.

"Just help me up the stairs. Then I'm good. I'll do my best to learn how to use the crutches," she assured him. "I'll be all right. I just can't wait to be prostrate," she groaned. "I wouldn't tell just anybody this, but the truth is, Adam, that I am beaten—just plain beaten. I'll probably bounce back, but today, right now, I am exhausted and on top of it all, entirely exasperated over the manuscript thing. In a million years, I'll never forget my shock when I found out that those twelve files really were drywall estimates!"

Very gingerly, with Sarah in tow, Adam went up the porch stairs. Sarah groaned with each step.

"I feel like I'm a hundred years old," she said.

"Well, Granny, let me ask you this: Will you be up for dinner with Daniel and Annette later, a rap session you might say? It was

Daniel's idea. He's off to California tomorrow, you know."

Sarah scrunched her face in thought.

"I think I have to say no. No dinner. I just can't."

"It won't be the same without the lead character in the story."

"Oh, Adam, I'm in no shape for chatting."

"Maybe after a good long rest?"

"I just don't think so."

"Well, hang on. I'll get the crutches."

A note was stuck under the doorknocker. Sarah reached for it and read it.

> *Annette is safe at home. We talked a long time, then I came back here. You were not here so I took Sarah's car home. One of the cops brought it from Payce. I hope that was okay. Her purse and stuff are in the house. Daniel.*

"Well, that's good," Adam said upon reading the note. "I'm relieved your car is back and I'm glad he got to go home. It would have been a long wait."

Sarah turned the key in the lock and opened the door, taking her first limping step inside. When she turned, Adam had his hat off and was pushing his fingers through his hair. She started to go in, but then had something more to say.

"I'm not sure I'll ever want to talk about *The Street of Petetra* again," she said, "or anything else written by that old man as long as I live. It has put an ugly taste in my mouth."

"You think you're done looking?" he asked simply, moving his hat into its proper place.

"For the books?"

"Yep."

Of course she was done looking. Where else on earth could she look? The plain and simple truth was that they had scoured the house—as had Robert and Raymond—and found absolutely nothing. Would they ever know if Chip had held those manuscripts in his hands, or for that matter, knew anything about them at all? Probably not.

"You know, I was so sure. I can't describe the certainty that drove me to text you from that Escalade. I was sure; but I was wrong. I'm horribly disappointed. I sincerely mean it when I say I am raising the white flag. Do you blame me?"

"No."

"There's nothing left to pursue."

"I know. We're at the proverbial brick wall, but...."

"Are you telling me, Adam Cook, that you're not giving up?" Sarah interrupted.

"I'm just saying that I'm not shutting the door," Adam said, handing the crutches to her. "It'd be a shame to let Chip down—and Herman—if they laid plans for getting those books out."

"Adam, there is not an inch in my house, or the shed, or behind the drywall, for that matter, that we have not diligently searched. If Chip ever had them in his hands, he did something with them besides leaving them here. They're not here! You and I both know that! They're ashes, Adam!"

"I know, I know. I'm thinking that you're right, but when I get to this point, I'm always hard on myself because it always turns out that I missed something...you know how you sort of O.D. on things when you are up to your nose in them for so long?"

"Well, count me out. I'm walking down another path. If I were you, I'd do the same thing."

"Once you really get to know me, you discover that I hardly ever shut the door on a good case!" Then he smiled that smile. "Now, Mrs. Finfield, go in," he said so kindly, maintaining his grip on her arm, "turn it all off for now. You've got a trip south of the border coming up just around the corner. Sarah, you need to get back on your feet—literally."

"Quite funny," she groaned. "The trip has been very much in the front of my mind. I'm looking forward to it...and at the same time, somewhat nervous."

"Go in and take care of Sarah Finfield," Adam repeated. "Take your pain meds. Escape to your nice new room. Go to sleep. Sleep will paint everything bright and hopeful. Sleep knits up the raveled sleeve of care. It is the death of each day's life, sore labor's bath, the balm of hurt minds."

"How is it that you are quoting Shakespeare?" she wondered aloud, her forehead wrinkled with questions.

"Oh, I've been involved with Shakespeare here and there in school. We did scenes from Macbeth in my senior year. I stored a few of those good lines up here." Adam tapped his forehead. "Not many, but some. Now, Mrs. Finfield, off you go. Your raveled sleeve of care will be entirely mended after a good long nap."

"I'll do my best, but keep in mind that I have been the main character in a very nasty nightmare."

Amused, Adam responded, "Well now, Sarah, go in and play the lead role in a pleasant dream. Go do what your friend is telling you to do. I'm heading over to the garage door. I'll get that closed up. You...you...you are off to slumberland."

Adam was a fine fellow, Sarah knew. Well, hadn't he told her that the first time they met? "You seem like a nice guy," she had said that very first day they talked in the great room about the broken door. She would not ever forget his mischievous grin and his reply: "I **am** a nice guy."

"Thanks for everything. Really. You know I mean it." She situated the crutches under her armpits. "It's just as you said, carpenter...you really are a nice guy."

Attempting to control the crutches, she removed her key, stepped inside and closed the door—or nearly closed the door. Adam pushed it open just a bit and looked in through the crack.

"One more thing, Mrs. Finfield," he said, smiling broadly, "I bet that someday when you're looking for a nail clipper, you're going to run into...*Brave Bonnie Augustine!*"

CHAPTER 28

It was now four o'clock, or sometime close depending on the choice of clock. Sarah heeded the mantel clock and disregarded the announcement of the cuckoo that came a few moments later. Her nap behind her and her foot propped up and resting on a large plaid pillow on the cedar chest, she was quite aware that had it not been for the delirious satisfaction of watching squad cars exit her property with Robert and Raymond in tow, tidily handcuffed and apprised of their rights, the agony over the missing manuscripts would even now be nearly unbearable. The Payces, nevertheless, were off to jail!

"Mrs. Finfield's alive and well, alive and well…" she sang absentmindedly, her thoughts still on the distasteful relationship with the Payces. It had been an unbidden renewal that took place at Mildred's graveside service and that had plagued her since mid-May. Already in the Slough of Despond at that time, still grieving deeply at the loss of Chip, she had endured the worst of treatment from the worst of men. Their wickedness, nevertheless, had caught up with them and Sarah was glad.

She decided, sitting like an invalid in her lovely family room, that she would shun spending even a moment of her valuable time or energy thinking about them. Trials and court battles were no doubt ahead, but for now, Sarah washed her hands of them—figuratively. No longer would they—or could they—control her on any level.

They would be out on bond, most likely. Sarah supposed they could be stupid enough to harass her further; they could—if they thought she was in possession of the manuscripts. Might they make another attempt to enter her house? They could, she decided. In their greedy little minds, Herman Lichten's masterpieces belonged to them. *"Little do they know—or will they know,"* Sarah thought, *"that it seems that there just aren't any masterpieces to be had!"*

In any event, the widow of Timber Lane was breathing freedom this afternoon, freedom from, in reality, many years of distasteful association with the Payces, and a pretty awful couple of months, in particular. She would meet them in court when the time came, but for today, she smiled at the thought of them incarcerated. *"Hmm,"* she thought, *"I like that word! In-car-cer-ated."* She was sure they were where they belonged. Undoubtedly they deserved to be there for a lot of reasons—but, at least for what they had done to her. That was good. What was not good was Richard's apparent escape. "Richard gets off scot-free...again," she said aloud, "or so it seems at the present. That...does not make me a happy camper."

Sarah stopped for a moment in her reflections and took time to eat the lunch she had prepared—not a half of a peanut butter and jelly sandwich—no, instead, a cup of chicken soup, a warmed up ham and cheese sandwich, and chips. How tasty it was! How wonderful to be sitting in her pleasingly restored great room! How wonderful, too, to have the drapes pulled back after so long and to enjoy the views surrounding her home! Was this not a momentous day in her life? The dread gray was gone, not only with the opening of the drapes, but also with the opening of her heart and spirit.

God had done that, but Sarah was suspicious that He had brought it about by dispatching a special angel to patiently oversee her healing. Her Yellow Pages angel! She recalled his sincere concern about her ankle and pondered the fact that he had shunned the claiming of the prize to first assure her wellbeing. Sarah frowned. She would have liked it better the other way around! Well, no matter, it all turned out to be a fruitless endeavor anyway. She frowned again. "What a horrible letdown!" she said aloud.

She shifted positions. She must do something about the pain. She would get more ice. And she would get another pain pill. Stepping carefully, she made her way to the master bath and returned to her perch on the couch with a new ice pack, a dose of pain killer—and her Bible.

The day was partly cloudy, as the weathermen love to say, and very hot; but Sarah loved hot. The south wind blew in through the front windows, tousling the sheers—crushed voile that had not felt a breeze for over a year. A twinge of guilt stung her as she thought of the long wasted months hiding behind the thick drapes. How dark and ominous had been that room for far too long!

The field across the road stretched across gently sloping hills, bordered with a mass collection of various wild flowers, bushes and small trees. The corn was high this year. Sarah watched as all of it swayed in the summer wind. The view out the front—looking south—was Sarah's favorite.

"Oh, I wish I could go for a walk!" she said aloud, stretching her arms high above her head. "What a nice day it would be for a walk!" Disgruntled, she wriggled herself into a better way to be comfortable. What a bummer! The outdoors was beckoning her and she could not respond! She must stay off of her foot!

She sat and pouted. She heard the whistle of a freight train as it rolled through town miles away. It, too, beckoned her. Suddenly, without warning, a notion came. Not normally impetuous or reckless, Sarah made a quick decision to do exactly what her heart was telling her to do, sprained ankle or not.

Using her crutches, she made her way to the hall mirror, refastened her barrette, and tucked in her light blue blouse. Then she grabbed her purse, which the police had retrieved from the Payce building along with her BMW, locked up the house and made her way to her car. Yes, Sarah Finfield was taking flight, unwilling to be chained by an injured ankle! Away she drove, with a word of thanks: "Thank you, Lord, that it's my left foot that is bad."

Sarah took her time winding down the country roads, purposely being sure to take Beaver Woods Trail, the only winding and hilly road in the area. On and on she drove, lost in its beauty and in a myriad of memories of days gone by. The glory of the ride took her mind away from her ankle pain. There was the pond; she and Chip had often fished there after a hard day's work. There was the lovely red barn at the top of the sloping hill, and the perfectly spaced evergreen trees bordering the long driveway. She scanned the fenced-in meadows for the horses but they were missing from the scene.

It was the beauty of the road and the delight of remembering such rides with Chip that had influenced Sarah to take this route; but it was not the only reason. Just a few miles down from the picturesque farm, she at last came to a weathered wrought iron fence with a wrought iron gate. She turned right and drove in beneath the brass words above: **WESTFIELD CEMETERY.**

Somehow, once inside, she knew exactly where to go—and that was no easy matter since the gravestones stretched over many acres. Up and around she drove, into a place of sights and sounds that had inwardly and privately haunted her for fifteen months. Halfway up the hill she pulled partially into the grass by the side of the road. It was the right spot; she had found it without a search. Out under the trees, the towering oak trees, she walked quietly toward the headstone that had once repulsed her, her crutches knocking on the hard earth with each step. There she stopped.

Four headstones stared back at her. Unlike the other dreadful visits to this cemetery, Sarah stood where all four were in view.

Tears gathered in her eyes. Was it easier for her to stand here today than it had been in the midst of grief? No, but Sarah knew that this time, when it came time to leave and drive beneath the brass letters on the black gate, she would not be leaving under the influence of consuming grief.

There was no need for Sarah to inquire of herself, "Why did I do this? Why exactly am I here?" Though the idea of a trip to the place where Chip was buried had sprung up suddenly, out of the blue, she knew exactly why her path had ended here. So clear was the beckoning to put the past to rest and to move on, that she sprang into the one motion that would take her to the one place where that could happen. She had vowed to never again set foot in this cemetery; yet, today, here she was, Sarah Finfield, heeding the call of God to *press forward*.

Under the oak trees, the shade provided slight relief from the hot, hot day. The lazy wind tugged at her light blue flowing skirt and cooled her flushed face. For a moment, her eyes lingered on the grave of her father-in-law. Mr. Finfield had become like a father to her when she married Chip. The day they got married, he had told Sarah that Chip had found a treasure. What a nice thing to say to your new daughter-in-law! What a strong, kind man! And how she had admired Mildred! Sarah mused that till the day she died, she would never understand Mildred's devotion to such a hateful man as Richard Payce. Mildred's graveside service had been bleak. Coupled with the re-entry of the Payces into her life, the memory of it was anything but pleasant.

Now Sarah gazed at the third stone. Her current peaceful spirit did battle with the threat of weeping. Could they co-exist—peace and pain? Yes, was the answer, and with serenity of heart, she let the tears flow.

"Chip," she wept, "I've come to tell you that I perished with you on the day you died. I have languished in a self-constructed tomb for more than a year, unable to live without you." Sarah used the palms of her hands to wipe the tears from her cheeks. "I have stayed away from here because I have been angry with you—can you imagine that?—angry with you and angry with God, and could not bear the thought of seeing your name chiseled in a piece of stone above your head. But God has intervened in my life and I've come to tell you that I'm going to make it and that I'm moving on. I know that you are not here but have flown away to heaven to be with your Savior."

Sarah's hair whipped about in the warm wind. She wrapped her hand around it and pulled it forward. Her spirit calmed. For a few moments she stood pondering the grand life she had enjoyed with her husband.

"I can never forget you and you know I will always love you," she said with a smile.

There, on a beautiful summer day, a serene Sarah Finfield allowed her eyes to rest upon the gothic letters staring back at her from the cold, marble slab. The haughty finger of death had once etched similar ones upon her broken heart as well; but today, the glorious resurrection of Jesus Christ from the dead was responsible for a new heart of hope. She stood looking down upon the letters and read them aloud.

CHESTER "CHIP" ELLIOTT FINFIELD, II
May 15, 1975 – May 15, 2004

"I am the Resurrection and the Life," Sarah quoted aloud from memory. "He that believes in Me, though he is dead, yet shall he live." She wiped away new tears from her cheeks.

"That's you, Chip! That is you!" Sarah's voice was passionate and intense as she finished the verse. "And whoever is living and believes in Me will never die. That's me, Chip Finfield! Me!"

Fastening her eyes on the fourth headstone, she bravely smiled. "You'll have to wait a good while," she called out, joy replacing the weeping. "Don't be waiting around for me!" she called, passing it by as she started to the top of the hill. "Sarah Finfield is alive and well!"

On she hobbled until the valley was in view. What a lovely picture looking down on the quaint little town of Meredith Grange! She could now recall coming to this very spot more than a year before, and steadying herself against the black iron fence. Ah, yes, here, right here, she had purposed to die. Life, she had decided, would no longer be worth living. Chip was gone.

Today, as she laid her crutches on a tree stump and steadied herself against that same black iron fence, her heart was full of hope. She pulled her long brown hair in front of her left shoulder. She wanted to pray—and she would—but what exactly was it she wanted to say? This was a stepping-stone day, a day to reach for what was ahead, not dawdle in the past. It would not do to dwell any longer on what others had done to her. Those things were things of yesterday. At least, she would try! The horror of Chip's death must fade, too. She would see to it. She must leave the past behind—good and bad. Yes, this was a stepping-stone day!

"Oh, God, my Father," she fervently and passionately prayed, "thank you for lifting the awful gloom! I was sure it was here to stay. How can it be that I am overflowing with such joy today? Oh, Father, I want to come out from under the past and move ahead! Will you help me? Please, Father, help me." With her eyes lifted to the sky—toward the throne of God—Sarah called out to Him, "I love You more than anything, and I love You more than anyone. And, I love You more today than ever before. If you have something for me to do, I'll do it!"

Sarah Finfield lingered there, happy to be alive. Down in the valley, Meredith Grange bustled like all small towns. Cars and people moved unhurriedly around the square; a freight train brought Main Street to a halt; and church bells, ever so faintly, rang out their six o'clock hymn.

It was time to go. Down the hill Sarah went, off to a fresh start, now and then stumbling and finding the descent more difficult than the way up. Step by careful step she went, singing in time with the thump of the crutches:

> *Oh, Jesus, Lord and Savior, I give myself to Thee,*
> *For Thou in Thine atonement didst give Thyself for me.*
> *I own no other Master; my heart shall be Thy throne,*
> *My life I give, henceforth to live, Oh, Christ, for Thee alone.*

CHAPTER 29

"Staying two more weeks," the message on Adam's phone read. "Home on 9/21."

Adam was sitting in one of the wicker chairs on Sarah's front porch, drinking a cup of coffee, already bothered a bit by the presence of an unexpected **FOR SALE** sign in her front yard, when her message showed up on his phone. His hat and tool belt lay on the porch beside him. It wasn't that Sarah was obligated to inform him that she was putting the house up for sale; it was just the matter of courtesy. There had been no communication from Sarah Finfield for two weeks; Adam conceded that perhaps primitive conditions made contact impossible. Today, though, a message had gotten through. Sarah was to stay in Mexico two more weeks.

"Well," said Adam, slightly perturbed, "that gives me time to finish the deck, too…and then, I'm done."

A red Porsche drove by, far too fast for the health of the gravel road. It stopped, backed up, and stopped again at Sarah's drive.

"Hello, Mr. Adam Cook!"

Adam waved. It was Annette with her boyfriend, Tony.

"How are you?" she hollered.

A high-volume conversation was not Adam's style. A hearty wave, he hoped, would suffice. A lively chat took place in the car and soon Annette was running up the brick walk and Tony was on his way westward.

"Adam Cook! How are you? I haven't seen you for a long time. But that's not your doing. It's mine. I was in Costa Rica with my mother and father for a vacation. I just got back yesterday. How are you?"

"I'm doing fairly well, Annette. It's nice to see you again."

"Tony…oh, Tony…I wanted him to come and meet you, but he wouldn't come. You know, he's afraid that you're going to preach a sermon at him right here on Mrs. Finfield's front porch! That's because I told him I once saw a Bible in your truck." Annette laughed. "He listens to me, but he just doesn't want any preaching."

"Well, I'm glad you stopped by. I'm just about to finish up here."

"For good?"

"Yep."

"I got a letter from Daniel," said Annette, plunking down in the other wicker chair. "He says you and he talk a couple of times a week."

"A letter, eh?" Adam said with a bit of surprise. "That's pretty good. He's not a letter writer."

"It was nice—perfectly gentlemanly, you know. I guess he was more or less checking on me now that I am a Christian. He says, go to church, read your Bible, pray every day." She turned her chair to face Adam and then mischievously said, "He doesn't know that I went to Mrs. Finfield's church recently, so that takes care of one thing! And they gave me a Bible; that takes care of two!"

Adam chuckled.

"Only if you read the Bible and keep going to church!"

Annette sighed.

"And I have to pray if I'm ever going to get through to my dad. He does not—absolutely, does not—believe in God."

"Keep praying. I'll be praying, too. I bet what's going to do it is watching the change in your life."

"You think?"

"Yep, I do."

"I miss Mrs. Finfield. I was planning on lots of chats with her about all of this."

"She'll be a big help."

"I hear that Cary Grant and his brother are out."

"Yep, they are—out on bail."

"You think they'll go to jail?"

"They should. You never know though."

"I bet Mrs. Finfield was glad to get out of here."

"Yeah, I think she was."

"Isn't she coming home today or tomorrow?"

"She was supposed to, but she's staying a couple of extra weeks. Makes sense. No sense going all that way for two weeks."

"Is she going to be a missionary or something?"

"I...I don't know."

"Hmm. I was counting on spending time with her."

"She'll be back."

"I miss her a lot," Annette whined "I bet you miss her, too."

"You know, I think I do!"

"Of course you do. After all you two have been through side by side?" Annette went on dreamily. "I'll never forget watching you tenderly carrying her to the truck in the wee hours of the morning, in the glow of the headlights. I kind of figured that after all the time you've spent together, anyway, that you guys were... well, how should I put it...fond of each other?"

"Hold on, Annette. I am Mrs. Finfield's carpenter/contractor; she is my customer."

"But, that was quite a picture!" Annette said dreamily.

"You have to consider the circumstances," Adam said, attempting to clarify the matter.

"I can see your point—but I can see mine, too. You had one of those expressions like...*macho man!* Oh, I mean that in a really good way! It was like you were saying, 'I'm here to save you, my love!'"

Adam could not help but smile at Annette's foolishness.

"Anyway," she went on, "I'm not surprised that you miss her."

"We're friends, and yes, I do miss her. Now enough of that."

"And what do you know about this Scott thing?"

"What Scott thing?"

"You don't know about it?"

"Are you talking about her friend, the missionary?"

"Yes...the Scott thing. Do you see him as a threat?"

"How do you know about him?"

"Mrs. Finfield told me."

"And what did she tell you?"

"Well, she said they are longtime friends and that she is going to see his ministry...is that what it's called?...in Mexico."

"And that she is."

"Are you worried?"

"I told you what the deal is between Mrs. Finfield and me. Now let's change the subject."

"Well, you probably don't know that I saw you parked across the field over there many a night, I'm supposing, with her safety in mind."

Taken by surprise, but not unnerved, Adam inserted a long pause before continuing the conversation.

"So, Annette, what's going on with you?" he inquired, cleverly— he thought—moving away from the previous subject.

"Are you surprised to know that someone knew you were watching over there?" Annette probed further.

"I guess, a little. Now, what's going on with you."

"I really, really want to go to college, but…hey, Adam, you keep changing the subject."

"That's because the subject is a private one."

With a deep sigh, Annette stood.

"Let me just say this: I hope I find a man who treats me like you treat her. You have really watched out for her! I've observed more than you might guess," she teased. The Red Flash appeared once again. "Well, there's Tony. He said he'd give me five minutes. Isn't that just like a man!"

"It's nice to see you," Adam said, standing up. "I've been wondering about you."

"I'm glad to see you, too. You and Daniel will always be beloved friends to me. I'll invite both of you to the wedding if I marry Tony. In fact, I'll invite Daniel **and** Mr. and Mrs. Adam Cook!"

Tony came, Annette went. Adam shook his head in wonder.

"Mr. and Mrs. Adam Cook! Macho man," he mumbled under his breath. "I must have a chat with Daniel!"

He sat down again, but just for a moment, and then, with a shove off his thighs, he stood and stretched, picked up his belt and fastened it around his waist. Reaching down for his hat and setting it on his head, he headed into the house. The floors were done—sanded and re-stained and varnished once again—thanks in part to Rico. He shook his head, marveling at their beauty.

"Nice floors," he declared to himself, "but what a grueling job!"

Now came the task of a final clean-up of any remaining powdery sawdust. He grabbed a face mask from his toolbox and put it on. Dust would be everywhere, he knew from experience, even though the major cleanup was done. One by one, he gingerly tore down the plastic sheets that covered each wall, floor to ceiling, folding them carefully inward and compactly, and placing them in a barrel. The plastic tightly wrapped around the furniture he would not remove—not yet, at least. Since hardwood covered the entire main floor—except for the kitchen—and because of the high ceilings, the chore took him close to three hours. No matter how carefully the house had been guarded against the dust, there would be, he knew, more clean-up even after the removal of the thin plastic tarps.

He set to work vacuuming and wiping down…and thinking. More than three weeks had passed since the arrest of Robert and Raymond Payce. As expected, they were out on bail the next day, but back in the next, charged with kidnapping, breaking and entering, and malicious trespass. They were, at present, again out on bail. Soon a trial date would be set. They would most likely be locked up for a good long time, unless Richard the Great and Powerful was mighty enough to invoke some sort of magic to keep that from happening.

It irked Adam—and infuriated Sarah—that Richard would suffer no penalty for his many crimes and injustices, to say nothing of his masterminding of such a vile plot steeped in greed against the widow. Sarah, greatly perturbed, had detailed to Adam what she could recall of the very incriminating information she had viewed on the monitor, file by file, information that Chip had gathered as a result of his suspicions. All lost! It nearly had been in her grasp! Now, the incriminating evidence, no doubt, had been expunged from every inch of the executive offices. It was quite probable that the publishing mogul and his enterprise would remain intact—at least for now.

"He that does wrong will receive for the wrong which he has done," Adam quoted from the Bible, "and there is no respect of persons." He admonished himself not to fret because of evildoers.

On he worked, vacuuming and sweeping, thinking and praying, remembering the whole sordid story from the very beginning.

"It has not ended well, has it, Adam?" Sarah had said a few days before she left. "I am very angry that Richard Payce has again escaped culpability for his evil. Robert and Raymond will take the heat, but Richard," she said with theatrical inflections and with an equally dramatic wave of her hand in the air, "is free as a bird!"

"The tale does not have a final chapter yet, my dear," Adam had reminded her. "We'll just have to wait and see about Richard Payce."

How long ago that all seemed and how it had predominated the headlines! Timber Ridge had experienced a torrent of correct, as well as disgracefully inaccurate, accounts of the story. The Town Gossip—Mr. Dickerson—did much to aid in that. Since he was Mrs. Finfield's neighbor, he had an inside track, he figured, and he embellished the truth whenever he could! Mrs. Finfield had gratefully escaped to the airport, the first leg of the journey to Scott Dolan.

It had seemed more proper than not to be absent from the Timber Lane house the day she left, Adam had decided. He was Sarah's carpenter; really, there was no reason for him to be there to see her off. So, he had moseyed around the shop in the morning and then taken care of a couple of his long lost regular customers. Yet, Adam could not escape the truth; he had hated to see her go. Now, her absence was to be extended two more weeks.

Today would be a day of working feverishly, he had already resolved, in order to be entirely finished before Sarah's return. Now, that had all changed. Extra time had been thrust upon him. Still, he remained focused and by five o'clock, the bedroom section of the house had been cleaned. He stood at the foyer entrance to the family room, trying to decide whether to keep going or call it a day. Something urged him to press on.

"I'll at least do the kitchen tonight. That won't take long. Tomorrow I'll finish the family room. Next week I'll finish the deck. And then, I'm done...at least here at Timber Lane."

Very much at home in Sarah's exquisite home, he fixed a pot of coffee and when it was brewed, sat down at the very table where Sarah had woefully poured out her story to him on the morning after the devastating break in. Was that really only two months ago? It seemed more like a year!

Memories surrounding Sarah's ordeal would not go away as well as memories of his own side of the story—fishing and time with Daniel; the ride along the Mississippi River and his mind pictures of Melanie; his resolutions about Sarah; the first indication of trouble showing up on his little tracking screen; and the long, long ride home. Adam recognized himself as stable and solid, and even at this moment, here, under strange circumstances, sitting in the home of a widow who, in order to decide upon a carpenter, had *thrown a dart* at a section in the Yellow Pages, his thoughts were under control. He did not foolishly pretend that Sarah had not grown on him, that he felt no warmth towards her at all; yet, Adam was content. Was he affected by her relationship with the missionary—whatever that might be?" Perhaps, yet consistently, the prayerful and sincere words that each night paved the way for sleep were "I want what You want for my life." Yes, Adam was content.

Adam finished his coffee break, rinsed his cup, turned it upside down on a towel on the counter, turned the coffee pot off, and began work on the spacious kitchen, promising himself to be done by seven. He wiped down everything. Even the fronts of the appliances, though they had been sufficiently covered with plastic, had a film of dust clinging to them. This was not Adam's favorite thing to do! He admitted that he missed Sarah by his side. For two months they had worked on just about everything together, at first, as strangers, then as friends.

"It'd be nice to have a little help from Mrs. Lazarus right about now," he declared, not quite sure whether his words were jovial, sarcastic, or dejected. Chip's words at the front of Sarah's Bible, the ones about the joy of working together with her came to mind. Adam understood. Nevertheless, he forged ahead, alone, and by the designated hour, he was done, ready to go home. Tomorrow, bright and early, he would go at it again.

The next day came, a beautiful August morning, the temperatures moderated as a result of a passing shower the night before. Adam was experiencing relief from being one day away from completion. This was supposed to be Sarah's homecoming day; but the short text message of yesterday told of a different plan. She would not be coming home today, and Adam realized that there was a slim chance that she might never actually return to Timber Lane.

The widow's house had been entirely restored. Nothing—except for the final cleansing of the enormous family room—remained undone. The deck was still in need of repair, but the inside of the house was free of all reminiscent scars from the atrocious deeds of the Payces. The beautiful home was truly ready to be on the market. The For Sale sign told a long story and revealed the heart of the widow.

Adam went to work on the family room—without his usual joy at the job. At two-thirty, he felt hungry, but he did not want to eat; he was almost finished and wanted to go home. He ended the tedious task with a thorough cleaning of the mantel, the fireplace, and the area around it. With furniture polish he put a shine on the fine woodwork; he vacuumed the massive stones; and he carefully wiped off the eagle heads.

"And now," he declared aloud, "there is one more thing. I must try the eyes on this other eagle."

With the polishing rag thrown over his shoulder, he casually walked to the right side of the fireplace, pressed down on both eyes of the eagle, one at a time, and chuckled when nothing happened.

"Well," he joked, "that's that. That's been bugging me since that night! And with that, I declare the restoration of the Finfield house on Timber Lane finished! Done! Complete!"

Yes, Adam was done, and to prove it to himself, he gathered all his tools together and carted them to the truck. Then he went back into the house for one last look. With surging mixed emotions, he sauntered through each room, his fingers stuck down into his back pockets. This had been the most extensive inside job he had ever encountered; along with it had come the engulfing involvement in something he could never have anticipated...the physical and emotional welfare of his client. It bothered him somewhat that he had done precious little to keep Mrs. Finfield safe from the Payces. The line of his lips manifest a frown of displeasure, thinking of the ways in which things could have gone wrong the night she had been hauled off to Payce headquarters. Yes, it bothered him—and perhaps it would for months to come—but Timber Lane and River Road would soon be light years apart; he had done his best; the two people in this story would go back to walking down their separate paths.

He stood in the doorway of the office. "Nice office," he said "I like it a lot." A memory of the falling Bible brought a smile. He remembered his prayer for Sarah; he remembered the geese; he remembered that he had experienced a trace of discomfort at the sight of Scott holding Sarah in a fond farewell embrace; and he remembered kicking his tire.

"Good grief, Adam Cook, time to go. You are done."

Resolutely, Adam set, as it were, his face toward the intersection of Pitman and River Roads. He stopped by the kitchen door to look out on the deck; though its need of repair stared back at him, his initial zeal to tackle those repairs had disappeared. An odd emotion for Adam surfaced: he wanted to quit. The only thing that bound him to the deck touchup was his word to Sarah, but at this juncture in her life, the deck was the farthest thing from her mind. Well, he would keep his word and complete the job before she entered her home again, he knew.

Walking one last time into the little *Sarah Haven* fashionably arranged around the fireplace, he glanced over the room, almost in an effort to paint it indelibly in his heart. He visualized Sarah, drawn and pale, telling him to just "take his check and go home." His mind fast forwarded. In this room, this restored room, in his mind's eye he could now see Mrs. Finfield, herself restored, her countenance refreshed, and figuratively identifying with Lazarus. Adam wanted to store those visuals in his heart forever. But now, it was time to go.

To listen once more, though, to Chip's incredible setup suddenly seemed to Adam the only proper way to depart this house. All alone here today, he could enjoy it to the fullest. He could turn up the volume and he could direct the orchestra with a carpenter's pencil— something he always did when no one was around—and he could even brew another cup of coffee for the occasion. He loved music, but never before had he experienced it as magnificently as the night Sarah had played a record for him. Yes, this would be the perfect farewell. He pressed the eye of the eagle. Operating electronically, the shelf holding Chip's turntable glided slowly from its concealed place.

"That...is quite cool," Adam said, impressed all over again with the innovation. "I shall pull out a record at random and sit in a Sarah-chair and listen to whatever it might be." He pulled a record from the shelf. "Hmm, Symphony No. 9 by Antonin Dvorak," he read, stumbling with the pronunciation. "New World Symphony. As good as any," he decided. "Let's see what it's like."

With the soothing strains of the music flooding the room, he wandered about, drinking in the beauty of this home, scenes that would always serve as memories of a pleasant chapter in his life. As the closing strains of the symphony were ringing forth, Adam stood by the eagle, his eyes closed. He was enraptured with the hearing of such music, music he had never heard before. He lifted his carpenter's pencil and led the musicians to the grand finale.

"Amazing," he said softly. "Simply amazing."

He retrieved the record and holding it carefully, replaced it in its jacket, and put it back on the shelf.

"Time to go." He pushed down on the left eagle eye; Chip's turntable disappeared into the woodwork. Flippantly, as he started toward the door, he touched the right eye. As he took only a step or two, not in the slightest expecting anything to happen, he heard the sound of a smooth operating motor—a faint hum. He turned. Glancing this way and that, Adam's eyes were drawn to movement on the right side of the fireplace. A shelf emerged from the woodwork, one that exactly matched the shelf for Chip's turntable.

Adam stood perfectly still, processing this very unexpected occurrence. He chuckled. "How absolutely bizarre! Obviously, Sarah knows nothing of this!" He had asked her about the other eye and she had said, according to Chip, it did nothing; but then, Chip had been home those few days before his death, evidently working his head off, judging by the results. Perhaps this was part of his labors.

"Hmm. Now isn't this just crazy?" he said, frozen in place and shaking his head. "There, ladies and gentlemen, is a hidden…laptop!"

Adam chuckled again as he removed his hat and pushed his hair back. Slowly, he walked over to look at things more closely. The very slim laptop sat upon a finely constructed mahogany box and was settled into a docking station, the blinking lights telling Adam that all was alive and well. The setup was not unlike that of the turntable. He took time to examine things more closely and quickly discovered that what was under the laptop was more than just cosmetic.

"This is not a solid piece of wood," Adam astutely determined. "This is hollow." He examined the highly polished mahogany box more carefully. "It'd be easy to gloss right over this. It's a box."

It didn't take him long to figure out that the nicely carved piece of wood that ran down the middle of the box from top to bottom held a secret. Gently he tugged at it. It opened on hidden hinges revealing an electronic digital lock with numbers from 0 to 9 running in two vertical columns. He shut the door and went to sit down in one of the fine leather recliners, processing the enormity of this discovery and exactly what it all should mean to him with Sarah absent. Staring at the laptop arrangement, the range of reactions covered a very wide spectrum. Such a development was the farthest thing from his mind! Figuratively speaking, his feet were already sprinting toward home; realistically, he was experiencing the satisfaction of a completed job; emotionally, he had bidden Sarah Finfield goodbye; and furthermore, he had lain to rest any hope of ever finding the original Lichten manuscripts. Had he found them? It had been the first question in his mind at the sight of the emerging box, but the answer had come back—no, it could not be. It was not big enough for eleven manuscripts.

Now he sat gawking at a hidden cache no doubt recently put into place. *"Even Sarah doesn't know about this!"* He was staring at what appeared to be only a fancy and brilliantly engineered hideaway for one's computer! So, this is what Chip Finfield had been up to! He had been a busy man...dry walling the garage, sneaking around Payce headquarters, and installing—or at least completing the installation of a hidden spot for the missing laptop. In a million years, a thief would not be bright enough, first of all, to press the eye of the eagle in hopes of discovering anything at all, and secondly, if he got that far, to see it as anything but a laptop cabinet.

Adam's whole being was electrified! This discovery of all of this threw him back into the story. Everything was crystal clear to him, from *the eye of the eagle* to *remember this sequence*. There was not a doubt in his mind that if he were to put the numbers from the note in the Bible into that electronic lock, something significant would happen. Undoubtedly, the code would somehow open the box itself. Could he remember the sequence? In reality, the question was, "Should I mess with this at all or should I turn and walk out the door?"

Sarah would not care, he knew. In fact, she would urge him to investigate. She would remind him that he had been as embroiled in the whole thing as she was. So, easily persuaded, once again standing in front of the laptop arrangement, he accessed the numeric keypad, ready to enter the code. Sarah had memorized the sequence immediately; he had nailed it down a day or two later. Now he could not remember it.

"Come on, Adam, you're no slouch when it comes to remembering such things!"

For a few moments, he paced in front of the fireplace, trying different possibilities aloud. Finally, he thought he had it. 369152784, he keyed in. Nothing happened. He tried again, feeling sure that this time he had it right: 369152748. Click. The front of the box opened, revealing a safe.

Once again, Adam had to sit down. He was dumbfounded. He had uneasiness about lifting the contents from inside; this was Sarah's domain. Yet, he craved getting answers. Sarah was 2,000 miles away and not easily reachable. Considering his involvement in the whole picture, he gave himself permission—under the circumstances—to start in slowly and stop at the first hint of trespassing.

The small laptop by itself answered one question: What in the world was Chip doing during the midnight hours after the fire? Sarah had seen him diligently at work on a computer yet not one bit of evidence of that diligence had been found on any computer in the house. Undoubtedly, here it was…stored on this electronic notebook! Adam decided to leave the computer alone.

Herman's original writings could not be here—eleven handwritten manuscripts would need a larger hiding place. Adam lightly ruffled through the mass of papers, three criss-crossed stacks of nearly all 8 ½ x 11 documents. These stacks became Adam's quest, and he took them and placed them in three separate piles on the cedar chest before him. For sure, the manuscripts were not here.

Again, he did a quick flip through the pages. He hesitated. Should he be looking at this stuff or not? He would go through it quickly and ascertain the answer to that question. If it was personal, he'd boogey on out of there; if it had to do with the case, he'd keep going. He placed the first stack in his lap.

"Hmm, a lot of post-it notes," he said, somewhat surprised. "Interesting. And this very first one is shouting at me that Chip was looking forward to a bright future."

"Send check for Sarah's bd present," it read, with a smiley face in the corner. It was stuck to a page from a magazine, an ad for a very expensive bike. Hesitating to reflect on the little note, Adam thought through the ramifications of such a revelation. He shook his head. This whole thing was not over.

One by one, Adam turned over the pages that had been inside a manila folder. Some were single; some were stapled together.

"Finish ad," the next one read. It was the layout for an advertisement, most likely headed for the newspaper, announcing Finfield Publishing, Inc. *"Get the marathon information,"* read the next one. Looking at each one carefully, Adam sought for answers and insight. This stack pointed most decisively to a happy, purposeful Chip Finfield. Had he met with foul play? Adam's spirit churned.

He laid the folder to the side; what he was looking and hoping for was not in it. He picked up the next stack. He pushed back in the leather recliner, his attention momentarily diverted away from the contents of the safe. Thoughts of Sarah came again. They had done all of this together thus far; he wished she was there.

There were multiple articles covering the Wentworth Building fire, paper clipped together. Adam read them each carefully. A post-it note strategically placed on the top article read: *"Talk to this guy!"* An arrow pointed to the name of a man who had been interviewed by a reporter, a man who lived across the street from Payce's building. Adam pondered that for a moment. Evidently Chip wanted to find out if Harold Barkley had seen anything unusual, and evidently, he had never had the chance to do so. Adam wondered if it was too late to take up the task, it being more than a year later. He decided it was something he'd have to do.

Lost in his pursuit of gleaning information about the relation-ship between Payce and the Finfields, he kept going. Page after page in the second stack, document after document, met his scrutiny, and with each one, he understood better the dishonorable reputation the Payces had—at least as he had heard from Sarah Finfield. Recogniz-ing from Sarah's descriptions of the items she had zipped through at the office, pieces of evidence that Chip had amassed, it all began to make sense. Chip had made copies and carried them home, no doubt, in his briefcase. Adam wondered why he had left the files on his office computer. Was it because he wanted Richard to know that he knew or was it because he never had a chance to go back? Who could ever know the answer to that question? The information passing before Adam's eyes shocked him; he knew that because Sarah was familiar with the history involved, being able to spend unhurried time re-viewing all of it would shock her even more.

At the top of the third pile, there was a bright red alligator clip holding a few pieces together. Adam could see that the top one was a typewritten letter, unfolded, and stuck under the flap of an envelope. The little reminder on top read, "Get Sarah's okay." Adam undid the clip and glanced quickly at the letter. It was Chip's letter of resigna-tion. According to what Sarah had learned from Richard, the letter of resignation had, in fact, been submitted. Evidently he had gone ahead without Sarah's okay. Adam chose not to read it.

The Timber Lane carpenter, at that moment, nearly talked him-self into putting things back the way they were, stuffing it all back into the small safe, and waiting till Sarah returned. He wished that he could let her know about his find. He got up and walked around. Was he even doing the right thing by going through all of this in-formation? He had not unearthed anything personal or private; what he had examined had been case related, that is, apart from what was in the manila folder. It was uncharacteristic for him to cross over any line of invading someone's privacy. In fact, he was known to fault to the other extreme. Yet, hadn't he become part of this situation, almost like part of the family? Big brother, she had said. Yes, in a very real way, Sarah had allowed him to be drawn into her world, trusting him with nearly everything that had to do with her. He would keep looking and if necessary, apologize later.

He turned over the papers in the clip. The next item was a note—perhaps better put, a letter—in Chip's handwriting which Adam now recognized after the incident with the falling Bible. He, at first, did not pick up the letter; instead, he read the words from the page without moving it, each word an unfolding revelation.

> *Sarah, you know I will always love you. I could have saved that old man, but I missed the warning signs. I should have saved him. It is hard for me to think of facing another day with such guilt.*

It was The Note. Sarah had quoted enough of it for him to recognize it here. Adam stared into the air, amazed at this incredible turn of events. He read on.

> *Yet, all of this has sent me to my knees where I have cast my burden upon the Lord.*

Adam sat up and placed his hands on the arms of the chair, the note resting in his lap. The truth was dawning.

> *Yet, all of this has sent me to my knees. I have cast my burden upon the Lord. It is a big burden, Sarah, bigger than just the old man's death. I could be in danger, but perhaps not. Richard has gone from despising me to fearing me for what I know. He—and Robert—should be afraid! I have a new respect for how David felt when King Saul was bent on killing him. It is not a moment too soon for me to be leaving there. I am doing everything I can to tie up the loose ends up so that I can exit Payce, hook, line and sinker, by the end of tomorrow.*

Abruptly, Adam went to stand at the front window. With his hands on his hips, he gazed out past the porch and out to the field, now full of tall browning stalks of late summer corn. His mind drifted back to the day that Sarah had opened up about finding her husband in his car. With squinting eyes and a countenance of unfolding comprehension, Adam realized the truth about Chip's suicide note. That note had been a first draft. These opening lines sounded very close to that note and Adam was sure that something in the opening lines in that first draft was different from these. It had not been a suicide note after all!

He closed his eyes and wished that Sarah Finfield was standing next to him. He knew exactly what he would do.

CHAPTER 30

When Adam opened his eyes, he realized immediately that he had fallen asleep in the soft blue leather recliner; he also knew that someone was looking at him. He scrambled to clear his mind and when the fog lifted, he realized that Sarah was standing near the door, her purse slung over her shoulder, a carryon bag at her feet, and a stylish straw hat on her head—and she was looking at him. Hastily he attempted to collect his thoughts as he shoved forward in the chair.

He stood, took off his hat, pushed his fingers through his hair and replaced the Home Depot cap backwards on his head. *"Who should speak first?"* he wondered, a smile of chagrin on his face.

"You're home," he said somewhat sheepishly to Sarah who was looking lovelier than ever. "Did I get it wrong?"

"Yes, I'm home, Adam," she responded, sighing and placing her purse on the small table next to the door and removing her hat, "and no, you didn't get it wrong."

"Good," he warmly responded, "on both counts."

Sarah sighed. "I was glad to see your truck. I didn't like the idea of coming home to an empty house, especially one with a big old For Sale sign stuck in the front yard. I figured you'd be long gone."

"I am done," he said, "but not gone. You look...really good."

"Well, thanks."

"Nice hat."

"Really?"

"Yep. Really. The green matches your eyes."

"I bought it on the way home...from a young Mexican girl outside a coffee shop."

"You're tan."

She looked down at her arms.

"Yes. The sun is hot down there."

"You're tan and serene."

"If that is true, it's a miracle after such a trip home, from begin-

309

ning to end. Such madness. My feet are killing me even with these comfortable shoes. So much walking and running in the airport!"

"Maybe, just maybe, the new tranquility runs deep enough to deal well with such madness."

With a smile of appreciation for kind words, Sarah took steps toward the fireplace wall.

"The carpenter being kind again," she said.

"What brings you home early? I'm assuming it's early since your text said you were staying two more weeks till September 21st."

"I came home to sign papers giving my lawyer power of attorney. That was a big part of it. There's more."

This answer struck Adam as odd. At this stage in their friendship, Sarah was never vague. Yes, there must be more, Adam thought, but he held his peace.

"What is all this?" she asked, very curious.

"Sarah, I think God must have brought you home early and I mean that sincerely. Come sit. I have much to show you."

He moved to the loveseat and she sat down beside him.

"I am thoroughly exhausted," she told him, perhaps as a signal that she would not be up to lengthy conversation. "I need to run to my room for a few minutes." She gathered her things and retreated down the long hall. It was ten minutes before she returned to her place next to Adam.

"I don't like flying," she grumbled. "By the way, here is your check. I'm sorry I forgot to give it to you before I left. It's for four weeks." She handed him a folded check. "I like to travel by car, without time constraints. Rushing to the airport, going through all that rigmarole once you get there, switching planes, retrieving your car…it's like a lost day, in my mind. I've been at it since a little after four this morning. I really am worn out."

"I bet. Do you need to eat?"

"I will soon. Have you eaten?" she wanted to know.

Adam thought for a moment.

"You know, I don't think I've eaten anything all day. What time is it?"

"It's close to four."

"Well, I guess we need to get something."

"I'm sure there's a Papa Luigi's pizza in there. How's that?"

"We could go somewhere."

"Frozen pizza doesn't sound that good, eh?"

"It's just that after we're done here, I think you might like a ride and a dinner out. I know I would."

Sarah leaned back.

"I won't say no." She smiled. "Remember when I used to give you a hard time about going to eat?"

"You know, that wasn't so long ago. It seems like a year but it's only a couple of months."

"I know. I was thinking about that on the flight home."

"So much has happened in that short time."

"Just since May."

"Sarah, you see all of this? You need to take a look. But first, did you notice the fireplace?"

She shook her head.

"Look there."

"What is that?" she asked, very perplexed. "What is that, Adam? It looks very much like the other side."

"It does and it opens the same way...except it's the right eye of the left eagle that opened this!"

"What!"

"Chip was very busy. He must have been working on this, too."

"He did say, 'Not yet' when I asked him a long time ago about the other eye. Another project while I was gone. Hmm. And what do you know, Chip had another laptop. I don't believe it!"

"That's part of it but look below. There's a safe."

"A safe?"

"Look over there."

Rising slowly, and with wide eyes, Sarah walked to the protruding shelf and box.

"What in the world? I had no idea there was a safe here."

For a few minutes, Adam gave Sarah his take on the existence of the safe and shared how it came to be that he found it.

"Watch," he said, pressing the eye once again. The compartment slid silently back into place. "It's the eye of the eagle, Sarah!" he declared with an air of finality. "Chip's note, Sarah! It was the eye of the eagle after all."

"I'm flabbergasted! How could you get the safe open though? You have to have some kind of code to enter into the key pad."

With one more touch to the eagle's eye, the hidden compartment appeared again.

"You can open it. Open the little door. Then think back, Sarah."

She quickly grasped his meaning and muttered, "Oh...my...goodness!" She entered the mysterious code slowly, one number at a time...369152748. The front of the box opened and the safe stood staring her in the face. She looked at Adam, wrinkles in her forehead, and said, "This is very hard for me to believe."

"You were gone; he tied up his loose ends!"

"He was an extremely busy man," she said, still very much in shock. "Adam! The manuscripts! They're here?" Sarah sat down slowly, hope in her eyes as she stared at her carpenter.

"No, Mrs. Finfield, they are not here. Their whereabouts are still a mystery."

"You're kidding."

"No. I'm not. But Sarah…."

"You're kidding."

"No. No manuscripts. But there's stuff in here you'll want to see," he said, returning to the loveseat, "a whole lot of stuff. Come, sit, Sarah." He reached for the stack of papers. "This answers a lot of questions, even for me," he said, handing them to her, "and undoubtedly will answer a whole lot more when you are the one doing the poking around."

Adam took Sarah through the papers in the exact order he had attacked them, feeling that Chip's letter should come last. Holding in her hands, the copies of Chip's collection of evidence against Richard Payce—and surprisingly against Robert as well—rewarded her with supreme satisfaction. What it all would eventually mean to her—and to them—she did not know; at least, though, she knew that Chip's labors had not been in vain.

"I wonder why he left them on his work computer."

"I wondered the same thing. Maybe he just didn't finish all that he wanted to do and had plans to go back the next day. Are people around there on a Saturday?"

"The presses are running but the offices are mostly empty."

When the first two stacks were viewed and discussed enough to straighten them into neat piles and set them aside on the chest, Adam situated himself in the loveseat so that he could watch Sarah proceed. She read the resignation letter out loud and stopped for a moment to ponder Chip's words. "He ended up just giving it to them anyway," she said as she placed it upside down on the table beside her. Adam took note of her composure and wondered if it was actually composure or an outcome of her two weeks with the missionary. It was more the air of a widow ten years down the road.

"I'm glad he went ahead and gave it to them, for whatever reason. It does my heart good to know that he knew that they knew. Too bad he never got to enjoy one day of his new enterprise."

Adam said nothing.

"No manuscripts, though, huh?"

"No, I'm afraid not."

"Well, that pretty well puts an end to that and I'm glad."

"I was disappointed."

"You should face up to it and close the door on this case, Mr. Private Eye."

"Perhaps."

Sarah sighed and went on.

"A letter from Chip," she said recognizing Chip's writing. "Did you read this?"

"I read just a bit of it. I...I struggled with looking at any of this, but I sense that you see me as part of the big picture, as part of the investigation, so to speak. I thought you wouldn't be home for two weeks and that there might be something...."

Sarah laid her hand on his arm.

"You don't need to explain," she said, shaking her head. "Really, Adam, I have come to see you as family. You've been as deep into this whole thing as I have. So don't badger yourself."

"I read a bit and then couldn't process anything else. I saw a couple of things, read a couple of things, got up and walked around in a highly emotional state, sat down in that chair over there and went into a deep sleep—right where you found me."

"It's unlike you."

"What, to fall asleep in a chair?"

"No, to be in a highly emotional state."

"I guess I'm involved in this more than I realized."

"Well, at this moment, I'm glad you're involved and that you're here while I read this letter."

She took the letter and began to read silently. Adam leaned against the heavy arm of the loveseat, his head resting on his hand, one ankle, as was his way, crossed over his knee. He watched to see her reaction to the first paragraph. She turned to look at him and simply said, "You read this, right?"

"Like I said, just a bit of it."

"You realize...."

"I do. It is what stopped me in my tracks."

Sarah began again at the top, reading aloud.

Sarah, you know I will always love you. I could have saved that old man, but I missed the warning signs. I should have saved him. It is hard for me to think of facing another day with such guilt.

She stopped.

"This...is the note," she said, trying to process things in her mind. "Adam, this is the note! This says the same thing as the one that floated to the garage floor that day!" Her voice was full of wonder. "I'm pretty sure, though, that this wording is different. That note said, um...'I can never face another day with such guilt.' I remember that now," she whispered. "Oh, my goodness! That note was just the beginning of a note, like...a first draft. I'm wondering, since I haven't gone near his car since that day, if maybe there's a pile of stuff or a bag of garbage there that he was going to throw out. In fact, Adam, there is! The night that sweet Annette rescued me, I remember a bunch of papers and junk mail scattering to the floor from the passenger seat! Chip kept his car meticulously clean! He was going to throw that note out!"

Slowly, she turned her face toward Adam. "Do you know what this means?"

"I know what it looks like it means," Adam said, somberly shaking his head. "It looks as though your husband did not kill himself. We've had growing suspicions, you and I, but perhaps we now know the truth." Adam was contemplative. "Read the rest," he urged, "perhaps things will be plainer by the end of the letter."

"I don't want to think about the other possibility right now," was her reply. "I just can't process it. Can you?"

"Keep going. Things may get clearer as you continue."

Sarah arose with the letter in hand, and began to walk back and forth in front of the fireplace, softly reading her husband's handwritten letter.

Sarah, you know I will always love you. I could have saved that old man, but I missed the warning signs. I should have saved him. It is hard for me to think of facing another day with such guilt.

Yet, all of this has sent me to my knees. I have cast my burden upon the Lord. It is a big burden, Sarah, bigger than just the old man's death. I could be in danger, but perhaps not. Richard has gone from despising me to fearing me for what I know. He—and Robert—should be afraid! I have a new respect for how David felt when King Saul was bent on killing him. It is not a moment too soon for me to be leaving there. I'm doing everything I can to tie up the loose ends up so I can exit Payce, hook, line and sinker, by the end of tomorrow.

"They killed him," Sarah announced quietly, her jaw firmly set, "or they had someone else do it. I have no doubts now."

Though Adam shared her viable suspicions, he said nothing. Sarah read on.

Why is he after me? Because what I know about him—and Robert, for that matter—is a threat to him. If the facts ever emerge, they will at least go to jail for a long time, but it's worse than that. Well, I have all the evidence needed now (but I won't tell you how I got it). It would be wrong of me to know what I know and not take it to the proper authorities. I will do that next week, God willing.

Tomorrow morning, I will put several things on Richard's desk: A contract signed by Herman Lichten for Petetra with a corrected royalty amount (that is a separate story), two other contracts (explanation later) and my resignation.
Chip

"Why would he write this to me if he knew we would see each other on Saturday?"

"I'm thinking he really was almost expecting trouble. Maybe it's like a *just-in-case* kind of thing. His mention of David and Saul is interesting."

"He really does sound scared."

"Knowing what we do now about your distant relatives, Sarah, we can understand that, right?"

"Not funny. Not my relatives." She turned Chip's note over and took the next paper. "I'm not sure I'll ever understand all of this."

"Maybe someday it will all make more sense."

"I hope so. This paper is a copy of an email. Hmm. It looks like...hmm. This was sent to me the night before he died. Actually, it was sent very early Saturday morning. It was sent to me at 3:27 a.m. I never got this, Adam. I never saw this email."

"You sure?"

"Yes, I'm positive."

"Did you check your email that morning? Maybe while still in Boston?"

"I didn't. It was Saturday. I left my hotel at 5:00 a.m.! I never saw this. I never saw this, Adam," she said, scanning it quickly.

"Well, I know that you looked at your email since then. We talked about those emails."

"I never saw this one, though, and that is because it was sent to my Kerrigan address. This email was sent to Kerrigan! It would make sense. I was still working for Kerrigan—though I quit that day—and Chip would assume that I'd check there for mail. He intended for me to read this a year ago, no, more than a year ago. I'm not so sure I want to read it now." With a voice full of emotion, she said, "I'm not sure I should." She looked at Adam for an answer. "Should I?"

"Read it, Sarah. I'm thinking things are going to become much clearer by the time you're done."

"I will, but this is all very confusing. Here goes."

> *Saturday morning. 3:00 a.m.*
> *Sarah, I hope you will forgive me for such an email. I just think I should write everything down, just in case.*

"In case of what though, Chip?" she asked aloud. "In case of what?" She continued to read.

> *If something should happen to me, you will need to know the things you read in this letter.*

"My goodness! He really was expecting trouble!"
"Keep going."

> *Don't get me wrong. I absolutely plan on celebrating my birthday with you later! What is in this email is just for just-in-case. OK? (By the way...do I get to pick where we go for dinner? ☺)*

> *OK. Here we go. Sarah, something unusual happened a little while ago. I wished you were here. I really needed you. I called you a couple of times but I could not get you and your voice mail was full. So I'm writing.*

"Ohhhh!" Sarah groaned, looking up at the ceiling. "Why do I let my box get full?" Agitated, she went on.

> *At 9:00 last night, I had chest pains. Can you believe that?*

"Chest pains! Chest pains!" she half shouted, jumping up and walking briskly to the front windows. There she paced back and forth, the letter still in her hands. "Chest pains?" she whispered. She went to the piano and sat on the bench. She read more.

> *They did not last long but they put me on the floor. It scared me, but then they went away. When you get home, we'll go see the doc. You know I must be worried for me to say I will go to the doctor!*

"Chest pains! He never had chest pains!" she burst out. "Chest pains that put him on the floor?" she sputtered, once again walking to stand before the fireplace. "What is that all about? Adam, what is that all about? He was only 29 years old! Why don't men go to the doctor! Why, Adam? Why don't men like to go to the doctor? I don't want to think this, but if two people really love each other, wouldn't they do everything possible to live as long as they can? Why, oh, why do men refuse to go to the doctor!"

Adam remembered nearly cutting off his finger and how adamant Melanie had to become in order to get him to the emergency room. He had almost bled to death by the time they finally got there. Such silent treatment he had gotten from his wife for a good while!

Tears welled up in the carpenter's kind eyes. Attempting to calm her, he said, "Chip loved you very deeply, Sarah. You must never doubt that. You must take it from me."

"I will never understand it. I will never, never understand it." She hesitated, deep in thought. "I wonder how life would be right now if I had gotten this email."

The revelation of severe chest pains introduced new questions about the cause of Chip's death. Just a few sentences before, Adam had confirmed, in his own mind, the hunch that the Payces had somehow been responsible. Now, suddenly and without warning, a new, very strong possibility had come to light. A twenty-nine year old dying of a heart attack is rare, but for one who discloses in a letter to his wife that he had chest pains of such magnitude, the odds would be greater! But the carpenter held his peace and the Timber Lane widow, it seemed, would soon have more to say.

Her face and demeanor contemplative, Sarah gracefully sat down on the blue leather recliner directly across from Adam. With her head leaned back, she stared at the beamed ceiling—or perhaps past it—out into the blue sky, and into the glory of heaven. Tears, only a few, rolled down into her hair. Young Chip had gone to be with Christ. Life would never be the same, yet, Sarah Finfield had learned better than ever in the last weeks how to hope when there is no hope.

The beautiful chimes of the mantel clock rang out—four forty-five, they said. The soft tick tock of the clock went on, silently, faithfully. Sarah was thinking, now with her eyes closed, weighing the message of her husband's letter against the events of the past year, especially the last two months.

"Adam," she said at last, quietly introducing a discussion that would be hushed and solemn, "do you realize that in the last 30 minutes or maybe an hour, I have been confronted with three extremely strong possible causes for Chip's death?"

"I know."

"I have lived more than a year under the dark cloud of suicide, sure that it was suicide; then, for the last month, I have been suspicious that the Payces had him killed; today, at one point in the letter, I was sure that they had; and now, a few minutes later, here I am faced with the possibility that he had a heart attack!" Her eyes yet closed and her head still leaning against the back of the recliner, Sarah went on. "This is all like something from a novel."

"You know, it really is."

"Chip did not take his own life," she peacefully announced. Such serenity was in her voice! Such a changed Sarah Finfield! How strong and confident she seemed! "Those papers in that pile right there are full of his hopes and his plans for the future. He was getting a bike for me because we were planning a trip up north that summer. He was gathering information on the marathon because both of us were going to run that fall. He had an ad ready for the paper and wanted me to check it. He was excited about Finfield Publishing, and who knows, maybe even doing Herman's other books. Who knows? But, Adam, I should have known better about Chip. I should never have believed that he took his own life. I knew him better than that."

Chip's email was still in her hands as she arose from her chair and walked around to stand behind the recliner. She was facing Adam as she went on.

"Do you think he could have had a heart attack?" she asked softly, her arms folded, her tanned face filled with bewilderment. "Chip would not consider a doctor's visit unless it was pretty awful. I am sure of that beyond a doubt. Maybe...."—Sarah was sorting things through—"maybe he went out somewhere in the morning and either on the way out or coming back home, had an attack that didn't take him right away. Instead, the carbon monoxide dealt the final blow. Could that be? Do you think that could be? Oh, Adam, I'm just thinking out loud."

It was a right moment for Adam to administer kindness and

comfort; he made his way to where Sarah was standing and put his arm around her shoulder.

"I think that what you're saying is actually very possible."

"What in the world do I do about it?" she asked greatly stressed by this quandary.

"Well, the first thing that comes to my mind is that we should talk to your lawyer. Maybe that should be first, but then, too, it would probably be a good idea to talk to your pastor. I don't know…maybe when all is said and done, Chip's doctor would have to be in on something like that."

Sarah turned and hugged Adam.

"Such good ideas, Adam," she said. "Yes. Those are good."

"You'll get through this," he said, gently moving her away.

She studied his face and then said, "I'm still counting on you to not be very far away."

"I'm in it with you," Adam answered, feeling some guilt at saying so after his resolve to *go down a different path.*

"How incredibly good God was to me to bring me such a friend. I can hardly put into words how much you mean to me. What would I have done without you?"

Adam went to stand before the casement windows facing west and watched the golden grain sway in the wind like waves of the ocean. *"Dad, you have to tell Sarah the truth."* Daniel's words revisited him. For the first time since struggling through a conversation with Mrs. Finfield about her bashed-in garage door, Adam owned up to the truth, deep down in his soul, where decisions of great magnitude are made—he loved Sarah Finfield. Sarah, nevertheless, having no way to know Adam's heart at that moment, moved on with the letter.

(I am dashing this off so that I can lie down and get some sleep yet tonight.)

To go on, God definitely used those pains to nudge me to do a couple of things. I wrote to Jeff and Char and speaking for both of us (I knew you would support me in this), I told them that I was so sorry for not taking steps for reconciliation, and for five years of ridiculous pride.

I didn't tell them about Liselle Elena. They don't need to know. I asked them to come to Timber Ridge soon. I'm telling you, Sarah, the thought of dying and not having that straightened out was terrible. I had to write.

The reading ceased for the moment. From where he stood at the window, Adam turned to look at Sarah. He knew precisely what she was thinking. Her eyes were upon the wall behind the piano, upon an oil painting of a tall ship off on a journey somewhere; but her stare went far beyond the gray waves and the billowing sails. Her tightened lips and a toss of her head gave her away; her bitterness was still alive and well. Without a word, she took up reading where she had left off.

> *And I wrote to my mom. I apologized for not taking better care of her. What more could I say? I wonder if she is as content as she tells me and I wonder if she really understands what I am trying to say. It makes me sick at my stomach to think that my mother is married to such a man.*

> *I am going to mail both letters in the morning. I'll pick up stamps, too. We need them. Then, I will come home and wait for you! You must never go away again!*

"I was right," she murmured. "He did go out. Somewhere there's a book of stamps that wasn't there when I left for Boston." She went on.

> *When you get home, we'll go to the doctor and we'll have lots of time to talk. Don't worry about the chest pains. I'm sure it's all okay. Anyway, I worry, too, when you're flying home! I'm never happy until you're on the ground again!*

Taking a seat on the ledge before the fireplace, Sarah, for a moment, let her hands—and the letter—rest in her lap.

"If I would have gotten this email, I would have called him and would have insisted that he go to the hospital. He says not to worry about the chest pains, but for some reason—and we know that God makes no mistakes—I never got this, and here I sit, a widow. This is all very hard for me."

"Is it better for me to be here or to go, Sarah?" Adam asked for her sake. "Maybe it'd be easier for you if I wasn't here."

"No! No. No, I'm glad you're here. You must stay. Will you stay? I want you here. I can go on." Pulling herself together, she straightened and bravely announced, "This is the new Sarah, remember? I will keep reading."

I told you on the phone that I had things to show you when you get home. I've held off telling you about this while I figured out exactly what to do, but the night I was with Mr. Lichten, he told me that he had written eleven more books besides The Street of Petetra."

Sarah arose in slow motion, her whole being radiant with anticipation of good news.

"I know you are as shocked as I was, but you will be even more shocked at this bit of news. In a strange twist, the eleven manuscripts belong to me...us. I have them. He was going to move the very next day and wanted them temporarily safe. Of course, neither of us would have ever suspected such a turn of events. I'm sure my friend, Herman, wasn't counting on dying in a fire that night! Nevertheless, I am grateful that for some odd reason, he wanted me to take them that night, and am in a bit of awe that he insisted on it. Otherwise...well, you know. His manuscripts are legally ours, but this could mean immeasurable trouble if Richard finds out. We must do everything carefully and legally correct."

"But where are they, Chip!" spouted Sarah, sounding very much like she expected an answer. Exasperated, she hurried on with the letter.

Night and day since you left, I have been working my head off to map out an undetectable plan to hide them and keep them for the future, because I am sure the Payces would stop at nothing to gain possession. They would ransack this house without a blink, to say nothing of possible personal violence to me or even you.

Richard will fight us for them when he finds out about them. Hopefully that will be long after my contract details with him run out. He does not know the books exist right now, but when he does, we'll have to keep in mind that he is a greedy, ruthless man and will fight us for them and will stop at nothing to get them and remember, he has the bucks to try. I have been assured, however, that we would win.

Look and chuckle at the contract below this email. It is perfectly legal! I went to see Bill Crombie yesterday and he says it's as legal as the Constitution!

So the manuscripts are ours, ours to publish when I am clear of Payce Publishing legalities. I will show you where they are when you get home. You'll be surprised.

With wide eyes and a "you've got to be kidding me," Sarah got up from the fireplace ledge and plopped down into the loveseat. She pressed her fingertips to her forehead, and scrunched her eyes shut. "No. No. No. No. Tell me...please tell me that I did not just read what I just read."

Adam wanted to laugh heartily but it seemed highly inappropriate at the moment. He searched Sarah's face for her mood and response to all of this.

"I cannot believe this!" she cried, her hands pressed against her cheeks. "The evidence has gone to the grave!"

"Yes...but no, Sarah." Adam briskly left his place before the front windows and went to stand behind one of the recliners. He rested his arms on the back. "Sarah, it tells me that we missed them! He hid them somewhere around here!"

Sarah was irritated and could hardly speak. She attempted a sentence two or three times but ended up with plopping her hands in her lap each time.

"This tells us a lot," Adam said, moving to sit next to her.

"Adam," she said, annoyed, "it tells us absolutely nothing. I think you know that as well as I do. You are a disgusting optimist!"

"No, Sarah," Adam said, suppressing a laugh, "if Chip said he would show them to you when you got home, then they are here. Where else could that be? We're missing something. I never asked you about a lock box. Do you have a lock box?"

"Yes, I do," was her curt reply.

"When's the last time you looked into it?"

"Once since he died and there are no manuscripts in it!"

"Could Chip have gotten another one? Have you looked through your papers, like banking papers?"

"I'm not discussing this anymore." She softly stalked into the kitchen. "I'm over the edge with confusion," she hollered. "I vowed a couple of weeks ago that I am through with all of it. I don't know what to make of this and I'm not in the mood," she said emphatically, "to pursue it further."

She returned with two glasses of ice water. "I'm so agitated and I wonder what I would have done if I would have had to do this alone back then and in the frame of mind I was in after he died? This is all so preposterous. So preposterous!" With a sigh, Sarah added quietly, "If I would have known I was coming back to this, I might have stayed in Mexico!"

"I'm glad you didn't. I wouldn't have known what to do with all of this. You needed to be here. Now, keep going, Sarah."

They both sat down on the fireplace ledge. Adam silently read the rest of the letter with her.

I have been lost without you, Sarah Finfield. You may think that I am a bulwark, but I am only strong when you are beside me. I am full of joy at the thought of you leaving Kerrigan and coming with me on this new journey. Thank you for your incredible support during these days of getting the company in place. I'm sure there is not another man alive blessed with such a strong and loving wife, one that can make a man laugh at the storms of life and hope when there is no hope.

Sarah's carpenter understood. Had Sarah looked at him at that moment, his expression and his smile would have given the truth away.

My heart is telling me that you and I will have a long, incredibly awesome journey together; but, I have just knelt before Almighty God and asked Him to take special care of you if that is not meant to be.

In every letter I have ever written to you, I have included this phrase: You know that I will always love you.

You know that I will always love you.
Chip

Unexpectedly, and rather abruptly, Sarah got up and left her cozy haven, laying the letter on the cedar chest. Adam heard her footsteps down the hall and then, the closing of her bedroom door. He sighed. Sarah was hurting, he assumed, and no wonder. Going through all of the contents of the new-found safe had been grueling!

He walked to the foyer. There he stopped to pray. Was it time for him to go or was it best for him to stay? This was the closest of friends in the most awkward of circumstances. They were friends but they were still carpenter and client; they were friends but ones of a very short duration. Adam felt he knew Sarah pretty well by now and yet, what was his role at a moment such as this? If he were her husband or fiancé, or even an actual big brother, how different it would be! Instead, his proverbial hands were tied. He could not run to her side.

After an absence of about five minutes, Sarah appeared once again, holding something tightly in her hand. Her eyes were down and she said nothing for a few moments. Then, she looked up and made eye contact.

"Here," she said, thrusting the object into Adam's masculine hand. "Read the inscription."

Down deep, somewhere in Adam's inner spirit, he chuckled. Sarah had not gone to weep or to take cover; Sarah had gone for her wedding ring. Privately chagrinned, he read what had been inscribed at Chip's request: *I will always love you.*

"Why don't you wear this anymore?" he asked, gazing deeply into her teary green eyes.

"It falls off my finger. I guess I've lost a little weight." She went on, confused and hurt, speaking very softly, "If he loved me, why didn't he rush to the doctor?"

"Sarah," Adam said meaningfully, taking her hand and gently wrapping her fingers around the ring, "doubt thou the stars are fire, doubt the sun doth move, doubt truth to be a liar, but never doubt thy love."

Leaning her head slightly to one side, an inquiring smile appeared through the storm on her face.

"What did you just say?"

Adam slowly and lovingly repeated the line from Hamlet's letter to Ophelia. "I said, 'doubt thou the stars are fire…doubt the sun doth move…doubt truth to be a liar, but Sarah Liselle Finfield, never doubt thy love.'"

Now she cast a skeptical sidelong glance at him.

"How is it that you said that to me?"

"Never mind that. Just remember those words…and on the other subject…you need to start eating better. Time to take care of Sarah." He kept her hand in his for as long as he dared; then, he released it slowly.

"Let's go through the rest of the papers," he suggested. "Did you finish the email?"

Sarah put the ring on her thumb and walked to the couch, pondering the words from Hamlet in her heart and the depth of the man who had just spoken them. She retrieved the email and sat down.

"Hmm, there's a little more to the email," she said. "Just a bit. Just a P.S. Here, listen."

P.S. I'm sending you on a treasure hunt! Just in case you get home before I do, look in your Bible. I left two clues for you. I know you'll figure it out in a minute! You are the smartest woman I have ever known!

First a chuckle, then an increasing hearty laugh burst forth from Sarah's carpenter, and it did not end quickly. Sarah looked up at him and shot back a smile of unbelief.

"Well," Adam said, still laughing, "go look!"

"No way! You go. It's next to my recliner. I'm in shock!"

The Sarah Liselle Finfield Bible really, truly held within its pages another note from Chip. Sarah would not take it from Adam when he held it out to her.

"You read it," she scowled in jest. "I cannot! I am so frustrated. Can you believe this?"

"Well, look. Look, Sarah, All it says is 'Ezekiel 8:7 and 8 (NLT)'. Oh, he's particular! He wanted you to read in the New Living Translation. Do you even have one?"

"I think I do," she growled, rolling her eyes. "It would be on the same shelves that fell on you that day."

Finding the whole thing very funny and laughing as he went, Adam went to retrieve the Bible and hurried back. He put it in Sarah's lap.

"You look it up, Adam! Will you? I can't."

Adam could not contain his laughter as he paged his way to Ezekiel. "Here. Here, listen," he said, still finding the whole situation very funny. "'Then he brought me to the door of the Temple courtyard where I could see a hole in the wall. He said to me, 'Now, son of man, dig into the wall.' So I dug into the wall and found a hidden doorway.'"

"Oh...my...goodness," Sarah grumbled. "This whole thing was a game! This was a treasure hunt!" she hollered, rising to her feet. "My husband was sending me...on a treasure hunt to find...his new contraption! I...can't...believe it. And Clue No. 2, ladies and gentlemen!" Sarah announced with dramatic flair and with a theatrical wave of the hand, "'This is the key: The Eye of the Eagle. If you remember that, the rest will be easy. Memorize this sequence. 369152748.'"

Adam could hardly talk. He got up and walked around, finding the whole treasure hunt idea hilarious. His merriment put a smile on Sarah's face.

"Would you have figured it out?" he asked through his laughter. He sat down across from Sarah in one of the recliners, still chuckling. "Would we have?"

"If we would have known it was a treasure hunt, yes! But no, we're sleuthing and snooping and solving on the phone, losing sleep, and looking through hundreds of albums and absolutely sure that 'the eye of the eagle' was a clue, thinking it would lead us to the manuscripts!"

Now Sarah burst into laughter. "Annette and I had records all over this floor! And poor Annette, sitting right there and telling me that she loved doing it because she is Annette Cappetti, Private Eye! It's a comedy! It's a downright comedy! I never, never saw this email! Ezekiel 8:7 and 8...," she groaned, "in the New Living Translation, no less!"

Neither Adam nor Sarah ventured into the *what ifs* of this entirely bizarre situation. Truly, life most likely would have taken a different turn if Chip's email of May 13th, sent at 3:27 in the morning, would have made its way to his wife, Sarah Finfield; but it had not. It was a moment to keep in mind the sovereignty of God. It was moment to at last experience the blessing of joy and laughter and the balm that comes from the funny side of life.

A few more papers lay beneath Chip's letter, and still feeling jovial and cheerful, they sat themselves down once again on the loveseat. There they found a ragged sheet of paper, a page torn from an old phone book, handwritten by Herman, the perfectly legal contract that Chip had referred to, a contract between the famous author, Herman Lichten, and his friend, Chip.

This is a contract dated this day, May 12, 2004 at 8:45 p.m. between Finfield Publishing, Inc. and Herman Lichten for the publishing of eleven (11) fiction novels authored by Herman Lichten. Royalty percentage = 10%.

I, Herman Lichten, surrender ownership as long as is necessary to Chester Elliott Finfield, President of Finfield Publishing, Inc. and request they be removed from these premises and held in safekeeping until I am able to retrieve them. It is my intention that at some future date, Finfield Publishing, Inc. will take charge of the publishing of all eleven books.

THE RESURRECTION OF SARAH FINFIELD

All royalties will be deposited directly to Herman Lichten's account at LaSalle National Bank in Chicago. In case of death, all royalties will be paid equally to the seven Home on the Range Homeless Shelters currently in existence. Headquarters in Galveston, Texas.

Signed Herman Lichten 5/12/04
Signed Chester Elliott Finfield, II 5/12/04"

"Will this day never stop handing us surprises?" Sarah wondered aloud.

"I, for one, am liking some happy surprises. What an incredible way to end this whole Eye of the Eagle thing." He laughed again. "That was hilarious!"

Almost done now, weary but cheerful, Sarah and Adam hovered over the last document. Below the contract was a list of Herman's novels. Sarah stood and faced Adam and read them aloud and slowly, flourishing each name with dramatic inflections.

"*The Dishonor of Sir Quiglee; Rachel's Flute; Brave Bonnie Augustine*...how does someone ever think up such stories and such interesting titles? Here's more: *Silver Cobblestones; Trumpet of Dunne Castle.*" Some sound like they take place centuries ago, like that one, but this one, this one down here, *The Invisible Needle* and, for that matter, *Frozen Light Years*, they are probably more like *The Street of Petetra*, more futuristic."

"Is that it?"

"No, there's a couple more. *The Golden Stairs of Morrow Cliffs, Juniper's Resolution*, and *Lantern in the Valley*. Oh, wait, did I say *Queen Carmella?*"

"I don't think so."

Smiling and drained, Sarah exclaimed "Oh! They all sound so awesome! My imagination runs wild with each one of those titles. I guess I will always have a smidgeon of hope that someday, like you said, Mr. Staunch Optimist, I really will run into *Brave Bonnie Augustine*. It sounds like my kind of book."

"I still think you will."

"Yeah, whatever."

"And when we do, I'm going to read that *Invisible Needle*. The thought occurs to me though, sitting here listening to you reading those titles, now wouldn't it be something if you sell this house, and the buyers decide to add a room on the back or put a second story on, and they make an amazing discovery in the walls somewhere!"

At first, Sarah laughed; then she rolled her eyes.

"You really do think they're here."

"I really do. But, never mind. It was just a strange thought that came to me out of nowhere. I hope you get to read your Bonnie Augustine book and that I get to see what the invisible needle is all about."

"Do you like to read, Adam?"

"I do, but I'm not a lover of castle-in-the-sky books."

"I love to read! And I would be ecstatic to read anything written by the genius who wrote *The Street of Petetra*! Actually that book is not a castle-in-the-sky book at all! It is truly exciting and mysterious! Unfortunately though, it does not appear that I will ever have that opportunity to hold another Lichten book in my hands."

"I may be a disgusting optimist, but you, my dear, are an equally resolute pessimist! Now, Mrs. Finfield, about dinner... what do say we go out somewhere."

"I am so wiped out, but Papa Luigi just doesn't sound quite right after all of this," Sarah agreed.

"I'm going to run home and shower and I'll come back for you, let's say, at 6:00. How's that?"

"Are you sure?"

"I'm sure. If you'd rather rest a little, I can come at 7:00ish."

"That actually sounds better. I'll lie down a bit and I want to change out of these clothes and freshen up."

"I'll make reservations for 7:30."

"I can meet you there. I'll meet you there. That way you won't have to drive all the way over here."

The tall, blond carpenter told Sarah his thoughts on that with one short shake of his head—and an Adam Cook smile.

"Okay, I'll be ready," she said, already moving toward her room. "Seven o'clock sharp."

"Wear the hat."

CHAPTER 31

Stonegate was the destination Adam had in mind, and Sarah caught on when the truck turned on to Meridian; Meridian was only a block long and boasted a row of high-end brightly colored town-homes on both sides of the street, a jewelry store, and two restaurants. Stonegate was one of them. It was Timber Ridge's classy spot to eat.

Tan and revived, Sarah climbed down from the truck without waiting for Adam's assistance. She wore a dark brown mid-calf skirt and a short sleeved white blouse, sterling silver beads around her neck and delicate earrings that matched—her only souvenirs from Mexico. Her hair, for the first time since Adam had laid eyes on her, was not in a barrette. Instead it hung, dark and shiny, and perfectly straight, halfway down her back; the straw hat was like a crown on the head of beautiful Sarah. She smiled at Adam in his tan sports jacket, white shirt and rust colored tie as he opened the door of the restaurant."

"Are you Adam Cook, the carpenter?" she dramatically teased.

"No," he said, "I am a Yellow Pages angel!"

"I hardly recognize you without your Home Depot hat!"

"I might say the same thing about you. That's a **very** nice straw hat. You are elegant."

Elegant? How nice that sounded! It had been Chip's word for her but the days since his death had held no yearning for elegance. Tonight, though, she took note of the smile that Adam's descriptive word for her had put on her face.

They were seated immediately. Adam had called for reservations. Their table was in the middle of the large dimly lit room. Flickering candles cast their glow on the goblets and fine silverware everywhere. A tuxedoed man was playing a white piano on a white platform, hanging by white chains from the ceiling. Water trickled over the edge of a high stone wall and splashed into a lighted pool. A very handsome waiter poured their water, showing off his expertise by pouring it from high above their heads without losing a drop. The guests were in a good mood, talking and laughing.

Adam felt the same. It was nice to dress up once in a while, to go somewhere special, to order something scrumptious to eat, to splurge. And it was even more pleasurable to enjoy it all with a close friend tonight—Sarah Liselle Finfield.

"I've never been here before," he said, taking a quick look around.

"Do you remember that Chip and I were here celebrating the new company the night of the fire?"

"Yep. That's why we're here. It's another celebration."

"And what are we celebrating?"

"The same thing you were celebrating with Chip."

"Finfield Publishing?"

"The company is yours. Chip set it up for you to be equal part-ners, right? "

"Yes. Yes, he did."

"And you could very well have all the business you need for a long, long time to come, if…when the manuscripts are found, right?"

"That's true, my overly optimistic friend. You just don't give up, do you. Well, Adam, I haven't given one thought to going on with the company. That's strange, I suppose."

"Up till now you haven't had reason to. Besides, you've been climbing out of a hole, fleeing for your life, putting your house back together. Sarah, I see that to a great degree, you have regained your strength and now you're standing at the threshold of a successful venture. Everything seems to be in place."

Sarah seemed relieved that the waiter chose that moment to ap-proach the table. They really were not ready, but she looked at Adam and said, "Is it all right if I pick the appetizers?"

The conversation, of necessity, ceased. It was time to peruse the menu, and when they had made their choices, they chatted about prime rib vs. filet mignon and about the good lobster and the bad lobster they had experienced. The appetizers came. Adam prayed so sincerely.

"Just want to thank you, dear Father, for this food and for all Your goodness to us these past months. In Jesus' name, Amen."

Slowly, quietly, calmly they ate their dinner and talked of a thousand things—the contents of the new-found safe, the kicked-in door, Annette and the Jaguar, the Night of the Drywall, Sarah's visit to River Road, Glen Lichten and his sunglasses, and on and on. It was as pleasant as the sharing of a perfect meal in a perfect setting could be. Great respect for each other was present. Through deep waters the two of them had gone together. Tonight was more than a celebration; it was a commemoration of a forever friendship.

"One thing I'll never forget is Chip's treasure hunt! Oh, my goodness!" Sarah laughed. "That was very funny...and unexpected. We had a good laugh over that whole thing."

"Been a long time since I laughed that hard. Good medicine. I think it was partly because going through all that stuff was so intense."

"Adam," Sarah said, leaning toward him, "it's all there."

"What's all there?"

"All the copies of the incriminating evidence that no doubt does not exist anymore at Payce. I did a quick look-through after you left today and there is a lot of stuff in those piles. Not surprisingly, there's a section that covers only Robert. I'm pretty sure I figured out what happened that night and why he craftily and hastily deleted that folder. It has been coming to me a little at a time. Do you want to hear?"

"You mean about the missing scan files?"

"Yes."

"Sure."

"I think that Chip and Robert ran into each other that night...probably congenially. Chip was leaving around midnight, Robert was coming—why, that late, I have no idea. The entry log for the 13th did not show Robert entering the building because he came right after midnight! If Andrew would have checked the entry log for the 14th as well as the 13th, I'm pretty sure Robert's name would have shown up. There is the solution to part of the mystery. So, he comes in, says hi to Chip, sees Chip finishing up at the scanner...."

"Chip, no doubt, was not expecting him!"

"No, and it probably freaked him out. Anyway, Robert wonders what Chip is doing, checks the scan log and finds file after file of incriminating evidence against him as well as his father. He deletes them, thinking that's the end of it. After all, Chip left shortly after he was done scanning. He didn't count on the fact that Chip was copying every bit of it to his hard drive. Then, a year later, the manuscripts come to light, Richard launches an investigation, drags me there to look for those manuscripts, oblivious to the truth, and lo, and behold, the **RICHARD** and the **ROBERT** files show up instead. I will never forget his curse when he saw that screen! He wasted no time getting rid of it all!"

"He is a pretty bad guy, it appears. So, you looked through it all now?"

"Just a quick skim through. Perhaps I'll give it all to the lawyer and let him deal with the criminal side of it. Are you familiar with the Cassidine conspiracy?"

"No, can't say that I am. I recall a Cassidine murder. That's all."

"Robert was involved in that! It was a hostile double takeover plot. Can you believe that he was involved in that? He was going to oust Richard! Well, enough of that. Anyway, there were a couple of things scribbled about Chip and Herman and about some talks about God."

Adam reached over and touched Sarah's arm.

"What do you say we don't talk shop anymore tonight? What do you say?"

"I guess that's a good idea." Sarah rested against the back of her chair. "I am in need of some peace and calm."

"What about your trip?" asked Adam. "Well, not the trip itself, but your time down there."

"It was so good. I stayed with a family with three daughters, all teens, in a house with two bedrooms. Two bedrooms is like a castle in that village. That, I must admit, was not easy! Anyway, every day, my job for a week was to hold something like a vacation Bible school for the orphans. There were twenty-four children ages four through fourteen. Thanks to quick Spanish lessons in the evenings, I was able to teach them songs and verses; we did crafts; I played the piano—if you can call it that; I wiped their noses, if you know what I mean."

"You handled that whole group by yourself?"

"I had a helper who spoke Spanish, but I was the one in charge. I've worked with kids before. I love working with kids." Sarah hesitated for a long moment, and then, not looking at Adam, she softly announced, "I'm going back."

These were words Adam did not want to hear, but oddly, for some reason, ones that did not surprise him. One did not have to be terribly astute to see that the trip had been good for the widow. And had she not told him once that she would have gone to the ends of the earth with Scott? *"What though,"* he mused, *"does 'going back' mean?"*

"Going back to the same place?" he asked with a wrinkled forehead.

"I think so. It appears that way."

Adam wanted so much to blurt out a question—any question—about Scott, just so he could take Sarah's temperature, so to speak; but how out of place it would sound at this point.

"The mission board is reviewing my situation. In fact, I will meet with them on my way back."

"Wow," Adam said quietly. He wiped his mouth with his napkin and folded his hands in his lap. "When are you leaving?"

Sarah appeared ill at ease. She looked away from him, her face a picture of the contemplation going on inside of her. It did not escape Adam's eye. He was mostly prepared for what the answer would be.

"I'm leaving tomorrow," was her almost apologetic reply. "In the afternoon. My plane leaves at 5:12."

"Well, that's...." He hesitated to choose his words wisely. "Well, Annette will be disappointed about that."

"Ohhh, have you seen her?"

"Yep, yesterday she stopped by. They just got home from vacation. She mentioned that she thought you were coming home today and was disappointed that you were going to be gone another two weeks. Bubbly Annette! She says she had hoped you and she could be spending some time together. You probably don't know that she went to your church a week or so ago."

"She did? Oh, dear. I'll call her. I know her number well, if you remember. I'll ask her to come down in the morning. I must see her."

"So, it's south of the border for you again. What do you think, Sarah? Are you ever coming back...I mean to stay?"

Sarah rested her chin on her palm and answered him gently.

"You are perceptive, Adam. You must be recognizing the fact that Sarah Finfield making two back-to-back trips anywhere in the world must mean something."

"You forgot another important factor," Adam responded.

Sarah waited to hear what that might be.

"The For Sale sign in your front yard," he said, fingering the stem of his water goblet. "That's significant."

"Yes, I suppose that's true. You know, though, how I have fought with the pain of living there."

"Yes, but you are greatly healed now."

"That's true, too. The sting really is greatly lessened—especially now after discovering the things we just did. But everything seems to be pointing to it being the right time." Sarah laid her fork on her plate. "To answer your question, I don't know. Am I ever coming back? I don't know. Believe me, I am just waiting on the Lord to open or shut doors. It almost sounds trite to say that after a year of closing Him out; but it's the faint desire of my heart to wait on Him. Tonight, with what I know, I would say I will soon be a former Timber Ridge resident. Yet, Adam, I am in a valley of unrest and uncertainty. It is all I can tell you. All I know for sure is that I'm going back to Villa de Tututepec for another short term missions trip, but not on the village jaunts with Scott."

Adam remained quiet. He was hardly ever flustered and never felt pressed to reply hurriedly. His casual demeanor gave him the opportunity to think things through before answering or reacting. Thus, he sat tonight, across from the widow who was, at least, his dear friend, interpreting Sarah's sketchy answers: The arrangement with Scott and Sarah working together in that area without being married had, most likely, posed a great problem. The mission board had acted quickly, and, in Adam's mind, wisely. To carry the conclusion a step further, though, brought questions to the carpenter about a possibility of a wedding on the horizon. Such a consideration disquieted him, not for reasons of jealousy; no, it mostly bothered him because he knew that his friend, the widow, was healed, but not nearly enough to make such a momentous decision. She would be marrying someone who, during the last ten years, had been in touch with her once—a basically surprise visit to her home—and then, for two weeks in Mexico, and someone who, in Adam's mind, had wounded her deeply once before. She would move away from everything familiar. Sarah's world and all that was therein might very possibly change abruptly. Nevertheless, he knew her well enough to know that she perceived herself as sufficiently resilient to do it; his perception was that Mrs. Finfield was still seeking escape.

"Well, I'm glad to hear you're praying about all of it. God will lead you. You know, He will make it undeniably clear to you, if that's what you want."

"Oh, it is. I feel strong and ready. I like what I was doing down there. It's a beautiful area and I love those kids, especially the teens, but I really am being careful. What do you think? Just knowing what you know about this situation and about me, what do you think about all of this? What do you think I should do?"

Adam noticed the absence of any mention at all of Scott, let alone any hint of fondness toward Missionary Dolan. He looked up from his food and after hesitating just a moment, he said, "I remember telling you once that I am your carpenter, not your counselor. I still see it that way."

"But you are more than my carpenter now." Sarah reminded him convincingly. "Remember? I pronounced that we are friend and friend. Do you recall?"

"I do and we are. Happily, that is true; yet, I'm not in a position to be your counselor on the subject of you and Scott."

"And what about on the subject of me and the missionfield?"

It was the kind of moment that necessitates careful forethought before answering; Adam hesitated, looking squarely at Sarah, as he did so. He took a long drink of ice water. As he set down his goblet, a smile, not so much on his lips as in his eyes, accompanied his answer.

"As I see it, Sarah, they are one and the same," was his reply—and the end of the subject, as far as he was concerned. He sought for a way to move the conversation elsewhere.

"I think I understand what you're saying," she said pensively. She sighed and cocked her head. "And what, Adam Cook, are you going to do now?" asked the widow, unintentionally changing the subject. "Is your answer still the same on the in-law's house?"

"I'm going to fix your deck and I'm going to stain it...and I must still say no to the Simpson Bell job. It's just not working out." He grinned. "Hey," he said, "aren't you going to finish your food?"

"I can't believe you're asking me that. By now, you should know."

"I do. Still this is a special night and awesome food. You should take full advantage. If you ever want that ring to fit your ring finger, you're going to have to kick back and enjoy eating again!"

"I keep telling you that I will, but I don't. I will. Soon."

"As for me and my plans," Adam said, picking up where he left off, "I've got a job right down the road from your in-law's house, oh, about a mile. I'm putting up a pole barn. They've been after me for it for six months now. And...there's some other jobs coming my way. I've put a lot of people on hold during these months."

"I know. I'm sorry."

"Oh, don't be. I've taken care of the important stuff. And along with the hammer and nails stuff, I think I'll take up reading *The Street of Petetra*."

"Great! It's very good. For me, so fond of Shakespeare, it's pretty amazing that I was so enraptured with it! Lichten had a noteworthy ability to write. It is excellent literature."

"Do you write, Sarah?"

"Yes, somewhat. I love to write—at least I used to—but I'm not sure that I'm any good."

"What do you write?" Adam asked, stretching out his legs and folding his arms.

"Children's books."

"Published?"

"Oh, no."

"You can publish them now! I know a good publisher! Hey,

someday I'd like to see something you wrote."

"Char is the writer. Her books are published...Christian novels."

"No kidding. It must run in the family. Are you two in touch yet?"

"No. I finally just read her letter from a year ago. On the plane. And I read one that I got a week or so ago. It was not a pleasant task. This thing has been very hard for me."

"I can tell."

"Would you like to read them?"

"No. No, I don't need to do that. But tell me about them."

Sarah became noticeably unsettled and a bit fidgety, but she proceeded to briefly describe the contents of Char's mail.

"Well, I read Letter No. 1 from a year ago first. It was filled with sympathy having just heard about Chip's death from a mutual friend out there in California. I know she tried to call me several times, but...I was not answering my phone, as you know. And then, she thanked me that we—Chip and I—wrote to make things right between our two families. I, of course, as you know, was not in on the writing of that letter, and really, not the sentiment either. Well, anyway, then, she told me that Jeff is losing his eyesight. If I would have known that, perhaps I would have been warmer that day outside the cafe, but I'm not sure even about that.

"That's why they were on the road that day, a year later. He had an appointment with one of the top eye doctors in the country. I guess his eyesight is deteriorating pretty rapidly. They had driven to Dubuque for a vacation—that's where his family lives—and the condition suddenly worsened. Someone—a neighbor or someone—told them about this doctor in Chicago, they called him and by a miracle, got an appointment almost right away. They hopped in the car, left the kids with grandma, headed for Chicago, and by a strange turn of events, ran into me."

"That **was**...a very strange turn of events. So, I assume that was Jeff in that car she ran back to."

"He's the one that saw me first."

"But he didn't want to talk to you, right?"

"He did not and does not." Sarah pulled two envelopes from her purse. "It's not a nice situation," she added with a woeful shake of her head. Choosing the letter written on apricot colored stationery, she looked through it until she found the right spot. "Let me read this part to you since you were there to witness our meeting outside the café. I think you'll appreciate this. She writes,

THE RESURRECTION OF SARAH FINFIELD

*How strange are the ways of God at times! You couldn't
make up such a story for a novel! The lady who stopped to see
if we needed help with our flat tire told me about Silver
Moon Café. She began to give me directions. I said, "Oh, I
know exactly what road you're talking about. I used to live
not too far from here." She said, "Oh, I saw the California
license plates. Where did you live when you were here?" I told
her that I had lived in Timber Ridge for about three years.
She exclaimed something about having a friend who lives
there. I asked her who that might be. She said, "Sarah Finfield."*

*Can you imagine my utter shock? I gasped, "You're kidding.
That is my big sister," I said. How strange it all was! She
went on to tell me that she has known you since you started
attending their church and then got married, and in fact, was
your wedding coordinator. I told her, "Then you and I have
been in the same room at least once! I was Sarah's matron of
honor." We remembered each other, only slightly, but still,
how very comforting to have just that single thin thread of
being in touch with you. I can only remember her first name.
Esther.*

*Sarah, she told me about your baby. I pretended that I knew,
but you will never know how such news crushed my spirit. I
am immeasurably sorry. I wish that I could say that "we" are
immeasurably sorry, but Jeff is still in the clutches of bitterness. When we heard of Chip's death and the way it happened, I was devastated, partly because of his death, but more
so because you and I were estranged and I could not be there
with you.*

*How kind of our loving and powerful God to see to it that
our paths crossed.*

"There's more," Sarah said after a deep sigh, "but that's the long
and the short of it."

"What are you going to do about it?"

"Jeff will never let her come here."

"You can go there."

Sarah opened her purse and carefully slid the letter down into one of the pockets, musing on Adam's words.

"I...I don't know."

"What don't you know?"

"I don't know if I can do that."

Adam leaned forward with his elbow on the table and rested his cheek against his fist. His eyes lingered on the tiny flame in the middle of the table and then moved to Sarah's face which was showing a faint but distinct resistance.

"I said that I'm your carpenter and not your counselor, but I'm going to tell you what I think on this one." There was no reprimand in Adam's tone; instead, his voice teemed with quiet entreaty. "Char is your sister! By your own admission you have been close. If you don't run toward reconciliation, in ten years you will have missed her life, her joys, her sorrows, her children and all their good happenings, and she will miss out on yours." Adam inserted a poignant pause. "In ten years, you cannot go back and regain that lost time. In fact, if you don't take care of it right away, you'll miss a day, and then, another day. No, Sarah, in my book you have no alternative. This comes first before anything else you might have in your head. Your sister's words are steeped in regret and forgiveness!" Adam took a deep breath. "Do you not think that this would be what Chip would want?"

"I know it is what he would want. Chip was a better man than I—better and kinder."

"Sarah," said Adam, now with that hint of reprimand in his voice, "you are one of the kindest people I have ever met and I'm pretty sure you will do the right thing." The carpenter's words became emotional and passionate as he spoke just above a whisper. He shook his head slowly, his face now moved closer to hers. "How grand is the verse in Ephesians that says, 'Be kind one to another.' Kind, Sarah. Kind. Tenderhearted...forgiving one another...like God... like God who for Christ's sake has forgiven us.'"

Tears brimmed in Adam's eyes, not enough to fall down his cheeks, but enough to tell the story of Adam Cook. Sarah sat stock still, her eyes moving from the waning candle to the water flowing in slow motion down the stone wall. Her lips tightened. Adam had seen that look on her face before. The diagnosis of the counselor? The heart of Sarah Finfield was not yet wholly mended.

"Can we go?" Sarah asked, not unkindly, but as more of an expression of extreme uneasiness.

"We can...and we should."

How dark the country roads seemed tonight and yet a near

three-quarter moon hung high in the sky! The silver truck went slowly toward Timber Lane and Sarah knew that Adam was deliberately taking his time. They had, tonight, talked their way through their lives since they had met several months before, finding the humor and the lessons in much of it. It had been a night of tying up the loose ends that come to be when two people from different worlds become friends. Even the stories of the last three months were refined as they told them from their vantage point. Now, in the drive home, Sarah was experiencing some of the same aversion to Adam's intrusion into the private part of her life that she had felt a couple of times before.

"Hey," Adam spoke into the darkness and the silence, "let's be friends. It was a wonderful dinner and a whole lot of fun being with you. You've got to just take my advice or leave it. I don't claim to be right all the time. You know that. Yet, in this case, I really don't think there is another way."

He reached over and put his hand on hers for just a moment.

"I lost my baby," she softly scowled. "We lost our hope. You cannot understand that."

He sighed.

"You know, Sarah," he said softly, "I can." Releasing her hand and placing his at the top of the steering wheel, he went on. "Do you remember telling me once that you liked my truck?"

"Yes? Does that have something to do with **this** subject?"

"Be nice. I'm just asking if you remember."

"I remember. I said, 'Your truck is nice.'"

"Exactly. Do you remember what I said?"

Sarah remembered mostly her terrible frame of mind that night. "You said something about there being a story attached to it."

"Correct. And I'm about to tell you that story right now." The story, however, did not begin immediately; only after a long stretch of country road and a profoundly deep sigh, did Adam begin. "Daniel once had a sister. When Daniel was six, Sarah was four."

Instantly, the photo of the little blond girl near Adam's door popped into Sarah's mind. Slowly she turned toward Adam. He felt her gaze. He continued his story, not dully, but as a gifted storyteller, painting his sentences with meaningful color.

"One day Daniel and Sarah were playing by the pond, on the side near the road. Every day they played in the same place. It was a favorite spot. There was a sandbox and a swing set and a little dock sticking out into the water. Melanie was ten feet away, working in the garden. She heard a tractor and looked up. It was the teenaged son of our neighbor who lived behind us down the road. Dustin went through our fence like it was toothpicks, down the hill, straight for the kids. Melanie screamed and ran, but it was too late. One of those big old tractor tires hit our darling little blond curly headed daughter and we lost our baby and we lost our hope."

Now the tears fell down Adam's cheeks—tears of memory and tears for Sarah. His voice faltered.

"Dustin had been drinking," he emotionally whispered. "Sixteen years old and just come from a beer party with his friends in one of their barns. The tractor actually ended up in the pond. When I got out there after hearing Melanie scream, this is what I saw: Dustin sitting on his tractor in the water at the edge of the pond, dazed; Melanie, holding a lifeless body in her arms; and Daniel, pulling on his sister's arm and saying, 'Wake up, Sarah! Wake up!'"

"Why did you never tell me this, Adam?" she said, hardly able to speak.

"There came a day when I had to stop talking about it. I had to let it go," he said with restrained sobs.

"Daniel was saying what?" Sarah asked after a few moments.

"'Wake up, Sarah, wake up!'"

"Sarah?"

"Yep. Sarah."

Except for the deep sigh that came from Adam's soul—and the drone of the diesel engine—no sound could be heard inside the cab of the truck. Sarah had much to ponder. Finally, she became inquisitive. What was the story of the truck?

"H...How does this tie into your truck?" she asked meekly.

"Dustin's father was overcome with grief. He adored little Sarah. They were friends. Now, he felt responsible for her death. He hid away in his house and would talk to no one. One day, about a month after the funeral, Melanie and I walked through our acreage, past the pond, and through the field toward the Nielsen's house. Melanie really didn't want to go. We were both devastated beyond words, but with the love of our friends and talks with the pastor and long talks between the two of us, she finally agreed to go.

"There was a little gate that Mr. Nielsen had built so that the kids could come to see him whenever they wanted to. We went through that gate and up the hill, up onto their back porch and knocked on the door. That afternoon, we sat with the Nielsens and told them that they had our complete forgiveness—and that Dustin had our complete forgiveness."

Now Adam was crying, struggling to continue.

"We told them about the forgiveness of Jesus. That was all. Then we went home. One day, they came to see us and asked if they could go to church with us—it was now and then at first, and then, all the time—and then, almost every Sunday for a very long time, we had dinner together after church.

"Mrs. Nielsen died five years ago and, let's see, almost two years ago, Mr. Nielsen died. When his will was read, he had left $45,000 for Melanie and me to buy a new truck. My rickety old truck had been the brunt of many a joke between us. In his will, he said, 'For the forgiveness of an unforgivable wrong, and for sharing the news of God's forgiveness, I bless my neighbors, Melanie Joy and Adam Benjamin Cook, with money in the amount of $45,000 to buy a new truck. Put that old truck out to pasture, Adam Cook,' he wrote. And so, I did. And that...is the story of the truck."

Now it was Sarah's turn to reach out and lay her hand on the arm of her friend.

"I don't know what to say." Her words did not come easily. "I'm so sad for you, Adam. I had no idea. I believe you when you say that you finally let it go. It's like you." She paused and then asked, "Your little girl's name was Sarah?"

"Yep. You probably never noticed what it says on the tailgate because it was always down."

"What does it say?"

"It's what we named the truck. Silver Sarah."

"Silver Sarah?" she repeated. "I never saw that. I can hardly believe this." She pulled out a tissue and wiped her eyes. "What happened to Dustin?"

"Two years' probation because of his age. Still messed up in his late twenties, I think. He's in Alabama, last I heard."

There was nothing to say, not for a while at least. Sarah replayed his tale of woe in her mind, this time impressed with his walk with God. Verses in the Bible actually governed his thinking. If God said to forgive, then Adam forgave. God said to be tenderhearted and kind; Adam said, "Okay, God." And now, without meaning to, here on the road home, he had preached a poignant sermon with just a short story and a tad of personal witness.

"You're an excellent man and a darn good counselor, Mr. Cook," she declared softly and kindly.

Miles passed in silence. Both were lost in their own world of thought. Life calls for times of complete silence, stretches of introspection and serious checking to see if life is all about you or all about those around you...and our great God.

"I need to call my sister," Sarah faintly murmured at last, "and I will somehow see her."

"Good!" Adam said, himself regrouping. "Now, Sarah Finfield, before you run off to Mexico again, let's be at peace and glad of heart. With mirth and laughter let old wrinkles come!"

"Merchant of Venice. Gratiano to Anthonio. How is it, Mr. Cook that you are suddenly quoting Shakespeare?"

"I'm not suddenly quoting Shakespeare. I'm just suddenly quoting Shakespeare in your presence, and that is because I only noticed your six volume set of all his works when I tore the plastic down the other day. You may be surprised that along with a major in business, I minored in English Lit. in college, and as a result of that, I became a fan of Bill...Bill Shakespeare, that is."

There was gentle laughter now, and ease. The air had been cleared and Sarah Finfield and Adam Cook were best friends.

"Did you know that those beautiful leather books—and the piano—were my Christmas gifts from Chip the year before he died? Wow! It sounds so strange to just say, 'he died.'"

"It sounds good even to me."

"I think it's okay to say that, don't you, even though it may be a while before I know for sure."

"You bet it's okay. It's more than okay. It's true. I'm sure of it."

They were almost home now, their friendly chatter replacing all the gloom and fear, distress and confusion of the day, and even that of the past few weeks.

"Stay there," Adam gently ordered Sarah as he turned off the ignition. "I'll get the door."

First the foyer light was turned on; then Sarah flipped the switch in the family room. She laid her purse on the trestle table in the foyer and started towards the Sarah Haven. Adam took her arm and held her back.

"Will you do something for me?"

With grand composure, Sarah looked into his face and waited to hear his request.

"Play something for me on the piano."

Sarah responded self-consciously. She shrugged and chuckled.

"I haven't played for fifteen months...more than fifteen. I'm not sure I can play anymore."

"You played in Mexico."

"Yes, and I gave you a hint of how that went!"

"Will you just play something? Play something you know. Can you play Moonlight Sonata?"

"Once upon a time."

Sarah went to the piano. Adam turned out the bright light that hung from the center beam of the great room and made his way to the front window, and as the August moon was sending its brilliant beams into the house on Timber Lane, the slow, melodious strains of Beethoven's glorious composition sounded from the magnificent grand piano. The light from the foyer transformed Sarah into a haloed silhouette. Suddenly the music stopped.

"I have to get the music, Adam, and I'll have to turn on the piano light. I'm entirely out of practice!"

Soon, under the glow of the little light above the music, Sarah started in again. Adam sat down in a high back chair, watching her from the corner of the room. He allowed himself to be honest deep in his heart: *How beautiful she is! Tan and poised and just plain lovely! How strong! How weak! How warm and confident! Nice hat. Just a good lookin' kid. That's all there is to it.*

He stood at the end of the first movement, assuming that, like most folk, it was all she knew. Sarah, though, went on to the second movement, her fingers flying, her face aglow. Adam sat down again and did not move until she had played all three movements; then, with the moonbeams landing upon his shoulders, enraptured with the composition, with the piano...and with the performer, when the last faint sounds of the piano strings died away, he stood. Sarah sighed and laid her hands in her lap.

"You keep making me open up doors to one little locked room after another. This was my birthday wish, you know."

"What was?"

"That someday soon, I would sit down and play once again."

"Hmm, your 'safe' wish, eh?"

"I knew it would happen. I just didn't know how or when."

"Well you got your wish...and I got mine. I wanted to hear you play. You are no amateur, Sarah!" Adam's heartfelt praise came from his place near the window. "If this is how you sound after a long absence from the piano, how will you sound after some practice?"

"Are you always kind, Adam?"

"I'm an angel, remember?"

"You are."

In the pale light, Adam strolled unhurriedly toward the piano. "Scoot over," he said, touching her arm. "Let me pull the bench over so I can sit."

Sarah folded the music and laid it on the floor beside her. She laid her straw hat with the textured green ribbon in her lap, pulled her hair back away from her face and let it fall down her back, and then donned the hat once again.

"Do you sing, Mrs. Finfield?" Adam inquired of the widow.

"Hmmm…I guess it depends on who you ask. Do you?"

"I asked first," he playfully responded.

"But do you?"

"I used to sing in the men's quartet, but now the young guys have taken over. It's fine with me. I don't sing, really. I like to. Anyway, do you know an old song called, 'Day by Day'?"

"Do you mean, '*Day by day and with each passing moment?*'"

"That's it."

"Wow. It's an oldie. It was pretty popular at college."

"It was popular everywhere, I think. Will you sing it?"

"Will you sing it with me?"

"No, not this time. You sing."

"You said once before…no, not this time. Remember?"

"No."

"When you gave me the birthday cupcake I asked if you were going to sing and you said…."

"You mean the day you made your *safe* birthday wish?" He smiled. "I did, didn't I. Well, okay. Next time. For tonight, you sing. It's one of my favorites. I'll just sit back and listen."

She most assuredly knew the song. Softly and with a quiet spirit, with Adam by her side, she sang the song that many years before had touched her life…and his…for the good.

> *Day by day and with each passing moment,*
> *Strength I find to meet my trials here.*
> *Trusting in my Father's wise bestowment,*
> *I've no cause for worry or for fear.*
>
> *He whose heart is kind beyond all measure*
> *Gives unto each day what He deems best;*
> *Lovingly, it's part of pain and pleasure,*
> *Mingling toil with peace and rest.*

"You sing, Sarah," Adam stated emphatically after taking a deep breath. "If anyone ever asks you again…tell them *yes.*"

"It is Adam Cook being kind again," she responded, and as she spoke, she began to stand up. Adam caught her by the arm and pulled her back to the bench.

"Sarah, I have something to tell you." He drew in a deep breath, calling upon it to impart courage and wisdom. The next moments, he knew, would be like tiptoeing across a minefield of eggshells. The woman beside him had her eyes on the other side of the globe, as it were; a godly missionary—a new widower, himself—was waiting at the arrival gate, so to speak; the widow was a mix of strength and frailty, in a water and oil state, you might say; folk would raise their eyebrows, most likely; and, the only relational words that had ever left Sarah's lips as it had to with Adam Cook were *angel* and *big brother*. Obstacles they were, yet Adam was not to be deterred.

He began, taking her off guard with his first words: "'I know of no way to mince it in love but directly to say, I love you.'"

Glancing quickly his way and duly perplexed, Sarah found herself sorting through Adam's meaning.

"H...Henry V.," she stuttered. "Henry V. Act V." She searched Adam's handsome face. It gave him away.

"I took a chance," he said, returning her glance and smiling. "You know your Shakespeare."

"Adam...."

"Please, Sarah, let me finish." He positioned one elbow on the music ledge, his head resting upon his hand, his gaze upon her. She turned away. The piano light cast a glow downward, creating shadows on their faces. Sarah stared at the piano keys. "I have fought this," Adam continued. "I have fought it fiercely, but not anymore, and I don't know any other way to do this but directly to say, 'I love you.' I know that I love you, Sarah, because I can't imagine the rest of my life without you. You might, then, question my love for Melanie, and that would be a reasonable, even levelheaded, question. What quality of love is there in a man who would wish to marry again in a little more than a year after claiming a flawless marriage to his first wife? It is because of that very marriage, Sarah, and because I tasted the love of the grandest woman on earth. Only a fool would not hope for it again.

"I'm free as a bird to speak to you of this because I'm in the dark about what's going on inside of you. When you told me tonight that you're leaving tomorrow, I knew I couldn't let you go without telling you how I feel."

Sitting up now, he tenderly placed his hand beneath her chin and turned her face towards his and with unmistakable intention, finished his romantic proposal, his face very close to hers.

"I'm asking you to marry me, Sarah Liselle Finfield...not necessarily today, not necessarily tomorrow, but not a long way off either. Sarah, Sarah, Sarah, how you have captivated me!" he went on, gazing into her beautiful green eyes. "You are lovely and inspiring. I want you to be my wife and I want to be your husband—caring for you, admiring you, and loving you.

"There. I'm done," he said, firmly taking her lovely tanned hand. "I have confessed what is in my heart. Will you marry me, Sarah?"

For a moment she studied his face and then turned away. She looked down at her hand, still in Adam's; then, she ever so gently took it from his grip and folded both hands in her lap.

"Adam," she said just above a whisper, striving to speak with a controlled voice—and without making eye contact, "Scott...has asked me to marry him."

The carpenter was not shocked; nevertheless, her words jolted his heart—though he did his best to regain his emotional footing quickly. Had he not gone into this declaration of love knowing full well that a Dolan/Finfield wedding could be in the works? Still, her words were not the ones he was longing to hear. He sighed. He knew exactly what needed to be said, yet he waited a few starkly silent moments before going on.

"I'm not really surprised. What was your answer?"

Sarah, too, took time before answering.

"I told him that I couldn't possibly give him an answer after only being with him two short weeks; but I also readily—and gladly—agreed to return to Mexico so that we could be together and talk."

Adam left her side and walked once again to stand at the window where the moon illuminated his face.

"Well, Sarah, I actually realized that such a thing might be true; but I made up my mind not to let you go without telling you what is in my heart. No matter what the future holds, I'm glad I did. Every night, I climb into bed, lay my head on the pillow, and say, 'Father, I want what you want for my life.'" He stopped and turned unhurriedly, his eyes fixed upon her shadowed, enchanting face. "I'm hoping that includes you, Sarah Liselle."

Adam moved from where he was standing and walked around to the other side of the bench. He reached down, lifted the straw hat from her head, ruffled her hair lightly, placed a lingering kiss upon her shiny hair, and then replaced the hat. He drew in a deep breath.

"You're the prettiest girl at the party, Mrs. Finfield," he said.

The mantel clock chimed nine thirty. At nine thirty three, the carpenter's truck turned onto Timber Lane.

∾∾∾∾∾

In the dark and dimly lighted and forsaken neighborhood of

Wentworth Street and First Avenue, a fine carpenter, dressed in a tan sport coat, his tie loosened at the collar, climbed into his truck and started the engine. The famous clock on the old shoe factory showed a bit after ten thirty. He slowly pulled from his parking spot.

Sure enough, Harold Barkley had seen it all; yet, he was not willing to talk, that is, at first. Nevertheless, drawing on all the toughness he could muster, Adam Cook had convinced him of the advantages of talking to him rather than ever meeting up with Richard Payce. Harold told all. If he lived long enough to see the trial of the publishing tycoon, his testimony would implicate the Payces, of arson, at least. Harold's description of the two who entered and exited the building after Herman left for Smitty's was explicit: A man who seemed to look like Cary Grant and a roly-poly man that he called Father. The two, Harold Barkley told Adam, had left in a hurry under cover of an unusually dark night. Had he seen Herman Lichten return? No, he had not.

Mr. Barkley presented Adam with a first-hand account of the explosion and fire—from his point of view. It had shaken his building, too, and had broken every pane of glass. It came not ten minutes after the men left. It was all very strange, Harold admitted to Adam.

The old man left first and five minutes later—or less—came the two men dressed in suits. Had they not left stealthily and in great haste, he never would have thought the fire to be more than just "that old building finally meeting its demise." But he had seen them and he had suspicions right from the start. No one ever thought to ask him, he guessed, if he had seen anything. That was a year ago. Now, he told Adam, it had sort of gone from his mind.

Adam left after he informed Harold that the police would no doubt be stopping by. Now in his truck, as he meandered down the streets of the rundown part of town, Adam's concentration was far from being fixed upon the story of Payce and Barkley. Talking to Harold had been encased within parentheses—on one side, a marvelous evening with Sarah ending in his declaration of love, and on the other side, an emotional aftermath stemming from her refusal—no, not a refusal, but rather, an announcement—one he would have preferred never to have heard.

He pointed his truck toward the interstate and when it came time to choose East or West, he headed to where the sun sets. Without concern for the hour or the miles, he drove through the night, drawing once again on the therapeutic benefits of a jaunt in his truck. The memory of every moment since the day he introduced himself to Sarah Finfield at the front door of Timber Lane until tonight went through his mind, step by step, in nearly chronological order.

The night passed quickly at first, but physical and emotional weariness began to set in and Adam found himself watching desperately for the pale dawning of the morning in his rear view mirror. At 5:30 a.m., he witnessed the rising of the sun between two buildings—a bank and a bakery—as he stood waiting for his gas tank to fill. The letters high atop the bank glowed in the rising sun: First National Bank of Omaha. He was in Nebraska. He didn't care; it really was not far enough.

Now, as he once more headed west, the daylight gave him freedom to think, unlike the hours of darkness which, in his wearied state of mind, required almost full concentration on driving. How had this happened to him, this fervent love for Sarah? He had not seen it coming. He had kept Melanie in a safe spot while engulfed in protecting Sarah and restoring order in her life in the worst of circumstances. Where had love for the widow come from? She had been his client, his customer, then, friends, but only friends. Now, it was true, the friendship had blossomed; but when and where had love stolen into the story?

He traveled on not considering the time of day or where exactly he was on the map, besides somewhere in the middle of the United States. His thoughts were on the lovely widow of Timber Lane, and on the strong probability that she would soon slip through his fingers. Ah, no! Things do not slip through the fingers of those who know and love Almighty God. He gently takes them and replaces them with something better.

Well into Nebraska, the pace slowed considerably as the driver of the Adam Cook Carpentry truck settled down in his spirit. Still his heart was stirred with love for Sarah, but now his love for God began to come into view much like the dawn of the day had done. A life with Sarah might not be in the category of *God's Best* for him; that was a strong possibility and he struggled with that. Yes, he had prayed the same prayer each night before bed for years, on his knees, never wavering in sincerity: "I really do want what you want for my life—no disclaimers." Adam recognized the difference between all those nights and now.

"This, I guess, is when I find out if I really meant it."

By the time Adam drove into Cheyenne, WY, he was fatigued and drained. He was worn out, so much so that at 6:40 p.m., he fell asleep in his truck in the parking lot of a closed medical building. Four hours later, he awoke. It was September 8th.

He checked his phone. There were no calls from Sarah.

CHAPTER 32

The deck was finished. The lawn had been mowed one last time, at least by Adam. The **FOR SALE** sign, still in the same place it had been for a month, had been updated. **SOLD**—the diagonal banner read. Inside the house, Sarah's key sat in the middle of the kitchen table with a short note.

Sarah had sent an unnerving text message that began with the word "Wedding," and apologetically went on to ask Adam to please take the Jaguar to his house temporarily; the contents of the house would be placed in storage by the movers on the last day of September. He had responded with a simple, "Sure," but his answer went against his heart's determination to walk away fully from the world of Sarah Finfield. He had put the finishing touches on the deck and had given the waterfall a facelift; with some pruning and edging, the grounds now looked nicely manicured. Hot and sweaty, Adam had completed the tasks while simultaneously grappling with just how one carries on after such an abrupt ending to a pleasant episode of life. Some of the time he was mentally robust and actually energized about the next phase before him, but he knew that as long as he was tied down, to any extent at all, to 12006 Timber Lane, a true recovery could not begin.

So, in a rather hurried frame of mind, he wrapped things up, working toward that final climb up into his truck—into Silver Sarah. He hesitated for a moment before pulling the kitchen door closed, thinking through his words on the note. Once the door was shut, there would be no opportunity to revise his short message; Sarah's house would be forever inaccessible.

All is done. Glad to see that you are doing well. It has been quite a ride. May God bless you with the best of His blessings in the future. Adam, Y.P.A.

Chastising himself for spending too much time deliberating, he gave the door a decisive yank. A chapter in the life of Adam Cook had now truly come to an end.

こうこうこうこうこう

September 30th appeared as it always does after the 29th, but today was the day Sarah's house was to be emptied. Had it not been for an unexpected stopover at O'Hare for Daniel, Adam felt pretty sure that even though he had severed the ties to the place, he would have been drawn to be at the Timber Lane house just to guarantee a smooth operation. The call from Daniel, however, rescued him from himself, and resulted in a joyful scurry through rush hour traffic to spend two hours with his son, and as he drove, there was a smile on Adam Cook's face rather than the normal wrinkled brow of late. *"I am suspicious of God in this unexpected stopover,"* he mused on his way to the airport. *"It is just like Him to send me a Special Delivery on a hard day."* It would be good to see Daniel. Nothing in the whole world would have the healing effect on his wounded heart as would a couple of hours with his own flesh and blood.

The two chatted quietly in a sandwich shop, so glad to be together. Adam listened as Daniel told as much of his secret orders to leave immediately for Japan as he could. He would return in six months and then after one more year, be done.

"So, Dad, what's happening since I talked to you the last time?"

"I'm actually done...finished...at Timber Lane. Getting calls from some of the old customers!"

"Well, that's good, right?"

"Yep. Hey, I made something for you." Adam reached into his shirt pocket and retrieved the little gift that he had planned to send to his son. "I'm glad I remembered it. I was going to send it but this is better."

Daniel chuckled as he looked at the keychain. "Scrabble letters, eh?"

"Yeah, Scrabble letters just glued around a little wood cube. Do you see what it says?"

"Uh, um...uh, it says 'NAILED.' What's that all about?"

"No, Daniel, it says 'DANIEL!'" Adam said, reaching for it.

"Just kidding, Dad. I know it says 'DANIEL.'"

"Hmph. You got me. You're right though! It does say 'NAILED!' That's a riot. I thought you'd appreciate a reminder of our recent games," Adam joked.

"You should have made one that says 'CONTENT.'" He attached it to his key chain.

"I thought of it. One too many letters."

There was little talk of Sarah; that subject had been sufficiently talked out in their phone calls. Today, it seemed, both Adam and Daniel had put it behind them. Only as the dad and son, so bonded in spirit, stood at the gate, saying their goodbyes, was her name spoken.

"I'm sorry I bugged you about Sarah, Dad," Daniel contritely told Adam. "I've been feeling guilty about probably making it all harder for you."

"Hey, I told you before, I'm content."

"I'm sorry that she slipped through your fingers."

"Things don't slip through the fingers of Christians, Danny Boy. God gently takes them," Adam said peacefully, with firm conviction, his eyes slightly wet with tears, "and most of the time...no, all the time...He replaces them with something better."

"That's really cool, Dad. You are a wise, wise man. I guess I don't need to ask you if you're going to be okay."

"I am."

"Are you worried about her?"

"I am."

"Well, it's like I told you in the truck on the way to our fishing trip, you've got to let go and trust God, only this time, you really need to let go."

Adam put his arm around his son's neck and pulled him close, lingering there for a few moments.

"Hey, you bring me so much joy, son. Be safe. I'll see you soon."

It would take a hasty run for Daniel to make it to the gate in time, but he stopped in the middle of his jaunt and turned to say one last goodbye. He saluted, and then resumed his run.

రాళ్లు రాళ్లు రాళ్లు

On an October afternoon, the 19th to be exact, Adam worked rigorously at chopping wood for the winter. Now and then, he stopped to think on the life he had lived here on River Road, even allowing memories of the horrid day of the accident to surface. The sky was deep aqua, the color one expects on a crisp fall day. Except for some oaks, the trees were nearly bare. The pond was blue like the sky. The Nielsen house, with its fresh coat of white paint, looked lovelier than ever up on its little hill. He removed his hat. The cool wind felt good as it rumpled his hair. Just a little more wood to be chopped and he would be done.

He sat down in the lawn chair, replaced his cap, and reached for his thermos of coffee. At this exact spot, Melanie had been standing the day they lost little Sarah. *"How is it,"* he thought, *"that you can go on after such a thing? How is it that life does not just plain grind to a halt when you lose your little girl in such an awful tragedy?"* He could never forget the scene as he had come upon it that day. How could he be going on with life, building and fixing, going to church, chatting and laughing with his friends, when a mere 13 years ago such a heartbreak had fallen upon them?

The answer was in his heart. It had been there from the first glimpse of the catastrophe until this very moment: God is everything He claims to be in His Word.

"Well, Adam Cook," he said out loud, "get goin' and get this job over and done with!"

His phone vibrated and he set down the ax. He struggled to pull the phone from his front pocket. There was a text message from Sarah Finfield. Seeing her name on his phone took him off guard, simply because he had successfully run a campaign to slowly diminish the hours she was in his thoughts; Adam had learned to busy himself amply to halt the constant thinking about her. He opened his phone and went to the message.

"I never thought I could love again," it read.

What first came to mind were the words, *"How nice for Sarah!"* The next thought was, *"How…could she ever send such a message?"* Had he really not gotten to know her at all? Perhaps he had missed a part of her—a flaw, maybe—a characteristic that kept her from understanding passion and hurt. Evidently she had not gotten it, his declaration of love, and still considered him *The Yellow Pages Angel* or worse yet, her *big brother!* Adam wished he could retrieve his note sitting on her kitchen table and erase the silly initials after his name.

He looked at the message on his phone again. His reaction bothered him. Why was he so upset? The answer dawned slowly. Evidently, Sarah meant it when she declared that they would always be good friends. How possible that had seemed at that moment! Now Adam was quite sure that he could not endure ongoing news of her.

Back to woodcutting he went, taking out his irritation and confusion on the pieces of tree trunk. He vacillated between spouting his resentment and having a talk with his Heavenly Father. He decided to do both.

"Father, You've got to help me out. You know that I was doing fine until this. Such a message, Lord! I have the right to be upset here, don't I? I need help! I need Your help. Please help me to conquer this, okay?"

The four o'clock sun fell upon Adam's cheeks as he sat on the back stairs, extremely exhausted from the afternoon's long stretch of hard physical labor. He did his best to disregard Sarah's message; finally, he pulled his phone from his pocket again and intentionally deleted it. Feeling a little stiff, he arose and went into the house, took a Coke from the refrigerator, and headed to get the mail. A car was coming down River Road; that was not unusual but the fact that it stopped at Adam's gate, was. It was a hotel courtesy car. His expression was inquisitive. Someone was getting out of the passenger side.

Sarah Liselle Finfield, poised and beautiful, walked leisurely around the back of the car as it drove away, dressed in a long, light-weight taupe coat, a brown turtleneck showing above the collar, and on her head, the green and brown straw hat Adam had adored. She slung the long strap of her brown leather purse over her shoulder and slowly sauntered toward the very surprised carpenter.

"Howdy," she said with a delicate smile, holding her hat in place.

"Sarah."

"I've come for the Jaguar," she declared cheerfully, coming to stand near him at the mailbox. The fragrance of a fine perfume accompanied her. *"Jasmine,"* he mused.

"I thought you were on the other side of the world."

"I was."

A very rapid battle took place in the mind of Adam Cook as he tried to decide whether to just go fetch the Jaguar or offer Sarah a seat on the front porch...and a Coke.

"Are you in a hurry?" he said, not fully sure what he hoped her answer would be.

"Not really," she replied.

"Come on, then, let's have a Coke together on the porch."

"I'd like that," she agreed.

Taken with how beautiful Sarah looked—and knowing full well that he could not tell her so—Adam, still in his plaid shirt, the sleeves rolled up, and wood chips clinging to his jeans, walked slowly through the house, soundly exhorting himself: "Be still, Adam Cook. Keep your head on straight."

"How are you doin'?" he asked upon returning with her soda. He moved the chairs to be facing each other.

"Let's sit on the steps, okay?" she suggested. "Do you mind?"

First Sarah sat and then Adam sat beside her, drinking in the beauty of a woman not quite so thin and drawn as at their last encounter, vibrant and even more poised than ever. She looked well and healthy...and happy.

"I'm doing very well. Can't you tell?"

"I can. When did you get back?"

"I've been back a little while. Did you get my message?"

Of course, he had, but how to handle an unexpected conversation on the topic was another issue. He took note of the knot forming in his stomach.

"Yep," he said, struggling with what more to say. "It...was not exactly the easiest message in the world, you must know. Yet...I can't help but be happy for you and Scott." Adam's words came slowly, with the characteristic pauses between thoughts. "It's okay. I'm glad you're able to love again, as you put it. It's a good thing, Sarah. Really. I mean that. You're young and it makes sense for you and Scott to have found each other again, so to speak."

"I have something for you to see." Sarah pulled a fine off-white envelope from her purse and handed it to him.

"What is this, Sarah?"

"It's the wedding invitation—and you're invited."

Adam leaned against the stair railing, stretched out his legs, and laid the invitation on the step between them. In unbelief, he stared at the yard light near the road searching for civility and for words to speak to the woman beside him. Then he turned to look at her.

"Why would you do this?" he said, exasperated, his expression a mix of perplexity and displeasure. "I remember you once telling me that I didn't know you very well. It appears that you were right." With a slight, slow shake of his head, he said, "I guess I don't." He stood and walked to the bottom of the stairs and then faced her. "If you remember, on that same day I told you that you must not know me well, either. Do you remember?"

She nodded and said, "I remember."

"Do you not know that this would hurt, Sarah, being invited to your wedding? Do you honestly think I would even consider going? You must think I'm made of steel or something. Why would you do this? Because we are friends? A friend wouldn't do this to a friend."

"But a friend would do this *for* a friend."

"Would they?"

"I would. Is it so strange that I would like you to be at my wedding after all that we've been through together?" She sighed. "Adam, if you really don't want to read it, it's okay."

He stuck his fingers into his front jeans pockets and stared down at the sidewalk for a good long time, regrouping; then, reluctantly, and with eyes now on Sarah's face, he motioned for her to hand the cream colored envelope to him. Slowly, he pulled the invitation from inside. He was not pleased, but at the entreating eyes of Sarah, he opened it and silently read.

Sarah Liselle Finfield

and

Adam Benjamin Cook
request the honor of your presence
at their marriage
on Saturday, October 29, 2005

There was more, but he stopped. Adam squinted at the page and then without lifting his head, moved his eyes to meet Sarah's. She saw the tiny, tiny smile of confusion on his lips even before he knew it was there and she smiled back at him, coyly. She removed her hat, hung it on the post next to her and began a slow, easy walk down the stairs toward Adam.

"Will you come?" she asked, a twinge of teasing in her voice.

Adam studied her bright face as she spoke. "I don't understand this, Sarah."

"Why? What's not to understand? You're invited to be at the wedding of Sarah Liselle Finfield and Adam Benjamin Cook."

He stood stock still, a thousand thoughts darting in and out of his unsettled mind.

"Were you not to marry Scott in the very near future?" he asked after a few moments. "Did you not text me with a simple message, 'Wedding,' and another telling me that you never thought you could love again?"

"Adam," Sarah said earnestly, now standing before him, "it is not Scott who has revived my love." Unfalteringly, she took his hands in both of hers and spoke to him serenely. "It is **you**. When I texted you, I was speaking of **you**... intentionally misleading you, hoping to come and surprise you."

"You succeeded."

"How else could I have done it," she animatedly said, her voice just above a whisper, "just barge in and tell you that I've reconsidered and my answer is now *yes?* I was a little nervous about that! Besides...I wanted to tell you in the most special way that I could think of, something that you would never forget."

"I think you've succeeded," Adam said again, still attempting to put the pieces together.

"Oh, Adam, the words you spoke to me that night at the piano after such a good evening together have not left my heart, not once, even though in a confused and somewhat unsteady frame of mind I went ahead with plans to marry Scott, and I suppose not too far down the road."

Adam's expression cast a question mark at her.

"What...did he stand you up again?"

"No. I beat him to it."

"And what does that mean?"

She did not answer. Adam paused and then asked his next question. "Why did you do that?"

"Two reasons," she said, her voice steady as she spoke the whole crux of the matter. "He said all the wrong things and you said all the right ones."

Adam let out a frustrated sigh, remaining silent an uncomfortable length of time. At last, he spoke.

Gently grasping her shoulder, he called upon her to make things clear. "Be patient with me here, Sarah. You know me. I'm gonna need a little more information."

"Okay, but really, all you need to know is that I love you, Adam, and I accept your proposal of marriage." She laughed lightly. "I guess. though, I'm taking a lot for granted."

"Sarah, tell me what happened," he softly said, moving his hand for a moment against her cheek. "I need to know."

"Well," she said, after taking a long and very deep breath, "basically...almost in the act of putting a ring on my finger, Scott said, 'I hope we're doing the right thing,' if you can grasp such a thing. You, on the other hand, told me that you couldn't imagine living the rest of your life without me. Do you catch the catastrophic difference? So, right there, in that restaurant in Mexico City, our wise God—I'm sure it was Him—put up a big, red, six-sided Stop sign right in between Scott and me." She hesitated for a moment and then kind of whispered her next words. "Before the ring ever made it to my finger, I stopped him—just like that."

Adam looked down and held up his hand.

"Wait, wait, wait, Sarah. This is going very fast. Don't get me wrong, I like fast, but sometimes I listen kind of slow. What does it mean—'I stopped him, just like that'?"

"I stopped him, just like that, and said, 'Scottie, this just isn't a good thing. I know it and I think you do, too.' Then I said all the things someone says when they're sorry for making a mess of things and I swore to him that I was not paying him back. I gave him my full forgiveness for standing me up years ago which, to be honest, I really had never done."

Adam brushed off his jeans and then sat down on a lower step. He motioned for Sarah to sit beside him. He reached for her hand and requested that she tell him everything.

"Okay. Everything. By the way," she said, looking sheepishly at him, "I didn't tell him about the stop sign."

There was a faint smile in his eyes as he responded. "That was probably wise."

"Well, anyway, we had a good long and healthy talk after the engagement ring episode, Scott Dolan and I did. He told me that he ended the relationship in college because he never discerned a missionary heart in me."

"What exactly is a *missionary heart?*" Adam asked skeptically, "and why didn't he tell you that then instead of dropping you like a hot potato an hour before the wedding?"

"Well, he sort of did, I guess. He told me that being in love wasn't enough and that it appeared that I was going to be a missionary because he was going to be a missionary. He was right about that, but I still don't see that as a bad thing. But that being said, I'm pretty sure he didn't tell the whole truth and nothing but the truth. He didn't mention Missions Major Chloe Kelleher waiting in the wings. I just found out that they got married three months later. Well anyway, it's clear to me that both times I was going to go to a far off land with my *missionary heart,* it was for the wrong reasons."

"I've been worried, Sarah."

"I guess you had reason to be."

"I didn't want you to be hurt again."

"I'm quite certain that this Mexico thing was an escape for me. I had no clear call from God to go to Mexico; no," she moaned, "...this lonely widow was hearing the voice of a lonely widower with two children." Sarah hesitated suddenly, looking up into the sky. "Isn't this just a beautiful day?" she exclaimed. "I love the sky in the fall. It's turquoise! It's absolutely cloudless!" She closed her eyes. "How good to be alive! I'm glad to be alive and I'm glad it's not raining!" she said, turning to Adam and taking his arm. "How would I have been able to tell you all of this under an umbrella!" She laughed. Her face sparkled. "Not very romantic, that's for sure!"

"Ah, Sarah," he softly said, 'it's nice to hear you laughing."

"You have no idea how wonderful it is to be laughing and...and loving the outdoors again! It tells the whole story."

"Let's walk, Sarah Liselle," he said just above a whisper. "I want to hear the whole story."

"Such a good idea! Let me get my hat."

Down River Road they went, saying nothing for a great stretch of road. Indeed it was a classic fall day. Browns had begun to replace the greens all around them. The hot and muggy days were gone; now crisp moderate days took their place. A brisk wind stirred up the dry autumn fields and occasionally whipped up the gravel dust, swirling it on the road ahead of them. It was a perfect day for walking and talking with a friend.

Sarah and Adam slowly ambled in step with each other, looking ahead most of the time; now and then their eyes met, and now and then they stopped and talked face to face in the middle of the road.

"You asked me before when I got back and I told you, 'a little while ago.' Actually, I got back on October 1st."

Adam interrupted. "October 1st? Here?"

"Back to the good old U.S. If things would have gone as originally planned, today would have happened on October 1st. But I longed to be sure. I decided to wait on the Lord and go slow. It was not an easy decision, believe me. I had come back just aching to rush right over here that day, but I knew that it was not the best way. I stayed at the hotel, much of the time on my knees entreating God to clarify His will in this thing. And I fasted...and researched, too."

Adam wanted to ask what exactly one researches when trying to ascertain matters of love, but the answer came without asking.

"I have had delightful visits with my pastor and yours." She folded her arms, pleasant peace upon her face.

"You've spent time with Pastor Pruitt?" he inquired, surprised.

"Twice with him and once, dinner with him and Pamela."

Now Adam halted their walk and turned to face her. He smiled and looked at her in amused unbelief. "You—had dinner with Tom and Pam?"

"Yes! A delightful dinner!" she responded spritely. "I had to find out if you are as wonderful as it seems. And you must know that they told me a lot of stuff."

"I bet." Adam took up walking again, casually putting his arm around Sarah and resting it on her shoulder.

"What a man you are...unless they were lying!" Sarah stopped as she struggled to tame her hair and her hat in the wind. "I heard about the Troopers that you started after Melanie died," she said. "You never told me about them."

"No. There was no reason to, I guess."

"And you know what else? He shared something very interesting with me."

"Hmph. I bet. In fact, I bet I know what's coming."

"He told me that you have been talking and talking to him about the need for the teen girls to go, too, to help in the orphanage but that you did not feel free to take them without female supervision...and what a problem that posed! He said you have been fairly exasperated."

"Hmm. He told you all that, did he?"

"Yes, and it was part of my confirmation." Excited and spirited, in a way Adam had never witnessed in the widow, Sarah spoke with great enthusiasm. "I'd **love** to go, Adam! I'd **love** to take a bunch of girls to Honduras! I'd **love** to do a short missions trips there and minister in that orphanage with ten awesome teen girls! I've wished for such a thing long before I ever met you."

"You have?"

"Yes, I have. I always yearned to go on a short missions trip with kids, maybe college kids, but Chip never did think those trips were a good idea for some reason. There's more to say on that, but for now, let me go on with...the rest of the story."

Settling down a bit now, Sarah picked up where she had left off.

"I met with my pastor, too. I had to. I knew I needed to." She sighed and went on. "I've always been a very capable and sensible person—mostly—and yet, as I evaluated myself on the plane coming home, I realized that my recent decisions have not shown that to be so. I decided to get some needed counsel for myself and to find out what he thought about...well, about you and me."

She stopped and detained him. Then she turned to face him.

"Adam," she said, "I came here today after all of that, and I have the peace that passes understanding about coming to you and speaking my heart. Like I said before, Sarah Finfield did not have her head on straight when she trekked off to Mexico. Sarah Finfield was escaping. And you know what? I think you knew that."

Adam nodded slowly. "I did, but I couldn't say anything."

Looking hard into Sarah's face, with wrinkled brow and holding her lovely hand in his large rough ones, he asked for an answer to his burning question: "And how is it that Sarah Finfield is sure about spending the rest of her life with me?"

Sarah turned so that the east wind would aid her in the fight to keep her hair out of her face. "The answer to that question," she said, holding onto her hat, "is quite clear to me. My dear friend, Adam, I will marry you because there are no doubts in my mind or heart about your love for me. Can you even imagine how your words and actions—not just at the piano, but at the restaurant and in the truck driving home—how they lingered with me even as I boarded the plane for Mexico and the whole time I was there? The strange reality is that I believe that I have slowly grown to love and trust you bit by bit since the day we met and didn't realize it."

Sarah's hair was annoying her greatly. She stopped, handed the hat to Adam, found a hair clip in her purse, and pulled her hair up into a knot that would fit very nicely beneath the hat.

"There! My hair was driving me crazy!" she cheerfully exclaimed. She plunked the hat on her head. "Ah, yes!" she said, taking up their walk once again, "that is much better!" Now, holding on to her lovely straw hat, she went to stand directly in front of Adam. There she finished her declaration.

"Adam. Adam. You are no second prize," she lovingly said, her eyes sparkling. "You are a first prize man! I am standing in the middle of River Road with an amazing man and have not a doubt in the world about his genuine love for me. You told me in the glow of the piano light that you had known the love of the grandest woman on earth and that only a fool would pass up a chance at that again. I can say the same thing!" she fervently avowed. "You are an excellent man! Only a fool would pass up the chance to spend her life with someone like you."

She leaned her forehead against his shoulder; he spread his strong, rugged hand behind her neck.

"And I am no fool," she declared ever so softly.

CHAPTER 33

When at last, they reached the foot path to the river, Adam took Sarah's hand, and together they walked until they came to a little bridge that crossed over to the other side. It was cooler here beneath the tall trees, and serenely beautiful.

"You've been here before," Sarah said. "I can tell."

"See that tree trunk over there? That's where I fish."

"No wonder. It's incredibly awesome in here!" she said, looking around and leaning up against the bridge. "It looks like maybe that path climbs to somewhere. Right?"

"Yep, it does. It's a good climb to the top—sometimes a little treacherous, but there's a prize when you get to the top...an incredible view. I think I can see Cheyenne, Wyoming from up there," he said, softly laughing.

"Maybe someday soon we can make that climb together," Sarah suggested with peace and confidence coming through her whole manner. "I'd love that."

Adam left his spot leaning against the other side of the bridge and walked to Sarah. There he stood in front of her. He took her hands in his. He said nothing. At first. Instead, he studied every part of her fine face, and looked into her emerald eyes, searching her soul.

"Do you love me, Sarah?" he asked very simply, his face overflowing with his deep love for her.

The soft squint of the eyes, the slight tilt of her head, and the expression on the face of Sarah Liselle, the quiet, staid widow of Timber Lane, told it all, but she pulled their hands into a clasp between them and there on the rickety wooden bridge over the White Rock River, tenderly spoke the words that were in her heart.

"I love you, Adam Cook, and I want to be your wife," she said convincingly."

How quiet it was, except for the sound of the river rushing over the rocks and the joyful melody of a robin's evening hymn. The late afternoon sun found a few openings in the tree branches to shine

361

through upon the romantic scene and put a sparkle on the bubbling water.

There was a pause—not an awkward pause, yet enough time for Sarah to choose her words well. "I need for you to know that this is no frivolous escapade on my part, nor is it an escape," she said, tears gathering in her eyes. "You have grown on me and I trust you and respect you highly. I thought it was just admiration, but then, my vision cleared and I recognized that it was love. You are such a man of character. By the way," she laughed softly, "you got an A+ from your pastor."

"I pay him well," Adam said, grinning.

"Adam, you are such a man of kindness...and, mostly, such a man of God. Your walk with God has stirred me. I will never forget your prayer for me the night I told you about Char, nor your exhortation about kindness and forgiveness at the restaurant. Dear Adam, there is not a speck of apprehension in confessing my love for you.

"Now," she said, making a frolicking move to take up walking again, "I guess I'm taking a lot for granted." Adam reached out and pulled her back. She smiled. "Perhaps," she teased mischievously, "I shouldn't just assume that you still feel the same way about me as you did sitting next to me on the piano bench."

The carpenter of Timber Lane slowly shook his head, looking into her green eyes, and smiling. Then, with both of his rough hands on either side of her face, Adam drew the elegant widow close and kissed her, a kiss that needed no explanation. "I love you more," he said, before kissing her again, his voice husky and emotional. He put his arms on her shoulders and gazed upon her beautiful face and into her lovely eyes, and with a slight, amused shake of his head, said, "Somehow...I love you more."

He pulled her close, remembering his prayer to God on County Road B in the wee hours of the morning.

"Thank You, Father. You are good to me," he silently prayed.

"I didn't know what to expect," she whispered in his ear. "I had to take a chance."

"Silly girl," Adam replied. "I've loved you for a very long time, Mrs. Finfield."

"Now, Adam, we've only known each other four months," Sarah chided him lightheartedly.

"It's the quality that makes me say that, Sarah, not the quantity. Four months of you is...a lifetime."

Adam gently removed Sarah's straw hat and removed the clip holding her hair in a messy little bunch at the top of her head. Then he ruffled it until it cascaded down her back. He pulled some of it to fall in front of her shoulders. The fragrance of jasmine, faint and sweet, hovered in the crisp river air. Annette's description of him on County Road B—*macho man*—came to mind and Adam was sure that it was happening again.

"Will you marry me?" he asked, placing her very nice hat once again upon her head.

"Yes."

He kissed her again and again.

"Soon?" he asked.

"You saw the date."

"That was a real date?" he asked, holding her away from him.

She sighed. "Yes, it is the last weekend that Pastor Samuelson will be pastor at my church and it is the only Saturday that Char can make it before next January!"

Adam could not help himself. He laughed gustily there in the quiet woods.

"So then, my sweet conniving fiancé...a week from Saturday we will marry?"

Sarah freed herself from his embrace.

"Yes. I'm thinking that we have to! I don't have anywhere to live!" she answered with delight. "Well," she went on with a sigh, "I guess that's really not true. I've still got Chip's folks' house."

Adam shook his head very slowly, leaving no doubts as to his verdict on that idea.

"October 29th it will be. Ten days of living out of a hotel will not be so bad, right?"

"I can do that."

"Come, sweet Sarah Liselle. Let's walk again."

Over the bridge, down the path that bordered the other side of the river, out into a grassy meadow they walked, Adam with his arm around Sarah's shoulder, Sarah with her hand holding her hat down.

"It seems to me that you once told me that my place seemed like home," Adam said. "In fact, I can almost quote you. They were nice words. You know...those kind Sarah-Finfield words."

"What did I say?"

"You said, 'I like this place, Adam. It's like...well, it's like home.'"

"I meant those words. I have loved my ranch house, but that day, when I gazed upon your home and the whole setting, I knew in my heart that a person would be blessed to be able call it home."

"You will think of Pitman and River Roads as home?"

"I already do," she announced softly. "I already do."

"Ah, Sarah! Such a woman you are! If I had to choose a woman to be my wife," he jested, "it would be you!"

"Sorry. I'm spoken for."

"Yes, you are."

"How odd this all is," Sarah said, keeping step with Adam. "It appears that God was paving the way, even back then when I commented on your lovely house."

"Well, perhaps, but He gave me a scare, that's for sure. I had a hard time that night at the piano when you brushed me off."

"I'm sorry," she groaned so apologetically. "Sarah did not have her head on straight quite yet. What did you do when you left?"

"What do you think I did?"

"Uh, did you go for a ride?"

"Yep. I took a drive in the truck and had a long, long conversation with the Lord."

"I should not have had to ask. Where did you go?"

Adam took Sarah by the hand.

"Want to keep walking?"

"Sure, but I thought maybe you'd like to take the Jag for a spin!"

He laughed quietly.

"We could do that, I suppose."

"We could walk for a while more. I love to walk in the fall. Then later, let's go wherever it was that you went that night."

Adam laughed quietly again.

"Are you up for a trip to Cheyenne, Wyoming?"

"What!"

"Never mind that. Come on, Sarah Finfield. Let's walk to the grove and then take the shortcut back."

"Tell me you didn't really go all the way to Cheyenne."

"I had to. It took that long to straighten my head out."

On they walked, in step with each other, Sarah's hat in one hand now and the other in the grip of her *first prize man*. A flock of geese flew overhead in perfect formation. Sarah and Adam both looked up and took time to watch them in their flight.

"That's incredible!"

"The geese? It's awesome!"

"No, your very long journey to the west!"

"Well, it's a little indicator of the condition of my heart."

Sarah stopped to gather up some blue cornflowers.

"I need to 'fess up to you," she said, looking up at Adam.

"What? Another Sarah Finfield confession?"

"Yes, another one," she groaned, joining him once again.

"Confess Sarah," he urged her. "I'm listening."

"I need to 'fess up to you that you nearly conquered me with your magnificent proposal." Speaking now with great fervor, Sarah said, "It was like...like...something you'd read in a passionate romance novel! It could not be simply shrugged off because, in reality, everything I know about you substantiated your every word."

"Magnificent proposals come easy when there's someone like you at the other end. Had you not told me of Scott's proposal, I would have ended the evening differently. It seemed rather cold to kiss you on the head and walk out. That's not what I wanted to do."

"You didn't just walk out. You said I was the prettiest girl at the party. *Then* you walked out. I've heard you say that before. What's the significance of that?"

One of those Adam chuckles was her answer.

"Come on, tell me."

"Well, okay. I guess I can tell you now. One night after a party at someone's house, on the way home, Daniel—who was only four at the time—said, 'Daddy, you know how to pick 'em. Mommy was the prettiest girl at the party...and the most nicest.' So, that just became our way of describing a splendid woman."

"Four years old, huh?" Sarah said, now clinging to Adam's arm. "Already noticing. Hmm."

"Well, now it's my turn to 'fess up," Adam said. "You ready?"

"Oh, yes! Misery loves company."

"Well, on The Night of the Drywall, when I pulled my truck up on that dark country road, and I found out that you were all right— except for the ankle—when I lifted you into my arms and carried you to the truck, I knew then."

"You knew what?"

"That I loved you. I fell really hard for you that night."

"I had no idea."

"You do now," he said, squeezing her arm against him.

The sun hung low over the great farms in the distance. In less than an hour it would be off to the other side of the world. The two made their way north to the grove and south down the shortcut to Adam's house...soon to be the home of Adam and Sarah Cook.

The conversation was different today than it had been over dinner at Stonegate. There they had been friends; now they were lovers. With sweet communion they walked together as one and they chatted warmly about everything that has to do with spending life together as man and wife.

❧ ❧ ❧ ❧ ❧

Adam could not help but smile. He was getting his first try at handling such a car as Chip's Jaguar. Sarah sat joyfully beside him, her hand on his brawny arm.

"Adam, I have just one more thing to ask you."

"And what's that?"

"What in the world did Daniel say to you the night he came home!" she griped.

Cruising along now, taking a lengthy stretch of Halliday Road north, Adam put his arm around Sarah and pulled her a little closer.

"You...are a character. You just won't let that alone, will you."

"I told you that I have a tough time with curiosity."

"I guess I can tell you now," he said with another of his famous chuckles. "I had told him that it was kind of lonely out here now, with Melanie and him gone, and he asked me—sort of choking on his words—'Yeah, well who was that gorgeous woman in the BMW?' And then he got down real close to my face and told me very soberly, 'Dad, don't let that beautiful woman slip through your fingers.'"

Sarah laughed heartily. "Oh, that's too funny! He was playing Cupid! It must run in the family, this angel thing."

"Hadn't thought about that. He would not accept my explanation that you were my client and I was your carpenter...and perhaps he was right."

"You called me that night to check on me, remember?"

"I know. It appears that I was falling for you long before the County Road B midnight rescue. In fact, Sarah, the day Scott came, the day I saw the *Sarah Liselle Finfield* Bible...remember that day?...I knew something was up when I got out to my truck and kicked my tire before getting in. I am not the type to kick my tire!"

How wonderful to be together, laughing and anticipating a day not too far off when they would be together for the rest of their lives.

"That's pretty early on!" Sarah commented.

"I'm pretty sure that I didn't connect the dots until much later, but looking back, I know something was up!"

"I have to say that it crossed my mind—for a split second—that you might be interested, the night you called. Well, anyway, won't it be fun to tell Daniel the news. Where are we going, Adam Cook?"

"Want to go to Cheyenne?"

"You mean...?"

"Sure! Let's go to Cheyenne and get engaged!"

"You mean...? Adam, are you serious?"

"Sure! Why not? Let's up and go right now. We'll just take our time...uh, it's about six now...we'll stop and eat along the way and just drive slow and we'll talk all night and get there in the morning."

"That's just crazy!" Sarah declared.

"What a great way to get engaged! Never to be forgotten! Should we take this or the truck?"

"I'd say that it depends on your mood, Mr. Cook. If you want to mosey along comfortably, we should take the truck, but if you feel like sailing and having fun on those long stretches of interstate in the black of night, then let's take the Jag."

"Hmm. That's a hard one."

"Then, let me make the choice for you. Let's take Silver Sarah. I think we'll both be better off with the comfort of the truck on an escapade like this!"

"Then it's settled. We'll go back, get the truck, drive all night, look at rings in Cheyenne, put one on your finger that stays there, and then come back home and get married on Saturday, the 29th as planned by Wedding Planner, Sarah Finfield! Sarah, Sarah, you are alive and well."

"I am."

"I suppose you've lined up Daniel, too."

"No, you should be the one to tell him. Besides," Sarah said mischievously, "I didn't have his number!"

"I like the way you think, Mrs. Finfield. Ten days isn't such a long wait. Just a few people, right?"

"Yes, for sure. I did get in touch with Annette, though."

"Ah, yes, we must not forget Annette. Someday I'll tell you what she had to say about you and me."

"Someday?"

"Yep. Gotta keep you curious." Adam reached for Sarah's hand and held it tight. "I'm glad Char will be there."

"I spent three days with her, Adam," Sarah said, tears gathering in her eyes. "Thank you, my dear counselor."

"You're so welcome, my sweet Sarah. It sounds like you got a lot done in a little amount of time."

"Sarah Finfield is back."

"Yes, she is, and I, for one, am loving it!" he shouted, ruffling her hair. "Now, Mrs. Finfield, you and I, we've got a lot of catching up to do and a lot of planning. You know that, right? We'll have lots of time for that on our exciting trip to the west. You ready?"

"I'm game, but just so you know, I have to be at the house by tomorrow night for some last minute clean up. Closing is on Friday."

"I thought that it was all over with."

"It was postponed. For two weeks," Sarah groaned.

"It's not empty?"

"Almost. Just some stuff in the shed and the basement that I need to put out at the road for pickup. And a little in the garage, too."

"No problem. We'll be back tomorrow night—tired, but happily engaged!"

"We could run over there now. I'm sure it's not going to take more than an hour."

"Good thinking, Mrs. Finfield. How I love you, Sarah! I wish we were running off to get married!"

"I've been thinking the same thing!"

Timber Lane was empty. It seemed like it had died and the soul had flown away to a far off land. The beauty of the house had not diminished since Adam saw it last, but the warmth and cordiality had departed. The two walked through the cold and empty house in a final farewell to a special place in their hearts, their footsteps and voices echoing in the hollow rooms. For Sarah, this was a welcomed event; she had wished it sold for many long months.

"Well, point me in the right direction," Adam said.

"There are a bunch of empty boxes in the shed, ones that didn't get used in packing. Could you take them to the road? I'll run down to the laundry room and get that stuff."

"Then is that all?"

"No, the movers left some things in the garage. All the stuff in the middle of the garage floor goes to the road, too. It's more boxes, tarps and some other stuff...I can't recall exactly."

Adam broke down the boxes and removed them from the shed, tidied up a bit and swept the floor.

"We could just burn all this stuff," he said to himself, jockeying the boxes as he carried them to the road. Sarah joined him with two garbage bags of laundry items.

"I left some detergent down there. I hope the Foxes don't mind."

"They shouldn't. It'll be like a little extra help on the mortgage." Adam smiled and put his arm around his wife-to-be. "The stuff in the garage...is that it?"

"Yes! And I couldn't be happier!"

"This is an unusually exquisite house, you know," he declared, stopping to take one last look, his arm around the widow. "I fell in love with it the first day I came. It is unusually exquisite."

"It was. It means nothing to me now. It has meant nothing to me for a long time. Nothing."

"I think that it was reviving a little for you lately, no?"

"I can't deny that, I guess. I've had some enjoyment once again, reading in my little haven. But today, I have no sorrow at passing it on to someone else...an architect and his wife, no less." She turned toward Adam for a hug. "I'm ready for a new chapter."

"Come on then. Let's get going."

With everything at the road, Sarah grabbed a broom and gave the garage floor a thorough sweeping. Impatiently, Adam paced slowly along the back wall.

"You leaving this rake and the dustpan?"

"I think so," Sarah replied. "Why would I need them now?"

"I wonder why these garden tools are here. Everything else is in the shed." Adam was getting restless, wanting to get going.

"Maybe the realtor was dealing with the leaves on the deck."

"Do you want me to take them back to the shed?"

"No. They're fine there."

"The drywall looks pretty good, eh?"

"Oh, it does! Thanks to your expertise! I meant to say something to you. You can't even see where you cut into it."

"No one would ever know we were snooping around behind it!"

"What a night—well, actually, what a morning that was! I'm almost done here. I can't figure out what this glass is from. Why wouldn't the movers clean this up? I think I'll register a complaint."

"Hey, Sarah, are you leaving all this paint here?" Adam asked, peering into the cabinet.

"Yes, I'll leave it. All of it matches somewhere in the house."

"This cabinet is full of paint cans—15, 20—some of it looking pretty ancient...like this one. It sounds empty."

"Well, pull out the ancient ones and set them by the mailbox."

One by one, Adam pulled down the old cans of paint.

"What's with all these cereal boxes in behind the paint?"

"What cereal?" Sarah asked, pushing the last bit of debris into the dustpan.

"There's boxes of cereal in this cabinet shoved behind the paint."

"Cereal? Boxes of cereal? I know nothing about cereal in the paint cabinet. I know I didn't put it there."

"There's a bunch."

"I haven't the slightest idea why Chip would buy a lot of cereal and put it in there! It had to be him." She shook her head. "That is very strange. Well, let's just toss it. Here, take this trash bag. One should be enough. Then just take it all out to the road, okay?"

Adam took down a box of raisin bran and shook it.

"Sarah," he murmured mysteriously, "these are not new boxes. This one is open but no cereal."

"You're kidding. Why on earth would Chip....?"

"Wait, Sarah," Adam interrupted, "something else is in here."

"Something else? Like what?" The broom fell to the floor.

"Look inside, Adam Cook!" Sarah cried, rushing to where he stood reaching down into the box. He laughed with great joy!

"Oh, ho, ho! I have a strange feeling about your box of raisin bran, Mrs. Finfield!"

It was *Brave Bonnie Augustine!* Holding the manuscript high above his head, Adam laughed heartily.

"It's your *Brave Bonnie Augustine!*" he announced to the jubilant Mrs. Finfield, holding it out to her. Sarah took the manuscript, tied together with a shoestring, and danced jubilantly around the empty garage floor. Adam, amused and pleased at the joy of the widow, retrieved the remaining boxes—ten more, to be exact—and lined them up on the ledge near the kitchen door.

"We almost missed them, Mrs. Cook!" he said, catching her arm in one of her twirls. He held up the empty garbage bag. "This close!"

It was the very last sentence in the very last chapter of *The House on Timber Lane*, and *The Mystery of Sarah and the Lost Manuscripts*. And...it was the beginning sentence in the first chapter of Finfield Publishing, Inc.

"I thought you said you checked everything in the garage," quipped a smiling Sarah as they entered the kitchen.

"And I thought you said there was nothing but paint in that cabinet," offered Adam as a comeback.

The garage was locked, the key placed on the kitchen table, and then, with a pull on the door and the sound of a lock, Sarah Finfield and Adam Cook left Timber Lane forever.

"Off to Cheyenne we go."

"Are you serious? That's a long way to go to get engaged!"

Adam spoke softly and with great affection—and with just a touch of his famous mischievous grin.

"I'm just thinkin' how I'll have you all to myself for 14-plus hours. And think about it, Sarah, won't it be a great story to pass down to the kids and the grandkids?"

It was the first sentence in the first chapter of *The Life and Times of Sarah Liselle and Adam Benjamin Cook*.

Adam turned toward the interstate and when it came time to choose East or West, he headed to where the sun sets.

CHAPTER 34
EPILOGUE

The wonderful aroma of French vanilla coffee was everywhere. Border's was decked out with Christmas decorations, the mood greatly influenced by the overhead holiday music. The bookstore was overflowing with customers, some smiling, some showing signs of celebrating in the Grinch mode. Near the coffee bar sat four friends, talking and laughing and making much too much noise for the people engrossed in their computers, books or magazines. It did not matter, though. This was a special occasion.

At the entry of the bookstore, there stood an easel with a large poster board resting on its ledge. Next to the advertisement were many stacks of handsome hard cover books; their jackets portrayed a castle on an exceedingly high mountain and in the foreground, a close up of the menacing face of a knight. *The Dishonor of Sir Quiglee* was the title; Herman Lichten was the author; Finfield Publishing, Inc. was the publisher.

For the four friends, this was a reunion and a celebration. Mr. and Mrs. Cook—Adam and Sarah—tanned and tired, had just returned with twelve teens from a short term missions trip in Honduras; Daniel Cook was settling back into Timber Ridge—at least temporarily—as an *almost* civilian; and Annette Cappetti, home on Christmas break from college bubbled over with words of relief that finals were behind her. That was the reunion part. The celebration was the introduction of Herman's second book. As the four sat together, enjoying Border's coffee, tea and goodies, they watched with delight as one after the other, folk stopped to pick up a copy, leaf through the book, and then carry it to the counter.

No one knew who the foursome was; for all anyone knew, they were just four noisy people sitting in the corner. A multitude of shoppers milled around them, coming, going, retrieving a new magazine, replenishing their coffee cups, bumping into one another and into those sitting at the round tables. Such a large crowd meant a long wait for a table, for some. Should the foursome move and let someone else sit down? No. A long year had gone by; the tales that each had to tell of their year apart had to be told in their entirety; and memories of a difficult time, a triumphant time, needed to be reminisced once again.

Sarah's venture into the publishing world had been a success. Adam, though he continued his construction endeavors, found himself pulled into her world extensively—and was liking it more each day. Daniel, still looking strong and still handsome as ever, weeks away from being done with the Marines, could not help smiling at the sight of his dad and Sarah sitting close and holding hands. "The lovely lady of Timber Lane," he mused, "and McGyver."

How grown up Annette seemed now—with her long hair and glasses—as she looked across at Adam, Sarah and Daniel and spiritedly told tales of dorm life and cafeteria food, chapel services and finals! Her scintillating tales brought on laughter...and joy. Adam sat back, his arms folded, and marveled at how God had used the ugly summer of 2005 to bring about a whole cluster of miracles.

"Why don't you go over there and just kind of...casually...tell all those people who you are, Sarah?" Adam joked. "Look at all those people. You're famous!"

"I'm not famous," she said. "Herman is famous! His book is famous! It is very sad to me that he's not around to see this."

"And we must not forget that the Payces are famous!" Annette interjected.

"Or infamous," Daniel corrected.

Truly, the Payces, by that time, a year and a half or so since the night of the abduction—or the Night of the Drywall, as they had lightheartedly named it—were indeed infamous. All three were in prison. Between the three of them, a staggering list of charges had put them away: Arson and manslaughter in the case of Herman Lichten and the Wentworth Building fire—based on their testimony that they believed the building empty; kidnapping; breaking and entering; malicious trespassing; and in a surprise case against Robert, conspiracy to commit murder—among other things. His hasty purging of the **ROBERT** folder had not saved him; Chip's hard copies put him away for twenty years for his part in a hostile takeover conspiracy along with Joel Cassidine, III that had led to the murder of Joel Cassidine, Sr., president of the publishing company with his name. (The trial brought to light that the takeover plan was a dual one:

Thomas and Robert were both plotting to remove their fathers from the picture!)

Father Payce, heretofore unscathed in legal battles, fought long and hard on behalf of himself to stay on the outside—and nearly succeeded; but his evil deeds to more than just Sarah Finfield converged to prove him a criminal. His incarceration had finally come to pass on December 12, 2006—two days before this happy Border's reunion! Many people, it turned out, were relieved and felt safer with him behind bars. Payce Publishing somehow escaped demise in the midst of all the mayhem; however, Herman Lichten's second book—and the remaining ten—ended up out of its hands.

"I say, let's go to dinner," Adam declared, slapping his knee. "I'm buying." He smiled at Sarah. "How about it?"

"Sure!"

"Where?" Daniel wanted to know.

"Stonegate...our official place for celebrating! We need to all go home and get dressed up—and I'm meaning, real dressed up—for the first annual Cook Christmas get together. Let's say seven."

"Could one of you drive me home? I'm stranded these days now that Tony and I are...well, you know. Can someone drive me home now?" Annette wanted to know.

Daniel stood. "I'll take you. How'd you get here? Are you here straight from school?"

"Thank you, Daniel. And, yes. Emily just dropped me off after a five-hour ride through a near blizzard!"

"Well, come on. I'll take you and come and get you later."

"No, Daniel. That's way out of your way coming from out in the boonies where you live. I'll have Dad drive me to Stonegate."

"I'll be glad to get you," Daniel said, "and I'll drive you home."

"I'm thinking I should have him drive me anyway. You know why?"

"Why?"

"He told me he has something really important to tell me. Strangely, he and I are turning into friends! Believe it or not, he and I have been emailing back and forth and guess what about?"

"What?"

"About God and Creation! It has been very cool! I sent him a book and believe it or not, he's reading it! So, if you don't mind, Dad will drive me there, but I accept your offer of a ride home, now and after dinner. Remember when we only had to walk 200 steps to my house? That seems like a hundred and twenty years ago!"

Grabbing her suitcase, purse and caramel latté—now a college coffee drinker—Annette started after Daniel; then she stopped, dropped everything right where it was, crowd or no crowd, and ran back to give Sarah a loving hug.

"I owe you, Mrs. Finfield. Look at me. Would you even know it's the same person as the one that pounded on your door that first day?"

"You are not! You don't even look the same, let alone all the wonderful changes in your life. You don't owe me, though; God gets all the glory for the precious woman that you are now."

"That's true, but I'm grateful to you, too. I'm sorry that I got so delinquent with the letters. College life is a lot different than I could have guessed."

"You did good with letter writing! I loved your letters. We'll talk more later, okay?"

Daniel wormed his way back to the table, pressing Annette to hurry. He retrieved her suitcase and started once again for the door.

"Coming?" he asked.

"Coming. Just a second."

She moved to stand next to Adam and bent down to give him a hug as well.

"Thank you, too, Adam Cook...Mr. Macho Man!"

With a toss of her head and a smirk, she hurried to catch Daniel.

"Did you hear that?" Adam asked his wife.

"Yes. What's that all about?"

"Hmm. I'll tell you later," Adam replied. He leaned back and put his arm around his wife.

"Lots of good things happening, eh? It's still hard for me to believe all of it," he said very softly, watching Daniel and Annette make their way through the crowd and out the door. "And just sitting here with you is such a treasure, I hope you get that. I thought I was content being alone. Well, in a way, I was content." He smiled. "I guess I'm just more content now. God has made me a happy man, Sarah Cook."

"Time to go, my Yellow Pages angel," Sarah said, taking his hand. "It's getting really crowded in here. Someone just stepped on my toe! Let's go."

"Let's stop at the Lichten display."

"Why?"

"I want to buy a copy of *The Dishonor of Sir Quiglee.*"

"Why, Adam?" she asked, somewhat bewildered.

"Oh, I'm ready for some more Herman Lichten," he mumbled, picking up a copy of the book.

"For $19.95! You can just go home and pull down the Cheerios box and read for free!"

They both laughed.

"Don't you just get such a good feeling, though, holding a hard copy in your hands?" Adam pensively asked. "Another whole story lies hidden in between the two covers of this book, a story that these people will never know." He replaced the hard cover novel and facing her, rested his arms on her shoulders. "Tell me, Sarah Cook, when you think back on those days when we were searching for the manuscripts and doing battle with the Payces, what is your one best memory?"

"Oh, dear. I'd have to think about that. I'm sure I know what yours would be."

"Tell me what you think it is."

"It had to be reaching down into that raisin bran box and finding more than raisin bran! Right?"

"Nope. It's on the list but down a bit. Remember my old adage: People first; then things."

"Well...then for sure it has to be something about our romance."

Adam laughed, his hands now clasped behind her neck.

"High on the list. Yes, very high. But not at the top."

"Okay, I give," Sarah conceded.

With a smile, Adam drew her to him. "Come closer or you'll miss it. It's noisy in here."

Sarah happily yielded.

"Here's my best memory. It happened on the day the new furniture arrived and you finally opened up about Chip's death. Do you remember what you said when you finished?"

"Yeah, I do." Yes, she remembered it well. She nodded.

"You said, 'I just caught a faint glimpse of how Lazarus must have felt when Jesus called his name." For a moment, Adam hesitated, thoughtfully choosing words to best define how her magnificent statement that day had impacted him. "I looked across the room at you, my heart filled with gladness, and knew that I had just witnessed...in a very real way...the resurrection of Sarah Finfield!" He kissed her, right there in front of all the shoppers reaching around them for a copy of Herman Lichten's second splendid novel. "Come on, my elegant Mrs. Cook, off to Stonegate! Let's celebrate!"

Hand in hand, they moved through the crowd, Adam leading the way. Overhead, the song about the partridge in the pear tree was playing merrily.

ABOUT THE AUTHOR

Sharon Diane Brock was born and raised on the northwest side of Chicago. At Midwest Bible Church, she came to know Christ as Savior at age 11. After high school, she attended Moody Bible Institute as a Missionary/Biblical Languages student, and in 1996, graduated from Judson University in Elgin, IL with a B.A. in Business Management.

She discovered her love for writing before she was yet a teen. During the Woodstock, Illinois years of her marriage to Ken Heldman, and the raising of five children—Nate, Matt, Ginger, Georgia and Angela—she wrote many stories, some that still reside on a shelf in their handwritten form. Only in the 90s did she begin to keep her new books in computer files, and only recently has she decided to publish them. She has written five Christian romance novels, one for each of her children; a little bit of each of them is woven into the stories.

The Resurrection of Sarah Finfield, a romance/mystery novel, is the story of a distraught young widow caught up in a perplexing mystery. Chronologically, it is the fourth novel that she wrote and was actually started a good while before Ken's death in 2006. Someday soon, the other four will be available as well!

∂ ∂ ∂ ∂ ∂

ALSO BY SHARON HELDMAN
There Was a Great Storm. There Was a Great Calm.

The night before they were to happily retire to a lovely farmhouse in Petersburg, IL, Sharon and Ken stayed in a motel, their belongings loaded on two moving vans, ready to take off the next morning. Early on August 31, 2006, God called Ken home as he slept. A steady series of significant storms, some immediate, swept into Sharon's new life as a widow. The journey was often tumultuous and sometimes seemingly hopeless, but over the sound of the pounding waves and the howling tempest, she heard a voice saying, "Peace be still." Within these pages lie the tale of grief and pain, hope and victory, and of a new and unique voyage with our faithful God…"to the other side of the lake."

Available on amazon.com.